FOOD AND DRINK IN IRELAND

First published in 2016 by

ROYAL IRISH ACADEMY
19 Dawson Street,
Dublin 2,
Ireland
www.ria.ie

ISBN 978-1-908996-84-8

Originally published in 2015 as *Proceedings of the Royal Irish Academy, Section C*, Volume 115.

Typesetting by Datapage International Ltd.
Printed in Ireland by Sprint-PRINT

FOOD AND DRINK IN IRELAND

Edited by Elizabeth FitzPatrick and James Kelly

Contents

Preface

Food and Drink is the second thematic volume to be published since the decision of the editorial board of *Proceedings* in 2007 to bring out an occasional thematic volume addressing a fundamental theme in Irish life. Like its predecessor, *Domestic Life in Ireland* (*Proceedings of the Royal Irish Academy*, 111C), which was published in 2011, the current volume favours the multi-disciplinary approach that is one of the defining features of the journal. It aspires thereby to provide a forum for new ideas and for syntheses of established approaches and findings. In keeping with the remit and tradition of the journal to explore the Irish past in *la longue durée*, it addresses food and drink between the Mesolithic and the present.

As Stephen Mennell's 'introduction' to this collection points out, despite the long tradition of collecting and assembling recipes and the cultural potential of printed cookery books, awareness of the rich and revealing potential of the history of food and drink is a comparatively recent development. The decision of Louis Cullen in 1981 to devote two chapters in his vastly influential exploration of the emergence of modern Ireland to 'diet in a changing society' and 'hospitality and men' was crucial in this respect, because it brought food and diet into the Irish historical mainstream.[1] It did not, to be sure, herald a flood of publications on these or allied subjects. The history of alcohol consumption, for example, remained anchored in a world that answered more visibly to the politics of social control than to the new perspectives presented by sociability, conviviality of sociability.[2] However, it did pave the way over time for more ambitious work, since as well as Regina Sexton's helpful short survey, which appeared in 1998,[3] the publication by Oxford University Press in 2001 of *Feast and famine: a history of food in Ireland, 1500–1920* by Leslie Clarkson and E. Margaret Crawford can justifiably be identified as a milestone, less for the novelty of its findings, than for the breadth of its conclusions, its temporal range and the eclectic range of sources upon which it draws.[4] It certainly highlighted the riches to be gleaned from parliamentary enquiries and official surveys, which Ian Miller has

* doi: 10.3318/PRIAC.2015.15

[1] L. M. Cullen, *The emergence of modern Ireland, 1600–1900* (London, 1981).

[2] Colm Kerrigan, *Father Matthew and the Irish Temperance Movement* (Cork, 1992); Paul A. Townsend, *Father Matthew, Temperance and Irish identity* (Dublin, 2002); Diarmaid Ferriter, *A nation of extremes: the Pioneers in twentieth-century Ireland* (Dublin, 1999).

[3] Regina Sexton, *A little history of Irish food* (Dublin, 1998).

[4] Leslie Clarkson and E. Margaret Crawford, *Feast and famine: a history of food in Ireland, 1500–1920* (Oxford, 2001).

demonstrated still more authoritatively and in greater detail in his recent pioneering engagement with the way in which science, medicine and social reform intersected to shape attitudes to food and diet in the later nineteenth and early twentieth centuries.[5]

This is a most important development because for all their intrinsic interest as subjects in their own right, food and drink are still more revealing archaeologically and historically of the societies, peoples and eras in which they are located when they are appealed to amplify and to illuminate broader societal behaviours and tendencies. This is something that Irish archaeology does particularly well. The archaeological essays in this volume introduce several new themes around food-related behaviour and culinary material culture, supported by innovative theoretical frameworks and breakthroughs in scientific methodologies. Complexity has been recognised as a feature of Mesolithic diets and foodways, with belief exercising an influence on food consumption and identified in the archaeological record as specific rituals and patterns of discard. The potential of stable isotope analysis on lipid residues has been realised in its initial application to Irish Neolithic ceramic vessels. This method has revealed that vessels were used mainly to process dairy fats and other foodstuffs, thereby providing new insights into diet and food procurement among the earliest farming communities on the island and marking a beginning to the research journey needed to understand more fully the place of food and drink in prehistory. The fact that Ireland was the most prominent user of pyrolithic technology during the Bronze Age, as evidenced in the extensive survival of burnt mounds or *fulachtaí fia* in the Irish landscape, has encouraged new thinking about social bonding during that period. The image presented is one of small family groups food-sharing and hosting feasts around these cooking sites.

Sophisticated ways of thinking about foodways in medieval Irish society show that there was restricted access to particular foods based on grade and status. The Middle Irish law tracts of the seventh and eighth centuries enshrined those proscriptions, while in the period 1100–1600 access to hunted foods such as red deer, fallow deer, hare, rabbit and wild pig was a marker of status and means of mediating social relationships. Where plant foods are concerned, archaeobotanical research has confirmed an abundance of native seasonal fruits in the Irish urban medieval diet and some of the earliest physical evidence for imported exotic foodstuffs such as fig, grape and walnut. It has proven to be groundbreaking too in recognising chronological and geographical variation in crop use which otherwise cannot be gleaned from documentary sources.

The social meaning that can be derived from food research has also been demonstrated by historians working in other jurisdictions. The significance and impact of Rebecca Spang's reconstruction of the 'invention of the restaurant' in late eighteenth-century France has served not only to illuminate

---

[5] Ian Miller, *Reforming food in Post-Famine Ireland: medicine, science and improvement, 1845–1922* (Manchester, 2014).

the emergence of one emblematical modern institution in a new and novel way, but also to encourage greater inquiry into the concept of public and private space which is central to the influential interpretative models associated with Jürgen Habermas and Norbert Elias.[6] This is not an arena with which the essays in this volume engage directly, for the simple reason that insufficient work has yet been completed to permit the application of a purely theoretical approach, and because of the utility of an empirical methodology. Yet all contributors eschew simple reconstruction in favour of an attempt to relate consumption, be it of food or drink, which provides the collection with its thematic frame of reference, to the social world in which they occur, and to engage in new and novel ways with the evidential record that remains. Mention has already been made of the usefulness of official inquiries for the reconstruction of diet and consumption patterns in the nineteenth and twentieth centuries. Prior to this period, outside of a handful of carceral institutions, the state seemed little interested in what people consumed, but this does not mean that diet is a subject closed off to inquiry. The analyses ventured by Madeline Shanahan and Regina Sexton of receipt books permits a revealing investigation of diet and dining patterns that underlines the extent to which early modern Ireland conformed to British and European norms, and how this and other forms of evidence allow us to identify how deeply these dining patterns percolated societally. The value of the press as a source, both for public (restaurant) dining and the varieties of alcohol that were available for purchase in the eighteenth century offers another reminder of the responsiveness of even the most ostensibly unpromising sources to focused interrogation, and of the dramatic shifts in diet that have occurred across the millennia that people have lived and consumed on this island.

It may be that for many it is the explanation of the current patterns of preparation and consumption that are of most immediate interest. There is, to be sure, much to ponder in the emergence of tea as the most popular liquid consumable, of the rise and fall and rise again of various varieties of alcohol (wine, beer and whiskey most obviously, but also rum, port and gin) consumption, but these cannot be separated from the emergence of the restaurant, which is explored by Máirtín Mac Con Iomaire, and the emergence of the kitchen as a separate defined space in the twentieth century, which is the subject of Rhona Richman Kenneally's contribution. And, of course, there is the symbolic and sociable use of food and drink. The centrality of the public and alcohol to homo-sociability in modern Ireland is acknowledged in Diarmaid Ferriter's essay. What is less well established is its centrality to patterns of behaviour with roots deep in the early modern period, in patterns of public commemoration and private sociability. This is considered by

---

[6] Rebecca Spang, *The invention of the restaurant: Paris and modern gastronomic culture* (Cambridge, MA, 2000).

James Kelly's essay, which expands on the historiography which had established that sociable feasting was integral to the medieval world.[7]

The essays that comprise this collection have aspired to do more than present an introduction to the variety of perspectives that food and drink offer on the history of consumption and human behaviour on the island of Ireland between the Mesolithic and the present—they have conceptualised the complex relationships between human society, and food and drink. Yet, the authors remind us that much more needs to be done on this topic, and in their respective contributions they have planted seeds for future directions in food and drink research.

This volume would not have been possible without the dedication and commitment of all of the contributors to whom the editors acknowledge their indebtedness. It is a reminder of what can be achieved when scholars with different backgrounds, working with different types of evidence, come together with a common purpose.

Elizabeth FitzPatrick and James Kelly

---

[7] Katherine Simms, 'Guesting and feasting in Gaelic Ireland', *Journal of the Royal Society of Antiquaries of Ireland* 108 (1978), 67–100; Catherine O'Sullivan, *Hospitality in medieval Ireland, 900–1500* (Dublin, 2004).

Introduction

This book is the most ambitious and comprehensive academic study of the history of food and drink in Ireland that has ever been published. It is admirably long term in its scope, beginning with the Mesolithic inhabitants of the island and stretching right up to the Irish restaurant scene of the early twenty-first century. It is also interdisciplinary, the outcome of collaboration between archaeologists, historians, natural scientists, a sociologist if you include me, and, yes, cooks.

It is curious that the history of food, drink and cooking remained for a very long time—and emphatically not only in Ireland—the domain of enthusiasts and mainly amateur historians. Cookery books were among the earliest to appear in most of the vernacular languages of Europe during the decades after the invention of moveable-type printing. These, and the manuscript sources that preceded them, did not escape the attention of antiquaries and bibliographers. For example, as early as 1780, Samuel Pegge published his edition of *The forme of cury*, containing recipes from the court of King Richard II of England (1377–99).[1] In 1790, the Reverend Richard Warner republished that manuscript, along with several others from the late Middle Ages, in his handsome folio *Antiquitates Culinariae*.[2] Still more were collected in Frederick Furnivall's *Early English meals and manners*.[3] Similar manifestations of interest are evident in several other European countries, especially in France, where national pride in *la cuisine française* is clearly evident from the mid-seventeenth century. Georges Vicaire's *Bibliographie Gastronomique* of 1890 runs to almost a thousand pages and includes books in a number of European languages.[4]

In the twentieth century, one thread in food studies was work by historically orientated nutritionists and nutritionally orientated historians. Examples include *Histoire de l'alimentation et de la gastronomie* by the French medical man Alfred Gottschalk, *The Englishman's food* by Sir Jack Drummond and his wife Anne Wilbraham, who were nutritionists by training, and *Plenty and want* by the nutritionally expert social historian John Burnett.[5] And a final

---

* doi: 10.3318/PRIAC.2015.16

[1] Samuel Pegge (ed.), *The forme of cury* (London, 1780).

[2] Richard Warner, *Antiquitates Culinariae, or Curious tracts relating to the culinary affairs of the Old English* (London, 1790; facsimile edn London, 1981).

[3] Frederick J. Furnivall (ed.), *Early English meals and manners* (London, 1868).

[4] Georges Vicaire, *Bibliographie Gastronomique* (Paris, 1890; facsimile edn London, 1978).

[5] Alfred Gottschalk, *Histoire de l'alimentation et de la gastronomie depuis la préhistoire jusqu'à nos jours* (2 vols, Paris, 1948); J. C. Drummond and Anne Wilbraham, *The Englishman's food: a history of five centuries of English diet* (London, 1939); John Burnett, *Plenty and want: a social history of diet in England from 1815 to the present day* (London, 1966).

thread worth mentioning is that of the 'scholar-cooks'—cookery book writers whose pursuit of recipes is grounded in serious historical research and whose writings, in my own experience, often contain insights worthy of historical investigation. Prominent examples from Britain are Dorothy Hartley, Elizabeth David, Jane Grigson and Alan Davidson, all of whose works also exhibit substantial literary quality.[6] The scholarly investigation of old recipes continues, as can be seen in Madeline Shanahan's study of Irish manuscript recipe books in this volume.[7]

This is only to hint at what was already an extensive literature. Yet, although such trends rarely have a precise beginning, the academic study of the history of food and drink may be said to have commenced its 'take off into self-sustained growth' following Fernand Braudel's celebrated call, in the *Annales* in 1961, for a 'history of material life and biological behaviour'.[8] This was especially influential because the leaders of the *Annales* School of historians from Marc Bloch and Lucien Febvre onwards encouraged collaboration with social scientists, and their journal was read by anthropologists, archaeologists and sociologists as well as historians. At least partly as a result, by the 1980s the growing body of research in the history of food and eating had spilled over into more theoretically orientated writing in anthropology by—notably—Mary Douglas, Jack Goody, Sidney Mintz and Marvin Harris, and in sociology by Anne Murcott and (if modesty does not forbid) me.[9]

Archaeologists have for a long time been an exception to the general rule of relative academic neglect of food habits. Utensils for cooking and eating, hunting equipment, and artefacts associated with cultivation, have been

---

[6] Dorothy Hartley, *Food in Britain* (London, 1954); Elizabeth David, *Italian food* (London, 1954), *French country cooking* (London, 1951), *English bread and yeast cookery* (London, 1977), *An omelette and a glass of wine* (London, 1984), etc.; Jane Grigson, *Charcuterie and French pork cookery* (London, 1967), *English food* (London, 1974), etc.; Alan Davidson, *The Oxford companion to food* (Oxford, 1999).

[7] See Shanahan's essay, pp. 197–218 below.

[8] Fernand Braudel, Robert Philippe, Jean-Jacques Hémardinquer and Frank Spooner, 'Vie matérielle et comportements biologiques—Bulletin No. 1', *Annales E–S–C* 16: 3 (1961), 545–74.

[9] See: Mary Douglas, 'Deciphering a meal', *Daedalus* 101:1 (1972), 61–81, and 'Food as an art form', *Studio International* September (1974), 83–8; J. R. Goody, *Cooking, cuisine and class: a study in comparative sociology* (Cambridge, 1982); Sidney Mintz, *Sweetness and power: the place of sugar in modern history* (New York, 1985); Marvin Harris, *Good to eat: riddles of food and culture* (London, 1985); Anne Murcott (ed.), *The sociology of food and eating* (Aldershot, Hamps., 1983) and *The nation's diet: the social science of food choice* (London, 1998); Stephen Mennell, *All manners of food: eating and taste in England and France from the Middle Ages to the present* (Oxford, 1985; revised edition, Champaign, IL, 1996). A survey of social scientific work on food up to the early 1990s can be found in Stephen Mennell, Anne Murcott and Anneke H. van Otterloo, *The sociology of food: eating, diet and culture* (London, 1993). A more up-to-date, theoretically informed survey of the literature is in the pipeline: Alejandro Colás, Jason Edwards, Jane Levi and Sami Zubaida, *Food, politics, and society: social theory and the modern food system* (Berkeley, CA, forthcoming *c.* 2017).

recovered during archaeological excavations. Recent scientific advances have made it possible to investigate ancient diets in more detail,[10] and indeed pushed back the field of research into the domain of palaeoanthropology—even before the biological evolution of the current form of human being, *Homo sapiens sapiens*. Richard Wrangham has argued that *Homo erectus* emerged about two million years ago through the ability of its immediate hominid predecessors to cook food.[11] His case rests mainly on considerations of biological evolution. Cooking increased the nutritional efficiency of food, with the development of a smaller, more effective digestive tract which, by using less energy itself, permitted the growth of a larger brain. The brain is what Leslie Aiello and Peter Wheeler have labelled 'expensive tissue'[12]—running the human brain demands a much greater proportion of the energy that the body derives from nutritional input than the brain of any other animal.

All the same, Wrangham's evolutionary focus may, it can be argued, put the cart before the horse. It has long been recognised that no other mammal apart from human beings and some of their hominid ancestors possess the means to maintain body temperature other than by eating. Humans can keep themselves warm around a fire. More than that, human beings hold a *species monopoly* of the active use of fire; once stated, that may seem obvious, but it was not obvious until Johan Goudsblom drew attention to it.[13] Insufficient attention has been paid to the implications of this human monopoly. Yes, the ability first to capture naturally occurring wild fire, then to tend it in order to keep it going, and eventually to light fires at will was connected both with keeping warm and with cooking food. But, as Goudsblom has shown, the active use of fire came to play a central part in the long-term *interweaving* of processes of *biological evolution* and processes of *social development*. The active use of fire involves overcoming fear: although fire remains forever dangerous, through the exercise of care and foresight the danger can be managed. Safety in the handling of burning wood requires the development of both manual and mental skills—the development of the hand and the brain cannot be separated. Keeping a fire going also required foresight routinised in the form of *social organisation*: fuel had to be gathered regularly, and some sort of rota to keep watch over the fire was also necessary. Moreover, the human species monopoly over the use of fire changed the balance of power between human beings and other animals: fire not only frightened other animals away, but made them more vulnerable (with implications for human diet) to more elaborate forms of hunting—and the

[10] See for instance the essays by Jessica Smyth and Richard Evershed, and by Susan Lyons, pp. 27–46 and pp. 111–66 below.

[11] Richard Wrangham, *Catching fire: how cooking made us human* (New York, 2009).

[12] Leslie Aiello and Peter Wheeler, 'The expensive tissue hypothesis: the brain and the digestive system in human and primate evolution', *Current Anthropology* 36:2 (1995), 199–221.

[13] Johan Goudsblom, *Fire and civilization* (London, 1992); see also Goudsblom's chapter 'Fire and fuel in human history', in David Christian (ed.), *The Cambridge world history* (Cambridge, 2015), vol. I, 185–207.

use of fire sticks in more complex hunting strategies[14] was also linked to the further development of the brain and the capacity for foresight and social coordination. Finally, cooperation in activities related to food and eating acquired a rich array of social meanings.

Thus the study of food deserves a more prominent place than it usually holds in historical literature, where it is less prominent and certainly less prestigious than political or social history. Yet, as several of the essays in this volume demonstrate, the production, cooking and consumption of food have always been an important aspect of social life, and are often strongly linked to politics and inequalities of power too. This is evident as early as the Mesolithic; as Graeme Warren writes in the opening chapter,

> Food is, and always has been, central to social life. Food maintains individuals and societies, and the archaeological study of food offers potential to understand past social identities. Food is a powerful symbol because it is consumed and because it is of overwhelming everyday significance in small-scale societies, be they hunters or farmers: it is 'what matters most to most people for most of the time'.[15]

That last point scarcely needs emphasis in Ireland, the most distinctive feature of whose food history is that it was this country that suffered the last catastrophic famine in Western European history, following the ravages of potato blight in the 1840s.

Yet, except in such extreme circumstances as famine, it has been noted that no human society consumes everything of potential nutritional value that is available in its environment. Few human groups (apart from, it is said, soldiers in training for recruitment into Britain's Special Air Service or SAS) have been able calmly to contemplate eating earthworms. Patterns of food avoidance vary markedly from country to country and from social stratum to stratum. For archaeologists, evidence of food discarding is important in showing both what was eaten in the distant past and what was not. In modern times, changes in food avoidances can be traced more accurately. Taste for foods that were once significant elements in diet has sometimes declined decisively. The case of offal is a good example. It seems to be the case not only that some foods are what economists call 'inferior goods'—that is, foods (like potatoes) of which consumption declines as increasing income makes possible their substitution by more highly valued foods—but also that they become invested with feelings of positive repugnance. Interestingly, a food such as tripe, once commonly eaten by the poor, falls off the menu at the foot of the social pyramid, but then reappears at the top in the best restaurants. (The trend against the consumption of offal is much more marked in the United States of

---

[14] Including in fishing, as Graeme Warren indicates in his essay; see p. 18 below.
[15] See Warren's essay, p. 1 below.

America (USA) than in France, with Britain and probably Ireland somewhere in between but nearer the American pole.)[16]

Some food avoidances are ritualised in religious prohibitions, as in the cases of pork for Jews and Muslims, and beef for Hindus, although cases of this kind do not much feature in the food history of Ireland.[17] One specific religious intervention in the diet of the people of Ireland was the obligation in the Catholic tradition to abstain from meat during Lent, and indeed the doctrinal view of Fridays as year-round penance days when Catholics were supposed to refrain from eating meat.[18] Apart from that, where religion has often been thought to play a part in people's eating habits in these islands is in the churches' attitudes towards the *enjoyment* of good food. More specifically, it has frequently been suggested that English cookery was 'stunted' by the victory of the Puritans in the civil wars of the seventeenth century.[19] Serious historical evidence for this is weak. For one thing, the Puritans did not 'win'—the monarchy was restored in 1660, and Dissenters were subject to civil and political discrimination. Asceticism continued to be a strand in the religious currents of these islands, but history is written by the victors, and the general killjoy attitudes of seventeenth-century Puritans have been exaggerated. True, they strongly opposed drunkenness, but they were not unique in that—as the campaigns of Father Matthew in Ireland a century and a half later serve to remind us.[20] What is more probably the case is that by the nineteenth century, in the spirit of the age *all* the Christian denominations preached what E. P. Thompson called an 'all-embracing "Thou Shalt Not"'.[21] This appears to apply to both islands; it fits better with what we know about the dominant Roman Catholic church's asceticism in nineteenth-century and early twentieth-century Ireland. It also fits better with something that is absent from this

---

[16] See Mennell, 'An excursus on offal', in *All manners*, 310–16.

[17] Anthropologists of the structuralist persuasion like Mary Douglas tended to treat such prohibitions as rationally inexplicable; in *Good to eat*, Marvin Harris offered developmental or 'materialist' explanations for several such cases, including those of pork and beef.

[18] This tradition by no means disappeared from Protestantism after the Reformation, though the justification for it did. In the Church of England's *Homilies* of 1562, congregations were instructed to observe the fasts not for religious but for political reasons: 'as when any realm in consideration of the maintenance of fisher-towns bordering upon the seas, and for the increase of fishermen, of whom do spring matriners to go forth upon the sea, to the furnishing of the Navy of the Realm, whereby not only commodities of other countries may be transported, but also may be a necessary defence to resist the invasion of the adversary'. See *Certain sermons or homilies appointed to be read in churches in the time of Queen Elizabeth of famous memory* (London, 1687), 300. The *Homilies* are formally anonymous, but were mainly written by Archbishop Thomas Cranmer,

[19] See Mennell, *All manners*, 103–08.

[20] See Diarmaid Ferriter's essay, pp. 350–1 below.

[21] E. P. Thompson, *The making of the English working class* (Harmondsworth, Middx, 1968), 411.

collection, namely signs of markedly different culinary cultures in the predominantly Catholic Republic and the majority Protestant Northern Ireland.

So is there any such thing as a distinctively Irish national cuisine, or Irish culinary culture? Probably not. What we think of as 'national cuisines' were a relatively late arrival on the European scene. Even Italian cuisine, which we regard as one of the most distinctive in western Europe, did not begin to take its present shape until long-distance international trade was regularised: imagine Italian food without pasta (probably adopted from China) and the tomato which, with its botanically close relative the potato, is one of the most obvious imports through the 'Columbian exchange'. Before Columbus, it has been observed, the cabbage was a staple from Sicily to Scotland. Even the 'French bean' has American origins. That is not to deny the probability that all parts of Europe had *regional dishes*, or that these regional differences seem to have survived more markedly in countries like Germany and Italy that were unified as states only in the nineteenth century.[22] The local or regional specialities were often feast-day dishes that were cooked for a few special occasions in the year. It was these special dishes—such as the famous cassoulet of Castelnaudary—that French gastronomes like Curnonsky, de Croze and Rouff collected in the early decades of the twentieth century as 'the gastronomic treasure of France'.[23] Soon complaints were heard that in Paris 'everything is available all the time'—an early example of the now ubiquitous dissatisfaction at the disappearance of the seasonality of the diet in the supermarket age.

Yet it is misleading to think of 'country cooking' as the foundation of haute cuisine even in France. One mark of 'fine dining' is the sheer variety of ingredients that go into it, and that is the product of urban markets rather than of rural tradition. A second mark is its labour intensiveness: it is expensive cuisine not only because it makes use of costly ingredients, but also because dishes often require many stages of preparation in well-staffed kitchens. It is no accident that we use the expression 'haute cuisine', or that French is more generally the language of cookery. French cuisine achieved a kind of culinary hegemony in Western Europe from the seventeenth century onwards, and by the nineteenth century its dominance had spread to North America and to other parts of 'Europe overseas'. I have argued that French haute cuisine took shape in the absolutist court of the ancien régime, mainly because for the French aristocracy deprived by (especially) Louis XIV of independent power and social function, conspicuous consumption—competitive virtuosity in rank-related houses, décor, equestrianism, music and art as well as food—became central to their social identity. The models set at court were emulated by lower but rising

---

[22] For Germany, see for example Horst Scharfenburg, *The German kitchen* (New York, 1989).

[23] Curnonsky (pseud. of Maurice-Edmond Sailland) and Marcel Rouff, *La France gastronomique: Guide des merveilleuses culinaires et des bonnes auberges françaises* (Paris, 1921–); Curnonsky and Austin de Croze, *Le Trésor gastronomique de la France* (Paris, 1933).

strata. Of course, other countries had court societies too, though the Versailles-like royal and ducal palaces that tourists visit today testify to the influence of French models. By Napoleonic times, when Parisian restaurants took over the function of culinary competiveness driving culinary innovation, 'path dependency' had made French leadership hard to dislodge for two centuries.[24] The upper reaches of society in many countries long remained French culinary colonies.[25]

So often, trends in culinary culture subtly reflect changes in the distribution of power in society more widely. England appeared to be on a similar trajectory towards an absolutist monarchy—and there appeared 'courtly' cookery books on the French model—until the Civil Wars of the seventeenth century nipped the development in the bud. After the Restoration in 1660, the great landowners retained their regional power bases and many of their old social functions. They lived large parts of the year outside London, eating the products of their own lands. Of course, some symptoms of conspicuous consumption can be found, but it was not so central to upper-class social identity as it was in France.

In this and many other respects the history of food in Ireland—the Famine apart—is not radically different from that of England. That is not offered as a criticism. Both countries have much in common with these parts of Western Europe where the trickle-down effect from court was weaker than in the special case of France: for example in the Netherlands, the urban *regenten* ('regents') rather than the courts of the *Stadhouders* were the model-setters, while in Germany a considerable cultural gulf developed between the *Bürgertum* ('middle class') and the numerous courts (which for a long time remained French-speaking).[26] So what we think of as typical German food is *gutbürgerlich* ('home cooking'), and Dutch food in the past often made English 'plain cookery' look quite elaborate.

In these islands, differences between social strata have been more evident than national differences—with the added complication that in Ireland for a long time the social elite actually *were* English. From her long and richly detailed study of food culture in pre-Famine Ireland, Regina Sexton concludes that

> The elite consumption cultures of the wealthy classes were received, directed and guided by British, and to a lesser extent, European norms. Wealthy gentry women embraced British styles of cookery and brought

---

[24] Mennell, *All manners*, 108–44; Rebecca Spang, *The invention of the restaurant: Paris and modern gastronomic culture* (Cambridge, MA, 2000).

[25] On this, see also Priscilla Parkhurst Ferguson, *Accounting for taste: the triumph of French cuisine* (Chicago, IL, 2004).

[26] See Stephen Mennell, 'Eten in Nederland', *De Gids* 150:2–3 (1987), 199–207 (the unpublished English original, 'Eating in the Netherlands' is available at http://www. stephenmennell.eu/publications/journalArticles.php (last accessed 10 August 2015)); and Eva Barlösius, 'Soziale und historische Aspekte der deutschen Küche', Afterword to Stephen Mennell, *Die Kultivierung des Appetits* (Frankfurt am Main, 1988), 423–44.

dishes that were strongly imbued with a British sense of identity and tradition to their homes and estates.[27]

As for the lower classes, the picture is largely of stagnation. Again, this is not unusual: even in France, as Marc Bloch remarked, 'on the eve of the Revolution, in contraposition to a bourgeois and even artisan diet which had already undergone appreciable development, the everyday food of the peasant remained singularly archaic'.[28] In Ireland after the Famine, according to Ian Miller, the story was one less of stagnation than actual nutritional decline.[29] Frank Armstrong continues the story into post-Independence Ireland, when—even if decline were halted—the sheer ordinariness of domestic cooking in the Irish countryside persisted. However, this picture of a diet dominated by bread and tea, cabbage and bacon is hardly more depressing than how Raymond Postgate colourfully described food in British hotels (and by implication much of domestic cooking) up to the mid twentieth century: 'there was a sort of Maginot Line of forbidding, unfriendly hotels, offering stringy over-cooked meat in tiny portions, sodden vegetables, and saccharined or tinned fruit with packet custard ...'.[30] Not surprisingly, Miller recounts the beginnings of cookery classes intended to improve the skills of Irish housewives. Not surprising, because such classes were spreading at about the same period in Britain, Scandinavia, the Netherlands and the USA. They often had a *de haut en bas* ('from top to bottom') character, as recounted by Magdalen Pember Reeves in her report on Fabian ladies' initiatives among the very poor in early-twentieth-century Lambeth.[31] A different twist to the story of cookery classes intended to 'improve' domestic cookery is provided by Rhona Richman Kenneally, who shows how in the 1950s organisations like the ESB, ICA and RDS[32] engaged a new mechanism for the purpose: the pursuit of social distinction.[33] Again, there are parallels with Britain, where at the same period women's magazines ran columns on what they called 'hostess cookery'[34]—more or less explicitly understood as a form of competitive culinary 'showing off'. Court society had come to the middle classes!

Great restaurants also came to Ireland in the twentieth century. In one of the final essays, far from the ambience of cabbage and bacon, Máirtín Mac Con Iomaire charts the success of some leading exponents of haute cuisine on this island. As a fairly recent blow-in—I came to live in Ireland in 1993—I was surprised to learn how early international recognition had come to

---

[27] See Sexton's essay, p. 306 below.

[28] Marc Bloch, 'Les Aliments de l'ancienne France', in J. J. Hémardinquer (ed.), *Pour une histoire de l'alimentation* (Paris, 1970), 231.

[29] See Miller's essay, pp. 307–23 below.

[30] Raymond Postgate, 'Preface', in *The good food guide, 1963–64* (London, 1963), xiii.

[31] Magadalen Pember Reeves, *Round about a pound a week* (London, 1913).

[32] That is: the Electricity Supply Board, the Irish Countrywomen's Association and the Royal Dublin Society.

[33] See Richman Kenneally's essay below pp. 325–47.

[34] Mennell, *All manners*, 257.

long-surviving Dublin restaurants like Jammet and the Russell. Less surprising was that they were bastions of *grande cuisine* in the style of Escoffier, whose name is synonymous with the codification of French cuisine in the age of the first great international hotels. Not until the nouvelle cuisine revolution of the 1960s, led by people such as Paul Bocuse and the Troisgros brothers, was the relatively heavy Escoffier dispensation overthrown. Even today, French influence is evident in the recent crop of Irish Michelin-starred restaurants: Patrick Guilbaud (obviously), Kevin Thornton and the Rankins. Even the Allen dynasty at Ballymaloe, Co. Cork, are not exempt from French influence. Mention of Ballymaloe, though does point to something that has changed since French haute cuisine was taking shape in the early modern period. The Allens pride themselves on sourcing their ingredients locally as far as possible, and growing quite a lot themselves; but today, with what has been called 'total urbanisation', it is no longer impossible for there to be great restaurants deep in the countryside.

One final thought arises from this comprehensive long-term history of food and drink in Ireland. There is no shame now in not being able to identify an Irish 'national cuisine', for pretty well all national cuisines have subtly merged into each other. I reflect that even when it was published 30 years ago, my book *All manners of food* was fast becoming an historical document. Since about 1980, the age of national cuisines has passed. We have witnessed the internationalisation of cooking and eating (or perhaps one should say not-cooking and eating). In every country in Europe and beyond, mass catering and fast food outlets have become normal. Most cities have a wide range of 'ethnic' restaurants, and they have gradually influenced each other through the development of 'fusion food'. Even at the pinnacle of the culinary hierarchy of prestige there is more emphasis on the brilliance of innovative individual chefs than on their location within national traditions. In all these respects, Ireland is part of the modern world.

Stephen Mennell, MRIA
University College Dublin

'Mere food gatherers they, parasites upon nature …': food and drink in the Mesolithic of Ireland

Graeme Warren*

School of Archaeology, University College Dublin, Belfield, Dublin 4

[Accepted 6 November 2014. Published 6 April 2015.]

Abstract

This paper reviews evidence for food and drink in the Mesolithic of Ireland (*c.* 8000–4000 cal BC). Evidence for past food is subject to systematic biases, including the nature of preservation and changing analytical methodologies as well as changing attitudes to wild foods. These biases are reviewed and evidence for Mesolithic foodways in Ireland is outlined. The closing discussion is structured around a simple *chaîne opératoire*: from food procurement, production and consumption through to its discard. The evidence suggests a level of complexity to Mesolithic diets and foodways, including evidence of the influence of belief on diet.

Introduction: wild food for thought

Food is narrowly defined as a substance that is consumed and maintains life in terms of energy and nutrition. It is much more than this, however, to those who procure, prepare, consume and discard it, often working with others as they do so. Food is, and always has been, central to social life. Food maintains individuals and societies, and the archaeological study of food offers the potential to understand past social identities. Food is a powerful symbol because it is consumed and because it is of overwhelming everyday significance in small-scale societies, be they hunters or farmers: it is 'what matters most to most people for most of the time'.[1]

Our attitudes to food reveal widespread cultural prejudices. For example, hunter-gatherers are widely perceived as being part of nature rather than being able to transform it to their ends. Their diet is seen as reflecting this:

> Not for them the vain effort to extract tilth from an unwilling soil, or metal from a stony rock. Not for them a wrestle against principalities and powers. Mere food-gatherers they, parasites upon Nature: content with the molluscs of the shores, with trapped birds or captured fish. Thus easily satisfied, they made no effort to explore the interior of the country, where all was unknown and full of dread …[2]

* Author's e-mail: graeme.warren@ucd.ie
doi: 10.3318/PRIAC.2015.115.09

[1] Felipe Fernández-Armesto, *Food: a history* (London, 2002), xiii.
[2] R. A. S. Macalister, *Ancient Ireland: a study in the lessons of archaeology and history* (London, 1935), 8.

In R. A. S. Macalister's 1935 description, hunter-gatherers simply consume wild food rather than produce their own through agricultural labour. Their diet is conflated with their desires and agency: 'easily satisfied' by the food they can 'trap' and 'capture' they never change Ireland, and never take ownership of it. Ironically, this 'old master narrative of progress, in which changes in food production . . . marked supposedly ameliorative stages' in social development, is challenged by the deleterious effects of industrialised food production on our health and environment.[3] The emphasis on 'wild' food also highlights the problems caused by an analytical dichotomy of hunter-gatherers and farmers. Hunter-gatherers are often considered to simply extract resources, whilst farmers manipulate ecological relationships in order to produce food, especially those involving domesticated species. Many societies, however, do not fit into this classification, and are understood as 'food producers' who actively manage and manipulate different aspects of their environments in order to produce food and other resources. Such communities construct ecological niches within which plants and animals can develop, but these resources are not domesticated or wild in any meaningful sense.[4] For example, 'wild' boar (*Sus scrofa*) was an important food source for the Mesolithic population of Ireland (see below). But 'wild' boar was probably imported to the island by Mesolithic colonists, and appears to have been managed by those communities, not least through patterns of culling.[5] Such introductions may have been especially significant given the restricted range of Ireland's native flora and fauna, with key large mammals such as ungulates and aurochs absent in the early Holocene (see below for discussion).

Our attitudes to the kinds of 'wild' food available are conditioned by cultural ambivalence. High cuisine emphasises the values of 'gathered' foods and numerous books advise how to forage for 'food for free'.[6] However, people in the twenty-first century are not familiar with the range of wild food that can be found in Ireland, nor how to process these resources.[7] We are highly selective in our dietary imagination: modern Europeans choose not to eat many insects, although other cultures do, and insects could have formed part of the Mesolithic diet.[8] The excitable media coverage of the recent discovery that toads were consumed in the Mesolithic of England highlights impoverished

---

[3] Felipe Fernández-Armesto and Daniel Lord Smail, 'Food', in Andrew Shryock and Daniel Lord Smail (eds), *Deep history: the architecture of past and present* (London, 2011), 131–59: 132.

[4] Bruce Smith, 'Low-level food production', *Journal of Archaeological Research* 9 (2001), 1–43.

[5] Graeme Warren, Stephen Davis, Meriel McClatchie and Rob Sands, 'The potential role of humans in structuring the wooded landscapes of Mesolithic Ireland: a review of data and discussion of approaches', *Journal of Vegetation History and Archaeobotany* 22:5 (2014), 629–46.

[6] Richard Mabey, *Food for free* (London, 1972).

[7] Ray Mears and Gordon Hillman, *Wild food* (London, 2007).

[8] Brian Morris, 'Insects as food among hunter-gatherers', *Anthropology Today* 24 (2008), 6–8.

expectations of Mesolithic diets.[9] Recent analyses of ceramic residues from Baltic hunter-gatherer sites demonstrate the use of spices and flavourings of limited calorific value demonstrating that Mesolithic food was not determined solely by calorific need, but by dietary preference and choice.[10] Not all substances consumed are ingested for strictly nutritional purposes: wild resources may have served functions as narcotics or medicines as well as flavour; they may have been eaten because to do so was perceived as transferring some property (such as strength, power or vision) to those eating them.

In common with the Mesolithic of many areas, analyses of the plants and animals from archaeological sites in Mesolithic Ireland have tended to consider subsistence practices rather than the importance of food and drink,[11] treating the range of species present as evidence for site seasonality and mobility strategies as well as demonstrating how a hunter-gatherer society adapted to their environment. This focus is important, but should not displace our attention from the other ways in which food maintained people and society: new approaches to the archaeology of food and power, food and gender, and food and symbolism, for example, have become significant[12] but are not widely discussed in the Mesolithic literature.

The primary focus of this paper is food not drink. What Mesolithic communities drank is rarely discussed in the literature—perhaps because it is not considered interesting in terms of subsistence strategy. Whilst water was (presumably) a staple, there are many herbal teas or infusions that can be created from foraged plants, especially given evidence for the use of thermal processing technologies (see below), which may have had medicinal or narcotic properties. Cleavers (*Galium aparine*) has been identified from Mesolithic contexts at Belderrig, Co. Mayo[13] (see Fig. 1 for location), and has traditionally been used as a tea with claimed health/medicinal benefits. Fermented fruit or honey drinks may have been attractive for their alcoholic content, and have been argued to have played a role in hunter-gatherer ritual in prehistoric Europe.[14]

---

[9] Mark Brown, 'Frogs' legs may have been English delicacy 8,000 years before France', *Guardian*, 16 October 2013, available at www.theguardian.com/science/2013/oct/15/wiltshire-dig-frogs-legs-eaten-british-before-french (last accessed 22 February 2015).

[10] Hayley Saul, Marco Madella, Anders Fischer *et al.*, 'Phytoliths in pottery reveal the use of spice in European prehistoric cuisine', *PLoS ONE* 8:8 (2013), e70583.

[11] Nicky Milner, 'Subsistence', in Chantal Conneller and Graeme Warren (eds), *Mesolithic Britain and Ireland: new approaches* (Stroud, Glos., 2006), 61–82.

[12] Katheryn Twiss, 'We are what we eat', in Katheryn Twiss (ed.), *The archaeology of food and identity* (Carbondale, IL, 2007), 1–16: 4.

[13] Footnotes are provided for specific points of evidence, otherwise, full references for all sites discussed are provided in the appendix.

[14] Patrick McGovern, *Uncorking the past: the quest for wine, beer and other alcoholic beverages* (London, 2009).

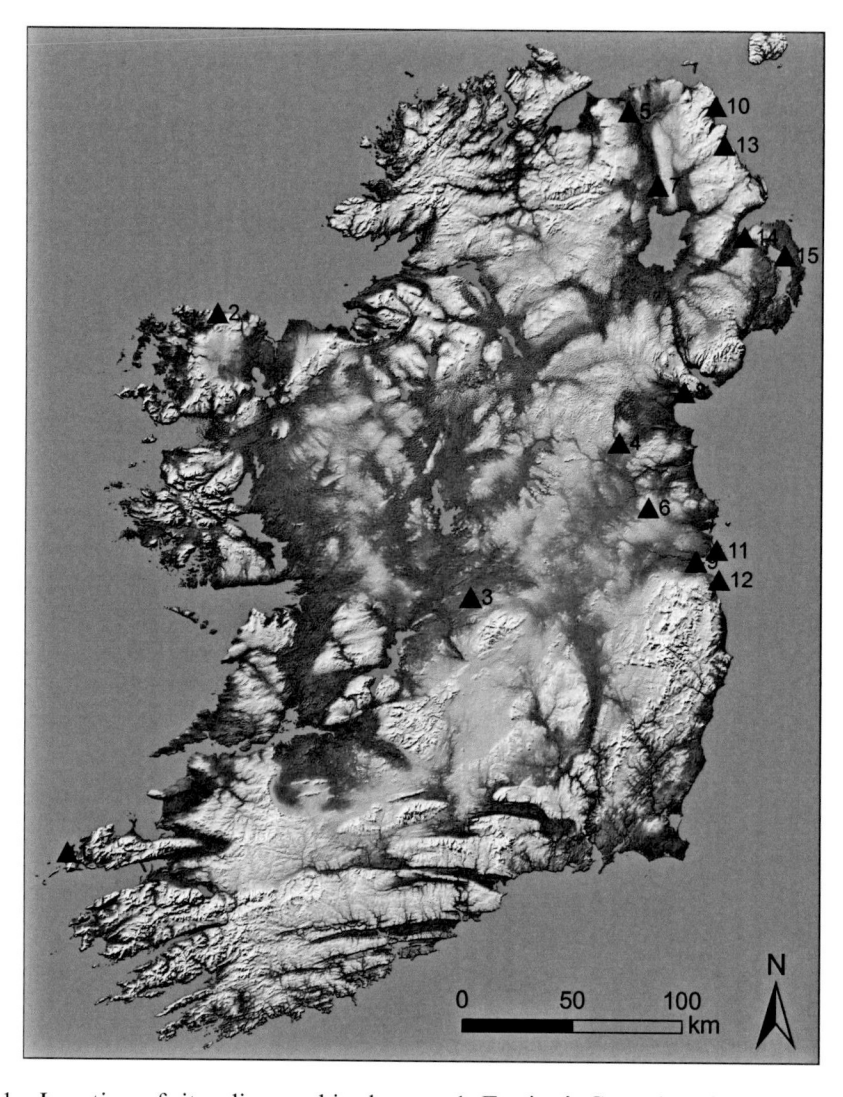

FIG. 1—Location of sites discussed in the text: 1: Ferriter's Cove; 2: Belderrig; 3: Lough Boora; 4: Moynagh Lough; 5: Mount Sandel/Castleroe; 6: Clowanstown; 7: Newferry; 8: Rockmarshall; 9: North Wall Quay; 10: Cushendun; 11: Sutton; 12: Dalkey Island; 13: Bay Farm; 14: Glendhu; 15: Kilnatierney. (Satellite image courtesy of NASA; see http://visibleearth.nasa.gov)

Evidence for food in Mesolithic Ireland

The evidence for food in the Mesolithic of Ireland is problematic. Some limitations derive from the nature of the evidence, but others result from the approaches that have been taken. Accounts of food build on a combination of data: the direct archaeological remains of plants or animals; a small number of human skeletal analyses that provide information on the diet of individuals; as well as other archaeological evidence of cooking features, or discard practices, etc.; information about the environment; and, in many cases, common sense and unexamined analogy. Site location is often seen as providing a very substantial clue as to the types of food procured and consumed on site: thus sites located near rivers are assumed to reflect the importance of fish even in the absence of direct evidence of fish.[15] The dangers of circularity are clear.

Plant and animal remains provide important information about food but must be approached with caution. Setting aside questions of preservation and recovery, in many cases we are not necessarily finding the evidence of meals, but of discarded resources—parts of which may have been eaten, but other parts may also have served other roles: exploited for fur, feathers, tendons or fibres, for example, or in the case of shellfish, used as bait for fishing. Separating out the use of different resources is complex.

There are hints of structured discard routines, and, at many sites, food waste was being discarded into fires (see below for discussion). As such, the plant and animal remains that we discover are not a direct reflection of a meal, but of decisions on how to discard materials following a meal. This distinction is important, because we don't understand the cultural logic surrounding the deposition of food waste, and we can't be certain that what we find is all of a meal or simply part thereof.

Faunal and plant remains are also often found in temporally aggregated deposits—a shell midden or occupation soil, which accumulated over time. As such, their relationship to the diet of an individual is not clear. There have been comparatively few excavations which have been able to examine the formation of such deposits and identify discrete episodes of consumption and discard: Ferriter's Cove, Co. Kerry, is an important exception, and is discussed below.

As well as possible food remains, information on diet comes from individuals. Carbon and nitrogen isotopes in human bone provide evidence of the protein component of diets over approximately the last ten years of life (see below for a detailed discussion). Analysis of teeth wear, dental calculus and tooth formation could also provide information about diet. Stone tools have also been used to provide some information about site function and subsistence, for example with the suggestion that the characteristic larger blade and flake technologies of the Later Mesolithic period may have played an important role in constructing and maintaining food-procurement technologies such as fish traps.[16] The ongoing research of Aimée Little provides a substantial review of the role of lithic technologies in subsistence and craft activities,[17] however, in advance of full publication, this material is not reviewed in detail here.

---

[15] Aimée Little, 'Fishy settlement patterns and their social significance: a case study from the northern Midlands of Ireland', in Sinead McCartan, Rick Schulting, Graeme Warren and Peter Woodman (eds), *Mesolithic horizons: papers presented at the Seventh International Conference on the Mesolithic in Europe, Belfast 2005* (Oxford, 2009), vol. 1, 698–705.

[16] Peter Woodman and Elizabeth Anderson, 'The Irish Later Mesolithic: a partial picture', in Pierre Vermeersch and Philip Van Peer (eds), *Contributions to the Mesolithic in Europe* (Leuven, 1990), 377–87.

[17] See www.york.ac.uk/archaeology/staff/research-staff/aimee-little/ (22 February 2015).

An overview of the evidence for woodland disturbance and management has recently been presented by Graeme Warren *et al.*[18] and is not repeated here.

Tim Denham argued that the global study of early agriculture and the transformation of food at this time had been revolutionised by microfossil and molecular techniques.[19] Unfortunately, such techniques are still rare in Ireland.[20] ZooMS (ZooArchaeology by Mass Spectrometry) provides genus or species identification of small fragmentary bone[21] but has not, to my knowledge, been applied in Ireland. Little use is made of starch or phytolith data,[22] whilst the absence of ceramics means that some residue/lipid approaches are not available. Increasing application of innovative field and laboratory analyses over the next decade will transform the evidence for Mesolithic foodways in Ireland.

Are you what you eat? Evidence for diets from human bones

Direct chemical analysis of human bones from Mesolithic Ireland indicates that different people ate varied diets (Fig. 2, Table 1). $\delta13C$ values provide a crude approximation of the source of the dietary protein, with values of *c.* -12% $\delta13C$ purely marine and *c.* -20% purely terrestrial.[23] Interpretation of this data is difficult, especially when freshwater fish are involved in the diet.[24] Twelve Mesolithic human individuals have been analysed, with the age of individuals from Sramore, Co. Leitrim, and Stoney Island, Co. Galway, contentious.[25] Taken at face value, the data suggests diversity in diet. Some individuals, whose bones were deposited near the coast, had diets with a very significant emphasis

---

[18] Warren *et al.*, 'The potential role of humans in structuring the wooded landscapes of Mesolithic Ireland'.

[19] Tim Denham, 'Early agriculture: recent conceptual and methodological developments', in Tim Denham and Peter White (eds), *The emergence of agriculture: a global view*, One World Archaeology Readers (London, 2007), 1–25: 11ff.

[20] Graeme Warren, 'The adoption of agriculture in Ireland: perceptions of key research challenges', *Journal of Archaeological Method and Theory* 20 (2013), 525–51.

[21] Michael Buckley, Matthew Collins, Jane Thomas-Oates and Julie C. Wilson, 'Species identification by analysis of bone collagen using matrix-assisted laser desorption/ionisation time-of-flight mass spectrometry', *Rapid Communications in Mass Spectrometry* 23:23 (2009), 3,843–54.

[22] James Eogan, 'Back to the old grindstone', *Seanda* 3 (2008), 60–1 for a Late Neolithic case study.

[23] Reliable nitrogen values are not available in the public domain and are therefore not discussed here.

[24] Christopher Meiklejohn and Peter Woodman, 'Radiocarbon dating of Mesolithic human remains in Ireland', *Mesolithic Miscellany* 22 (2012), 22–41: 23, describe the 'confounding issues' of interpretation.

[25] The Sramore and Stoney Island burials are discussed by Meiklejohn and Woodman, 'Radiocarbon dating of Mesolithic human remains in Ireland', 33. The Sramore individual is considered to lie on a Mesolithic/Neolithic interface and, as it lacks any other archaeological context cannot be safely assigned to either period. The Stoney Island individual has returned a range of incompatible dates from the Mesolithic and the end of the fifth millennium. Meiklejohn and Woodman urge caution in considering its date. Both sites are included here but demarcated by colour in Figure 2.

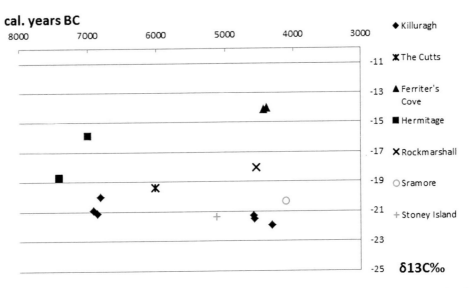

Fig. 2—δ13C‰ from Mesolithic (black) and possibly Mesolithic (grey) human skeletal materials in Ireland. All data from Christopher Meiklejohn and Peter C. Woodman, 'Radiocarbon dating of Mesolithic human remains in Ireland', *Mesolithic Miscellany* 22 (2012), 22–41, with the exception of Stoney Island and Sramore, both pers. comm. Thomas Kador. Dates are midpoints of calibrated ranges with no correction for marine-reservoir effect: individuals with significant marine components in their diets are likely to be younger than these dates by *c.* 300–400 years. For discussion of the controversial dates of Sramore and Stoney Island, please see footnote 25.

on marine resources (Ferriter's Cove), but other bones from similar locations, such as the individual whose femur was found in the Rockmarshall, Co. Louth, midden, had a mix of terrestrial and marine proteins. A Mesolithic dog from Dalkey Island, Co. Dublin (henceforth, 'Dalkey'), had a strongly marine diet (–13.71‰ δ13C, even more marine-based than the Ferriter's Cove

TABLE 1—Data used in the construction of Figure 1.

Site name	Lab. code	C14 age	Error	δ13C‰
(The) Cutts	UB-7562	7157	43	−19.4
Ferriter's Cove	OxA-4918	5545	65	−14
Ferriter's Cove	OxA-5570	5590	60	−14.1
Hermitage	Beta-214237	8070	40	−15.9
Hermitage	Beta-214236	8350	40	−18.7
Killuragh	OxA-6749	5455	50	−21.9
Killuragh	GrA-27180	5700	40	−21.5
Killuragh	OxA-6752	5725	55	−21.3
Killuragh	GrA-2433	7880	60	−20
Killuragh	GrA-27215	7955	45	−21.1
Killuragh	GrA-2434	8030	60	−20.9
Rockmarshall	OxA-4604	5705	75	−18.1
Sramore	UB-15772	5227	36	−20.4
Stoney Island	UB-15765	6168	31	−21.4

individuals).[26] However, individuals from inland contexts, including those from Killuragh Cave, Co. Limerick, the Cutts, Co. Derry, and possibly Sramore and Stoney Island, show little evidence for marine influence. It is important to note that the remains of the individual from the Cutts is an ulna sharpened into a bone point:[27] the relationship between place and context of deposition of human remains and the life of an individual may be very complex.

Given the small sample size, it is difficult to assess whether meaningful trends exist across time and space or between individuals in this data. In 1999 the data available meant that Peter Woodman was able to ask 'was it actually possible for some Mesolithic communities to subsist exclusively in the interior of Ireland?';[28] it now appears that some were not reliant on marine foods.

Leftovers: evidence from plant and animal remains

The following sections review data for the use of plants and animals, based on a systematic review of faunal remains. Data on plants was recently reviewed by Meriel McClatchie and is summarised here.[29] Important assemblages from Baylett, Co. Donegal, and Derragh, Co. Longford, are still undergoing analysis and are not considered in detail. All identifications are taken from the original reports unless otherwise stated. Many of these data are from older excavations. Dalkey is especially problematic in terms of its chronology and is only included here as a 'possible' example unless individual bones have been dated. Data are presented in Tables 2–5 and the appendix.

Mammals

Ireland was an island in the early Holocene and its native flora and fauna is restricted in diversity in comparison to other parts of Europe. This includes large mammal species, such as red deer (*Cervus elaphus*)[30] and auroch (wild cattle, *Bos primigenius*), which were important parts of the Mesolithic diet elsewhere. Milner lists twelve non-domesticated fauna from Star Carr, northern England,[31] in contrast to the six species identified from Ireland (Table 2, one of which is a marine species, and would not have been found at Star Carr). The limited range of mammals in Table 2 partly reflects the fact that the earlier excavations that form a key part of the Mesolithic record in Ireland rarely

---

[26] Peter Woodman, 'Ireland's place in the European Mesolithic: why it's ok to be different', in McCartan *et al.* (eds), *Mesolithic horizons*, xxxvi–xlvi: xl.

[27] Meiklejohn and Woodman, 'Radiocarbon dating of Mesolithic human remains in Ireland', 27.

[28] Peter Woodman, Elizabeth Anderson and Nyree Finlay, *Excavations at Ferriter's Cove, 1983–95: last foragers, first farmers in the Dingle Peninsula* (Bray, 1999), 143.

[29] Warren *et al.*, 'The potential role of humans in structuring the wooded landscapes of Mesolithic Ireland', 632–4.

[30] Ruth Carden, Allan D. McDevitt, Frank E. Zachos, *et al.*, 'Phylogeographic, ancient DNA, fossil and morphometric analyses reveal ancient and modern introductions of a large mammal: the complex case of red deer (*Cervus elaphus*) in Ireland', *Quaternary Science Reviews* 42 (2012), 74–84.

[31] Milner, 'Subsistence', 72.

TABLE 2—Mammal remains from Irish Mesolithic sites.[a]

Species		Bay Farm	Belderrig	Castleroe	Clowanstown 1	Cushendun-Deposit E	Ferriter's Cove	Kilnatierney	Lough Boora	Mount Sandel	Moynagh Lough	Rocknmarshall	Sutton	Dalkey Island (possible)
Indet.														
Boar	*Sus scrofa*		P	P	P	P	A	P	A	A	P	?	P	*P*
Grey seal	*Halichoerus gryphus*											?		*P*
Brown bear	*Ursus arctos*										P			*?*
Otter	*Lutrinae*										P			
Wild cat	*Felis sylvestris*								P					
Hare	*Lepus capensis*						P			P	P		C	
Domesticates?														
Cow	*Bos*				?		P							*P*
Sheep	*Ovis aries*						P							*P*
Dog	*Canis familiaris*								P	P		P	P	*P*
Indet.		P												
Cetaceans														
Dolphin												P		*P*
Porpoise	*Phocoena phocoena*											P		

Abbreviations: A = abundant (*n* >2, 30–100%), C = common (*n* >2, 10–29%), Indet. = indeterminate, P = present (<10%, or frequency not specified).

[a] For references for sites and discussion of any "?" attributions in the table, see the appendix. Note that the boar and seal from Dalkey Island are directly dated; all other Dalkey evidence is only possibly Mesolithic and is highlighted in italics.

TABLE 3—Bird remains from Irish Mesolithic sites.[a]

Species	Family/Order		Castleroe	Ferriter's Cove	Lough Boora	Mount Sandel	Rockmarshall	Sutton	Dalkey Island (possible)
Bird (indet.)			P	P			P	P	*P*
Golden/white-tailed eagle	Accipitridae	*Aquila chrysaetos/Haliaeetus albicilla*				P			*P*
Goshawk	Accipitridae	*Accipiter gentilis*				P			*P*
Teal/garganey	Anatidae	*A. crecca/A. querquedula*			P	P			
Mallard	Anatidae	*Anas platyrhynchos*			P	C			
Wigeon	Anatidae	*Anas penelope*				P			
Ducks (indet.)	Anatidae	*Anatidae*							*P*
Guillemot	Charadriiformes	*Uria aalgae*		P					
Razorbill/guillemot	Charadriiformes	*Alca torda/Uria aalge*							*P*
Puffin	Charadriiformes	*Fratercula arctica*							*P*
Herring gull	Charadriiformes	*Larus argentatus*		P					
Rock dove	Columbidae	*Columba livia*				?			
Wood pigeon	Columbidae	*Columba palumbus*			A	A			
Jay	Corvidae	*Garullus glandiarus*			C				
Peregrine	Falconiformes	*Falco peregrinus*			P				
Red-throated diver	Gaviidae	*Gavia stellata*				P			
Passerine (indet.)	Passeriformes			P					*P*
Thrush	Passeriformes	*Turdus sp.*			P	C			
Coot	Rallisae	*Fulica atra*				P			
Woodcock	Scolopacidae	*Scolopax rusticola*				C			
Snipe	Scolopacidae	*Gallinago gallinago*				C			
Owls	Strigiformes	*Tytonisa/Strigidae*			P				
Gannet	Sulidae	*Sula bassana*		P					
Grouse	Tetraonidae	*Lagopus/Lyrurus*			P	P			
Capercaillie	Tetraonidae	*Tetrao urogallus*				P			

Abbreviations: A = abundant (*n* > 2, 30–100%), C = common (*n* > 2, 10–29%); indet. = indeterminate, P = present (<10%, or frequency not specified).

[a] For references for sites and discussion of any "?" attributions in the table, see the appendix. Note that the boar and seal from Dalkey Island are directly dated; all other Dalkey evidence is only possibly Mesolithic and is highlighted in italics.

recovered evidence of smaller animals, but also indicates both the impoverished range of native mammalian fauna in Ireland.

As noted above, boar was most likely introduced into Ireland by Mesolithic communities and appears to have been an important food, being present on all sites where species identifications were possible. The age and sex of boar faunal assemblages indicates some form of selective hunting or management of the 'wild' boar population.[32] Recent ancient DNA work has shown that supposedly 'wild' boars from fifth millennium Ertebølle hunter-gatherer contexts in Northern Germany were actually from domesticated pigs

---

[32] Finbar McCormick, 'Mammal bone studies from prehistoric Irish sites', in Eileen M. Murphy and Nicki J. Whitehouse (eds), *Environmental archaeology in Ireland* (Oxford, 2007), 77–101: 79–82.

TABLE 4—Fish from Mesolithic Ireland.[a]

Species		Belderrig	Castleroe	Liffey Estuary	Cushendun-Deposit E	Ferriter's Cove	Kilnatierney	Lough Boora	Mount Sandel	Moynagh Lough	Newferry	Rockmarshall	Sutton	Dalkey Island (possible)
Fish (indet.)														
Bass	*Dicentrarchus labrax*			P									P	*P*
Cod family	*Gadidae*	P	P		P	C			P					
Conger eel	*Conger conger*	C	P		P	P								
Eel	*Anguilla anguilla*					P		A	P		P			
Flatfish, right sided	*Pleuronectidae*													
Flatfish, small	*Pleurovectus platbessa,* possibly *Solea?*						C					P		
Flatfish, tope	*Pleurotremata (? Galeus)*					P			P			P		*P*
Flatfish, plaice/flounder	*Pleuronectes platessal Platichthys flesus*													
Gurnards	*Triglidae*					P								
Haddock	*Melanogrammus aeglefinus*					P								
Herring	*Clupea harangus*					P								
Ling	*Molva molva*					P								
Mullet	*Mugil sp.*					P						P		*P*
Perciformes order		C												
Saithe	*Pollachius virens*	(p)	P			P								
Salmonids											P			
Salmon	*Salmo salar*					P			A					
Trout	*Salmo trutta*							A	A					
Sand eel	*Ammodytidae*						P							
Scad	*Trachurus trachurus*					P								
Sea bass	*Dicentrarchus labrax*													
Sea bream/porgies	*Sparidae*					P								
Shark-type species	*Elasmobranches*					P								
Thornback ray	*Raja clavata*					P								
Whiting	*Merlangius merlangus*					A								
Wrasse	*Labridae*	C				A	A							*P*

Abbreviations: A = abundant (*n* > 2, 30–100%), C = common (*n* > 2, 10–29%), indet. = indeterminate. P = present (< 10%, or frequency not specified). (p) = possible.
[a] For references for sites and discussion of any '?' attributions in the table, see the appendix. Note that the boar and seal from Dalkey Island are directly dated; all other Dalkey evidence is only possibly Mesolithic and is highlighted in italics.

TABLE 5—Shellfish species recorded from more than one site.[a]

Species		Ferriter's Cove	Glendhu	Kilnatierney	Rockmarshall	Sutton	Dalkey Island (possible)
Saddle oyster	Anomia ephippium			P	P	P	P
Whelk	Buccinum undatum			P	P	P	
Cockle	Cerastoderma edule	P	P	P	P	P	P
Variegated scallop	Chlamys varia			P	P	P	
Razor clam	Ensis/Solen sp.			P	P	P	
Top shell	Gibbula magus tuberculata/pennanti/umbilicalis	P				P	
Periwinkle	Littorina littorea	P		A	C	P	P
Flat periwinkle	Littorina obtusata	P		P		P	P
Thick top shell	Monodonta lineata			P		P	P
Mussel	Mytilus edulis	P		P	P	P	
Netted dog whelk	Nassarius reticulatus	P			P	P	
Dog whelk	Nucella lapillus	P		P	P	P	P
Sting winkle	Ocenebra erinacea	P			P	P	
Oyster	Ostrea edulis	P	P	A	C	P	P
Carpet shell	Tapes decussates/Paphia decussata	P		P	C	P	
Limpet	Patella vulgata	A		P	P	P	A
Great scallop	Pecten maximus			P	P	P	P

Abbreviations: A = abundant ($n > 2$, 30–100%), C = common ($n > 2$, 10–29%); P = present (0–10% or unspecified).
[a] For references for sites see the appendix. Note that the boar and seal from Dalkey Island are directly dated; all other Dalkey evidence is only possibly Mesolithic and is highlighted in italics.

exchanged with LinearBandKeramik farmers.[33] Given evidence for the import of domesticated cattle to Ireland in the late fifth millennium and that some of the later Mesolithic boar from Moynagh Lough, Co. Meath, have previously been argued to be similar in size to large domesticated pigs,[34] it is possible that some of the boar present in later Mesolithic contexts may also be domesticated not wild.

Dalkey is the only site with evidence for seal, despite many sites being located in areas where seals are common today. The absence of evidence for seal may reflect specific seasonal use of individual sites at times when seals were not present[35] but it provides a very strong contrast with Mesolithic Scotland, where

[33] Ben Krause-Kyora, C. Makarewicz, A. Evin, *et al.*, 'Use of domesticated pigs by Mesolithic hunter-gatherers in northwestern Europe', *Nature Communications* 4 (2013) 1–7.
[34] Finbar McCormick, 'Hunting wild pig in the Late Mesolithic', in Helen Roche, E. Grogan, J. Bradley, *et al.* (eds), *From megaliths to metals: essays in honour of George Eogan* (Oxford, 2004), 1–5: 3.
[35] Woodman *et al.*, *Excavations at Ferriter's Cove*, 136.

some sites show heavy exploitation of seals, including examples where just the skin and fat were used.[36]

Hare is found on three sites and at Moynagh the skeletal evidence suggests that it was used primarily for meat, not furs.[37] Otter and wild cat are also present on individual sites.

Bear was found at Moynagh Lough (and possibly Dalkey); at Moynagh Lough, Finbar McCormick describes marrow extraction from bear bones and raises the possibility that just skins and paws were present.[38] It is interesting that bears appear to have been eaten. Bears were the largest and most dangerous animals in Mesolithic Ireland, and hunting, killing and dismembering one was not a trivial task. It is worth considering why bear was being consumed, assuming that this may have been driven by more than simple calorific need and that there were easier meals available. In many cultures, eating food is considered a way of taking on, or embodying, some of the properties of the substance consumed. Given that there is evidence of captive bears in Mesolithic Europe and that bear may also have played an important role in symbolic understandings of the world,[39] it is possible that consuming bear was a way of people taking on the behavioural properties (strength, power, etc.) of the bear.

A small number of bones of domesticates are present. Dog is assumed not to have been part of the diet, and may have served a number of functional and symbolic roles in Mesolithic society. Cattle bones at Ferriter's Cove are argued to represent contact with Neolithic communities. A limb bone shaft from Sutton, Co. Dublin, dating to *c.* 5600 cal BC had originally been identified as *Bos* but Woodman *et al.* argue that as this is unlikely to be a date for native *Bos primigenius*, that it is most likely a misidentification and that the bone may have come from a bear.[40] They also raise the possibility that it was a 'chance incursion of an auroch from Wales'. This might be evidence of the importation of unusual food and this bone would be an interesting candidate for ZooMS analysis.

There is limited evidence for use of cetaceans: a porpoise mandible from Rockmarshall, a cetacean bone from Bay Farm, Co. Antrim, and a dolphin from Dalkey (not certainly Mesolithic). Van Wijngaard-Bakker records

---

[36] Clive Bonsall and Catriona Pickard, 'A different kettle of fish: food diversity in Mesolithic Scotland', in Dave Collard, Jim Morris and Elisa Perego (eds), *Food & Drink in Archaeology 3* (Totnes, Devon, 2012), 76–88: 85.

[37] McCormick, 'Hunting wild pig in the Late Mesolithic', 3.

[38] McCormick, 'Hunting wild pig in the Late Mesolithic', 4.

[39] Louis Chaix, A. Bridault and R. Picavet, 'A tamed brown bear (*Ursus arctos* L.) of the Late Mesolithic from La Grande-Rivoire (Isère, France)?', *Journal of Archaeological Science* 24 (1997) 1,067–74; Peter Jordan, *Material culture and sacred landscape: the anthropology of the Siberian Khanty* (London 2003).

[40] Peter Woodman, Margaret McCarthy and Nigel Monaghan, 'The Irish quaternary fauna project', *Quaternary Science Reviews* 16:2 (1997), 129–59: 155.

cetaceans from Curran Point, Co. Antrim, but Movius states that these are derived.[41] This is in contrast to Scotland, where whale bones are presumed to indicate the consumption of stranded, not hunted, whales.[42]

Birds

Bird remains have been found mixed with other animal bones on a number of sites (Table 3) and are assumed to have been eaten because of the ways they have been processed or discarded.[43] Sometimes they seem to have made only a minor contribution to the diet,[44] but this is not always the case. Many are good food;[45] pigeons, woodcock and snipe or the ducks from Mount Sandel and Lough Boora, Co. Offaly, for example. Grouse and capercaillie are also good eating, but are also aggressive and visually striking birds, especially the violent and territorial capercaillies. Gannets and guillemots have been eaten historically and gannet fat has medicinal purposes. Whilst there is no direct evidence for the use of bird eggs, eggs are nutritious and can be abundant.

Whilst it is problematic to use the modern abundance of birds as a guide to the early Holocene, some of the species are likely to have been rare. Birds of prey at Mount Sandel and Lough Boora (as well as possibly at Dalkey) include owls, large eagles and peregrine falcons. Birds of prey are not usually considered good eating (although young eagles are sometimes considered edible) but are visually striking and hold strong symbolic associations. Owls were especially rare in Ireland because of the paucity of small mammals,[46] and the presence of one at Lough Boora is therefore notable. The owl has been described as having a 'universal' association as an 'emblem of malevolence and death'.[47] The peregrine falcon's 'exceptional proficiency and strength as a predator'[48] has long been recognised. The white-tailed eagle is the largest eagle in Europe and is surprisingly common in archaeological assemblages: it is the second most common bird on Mesolithic and Neolithic sites of the Rhine basin, where it was

---

[41] Louise van Wijngaarden-Bakker, 'Faunal remains and the Irish Mesolithic', in Clive Bonsall (ed.), *The Mesolithic in Europe: papers presented at the third international symposium, Edinburgh 1985* (Edinburgh, 1990), 125–33; Hallum Movius, 'Curran Point, Larne, County Antrim: the type site of the Irish Mesolithic', *Proceedings of the Royal Irish Academy* 56C (1953–4), 1–195: 169, fn1.

[42] Bonsall and Pickard, 'A different kettle of fish', 85.

[43] See, for example, Wijngaarden-Bakker, 'Faunal remains and the Irish Mesolithic'; see also Woodman *et al.*, *Excavations at Ferriter's Cove*, 90.

[44] Woodman *et al.*, *Excavations at Ferriter's Cove*, 92.

[45] Historical and comparative data on birds, their uses and folklore from Mark Cocker and Richard Mabey, *Birds Brittanica* (London, 2005).

[46] Derek Yalden and Robert Carthy, 'The archaeological record of birds in Britain and Ireland compared: extinctions or failures to arrive?', *Environmental Archaeology* 9 (2004), 123–6: 125.

[47] Cocker and Mabey, *Birds Brittanica*, 283.

[48] Cocker and Mabey, *Birds Brittanica*, 146.

used for awls, beads and pendants.[49] A white-tailed eagle from Hüde I, Germany, developed *periostitis ossificans*—a form of osteomyelitis—from the repeated plucking of feathers from its tail: this is presumably a captive or tamed bird.[50] Sea eagles were also used in the Neolithic of Orkney, Scotland, famously from the 'Tomb of the Eagles' at Isbister, but also placed in the closure deposits of a settlement at Links of Noltland. Luc Amkreutz and Raymond Corbey argue that most of the use of the eagle relates to its powerful symbolic importance and association with hunting. It is not clear that birds of prey were eaten in Mesolithic Ireland, but their presence in faunal assemblages certainly raises that possibility (it is possible that these birds were present as tamed/ captive individuals). Given the rarity of these birds, their likely symbolic importance, as well as the lack of historic consumption of these animals, it is possible that consuming these birds was more a way of consuming their behavioural and symbolic characteristics (possibly including their prowess as hunters, as swift and sharp-eyed, as dangerous) than their calorific value. As such, they point towards complex cultural understandings of what food is.

The significant presence of the jay at Lough Boora should be noted. Jays are not regarded as good eating, but have long been kept as pets: like many corvids they are intelligent, communicative birds. Their distinctive plumage is one of the most bright and distinctive among native birds and has been widely exploited for varied decorative and functional purposes, especially the azure primary coverts 'which were particularly popular with Irish salmon fisher-men'.[51]

Fish

Mesolithic sites are often located in lacustrine or riverine settings, which, coupled with the restricted terrestrial fauna of Ireland, led to emphasis on the significance of fishing: the so-called 'fish and flake' narratives of Mesolithic Ireland.[52] A range of fish (freshwater, marine and anadromous) has been identified from Irish Mesolithic sites (Table 4). Given the variation in the numbers of bones in different species of fish it can be problematic to equate an abundance of bones with the importance of the species[53] but some patterns are apparent.

In common with the terrestrial fauna, a comparatively small number of freshwater fish colonised Ireland in the Holocene, with many species important

---

[49] Luc Amkreutz and Raymond Corbey, 'An eagle-eyed perspective: *Haliaeetus albicilla* in the Mesolithic and Neolithic of the Lower Rhine area', in Harry Fokkens, Bryony Coles, Annelou van Gijn and Jos Kleijne (eds), *Between foraging and farming: an extended broad spectrum of papers presented to Leendeert Louwe Kooijmans*, Annalecta Praesitorica Leidensia 40 (Leiden, 2008), 167–81.
[50] Amkreutz and Corbey, 'An eagle-eyed perspective', 173.
[51] Cocker and Mabey, *Birds Brittanica*, 399.
[52] Little, 'Fishy settlement patterns and their social significance'.
[53] Woodman *et al.*, *Excavations at Ferriter's Cove*, 87.

elsewhere in Europe, such as pike, absent.[54] The 27 different fish species identified in Mesolithic contexts in Ireland compares to 48 from Mesolithic Denmark and 50 from Mesolithic Portugal.[55] In general, the diversity of fish species reflects the diversity of habitats—sometimes very local to the site: at Belderrig, for example, conger eel and ballan wrasse are still fished from rocky pools immediately beside the site. In keeping with other areas of north-western Europe, most of the fish data implies in-shore fishing using nets or traps rather than deep-sea fishing.[56] Some riverine fish appear to have been particularly important resources, especially migratory salmonids and eels.

Molluscs

A wide range of species have been recovered, and Table 5 simplifies this by presenting only those species found on more than one site. Shellfish are sometimes assumed to provide dietary variation, in terms of vitamins and minerals, rather than forming a staple,[57] but also provided a seasonally predictable and easily harvested resource. Different sites have different combinations of shellfish, reflecting variation in local environments. Oysters, limpets, periwinkles and carpet shells were key species, supplemented by others: for example, oyster, periwinkle and mussel were significant at Baylett.[58]

Land snails were recovered from Kilnatierney, Co. Down, and may also have formed a useful resource, with some recent claims that they were deliberately farmed by Mesolithic communities.[59]

Plants

The potential significance of plants as a foodstuff for Mesolithic communities has been downplayed. Changing sampling strategies and analytical methodologies are leading to a realisation that plants were an important part of the diet

---

[54] Sheila Hamilton-Dwyer, 'Exploitation of birds and fish in historic Ireland: a brief review of the evidence', in Murphy and Whitehouse (eds), *Environmental archaeology in Ireland*, 102–18.

[55] Igor Gutiérrez-Zugasti, S. Andersen, A. C. Araújo, *et al.*, 'Shell midden research in Atlantic Europe: state of the art, research problems and perspectives for the future', *Quaternary International* 239 (2011), 70–85: 81.

[56] Catriona Pickard and Clive Bonsall, 'Deep-sea fishing in the European Mesolithic: fact or fantasy?', *European Journal of Archaeology* 7 (2004) 273–90.

[57] Emily Murray, 'Molluscs and middens: the archaeology of "Ireland's early savage race"?', in Murphy and Whitehouse (eds), *Environmental archaeology in Ireland*, 119–35.

[58] Nicky Milner and Peter Woodman, 'Deconstructing the myths of Irish shell middens', in Nicky Milner, Oliver Edward Craig and Geoff Bailey (eds), *Shell middens in Atlantic Europe* (Oxford, 2007), 101–10.

[59] Adele Grindon and Angus Davison, 'Irish *Cepaea nemoralis* land snails have a cryptic Franco-Iberian origin that is most easily explained by the movements of Mesolithic humans', *PLoS ONE* 8:6 (2013), e65792.

for Mesolithic communities: for example in the 'hazelnut economy' of northern Germany.[60] The archaeobotanical evidence for the exploitation of plants in Mesolithic Ireland is more extensive and richer than is widely supposed and demonstrates that a wide variety of nuts, roots, fruits and seeds were utilised.[61]

Hazelnuts (*Corylus avellana*) are found frequently in large quantities, and whilst taphonomic factors may potentially overemphasize the role of hazelnuts, they are known to have formed a very significant resource in other parts of Europe. Fruits, including pears/apples (*Pyrus/Malus* spp.), crowberries (*Empetrum nigrum*), blackberries (*Rubus fruticosus*) and guelder rose berries (*Viburnum opulus*) would have provided important seasonal variation. White water-lily (*Nymphaea alba*) and yellow water-lily (*Nuphar lutea*) seeds are present on a number of sites, sometimes in significant quantities, and could have been eaten in a variety of ways (see below). Tubers include the lesser celandine (*Ranunculus ficaria*) and members of the sedge (*Cyperaceae*) family. Seeds of vetches/peas (*Vicia/Lathyrus* spp.), cleavers (*Galium aparine*) and bedstraws (*Galium* spp.) are also present. There is no evidence for the collection of seaweed, unlike in Scotland,[62] but the small number of modern archaeological analyses of shell assemblages which may provide proxy evidence for seaweed exploitation should be noted.

The experience of food: from procurement to discard

Having considered the range of foodstuffs available, we can consider something of the experience of food. Much of what archaeologists discuss is rather abstracted from the immediate sensual experience of food. As Nicky Milner comments, our accounts are often oddly sterile: 'with no rare steaks or sizzling fat'.[63] The experience of food would have varied through the seasons and through the life of an individual. Mesolithic food in Ireland was highly seasonally varied—with particular tastes most likely strongly associated with particular times. Food also changed over the human lifetime, including key nutritional changes such as weaning, or changes in diets associated with rites of passage or movement between communities. Periods of sharp dietary stress were probably common. Some, at least, of these lifetime experiences of food can be approached through skeletal and chemical analysis, and this should be a priority for future research. We can also approach the experience of food through considering the sequence of activity involving food—from

---

[60] Daniela Holst, 'Hazelnut economy of early Holocene hunter-gatherers: a case study from Mesolithic Duvensee, northern Germany', *Journal of Archaeological Science* 37 (2010), 2,871–80; Steven Mithen, Nyree Finlay, Wendy Carruthers, *et al.*, 'Plant use in the Mesolithic: evidence from Staosnaig, Isle of Colonsay, Scotland', *Journal of Archaeological Science* 28:3 (2001), 223–34.

[61] Warren *et al.*, 'The potential role of humans in structuring the wooded landscapes of Mesolithic Ireland', 632–4; see also Rachel Maclean, 'Eat your greens: an examination of the potential diet available in Ireland during the Mesolithic', *Ulster Journal of Archaeology* 56 (1993) 1–8.

[62] Bonsall and Pickard, 'A different kettle of fish', 82–3; Woodman *et al.*, *Excavations at Ferriter's Cove*, 100.

[63] Milner, 'Subsistence', 77.

procurement, production, consumption and finally deposition. Different aspects of the *chaîne opératoire* of food[64] are sometimes hard to differentiate, and are treated here as heuristics.

Food procurement

Trapping, hunting or collecting has been prominent in the literature in a general sense. However, there are also more intimate glimpses of food procurement: the evidence for torches in association with fishing locations for example at Derragh and Clowanstown, Co. Meath, perhaps suggesting 'burning the water'—using torches at night to bring eels or salmon to the surface.[65] At Ferriter's Cove, limpets were collected at full moon and the selection of only larger oysters at Kilnatierney suggests either collection at the lowest of tides, or wading or diving.[66] Here the link between the tides and food procurement reminds us that aspects of food procurement, and therefore social life were structured around the temporality of tides, and ultimately the moon, not just day and night.[67]

The evidence is silent about the moments of capture: the death throes of a fish drawn from water, or the struggles with a bear or boar. There is substantial evidence, however, of investment of time and labour in preparing equipment for food procurement, especially in terms of fishing. There is evidence for the use of nets, hooks, spears, boats and traps. Many of these would have been time-consuming articles to manufacture, especially those involving cordage, and preparing for food procurement would have been a key task for many individuals. Far from being 'parasites', or 'easily content', Mesolithic communities in Ireland spent considerable periods of time developing technologies and resources that allowed them to procure food.

The procurement of food also generated senses of time. The preparation of hazel weirs for trapping fish on the River Liffey, Co. Dublin,[68] was an investment of time and energy in selecting and felling the appropriate stakes and weaving them together. The stakes themselves resulted from opportunistic coppicing—long-term patterns of returning to the same places and searching

---

[64] Katheryn Twiss, 'The archaeology of food and social diversity', *Journal of Archaeological Research* 20 (2012), 357–95.

[65] Little, 'Fishy settlement patterns and their social significance'.

[66] Woodman *et al.*, *Excavations at Ferriter's Cove*, 100. Emily Murray, 'A late Mesolithic shell midden at Kilnatierney near Greyabbey, Co. Down', *Journal of Irish Archaeology* 20 (2011), 1–18: 13.

[67] Antony Pollard, 'Time and tide: costal environments, cosmology and ritual practice in early prehistoric Scotland', in Antony Pollard and Alex Morrison (eds), *The early prehistory of Scotland* (Edinburgh, 1996), 198–210.

[68] Melanie McQuade and Lorna O'Donnell, 'Late Mesolithic fish traps from the Liffey Estuary, Dublin, Ireland', *Antiquity* 81 (2007), 569–84; Melanie McQuade and Lorna O'Donnell, 'The excavation of Late Mesolithic fish trap remains from the Liffey Estuary, Dublin, Ireland', in McCartan *et al.* (eds), *Mesolithic horizons*, 889–94.

for appropriate sized and shaped pieces of wood.[69] In returning to previously worked woodland, and interacting with a woodland that was already shaped by the actions of previous years and previous generations, people encountered a different sense of time. Placing the traps was often determined by the times of tides. These senses of time and place may have given rise to associations between communities and particular food procurement locations. Woodman suggests that in places with limited access to good fishing grounds '(t)he limiting factor would probably have been points of access, and if "fixed engines" were used then it is possible that each point of access would have been controlled by a small group or even an extended family'.[70] Senses of time and community were generated through food procurement.

Food processing

Once resources were gathered, hunted or collected from traps, they needed to be turned into an edible form. Many resources, of course, required little or no processing—berries munched from the hand; cockles swallowed raw from their shells at Ferriter's Cove; or blood or delicate internal organs taken raw from a steaming corpse. Processing, however, is central to the human experience of food and the transformation of a resource into food and might include butchery or either thermal or non-thermal processing.

Evidence for butchery is comparatively rare. At Moynagh Lough, pig skull cases and bones were being smashed in order to remove the brain and marrow, presumably to eat these fat-rich, nutritious parts. McCormick comments that '(t)he acute fragmentation of the assemblage indicates that a considerable effort was made to remove all edible parts from the carcass'.[71] Tendons were removed, presumably for craft use. At Ferriter's Cove, boar were brought whole to site and then butchered.

Food can be processed through thermal or non-thermal techniques.[72] Non-thermal techniques include pounding and soaking, and can be key to making a resource edible. Sometimes these non-thermal processes were lengthy: water-lily seeds, for example, which are known from a number of Mesolithic sites, would have been soaked for at least two weeks.[73] The significance of non-thermal processing techniques is under-researched, and many coarse stone tools may have played a key role in these tasks.

Thermal processing involves the application of heat, and hearths and evidence of burning are common; from short-term, informal hearths, to highly

---

[69] Warren *et al.*, 'The potential role of humans in structuring the wooded landscapes of Mesolithic Ireland', 635–7.

[70] Peter Woodman, *Excavations at Mount Sandel 1973–77, County Londonderry* (Belfast, 1985), 161.

[71] McCormick, 'Hunting wild pig in the Late Mesolithic', 2.

[72] Rachel Carmody and Richard Wrangham, 'The energetic significance of cooking', *Journal of Human Evolution* 57 (2009), 379–91.

[73] Mears and Hillman, *Wild food*, 126.

structured fire settings, through to clearance and redeposition of residues from fire. Fire could have been used to cook food directly, to smoke it or via a variety of pyrolithic (hot rock) technologies. Alan Hawkes[74] argues that pyrolithic technology was used primarily for dry roasting, baking and sometimes steaming in the latest parts of the Mesolithic, and that large-scale boiling of meat was a key feature of the Neolithic in Ireland. Little has argued that fire-cracked rocks may also have been used in cooking plant food, possibly in formal fire pits, at Clonava Island, Lough Derravaragh, Co. Westmeath.[75] Storage has often been assumed, especially in terms of the smoking of migratory fish such as salmon,[76] and the possibility of storing hazelnuts.[77] Both processes may involve the careful management of fire.

Some sites have formal fireplaces, such as the deep fire pits located centrally within the Mount Sandel buildings. Here, fireplaces appear to have been cleaned and their contents distributed into other pits and features on site (see below for discussion). Informal fire settings are associated with food at a number of sites. At Kilnatierney a simple fire setting comprised a charcoal spread on the surface of an oyster midden that overlay a low subcircular depression, which contained ash, burnt shells and burnt pig and fish bones. Some of the fish were small and are argued to have been cooked on skewers or hot rocks.[78] Similar informal hearths were found in the midden at Rock-marshall and on other sites.

Food processing is sometimes considered in strongly gendered terms. Eileen Murphy's reconstructions of gendered spaces within the Mount Sandel houses, for example, strongly correlates food-processing activities with female space within the building.[79] Nyree Finlay is sharply critical of such approaches, suggesting that they essentialise particular tasks, and fail to consider the more complex ways in which different genders were constructed and maintained through the intersection of many different aspects of activity.[80]

---

[74] Alan Hawkes, 'The beginnings and evolution of the *fulacht fia* tradition in early prehistoric Ireland', *Proceedings of the Royal Irish Academy* 114C (2013), 1–51
[75] Aimée Little, 'Clonava Island revisited: a story of cooking, plants and re-occupation during the Irish Late Mesolithic', *Proceedings of the Royal Irish Academy* 114C (2014), 35–55.
[76] See, for example, extensive discussions in Woodman, *Excavations at Mount Sandel.*
[77] Anne McComb and Derek Simpson, 'The wild bunch: exploitation of the hazel in prehistoric Ireland', *Ulster Journal of Archaeology* 58 (1999), 1–16: Anne McComb, 'The ecology of hazel (*Corylus avellana*) nuts in Mesolithic Ireland', in McCartan *et al.* (eds), *Mesolithic horizons*, 225–33.
[78] Murray, 'A late Mesolithic shell midden at Kilnatierney', 1–18.
[79] Eileen Murphy, 'Possible gender labour divisions at the Mesolthihic site of Mount Sandel, Co. Londonderry, Northern Ireland', *Kvinner Arkeologi Norge* 21 (1996), 103–24.
[80] Nyree Finlay, 'Gender and personhood', in Conneller and Warren (eds), *Mesolithic Britain and Ireland*, 35–60.

Food consumption

Given the social significance of food consumption, it is ironic that our accounts are at their most sterile when it comes to considering the location, context and audience of food consumption. At times the differentiation of procurement, processing and consumption was limited: the simple hearth at Kilnatierney, discussed above, was a place for cooking and eating. At Ferriter's Cove, 'discrete deposits of discarded or burnt shells are associated with the remains of other food waste: dumps of charred hazelnut shells, crab claws and fish bones'[81] are argued to be separate 'snacking events'. But in many cases, the scale and character of the consumption event is unclear. The possibility of feasting in the Mesolithic of Europe has been discussed widely recently,[82] but there is little compelling evidence from Ireland. Sarah Cross argued that Late Mesolithic shell middens were evidence of large scale feasting, with an easily harvested and abundant resource of marine foods facilitating 'large groups of people getting together at the same place for many years and then moving on'. Woodman dismisses this argument, pointing out that many of the hearths at sites like Rockmarshall are small and informal in character rather than being associated with feasting.[83]

Food discard

The discard of food is comparatively well-manifested in the archaeological record, but our approaches to what this evidence represents have sometimes been simplistic. Whilst we have been able to identify spreads and dumps of material containing food waste, as for example in Woodman's highly detailed analyses of Mount Sandel,[84] ethnographic and archaeological approaches have shown that in many cultures, food remains are rarely considered as simply rubbish, and are manipulated and transformed according to complex symbolic schemes and social strategies.[85]

There are hints of structured patterns of activity involving waste. At Kilnatierney, Lough Boora, Moynagh Lough and Mount Sandel, the presence of animal remains in fires, sometimes heavily burnt beyond what seems likely in terms of food preparation, was noted by faunal specialists. Fire therefore appears to have been used as a way of disposing of food waste in both the Early

---

[81] Woodman *et al.*, *Excavations at Ferriter's Cove*, 101.

[82] Preston Miracle, 'Mesolithic meals from Mesolithic middens', in Nicky Milner and Preston Miracle (eds), *Consuming passions and patterns of consumption* (Cambridge, 2002), 65–88; see also Milner, 'Subsistence'.

[83] Sarah Cross, 'Competitive feasting in the Neolithic', *Archaeology Ireland* 15 (2001) 11–13: 11; Peter Woodman, 'Mesolithic middens—from famine to feasting', *Archaeology Ireland* 15 (2001) 32–5:

[84] Woodman, *Excavations at Mount Sandel.*

[85] See Ian McNiven, 'Ritualized middening practices', *Journal of Archaeological Method and Theory* 20 (2013), 552–87.

and Later Mesolithic: and this may be one reason for the dominance of the taphonomically robust charred hazelnut shell. Finlay argues that fire 'played a transformative role in (the) discard practices adopted' in the Mesolithic of Ireland, being part of a 'process of transubstantiation'.[86] The deposition of cremated human bodies at Hermitage, Co. Limerick,[87] provides further evidence of the significance of fire as a transformative element in Mesolithic routines, and makes links between classes of evidence (food remains and the treatment of the human body) that we often keep separate.

Shell middens result from a strategic discard of food remains, but our understandings of the processes of midden formation are still coarse-grained. Few middens have been excavated recently and, as in other areas of Europe, 'many questions remain unanswered' about shell middens.[88] The larger shell middens tend to dominate our understanding, but many middens are smaller, and some sites, such as Ferriter's Cove, are characterised by small, discrete deposits of shells, often < 1m in diameter. Woodman *et al.* comment that 'it may have been more usual to consume smaller quantities of shellfish that did not leave a distinctive archaeological record'.[89] At Ferriter's Cove, some of the larger midden deposits are not just an accumulation of the small events, but have different compositions, and are argued to have resulted from different activity: baiting for fishing, or different groups or contexts for consumption. As Ian McNiven argues, the presence of visible deposits of food waste provides the potential for later action—to add to, or avoid, such areas.[90] Middens arise from decisions about what was appropriate and much more work is needed on Mesolithic shell middens from this perspective. Our very category of shell middens also requires further consideration. Shell middens are a product of particular histories and taphonomic processes, but are linked to Mesolithic 'occupation soils' or 'dumps' and 'spreads', often also including food waste.

Finally, in terms of deposition, we should note that most food that is consumed ends up passing through the human digestive system and needs to be disposed of somewhere. The presence of intestinal parasites at the Mesolithic site of Goldcliff, Wales, has been used as evidence for the existence of toilet areas on site.[91] Cultural attitudes to such food waste are likely to have provided a key structuring principle to the experience of the spaces near where people lived.

---

[86] Finlay, 'Gender and personhood', 52; Nyree Finlay, 'Futile fragments?—some thoughts on microlith breakage patterns', in Nyree Finlay, Sinead McCartan, Nicky Milner and Caroline Wickham-Jones (eds), *From Bann Flakes to Bushmills; papers in honour of Professor Peter Woodman* (Oxford, 2009), 23–30: 24.

[87] Tracy Collins, 'Hermitage, Ireland: life and death on the western edge of Europe', in McCartan *et al.* (eds), *Mesolithic horizons*, 876–9.

[88] Gutiérrez-Zugasti *et al.*, 'Shell midden research in Atlantic Europe', 74, 83.

[89] Woodman *et al.*, *Excavations at Ferriter's Cove*, 136.

[90] McNiven, 'Ritualized middening practices'.

[91] Martin Bell, *Prehistoric coastal communities: the Mesolithic in Western Britain* (York, North Yorks., 2007).

Conclusion

This review has highlighted areas of complexity in our understanding of Mesolithic food; as well as many areas for further research, not least in the application of new approaches in order to increase the data available to us.

Mesolithic diets in Ireland appear to have been varied, although the causes and character of this diversity are not well understood. Some individuals, at least, relied heavily on marine resources, whereas others did not. The potential existence of intercommunity variation, or change across the lifespan of an individual cannot be assessed. Different archaeological sites indicate a reliance on slightly different resources; often reflecting the variation in local environments.

The relative paucity of Ireland's native flora and fauna is manifest in the range of species exploited. This is especially notable in terms of the mammals, particularly large ungulates and aurochs. It is also apparent in the range of fish species present. This lack of diversity must have been a key difference between the Mesolithic experience of food in Ireland and that in other parts of Europe. Put simply, the dietary routine for Mesolithic communities in Ireland was different than their neighbours in Britain and on the continent. Given that these communities were in contact during the Mesolithic, these differences would have been noticed; and given the centrality of food to social life, it is likely that these differences were considered important.

Food-related activities formed the dominant rhythms of Mesolithic lives and may have involved importing and managing resources, it certainly involved substantial investments of time and energy in developing technologies to procure food. Processing and discard practices created particular kinds of places. In some senses then, we can see the actions of Mesolithic communities in Ireland as actively creating particular kinds of food-bearing ecologies. The presence of herring gull, 'arch exploiters of human opportunities',[92] in association with small deposits of shell and animal/fish at Ferriter's Cove, for example, might suggest that the long-term co-evolution of seagull and human habitats.

The procurement of food, its preparation and consumption also generated particular kinds of people. The rhythms of food routines, the associations with place developed through long-term use of resources, shared meals, specific rituals and patterns of discard all generated senses of community, time and space—although these are hard for us to discuss in detail. There are occasional glimpses of Mesolithic world views manifest in our food evidence. The consumption of bear and birds of prey raises the possibility that species were being eaten not just for their calorific content but because they were considered to hold properties that were of value to Mesolithic communities. Far from being 'easily satisfied' by the food available to them, Mesolithic communities in Ireland had rich traditions of food and food-related behaviour.

---

[92] Cocker and Mabey, *'Birds Brittanica'*, 238.

Acknowledgements   Julie Rossi provided invaluable research assistance—I am very grateful for her help. Thanks to Thomas Kador, Aimée Little and Meriel McClatchie for helpful comments on drafts. Thomas Kador also kindly shared data from his Mesolithic skeletal research. Thanks to Chris Meiklejohn and Peter Woodman for discussion and clarification of the isotope data. Lucy Hogan's precise and careful editing greatly improved the text. Despite all of this assistance, any errors, misunderstandings and opinions are solely my responsibility.

Appendix

Bay Farm

Peter Woodman and Gina Johnson, 'Excavations at Bay Farm 1, Carnlough, Co. Antrim and the study of the "Larnian" technology', *Proceedings of the Royal Irish Academy* 96C (1996), 137–235: 187: one cetacean bone. The date is not clearly stated, but as it is distinguished from two bones from 'disturbed levels' it is probably Mesolithic(?).

Belderrig

Unpublished data in the possession of the author.

Castleroe

Peter Woodman, *Excavations at Mount Sandel 1973–77, County Londonderry* (Belfast, 1985).

Clowanstown 1

Matt Mossop and Emma Mossop (eds), 'M3 Clonee—north of Kells. Contract 2 Dunshaughlin—Navan. Report on the archaeological excavation of Clowanstown 1, Co. Meath. Ministerial directions no. A008/011 E3064', unpublished excavation report, 2009. Boar from this context is dated to 4300–4000 cal BC. Bos from Context 17 may be Mesolithic or Neolithic.

Cushendun—Deposit E

Hallam Movius, Knud Jessen, Nora F. McMillan and F. L. W. Richardson, 'An early post-glacial archaeological site at Cushendun, County Antrim', *Proceedings of the Royal Irish Academy* 46C (1940), 34–8.

Dalkey Island

G. D. Liversage, 'Excavations at Dalkey Island, Co. Dublin, 1956–1959', *Proceedings of the Royal Irish Academy* 66C (1968), 53–233; see also Peter Woodman, Margaret McCarthy and Nigel Monaghan, 'The Irish quaternary fauna project', *Quaternary Science Reviews* 16 (1997), 129–59. With the exception of directly dated seal and boar bone (see Woodman *et al.*, 'Irish Quaternary Fauna Project'), data from Dalkey is very hard to confidently assign to a specific period. Bear, possibly, from Dalkey: one bone, initially identified as bear was later argued to be seal (Woodman *et al.*, 'Irish Quaternary Fauna Project'), but there is also an undated bear canine.

Ferriter's Cove

Peter Woodman, Elizabeth Anderson, Nyree Finlay, *Excavations at Ferriter's Cove, 1983–95: last foragers, first farmers in the Dingle Peninsula* (Bray, 1999).

Glendhu

Peter Woodman, 'Excavations at Glendhu, Co. Down', *Ulster Journal of Archaeology* 48 (1985), 31–40.

Kilnatierney

Emily Murray, 'A late Mesolithic shell midden at Kilnatierney near Greyabbey, Co. Down', *Journal of Irish Archaeology* 20 (2011), 1–18.

Liffey Estuary (North Wall Quay)

Melanie McQuade and Lorna O'Donnell, 'Late Mesolithic fish traps from the Liffey Estuary, Dublin, Ireland', *Antiquity* 81 (2007) 569–84.

Lough Boora

Michael Ryan, 'Lough Boora excavations', *An Taisce* 2 (1978), 13–14. Michael Ryan, 'An early Mesolithic site in the Irish midlands', *Antiquity* 54 (1980), 46–7. Louise H. van Wijngaarden-Bakker, 'Faunal remains and the Irish Mesolithic', in C. Bonsall (ed.), *The Mesolithic in Europe: papers presented at the third international symposium, Edinburgh 1985* (Edinburgh, 1990), 125–33.

Moynagh Lough

John Bradley, 'Excavations at Moynagh Lough, County Meath', *Journal of the Royal Society of Antiquaries of Ireland* 121 (1991), 5–26; Finbar McCormick, 'Hunting wild pig in the Late Mesolithic', in Helen Roche, E. Grogan, J. Bradley, *et al.* (eds), *From megaliths to metals: essays in honour of George Eogan* (Oxford, 2004), 1–5.

Newferry

Peter Woodman, 'Recent excavations at Newferry, Co. Antrim', *Proceedings of the Prehistoric Society* 43 (1977), 155–99.

Rockmarshall

Frank Mitchell, 'An early kitchen-midden in County Louth', *Journal of the County Louth Archaeological Society* 11 (1947), 169–74; Frank Mitchell, 'Further early kitchen-middens in County Louth', *Journal of the County Louth Archaeological Society* 12 (1949), 14–20; see also Woodman *et al.*, 'The Irish quaternary fauna project', 129–59. Dog bone from Rockmarshall is a worked bone point. Emily Murray ('Molluscs and middens: the archaeology of "Ireland's early savage race"?', in Eileen Murphy and Nicki Whitehouse (eds), *Environmental archaeology in Ireland* (Oxford, 2007), 119–35) states that seal was recovered from Rockmarshall, but this is not identified in the reports.

Sutton

Frank Mitchell, 'An early kitchen-midden at Sutton, Co. Dublin', *Journal of the Royal Society of Antiquaries of Ireland* 86 (1956), 1–26; see also Woodman *et al.*, 'The Irish quaternary fauna project', 129–59.

The molecules of meals: new insight into Neolithic foodways

JESSICA SMYTH

Department of Archaeology and Anthropology, University of Bristol, Bristol, BS8 1UU, United Kingdom

RICHARD P. EVERSHED

School of Chemistry, University of Bristol, Bristol, BS8 1TH, United Kingdom

[Accepted 14 October 2014. Published 20 April 2015.]

Abstract

Details of daily life such as food and drink can be difficult to capture in prehistory, especially on an island with a temperate climate and covered mainly by acidic soils: plant remains will only survive through charring or water-logging, whilst animal bone frequently dissolves unless calcined. At the molecular level, however, a host of biochemical and isotopic signatures exist indicating what our prehistoric antecedents ate and drank. The most robust of these biomarkers are lipids, commonly found absorbed into the clay matrix of pottery vessels—the residues of meals sometimes many thousands of years old. The wet, acidic conditions that accelerate the decay of so much prehistoric organic matter fortunately preserve these lipid residues exceedingly well. This paper details the results of a recent programme of molecular and compound-specific stable isotope analysis on lipids from nearly 500 Irish Neolithic vessels, providing unparalleled insights into the diet, and food procurement and processing activities of our earliest farming communities.

Introduction

'...the sober fact seems to be that from prehistoric times to the close of the 17th century corn and milk were the mainstay of the national food'.[1] A. T. Lucas's in-depth and scholarly review of Irish food products, quoted above, which has been acknowledged elsewhere in this volume, provides an unparalleled source of inspiration and information for those interested in past foodways and is an obvious starting point for any consideration of food and drink in Ireland. Yet, in terms of prehistory, and the Neolithic in particular, the above was an undeniably lofty claim at the time it was written (in 1960); Lucas had only a

* Author's e-mail: jessica.smyth@bristol.ac.uk

doi: 10.3318/PRIAC.2015.115.07

[1] A. T. Lucas, 'Irish food before the potato', *Gwerin* 3:2 (1960), 8–43.

small pool of published data from which to draw, most notably the important excavations at Lough Gur, Co. Limerick[2] and some early palynological and plant macrofossil work.[3] There could be no way to properly assess whether or not cereals and dairy products were the 'mainstay' of the prehistoric diet, and this is reflected in Lucas's paper—just a few sentences on prehistoric foods in over 30 pages of text.

More than a half a century later, we are much better placed to test the veracity of Lucas's claim or the plant-based component of it at least. Recent research into the nature and timing of agriculture in Ireland has resulted in the collation and analysis of a high resolution data set of Neolithic plant macrofossil remains, currently one of the largest of its type from any individual European country.[4] Issues of taphonomy notwithstanding,[5] a relatively wide range of plant foods have been detected, with early farming communities consuming fruits such as crab apple and blackberry, tubers, leafy greens and flax seeds. Cereal remains were found to be present on more than three quarters of the sites analysed, second only to hazelnut shell fragments in their ubiquity (albeit mostly in small quantities). The data set also highlights interesting regional preferences in cereal cultivation, such as the paucity of einkorn across early Neolithic Ireland, Britain and possibly northern France, an area already argued to be connected on the basis of pottery styles.[6] At a different scale, there is a striking contrast between the preference for emmer wheat on Irish sites and

---

[2] Seán Ó Ríordáin, 'Lough Gur excavations: Neolithic and Bronze Age houses on Knockadoon', *Proceedings of the Royal Irish Academy* 56C (1953/4), 297–459; Gabriel Cooney, 'In Retrospect: Neolithic activity at Knockadoon, Lough Gur, Co. Limerick, 50 years on', *Proceedings of the Royal Irish Academy* 107C (2007), 215–25.

[3] Knud Jessen and Hans Helbaek, 'Cereals in Great Britain and Ireland in prehistoric and early historic times', *Det Kongelige Danske Videnskabernes Selskab Bioligiske Skrifter* 3:2 (1944), 1–68; Hans Helbaek, 'Early crops in southern England', *Proceedings of the Prehistoric Society* 18 (1953), 194–233: 48 ff.

[4] Nicki J. Whitehouse, Rick J. Schulting, Meriel McClatchie, Phil Barratt, T. Rowan McLaughlin, Amy Bogaard, Sue Colledge, Rob Marchant, Joanne Gaffrey and M. Jane Bunting, 'Neolithic agriculture on the western fringes of Europe: a multi-disciplinary approach to the boom and bust of early farming in Ireland', *Journal of Archaeological Science* 51 (2014), 181–205; Meriel McClatchie, Amy Bogaard, Sue Colledge, Nicki J. Whitehouse, Rick J. Schulting, Phil Barratt and T. Rowan McLaughlin, 'Neolithic farming in north-western Europe: archaeobotanical evidence from Ireland', *Journal of Archaeological Science* 51 (2014), 206–15.

[5] The vast majority of plant remains were preserved through charring, with water-logged remains occurring at only three sites.

[6] Alison Sheridan, 'From Picardie to Pickering and Pencraig Hill? New information on the "Carinated Bowl Neolithic" in northern Britain', in Alasdair Whittle and Vicki Cummings (eds), *Going over: the Mesolithic-Neolithic transition in north-west Europe* (Oxford, 2007), 441–92; Alison Sheridan, 'The Neolithisation of Britain and Ireland: the "big picture"', in Bill Finlayson and Graeme Warren (eds), *Landscapes in transition,* Levant Supplementary Series 8 (Oxford and London, 2010), 89–105.

the predominance of barley in Scottish Neolithic assemblages, particularly on sites along the Atlantic coast, which may represent a response to more challenging local growing conditions.[7] Such examples serve as good reminders that food habits can be formed by cultural as well as environmental factors.

In terms of animal products, Lucas was able to point to the consumption of beef in the Neolithic, noting that any attempt to assess the relative importance of meat in prehistory needed to integrate quantification of animal bone with the duration of each site and its likely number of occupants. This sensible observation has remained more or less in the abstract however; while the number of Neolithic sites yielding faunal remains has certainly increased since 1960, the preservation of bone is on the whole extremely poor and few detailed analyses of animal exploitation across different sites and different species can be made.[8] Nevertheless, sufficient faunal remains survived the acidic soil conditions for occasional species identifications to be attempted, confirming the presence of the aforementioned cattle as well as pig and sheep/goat in Ireland. Many of these bone fragments have been recovered from domestic contexts such as house slot trenches and post holes and/or have been subjected to high temperatures, making it likely that food remains are represented. To date, the largest faunal assemblages have been recovered from non-domestic settings and there is some indication that ceremonial events or large gatherings provided the setting for the consumption of large quantities of beef. At Ashleypark, Co. Tipperary, the remains of three mature cattle were found among the stone cairn sealing the burial chamber of a Linkardstown-type burial mound. The bones were disarticulated, in many cases split or broken for marrow extraction, and occasionally displayed butchery marks. These were interpreted as the remains of food consumed during the sealing of the chamber.[9] At Kilshane, Co. Meath, the recent excavation of a small Middle Neolithic enclosure has yielded an assemblage of nearly 4,000 cattle bone specimens from at least 58 animals. The carcasses had been disarticulated and defleshed, providing tonnes of meat, and are thought to have been

---

[7] R. R. Bishop, M. J. Church and Peter Rowley-Conwy, 'Cereals, fruits and nuts in the Scottish Neolithic', *Proceedings of the Society of Antiquaries of Scotland* 135 (2009), 47–103. Emmer wheat was dominant at a number of Early Neolithic rectangular house structures in Scotland. Emmer wheat was also the dominant crop at smaller Early Neolithic Irish rectangular houses.

[8] Finbar McCormick, 'Mammal bone studies from prehistoric Irish sites', in Eileen Murphy and Nicki Whitehouse (eds), *Environmental archaeology in Ireland* (Oxford 2007), 77–101; Rick Schulting, 'On the northwestern fringes: earlier Neolithic subsistence in Britain and Ireland as seen through faunal remains and stable isotopes', in Sue Colledge, James Conolly, Keith Dobney, Katie Manning and Stephen Shennan (eds), *The origins and spread of stock-keeping in the Near East and Europe* (Walnut Creek, CA, 2013), 313–38.

[9] Finbar McCormick, 'The animal bones', in Con Manning, 'A burial mound at Ashleypark, Co. Tipperary', *Proceedings of the Royal Irish Academy* 85C (1985), 61–100: 89–94.

deposited in the enclosure ditch on a few separate occasions over a relatively short period of time.[10]

Fish is all but invisible in Neolithic Ireland. Given the poor preservation of larger and more robust mammal bone, it is perhaps no surprise that there is little direct evidence for the consumption of aquatic resources. Nonetheless, hints of a contribution of aquatic foodstuffs to the diet do occasionally appear in the archaeological record: the Early Neolithic houses at Monanny, Co. Monaghan, for example, were located just metres from a tributary of the River Glyde, part of a river system well known today for its salmon, sea trout, brown trout and eel,[11] and what seems to be a Middle Neolithic fish weir has also recently been recovered from the palaeo-shoreline of the Liffey Estuary.[12]

Currently, the chemical signatures from prehistoric human bone provide the clearest indicator of the types of resources (that is, terrestrial or marine), favoured in the Neolithic. There are bulk carbon and nitrogen stable isotope measurements on over 30 individuals from Ireland[13] and a coherent picture is emerging: there was no significant contribution (i.e. more than *c.* 5–10%) of marine foods to the overall dietary protein intake of Irish Neolithic communities. This does not rule out the periodic use of marine foods, although the fact that a low marine protein contribution—including individuals in coastal locations—contrasts so sharply with the preceding Mesolithic[14] does suggest that attitudes to food shifted dramatically at the advent of farming, something also recorded across Britain.[15]

---

[10] Finbar McCormick, 'The animal bones from Kilshane', in Finola O'Carroll, Matt Seaver, Richard Clutterbuck and Donal Fallon (eds), *The archaeology of the N2 Road Scheme: travels through time from Finglas to Ashbourne* (Dublin, in press).

[11] Fintan Walsh, 'Archaeology of two townlands (part 1): from Stone Age settlers to 19th-century farmers at Monanny and Cloghvally Upper, Co. Monaghan', *Clogher Record* 20 (2011), 500–20.

[12] Melanie McQuade, 'Gone fishin'', *Archaeology Ireland* 22:1 (2008), 8–11; Melanie McQuade, 'Spencer Dock, North Wall Quay, Dublin. Prehistoric fish traps', in Isabel Bennett (ed.), *Excavations 2007: summary accounts of archaeological excavations in Ireland* (Dublin, 2010), 119–20.

[13] Peter Ditchfield, 'Stable isotope analysis', in Ann Lynch (ed.), *Poulnabrone, Co. Clare. Excavation of an Early Neolithic portal tomb* (Dublin, 2014), 86–92; Rick Schulting, Eileen Murphy, Carleton Jones and Graeme Warren, 'New dates from the north, and a proposed chronology for Irish court tombs', *Proceedings of the Royal Irish Academy* 112C (2012), 1–60; Schulting, 'On the northwestern fringes', 327–30. Additional stable isotope analysis of human remains from Knowth is forthcoming.

[14] Peter Woodman, 'The exploitation of Ireland's coastal resources—a marginal resource through time?', in Manuel Ramón González Morales and Geoffrey Clarke (eds), *The Mesolithic of the Atlantic façade* (Tucson, AZ, 2004), 37–55; Schulting, 'On the northwestern fringes', 331. Salmon also has a marine isotopic signal, that is enriched isotope values, and is included as a 'marine food'.

[15] Michael Richards, Rick Schulting and Robert Hedges, 'Sharp shift in diet at onset of Neolithic', *Nature* 425 (2003), 366; Rick Schulting and Michael Richards, 'The wet, the wild and the domesticated: the Mesolithic–Neolithic transition on the west coast of Scotland', *European Journal of Archaeology* 5:2 (2002), 147–89; Rick Schulting and

Food at a
molecular level

These well-established traditions of faunal and plant macrofossil analysis, together with the more recent utilisation of isotope analysis on unburnt human bone, have clearly provided important information on consumption practices in the Neolithic. Nevertheless, the variable survival of prehistoric organic remains (common to most archaeological contexts and regions) and the susceptibility of bone to soil acidity (especially true for Ireland) mean that they can only ever provide a partial picture. How might we go about building on these techniques? Pottery vessels are of course regularly used for storage, cooking and consumption, and it makes sense to scrutinise these more closely for information on past diet.

Potsherds are also a relatively plentiful archaeological resource, and are more easily identified and more likely to be retained during excavation than, for example, plant remains (or soil samples containing plant remains) that can frequently be under-sampled. Another advantage is that pottery is generally diagnostic, whereas animal bone and plant remains first need to be assigned to the Neolithic through direct dating or through association with a secure context of Neolithic date (and even with the latter approach, material can still be found to be intrusive).[16]

The scientific examination of residues adhering to pots was first attempted in the late nineteenth and early twentieth centuries[17] but it was only with the increased refinement of chemical separation and fingerprinting techniques, and in particular the development of compound-specific stable isotope analyses from the 1990s onwards, that the full potential of the molecular information in residues adhering to and absorbed within pottery vessels could be tapped. The hydrophobic nature of lipids means that their susceptibility to decay is small in comparison to other organic molecules and hence organic residue analysis has mainly focused on lipid identification. Lipid molecules survive particularly well when absorbed into the clay matrix of unglazed pottery vessels during the processing of commodities, remaining relatively well protected from microbial attack and degradation over

Michael Richards, 'Radiocarbon dates and stable isotope values on human remains', in Anna Ritchie (ed.), *On the fringe of Neolithic Europe* (Edinburgh, 2009), 67–74. Supporting evidence from zooarchaeological and pottery lipids data is also outlined in Lucy Cramp, Jennifer Jones, Alison Sheridan, Jessica Smyth, Helen Whelton, Jacqui Mulville, Niall Sharples and Richard Evershed, 'Immediate replacement of fishing with dairying by the earliest farmers of the NE Atlantic archipelagos', *Proceedings of the Royal Society* 281B (2014), doi:10.1098/rspb.2013.2372.

[16] See for example, the pea (*Pisum sativum L.*) remains recorded in a Neolithic deposit at Castletown Tara 1, Co. Meath, subsequently dated to the medieval period (see McClatchie, 'Neolithic farming in north-western Europe', 208), and the faunal remains from a number of recently dated Early Neolithic court tombs, all of which yielded determinations falling in the second millennium AD (see Schulting, Murphy, Jones and Warren, 'New dates from the north', 1–60: 9).

[17] See references in Martine Regert, 'Analytical strategies for discriminating archeological fatty substances from animal origin', *Mass Spectrometry Reviews* 30 (2011), 177–220.

archaeological timescales. Even so, experimental work has shown that only a small fraction of the lipid originally absorbed into vessels survives burial.[18] Trace amounts of lipid (>5µg/g potsherd) can nevertheless be analysed in the laboratory. As will be discussed in more detail below, most of the Irish potsherds analysed contained lipid concentrations far in excess of this figure. To successfully identify the original contents of prehistoric pots from these absorbed residues, it is essential that the composition of archaeological lipid mixtures is compared with those from modern reference materials. As such mixtures invariably represent the degraded lipid component of ancient commodities, interpretation must also be based on a sound knowledge of how lipids break down and change over time and with processing (e.g. heating). Extensive experimental work with modern reference materials thus goes hand-in-hand with analysis of archaeological materials.[19] Given the above, what kinds of molecular evidence for food might we expect to recover?

Animal fats

The most common compounds detected in archaeological potsherds are those from degraded animal fats. Fresh animal fats, such as those in meat and milk, are composed almost entirely of triacylglycerols (TAGs), a lipid molecule consisting of three long-chain fatty acids joined to a glycerol 'backbone'. Over time and/or with processing, TAGs break down to diacylglycerols (DAGs), monoacylglycerols (MAGs) and, finally, single chains of free fatty acids, most of which are sixteen or eighteen carbon atoms in length ($C_{16:0}$ and $C_{18:0}$). A degraded animal fat will typically contain low concentrations of TAGs, and slightly higher concentrations of DAGs and MAGs, with $C_{16:0}$ and $C_{18:0}$ fatty acids dominating (Fig. 1). The range of TAGs present in a lipid residue can give an indication of the origin of animal fats, as fresh milk and meat fats are characterised by wide and narrow distributions of TAGs, respectively,[20] although the more robust criterion is to distinguish between fats based on the stable carbon isotope ($\delta^{13}C$) values of their $C_{16:0}$ and $C_{18:0}$ fatty acids. Differences in the diets of ruminant and non-ruminant animals (e.g. cattle,

---

[18] Typically *c.* 1%; Richard Evershed, 'Experimental approaches to the interpretation of absorbed organic residues in archaeological ceramics', *World Archaeology* 40 (2008), 26–47.

[19] Evershed, 'Experimental approaches'; see also references in Jessica Smyth and Richard Evershed, 'Pottery, archaeology and chemistry: contents and context', in Alasdair Whittle and Penny Bickle (eds), *Early farmers: the view from archaeology and science* (London, 2014).

[20] The former typically with TAGs of carbon chain length C_{28}–C_{54}, the latter C_{44}–C_{54}, although the selective decay of shorter-chain TAGs in milk can lead to a distribution of TAGs resembling that of meat fats; Stephanie Dudd and Richard Evershed, 'Direct demonstration of milk as an element of archaeological economies', *Science* 282 (1998), 1478–81.

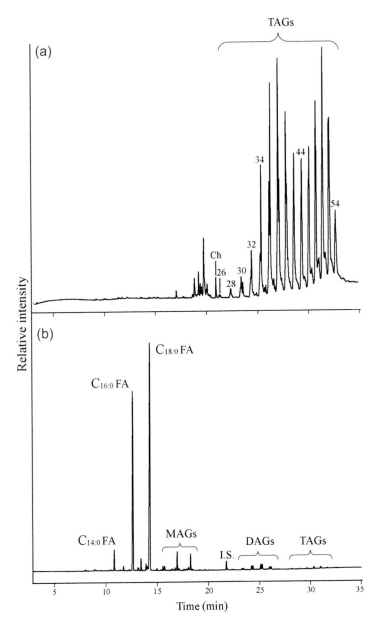

FIG. 1—Chromatograms showing the lipid components characteristic of (a) a fresh animal milk fat (the numbers in this chromatogram are TAGs of carbon length 26–54); and (b) a degraded, archaeological milk fat from sherd 03E0157:37:36 (BRG-1), part of a Middle Neolithic broad-rimmed vessel from Balregan, Co. Louth. (Ch = cholesterol; Cx:y = free fatty acids of carbon length x and degree of unsaturation y; FA = fatty acids; MAGs = monoacylglycerols; DAGs = diacylglycerols; TAGs = triacylglycerols; I.S. = internal standard (C_{34} n-alkane).)

sheep and goat versus pig) and variations in their metabolisms and physiologies result in different $\delta^{13}C$ ranges for their fats, meaning that lipids derived from the meat fats of ruminants and non-ruminants, and from the meat and milk of ruminants, can be successfully distinguished.[21] These $\delta^{13}C$ ranges have again been verified through experimental work, with a database of reference values generated from modern animals with a diet and environment matching prehistoric conditions as closely as possible. In addition, the heating of animal fats can be detected through the identification of ketones, which are lipid compounds that can form when the $C_{16:0}$ and $C_{18:0}$ fatty acids in pottery are heated in excess of 300°C in the presence of the metal salts present in some pottery clays.[22]

Plant lipids

Lipid compounds originating from plants, such as long-chain alkanes and alcohols, plant sterols and wax esters, are also detectable in residues from pottery vessels. However, most plants contain substantially lower lipid concentrations than animal products. Surviving plant lipids are thus present in relatively small quantities and tend to be 'drowned out' by animal lipids, which will dominate a lipid mixture if both types of commodities have been processed in the same pot (Fig. 2). Experimental work has shown that the concentration of fat absorbed into vessel walls after five boilings of meat is *c.* 150 times the concentration of lipid deposited after ten boilings of vegetable leaves.[23] While significant concentrations of plant lipids are regularly observed in pots of medieval date onwards, the percentage of Neolithic potsherds found to contain noticeable concentrations of plant-derived lipids remains very low, at *c.* 5%.[24] Certainly, the cooking of vegetables in the Neolithic may not have necessitated their boiling in pots, but it seems unlikely that such a small proportion of vessels was used to process plants. Taphonomic factors may be in

---

[21] For more detail see Jessica Smyth and Richard Evershed, 'Milk and molecules: secrets from prehistoric pottery', in Bernice Kelly, Niall Roycroft and Michael Stanley (eds), *Fragments from lives past* (Dublin, 2014), 8–9.

[22] Specifically, ketones containing 31, 33 and 35 carbon atoms. Ketones are also a component of plant lipids and can be distinguished by their $\delta^{13}C$ values, which are more depleted in plants. Richard Evershed, Andrew Stott, Anthony Raven, Stephanie Dudd, Stephanie Charters and Ann Leyden, 'Formation of long-chain ketones in ancient pottery vessels by pyrolysis of acyl lipids', *Tetrahedron Letters* 36 (1995), 8875–8; Anthony Raven, Pim van Bergen, Andrew Stott, Stephanie Dudd and Richard Evershed, 'Formation of long-chain ketones in archaeological pottery vessels by pyrolysis of acyl lipids', *Journal of Analytical and Applied Pyrolysis* 40–1 (1997), 267–85.

[23] For example, *Brassica* leaves contain relatively high concentrations of leaf wax, but fatty meat contains several orders of magnitude higher concentrations of TAGs; Evershed, 'Experimental approaches', 30–1.

[24] Mark Copley, Rob Berstan, Stephanie Dudd, Vanessa Straker, Sebastian Payne and Richard Evershed, 'Dairying in antiquity. III. Evidence from absorbed lipid residues dating to the British Neolithic', *Journal of Archaeological Science* 32 (2005), 523–46: 529; Anna Mukherjee, 'The importance of pigs in the later British Neolithic: integrating stable isotope evidence from lipid residues in archaeological potsherds, animal bone, and modern animal tissues', unpublished PhD thesis, University of Bristol, 2004. In

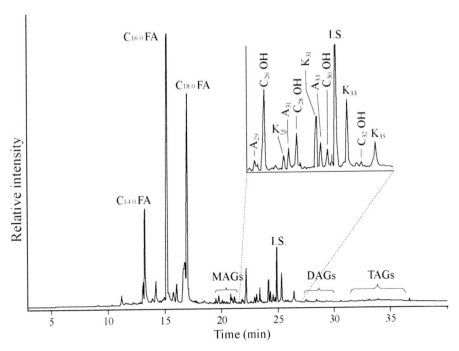

Fig. 2—Chromatogram of a lipid extract from a sherd (DY34) found at Danebury Iron Age hillfort, Hampshire, United Kingdom, containing lipids characteristic of degraded animal fats (triacylglycerols (TAGs), diacylglycerols (DAGs), monoacylglycerols (MAGs) and fatty acids (FAs)) and plant waxes (long-chain alcohols and alkanes—A_x represents n-alkanes of carbon chain length x; $C_x OH$ are n-alcohols of carbon chain length x). Ketones (K_x, of carbon length x) can be indicative of both animal and plant lipids, but those of carbon length 31, 33 and 35 are more likely to have formed from the $C_{16:0}$ and $C_{18:0}$ fatty acids dominating degraded animal fats. From Mark Copley, Rob Berstan, Vanessa Straker, Sebastian Payne and Richard Evershed, 'Dairying in antiquity. I. Evidence from absorbed lipid residues dating to the British Iron Age', *Journal of Archaeological Science* 32 (2005), 488.

play, with plant lipids—already in relatively low abundance—lost from pottery vessels over time.

The most abundant and commonly detected plant lipids are the waxes from leafy vegetables. The remains of such vegetables are not usually detectable via plant macrofossil and pollen analyses, and so these lipids provide important additional evidence for plant use and consumption in the past. Plant leaf waxes are characterised by a distribution of compounds with long carbon chains, such as odd-numbered alkanes (C_{25}–C_{33}), even-numbered alcohols and aldehydes (C_{20}–C_{34} and C_{24}–C_{28}, respectively), and esters (C_{39}–C_{52}). Abundances of these compounds vary between plant species and different ratios can sometimes be

medieval pottery vessels from Britain, evidence for the cooking of leafy vegetables is common, for example Richard Evershed, Carl Heron and L. J. Goad, 'Epicuticular wax components preserved in potsherds as chemical indicators of leafy vegetables in ancient diets', *Antiquity* 65 (1991) 540–4.

used to narrow down plant sources, although such an approach is made difficult by the mixing of commodities in vessels. Occasionally, plant leaf waxes consist of just a few compounds and can be more readily distinguished; the leaf wax of the genus *Brassica* for example comprises mostly the C_{29} alkane nonacosane and its oxygenated derivatives, nonacosan-15-one and nonacosan-15-ol. The presence of these three compounds can indicate the processing of vegetables such as cabbage, turnip, kale and broccoli; although to date they have only been detected in pots from the early medieval period onwards. Several of the compounds present in leaf waxes are also present in animal waxes and the two sources can successfully be distinguished by their $\delta^{13}C$ values, which are significantly more depleted in plants. Stable carbon isotope analysis can also be used to distinguish between C_3 plants (e.g. wheat, rye, barley, legumes and tubers) and C_4 plants (e.g. sugar cane, maize, sorghum and dryland grasses), although the latter were only introduced to Ireland and Britain in recent centuries and did not contribute to the diet of prehistoric populations.

Beeswax

Beeswax is another commodity sometimes detected in pottery lipid residues. Fresh beeswax is characterised by long-chain odd-numbered alkanes, even-numbered fatty acids and even-numbered wax esters, these last compounds partially degrading over time to form long-chain even-numbered alcohols and additional fatty acids and alkanes.[25] In food terms, the presence of beeswax can indicate that honey was being used to sweeten or ferment other commodities. However, beeswax may have had other non-food uses, for example, as a vessel sealant, as the active ingredient in medicinal or therapeutic products, or as fuel for lamps.[26] Interestingly, beeswax traces from British Neolithic vessels occur more frequently on their own than as part of mixtures of commodities, suggesting that beeswax was applied as a sealant, or that vessels were used solely for honey or beeswax processing.[27]

---

[25] Richard Evershed, Sarah Vaughan, Stephanie Dudd and Jeffrey Soles, 'Fuel for thought? Beeswax in lamps and conical cups from the late Minoan Crete', *Antiquity* 71 (1997), 979–85; Martine Regert, Sylvie Colinart, Laure Degrand and Oreste Decavallas, 'Chemical alteration and use of beeswax through time: accelerated ageing tests and analysis of archaeological samples from various environmental contexts', *Archaeometry* 43 (2001), 549–69.

[26] Carl Heron, Nadia Nemcek, Kath Bonfield, D. Dixon and B.S. Ottaway, 'The chemistry of Neolithic beeswax', *Naturwissenschaften* 81 (1994), 266–9; Stephanie Charters, Richard Evershed, Paul Blinkhorn and V. Denham, 'Evidence for the mixing of fats and waxes in archaeological ceramics', *Archaeometry* 37 (1995), 113–27; Evershed *et al.*, 'Fuel for thought', 981.

[27] Copley *et al.*, 'Dairying in antiquity. III', 529. A similar trend was seen at Iron Age and Bronze Age sites in Britain where a total of three out of five sherds contained beeswax only: Mark Copley, Rob Berstan, Stephanie Dudd, Vanessa Straker, Sebastian Payne and Richard Evershed, 'Dairying in antiquity. I. Evidence from absorbed lipid

Fish lipids

Marine and freshwater fats and oils are characterised by distributions of long-chain polyunsaturated and monounsaturated fatty acids. These compounds degrade rapidly and do not generally survive archaeological timescales. However, some of the degradation products themselves are very stable and can be detected in lipid residues in prehistoric pots. Although degraded, these compounds preserve the characteristic features of the original fatty acids and can thus act as reliable proxies for the presence of aquatic fats and oils. Vicinal dihydroxy acids and v-(o-alkylphenyl)alkanoic acids (APAAs) are two such degradation products for which one can scan. The former are created spontaneously through oxidation at room temperature, but the latter require heating for formation and provide an additional indicator of heating or cooking.[28]

Lipids from Irish Neolithic pottery

Sample selection

The primary aim of the sampling strategy was to bring together a range of pottery assemblages representative of the Irish Neolithic that is from the early fourth to the mid-third millennium cal BC. Currently, the period can be divided into three broad phases—early, middle and late—that are defined by changes in domestic architecture, monuments and artefact types (including pottery). Assemblages diagnostic of these three phases were thus selected to test whether there were discernible differences in vessel use through the period. Assemblages from different types of sites were also chosen, such as causewayed enclosures, houses and pit complexes, and from different parts of the island, to examine whether site function and geography also had an impact on what pots contained (Fig. 3).

As the percentage of sherds yielding appreciable lipid concentrations (>5µg of lipid per gram of powdered potsherd) can vary greatly from site to

---

residues dating to the British Iron Age', *Journal of Archaeological Science* 32 (2005), 485–503; Mark Copley, Rob Berstan, Vanessa Straker, Sebastian Payne and Richard Evershed, 'Dairying in antiquity. II. Evidence from absorbed lipid residues dating to the British Bronze Age', *Journal of Archaeological Science* 32 (2005), 505–21.

[28] Vegetable oils are often high in triunsaturated fatty acids (predominantly $C_{16:3}$ and $C_{18:3}$) and can form APAAs when heated. However, vegetable oils do not contain the $C_{20:3}$ fatty acid and the detection of C_{20} APAAs in a lipid residue is thus particularly important in reliably assigning an aquatic source. Two isomers of the $C_{16:0}$ fatty acid—4,8,12-TMTD and phytanic acid—are also very prevalent in aquatic products and their presence is used to further support classification. The origin of compounds can be further tested by stable carbon isotope analysis, with marine fats and oils exhibiting higher $\delta^{13}C$ values than terrestrial species.

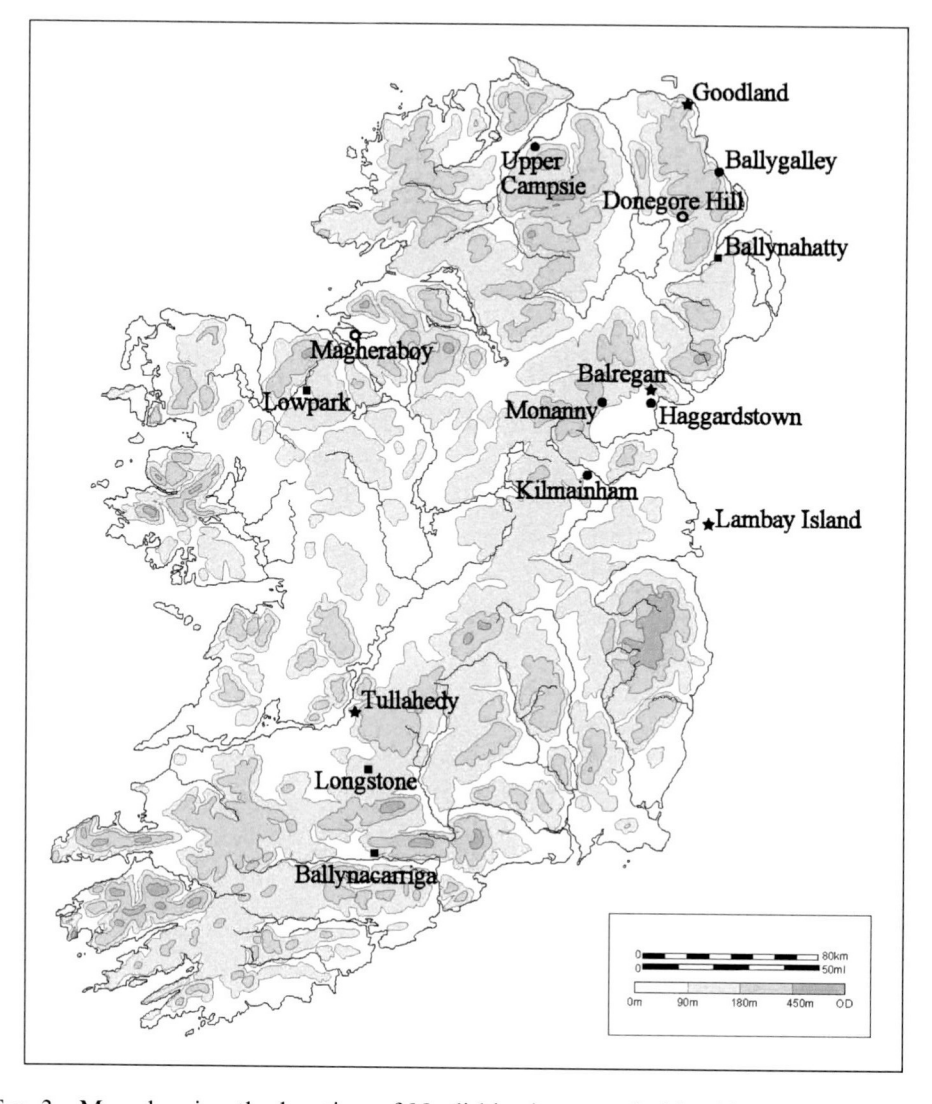

Fɪɢ. 3—Map showing the location of Neolithic sites sampled in this study. Circles = Early Neolithic sites (open—causewayed enclosures; filled—houses); stars = Middle Neolithic sites; squares = Late Neolithic sites. (For further description see Table 1.)

site and from one sample subset to another, a sample size of 30 sherds, each representing a different vessel, ensures that a statistically reliable amount of data is obtained. However, adopting this criterion meant that megalithic monuments, which generally have small pottery assemblages, were not sampled in this study. Experimental work[29] has shown that lipids are most abundant in

---

[29] Stephanie Charters, Richard Evershed, L. John Goad, Ann Leyden, Paul Blinkhorn and Varian Denham, 'Quantification and distribution of lipid in archaeological ceramics: implications for sampling potsherds for organic residue analysis and the classification of vessel use', *Archaeometry* 35 (1993), 211–23.

TABLE 1—Sites and pottery assemblages sampled in this study.

Site	Description	Site/assemblage phase	Pottery type	No. of vessels	No. of sherds
Donegore Hill	Causewayed enclosure	Early Neolithic	Carinated Bowl	50	50
Magheraboy	Causewayed enclosure	Early Neolithic	Carinated Bowl	30	30
Ballygalley	House site	Early Neolithic	Carinated Bowl	35	35
Upper Campsie	House site	Early Neolithic	Carinated Bowl	34	34
Haggardstown	House site	Early Neolithic	Carinated Bowl	30	30
Monanny	House site	Early Neolithic	Carinated Bowl	33	33
Kilmainham 1C	House site	Early Neolithic	Carinated Bowl	27	27
Tullahedy	Enclosed settlement	Middle Neolithic	Modified Carinated Bowl	37	37
Lambay Island	Axe production site	Middle Neolithic	Carrowkeel bowl; ?Carinated Bowl	18	16, 5
Goodland	Enclosed pit complex	Middle Neolithic	Carrowkeel bowl; impressed ware	30	30
Balregan	Pre-henge activity	Middle Neolithic	Impressed ware; Grooved Ware	22	19, 3
Ballynahatty	Ceremonial complex	Late Neolithic	Grooved Ware; Carrowkeel bowl	23	21, 2
Lowpark	Pit and post complex	Late Neolithic	Grooved Ware	15	22
Ballynacarriga	?Settlement activity	Late Neolithic	Grooved Ware	30	30

the rim and upper body of vessels and these types of sherds were preferred, as were sherds weighing 5g or more, which allowed for re-sampling if necessary and easier manipulation when recording and cleaning. In total, some 454 sherds from 15 sites were sampled (Table 1).

Methods

The project methodology has been described in detail elsewhere[30] but is briefly outlined here. To begin with, the area of each sherd to be sampled was surface-cleaned with a modelling drill. A small portion (2–3g) of this cleaned area was chipped off and ground to a fine powder. Solvents were added to the powder to extract the lipids and the total lipid extract (TLE) was filtered and purified before being analysed using a gas chromatograph (GC), which separates out the lipid mixture into its individual compounds and displays the information as a

---

[30] Jessica Smyth and Richard Evershed, 'Milking the megafauna: using organic residue analysis to understand early farming practice', *Journal of Environmental Archaeology* (2015), doi: 10.1179/1749631414Y.0000000045.

gas chromatogram (see Figs 1 and 2). Compounds were then quantified and identified through comparison with internal and external standards of known concentration and composition.

If further identification of compounds was required, a second portion of the TLE was prepared and analysed via gas chromatography-mass spectrometry (GC-MS). The mass spectrometer ionises and breaks up the molecules in individual compounds as they emerge from the GC. This process provides both a molecular weight and a characteristic fragmentation pattern for each molecule, creating a 'fingerprint' from which the original compound structure is deduced.

To determine the origin of certain lipids, for example whether they come from terrestrial/marine or ruminant/non-ruminant sources, their $\delta^{13}C$ values are determined via gas chromatography-combustion-isotope ratio mass spectrometry (GC-C-IRMS). In this final step, fatty acids or other lipids that are to be measured are separated via GC, with compounds emerging sequentially, and are combusted to carbon dioxide before passing through the IRMS, which captures and separates the carbon stable isotopes ^{12}C and ^{13}C, quantifying the amount of each isotope in the target compound.

Results

GC screening revealed extremely good preservation of absorbed lipids in Irish Neolithic pottery. Over 90% of sherds yielded appreciable amounts of lipid residues. Lipid concentration varied somewhat from site to site, but the average was 350μg/g, noticeably higher than the average lipid concentration (*c.* 100μg/g) observed in archaeological potsherds from northern Europe and the Near East.[31] Nearly 60% of TLEs screened produced distributions of fatty acids and other acyl lipids consistent with degraded animal fats (Fig. 4). Intact TAGs and their degradation products, DAGs and MAGs, were observed in over 90% of these animal fats, further demonstrating the high level of lipid preservation. Comparable analysis of British Neolithic sites has shown that 54% of sherds from southern England and 87% of sherds from Scotland yielded lipid concentrations >5μg/g.[32] Such a difference is more than likely due to the acidic soils covering much of Ireland and Scotland, which seem to better preserve lipids.

During further scrutiny of TAGs in the Irish samples, the presence of C_{42}, C_{44} and C_{46} TAGs was often noted, compounds only detectable in

---

[31] Evershed, 'Experimental approaches', 28.

[32] Copley *et al.*, 'Dairying in antiquity. I', 525; Anna Mukherjee, Alex Gibson and Richard Evershed, 'Trends in pig product processing at British Neolithic Grooved Ware sites traced through organic residues in potsherds', *Journal of Archaeological Science* 35 (2008), 2059–73: 2063; Cramp *et al.*, 'Immediate replacement of fishing with dairying', supplementary info.

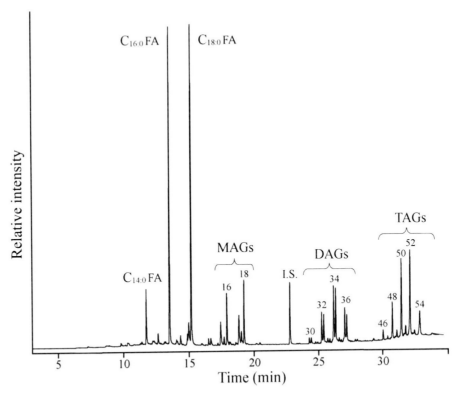

FIG. 4—Typical chromatogram of a lipid extract from Irish Neolithic pots, containing lipid components characteristic of a degraded animal fat. The sample shown is from sherd UPC-8 (112:46a) from the Early Neolithic house site at Upper Campsie, Co. Derry. (Cx:y = free fatty acids of carbon length x and degree of unsaturation y; FA = fatty acids; MAGs = monoacylglycerols; DAGs = diacylglycerols; TAGs = triacylglycerols; I.S. = internal standard (C_{34} n-alkane).)

milk fat.[33] Of the 212 samples carried forward for compound-specific carbon stable isotope analysis, nearly 90% were found to contain $C_{16:0}$ and $C_{18:0}$ fatty acids with $\delta^{13}C$ values consistent with those from reference milk fats, providing overwhelming evidence for the processing of dairy products in Irish Neolithic pots. Indeed, ruminant milk fats were the dominant fat observed in residues from vessels dating to all phases of the Neolithic (Fig. 5). Additionally, GC-MS analysis confirmed the presence of C_{31}, C_{33} and C_{35} ketones in approximately 40% of samples, indicating that many vessels (and the fats therein) had been heated to temperatures in excess of 270°C.

Milk and/or dairy fats were not the only animal products detected in the assemblages. Of the samples submitted for stable isotope analysis, 24 vessels (just over 10%) appear to have contained meat fats predominantly or a mixture of milk and meat fats (Fig. 5). There was less evidence for the processing of plants in pottery vessels, with compounds such as long-chain alcohols and

---

[33] Dudd and Evershed, 'Milk as an element of archaeological economies', 1480.

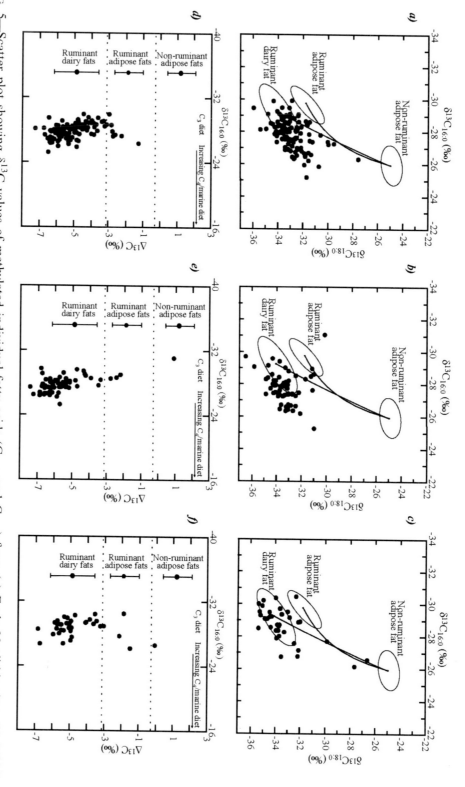

Fig. 5—Scatter plot showing δ¹³C values of methylated individual fatty acids (C₁₆:₀ and C₁₈:₀) from (a) Early Neolithic sites, (b) Middle Neolithic sites, and (c) Late Neolithic sites. These data are plotted against reference ellipses derived from modern United Kingdom animal fats that have been corrected for the contribution of post-industrial carbon. ((d)–(f)) The same data with Δ¹³C values (= δ¹³C₁₈:₀ – δ¹³C₁₆:₀) plotted against δ¹³C₁₆:₀ values–(d) Early Neolithic sites, (e) Middle Neolithic sites; and (f) Late Neolithic sites. The Δ¹³C proxy highlights the metabolic and biosynthetic characteristics of the animal fat source, and allows fats from animals raised on different diets in different environments to be distinguished. Ranges of the Δ¹³C values are based on a global database comprising modern reference animal fats from the UK, Africa, Kazakhstan, Switzerland and the Near East.

alkanes observed at low concentrations only occasionally. Likewise, there was no obvious sign of the compounds characteristic of beeswax in the sherds analysed. While further work needs to be carried out in this area, the apparent absence of beeswax residues in an Irish context raises interesting questions about the spread (anthropogenic or otherwise) of bee species in early prehistoric Europe. In terms of the utilisation of non-terrestrial resources, Irish Neolithic pots have not yet been screened for aquatic biomarkers, although it is worth noting that such biomarkers have been detected in less than 1% of pottery residues at over 40 Neolithic sites along coastal northern Britain, on the islands of Orkney, Shetland, North and South Uist, Lewis, and on the Isle of Man.[34]

Food traditions in the Irish Neolithic

Presence and prevalence of dairy products

The above results afford important new insights into food and drink in prehistory. They provide the first unequivocal evidence that dairying in Ireland began in the Neolithic and that it was being practised by some of the very earliest farming communities on the island. Such a scenario complements the evidence from Britain and continental Europe,[35] where it has been conclusively established that dairying predates the 'secondary products revolution' thought to have emerged during the Bronze Age.[36] Most significantly, given the poor preservation of Irish Neolithic faunal remains already described, the evidence provided by organic residue analysis is very unlikely to have been detected through other means.

A second aspect of these findings is that milk and milk products are not just early foods, but seem to be important foods, and that they remain important through the Neolithic. Pottery assemblages of Early, Middle and Late Neolithic date yielded the same strong dairy signal, as did assemblages from different parts of the island, and assemblages from different site types—such as enclosures, houses and ceremonial complexes.[37] That early farmers were doing other things with milk besides drinking it in its raw or 'ready-made' state is probably common sense, but this can be confirmed by the relatively high

---

[34] Cramp *et al.*, 'Immediate replacement of fishing with dairying', 3.

[35] See for example Copley *et al.*, 'Dairying in antiquity. III'; Mélanie Salque, Peter Bogucki, Joanna Pyzel, Iwona Sobkowiak-Tabaka, Ryszard Grygiel, Marzena Szmyt and Richard Evershed, 'Earliest evidence for cheese making in the sixth millennium BC in northern Europe', *Nature* 493 (2013), 522–5.

[36] Andrew Sherratt, 'Plough and pastoralism: aspects of the secondary products revolution', in Ian Hodder, Glynn Isaac and Norman Hammond (eds), *Pattern of the past: studies in honour of David Clarke* (Cambridge, 1981), 261–305.

[37] See Jessica Smyth and Richard Evershed, 'Milking the megafauna: using organic residue analysis to understand early farming practice', *Journal of Environmental Archaeology*, 2015.

percentage of vessels shown to have been heated to high temperatures. On a wider scale, the evidence from Ireland complements that gathered from across Britain and together they form a very strong, regionally distinct signal of high dairy production and consumption. Such strikingly similar culinary practices (and by extension animal husbandry practices)[38] can be viewed as another facet of the close cultural connections between these islands in the Neolithic, long recognised in styles of mortuary architecture and material culture. Indeed, that such overtly similar patterns of food consumption and animal husbandry might have originated from the same cultural source or sources becomes all the more plausible in the light of recent dating work on the adoption of agriculture across Britain and Ireland, which appears to have been a very rapid and dynamic process.[39]

The cooking and consumption of meat

There is relatively little evidence for meat being cooked in pottery vessels in the Neolithic, a behaviour or pattern that again continues through the period, and which provides quite a striking contrast to the pattern of meat consumption observed in residues from British Neolithic pots.[40] While the small fragments of calcined animal bone recovered from sites point towards alternative cooking methods, such as roasting on open fires or baking in pits, it remains impossible to quantify what scale of meat consumption this represented. Indeed, such is the strength of the dairy signal from the Irish vessels that we might usefully re-evaluate our assumptions about how much meat was consumed on a day-to-day basis, something not often made explicit in our prehistoric narratives.[41]

The kinds of meat and meat products preferred in the Irish Neolithic are equally difficult to interpret. Information that can be gleaned from the faunal record points to the consumption of cow, sheep/goat and pig, but the relative importance in the diet of the carcass products of each species remains elusive if one cannot reliably reconstruct a minimum number of individuals or similar calculation from site assemblages. Organic residue analysis can in theory offer some species-level differentiation, as the $\delta^{13}C$ values of lipids from non-ruminants and ruminants are sufficiently distinct from one another to plot

---

[38] Though perhaps diverging somewhat in the Late Neolithic, as reflected in the lipid residues from Grooved Ware vessels. See Cramp *et al.*, 'Immediate replacement of fishing with dairying', 4.

[39] Alasdair Whittle, Alex Bayliss and Frances Healy, 'Gathering time: the social dynamics of change', in Alasdair Whittle, Frances Healy and Alex Bayliss, *Gathering time: dating the Early Neolithic enclosures of southern Britain and Ireland* (Oxford, 2011), 848–914: 862.

[40] Copley *et al.*, 'Dairying in antiquity. III', 526–7; Mukherjee *et al.*, 'Trends in pig product processing', 2068–9.

[41] See, for example, various papers in Michael Parker Pearson (ed.), *Food, culture and identity in the Neolithic and Early Bronze Age*, BAR International Series 1117 (Oxford, 2003); Lucas, 'Irish food products', 14.

well apart.[42] However, this large isotopic difference between ruminants and non-ruminants also means that the mixing of even small amounts of one lipid source with the other—for example, the occasional cooking of pig products in a vessel used mostly for processing milk products and vice versa—will result in the $\delta^{13}C$ values of the predominant lipid source plotting outside of its reference range. This issue can be addressed, in part, by using a mixing model that estimates the varying proportions of different animal fats within a single vessel,[43] but ideally the results of isotope analysis are compared with the faunal assemblage to see how well the range proportions of different species correlate. Where there is no or insufficient morphological data on animal species, there is a risk that the consumption of ruminant meat will be overestimated and that of milk and non-ruminant meat will be underestimated, as mixtures of these latter commodities plot in the area of ruminant meat fats.

In an Irish context, where so many of the vessels have been used to process dairy fats, there is little risk of underestimating the consumption of milk products. However, caution must be exercised in interpreting the *c.* 10% of lipid residues with $\delta^{13}C$ values plotting within the range of ruminant and non-ruminant meat fats (Fig. 5). One scenario is that early Irish farmers were only occasionally processing pig products in pottery vessels. This may reflect wider consumption practices, or may mean that these animals were being cooked using different methods. A second scenario is that vessels used to cook pork were fairly regularly used to process dairy products, on separate occasions or perhaps as part of the same meal. Interestingly, both traditions would seem to diverge from culinary practices in Neolithic Britain, where there is a higher incidence of vessels being used solely or predominantly to process pig products.[44]

Conclusions

As tempting as it may be to hail the words of A. T. Lucas as happily prescient, we must stress that these results do not demonstrate that dairy products formed the main dietary component in the Irish Neolithic; this will be for ourselves and other researchers to test further, and to prove or disprove, in the future.

[42] There is potential for further differentiation among ruminants based on differences in their TAG lipids, although these are normally the first compounds that degrade and are lost from archaeological residues. See Sigrid Mirabaud, Christian Rolando and Martine Regert, 'Molecular criteria for discriminating adipose fat and milk from different species by NanoESI MS and MS/MS of their triacylglycerols: application to archaeological remains', *Analytical Chemistry* 79:16 (2007), 6182–92.

[43] This model utilises the percentage abundance of each specific fatty acid in fresh porcine and ruminant fats, and its associated $\delta^{13}C$ value; it is not possible to quantify exactly how much mixing took place during each vessel use and how often each vessel was subsequently reused; see Anna Mukherjee, Mark Copley, Rob Berstan and Richard Evershed, 'Interpretation of $\delta^{13}C$ values of fatty acids in relation to animal husbandry, food processing and consumption in prehistory', in Jacqui Mulville and Alan Outram (eds), *The zooarchaeology of fats, oils, milk and dairying* (Oxford, 2005), 77–92.

[44] Copley *et al.*, 'Dairying in antiquity. III', 526–7; Mukherjee *et al.*, 'Trends in pig product processing', 2068–9.

The dairy signal from lipid residues in Neolithic pottery may very well reflect only part of a broader spectrum of food procurement, preparation and consumption activities. Indeed, through the continuing development of analytical protocols[45] we are beginning to distinguish different ranges of lipid compounds, particularly those indicative of plant products and which may yet reverse their 'invisibility' in prehistoric pot residues.

With any questions of food and drink, quantification remains the outstanding issue, and is a particular challenge for archaeologically marginal environments, where differential preservation of organic remains can leave large gaps. Stable isotope analyses can give us some degree of clarity on the proportions of plant: animal, milk: meat, and terrestrial: aquatic resources that were consumed in the Neolithic, but there is no getting around the fact that all organisms—plants, non-human animals and humans—are a complex mix of chemical signatures constituted through a number of (invariably shifting) variables: where and how they grow, which can change over the course of a lifetime, and what they consume, which regularly includes one another. Nevertheless, what the lipid residues from Neolithic pots have allowed us to conclusively demonstrate is that dairy products were being consumed as soon as farming appears on the island. This finding alone has huge implications for our understanding of prehistoric farming practice, social organisation and settlement patterning, not to mention diet and health.[46] This study has also hopefully demonstrated the enormous potential of molecular-level archaeology to open up new windows on the past, particularly in an Irish context, where trace molecules are often all that survive. Increasingly aligned to a growing suite of micro-analytical, multi-proxy techniques, such as protein profiling, ancient DNA sequencing, and compound-specific stable isotope analyses, it is safe to say that investigation into food and drink in prehistory is only beginning.

Acknowledgements   The research leading to these results has received funding from the People Programme (Marie Curie Actions) of the European Union's Seventh Framework Programme FP7/2007–2013/ under Research Executive Agency grant agreement n°273462. Thanks are due to the staff of museums, university departments and commercial archaeology companies across Ireland who facilitated access to and sampling of pottery assemblages. Colleagues at the Organic Geochemistry Unit also provided enormous support and guidance throughout Jessica Smyth's Marie Curie fellowship. We are grateful to an anonymous peer reviewer for his or her helpful comments, and to the journal editors Elizabeth FitzPatrick and James Kelly for their invitation to contribute to the volume. Members of the Royal Irish Academy publications team, especially Lucy Hogan, are thanked for their patience and understanding.

---

[45] Marisol Correa Ascencio and Richard Evershed, 'High throughput screening of organic residues in archaeological potsherds using direct acidified methanol extraction', *Analytical Methods* 2014:6 (2014), 1330–40.

[46] See discussion in Smyth and Evershed, 'Milking the megafauna', 6–9.

Fulachtaí fia and Bronze Age cooking in Ireland: reappraising the evidence

ALAN HAWKES

Department of Archaeology, Connolly Building, Dyke Parade, University College Cork

[Accepted 9 March 2015. Published 13 May 2015.]

Abstract

This paper examines the technical aspects of indirect cooking using pyrolithic technology in Ireland with a particular focus on its application during the Bronze Age. The widespread distribution of burnt mounds (*fulachtaí fia*) is striking, suggesting that Ireland was the most prominent user of this technology in Bronze Age Europe. However, narratives related to these sites have long revolved around function, to the extent that the basic definition of this monument type has been called into question. This paper examines the use of these sites based on evidence from some 1,000 excavated examples in Ireland and provides new insights into the use of pyrolithic technology for cooking. The model proposed here is of open-air feasting/food-sharing hosted by small family groups, in a manner that was central to different types of social bonding.

Introduction

> The name *folach fiadh* is well known to the country people, and they bestow it on a heap of burnt stones, of which, as a rule, they know neither the origin nor the use.[1]

The consumption of food is universal and is one of the most fundamental activities in society, helping to establish and sustain social life. The sharing of food is a social act that creates and maintains different bonds and obligations within a group or community. The preparing of food is also a basic element of human life and is an activity indicative of the way in which people use a landscape. The contexts, whereby these cooking-related activities appear in the archaeological record, are widely diverse. In Bronze Age Ireland (*c.* 2000−600 BC), the cooking and consumption of food was carried out using both direct and indirect methods. Direct cooking methods involved roasting, boiling and

---

* Author's e-mail: alanhawkes@gmail.com

doi: 10.3318/PRIAC.2015.115.13

[1] Richard Smiddy, *The druids, ancient churches, and round towers of Ireland* (Dublin, 1873), 52.

baking on open fires—probably using ceramic vessels, spit structures or surface griddles—while indirect methods used a pyrolithic technology. The latter involved a process of heat transfer that centred on the use of hot stones immersed in water. Through thermal conduction, stones capture and hold the heat generated by fast-burning fuel that would otherwise dissipate before many foods could be cooked over open flames.[2] Hot stones, by their nature and relative non-combustibility, have the potential to capture and retain heat, which facilitates the cooking of a broad range of foods. The use of hot stones enabled prolonged cooking of food by roasting, steaming and boiling in different types of pits. Pit-cooking using hot stones, was also used in some parts of the world to chemically alter the structure of root foods and to increase digestibility.[3] Compared to other cooking methods, boiling is most likely to have yielded a greater proportion of potentially available calories/nutrients from a given piece of food.[4] Another important use of hot stones was to generate steam for sweat-bathing, a practice not only widespread in North America and the circumpolar region during prehistory and ethnographic eras but also in parts of medieval Eastern Europe.[5] Pyrolithic technology seems to have originated in Upper Palaeolithic Europe,[6] while it has also been recognised in central and western North America from at least 10,500 years ago.[7] Its use did not, of course, mean the replacement of older methods of 'direct' cooking. While more costly techniques, such as pyrolithic water-boiling (in terms of heat expended and labour invested), were occasionally used in certain societies, less costly, open-fire methods continued to be used for easily cooked foods.

---

[2] Aslton V. Thoms, 'Rocks of ages: propagation of hot-rock cookery in western North America', *Journal of Archaeological Science* 36 (2009), 573–91.

[3] Sandra L. Peacock, 'From complex to simple: balsam root, inulin, and the chemistry of traditional interior Salish pit-cooking technology', *Botany* 86 (1998), 116–28.

[4] Luann Wandsnider, 'The roasted and the boiled: food composition and heat treatment with special emphasis on pit-hearth cooking', *Journal of Anthropological Archaeology* 16 (1997), 1–48.

[5] Lawrence Barfield and Michael A. Hodder, 'Burnt mounds as saunas and the prehistory of bathing', *Antiquity* 61 (1987), 370–9.

[6] Hallam L. Movius, 'The hearths of the upper Perigordian and Aurignacian horizons at the Abri Pataud, Les Eyzies (Dordogne), and their possible significance', *American Anthropology* 68 (1966), 296–325; Yuichi Nakazawa, Lawrence G. Straus, Mauel R. Gonzales-Morales, David C. Solana and Jorge C. Saiz, 'On stone-boiling technology in the Upper Paleolithic: behavioural implications from an Early Magdalenian hearth in El Mirón Cave, Cantabria, Spain', *Journal of Archaeological Science* 36 (2009), 684–93.

[7] Alston V. Thoms, 'The fire stones carry: ethnographic records and archaeological expectations for hot-rock cookery in western North America', *Journal of Anthropological Archaeology* 27 (2008), 443–60; J. Johnson, 'Fire in the hole: archaeological analysis and interpretation of the Barnett Site (41 MI 77), a burned rock midden on Pecan Bayou in Mills County, Texas', unpublished MA thesis, Texas Tech University, 2009.

Although a non-water-boiling version of the technology may have been employed in Ireland during the fifth millennium BC, it is likely that the use of pyrolithic water-boiling technology did not become popular until the Neolithic. This is based on the identification of trough pits and domesticated faunal remains in excavated burnt mound/spread sites dating from the early fourth millennium BC. The overall chronology of the site type suggests that these new cooking techniques emerged as a consequence of the adoption of animal husbandry in Ireland.[8]

The method involved a process of heat transfer whereby water was boiled through the introduction of stones heated in a nearby fire. The heat transferred directly from the stones, raising the water to a temperature suitable to cook food. After numerous firings these stones were eventually shattered by the sudden cooling process, and gradually accumulated as a result of human action near the trough to form a low mound or spread that contained large amounts of charcoal. These are generally recognised as crescent-shaped mounds of burnt stone, or are exposed in plough soil as levelled spreads of burnt stone mixed with high levels of charcoal-enriched soil (Pl. I).

They can occur individually or in small clusters, and are generally located close to a water source. There is some variability within these sites when excavated, although generally the deposits of burnt stone are accompanied by a range of features that include sunken troughs which are often lined with wood or stone. During the Bronze Age the use of this particular technology became widely adopted in North Atlantic Europe, particularly in Ireland. These sites gradually became mythologised in Irish folklore[9] and were recognised by antiquarians and archaeologists as a class of monuments known as *fulachtaí fia*.

The most difficult aspect of interpreting the function of burnt mounds is identifying how the boiled water was utilised. The interpretation that they were cooking sites is perhaps the most widely accepted of the many theories. Here, the primary purpose of the site was to cook food by means of heat transfer from hot stones to water and then eventually to the food. Experimental work, most notably by Michael J. O'Kelly[10] at Ballyvourney, Co. Cork, confirmed that the typical features of an excavated burnt mound, namely a water receptacle, hearth and the burnt stone and charcoal, could indeed relate to the type of cooking processes described in Geoffrey Keating's *Foras Feasa ar Éirinn* (Pl. II).[11]

---

[8] Alan Hawkes, 'The beginnings and evolution of the *fulacht fia* tradition in early prehistoric Ireland', *Proceedings of the Royal Irish Academy* 114 C (2014), 89–139.

[9] Alan Hawkes, 'Medieval *fulachtaí fia* in Ireland? An archaeological assessment', *The Journal of Irish Archaeology* 20 (2012), 77–100.

[10] Michael J. O'Kelly, 'Excavations and experiments in Irish cooking places', *Journal of the Royal Society of Antiquaries of Ireland* 84 (1954), 105–56.

[11] D. Ó Drisceoil, '*Fulachta fiadh*: a study', unpublished MA thesis, University College Cork, 1980.

PL. I—*Top*: Typical horseshoe-shaped burnt mound at Turnaspidogy, Co. Cork (RMP CO081-044). (© National Monuments Service, Department of Arts, Heritage and the Gaeltacht.) *Bottom*: Reconstructed boiling trough and burnt stone mound at Rathbarry, Co. Cork. (© Alan Hawkes.)

This seventeenth-century text is the only source that associates the term '*fulacht*' with heating water by using hot stones:

And it was their custom ... with whatever they had killed ... to kindle ranging fires theron, and put into them a large number of emery stone;

Pl. II—The first cooking experiment carried out by M. J. O'Kelly at Ballyvourney, Co. Cork (after O'Kelly, 'Excavations and experiments in Irish cooking places', *Journal of the Royal Society of Antiquaries of Ireland* 84 (1954), 105–56). (**A**) Meat is wrapped in straw and placed into the trough, taking 35 minutes to bring 454 litres of water to boil. (**B**) It is allowed to cook for 3.5 hours after which time the meat is removed (**C**) and prepared for serving (**D**). (Reproduced by permission of the Royal Society of Antiquaries of Ireland.)

and to dig two pits in the yellow clay … put some of the meat on spits to roast before the fire; and to bind another portion of it with sugáns in dry bundles, and to set it to boil in the larger of two pits, and keep plying them with the stones that were in the fire … until they were cooked.[12]

Over the years, however, several commentators have questioned the use of *fulachtaí fia* as cooking places, with the relevance of early literary sources such as the above now in doubt. The terminology used to describe these sites

---

[12] Patrick S. Dineen, *The history of Ireland: Foras Feasa ar Éirinn by G. Keating* (London, 1908).

has also come under scrutiny. A connection with pyrolithic technology should no longer be considered appropriate, as medieval manuscripts such as the *Yellow book of Lecan* and the *Book of Leinster* refer to the word '*fulacht*' as cooking on a spit rather than a pit in the ground.[13] Based on similar sources, part of the 'cooking site' theory has been an assumption that burnt mounds represent seasonal hunting camps used over a long period. On this basis, these sites should occur in suitable hunting environments such as uplands and wetlands, and predominantly contain faunal remains from wild animals, neither of which is the case. The majority of sites occur in low-lying agricultural land, while the faunal remains from recent excavations are dominated by domesticated animals.[14] The radiocarbon evidence also questions the relevance of early literary sources as the great majority of these sites are a millennium or more earlier than the relevant texts. An analysis of the radiocarbon dates from Ireland demonstrates the use of pyrolithic water-boiling technology from the Early Neolithic onwards with a clear concentration of use during the Early to Middle Bronze Age.[15] It is likely that the literary sources record a mythologising of these ancient sites in early medieval Ireland. These Irish legends concerning burnt mounds emerged long after open-air water-boiling went out of use, when their actual purpose had been forgotten, but while they were still prominent and common features of the landscape. This may have led to some early exploration of these sites, possibly in the course of farming activity, which invited people to invent imaginative stories in order to explain these enigmatic mounds. Whether related to cooking on a spit or in a boiling trough, the term '*fulacht*' and its derivatives probably do refer to some type of cooking activity. The term was probably adopted by later writers who recognised an ancient form of cooking from their understanding of the visible remains.[16]

These questions concerning function have been clarified in recent years as the number of excavations of this site type has increased due to modern infrastructural developments such as road and pipeline schemes. Many excavators now favour multifunctional interpretations due to the ubiquity of the technology and the different possible applications of hot water. Where deposits of burnt stone are found, arguments have been made for a wide range of activities, including cooking, bathing, brewing, metalworking, tanning, dying, washing and the fulling

---

[13] Fergus Kelly, *Early Irish farming* (Dublin, 2000); John Ó Néill, '*Lapidibus in igne calefactis coquebatur*: the historical burnt mound tradition', *The Journal of Irish Archaeology* 12/13 (2005), 79–85.

[14] A. Tourunen, *Fauna and fulachta fiadh: animal bones from burnt mounds on the N9/N10 Carlow Bypass*, National Roads Authority Monograph Series No. 5 (Dublin, 2008).

[15] A. Hawkes, 'Prehistoric burnt mound archaeology in Ireland', unpublished PhD thesis, University College Cork, 2014.

[16] Hawkes, 'Medieval *fulachtai fia* in Ireland? An archaeological review', 87.

of textiles.[17] The discovery of hut structures at a number of these sites has been connected to the use of steam lodges or sweat houses.[18]

The cooking interpretation has been challenged on several grounds, including:

- Absence of food waste (animal bone and environmental remains) or any artefacts associated with the processing of food;
- The often ambiguous nature of surviving archaeological remains;
- Uncertainties about the relevance of early literary accounts of *fulacht fia* type sites;
- Alternative uses of hot water;
- The laborious nature of pyrolithic processes for the purpose of cooking;
- The practicality of using certain rock types (limestone) for cooking in water-boiling process.

Those who favour alternative explanations have highlighted the limitations of excavation evidence of the cooking hypothesis. As a technology, however, hot stones may have been first used for cooking (roasting/steaming/baking) during the Mesolithic period in Ireland.[19] It is, however, during the Early Neolithic that pyrolithic deposits associated with boiling troughs and domestic faunal remains were first used.[20] This practice continued into the Bronze Age, when the tradition was at its strongest.

The rapid adoption of pyrolithic technology, however, was not based on a search for more efficient cooking techniques, but rather in the social context of its use. As Katherine Wright observed 'meals are everyday rituals of profound importance in social life, structuring daily social intercourse and reinforcing cultural values'.[21] If cooking was indeed the primary function of *fulachtaí fia*, it should not be viewed as a mundane undertaking, but rather one that actively contributed to the constitution of social relations. It is only

---

[17] Stephen Jeffery, 'Burnt mounds, fulling and early textiles', in Michael A. Hodder and Lewis H. Barfield (eds), *Burnt mounds and hot stone technology. Papers from the Second International Burnt Mound Conference* (Sandwell, West Mids, 1991), 97–108; B. Quinn and D. Moore, *Fulachta fiadh and the beer experiment*, National Roads Authority, Monograph Series No. 6 (Dublin, 2009), 43–53.

[18] Barfield and Hodder, 'Burnt mounds as saunas and the prehistory of bathing', 370–9; James Eogan, 'Cleansing body and soul', *Seanda* 2 (2007), 38–9.

[19] A. Little, 'Tasks, temporalities and textures: reconstructing the social topography of an Irish Mesolithic lakescape', unpublished PhD thesis, University College Dublin, 2010; Peter C. Woodman, Elizabeth Anderson and Nicky Finlay (eds), *Excavations at Ferriter's Cove 1983–95: last foragers, first farmers in the Dingle Peninsula* (Wicklow, 1999), 125. Aimée Little, 'Clonava Island revisited: a story of cooking, plants and re-occupation during the Irish Late Mesolithic', *Proceedings of the Royal Irish Academy* 114C (2014), 35–55.

[20] Hawkes, 'The beginnings and evolution of the *fulacht fia* tradition in early prehistoric Ireland', 96.

[21] Katherine I. Wright, 'The social origins of cooking and dining in early villages of western Asia', *Proceedings of the Prehistoric Society* 2 (2000), 89–122.

through recent road and pipeline schemes, and other commercial archaeology projects that we can begin to identify and systematically address research topics concerning *fulachtaí fia*. This large body of data has the potential to address many long-standing research questions, particularly relating to site function, an area where there has been much controversy.

Burnt mounds and pyrolithic cooking in Ireland

The acidic nature of Irish soils is often used to explain the scarcity of faunal remains recovered from burnt stone deposits. Others have argued that the absence of animal bone at *fulachtaí fia* may have been the result of ritual disposal of bones after consumption or scavenging animals, or that this meat may have been butchered and consumed at another location.[22] Even where alkaline soils are conducive to the preservation of bone, the stone used for the pyrolithic process is often sandstone, which is acidic and so would affect the preservation of food waste.

An important development in recent years is the growing number of excavations that have produced animal bone, which has placed the focus once again on cooking. The current study has identified 263 sites out of 1,165 excavated examples with evidence of faunal remains. At 67 of these sites, the bone is described as burnt and it is often not clear whether it is animal or human, however the former is likely as human remains have only been recovered from a small number of *fulacht fia* sites in Ireland. This animal bone has been recovered from troughs (28%), pits (25%), mounds (32%) and other related features such as hearths, stake-/post-holes and deposits (12%). At 66 sites, bone has been obtained from more than two contexts on site, reducing the possibility that the material is intrusive. Therefore, a large proportion of animal bone finds from excavated *fulachtaí fia*/burnt mounds can be regarded as securely associated with the use of these sites.

Out of 14,789 animal bone fragments recovered from *fulachtaí fia* since 1950, 3,973 can be identified to species with 67% of the remains identified as cattle followed by sheep/goat (11%), pig (8%), deer (6%), dog (5%) and horse (3%). Some 9,546 fragments could not be identified to species due to the high degree of fragmentation caused by taphonomic processes or as a result of burning (Fig. 1). Burnt bone accounts for a proportion of these unidentified remains and was only found by the bulk-sampling of certain features and deposits. This is certainly not carried out at every *fulacht fia* and even when the number of samples taken is reported, the size of the sample processed is limited. The recovery of burnt bone can vary depending on the way in which the site was excavated and the sampling procedure. In many instances, the mound material might be removed rapidly, whereas features such as the trough were excavated with greater care. The different recovery techniques employed during excavation may also give rise to different interpretations. This is certainly a factor in

---

[22] E. Grogan, *The North Munster Project. Volume 1: the later prehistoric landscapes of south-east Clare* (Bray, 2005), 41; John Waddell, *The prehistoric archaeology of Ireland* (Galway, 1998), 177.

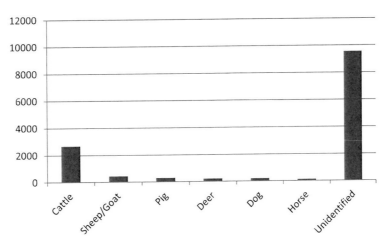

FIG. 1—Range of species identified from bone fragments recovered from excavated *fulachtaí fia* and burnt stone deposits in Ireland.

relation to *fulachtaí fia* investigated during road developments where, in many cases, only the base of features such as troughs and pits survive. The recovered faunal remains often survive in poor condition and assemblages are usually too small to put forward any reliable statistics on age/sex slaughter patterns. Most assemblages consist of less than ten fragments of bone, with the predominance of teeth reflecting poor preservation in acidic soil conditions (Fig. 2).

Not surprisingly, a larger number of bones were recovered from burnt mound deposits in alkaline environments, where limestone was used in the boiling process. This includes animal bone recovered from burnt mounds composed chiefly of limestone, including sites at Fahee South, Co. Clare; Inchagreenoge, Co. Limerick; and five *fulachtaí fia* excavated along the N18

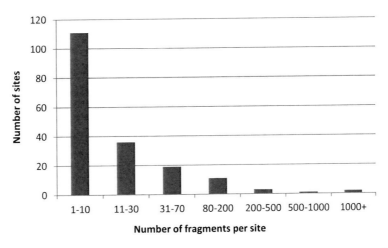

FIG. 2—Range of fragment assemblages recovered from excavated *fulachtaí fia* and burnt stone deposits in Ireland.

Oranmore to Gort Road Scheme.[23] This is significant as the caustic nature of limestone, when heated and immersed in water, has been used as an argument against the interpretation of such sites as cooking places.[24] It has been observed that the quantities of calcium carbonate produced in the heating of water would not be harmful if the meat was protected and wrapped in vegetation or straw.[25] Limestone also has varying chemical and geological components depending on the source, so some limestone would react differently to others. Recent excavation records confirm that limestone was commonly used in *fulachtaí fia* at sites with animal bone waste and must have been regarded as suitable for cooking purposes.

Larger animal bone assemblages at a number of sites contribute significantly to our understanding of *fulachtaí fia* as possible cooking places. For example, an estimated 1,000 fragments of bone were recovered from a number of sites, including Inchirourke, Co. Tipperary; Inchaquire, Co. Kildare; and Inchagreenoge.[26] The faunal remains from the latter site include cattle, pig, horse and sheep/goat. The range of skeletal parts suggests that the animals were slaughtered, butchered and eaten on the site, and the age ranges are typical of animals raised for both meat and secondary products.[27] Evidence of butchery marks has been recorded at some 30 excavated *fulachtaí fia* but such marks are rarely identified due to the fragmentary nature of the surviving remains. Interestingly, the most common finds recovered from burnt stone sites are flaked and modified stone tools, some of which can be dated to the Bronze Age. The present study indicates that 268 sites contained such material, sometimes in great quantity and, in a number of cases, with numerous waste flakes that indicate flint-knapping.[28] Moreover, the presence, in these sites, of numerous flint and chert scrapers, along with blades and their associated resharpening debitage, suggests that processes relating to the butchery of animals and the processing of their meat could have taken place.

For example, a red deer humerus showing marks of butchery at Balgeeth, Co. Meath, 'clearly represents the remains of a shoulder of venison

[23] Finn Delaney and John Tierney, *In the lowlands of south Galway: archaeological excavations on the N18 Oranmore to Gort National Road Scheme*, NRA Scheme Monograph 7 (Dublin, 2011), 44.

[24] Emer Dennehy, 'Hot property: the morphology and archaeology of Irish *fulachta fiadh', The Journal of the Kerry Archaeological and Historical Society* 8 (2008), 5–27.

[25] Eoin Grogan, Lorna O'Donnell and Penney Johnston, *The Bronze Age landscapes of the pipeline to the west: an integrated archaeological and environmental assessment* (Bray 2007), 98.

[26] Gary Conboy, 'A report on the archaeological excavations at Inchirourke, Co. Tipperary', unpublished report, Valerie J. Keeley on behalf of Tipperary County Council, 2009; Robert Hanbidge, 'A report on the archaeological excavations at Inchaquire, Co. Kildare', unpublished report prepared for Headland Archaeology on behalf of Kildare County Council, 2009.

[27] Grogan, O'Donnell and Johnston, *Pipeline to the west*, 282.

[28] Hawkes, 'Prehistoric burnt mound archaeology in Ireland', 344–8.

that was cooked at the site'.[29] Red deer was present in eight of the excavated *fulachtaí fia* along the Dunshaughlin Sewerage Scheme in County Meath and crudely smashed meat-bearing limb bones were present in all samples. The presence of long bones is associated with the exploitation of animals as a meat source, especially species such as cattle and sheep/goat.[30] This was the case at a cluster of *fulachtaí fia* excavated in the townlands of Kilbeg, Co. Westmeath; Caltragh, Co. Sligo; Caheraphuca, Co. Clare; Attireesh, Co. Mayo; Ballina-curra, Co. Limerick; and Athronan, Co. Meath. At Ballinrobe Demesne, Co. Mayo, the concentration of bones derived principally from the butchery of two cattle carcasses under two and a half years of age and the sample consists mostly of meat-producing upper limb bones.[31] Auli Tourunen observed that the processing of a large carcass can be divided into three different stages: slaughter (including skinning and removal of the horn cores), primary butchery (carcass dismemberment) and secondary butchery (preparation for cooking).[32] Further-more, she states that bones with little meat around them, such as skulls, jaws and lower leg bones are usually abandoned or discarded in the initial place of slaughter. Their presence at some excavated sites, however, indicates that animals may have been slaughtered on site and not introduced as processed carcasses. At Burrow or Glennanummer 2, Co. Offaly, butchered animal bone was recovered from a compacted burnt stone platform revetted by a number of timber planks.[33] This platform was separated from the trough suggesting it may have functioned as an area for the slaughter and butchery of animals. Some stake-hole clusters found at *fulachtaí fia* sites have also been interpreted as possibly forming tripod arrangements for the raised butchery of animals or for the collection of blood.[34]

Assuming that the representation of faunal remains reflects the economic and dietary situation, there is a clear indication of the importance of domestic cattle in the local economy during the Bronze Age. However, as was already stated, it is often not the only species present at *fulachtaí fia*, with other domestic and wild animals also used for food consumption. At sites such as Holdenstown, Co. Kilkenny; Sonnagh, Co. Mayo; and Correagh I, Co. Westmeath; pig dominated the assemblage with the latter site producing evidence of butchery in the form of a cut marks visible on the surface of the bone. Analysis of the faunal remains from Sonnagh showed that the pig jaw

[29] Margaret McCarthy, 'Animal bone report from excavations at Balgeeth, Co. Meath', unpublished report, CRDS Ltd on behalf of Meath County Council, 2010, 38.

[30] Finbar McCormick and Emily V. Murray, *Knowth and the zooarchaeology of early Christian Ireland* (Dublin, 2007), 21–3.

[31] Margaret McCarthy, 'Animal bone report', in Gerry Walsh (ed.), *Archaeological excavations on the Ballinrobe Sewerage and Sewage Disposal Scheme 1994* (Ballinrobe, 1995), 37–40.

[32] Tourunen, 'Fauna and *fulachta fiadh'*, 38.

[33] Tim Coughlan, 'A report on the archaeological excavations at Burrow or Glennanummer 2, Co. Offaly', unpublished report, Irish Archaeological Consultancy Ltd on behalf of Offaly County Council, 2009.

[34] Delaney and Tierney, *In the lowlands of south Galway,* 43.

fragments could have all come from a single adult male aged between seventeen and nineteen months, suggesting that the animal was slaughtered during the autumn of its second year.[35] Similar conclusions were drawn from the pig remains at Ballinrobe Demesne.[36] All of the animal bone remains recovered from *fulachtaí fia* excavated at Killoran, Co. Tipperary, in advance of the Lisheen Mines project were identified as sheep.[37] However, as these remains survived in poor condition and were predominately from denser bone such as teeth, this may be a reflection of acidic soil conditions.

The hunting of red deer also seems to have played a significant role and while many of the samples contain antler fragments, the use of locally available wild deer is reflected in the butchered post-cranial bones. At Coolroe, Co. Mayo, red deer form the major part of the assemblage, accounts for 81% of the identifiable bones. The sample consisted mostly of antler fragments from adult male deer. In all, 91 fragments of red deer were identified, including antler, teeth and post-cranial remains. The presence of three unshed burrs, two chopped humeri, a pelvis with clear chop marks and butchered post-cranial bones indicates that the deer were hunted and eaten.[38] At Kilmessan, Co. Meath, the base of an antler set was attached to one of the skull fragments indicating that red deer was hunted before the males lost their antler in late spring.[39] Red deer remains are generally scarce on Bronze Age sites, but have been recovered from 39 *fulachtaí fia* and are particularly common in Chalcolithic and Early Bronze Age contexts.

To date, no *fulachtaí fia* in Ireland have produced fish bone, which is surprising given the proximity of many sites to coastal areas, lakes, rivers and other large bodies of water. It has been suggested that pyrolithic technology was used in the cooking of marine molluscs in shallow roasting or steaming pits during the Late Mesolithic in Ireland.[40] The cooking of fish using a water-boiling technology during the Bronze Age is more difficult to establish. That said, fish bones recovered from a trough at Meur, Sanday, in the Orkney Isles is relevant, as the material within the trough was interpreted as a final deposit from the last boiling episode dated to 790–420 BC.[41] Boiling fish in this manner, however, may not have been practical given the process involved. Interestingly, pottery sherds recovered from Meur, displayed signs of having been immersed in water and are comparable to examples found at Tangwick burnt mound

---

[35] Richard Gillespie and Agnes Kerrigan, *Of troughs and tuyères: the archaeology of the N25 Charlestown Bypass*, NRA Scheme Monograph 6 (Dublin, 2010).

[36] McCarthy, 'Animal bone report', 38.

[37] Sara Cross May, Ciara Murray, John Ó Néill and Paul Stevens, *The Lisheen Mine Archaeological Project* (Dublin, 2005).

[38] Margaret McCarthy, 'Animal bone report from excavations at Coolroe, Co. Mayo', unpublished report, Richard Gillespie on behalf of Mayo County Council, 2012, 53.

[39] McCarthy, 'Animal bone report from excavations at Balgeeth, Co. Meath', 38.

[40] Hawkes, 'The beginnings and evolution of the *fulacht fia* tradition in early prehistoric Ireland', 96–7.

[41] Ronan Toolis, 'The excavation of a burnt mound at Meur, Sanday, Orkney', *Scottish Archaeological Journal* 29 (2005), 31–49.

excavated in Shetland.[42] This raises the possibility that ceramic vessels may have been placed within boiling troughs in order to prepare these resources. While similar practices may have taken place at pyrolithic sites in Ireland, there is currently no supporting archaeological evidence. It is likely that if fish was cooked, it would have been more efficient to do so on hot stones or in some form of earth oven or steaming pit. Ethnographic accounts illustrate how a variety of fish and shellfish could be cooked using hot stones in this manner.[43]

It might be assumed that the only evidence from excavated *fulachtaí fia* pertaining to cooking is the recovery of faunal remains. However, 'cooking' is a wide-ranging culinary term that incorporates many different foodstuffs and should not be viewed solely in relation to the preparation of meat. As discussed elsewhere, pyrolithic technology has been used in the past to cook a wide range of foodstuffs and given the use of hot stones for processing root foods in other cultures, the possibility exists that foods other than meat could have been processed using these methods in Bronze Age Ireland. Plant remains, however, are rarely recovered from burnt stone deposits and are less durable than bone, tending only to survive in ideal conditions. The discovery of charred and uncharred seeds and nuts at some excavated sites does indicate that plant gathering/processing/consumption may have been carried out at *fulachtaí fia*. Examples include Coolderry 2, Co. Tipperary, where a circular trough was divided in two by a single plank. A quantity of hazelnut shell was found in the smaller section of the trough.[44] The high volume of hazelnut shell present may indicate that it was being used at the site, rather than accruing naturally or accidentally occurring if hazel wood was being brought there. The excavator suggests that, as hazelnuts have an outer bitter skin, this could have been easily removed if boiled for a short period and immersed in cold water (blanched). Alternatively, the hazelnuts could have been boiled in order to extract the oil which could have been collected from the surface of the water.

Billy Quinn and Declan Moore have demonstrated through experimentation, that the use of hot stone boiling in a wooden trough is effective in the production of a highly nutritious beverage consisting of malted grain, water, yeast and herbal additives.[45] The success of the experiment combined with the suggestion that cereal grain may have been processed at *fulachtaí fia* using saddle querns of a type found in some sites led the authors to conclude that these sites functioned primarily as Bronze Age beer-processing sites. Although not supported by the discovery of processed cereals on these waterlogged sites,

[42] H. Moore and G. Wilson, 'Food for thought: a survey of burnt mounds of Shetland and excavations at Tangwick', *Proceedings of the Society of Antiquaries of Scotland* 129 (1999), 234.

[43] Thoms, 'The fire stones carry', 443–60; Wandsnider, 'The roasted and the boiled', 13–14.

[44] Patricia Long, 'A report on the archaeological excavations at Coolderry 2, Co. Tipperary', unpublished report, Headland Archaeology Ltd on behalf of Tipperary County Council, 2009.

[45] Quinn and Moore, '*Fulachta fiadh and the beer experiment*', 43–53.

this emphasises that discussions relating to cooking and *fulachtaí fia* should incorporate liquid-based food produce.

Some attempt has been made to provide positive evidence of cooking through residue analysis, a process which has shown some success in relation to Bronze Age ceramics. The technique has been used, for instance, to test for lipids and was carried out on a number of potsherds found in a burnt mound in the Western Isles, in North Uist.[46] The remains were found to contain residual fat, probably from sheep. No such studies have been undertaken in Ireland, where pottery is only rarely found in *fulachtaí fia*. Lipid analysis has been carried out on soil samples taken from the fills of a number of burnt mound troughs[47] but the results of these analyses have been disappointing and further research is required.

Aslton Thoms suggests that two kinds of alterations occur from the heating of stone.[48] Firstly, the stone undergoes a physical change—cracking and colour change. Secondly, the affected stone absorbs other materials such as food residues, charcoals and ashes which is attested to by the blackening of many stones uncovered during excavation. This creates the possibility that lipids may become trapped within the heated stone itself during the process as they would often be in direct contact with the meat itself or the fats which are being expressed. As a result of this, there is considerable promise in the identification of plant chemical signatures and microfossils lipids on fire-cracked stone associated with pyrolithic features.

Luann Wandsnider's study of food composition and heat treatment provides significant information with regard to the application of pyrolithic technology.[49] She explains that lean meats are boiled to restore moisture, which will assist the action of digestive enzymes. Moreover, fatty meat tissues may be boiled in order to promote lipid hydrolysis and to melt and express tissue lipids, which may then be recovered and used for other purposes. This was recently highlighted in relation to Irish water-boiling sites.[50] Experimentation has also demonstrated that fats generally rise to the surface of the water during boiling.[51] These may have been collected or skimmed off the surface as a secondary by-product and used for other purposes such as leather-processing, waterproofing of woollen garments, preservation, and possibly for making

---

[46] Ian Armit and A. Braby, 'Excavation of a burnt mound and associated structures at Ceann nan Clachan, North Uist', *Proceedings of the Society of Antiquaries of Scotland* 132 (2002), 229–58.

[47] P. Finch, 'Analysis of organic extractives from Demesne or Mearsparkfarm, N6 Kilbeggan to Kinnegad, Co. Westmeath', unpublished report, Valerie J. Keeley Ltd, 2007.

[48] Thoms, 'The fire stones carry', 452.

[49] Wandsnider, 'The roasted and the boiled', 15.

[50] Michael Monk, 'A greasy subject', *Archaeology Ireland* 21:1 (2007), 22–4.

[51] O'Kelly, 'Excavations and experiments in Irish cooking places', 122; Christy Lawless, 'A *fulacht fiadh* Bronze Age cooking experiment at Turlough, Castlebar', *Cathair na Mart, Journal of the Westport Historical Society* 10 (1990), 8.

rushlights.[52] The collection of these secondary by-products from troughs, however, cannot currently be supported with evidence, but remains a possibility.

Boiling meat is also seen as an efficient cooking method by which to conserve fat in meat and bone, as opposed to roasting it on an open fire, which can be wasteful.[53] Extracted fat could also have been used for nutrition when dealing with unpredictable food resources.[54] Evidence for marrow extraction is also evident from the excavations recorded; however, if bone is subjected to high boiling temperatures, marrow becomes molten and could melt through the foramen.[55] Boiling was an essential technique used to extract bone grease by Upper Palaeolithic hunter-gatherers in Europe. The process involved smashing the bone into small pieces and boiling it resulting in large numbers of small pieces of spongy bone accompanied by larger shaft splinters. The fragmentary nature of much of the bone remains from *fulachtaí fia* could account for this process taking place; however, this hypothesis remains tentative at best.

The number of animal bones recorded at *fulachtaí fia* in Ireland need not imply that the cooking of animals was of minor importance at these sites. The evidence from many recent excavations strongly suggests that cooking was the primary function of a large proportion of burnt mounds. The formal organisation of some sites (as evidenced from mound revetments and the deliberate placement of certain features), their often continuous use and separateness within the contemporary settled landscape, suggests that cooking perhaps took place within a cycle of feasting events and not as a daily routine.

Cooking facilities

A number of possible cooking features can be proposed for *fulachtaí fia* based on the surviving archaeological remains and parallels in the ethnographic and archaeological record elsewhere in mainland and north-western Europe. A. H. Smith described six basic types of 'cook-stone' facilities common in North America,[56] versions of which were used by hunter-gatherers throughout the Northern Rockies and beyond. These include: (1) an earth oven in a shallow pit with rocks heated therein; (2) an earth oven in a shallow pit with rocks heated in a nearby hearth; (3) a surface oven or hearth with rocks heated therein; (4) a steaming pit with rocks heated in a nearby hearth; (5) stone boiling in a pit with rocks heated in a nearby hearth; and (6) stone boiling in above-ground containers with rocks heated in a nearby hearth.

---

52 Monk, 'A greasy subject', 23.
53 Nakazawa, Straus, Gonzales-Morales, Solana and Saiz, 'On stone-boiling technology in the Upper Paleolithic', 684–93.
54 Nakazawa, Straus, Gonzales-Morales, Solana and Saiz, 'On stone-boiling technology in the Upper Paleolithic', 684.
55 A. K Outram, 'Bone fracture and within-bone nutrients: an experimentally based method for investigating levels of marrow extraction', in P. Miracle and N. Milner (eds), *Consuming passions and patterns of consumption* (Cambridge, 2002), 51–63.
56 A. H. Smith, 'Kalispel ethnography and ethnohistory', in W. Andrefsky, Jr, G. C. Burtchard, K. M. Presler, S. R. Samuels, P. H. Sanders and A. V. Thoms (eds), *The Calispell Valley Archaeological Project final report* (Washington State University, 2000) vol. 1, 410–46.

Pit features accompanying burnt stone deposits in Ireland may have functioned in a similar manner. Two types of cooking, differentiated by heat transfer, may be proposed namely moist-heat cooking and dry-heat cooking. Identifying the purpose of different pits is complicated by the considerable variation in size and morphology. This is illustrated by the multitude of diverse pits identified in recent years filled with deposits of burnt and fire-cracked stones. While these hot-rock cooking methods may have varied considerably, they generally involved some version of roasting, steaming or boiling. Repeated use of a given place also resulted in a large mound or mounds of waste-firing material and may sometimes contain multiple types of cooking apparatus. It is not uncommon for unlined pits of varying sizes to accompany timber-lined troughs. In many cases, these features do not display evidence for in situ burning making interpretation difficult. The occurrence of oxidised and burnt sediments, as well as charcoal, may be indicative of earth ovens or steaming pits. In contrast, the absence of evidence for in situ fires may be indicative of charcoal-less earth ovens, steaming pits and stone-boiling pits where hot stones were transported from adjacent hearths.[57]

Water-boiling troughs

Water-boiling troughs are generally sunken pits, usually located adjacent to hearths and often lined with stone or timber (Pl. III). The current study indicates that 1,482 pit features out of a total of 3,271 excavated in Irish

PL. III—A water-boiling experiment carried out in a reconstructed timber-lined trough. (Courtesy of Irish National Heritage Park, Ferrycarrig, Co. Wexford.)

---

[57] Thoms, 'The fire stones carry', 456.

fulachtaí fia between 1950 and 2010 can be interpreted as water troughs. Almost half (48%) are rectangular in plan. Seven different lining methods have been observed, including stone, planking, roundwood, wattle, clay, hollowed-out logs or a combination of these materials. A further 298 pits exhibit stake-holes, cutting the base and sides suggesting the presence of a former organic lining that no longer survives. These stake-holes can be interpreted as internal supports for wooden side walling. Eight hundred and fourteen trough pits are unlined although the use of an organic lining may have been more common than the archaeological record would suggest.[58] Problems of poor preservation make it difficult to quantify the frequency of wooden troughs, although this seems to have been the most common material used.

Twelve examples contain evidence for internal trough divisions or compartments, possibly used to separate materials from the fired stone during the boiling process. This was the case at sites such as Coolderry 2; Ballycroughan, Co. Down; Dromnevane, Co. Kerry; Gortaroe, Co. Mayo; and Currinah, Co. Roscommon.[59] These divisions have been noted in different trough forms composed of wattle, timber planks or stone slabs. The site evidence suggests that water filled both compartments therefore ruling out a connection with dry heat such as roasting. It is apparent that these trough divisions were an important and integral part of their function. However, as the actual nature of that function is elusive, one possible interpretation is that these divisions were constructed in order to separate hot stones and other debris from the food produce being cooked in the trough. For instance, at Gortaroe, the wattle partition marked a divide between the stone and peaty fills of the trough and between the preserved wood and the half with very little wood.[60] There was also a noted difference in the two separate fills of a stone-lined partitioned trough at Aughinida, Co. Cork.[61]

While water was heated in unlined pits, the addition of a timber or stone lining allowed for a more efficient way of water-boiling in that it maintained the pit structure in wet soil conditions and facilitated regular emptying of heat-shattered stone from the trough. The use of moss as bedding layers under plank bases may also have allowed for the filtering of water, which was tainted by

[58] Hawkes, 'Prehistoric burnt mound archaeology in Ireland', 124–6.

[59] Patricia Long, 'A report on the archaeological excavations at Coolderry 2, Co. Tipperary', unpublished report, Headland Archaeology on behalf of Tipperary County Council, 2009; H. W. M. Hodges, 'The excavation of a group of cooking-places at Ballycroghan, Co. Down', *Ulster Journal of Archaeology* 18 (1955), 17–28. Linda Lynch, 'A report on the archaeological excavations at Dromnevane, Co. Kerry', unpublished report, Aegis Archaeology Ltd on behalf of Kerry County Council, 2007; Richard Gillespie, 'Archaeological excavations on the Westport Main Drainage and Waste Water Disposal Scheme', unpublished report, Mayo County Council, 2001; Gillespie and Kerrigan, *Of troughs and tuyères* 133–7.

[60] Gillespie, 'Archaeological excavations on the Westport Main Drainage', 66.

[61] Ellinor Larsson, 'A report on the archaeological excavations at Aughinida, Co. Cork', unpublished report, Arch-Tech Ltd on behalf of Cork County Council, 2003.

surrounding boggy environments. Water channels are also associated with troughs and while some of these functioned as overflow drainage features, a number of troughs have been identified with accompanying pits at lower levels connected by short channels. These may have functioned as emptying receptacles, allowing standing or sullied water to be released from the trough pit and replenished with fresh water.[62] The placement of some troughs over and adjacent to natural springs would also seem to indicate a preference for fresh, clean water for operations within the trough. This demonstrates that some degree of planning/local knowledge may have been involved in the placement of pits, in terms of the capacity to identify suitable positions for their location.

Dry-roasting and steaming pits

Pits are the most common feature revealed at excavated *fulachtaí fia* and are often found in great numbers. They are also connected with a different class of site where dry heat was employed exclusively, with one or more pits and a small spread of waste-firing material the only archaeological features present. While lined pits functioned as water-heating receptacles, the insubstantial nature of other pit features on these sites makes it unlikely they were used for the purpose of boiling water. Pits cut into sandy soil at other sites would also have made water-boiling impossible without the use of a lining.

The interpretation of such pits is complicated by the fact that many of those identified were not in use at the same time and may have developed sporadically over the life of a site. The majority (70%) are circular or oval in plan. A total of 73 (4%) pits display evidence of burning/oxidisation at the base or are lined with stone suggesting they may have functioned as primitive ovens or roasting pits with an in situ fire, while other pits may have used an external fire to heat the stones (Pl. IV). This type of cooking generally involved an unlined pit in which hot stones were evenly distributed and covered by a layer of plant material that served as a base for the food produce. Additional layers of hot stones and plant material were then added, depending on the amount of food being cooked, before being covered by earth. A fire may also have been lit on the surface of the covered pit, depending again on the food type.

Steaming pits would have functioned in a similar manner to earth ovens, the only difference being a small hole in the earthen lid made by a small stick inserted into the pit prior to its filling. As the pit was covered over, the stick was removed. Water was then poured through the small aperture, which was sealed promptly to insure that steam and vapour did not escape. Thoms has written extensively on the use of hot rocks in western North America, whereby prolonged cooking is required to hydrolyse inulin-rich roots adequately, as well

---

[62] Rose M. Cleary and Alan Hawkes, 'Excavation of a *fulacht fia,* ring-ditch and medieval ditch at Carrigtohill, townland, Co. Cork', *The Journal of Irish Archaeology* 23 (forthcoming).

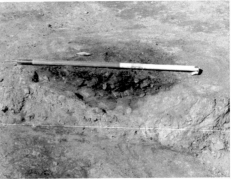

PL. IV—*Left*: Possible roasting pit filled with burnt stone at Kilbeg 4, Co. Westmeath. *Right*: Another possible roasting pit at Tinnock Lower, Co. Wexford. (Courtesy of Fintan Walsh, IAC Ltd and Kevin Martin, VJK Ltd.)

as to detoxify plant foods in order to render them more readily digestible and nutritious.[63]

Experimentation

The use of pyrolithic technology needs further explanation to help to put into context the application of cooking at these sites. This may provide a basis for the interpretation of archaeological remains representative of different cooking facilities. For example, useful data pertaining to how pits functioned at *fulachtaí fia* can be extracted from individual pieces of burnt stone.[64] Thermal-weathering studies have revealed information on how certain heat-affected stones may have been used. It is suggested that rapid cooling (associated with stone-boiling) causes more damage to a stone than prolonged exposure to heat (associated with a roasting oven). The latter was thought to cause less damage because it slowly returned a hot, expanded rock to its original form. It was, therefore, concluded that large rocks (larger than 10cm in diameter) were preferred in earth ovens and rock griddles because they stored heat for longer periods of time.[65] Small rocks (less than 10cm in diameter) were avoided in this cooking method because they had a higher ratio of surface area to mass, which caused them to lose heat more rapidly than larger stones.[66] Therefore, it was argued

[63] Wandsnider, 'The roasted and the boiled', 28

[64] Michael M. Jackson, 'The nature of fire-cracked rock: new insights from ethnoarchaeological and laboratory experiments', unpublished MA thesis, Texas A & M University, 1998; G. Dumarcay, A. Lucquin and R. J. March, 'Cooking and fire on heated sandstone: an experimental approach by SEM', in L. Longo and N. Skakun (eds), *Prehistoric technology 40 years later: functional studies and the Russian legacy*, British Archaeological Report (International Series) 1783 (Oxford, 2008), 345–54.

[65] R. Shalk and D. Meatte, 'The archaeological features', in R. F. Shalk and R. L. Taylor (eds), *The archaeology of Chester Morse Lake: the 1986–87 investigations for the Cedar Falls improvement project* (Washington, D.C., 1988), 8.1–8.58.

[66] Jackson, 'The nature of fire-cracked rock'. 94.

that small rocks were preferred for stone-boiling because of their better resistance to thermal shock and because they were easier to handle. Based on his own experiments, Michael M. Jackson argues that 'the length of time of exposure to high temperatures is more important to thermal weathering than is shock cooling'.[67] For him, the length of heat exposure rather than the rate of cooling causes the highest magnitude of thermal stress to a stone.

The dominance of sandstone in many burnt mounds is significant in this regard. Stephen Mandel observed that coarse-grained rock types are better in terms of the absorption and discharge of heat, whereas fine-grained rock types do not absorb heat in the same manner.[68] The temperature of the fire would also fluctuate depending on the fuel used, therefore, the reaction of some rocks to the heat and water could vary depending on external factors. The selection of sandstone highlights the attention given to different petrologies in terms of their thermal properties for the purpose of water-boiling. As observed by Jackson, the type of stone used is important because its strength will determine the response of a rock to the various types of cooking and heating facilities.[69] It is likely, therefore, that rocks were selected for durability and for their response to specific requirements.

John Ó Néill suggested that it may be possible to establish a direct relationship between the temperature of the fire in which the stones are heated and the volume of the stone required to heat water to cook the meat.[70] O'Kelly demonstrated that it took 35 minutes to bring 454l of water to the boil, and 3 hours and 40 minutes to cook a 4.5kg leg of lamb wrapped in straw. After this experiment, the amount of broken stone that had resulted from it was measured and found to be 0.5m[3].[71] Ó Néill demonstrated that at Ballyvourney, the total heat transfer required to cook meat was probably around 280°C, assuming that the hearth reached temperatures of around 600°C. He also acknowledged that this is not particularly helpful for discriminating between particular thermal regimes. While there is a known rate of increase of rock temperatures and water/stone ratio and the discolouration provided by fires in which the stones would be heated, the apparent ubiquity of hearths placed on humic soils makes a direct correlation between the volume of stone used and pit capacities quite complex.[72] An unknown factor in this analysis is the degree to which the stone deposit in the trough is representative of the final use of the pit. Once immersed in water, the stones required between five and ten minutes to transfer all their heat to the water. O'Kelly for instance had noted that once these stones had lost their heat, they could easily be extracted, reheated and

[67] Jackson, 'The nature of fire-cracked rock', 95.

[68] Stephen Mandel, 'Petrographical report on stone samples from Caltragh, Co. Sligo', unpublished report, Archaeological Consultancy Services Ltd on behalf of Sligo County Council, 2007.

[69] Jackson, 'The nature of fire-cracked rock', 95.

[70] John Ó Néill, *Burnt mounds in Northern and Western Europe: a study of prehistoric technology and society* (Saarbrücken, 2009), 67.

[71] O'Kelly, 'Excavations and experiments in Irish cooking places', 122.

[72] Ó Néill, *Burnt mounds in Northern and Western Europe*, 67.

reused. It is also difficult to establish how much of the trough was emptied after its final use.

Burnt stone equals *fulacht fia*?

The variations in size and layout of burnt mound sites excavated on infrastructural projects may partly be explained by post-depositional disturbance in more recent times. At the same time, one should acknowledge that the variations may be a manifestation of an adaptation of pyrolithic processes to changes in use for whatever reason (see below).[73] We can no longer view these sites as simply representing water-boiling activities associated with a single trough and a mound of burnt stone. Understanding the type of cooking depends on an ability to differentiate between different types of heating process, such as heat transfer by moisture where the heat is transferred through water, and dry heat where the heat is transferred through the air, as in an earth oven or roasting pit.

The most identifiable materials associated with pyrolithic technology are deposits of thermally altered stone and one or more pits associated with dry heat or water-boiling. In light of recent excavations, two main variants can be identified; burnt spreads/mounds that have troughs and those that do not. The former can be subdivided into sites with single troughs, multiple troughs, connected troughs, troughs with structures or sites with single pits, no pits or multiple pits. This allows distinctions to be drawn between the different types of site employing pyrolithic technology. It may be that the innate complexity of *fulachtaí fia* cannot be adequately reflected or accommodated within basic site classifications. The available evidence also makes classification difficult due to the disturbed nature of the archaeological record and limitations with respect to excavation extent. Notwithstanding this, there would appear to be a reasonably strong case to argue that some *fulachtaí fia* had different uses to others, and that this is not a clearly defined monument type but one with considerable variability in terms of practices and features.

Taking into account site disturbance and partial excavation, it is apparent from sites excavated as a result of infrastructural development that a high percentage of burnt stone deposits did not accumulate to such a height that they could be referred to as 'mounds'. As outlined by Susan Ripper and Mathew Beamish, there is a clear distinction between the heating of water and dry-roasting as one-off episodes leaving perhaps solitary pits with no related spread of burnt stone, and the formalisation of such a sites as mounds or 'monuments' that is intentionally defined, used, revisited and sometimes redefined over a period of time.[74] As troughs are marked by an accumulation of burnt stone, these mounds would have been visible in certain locations where they influenced the understanding of settlement space. The revisiting of *fulachtaí fia,* and specifically the reuse and relining of individual troughs, shows that the locations of these sites were an enduring element in the

---

[73] Hawkes, 'Prehistoric burnt mound archaeology in Ireland', 195–200.

[74] Susan Ripper and Mathew Beamish, 'Bogs, bodies and burnt mounds: visits to the Soar Wetlands in the Neolithic and Bronze Age', *Proceedings of the Prehistoric Society* 78 (2011), 173–206.

landscape, even if the activity at each site was episodic. Similarly, the construction of what might have been multiple numbers of cooking pits and/ or hearths at any given time could have invoked a sense of community around a persistent place in the landscape. The act of deposition itself may also have been significant as fired debris could have been mounded to deliberately mark a particular location. Equally, it may have been about connections to specific parts of the landscape and particular ways of doing things in those places. As Vicki Cummings observes in relation to shell midden deposits, it may have been about a connection to a place, a connection that may well have existed in relation to other sites but that was expressed in a different way.[75] This is not the case at other sites employing a similar technology for brief boiling or roasting episodes on a small scale. As a result, a case can be made for the use of sites over longer periods forming mounds as well as smaller sites leaving less significant deposits. This indicates that a number of distinctions can be made in relation to the site type as a whole.

These smaller deposits of fired stone and charcoal with an accompanying pit or pits were probably used for water-boiling, steaming or dry-roasting. Some sites are simply composed of isolated pits filled with deposits of burnt stone and charcoal, also indicative of pyrolithic processes, but are without substantial deposits of waste material. It has been demonstrated elsewhere that pits of this nature were used as ovens or roasting pits related to dry heat without the substantial use of water (see below). Similar sites have been found in Britain along comparable road, pipeline and other development schemes.[76] As such, these features have not been widely discussed as separate distinct entities in Britain and Ireland, with many simply being classified as 'burnt mound' or 'pot-boiler'. These site types do not represent the same level of communal social investment as other *fulachtaí fia,* but are still located in areas of persistent burnt-mound activity where larger, more sustained pyrolithic water-boiling and related processes took place. These lesser sites, employing the same technology must relate to less intensive use compared to the larger burnt mounds. This was the case at sites such as Coolfin 4, Co. Laois,[77] and Ardbraccan 3, Co. Meath,[78] where we see the remains of well-defined troughs with evidence of timber linings and no related mounds. At other sites where this social investment was not undertaken, small unlined pits were used for short-term boiling/roasting/

---

[75] Vicki Cummings, *A view from the west: the Neolithic of the Irish sea zone* (Oxford, 2009), 17.

[76] David Maynard, 'The burnt mounds', in Richard Cutler, A. Davidson and G. Hughes (eds), *A corridor through time: the archaeology of the A55 Anglesey road scheme* (Oxford, 2012), 122–9; Jane Kenney, 'Recent excavations at Parc Bryn Cegin, Llandygai', *Archaeological Cambrenensis* 157 (2008), 55–70.

[77] Ed Danaher, 'A report on the archaeological excavation of Coolfin 4, Co. Laois', unpublished report, Archaeological Consultancy Services Limited on behalf of Laois County Council, 2008.

[78] Matt Mossop, 'A report on the archaeological excavation of Ardbraccan 3, Co. Meath', unpublished report, Archaeological Consultancy Services Limited on behalf of Meath County Council, 2008.

steaming. This may imply that the size and lining of a trough pit partly depended on whether a particular location was deemed important enough for prolonged pyrolithic activity where sufficient resources were locally available. It is reasonable to suggest that these smaller pyrolithic sites were not used for larger communal-based gatherings, but may instead relate to smaller familial or even hunting-party meals organised on an ad hoc basis.[79] The latter may be supported by the recovery of wild animal remains such as those uncovered at sites such as Balgeeth (see above).

This suggests that some tasks, including the preparation and consumption of food, were not confined to any one category of burnt mound site, but took place at many different locations in combination with more specialised activities. At some of the larger burnt mounds, it is conceivable that the archaeological remains represent places that people returned to regularly over a long period. Although difficult to establish, they could represent the remains of a single family usage at a given time or a larger community.

Social context of pyrolithic cooking in Bronze Age Ireland

As Iona Anthony suggests, the function of burnt mounds need not necessarily be seen solely in terms of the practical use of these sites.[80] It is important to acknowledge the importance of these sites socially. For example, two sites might have the same primary use (cooking) but might have served different purposes (communal feasting or family feasting) within the community. These social contexts, along with the socialising component of these gatherings, should not be overlooked in relation to discussions on site function. Food played an essential role in assemblies, as it does in social circumstances today, and would not have been eaten simply for sustenance. Social groups select foodstuffs and organise meals in accordance with cultural norms, and the process may involve historically determined social patterns, such as how the food is prepared.

In this respect, the laborious nature of the process (to the modern observer) suggests that cooking food in this manner may have been largely social, connected to special events and feasting. A review of various experimental work and the historical and ethnographic evidence for similar practices provides an insight into the real time requirements for undertaking pyrolithic processes. This amounts to:

- Preparing a boiling apparatus (including lining if required);
- Collecting firewood and suitable stones;
- Preparation of raw food;
- Lighting of fires and heating of stones;
- Heat transfer process and maintenance of fire and water temperatures.

---

[79] Mathew Murray, 'Viereckschanzen and feasting: socio-political ritual in Iron Age central Europe', *The Journal of European Archaeology* 3:2 (1995), 125–51; Michael Dietler, 'Driven by drink: the role of drinking in the political economy and the case of early Iron Age France', *Journal of Anthropological Archaeology* 9 (1990), 352–406.

[80] Iona M. C. Anthony, 'Luminescence dating of Scottish burnt mounds: new investigations in Orkney and Shetland', unpublished PhD thesis, University of Glasgow, 2003, 67.

Ó Néill observed that, in total, this can represent anything from three to four hours to as many as seven or eight hours or more in duration, depending on the anticipated result.[81] This is a substantial amount of time (compared to everyday residential food production) for an activity that seems to have been undertaken on a sporadic basis. In that sense, burnt mounds may have represented significant places in which people engaged in different forms of social reproduction and the transfer of knowledge.[82]

Pyrolithic activity areas were open-air sites and almost exclusively unenclosed leaving the boundaries between where people lived and communal space (where burnt mounds typically occur) unstructured and highly visible. As Kerri Cleary has outlined in relation to external activity areas within Bronze Age settlements:

> there are less obvious ways in which settlements can be spatially organised, e.g. through the location of external hearths and pits ... which may have been equally important in creating social spaces where people came together to meet, undertake specific tasks and deposit particular artefacts.[83]

The use of these external activity areas as the foci for social activities could also be expanded to include pyrolithic sites, which are frequently found in the environs of settlements. Their exclusive occurrence in specifically designated areas within the settled landscape suggests a clear separation where particular places were selected for the application of pyrolithic technology, thereby creating socially distinctive spaces within the environs of settlement locations. As mentioned previously, the reuse and relining of individual troughs shows that the locations of these sites were a fixed and permanent element of the landscape, even if the activity at each site was episodic. In a few cases, it may be that localised fluctuations in water-table levels dictated the use pattern but these sites mostly functioned as a collective facility to be used as required in different social contexts.

Eoin Grogan in his work on the North Munster Project, and later in collaboration with Lorna O'Donnell and Penney Johnston, suggests that the sheer numbers of *fulachtaí fia* across Ireland indicate that they operated at a communal and possibly even a familial social scale, while their size suggests that they were the focus of relatively small groups.[84] In relation to cooking, they may have provided the context for gatherings of kin and neighbours in order to prepare and share food as part of a regular social round, probably on special days and occasions that engendered bonding within local communities, outside

---

[81] Ó Néill, *Burnt mounds in Northern and Western Europe*, 197.

[82] Ó Néill, *Burnt mounds in Northern and Western Europe*, 197.

[83] K. Cleary, 'Irish Bronze Age settlements: spatial organisation and deposition of material culture', unpublished PhD thesis, University College Cork, 2007, 288.

[84] Grogan, *The North Munster Project*, vol. 2, 138; Grogan, O'Donnell and Johnston, *Pipeline to the west*, 100–01.

the formality of other ceremonies and rituals that may have also taken place at these sites (see below). Wright suggests that storage and food preparation were highly visible activities and would have presented opportunities for social contact between different settlement areas, with the possibility that some facilities may have been shared by several groups.[85] While this should only remain speculative based on current evidence, it remains a possibility nonetheless.

By the Middle Bronze Age functionally and spatially distinct domestic sites were a common feature of the settled landscape. The widespread use of pyrolithic technology would imply that *fulachtaí fia* were an integral part of this settlement pattern. The location of many burnt mounds within these settlement locales, some immediately adjacent to habitations, might question their significance as communal feasting places.[86] Some may have operated on a small scale, where family groups prepared and shared food as part of a regular social round. However, as outlined by Ronan Toolis in relation to a burnt mound on Sanday, small landholding groups may not have had sufficient resources to produce meat for consumption on a regular basis.[87] The provision of communal feasts by different landholding units at different times, may have offered members of the wider community the opportunity to consume meat on a more frequent basis than that of which each individual landholding unit was capable. This would have maintained social cohesion through reciprocal relationships between individual groups within the wider community and may explain the deliberate planning and careful construction of some sites with stone-built hearths and large, lined troughs with substantial structural coverings (Pl. V). Examples such as Scartbarry and Carrignafoy, both in Co. Cork, Cloughjordan, Co. Tipperary, and Coolmoohan, Co. Cork, might have provided appropriate settings for communal feasts given the size of the water-boiling troughs capable of cooking large amounts of food during a single event.[88] The communal aspect of feasting is further supported by the spatial association of many *fulachtaí fia* with stone circles and other ritual monuments from later periods of the Bronze Age.[89] This suggests that the familial, 'domestic', 'communal' and 'ceremonial' use of the technology were not

---

[85] Wright, 'The social origins of cooking and dining in early villages of western Asia', 111.

[86] Moore and Wilson, 'Food for thought', 234; Mike Parker Pearson, *Bronze Age Britain* (London, 2005), 98; Grogan, O'Donnell and Johnston, *Pipeline to the west*, 100.

[87] Toolis, 'The excavation of a burnt mound at Meur, Sanday, Orkney', 45.

[88] William O'Brien, 'Aspects of *fulacht fiadh* function and chronology in Cork', *Journal of the Cork Historical and Archaeological Society* 118 (2012), 107–33; while this site is often referred to as a possible sweat lodge or sauna, it is more likely, based on other more convincing sweat lodges in the archaeological record, that this site was more akin to the production of greater quantities of food. Equally, these sites may have been associated with group bathing.

[89] Ed M. Fahy, 'A hut and cooking places at Drombeg Co. Cork', *Journal of the Cork Historical and Archaeological Society* 65 (1960), 1–17; Connie Murphy, 'The prehistoric archaeology of Beara', in William O'Brien (ed.), *Local worlds: early settlement landscapes and upland farming in south-west Ireland* (Cork, 2009), 13–20; Nick Hogan,

PL. V—*Left*: Large trough, hearth and structure at Scartbarry, Co. Cork. (Courtesy of Ken Hanley, National Roads Authority.) *Right*: Possible 'sweat lodge' at Rathpatrick, Co. Kilkenny. (Courtesy of Trish Long, Rubicon Heritage Services Ltd.)

mutually exclusive and all operated concurrently. These specialised structures should also, at least in part, be attributed to the cost of hosting competitive display feasts. Consumption of high-cost animals, lavish displays or deliberate deposition of particular objects are the hallmarks of competitive displays.[90] In addition to these structures with internal trough, there is also the possibility

---

'The Ardgroom landscape', in O'Brien, *Local worlds*, 69–86; Grogan, *The North Munster Project*, 136–8; Rose M. Cleary and Alan Hawkes, 'Excavation of a *fulacht fia*, ring-ditch and medieval ditch at Carrigtohill, townland, Co. Cork', *Journal of Irish Archaeology* 23 (forthcoming).

[90] Brian Hayden, 'Feasting and social dynamics in the Epipaleolithic of the Fertile Crescent', in Gonzalo Aranda Jiménez, Sandra Montón-Subías and Margarita Sánchez Romero (eds), *Guess who's coming to dinner; feasting rituals in the prehistoric societies of Europe and the Near East* (Oxford, 2011), 46.

that a number of dry-walled structures of the Middle to Late Bronze Age in some upland areas of the country were constructed for similar cooking activities.[91] A site at Garranes, in the Beara Peninsula, Co. Cork, provided evidence for two separate phases of activity that began with a typical *fulacht fia* using the hot-stone/water-boiling technique. This was replaced when a possible roofed structure was constructed over the site for use as a possible cooking house for dry-roasting.[92] The site provided clear evidence for a change in cooking methods, from open-air water-boiling during the Middle Bronze Age, to more specialised activity in a roofed structure during the Late Bronze Age, possibly involving dry-roasting.

The production of steam may have led to new applications of pyrolithic technology during the latter part of the Middle Bronze Age. While water-boiling, and to a lesser extent dry-roasting, remained important throughout the second millennium BC, the use of the technology for the creation of steam may have been limited to certain elements of society.[93] This evidence is very limited but a range of distinguishing characteristics may be tentatively identified. These include the presence of a large circular pit, *c.* 5m in diameter and internally cut by stake-holes indicating the presence of a tented structure. Examples include Rathpatrick and Ballykeoghan, Co. Kilkenny, and Burrow or Glennanummer,[94] sites that have been interpreted as the remains of sweat lodges where water was poured onto hot stones in order to create steam inside small tented structures. Given the rarity of such sites in the archaeological record, these facilities may have been used intermittently for special purposes throughout the year, possibly for ritual cleansing that had a seasonal aspect. The social aspect of the steam lodge is also important and may have been a focus for the gathering of specific groups at periods during the year. This is significant in terms of our wider understanding of the use of pyrolithic technology in prehistoric Ireland.

| *Fulachtaí fia* as feasting locations? | The significance of *fulachtaí fia* in terms of social gatherings may have been connected with feasting events linked to special occasions such as births, weddings, deaths and rites of passage, as well as religious festivities and significant events in the agricultural calendar. While the ethnographic and archaeological literature contains numerous accounts of feasting in other parts of the world, there have been few attempts to examine evidence of feasting in an Irish prehistoric context due to the limited excavation record and poor |

---

[91] William O'Brien, *Local worlds: early settlement landscapes and upland farming in south-west Ireland* (Cork, 2009).

[92] O'Brien, 'Aspects of *fulacht fiadh* function and chronology in Cork', 107–33.

[93] Catriona Gleeson and Gerry Breen, 'A report on the archaeological excavations at Rathpatrick, Co. Kilkenny', unpublished report, Headland Archaeology Ltd on behalf of Kilkenny County Council, 2006; James Eogan, 'Cleansing body and soul', 39.

[94] Gleeson and Breen, 'A report on the archaeological excavations at Rathpatrick, Co. Kilkenny'; Graham Laidlaw, 'Cleansing body and soul', *Seanda* 3 (2008), 26; Tim Coughlan, 'A report on the archaeological excavations at Burrow or Glennanummer 3, Co. Offaly', unpublished report, Irish Archaeological Consultancy Ltd on behalf of Offaly County Council, 2009.

preservation of animal bone remains. As a social phenomenon feasting is complex and often difficult to define.[95] In most cases, prehistoric faunal assemblages in Ireland do not provide clear indications of ceremonial feasting.[96] Mount has argued that the animal bone assemblage discovered in front of the passage tomb at Newgrange, Co. Meath, is indicative of feasting practices,[97] while similar practices connected to burial ceremony have been identified at a number of excavated megalithic tombs in Ireland.[98]

The feast is seen as being less frequent, undertaken outside the residential areas at some significant location and as following its own distinctive rules in relation to such matters as food choice.[99] Brian Hayden observed that feasting can be broadly defined as 'the sharing of special food on special occasions', while Katheryn Twiss defines feasts as 'occasions consciously distinguished from everyday meals, often by a greater number of participants and a larger supply of food'.[100] Furthermore, she suggests that the modes of preparation, the discarding of food waste and the locational framing of the event may also mark certain feasting occasions.[101] Certainly, *fulachtaí fia* would have been prime locations for such activities, as they were often separated from the home base (but within the environs of contemporary settlements), while the method of cooking is differently applied, notably the use of a pyrolithic technology using an indirect heat rather than a direct one.

The size of certain excavated troughs also (up to 5m in length) indicates large-scale boiling episodes for the cooking of large amounts of meat. Niall Roycroft observed that during the Bronze Age, small farming communities/ families with several small herds may have had a surplus of 10–20 beasts

---

[95] Katheryn C. Twiss, 'Transformations in an early agricultural society: feasting in the southern Levantine pre-pottery Neolithic', *Journal of Anthropological Archaeology* 27 (2008) 418–42; Michael Dietler, 'Theorizing the feast: rituals of consumption, commensal politics, and power in African contexts', in Michael Dietler and Brian Hayden (eds), *Feasts: archaeological and ethnographic perspectives on food, politics, and power* (Washington, D.C., 2001), 65–114.

[96] Finbar McCormick, 'Ritual feasting in Iron Age Ireland,' in Gabriel Cooney, Katharina Becker, John Coles, Michael Ryan and Susanne Sievers (eds), *Relics of old decency: archaeological studies in later prehistory* (Bray, 2009), 406.

[97] Charles Mount, 'Aspects of ritual deposition in the Late Neolithic and Beaker periods at Newgrange, Co. Meath', *Proceedings of the Prehistoric Society* 60 (1994), 433–43.

[98] Conleth Manning, 'A Neolithic burial mound at Ashleypark, Co. Tipperary', *Proceedings of the Royal Irish Academy* 85 (1985), 61–100; Carleton Jones, *Temples of the stones: exploring the megalithic tombs of Ireland* (Cork, 2007).

[99] Martin Jones, 'Eating for calories or for company? Concluding remarks on consuming passions', in Miracle and Milner, *Consuming passions and patterns of consumption*, 131–6.

[100] Brian Hayden, 'Fabulous feasts: a prolegomenon to the importance of feasting', in Dietler and Hayden, *Feasts: archaeological and ethnographic perspectives on food, politics, and power*, 28; Twiss, 'Transformations in an early agricultural society', 419.

[101] Twiss, 'Transformations in an early agricultural society', 419.

that were not worth feeding, or that could not be fed through the winter.[102] He proposed that *fulachtaí fia* may have been used for large-scale processing of butchered carcases. While evidence pertaining to the preservation of meat during this period is limited, the consumption of large amounts during a single event is nevertheless possible. It is more difficult to establish, however, whether this meat was consumed on site or taken elsewhere. The division of a carcass within a group could also have been used as a means of reinforcing social order at mealtimes, with higher-quality cuts restricted to those of higher social standing.[103] Anthony J. Pollard observes that 'animals are woven into the fabric of social life through their ubiquitous presence and involvement in the creation and maintenance of social relations as a medium of exchange, feasting and offering'.[104] Ethnographic accounts confirm that in many indigenous societies cattle symbolise wealth, power and prestige, and their meat was only consumed during feasting rituals.[105] It is noteworthy in this regard that cattle dominate the animal bone assemblages from burnt stone deposits of Bronze Age date in Ireland.

It has also been noted that there is a strong association between feasting and ritual activity. As Andrew Fleming observed, a ritual area should provide a focal point for the activities of the principals, and should ideally be large enough to hold the participants and preferably designed to circumscribe them in some way.[106] Owing to waterlogging at many burnt mound sites, the available working space may have been limited to a small number of people. Nevertheless, these spaces could still have been important to the performance of feasting ceremonies; indeed, the entire area around some troughs may have been symbolically charged. The identification of trackways and stone surfaces implies the movement of people around the central working space of a site, and the exclusive placement of the hearth and mound material on the shorter ends of the trough imposes limits on the movement of people in certain areas.[107] This may imply that these considerations had important bearings on the use of the surrounding space, particularly where large-scale feasting involved a large audience looking into the central working space. Such concerns regarding site organisation could go some way to explaining the reason for some burnt mounds being open at one end in a horseshoe formation.

---

[102] Niall Roycroft, 'A theory on boiled bull and burnt mounds', *Seanda* 1 (2006) 38–9.

[103] Finbar McCormick, 'The distribution of meat in a hierarchical society: the Irish evidence', in Miracle and Milner, *Consuming passions and patterns of consumption*, 25–31.

[104] Anthony J. Pollard, 'A community of beings: animals and people in the Neolithic of southern Britain', in D. Serjeantson and D. Field (eds), *Animals in the Neolithic of Britain and Europe*, Neolithic Studies Group Seminar Papers 7 (Oxford, 2006), 135–48.

[105] Gonzalo Aranda Jiménez and Sandra Montón-Subías, 'Feasting death: funerary rituals in the Bronze Age societies of south-eastern Iberia', in Aranda Jiménez, Montón-Subías and Sánchez Romero, *Guess who's coming to dinner*, 143

[106] Andrew Fleming, 'Vision and design: approaches to ceremonial monument typology', *Man* 7:1 (1972), 57–73.

[107] Hawkes, 'Prehistoric burnt mound archaeology in Ireland', 309–12.

Feasts are often marked by the production and display of commemorative items, which not only commemorate the feast but retain some of its ritual power.[108] The careful deposition of objects, as part of non-funerary rituals at the site may bear witness to such episodes taking place. The occurrence of votive offerings, such as hoards, foundation or closing deposits is a feature of the broader contemporary landscape in the Bronze Age.[109] While the types of objects found in hoards and votive deposits are rarely encountered at burnt mounds, evidence of special deposits at these sites is now evident in the archaeological record. These include items of stone, metal, animal and human bone and wood, some of which are comparable to structured deposition at Bronze Age settlements.[110]

The considerable effort required to carry out pyrolithic water-boiling implies high cost and hence importance of these possible feasting events for communities. It must be admitted, however, that the association of feasting and *fulachtaí fia* should be viewed with caution until confirmed by future excavations and scientific studies of faunal remains. No single data set is likely to be diagnostic of feasting, especially since many sites lack several of the material correlates described above. However, special occasions may have warranted gatherings for feasting and the importance of such events is supported by specialised structures, large troughs, animal bone assemblages and deliberate deposits from a number of sites.

Conclusion

While this paper considered cooking as the primary purpose of burnt mounds and pyrolithic processes in Bronze Age Ireland, other interpretations have emerged in recent years. The difficulty is that few can be supported by any firm empirical evidence, and through reiteration in the literature, many archaeologists have come to accept these ideas as established fact.

This paper has raised several points with regard to the use of pyrolithic technology in different social settings in Bronze Age Ireland. In the past, function was often conceived in terms of the evidence provided from the early literary sources, however there is now considerable archaeological evidence to support early suggestions that *fulachtaí fia* were used as cooking areas. A review of ethnographic studies of hot-stone cooking features provides possible points

---

[108] Twiss, 'Transformations in an early agricultural society', 424; Hayden, 'Feasting and social dynamics', 48.

[109] Joanna Brück, 'Houses, lifecycles and deposition on Middle Bronze Age settlements in southern England', *Proceedings of the Prehistoric Society* 65 (1999), 145–66; Kerri Cleary, 'Skeletons in the closet: the deposition of human remains on Irish Bronze Age settlements', *Journal of Irish Archaeology* 14 (2006), 23–42.

[110] Eoin Grogan, 'High and low: identity and status in Late Bronze Age Ireland', in V. Ginn, R. Enlander and R. Crozier (eds), *Exploring prehistoric identity in Europe: our construct or theirs?* (Oxford, 2014), 61–3; Alan Hawkes, 'The re-use of prehistoric burnt mounds in Ireland; the importance of social memory, identity and place', in D. Brandherm and G. Plunkett (eds), *Proceedings of the Bronze Age Forum 2013* (forthcoming).

of comparison, especially with regard to how various unlined pits may have served as cooking facilities. However, this should not exclude a small number of secondary uses, as the technology was also possibly connected with steam-bathing at different times during the Bronze Age. Our understanding of *fulachtaí fia*, and how they operated in the daily life and work routines of Bronze Age society, must also be placed against the nature of the excavated evidence of recent years. The archaeological excavation of burnt stone sites in Ireland has largely focused on the results from road and pipeline developments where sites have been severely damaged.

The rapid adoption of pyrolithic technology in Bronze Age Ireland was not based on a search for more efficient cooking techniques, but rather on the social contexts of its use. It has been argued elsewhere that pyrolithic water-boiling technology of the Early Neolithic may have operated on a communal level associated with specialised feasting activities.[111] It could equally be argued that some burnt mounds of the Bronze Age became a symbolic focus of group unity from the later third millennium BC. While small deposits of burnt stone with associated pits may be typical of ad hoc cooking episodes representing a different scale of pyrolithic activity, the larger mounds are marked by a higher level of labour mobilisation and possibly, some degree of inter-group coopera-tion. Instead of isolated hunting camps, we should expect these sites to be located within the environs of a contemporary settlement, with the occupants returning regularly. As a result it is possible to see the importance of the community in Bronze Age Ireland in the social dynamics of *fulachtaí fia* use and their presence in the landscape.

Acknowledgements   The author would like to thank Professor William O'Brien for reading earlier versions of this paper, and for his encouragement throughout my doctoral research. My thanks also to the National Roads Authority (NRA), the relevant archaeological companies and excavation directors who supplied information for this study and the National Monuments Service, Ferrycarrig National Heritage Park, Ken Hanley (NRA), Trish Long (Rubicon Heritage Services), Fintan Walsh (Irish Archaeological Consultancy Ltd) and Kevin Martin for permission to reproduce their photographs. Finally, I would like to thank the editors of this volume, the anonymous reviewer for their helpful comments and Lucy Hogan for her patience and support.

---

[111] Hawkes, 'The beginnings and evolution of the *fulacht fia* tradition in early prehistoric Ireland', 26.

'He is not entitled to butter': the diet of peasants and commoners in early medieval Ireland

CHERIE N. PETERS*

Department of Histories and Humanities, Trinity College Dublin

[Accepted 1 September 2014. Published 16 March 2015.]

Abstract

Hospitality was an important part of early medieval Irish culture and one of the ways this was expressed was through the preparation of meals for guests. Old and Middle Irish law tracts, written mainly in the seventh and eighth centuries, described the types of foods to which each level of free society in early medieval Ireland was entitled during these social visits and, as can be seen from the quotation in the title of this paper, certain restrictions based on grade and status applied. The legal entitlements of commoners to vegetables, dairy products, breads and, on the rare occasion, meats while in another person's home was neither the full range of foods available in early medieval Ireland nor the totality of the foods an individual might consume in their own home or during feasts. An investigation into these law tracts as well as Old and Middle Irish sagas, poetry, other literary compositions and ecclesiastical descriptions of a penitential or hermetic diet suggest a wider range of available foods, including fruits, fish and wild game that both peasants and commoners were likely to have consumed on a seasonal basis.

Introduction

Although a number of factors impact the types of foods individuals consume, like environment, availability, access and nutrition, in hierarchical societies, such as early medieval Ireland, diet is also, partially, influenced by a person's relative social status.[1] The quote from the title of this paper comes from the *c.* 700 Irish law tract entitled *Críth Gablach*, 'Branched purchase'.[2] This clause, amongst others, referred to the minimum entitlements of commoners and nobles when they were entertained as guests in another person's home. Although this law tract did not prescribe the exact foods individuals would

---

* Author's e-mail: petersch@tcd.ie
doi: 10.3318/PRIAC.2015.115.03

[1] See, for example, Marijke van der Veen, 'When is food a luxury?', *World Archaeology* 34:3 (2003), 405–27 and David Waines, '"Luxury foods" in medieval Islamic societies', *World Archaeology* 34:3 (2003), 571–80.

[2] Eoin MacNeill, 'Ancient Irish law. The law of status or franchise', *Proceedings of the Royal Irish Academy* 36C (1921–4), 265–31; Daniel Binchy, *Críth Gablach* (Dublin, 1941, repr. 1970); Liam Breatnach, *A companion to the Corpus Iuris Hibernici* (Dublin, 2005), 244.

have eaten at any one time, it allowed these guests to justly accuse their host of failing in his/her obligations if a named food, to which their grade was entitled, was absent.[3] While *Críth Gablach* and other, similar, law tracts focus mainly on free adult male landowners and their rights, some details regarding the entitlements of women and children are also included, providing an emic perspective of the very least any one grade had the right to expect for his/her ordinary meals. Furthermore, the association between certain foods and commoners or nobles indicated their relative status as 'luxuries'. Unfortunately, these law tracts do not provide any information regarding the food entitlements of peasants, as they were considered semi-free and not legally entitled to hospitality. There is some evidence to suggest, however, that the rights and responsibilities of some peasants may have been similar to those of low-ranking commoners.[4] Thus, the foods that commoners were able to request during hospitality will be used as a foundation for a wider investigation into the alimentary practices of both peasants and commoners.

Outside of the law tracts, certain goods associated with the nobility were also designated as 'luxuries' and these connections can similarly be used to identify the types of foods that were considered appropriate/inappropriate for peasants and commoners. An image of the *Suidigud Tigi Midchúarda*, 'The seating of the house of the mead-circuit', which survives in the *Book of Leinster* (*c.* 1160), expertly illustrates this principle. In this depiction, members of the king's household are carefully positioned around a banqueting hall, and both their proximate position to the king as well as the portion and quality of meat they were afforded were based on their grade and status.[5] Finbar McCormick has shown that the higher up on a cow's back the meat was, the greater status it was afforded; the king received the tenderloin and the queen a rump steak,

---

[3] Fergus Kelly, *A guide to early Irish law* (Dublin, 1988, repr. 1991), 139–40. In one twelfth-century tale of the 'first' recorded satire, as a guest, the poet, Cairpre Mac Edaine, received only three small dry cakes and on the morrow uttered a justified satire upon his host, the king, Bres Mac Eladain: Vernam Hull, 'Cairpre mac Edaine's satire upon Bres Mac Eladain', *Zeitschrift für Celtische Philologie* 18 (1930), 63–9. Similar penalties applied for the refusal of ecclesiastical guests, according to a seventh-century canonical tract: Ludwig Bieler, *The Irish penitentials* (Dublin, 1963), 172–3. If guests were fed rotten or nauseating food, varying penalties also applied: Daniel Binchy, *Corpus Iuris Hibernici: ad fidem codicum manuscriptorum recognovit* (6 vols, Dublin, 1978), vol. i, 180.34–181.4.

[4] Thomas Charles-Edwards, *Early Irish and Welsh kinship* (Oxford, 1993), 307–36.

[5] Trinity College Dublin (TCD), MS 1339, *Book of Leinster, c.* 1160, 29: Fergus Kelly, *Early Irish farming* (Dublin, 1997), 356; George Petrie, 'On the history and antiquities of Tara Hill', *Transactions of the Royal Irish Academy* 18 (1839), Antiquities, 25–232: plates 8–9. The same chart, with slightly different placements, is also found in TCD MS 1318, *Yellow book of Lecan*, late fourteenth early fifteenth century, col. 244, written mostly by Giolla Íosa, son of Donnchadh Mór of the Mac Fhir Bhisigh family, in the fourteenth century.

while the royal doorkeepers received the coccyx.[6] This division of food based on personal grade and status can also be found in a dish entitled the 'cauldron of restitution' (*caire aisic*), which appears in two twelfth-century Irish tales.[7] In each instance, individuals placed their forks into the cauldron and pulled out a meal that was 'sufficient for the company according to their grade and rank'.[8] Thus, the foods which people ate, or were seen to eat in early medieval Ireland, 'did not create social difference in this period but it was evidence of social difference and ... it helped [to] perpetuate that difference'.[9]

Who were peasants and commoners?

Before an in-depth discussion of the types of foods afforded to, and eaten by, peasants and commoners can begin it is perhaps best to clarify to whom exactly the terms 'peasants' and 'commoners' referred in early medieval Ireland between *c.* 680 and 1170.[10] The law tracts, written mainly between the seventh and eighth centuries by a combination of ecclesiasts and lay academics,[11] were 'text-books' composed in law schools and were used to guide judges through cases based on customary law. These texts offer a valuable perspective on social stratification, describing at least seven grades of commoners and a further three grades of semi-free peasants; many of these grades being, sometimes, further

---

[6] Finbar McCormick, 'The distribution of meat in a hierarchical society: the Irish evidence', in Preston Miracle and Nicky Milner (eds), *Consuming passions and patterns of consumption* (Cambridge, 2002), 25–31: 28.

[7] Whitley Stokes, 'The Irish ordeals, Cormac's adventure in the land of promise, and the decision as to Cormac's sword', in Ernst Windisch and Whitley Stokes (eds), *Irische Texte: Mit Übersetzungen und Wörterbuch* (4 vols, Leipzig, 1891), vol. iii, 183–299: 205–06, §§9–10. This saga centres around the king, Cormac Mac Airt, who supposedly reigned in the third century; but the text, as it survives, is most likely a twelfth-century composition, preserved in two fourteenth-century manuscripts, the *Book of Ballymote* and the *Yellow book of Lecan*: Vernam Hull, 'Echtra Cormaic Maic Airt, "The adventure of Cormac Mac Airt"', *Proceedings of the Modern Language Association* 64:4 (1949) 871–83: 871; John O'Donovan, *The banquet of Dun na n-Gedh and the battle of Magh Rath: an ancient historical tale* (Dublin, 1842); Ruth Lehmann, *Fled Dúin na nGéd* (Dublin, 1964). For the date of the text see, Máire Herbert, '*Fled Dúin na nGéd*: a reappraisal', *Cambridge Medieval Celtic Studies* 18 (1989), 75–87.

[8] O'Donovan, *The banquet of Dun na n-Gedh and the battle of Magh Rath*, 51–3.

[9] P.R. Schofield, 'Medieval diet and demography', in C.M. Woolgar, D. Serjeantson and T. Waldron (eds), *Food in medieval England: diet and nutrition* (Oxford, 2006), 239–53: 244.

[10] The date AD 680 has been chosen as the terminus post quem for this discussion as one of the earliest law tracts from early medieval Ireland, *Cáin Fuithirbe*, can be dated, on historical grounds, between AD 678 to 683, see, Daniel Binchy, 'The date and provenance of *Uraicecht Becc*', *Ériu* 18 (1958), 44–54: 51–4; see also Liam Breatnach, 'The ecclesiastical element in the Old-Irish legal tract *Cáin Fhuithirbe*', *Peritia* 5 (1986), 36–52.

[11] Liam Breatnach, 'Lawyers in early Ireland', in Daire Hogan and W.N. Osborough (eds), *Brehons, serjeants and attorneys: studies in the history of the Irish legal profession* (Dublin, 1990), 1–13.

subdivided (Tables 1 and 2).[12] Descriptions of social classes and their property qualifications, found mainly in status-based texts, could vary from school to school and thus from tract to tract, but they all saw themselves as describing island-wide custom rather than regional variations.[13]

The grades of commoners can be categorised as free landowning non-noble farmers of varying degrees of age and wealth, of which the three most well-known grades are: the *fer midboth* ('a man between [two] houses'), the *ócaire* ('young freeman') and the *bóaire* ('cow freeman', similar to the *ceorl* in Anglo–Saxon laws).[14] These grades were especially important, since a person's ability to participate in legal matters, such as a freeman's ability to make contracts with lords (*flathi*) in the socio-economic relationship known as clientship, differed depending on these divisions.[15] These clientship contracts, however, were only available to freemen (noble or commoner, not peasant). Although the law tracts offer less information about this social group, peasants

TABLE 1—Commoner grades listed in c. 700 *Críth Gablach* (from highest to lowest).

Aire coisring
Fer fothlai
Mruigfer
Bóaire febsa
Aithech ara threba a deich
Ócaire
Fer midboth.ii.
Fer midboth.i.

[12] See, for example, the grades of commoners outlined in eighth-century law tracts *Críth Gablach*, 'Branched purchase', and *Uraicecht Becc*, 'Small primer' in Tables 1 and 2. Both of these law tracts are translated in MacNeill, 'Ancient Irish law', 265–31; for the grades enumerated in *Críth Gablach*, see Binchy, *Críth Gablach*, 1, ll. 16–18, §4.

[13] Donnchadh Ó Corráin, 'Nationality and kingship in pre-Norman Ireland', in T.W. Moody (ed.), *Historical studies xi: nationality and the pursuit of national independence, papers read before the conference held at Trinity College, Dublin, 26–31 May 1975* (Belfast, 1978), available online at: http://celt.ucc.ie/nation_kingship.html (last accessed 25 January 2015).

[14] Thomas Charles-Edwards, '*Críth Gablach* and the law of status', *Peritia* 5 (1986), 53–73; Thomas Charles-Edwards, 'Kinship, status, and the origins of the hide', *Past & Present* 56 (1972), 3–33: 9. See also, Martin J. Ryan, 'That "dreary old question": the hide in early Anglo–Saxon England', in Nicholas J. Higham and Martin J. Ryan (eds), *Place-names, language and the Anglo–Saxon landscape* (Woodbridge, 2011), 207–23 and Patrick Wormald, 'Society: warriors and dependants', in Christopher Haigh (ed.), *The Cambridge historical encyclopedia of Great Britain and Ireland* (Cambridge, 1985; repr. 2000), 81–7: 84.

[15] Charles-Edwards, *Early Irish and Welsh kinship*, particularly chapter 8 on Irish clientship, 337–63.

Table 2—Commoner grades listed in eighth-century *Uraicecht Becc* (from highest to lowest).

Bóaire túise
Bóaire tanaise
Mruigfer
Fer midboth
Gairid
Flescach
Inol

(mainly the *fuidri*, tenants-at-will, and *bothaig*, cottiers) were also cultivators, but they were semi-free in the eyes of the law and, for the most part, did not own their own property, but cultivated land owned by lords, as labourers or sharecroppers (similar to the *coloni* in Carolingian Francia).[16] *Senchléithi* (serfs) were a group of peasants hereditarily bound to the soil (*adscripti glebae*) and considered a permanent asset of a noble's property.[17]

The extensive detail, regarding the grades of individuals, into which these law tracts delved, indicates an early medieval preoccupation with status, particularly the differentiation between commoners and nobles. This fixation may have been due, in part, to the fact that, outside of the law schools and their texts, it would have been difficult to discern a high-ranking commoner from a low-ranking noble or a high-ranking peasant from a low-ranking commoner.[18] The lawyers, therefore, introduced a variety of social cues, including the foods one was entitled to consume in another person's house in order to reinforce social differentiation. Consequently, these entitlements, though not representative of the total amounts and types of foods consumed by peasants and commoners, can be used as a dietary baseline for wider alimentary practices.

Unfortunately, these law tracts, as well as much of the contemporary secular and ecclesiastical literature, do not focus on the semi-free in society.

[16] See Charles-Edwards, *Early Irish and Welsh kinship*, 338–9, Paul Freedman, *Images of the medieval peasant* (Stanford, 1999), 9–10. Some *fuidri* may have possessed or held limited rights over kin-land, see Rudolf Thurneysen, *Irisches Recht. I. Dire. Ein altirischer Rechtstext. II. Zu den unteren Ständen in Irland*, Abhandlungen der preussischen Akademie der Wissenschaften, Philosophisch-historische Klasse, Nr 2 (Berlin, 1931), repr. in Patrizia de Bernardo Stempel and Rolf Ködderitzsch (eds), *Rudolf Thurneysen Gesammelte schriften* (3 vols, Tübingen, 1991–5), vol. iii, 233–55. See also, Charles-Edwards, *Early Irish and Welsh kinship*, 319–24.

[17] Charles-Edwards, '*Críth Gablach* and the law of status', 58–9; Charles-Edwards, *Early Irish and Welsh kinship*, 309; Gearóid Mac Niocaill, 'The origins of the betagh', *The Irish Jurist* 1 (1966), 292–8.

[18] This problem is particularly prevalent when modern archaeologists attempt to determine the status of an early medieval archaeological site when there is no linked historical association. For the types of social and economic clues that can be utilised, see Michelle Comber, *The economy of the ringfort and contemporary settlement in early medieval Ireland*, British Archaeological Reports, International Series, no. 1773 (Oxford, 2008).

As a result, this analysis will include both a wide variety of sources that relay information directly about commoners and those that indirectly describe a 'poor' diet. The Irish adjective *bocht* (poor) or in its substantive form 'poor man', along with its Latin equivalents, was used throughout Irish history in order to describe a restricted diet in both secular and ecclesiastical works. In the accompanying glosses to the eighth-century legal text *Cethairṡlicht Athgabálae*, 'The four divisions of distraint', for example, the rations for a cowherd (*buachail*), who was in fetters for failure to pay his debts, was, during 'the time of milk', described as 'the fill of a poor man's cup' (*lán eini in boicht*), the capacity of which was twelve hen's eggs or a Roman pint, *c.* six fluid ounces, and 'in the time of corn' he received a half-loaf (*urchaelán*), thin at both ends, in contrast to a round whole loaf.[19] The diet of monks and ascetics was also frequently associated with this type of 'poor' diet; St Columbanus, for instance, insisted, in his monastic Rule, that the food of monks should be poor (*vilis*).[20] The association between the ecclesiastical diet and the diet of a secular peasant, however, should not be exaggerated. In his Rule for monks, St Augustine noted that a monastic diet was simultaneously inferior to a secular nobleman's, but superior to a pauper's.[21] Furthermore, the surviving evidence attests that, although the ideal was 'poor' rations, many ecclesiastics consumed a broader diet, sometimes containing luxury goods.

Previous research into the study of diet in early medieval Ireland has focused on the two main activities for a settled economy, cereal growing and livestock rearing. A.T. Lucas, in his seminal work, 'Irish food before the potato', asserted that 'from prehistoric times to the close of the seventeenth century corn and milk were the mainstay of the national food'.[22] The otherwise excellent study denied meat any significant role in the diet of all socio-economic

---

[19] '*na dlegait biathad acht bochtan no urchaelan no bairgen huasallaithe cona handlonn*' Binchy, *Corpus Iuris Hibernici*, vol. ii, 363.26–7; trans. in W. Neilson Hancock, Thaddeus O'Mahony, Alexander George Richey and Robert Atkinson (eds and trans), *Ancient laws of Ireland* (6 vols, Dublin, 1865–1901), vol. i, 107: 'he is not entitled to any food except the 'bóchtan' or 'urchaelan' or cake of the noble feast with its condiment'. *Bochtan* is glossed '*lcha dlegait biathad s̄ lan eini in boicht*', Binchy, *Corpus Iuris Hibernici*, vol. ii, 364.4; trans. in Hancock *et al.*, *Ancient laws of Ireland*, vol. i, 107: 'he is not entitled to any food but the full of the poor man's [cup]'; see also Kelly, *Early Irish farming*, 577; The discussion of seasonal allotments ('the time of milk' and 'the time of corn') is found in the later commentary.
[20] G.S.M. Walker (ed.), *Sancti Columbani Opera* (Dublin, 1957), 124–5, §5 'Of food and drink'.
[21] George Lawless (ed.), *Augustine of Hippo and his monastic rule* (Oxford, 1987), 80–1, ll. 19–21, §5. Augustine specifically warns that paupers should not join a monastery in hopes of increasing the quantity or quality of his diet. A sentiment that was repeated by the thirteenth-century Humbert of Romans in a sermon to lay Cistercian brothers, Massimo Montanari, *The culture of food (La fame e l'abbondanza)*, trans. by Carl Ipsen (Oxford, 1994), 51.
[22] A.T. Lucas 'Irish food before the potato', *Gwerin* 3:2 (1960), 8–43: 8.

levels. More recently, Fergus Kelly's exhaustive *Early Irish farming* included both cereals and meats as the cornerstones of the medieval diet; importantly, however, he also argued for a potentially balanced diet, depending on seasonal and regional availability of nutritious fruits and vegetables.[23] Both of these studies, however, focused on the diet of nobles, mainly due to the prestige-based nature of many of the surviving sources. While Kelly's discussion included valuable information on restricted ecclesiastical diets and feasts, foods specifically related to the diet of peasants and commoners was often eclipsed by necessary generalisations. Recent archaeological and historical analyses have added to this growing dietary discussion by offering evidence for extensive fishing, fowling and gathering in early medieval Ireland. In order to obtain a clearer image of the diet of peasants and commoners, specifically, the prestige-based legal and literary tradition will, therefore, be counterbalanced by an analysis of literary descriptions of restricted diets and supplementary archaeological evidence.

The law tracts

Hospitality was a vital cultural institution in early medieval Ireland, for which every free law-abiding individual, 'regardless of his rank or profession', was eligible.[24] The seventh- and eighth-century Irish law tracts meticulously describe the types of foods to which each level of free society was entitled during these social visits. As can be seen from the quotation in the title of this paper, certain limitations applied to these meals, based on a person's grade and status; nobles were generally allotted the 'selection of the prime quality parts', while commoners often received the remainders.[25] The nourishment of guests, therefore, reinforced the social hierarchy through these dietary entitlements. Yet, when guests were absent from the meal and the social construct was removed, peasants and commoners had some freedom over the foods they chose to prepare and consume (excluding those foods that were reserved for high-ranking guests and for legal dues owed to lords, kings or churches). As a result, these entitlements offer a vital glimpse into the alimentary practices of peasants and commoners, but do not prescribe a complete dietetic regime.

The two key texts for food entitlements during hospitality are the previously mentioned *Crith Gablach* (*c.* 700) thought to have been produced in a law school near Meath/south Ulster and *Uraicecht Becc*, 'Small primer' (eighth-century), thought to have been produced in a *Nemed* law school in Munster.[26] The authors of these texts record in exhaustive detail luxury food items only due to the nobility on these occasions, as well as standard foodstuffs to which

---

[23] Kelly, *Early Irish farming*, 317.
[24] Catherine O'Sullivan, *Hospitality in medieval Ireland, 900–1500* (Dublin, 2004), 31.
[25] Anton Ervynck, Wim Van Neer, Heide Hüster-Plogmann and Jörg Schibler, 'Beyond affluence: the zooarchaeology of luxury', *World Archaeology* 34:3 (2003), 428–41: 432.
[26] Kelly, *A guide to early Irish law*, 246 (for *Uraicecht Becc*) and 246–8 (for *Crith Gablach*); see also, Binchy, *Crith Gablach*, xiv and Binchy, 'The date and provenance of *Uraicecht Becc*', 44–54 for information regarding some locations and events which help to date and possibly locate the texts.

commoners were entitled. A close reading of these two sources and their discussions regarding the entitlements of commoners will indicate that, although the anonymous authors of these texts approached the entitlements in different ways, allowing for some variety in social practice, they did, as Lucas asserted, focus, mainly, on rations consisting of cereals and dairy products; however, some fruits, vegetables and meat were also documented.

According to *Críth Gablach*, the food provisions appropriate to a visiting *fer midboth*, the lowest ranked commoner, were milk and cheese or cereals; the substitution of cereals for milk and cheese was likely to have been a seasonal allowance during the winter when stores of dairy products were at their lowest.[27] This law tract also specifically denies the *fer midboth* the right to request butter. While no particular reason was expressed, other than 'he is not entitled to butter' (*ní dlig imb*), the *fer midboth*'s inferior rank is the most likely basis for this prohibition, as higher grades of commoner, such as the *aithech ara threba a deich*, were entitled to request this particular dairy product.[28] The contemporary legal tract *Uraicecht Becc* likewise conveyes the provisions for a *fer midboth*, but it describes them exclusively as three loaves (*bairgin*); no seasonal substitutions are indicated.[29] The non-entitlement to butter, or, if *Uraicecht Becc* is to be relied upon, all dairy products, was the only limit specifically imposed upon the meal of a visiting *fer midboth*.

In the outline of the meals that the next commoner grade, the *ócaire*, was allotted while visiting someone else's home there emerges yet another distinction between *Críth Gablach* and *Uraicecht Becc*. According to *Críth Gablach*, an *ócaire* would have been presented with the same basic fare as a *fer midboth*, milk and cheese or cereals, with the same non-entitlement to butter.[30] He was, however, entitled to certain additional side dishes.[31] These supplementary

---

[27] First *fer midboth*: '*A bíathad [a] óenur, ass ⁊ grús nó arbur*', Binchy, *Críth Gablach*, 2, ll. 26–7, §6; 'his food-provision is for himself alone, milk and curds or corn', trans. in MacNeill, 'Ancient Irish law', 283, §66; second *fer midboth*: '*A bíatha[d] [a] óenur, ass ⁊ grús nó arbur*', Binchy, *Críth Gablach*, 2, l. 44, §7; 'food-provision for himself alone, milk and curds or corn': trans. in MacNeill, 'Ancient Irish law', 284, §69. MacNeill translated *grus* as curds, but it was translated in the *Dictionary of the Irish language* and by Kelly as cheese, and as such cheese will be the term used in this discussion, *Dictionary of the Irish Language*, available online at: www.dil.ie (last accessed 4 February 2015), s.v. *grus* (2) and Kelly, *Early Irish farming*, 326.
[28] Binchy, *Críth Gablach*, 2, l. 27, §6; trans. in MacNeill, 'Ancient Irish law', 283, §66.
[29] '*et teora bairgen a biathad*': Binchy, *Corpus Iuris Hibernici*, vol. v, 1610.23; 'and three [loaves] his food-provision': trans. in MacNeill, 'Ancient Irish law', 277, §34.
[30] Binchy, *Críth Gablach*, 5, l. 116, §10; trans. in MacNeill, 'Ancient Irish law', 288, §82.
[31] '*biathad deise dó di as ⁊ grús nó arbaimm*': Binchy, *Críth Gablach*, 5, ll. 115–16, §10. Though the nomenclature in *Uraicecht Becc* listed a *bóaire tanisi*, an analysis of grades and rank shows that the *bóaire tanisi* and the *ócaire* were the same grade. As such, all references will be made to the *ócaire* not the *bóaire tanisi*. See, for example, Neil McLeod, 'Interpreting early Irish law: status and currency. Part 1', *Zeitschrift für Celtische Philologie* 41 (1986), 46–65 and Neil McLeod, 'Interpreting early Irish law: status and currency. Part 2', *Zeitschrift für Celtische Philologie* 42 (1987), 41–115: 72–4.

items included a wooden mug of twelve inches filled with a thickened sour milk (*draumce*)[32] and 'a full-sized [loaf]' (*bairgen*) or 'two [loaves] of a woman's baking' (*di bairgin banḟuini*).[33] These 'loaves' of bread measured, roughly, twelve 'inches' (*ordlach*) in circumference and were as thick as 'a man's little finger' (*lútu laime fir*), according to the eighth-century legal tract *Cáin Aicillne*, 'Law of base-clientship'.[34] Generally, these loaves were produced from barley or oats, as both historical and archaeological evidence has shown that these were the most popular grains cultivated in early medieval Ireland, since wheat and rye require especially rich soil in which to grow and were, as a result, considered luxuries.[35] These two grains, barley and oats, furthermore, lack gluten, a necessary leavening agent, and indicate that these loaves would have been quite dense. The inclusion of sour milk and loaves of bread would seem to indicate that the *ócaire* was not restricted to milk and cheese or cereals, but could request a combination of the three. In *Uraicecht Becc*, on the other hand, the *ócaire* was listed as being entitled to five loaves (*bairgin*) and he was allowed either milk or butter.[36] The potential substitution, in this case, may not have centred on the season, although butter could be salted and preserved for winter, but upon the contents of the homeowner's larder. The choice, therefore, for milk or butter was, likely, not made by the visiting *ócaire*, but by the homeowner, who may have been of a similar grade and needed to reserve his butter stores for

---

[32] '*Cúad dá ordlach .x. di draumcu ar lemlacht cechtar n-aí*': Binchy, *Críth Gablach*, 5, ll. 116–17, §10; 'A noggin of twelve inches of *draumce* instead of new milk for each of the two': trans. in MacNeill, 'Ancient Irish law', 288, §82; Micheál Ó Sé, 'Old Irish cheeses and other milk products', *Journal of the Cork Historical and Archaeological Society* 53:2 (1948), 82–7: 86. Fergus Kelly called this a 'whey drink', Kelly, *Early Irish farming*, 328.

[33] '₇ *bairgen in(d)ruic nó dí bairgin banḟuini*': Binchy, *Críth Gablach*, 5, ll. 117–18, §10; 'and a full-sized [loaf], or two [loaves] of woman's baking': trans. in MacNeill, 'Ancient Irish law', 288, §82.

[34] For the circumference of the loaf see: '*Bargen trichat ungae mesl ar dá ordlach déc is cóir,/ acht ma gabthai gortae díbl dlegait in bráthair im nóin*', 'A [loaf] of thirty ounces, in measure by twelve inches (in size), it is just, unless a famine take it from them, the brethren should get it about nones': text and trans. in Joseph O'Neill, 'The Rule of Ailbe of Emly', *Ériu* 1 (1907), 92–115: 102–03, §31a. John Strachan also has an edition of this text and dates it to before AD 800: John Strachan, 'An Old-Irish metrical Rule', *Ériu* 1 (1904), 191–208: 192. For the thickness described in *Cáin Aicillne*, see: Binchy, *Corpus Iuris Hibernici*, vol. v, 1781.29 and Rudolf Thurneysen, 'Aus dem Irischen Recht I', *Zeitschrift für Celtische Philologie* 14 (1923), 335–94: 345, §6.

[35] See, for example, Michael Monk, John Tierney and Martha Hannon, 'Archae-obotanical studies in early medieval Munster', in Michael Monk and John Sheehan (eds), *Early medieval Munster: archaeology, history and society* (Cork, 1998), 65–75 and Finbar McCormick, Thomas Kerr, Meriel McClatchie and Aidan O'Sullivan, 'The archaeology of livestock and cereal production in early medieval Ireland, AD 400-1100', Early Medieval Archaeology Project, Report 5.1 (December, 2011).

[36] '*cuic bairgin la hais do l him,*': Binchy, *Corpus Iuris Hibernici*, vol. v, 1611.5; 'five [loaves] with milk for him or butter': trans. in MacNeill, 'Ancient Irish law', 277, §35. See also Binchy, *Corpus Iuris Hibernici*, vol. vi, 2327.19.

visits by higher-ranking individuals. While these two texts conflict over the amount of loaves or the type of dairy products appropriate for the meal of an *ócaire,* the character, cereals and dairy, remains the same.

As the grades of commoner progressed up the social ladder so too did the variety of food they were allowed to request while eating in another person's home. The higher grades of commoners listed in *Críth Gablach,* some of which do not appear in *Uraicecht Becc,* were allotted the same basic fare, but with vegetables or various meats as side dishes. The *aithech ara threba a deich,* according to *Críth Gablach,* consumed the typical milk and cheese or cereals, but he was also permitted butter on Sundays as well as 'a *serccol* of condiment with this, *duilesc* [dulse], onions and salt' (*serccol ta(r)rsain[n] la sodain–duilesc, cainnenn, salann*).[37] In the *Ancient laws of Ireland* the editors translated *serccol tarsain* as 'salted venison', but this was queried by Eoin MacNeill who, in his translation of *Críth Gablach* (above), left *serccol* untranslated and referred only, in his footnotes, to an 'official' translation of salted venison.[38] Fergus Kelly has interpreted *serccol* to mean a 'titbit, delicacy' and *tarsunn,* 'a relish', which applied to the dulse (a type of seaweed), onions and salt.[39] The translators of the *Ancient laws of Ireland* may have inferred venison in this particular instance as there are similar historical contexts in which deer meat constituted part of a 'poor' diet (see below).

The meals of the highest grades of commoners, according to *Críth Gablach,* the *bóaire febsa,* the *mruigfer,* the *fer fothlai* and the *aire coisring,* were entitled to meat, likely sourced from domestic livestock. The *bóaire febsa* was entitled to the same meal, milk and cereals, as the grades below him, but with the addition of, according to Eoin McNeill's translation, 'fresh or salted onions for condiment' (*firchainnenn nó saillte do tharsun[n]*).[40] MacNeill's translation was queried by Daniel Binchy who proposed, instead, that *saillte,* in this case, acted as a substantive and referred specifically to salted meat.[41] *Uraicecht Becc,* unfortunately, does not offer any clarification and, instead, outlines 'eight [loaves] for him with their condiment, and salt for their seasoning' (*ocht mbairgin do cona nandlunn ⁊ saland dia tarsand*).[42] The *mruigfer,* according to *Críth Gablach,* was always allowed to have 'butter with its condiment' (*imb do co tarsund*), as well as 'salted meat on the third, fifth, ninth, and tenth days, and on Sunday' (*sall dó i tr[e]isi, i cóicthi, i nómaid, i ndechmaid, in ndomnuch*).[43]

---

[37] Binchy, *Críth Gablach,* 6, ll. 149–50, §12; trans. in MacNeill, 'Ancient Irish law', 290, §86; Kelly, *Early Irish farming,* 304–05; 313.

[38] Hancock *et al., Ancient laws of Ireland,* iv, 309; MacNeill, 'Ancient Irish law', 290, §86, note 1.

[39] Kelly, *Early Irish farming,* 316–17; see also *Dictionary of Irish language,* s.v. *serccol(1), tarsand.*

[40] Binchy, *Críth Gablach,* 7, ll. 168–9, §13, trans. in MacNeill, 'Ancient Irish law', 290, §88.

[41] Binchy, *Críth Gablach,* 62, glossary, s.v. *saillte.*

[42] Binchy, *Corpus Iuris Hibernici,* vol. v, 1611.25–31; trans. in MacNeill, 'Ancient Irish law', 277, §36.

[43] Binchy, *Críth Gablach,* 8, ll. 205–06, §15; trans. in MacNeill, 'Ancient Irish law', 291, §90.

Both MacNeill and Binchy translated *saill* simply as salted meat, but, in a similar context, it could refer specifically to pork.[44] The *fer fothlai* was, likewise, entitled to salted meat while the *aire coisring* was allowed salted meat and titbits or relish.[45]

In these lists of potential meals, the luxury status of certain items is clear; salt was a condiment to which only the grades of an *aithech ara threba a deich* or above were entitled and salted meat, specifically domesticated livestock, was reserved only for the highest grades of commoner, suggesting that fresh meat was indeed a luxury consumed mainly by the nobility. The restrictions on butter, however, become much more interesting when viewed in light of another eighth-century law tract that differentiates between the types of lords in Irish society, based on the renders they received in clientship. A commoner, who had acquired enough wealth to start lending to other commoners, could become what was known as a commoner lord (*flaith aithig*) and was described as the lord 'who is only entitled to butter and seed[-corn] and live cattle' as renders from his clients, distinguishing him from noble lords who were entitled to ale, and various forms of salted and fresh meat.[46] While this description was, mainly, used to highlight the prestige of ale and meat, it simultaneously underlined that the status applied to luxury items, such as butter, was relative.

An important caveat to these itemised lists of food, of which a commoner was allowed to avail while in another person's home, was that certain restrictions on luxury or high-status items could, occasionally, be waived during periods of institutionalised caretaking, such as sick maintenance; a process, which involved the care and treatment of a wounded individual by the attacker. The two main law tracts on the types of food available to a wounded individual, *Críth Gablach* and *Bretha Crólige*, 'Judgements on sick maintenance', describe foods appropriate to both his illness and his status. *Bretha Crólige* maintains the restriction on butter for the *fer midboth*,[47] but relaxes this provision for other grades, such as the *ócaire* and the *bóaire febsa*.[48]

---

[44] See for example, a gloss in the *Thesaurus Palaeohibernicus* on *Broccán's hymn* in which *tinne* 'a flitch (of bacon)' is glossed *saille*: Whitley Stokes and John Strachan (eds), *Thesaurus Palaeohibernicus: a collection of Old-Irish glosses, scholia prose and verse* (2 vols, Cambridge, 1901–03), vol. ii, 339, l. 1, gloss no. 21. *Dictionary of Irish language*, s.v. *saill, tinne (2)*.

[45] *Fer fothlai*: Binchy, *Críth Gablach*, 11, ll. 270–71, §19; trans. in MacNeill, 'Ancient Irish law', 294, §94; *aire coisring*: Binchy, *Críth Gablach*, 12, ll. 300–01, §20; trans. in MacNeill, 'Ancient Irish law', 295, §99.

[46] Binchy, *Corpus Iuris Hibernici*, vol. v, 1772.34–1773.28; trans. in Thomas Charles-Edwards, *Early Christian Ireland*, 93.

[47] Neil McLeod, 'Crólige mbáis' in *Ériu* 59 (2009), 25–36: 33.

[48] *Ócaire*: 'imb i suidiu i treisi, i cóicthi, i nómaid, i ndechmaid, i ndomnuch', Binchy, *Críth Gablach*, 5, ll. 118–9, §10, 'butter, in this case, on the third, fifth, ninth and tenth day, and on Sunday', trans. in MacNeill, 'Ancient Irish law', 288, §82; *bóaire febsa*: 'imb(m) dó i ndeissi, i treisi, i cóicthi, i nnómaid, i ndechmaid, i ndomnuch', Binchy, *Críth Gablach*, 7, ll. 167–8, § 13; 'butter on the second, third, fifth, ninth and tenth day, (and) on Sunday', trans. in MacNeill, 'Ancient Irish law', 290, §88.

The inclusion of butter in a sick person's diet, almost regardless of status, may be indicative of the supplementary nutrients in this foodstuff. The ninth-century ecclesiastical document known as the 'Monastery of Tallaght' contains a story, which describes a group of saints seeking aid from heaven after witnessing penitents dying as a result of a strict penitential diet of bread and water. In response, an angel appeared and ordered the saints to 'mix some meal with their butter to make gruel, so that the penitents should not perish upon their hands(?), because the water and the bread did not suffice to support them' (*ni de min do chummusc doib aranim combed menadach arna toitsitis an aes pende immallama fobithin arna forfoelnangair int uisce ₇ int aran*).[49]

During sick maintenance, Binchy has argued, various members of commoner grades were also allowed to consume salted meat on Sundays between New Year's Eve and Lent and fresh meat between Halloween and New Year's Eve, although the exact days for the latter were not articulated.[50] The loosely worded section in *Bretha Crólige* simply notes that 'every freeman from a *fer midbad* up to an *aire ard* is entitled to fresh meat' (*alid carnai cach aire otha fer midbod connicc airig na(i)rd*), which the later glossators attempted to restrict solely to Sundays or festivals.[51] These relaxations reinforce the notion that, outside of hospitality, a commoner is likely to have consumed a wider variety of foods.

Women and children

The discussion, so far, has focused on foods to which men were entitled in certain situations in early medieval Ireland, as more evidence survives for their consumption than for their wives or their daughters. *Bretha Crólige* is one of the only contemporary sources that describes the food entitlements of sick women; a woman on sick maintenance was entitled to half of the food (*lethbíathad*) to which her husband was entitled.[52] A concubine, however, could only claim one-third or one-quarter of his food;[53] no mention is made of any compositional differences. The surviving sources offer very little information regarding any specific meals prepared for unmarried adult women of commoner grade. One reference, in the ninth-century 'Prose Rule of the Céli Dé', requires nuns who were menstruating to be given *brochan* (v.l. *brothchán*), a dish often reserved for invalids, made by heating milk with oatmeal and herbs.[54] Any law-abiding freeman was entitled to collect herbs for just such a concoction, even if the

---

[49] Edward Gwynn and W.J. Purton, 'The monastery of Tallaght', *Proceedings of the Royal Irish Academy* 19C (1911–12), 115–79: 157–8, §73.

[50] Daniel Binchy, 'Sick-maintenance in Irish law', *Ériu* 12 (1938), 78–134: 108–09.

[51] Daniel Binchy, 'Bretha Crólige', *Ériu* 12 (1938), 1–77: 22–3, §26.

[52] Binchy, 'Bretha Crólige', 24–5, §30, 44–5, §56; Binchy, 'Sick-maintenance in Irish law', 110.

[53] Binchy, 'Bretha Crólige', 44–5, §56; Binchy, 'Sick-maintenance in Irish law', 110.

[54] John O'Donovan, 'Prose Rule of the Céli Dé', in William Reeves (ed.), *The Culdees of the British islands, as they appear in history: with an appendix of evidences* (Dublin, 1864; repr. Somerset, 1994), 84–97: 93; Kelly, *Early Irish farming*, 349.

herbs grew on private property, according to one eighth-century law tract, *Di Astud Chirt ₇ Dligid*, 'On the confirmation of right and law'.[55]

Relaxations of, and exceptions to, the normal fare (unfortunately not discussed) were also acknowledged as appropriate during pregnancy. At this time a woman, and her child, require additional vitamins and nutrients, and this need was recognised in early Irish society. The vernacular ninth-century hagiographical text *Bethu Phátraic* documents one pregnant woman's quest for chives, while another legal tract shows that the smell of malt could trigger a pregnant woman's desire for ale.[56] In the latter case, a person was exempted from any liabilities incurred during the pursuit of ale for a pregnant woman. Ale, mostly brewed from barley, was also an important beverage in the winter, as it provided the consumer with vitamins and nutrients lacking when milk and other vegetables were in short supply.[57] Though the law tracts do not describe the consumption of ale by commoners on a regular basis, *Críth Gablach* insists that a *mruigfer* should always have a 'mug of beer [ale]' (*ian chorma*) available for guests and a 'vat in which a brew can be mashed' (*dabach' i(n) roinmdeltar bruth*) amongst his possessions, suggesting that much, if not all, of the brewing process could be accomplished domestically.[58] According to one eighth-century law tract, *Cethairslicht Athgabálae*, 'The four divisions of distraint', a man could be fined for withholding these longed-for foods from a pregnant woman:

> For the longed-for morsel, i.e. the longing of a pregnant woman, i.e. what she longs for not being given her, i.e. by her own husband, and it was through penuriousness or niggardliness the food was withheld on this occasion, or it was in wantonness. The fine which is for it has a stay of three days, i.e. body-fine.[59]

---

[55] '*Iosa brochain cacha muige*': Binchy, *Corpus Iuris Hibernici*, vol. i, 242.17–18; 'herbs for [an invalid's] broth from every plain', trans. in Kelly, *Early Irish farming*, 304, note 234.

[56] Kathleen Mulchrone, *Bethu Phátraic: the tripartite Life of Patrick* (Dublin, 1939), 120–1; Kelly, *Early Irish farming*, 257, 350; Binchy, *Corpus Iuris Hibernici*, vol. iii, 1068.3.

[57] Kelly, *Early Irish farming*, 333.

[58] Binchy, *Críth Gablach*, 7, l. 184, §15 and ll. 174–5, §14; trans. in Daniel Binchy, 'Brewing in eighth-century Ireland', in B.G. Scott (ed.), *Studies on early Ireland: essays in honour of M.V. Duignan* (Belfast, 1982), 3–6: 4. In certain cases, when ale was owed to a lord in clientship, part of the brewing process was done by the commoner, but the final product was produced by the lord's brewer (*scóaire*), Binchy, 'Brewing in eighth-century Ireland', 3–6.

[59] '*i mir mend .i. mian mna torrcha, .i. gan a mian a thabairt di, .i. ó á fir féin, ocus ar daigin secdachta no crunnachta ro gabadh im in mbiadh ann, no cumad ar daigin esba. Ocus a fuil ann ar treisi, .i. in coirpdire*', text and trans. in Hancock *et al.*, *Ancient laws of Ireland*, i, 180–1; text in *Corpus Iuris Hibernici* is arranged differently '*i mir mend .i. in coirpdire .i. o fir fein .i. mian mna torrcha. .i. gan a thabairt di, ₇ ar daigin secdachta ł crunnachta rogabad imin mbiad ann, ł cumad ar daigin espba; ₇ a fuil ann ar .iii.*', Binchy, *Corpus Iuris Hibernici*, vol. ii, 387.30, gloss, ll. 34–6. See also, Kelly, *A guide to early Irish law*, 154.

Brónagh Ní Chonaill has suggested that one of the reasons lawyers may have justified this fine was because a husband or partner might have withheld food intentionally in an attempt to cause the miscarriage of an unwanted child.[60] The absence of a specific list of foods apportioned to women on sick maintenance, or when on a visit to another person's home, suggests that they were likely to be entitled to the same type of foods as their husband, based on his rank, but in smaller quantities.

On the other hand, there is abundant surviving legal evidence for the types of foods that were considered appropriate for children, as detailed in a list of responsibilities for a foster-parent. Fosterage, in medieval Ireland, was an institution through which a parent gave his child, generally at the age of seven or possibly even at infancy, to another individual to be raised in the proper manner, based on the status of the father.[61] According to *Bretha Crólige*, all children in fosterage were given the 'soft fare of fosterage' (*maotbiad altruma*), explained by a later glossator as 'the yoke of eggs, butter, curds and [porridge]' (*in buidecan ⁊ im ⁊ maotla ⁊ lictiu*).[62] The types of condiments that were added to a basic porridge dish, however, were reflective of their father's grade in society, as another law tract, *Cáin Íarraith*, 'Law of the fosterage-fee', states 'porridge is given to them all, but the flavouring which goes into it differs' (*lite doib uile acht ni cosmuil tuma tet indte*).[63] According to *Cáin Íarraith*, the children of commoners were allotted 'porridge made with buttermilk or water' (*lite blaithighe no uisce*), although quantities were quite small, as they could only expect 'a bare sufficiency of it' (*a seangsaith doibh di*).[64] While the children of nobles were entitled to have fresh butter added to their dishes and the children of kings were allowed honey, the children of commoners were only entitled to have 'salted butter' (*gruiten*) added to their meal 'for flavouring' (*dia tumu*),[65] further reinforcing the luxury status of fresh versus salted foods. The discussion in *Cáin Íarraith* did not detail the differences between the grades of commoners, but it, clearly, attempted to distinguish the child of a commoner from the child of a noble or king based on their food entitlements while in fosterage. Thus,

---

[60] Brónagh Ní Chonaill, 'Child-centred law in medieval Ireland', in R. Davis and T. Dunne (eds), *The empty throne: childhood and the crisis of modernity* (Cambridge, in press), 1–31: 4, available at: http://eprints.gla.ac.uk/3812/1/Child2-Centred_Law.pdf (4 February 2015). See also, Hancock *et al.*, *Ancient laws of Ireland*, iii, 550–3.

[61] Ní Chonaill, 'Child-centred law in medieval Ireland', 11–12. See also Brónagh Ní Chonaill, 'The place of the child in medieval Irish and Welsh law', unpublished PhD thesis, Trinity College Dublin, 2011.

[62] Binchy, 'Bretha Crólige', 42–3, §52. Binchy translated *lictiu* as gruel, but both Ó hInnse and Kelly preferred a translation of porridge. The latter will be used in this thesis: Seamus Ó hInnse, 'Fosterage in early medieval Ireland', unpublished PhD thesis, University College Dublin, 1943, 15, §16; Kelly, *Early Irish farming*, 84; *Dictionary of the Irish language, s.v. littiu.*

[63] Ó hInnse, 'Fosterage in early medieval Ireland', 15, §16.

[64] Ó hInnse, 'Fosterage in early medieval Ireland', 15, §16; Binchy, *Corpus Iuris Hibernici*, vol. v, 1759.39–41.

[65] Ó hInnse, 'Fosterage in early medieval Ireland', 15, §16.

it must be remembered that the foods discussed in the law tracts do not necessarily represent the total foods consumed by children in early medieval Ireland.

It is clear that some of the seventh- and eighth-century law tracts, along with their glosses and commentaries, differed as to the specific foods appropriate for different grades of commoners when in other people's homes. What is consistent, however, is that, according to the jurists, the foods appropriate to commoners were not the same as those appropriate to nobles and kings, and that certain items were considered luxuries. Yet, a range of information from legal, literary, ecclesiastical and archaeological sources indicates that different grades of commoners, their wives and their children were not limited to these items within their own homes, during feasts or even when under certain legal constraints. For example, another one of the dishes to which the poor cowherd in fetters (discussed at the start of this paper) was entitled, is described as the 'bread of the noble feast, with its condiment' (*bairgen huasallaithe cona handlonn*).[66] A later glossator specified this as the bread eaten during 'Easter or Christmas or Sundays' (*casc l notlac l domnaig*).[67] Various hagiographical texts suggest that this feast bread was likely made of wheat; Finian of Clonard, who normally consumed 'a bit of barley bread and a drink of water' (*boim do aran eorna 7 deogh do uisce*), not unlike the meals listed above for commoners, was allowed to exchange this meal for wheaten bread and some broiled salmon on holy days or Sundays in one twelfth- or thirteenth-century vernacular *Life*.[68] Beyond these religious relaxations on the types of foods consumed, other foods such as pulse crops, vegetables, fruits, fish, fowl and meat, were all locally available, with certain regional variations. Although direct records of peasant or commoner consumption of these foods does not always survive, the extant literary and archaeological evidence indicates that these types of foods would have been consumed by a wide range of the population, *including* peasants and commoners.

Alternative sources for milk

As is clear from the discussion of the foods to which commoners, while in another person's home, were entitled, milk and dairy products were important to the early medieval diet. However, the variety of milk types available is often underrepresented in modern discussions. Three domestic animals were bred, either incidentally or wholly, for milk production: cows, goats and sheep. Dairy milk was, by far, the most common type of milk consumed in early medieval Ireland, yet the milk of both goat and sheep was discussed in legal and literary compositions. Unlike cows and sheep, goats are not often found in contemporary

---

[66] See above, note 19. This may also be an early reference to the use of 'trenchers', slices of bread used instead of plates at feasts and which were distributed to the dogs or the poor after the meal had finished: Thomas King Moylan, 'Dubliners: 1200–1500', *Dublin Historical Record* 13:3–4 (1953), 79–93: 89.

[67] Binchy, *Corpus Iuris Hibernici*, vol. ii, 364.7–8.

[68] Whitley Stokes (ed.), 'Life of Findian of Clonard', in *Lives of Saints from the Book of Lismore* (London, 1890), 81, l. 2734, trans., 229.

literature, nor are their bones found in high numbers on early medieval archaeological sites (although this might have more to do with problems in species determination). Yet, goat's milk was valued more highly than sheep's milk in some Irish legal material despite the fact that sheep were generally valued more highly; a twelfth-century commentary on the legal text *Bretha Éitgid*, 'Judgements of inadvertence', valued the milk of a female goat at one and a third of a penny,[69] while the milk of a sheep was valued at one-half or one-third of a penny.[70] For the animals themselves, however, a female sheep could be worth up to three scruples, while the highest value a female goat could attain was two scruples.[71] There is evidence to suggest that goats may have been given to clients by a lord in the economic arrangement known as clientship. Commentary to one eighth-century legal tract, *Di Dligiud Raith ₇ Somaine la Flaith*, 'On the due of fief and lord's revenue', describes the renders a client owed to his lord for the goat as 'a [twelve]-inch mug of [sweet cheese] the first year, a full *cúad* of butter the second, and the makings of two *ians* (of butter) the third year—[man-butter and woman-butter], [four] inches, of standard quality, [woman-butter], five of [man-butter]' (*cuadh da ordlach .x. in .c.bliadain do milsen, cuad lan imme in tanaise, Damna da neine in tres bliadain, ferim ₇ banimb, cethri ordlaigi indraic do baneim, a .u. do ferimb*).[72] Yet, part of the low value placed on sheep's and goat's milk in the contemporary sources may relate to their low milk yields; sheep and goats only produced, approximately, one-tenth the milk yield of cows.[73] One scholar has estimated that medieval sheep and goats only produced between 40 and 50 litres of milk a year, some of which needed to be reserved for the suckling of young.[74] This low yield suited domestic consumption of sheep's and goat's milk. Thus, although goat's and sheep's milk is likely to have played a role in the diet of commoners, as well as their lords, it remained a minor resource.

Pulse crops

Another minor resource in early medieval Ireland was legumes. While the invasion of the Normans increased the cultivation of pulse crops, both historical and archaeological evidence indicates that some parts of the country were already growing peas and beans in the early Middle Ages and that these

---

[69] '*pinginn ₇ trian pinginne ar scath a lachta*', Binchy, *Corpus Iuris Hibernici*, vol. i, 307.10–11; Kelly, *Early Irish farming*, 79.

[70] '*lethpingind arin lacht*', Binchy, *Corpus Iuris Hibernici*, vol. i, 307.6 or '*a aentrian arin lacht*', Binchy, *Corpus Iuris Hibernici*, vol. i, 307.7.

[71] See Kelly for the relative value of a penny and a scruple: Kelly, *Early Irish farming*, 76–9.

[72] Binchy, *Corpus Iuris Hibernici*, vol. iii, 920.28–32, trans. in Bette Crigger, '"A man is better than his birth": identity and action in early Irish law', unpublished PhD thesis, University of Chicago, 1991, 366, §11, with a few emendations based on Kelly's discussion of the text; Kelly, *Early Irish farming*, 78; Breatnach, *A companion to the Corpus Iuris Hibernici*, 295.

[73] Kathy L. Pearson, 'Nutrition and the early-medieval diet', *Speculum* 72:1 (1997), 1–32: 17.

[74] Pearson, 'Nutrition and the early-medieval diet', 17.

crops were, occasionally, directly linked to commoners.[75] In the eighth-century legal tract *Bretha Déin Chécht*, 'Judgements of Dían Cécht', the penalties for wounding members of different grades were associated with different crops. While injuries to kings and bishops were commensurable with different types of wheat and rye grains, the wounds of commoners were linked to oats, peas and beans: 'a grain of oats for a *bóaire* and every person of equal status corresponding to him' (*grainni coirce do boairig 7 cech gra(i)d cuma frisidngair*), while there was 'a pea for an *ócaire* and every person of equal status corresponding to him' (*graine pisi do ocairig 7 cach gra(i)d cuma frisidngair*) and 'a bean for a *fer midboth* and every person of equal status corresponding to him' (*graindi sebe do fir midboth 7 cech gradh cuma frisitngair*).[76] Pulse crops also featured in ecclesiastical diets; in his *Rules* for monks, St Columbanus included beans (*legumina*) in his list of acceptably poor (*vilis*), foods.[77] Archaeobotanical evidence, though limited, from a late eighth- to an early ninth-century phase of Talbot's Tower in Kilkenny and an early medieval farm in Boyerstown, Co. Meath, indicate consumption of peas.[78] Finds from the Viking-Age towns of Dublin and Waterford also contained evidence for legume consumption and are particularly important, since the Irish word *pónair*, used almost exclusively after the tenth century, derived from Old Norse *baunir* ('beans').[79] The cultivation of pulse crops were, however, subject to great geographical variation; rural sites in Leinster, for example, have the most archaeobotanical finds of legumes, while they are almost completely absent from the archaeological record in Connacht.[80] Thus, while pulse crops were part of the diet, they too were a minor resource.

---

[75] Michael A. Monk, 'Evidence from macroscopic plant remains for crop husbandry in prehistoric and early Ireland: a review', *The Journal of Irish Archaeology* 3 (1985–6), 31–6: 34; Aidan O'Sullivan, Finbar McCormick, Lorcan Harney, Jonathan Kinsella and Thomas Kerr, 'Early medieval dwellings and settlements in Ireland, AD 400–1100', Early Medieval Archaeology Project, Report 4.2 (December, 2010), 58.

[76] Daniel Binchy, 'Bretha Déin Chécht', *Ériu* 20 (1966), 1–66: 22–3, §2.

[77] Walker, *Sancti Columbani Opera*, 124–5, 126–7, §3.

[78] Nikolah Gilligan, 'Archaeobotanical assemblage of medieval Talbot's Tower, Kilkenny', Heritage office, Kilkenny Local Authorities, 2012, 13; L. Clarke, 'Report on the archaeological excavation of Boyerstown 3, Co. Meath,' excavation report unpublished, available at: http://www.m3motorway.ie/Archaeology/Section3/Boyerstown3/ (25 January 2015); Finbar McCormick *et al.*, 'The archaeology of livestock and cereal production in early medieval Ireland', 'Plant remains gazetteer', p20–8, available at: http://emap.ie/documents/EMAP_Report_5_Archaeology_of_Livestock_and_Cereal_Production_WEB.pdf (25 January 2015).

[79] Siobhan Geraghty, *Viking Dublin: botanical evidence from Fishamble Street* (Dublin, 1996), 32; John Tierney and Martha Hannon, 'Plant remains', in M.F. Hurley and O.M.B. Scully (eds), *Late Viking Age and medieval Waterford excavations 1986–92* (Waterford, 1997), 889; O'Sullivan *et al.*, 'Early medieval dwellings and settlements in Ireland, AD 400–1100', 55. See also Kelly, *Early Irish farming*, 249. The word *ponair* can also be found in a gloss on *Bretha Déin Chécht*, Binchy, 'Bretha Déin Chécht', 22–3, §2.

[80] O'Sullivan *et al.*, 'Early medieval dwellings and settlements in Ireland, AD 400–1100', 55.

Vegetables and fruits

Various supplements of vegetables and fruits were also likely to have been part of the regular diet of peasants and commoners. The eighth-century legal tract *Di Dligiud Raith ⁊ Somaíne la Flaith* noted that one of the services a client owed his lord was the preparation of a 'garlic feast' (*crimḟeis*), sometime before Easter;[81] failure to hold this feast resulted in a three *séoit* penalty fine.[82] Another eighth-century legal tract, *Di Astud Chirt ⁊ Dliged*, 'On the establishing of right and entitlement', entitled every free person in good legal standing in a *tuath* the right to 'wild garlic' (*crim allda*);[83] even though an accompanying gloss restricted this right to garlic found on common land.[84] Other vegetative plants were associated, more generally, with the poor. According to one story, found in the body of notes that accompany the ninth-century text of the *Félire Óengusso*, 'The martyrology of Óengus', St Columba desired to emulate a 'miserable/poor' (*trógnait*) woman by consuming a soup made solely from nettles.[85] Yet, when the saint asked his cook to prepare the meal for him, the cook added butter to the dish.[86] The addition of the butter may have been nutritionally necessary, but it simultaneously reaffirmed the relative luxury status of butter; although St Columba desired to consume the same meagre meal as a poor person, his nobility was affirmed by the addition of a prestige item.

In some cases, remains from archaeological sites can increase the amount and types of vegetables, not directly mentioned in the documentary sources, which were consumed by farmers. For example, the archaeobotanical remains from Viking-Age Dublin and early medieval rural sites, such as Ballynagallagh, Co. Limerick; Killederdadrum, Co. Tipperary; Lisnagun, Co. Cork; Raystown, Co. Meath; Boyerstown, Co. Meath; and Scart, Co. Kilkenny, contained the remains of wild radish, carrots and cabbage.[87] Some of these remains evidence consumption, notwithstanding that wild radish, in particular, was an invasive weed that occasionally contaminated the cereal crop (especially barley).[88]

---

[81] Crigger, 'A man is better than his birth', 356, §12; Binchy, *Corpus Iuris Hibernici, vol.* v, 1910.24.

[82] Kelly, *Early Irish farming*, 309; Binchy, *Corpus Iuris Hibernici*, vol. v, 1910.24; iii, 918.38–9.

[83] '*Cis lir rosuidigead rodilse cacha tuaithe ada comdilsi da cach recht hae aite | crim allda*': Binchy, *Corpus Iuris Hibernici*, vol. i, 241.19–20; 'How many things have been established as the inherent rights of every territory, and which are equally due to every person ... wild garlic': trans. in Hancock *et al.*, *Ancient laws of Ireland*, v, 483.

[84] '*.i. arna bi techtugud*', Binchy, *Corpus Iuris Hibernici*, vol. i, 241.32; 'which is not appropriated [i.e. held as common property]', trans. in Hancock *et al.*, *Ancient laws of Ireland*, vol. v, 485; *Dictionary of the Irish Language*, s.v. *techtugad*.

[85] Whitley Stokes (ed.), *Félire Óengusso Céli Dé: the martyrology of Oengus the Culdee* (London, 1905), 146–7, notes on the month of June.

[86] Stokes, *Félire Óengusso*, 146–7, notes on June.

[87] McCormick *et al.*, 'The archaeology of livestock and cereal production in early medieval Ireland', 'Plant remains gazetteer', p16, p27, p138, p157, p197, p210.

[88] Gilligan, 'Medieval Talbot's tower, Kilkenny', 14; Geraghty, *Viking Dublin*, 38.

Specific cultivated vegetables were also consistently mentioned in legal and literary texts. When sick, any law-abiding free person in early medieval Ireland was entitled to 'garden herbs' (*lus lubgoirt*) 'for it is for this purpose that gardens have been made' (*air is airi der[ō]nta lubgo[i]rt ar foichill notrusa*).[89] A gloss on this section, however, restricts commoners to honey (*mil*)—presumably because a beehive may have been kept in the garden—cultivated onions and *imus*. During Lent these limitations were applied to both nobles and commoners.[90] Conversely, this statement is contradicted in a later section of the text, which restricts commoners from consuming honey, cultivated onions and unlimited *imus*.[91] Commoners were, instead, only entitled to *imus*.[92] While it is unclear in the historical sources as to which plant is referred to by the term *imus* it is generally believed to have been some type of an umbelliferous plant, possibly wild celery.[93] Plants which were cultivated in gardens clearly acted as a source of food, but so did invasive weeds and wild plants which often grew around rural settlements; although these wild plants probably would have accounted for only a small portion of the diet.

Many varieties of fruits available in early medieval Ireland also found their way into the meals of peasants and commoners. One fruit, in particular, is discussed throughout early Irish literature: the apple. The 'wild apple tree' (*aball*), was listed amongst one of the seven 'nobles of the wood' (*airig fedo*) in the eighth-century law tract *Bretha Comaithchesa*, 'Judgements of neighbour-hood'.[94] Additionally, a common motif in some hagiographical texts was the transformation of bitter wild apples into sweet cultivated ones.[95] While most literary texts reserve the consumption of sweet apples for the nobility, other sources indicate a much broader range of consumers. The seventh-century law tract *Bechbretha*, 'Bee judgements', notes that if a fruit tree lay on, or near, the

---

[89] Binchy, 'Bretha Crólige', 22–3, §27.

[90] Binchy, 'Bretha Crólige', 22–3, §27, gloss number 3.

[91] Binchy, 'Bretha Crólige', 36–7, §45.

[92] '*ar ailid cac otrus humus(a) la Fēne ota airig etir da airic corigi fer midbod, aragair eslane nad comlui, aragair luge ndige nat fuiben fuile*', 'for every (person on) sick-maintenance in Irish law from an *aire itir dā airig* down to a [*fer midboth*] is entitled to [*imus*], which prevents sickness and does not stir it up, which prevents thirst and does not infect wounds', text and trans. in Binchy, 'Bretha Crólige', 36–7, §45.

[93] Binchy, in his edition of the text, translated *imus* as celery: Binchy, 'Bretha Crólige', 23, §27; 37, §45. This translation was followed by Donnchadh Ó Corráin, but he worried about the potential toxicity of the plant, Donnchadh Ó Corráin, 'Ireland c. 800: aspects of society', in Dáibhí Ó Cróinín (ed.), *A new history of Ireland: prehistoric and early Ireland* (Oxford, 2005), 549–608: 567. The *Dictionary of the Irish language* offered parsley as a possible alternative, but this was rejected by Fergus Kelly who instead proposed that *imus* referred to alexanders: *Dictionary of the Irish language*, s.v. *imus*; Kelly, *Early Irish farming*, 254.

[94] Fergus Kelly, 'Old Irish tree-List', *Celtica* 11 (1976), 107–24: 113.

[95] Alan Orr Anderson and Marjorie Ogilvie Anderson, *Adomnán's Life of Columba* (Edinburgh, 1961; repr. and rev. by M.O. Anderson, Oxford, 1991), 96–7, book ii, ch. 2.

boundary between two properties, any fruit which fell onto the neighbouring property was divided equally for three years.[96] In the fourth year the neighbour retained all rights to the fruit, but in the fifth year the cycle began anew.[97] Even if a commoner did not personally own property upon which an apple tree grew it was possible to obtain rights to the consumption of the fruit. Furthermore, one law tract indicates that wild apple trees sometimes grew on common land, yet, in some cases, it was possible to recognise private rights over trees, even on common land;[98] one reference in the eighth-century legal tract *Di Astud Chirt ₇ Dligid* described a 'wild apple (tree?)' (*fiad aball*), which, according to the gloss, had been appropriated by a lord, and strict penalties were enforced for stealing any of the fruit.[99] Common rights of consumption also applied to types of nuts. One Old Irish legal poem, dated between the seventh and the eighth centuries entitled any free person in good legal standing to 'a handful of ripe nuts' (*bas chnoe foísce*). [100] Nuts, particularly hazelnuts, could be eaten whole or 'crushed to form a kind of meal called *maothal*' which Eugene O'Curry described as a meal 'which consisted at first of nut meal and milk and afterwards of oatmeal, milk, cheese, etc.' [101]

Some early medieval sources also describe the distribution to and consumption of wild berries by the poor. In the ninth-century vernacular *Bethu Brigte*, Brigit is described as, twice, giving away baskets filled with apples and sweet sloes or plums (*arni cumrae*) to begging lepers.[102] These fruit-based donations to the poor, however, should not be considered typical fare, but instead were exceptional contributions to their diet by a gracious saint. There is also a story in the *Life* of Cóemgen of Glendalough in which a group of sick people were given blackberries to satisfy their cravings. Blackberries, in particular, are directly associated with commoners in one hagiographical text. In the *c.* twelfth-century *Life* of Senán, his father, Geirgeann, is described specifically as an *aithech* (literally translated as 'rent-payer', *aithech* was a popular term used to describe commoners) and his wife, Senán's mother, picks

---

[96] Thomas Charles-Edwards and Fergus Kelly, *Bechbretha* (Dublin, 1983), 103, notes to §12.

[97] Charles-Edwards and Kelly, *Bechbretha*, 103, notes to §12.

[98] 'im crand ngabala bis i ndithrib': Binchy, *Corpus Iuris Hibernici*, vol. ii, 395.23; 'an appropriated tree which is in the wilderness': trans. in Kelly, *Early Irish farming*, 407.

[99] Binchy, *Corpus Iuris Hibernici*, vol. i, 238.31. For the fine: '.i. na flatha .i. u.s. ind do rigaib cona comgradaibh; amal glas fiadan he': Binchy, *Corpus Iuris Hibernici*, vol. i, 238.34–239.1; 'of the chief, i.e. there are five 'seds' for it to the kings, with those of the same grade; it is like a wild herb', trans. in Hancock *et al.*, *Ancient laws of Ireland*, vol. v, 475.

[100] Daniel Binchy, 'An archaic legal poem', *Celtica* 9 (1971), 152–68: 157, l. 47; MacNeill, 'Ancient Irish law', 307–11.

[101] Geraghty, *Viking Dublin*, 44; Eugene O'Curry, *On the manners and customs of the ancient Irish* (3 vols, Dublin, 1873), vol. i, ccclxv–ccclxvi.

[102] Donnchadh Ó hAodha (ed.), *Bethu Brigte* (Dublin, 1978), 29, §§32–3.

blackberries by a well.[103] Archaeobotanical remains, though often hard to recover, from urban and rural sites in early medieval Ireland further indicate the consumption of strawberries, rowan berries, sloes and bilberries.[104] Fruits and vegetables, which grew around a commoner's property and in cultivated small gardens, were, therefore, exploited by a wide range of consumers in early medieval Ireland, including peasants and commoners; though the types and varieties of these side dishes would have depended, to a large degree, on the season and the geographical location.

Fish

This exploitation of natural resources also applied to the lakes, rivers and extended coastline in Ireland. The fish weirs of Strangford Lough, near Grey Abbey Bay and around Chapel Island in County Down, would have been filled with salmonids such as salmon and sea trout, flatfish such as flounder and plaice, mackerel, cod, grey mullet, skate and conger eels, while the Shannon Estuary contained many of the same fishes, including lampreys and shad.[105] These fish weirs were artificial barriers, of stone or wood, constructed in rivers or estuaries to 'deflect fish into an opening where they could be trapped in nets or baskets'.[106] According to the Old Irish legal tract, *Anfuigell*, 'Wrong judgement or decision', the size of these weirs could be restricted, in case they interrupted the flow of fish to other weirs further upstream or downstream.[107]

Land that had access to a river or estuary was highly valued, and often owned by high-status individuals or churches.[108] Yet, some glosses on the eighth-century law tract, *Cethairslicht Athgabálae* note that a *fine* (kindred) may

---

[103] Whitley Stokes (ed.), 'Life of Senán', in *Lives of saints from the Book of Lismore* (London, 1890), 54–74, trans. 201–21: 57, l. 1880 and ll. 1890-4, trans. 204, l. 1880 and ll. 1890-4; Pádraig Ó Riain, *A dictionary of Irish saints* (Dublin, 2011), 557–60.

[104] Geraghty, *Viking Dublin*, 36–42; McCormick *et al.*, 'The archaeology of livestock and cereal production in early medieval Ireland', 'Plant remains gazetteer', p113, p197, p217; since preservation was often achieved through charring, fruit remains are often difficult to find in the archaeobotanical record: Meriel McClatchie, 'The plant remains', in Rose M. Clery 'Excavations of an early-medieval period enclosure at Ballynagallagh, Lough Gur, County Limerick', *Proceedings of the Royal Irish Academy* 106C (2006), 58–66: 65.

[105] Aidan O'Sullivan, 'Place, memory and identity among estuarine fishing communities: interpreting the archaeology of early medieval fish weirs', *World Archaeology* 35:3 (2003), 449–68: 459.

[106] O'Sullivan, 'Place, memory and identity among estuarine fishing communities', 451.

[107] Whitley Stokes, 'O'Davoren's glossary', in Kuno Meyer and Whitley Stokes (eds), *Archiv für celtische lexicographie* ii (London, 1904), 206, §60; for the association between this section in O'Davoren's glossary and *Anfuigell* see Breatnach, *A companion to the Corpus Iuris Hibernici*, 165.

[108] Gearóid Mac Niocaill, 'Tír Cumaile', *Ériu* 22 (1971), 81–6, especially, 85.

have had common rights to fish weirs in early medieval Ireland[109] and, according to the eighth-century law tract *Di Astud Dligid 7 Chirt*, any free person in good legal standing was entitled to a 'single swift dip of a fishing-net in a stream'.[110] Additionally, some streams were freely accessible to all legal members of the community; Fergus Kelly noted one particular gloss from *Cethairślicht Athgabálae* which refers to a regulation on fishing-nets: 'i.e. of fish i.e. a common place which is for the community in water' (*.i. piscium .i. āit coitcend bīs don tuaith i n-uisce*).[111] Renting the use of fish weirs may also have been a possibility for those commoners who did not have direct water access. The early Irish law tract, *Coibnes Uisci Thairidne*, 'Kinship of conducted water', debates the legal ramifications of the construction of a mill race through a neighbour's land. If a neighbour (a) needed water for his mill and he had to go across his neighbour's (b's) land to reach a lake, river, or pond, this law afforded (a) the legal right to build on (b's) property, as long as (a) either paid (b) a fee or offered (b) usage of the mill.[112] These early medieval watermills could have ponded fish, which would have allowed a neighbour limited access to fishing;[113] they were not, however, specifically constructed for fish, and it is unclear whether or not they would have been consistently restocked for this purpose.[114] Yet, this law text also recorded that one of the entitlements which an heir could not alter was that of a neighbour's fishing weir on his property, provided a fee had been paid to their family.[115] It is possible, then, that, if the offer of payment and or usage was available for a mill race then the same might exist for a fishing weir: the owner of the land could have either been paid for fishing rights or received a share of the catch.

Shellfish offered another opportunity for peasants and commoners to add marine life into their diet. A cave in Kilgreany, Co. Waterford, for instance, may have been a seasonal habitation, where shellfish such as periwinkles, cockles, mussels, oysters and scallops were consumed.[116] Despite the lack of early medieval settlements around the area, Marion Dowd argued that the cave would have been a home to commoners, based on additional finds, including

---

[109] Kelly, *Early Irish farming*, 288; '*l in cora coitcend na fine*', Binchy, *Corpus Iuris Hibernici*, ii, 369.15; 'or the common weir of the *fine*'.

[110] Binchy, *Corpus Iuris Hibernici*, vol. i, 241.20–2; trans. in Kelly, *Early Irish farming*, 286.

[111] Text and trans. in Kelly, *Early Irish farming*, 287, citing Binchy, *Corpus Iuris Hibernici*, vol. iii, 888.15.

[112] David Binchy, 'Irish law tracts re-edited', *Ériu* 17 (1955), 52–85.

[113] Niall Brady, 'Mills in medieval Ireland: looking beyond design', in Steven A. Walton (ed.), *Wind and water in the Middle Ages: fluid technologies from antiquity to the Renaissance* (Tempe, AZ, 2006), 39–68: 51.

[114] Margaret Murphy and Kieran O'Conor, 'Castles and deer parks in Anglo–Norman Ireland', *Eolas: The Journal of the American Society of Medieval Studies* i (2006), 53–70: 55.

[115] Binchy, 'Irish law tracts re-edited', 68–9, §9.

[116] Marion A. Dowd, 'Kilgreany, Co. Waterford: biography of a cave', *The Journal of Irish Archaeology* 11 (2002), 77–97: 87.

small personal ornaments.[117] Shell middens, or mounds of accumulated shells, from early medieval Ireland, such as the one in Cork harbour, which stretched over 125 meters long and was up to two meters thick in some areas, coexisted with good agricultural land, and suggests that the collection of shellfish in the early Middle Ages, as in the Mesolithic period, was 'more than the product of a marginal lifestyle'.[118] Other middens, like those at the ninth-century cashel at Rinnaraw, Co. Donegal, can be found near settlements and are evidence of either the focus of a seasonal habitation 'designed to exploit the local marine resources' or a permanent home in which the occupants were dependent on both local pasturage and marine resources.[119]

The importance of fish in the diet of peasants and commoners in early medieval Ireland should not, however, be overstated. Recent scientific techniques, such as isotopic analysis on human skeletal remains from early medieval burials, can help to determine the types of foods eaten by individuals based on the fact that that 'different classes of food differ in their stable isotope ratio'.[120] Carbon isotopes can provide information regarding the 'ecosystem of the consumer, distinguishing between terrestrial versus marine niches' while nitrogen isotope ratios help to differentiate between herbivores, omnivores and carnivores.[121] Thus, lower levels of $\delta^{13}C$ can indicate a mainly terrestrial as opposed to marine diet, as was the case at the early medieval graveyard at Owenbristy, Co. Galway.[122] Recent isotopic analyses on skeletons from Fishamble Street and John's Lane in Viking-Age Dublin ascribe a mainly terrestrial diet to the inhabitants, but also point to 'some marine protein consumption';[123] some individuals moreover may have consumed 'relatively large amounts of marine products' within the last few years of their lives.[124] These conflicting results can represent both geographical variation (as Owenbristy is some distance from the coast), or a cultural preference. Although there is no 'typical' Viking diet, research from Scotland, England and Dublin

---

[117] Dowd, 'Kilgreany, Co. Waterford', 90.

[118] Peter Woodman, 'Mesolithic middens: from famine to feasting', *Archaeology Ireland* 15:3 (2001), 32–5: 33.

[119] Michelle Comber, 'Tom Fanning's excavations at Rinnaraw Cashel, Portnablagh, Co. Donegal', *Proceedings of the Royal Irish Academy* 106C (2006), 67–124: 108.

[120] Jonny Geber, 'Human remains from Owenbristy' in Finn Delany and John Tierney (eds), *In the lowlands of South Galway: archaeological excavations on the N18 Oranmore to Gort*, National Road Scheme Monograph 7 (Galway, 2011), 88–97: 91.

[121] Laurie J. Reitsema, Douglas E. Crews and Marek Polcyn, 'Preliminary evidence for medieval Polish diet from carbon and nitrogen stable isotopes', *Journal of Archaeological Science* 37:7 (2010), 1413–23: 1413–4.

[122] Geber, 'Human remains from Owenbristy', 91.

[123] Kelly J. Knudson, Barra Ó Donnabháin, Charisse Carver, Robin Cleland and T. Douglas Price, 'Migration and Viking Dublin: paleomobility and paleodiet through isotopic analysis', *Journal of Archaeological Science* 39:2 (2012), 308–20: 317.

[124] Knudson *et al.*, 'Migration and Viking Dublin', 317.

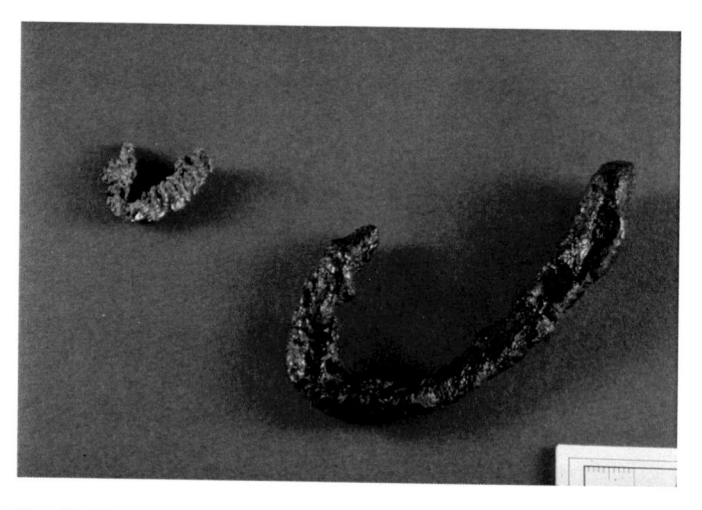

Pl. I—Iron fish hooks from Westness, Orkney, AD 800–1100. Reproduced with the permission of the National Museums of Scotland.

does indicate the consumption of marine foods by these disparate Viking groups (see Pl. I, fishing hook found in a child's furnished burial in Westness, Orkney).[125]

It is probable that farmers in early medieval Ireland, like farmers in medieval Icelandic communities, ploughed and harvested during the respective seasons, and, in the other months, focused more intensely on fishing to supplement their diet;[126] eels, for example, were regularly caught in the Shannon Estuary between October and November after crop harvesting in September.[127] After the growth of urban populations and improved methods of fishing in the tenth and eleventh centuries, however, fishing became more regulated and a source of great wealth and power.[128] During this time fish weirs, ponds, lakes and rivers fell increasingly under the power of a lord or the church, and were less likely to be owned by local commoners.[129] Nevertheless, the surplus of rivers and lakes in Ireland, as well as the surrounding coastline, allowed for a consistent small-scale consumption of marine life by local groups; the amount of fish in a commoner's or peasant's diet is likely to have depended on proximity to a waterway and his or her own resourcefulness.

Wild birds and domestic fowl

Enterprising peasants and commoners were also noted in the historical and archaeological record as consuming various types of wild birds. A blackbird, in one Middle Irish poem, lamented the loss of his wife and children at the hands

---

[125] Knudson *et al.*, 'Migration and Viking Dublin', 312.

[126] Robb Robinson, 'The common North Atlantic pool', in David Starkey, Chris Reid and Neil Ashcroft (eds), *England's sea fisheries: the commercial sea fisheries of England and Wales since 1300* (London, 2000), 9–17: 12.

[127] O'Sullivan, 'Place, memory and identity', 459; Kelly, *Early Irish farming*, 237.

[128] O'Sullivan, 'Place, memory and identity', 462.

[129] O'Sullivan, 'Place, memory and identity', 462.

of some cowherds (*buachalla*)[130] who, according to the eighth-century legal tract *Cethairṡlicht Athgabálae*, shared similar legal rights to slaves and peasants.[131] A quatrain from a poem, ascribed to Colmán mac Lénine, in the Middle Irish preface to *Amra Choluim Chille* listed blackbirds and a female commoner (*banathech*), in contrast to items of higher-value, such as swans and queens.[132] Excavations of a seventh- to ninth-century phase of a ring fort at Rathgurren, Co. Galway, indicated the types of birds likely consumed, including geese, small passerines, such as blackbirds, and seabirds, such as a Manx shearwater.[133] The latter was important for early medieval coastal ecclesiastical communities and pious laymen/women who may have substituted the Manx shearwater for the flesh of quadrupeds during holy days.[134] A part of the eighth-century law tract *Bretha Sén Forma*, 'Judgements on nets for bird-snaring', entitles any individual to trap a small bird (*minnta*), a heron (*corr*) or 'a hawk or other large bird of prey' (*séig*) on a neighbour's property, without first obtaining permission.[135] Some late legal commentary on this law tract notes that in some cases the owner of the land was permitted a portion of the catch;[136] if a bird was caught on land owned by a commoner, he was entitled to one-fifth of the flesh and two-fifths of the feathers.[137] It has been argued, by some scholars, however, that the meat obtained from some wild birds would

---

[130] Kuno Meyer, 'A Middle-Irish lyric', *The Gaelic Journal* 4 (1889) 42–3: 42, ll. 9–12.

[131] '*Ni mug. ni fuidir. ni fulla. ni augaire. ni buachail. ni crette cuaine*': Binchy, *Corpus Iuris Hibernici*, vol. ii, 363.23–4; 'No slave, nor *fuidir*, nor lunatic(?), nor shepherd, nor cowherd nor dog's-body (poet's apprentice)'. For more information on the *crette cuaine na filed*: Liam Breatnach, *Uraicecht na Ríar* (Dublin, 1987), 112–3, §18 commentary.

[132] Whitley Stokes, 'The Bodleian Amra Choluimb Chille', *Revue Celtique* 20 (1899): 31–55, 132–83, 248–89, 400–37: 40–41. See also, Maria Tymoczko, 'The semantic fields of early Irish terms for black birds and their implications for species taxonomy', in A.T.E. Matonis and Daniel F. Melia (eds), *Celtic language, Celtic culture: a festschrift for Eric P. Hamp* (Van Nuys, 1990), 151–71: 157.

[133] Sheila Hamilton-Dyer, 'Exploitation of birds and fish in historic Ireland: a brief review of the evidence', in Eileen M. Murphy and Nicki J. Whitehouse (eds), *Environmental archaeology in Ireland* (Oxford, 2007), 102–18: 107; Sheila Hamilton-Dyer, 'Fish and fowl bones', in Michelle Comber, 'M.V. Duignan's excavations at the ringfort of Rathgurreen, Co. Galway, 1948–9', *Proceedings of the Royal Irish Academy* 102C (2002), 137–97: 192–3.

[134] See, for example, the monastic community at Illaunloughlan, Co. Kerry: Emily Murray, Finbar McCormick and Gill Plunkett, 'The food economies of Atlantic Island monasteries: the documentary and archaeo-environmental evidence', *Environmental Archaeology* 9:2 (2004), 179–88.

[135] Stokes, 'O'Davoren's glossary', 460, §1480. On *Bretha Sén Formae* see Breatnach, *A companion to the Corpus Iuris Hibernici*, 308; Kelly, *Early Irish farming*, 189.

[136] Kelly, *A guide to early Irish law*, 106; Binchy, *Corpus Iuris Hibernici*, vol. vi, 2108.24–9.

[137] '*Mas ar ferannn na ngradh fene roinnled gin fiarfaigid l cu fiarfaigid, cuicedh feola ₇ da .u.eth cluime*': Binchy, *Corpus Iuris Hibernici*, vol. vi, 2108.28–9; 'If it is on the land of the commoner grades that it was trapped without permission or with permission, one-fifth of the flesh and two-fifths of the feathers [are owed]'.

have been tough and generally unpleasant; additionally, in the case of smaller passerines, the amount of available meat was limited.[138]

Peasants and commoners, however, did not have to actively hunt birds in order to consume fowl, as the historical evidence indicates that poultry was often kept on early medieval farmsteads.[139] The surviving historical evidence indicates that chickens, in particular, were kept, firstly, for their eggs and, secondly, for their flesh, as the value of a hen decreased considerably after it was no longer able to lay eggs.[140] Yet, these eggs were not always retained by the owner of the animal; the eighth-century legal tract *Dligid Raith ⁊ Somaine la Flaith* includes hens as one of the loans a lord could give to his client to cement a clientship contract and describes the reciprocal render as a twelve-inch mug full of eggs.[141] Since these hens were only expected to lay about 50 eggs a year, the client owed his lord a substantial part of its produce, limiting the amount of both eggs and fowl that commoners consumed.[142] Geese were also commonly consumed in early medieval Ireland, but a high status could be attached to their eggs in contrast to hens' eggs; the eleventh- or twelfth-century tale *Fled Dúin na nGéd*, 'The banquet of Dun na n-Gedh', describes a fight, which erupted between the high king, Domnall, and his foster son, Congal, king of the Ulaid, when Congal received a hen's egg on a plate as opposed to a goose's egg at a feast.[143] The outrage and war that ensued may have been due, partially, to size, as one quote from a lost legal text notes that a hen's egg was only four inches in circumference and five inches along the vertical axis.[144] While the dimension of the goose egg was not given, it can be accepted that it would have been much larger, relative to the size of the bird.[145] The higher perceived value of a goose egg may also have derived from its limited availability; unlike hens, that could lay for longer periods of time, geese normally only laid in summer.[146] Through

---

[138] Although it has been argued by Umberto Albarella and Richard Thomas that, in medieval England, the rarity of some wild birds increased the perceived status of the consumer regardless of the taste of the bird itself: Umberto Albarella and Richard Thomas, 'They dined on crane: bird consumption, wild fowling, and status in medieval England', *Acta zoologica cracoviensia* 45 (2002), 23–38.

[139] Kelly, *Early Irish farming*, 102–05.

[140] '*da miach ar circ cein dotas, Miach ar caileach cein niunas, lethmiach iarmotha*', Binchy, *Corpus Iuris Hibernici*, vol. v, 1609.38–9; 'two sacks for a hen while it is hatching, a sack for a cock when it is treading, half a sack thereafter', trans. in Hancock *et al.*, *Ancient laws of Ireland*, vol. v, 83.

[141] '*Somuine chirce: a aithgin, cuad da ordluch .x. lan d'uighe*': Binchy, *Corpus Iuris Hibernici*, vol. iii, 920.35–7; 'Render for a hen: it's restitution, a twelve-inch mug full of eggs'.

[142] Kelly, *Early Irish farming*, 104.

[143] O'Donovan, *The banquet of Dun na n-Gedh and the battle of Magh Rath*, 31.

[144] Stokes, 'O'Davoren's glossary', 461, §1484.

[145] See Dale Serjeantson, *Birds* (New York, 2009), specifically 165–83.

[146] Consequently the geese eggs in *Fléd Dúin na n-Gedh* were particularly hard to find since it was not the appropriate season: O'Donovan, *The banquet of Dun na n-Gedh and the battle of Magh Rath*, 16–17, particularly note 'm'.

the processes of domestic fowling, as well as trapping wild birds, it is clear, then, that peasants and commoners consumed both the meat and the eggs of these animals. While some of these smaller birds may only have played a seasonal role, others, like hens, which lay year-round, could have supplemented the normal milk and cereal fare.

Meat

In early medieval Ireland various types of domestic livestock (goats, sheep, cows and pigs) were slaughtered for their meat. The consumption of goats, in particular, was not common in the early medieval sources, and would seem to indicate that they were kept mainly for milk and secondly for meat (as noted above);[147] one condemnation in some Middle Irish satire likened an unfortunate individual to 'an evil, roasted goat' (*felgabar/fonaide*).[148] Sheep, on the other hand, were often consumed, but were prized in the literature more for their wool than their meat[149] and, unlike goats, sheep were frequently owned by commoners.[150] While wethers, castrated male sheep, were included in the food rents that a *fer midboth* owed his lord,[151] one ninth-century poem, the 'Lament of the old woman of Beare', indicates a more general consumption of mutton on special occasions, such as weddings.[152]

Beef, on the other hand, was noticeably lacking from most discussions in the law tracts regarding the foods that commoners could request. The importance of the cow in early medieval Ireland has been well established by modern scholars, such as A.T. Lucas, Fergus Kelly,[153] and by archaeozoologists, such as Finbar McCormick, who has shown that on many early medieval archaeological sites cattle bones clearly outweighed and outnumbered other domestic livestock.[154] There is some evidence, however, to indicate that peasants and commoners were likely to consume beef on special occasions. One of the tasks a client had to perform for his lord was to help with the harvest and groups of these commoners, commonly referred to as a band of reapers

---

[147] See above for the equal value attached to a she-goat's milk, flesh and kids.

[148] Roisin McLaughlin, *Early Irish satire* (Dublin, 2008), 142–3, §27.

[149] The seventh-century *Audacht Morainn*, for example, noted that a king should 'estimate sheep by their covering which is selected for the garments of the people' rather than by their meat: Fergus Kelly, *Audacht Morainn* (Dublin, 1876), 13, §44.

[150] *Ócaire*: Binchy, *Críth Gablach*, 4, ll. 89–91, §10; trans. in MacNeill, 'Ancient Irish law', 286, §77.

[151] Binchy, *Críth Gablach*, 3, ll. 71–6, §9; trans. in MacNeill, 'Ancient Irish law', 286, §73.

[152] '*Ní feraim cobra milis;/ ní marbtar muilt dom banais;/ is bec, is líath mo thrilis;/ ní líach droch-caille tarais*'.'I speak no honied [sic] words; no wethers are killed for my wedding; my hair is scanty and grey; to have a mean veil over it causes no regret': text and trans. in Gerard Murphy, 'The lament of the Old Woman of Beare', *Proceedings of the Royal Irish Academy* 55C (1952–3), 83–109: 94–5, §11.

[153] A.T. Lucas, *Cattle in ancient Ireland* (Kilkenny, 1989); Kelly, *Early Irish farming*, 27–66.

[154] Finbar McCormick and Emily Murray, *Excavations at Knowth: Knowth and the zooarchaeology of Early Christian Ireland* (Dublin, 2007); Finbar McCormick, 'The decline of the cow: agricultural and settlement change in early medieval Ireland', *Peritia* 20 (2008),

(meithel) were occasionally paid in food. An ox, for example, was prepared by Columba, for a band of reapers in the twelfth-century *Betha Choluim Cille*, 'Life of Colum Cille'.[155] In a similar story from the twelfth-century version of the 'Expulsion of the Déisi', however, the food prepared for harvest workers was loaves of bread, not beef.[156]

Unlike sheep, goats and cows, pigs were kept solely for consumption and, as noted above appeared in the dishes that a commoner could request while visiting (see Pl. II, pig about to be slaughtered). Similarly, the main dish

Pl. II—Detail of a miniature of a pig being slaughtered, in the calendar for December. © The British Library Board, Royal 2 B II, f. 6v.

210–25, Margaret McCarthy, 'The faunal remains', in Rose M. Cleary, 'Excavations of an early-medieval period enclosure at Ballynagallagh, Lough Gur, County Limerick', *Proceedings of the Royal Irish Academy* 106C (2006), 1–66: 54; Aidan O'Sullivan, *The archaeology of lake settlement in Ireland* (Dublin, 1998), 117.

155 Whitley Stokes, 'Life of Columb Cille', in *Lives of saints from the Book of Lismore* (Oxford, 1890), 20–33, trans. 168–81; II, 1055–63, trans. 179. For Máire Herbert's more recent edition of the text see: Máire Herbert, *Iona, Kells, and Derry: the history and hagiography of the monastic familia of Columba* (Oxford, 1988), 239, §60, translation 262–3.

156 Richard Best and Osborn Bergin (eds), *Lebor na hUidre: the Book of the Dun Cow* (Dublin, 1992), 137, ll. 4350–5; Vernam Hull, 'The later version of the Expulsion of the Déisi', *Zeitschrift für Celtische Philologie* 27 (1958–9), 14–63, §3, trans. 25, 46. A similar story of bread baked for labourers can be found in the twelfth-century anecdote, 'The quarrel about the loaf': T.P. O'Nowlan, 'The quarrel about the loaf', *Ériu* I (1904), 128–37: 132–5.

served at most feasts during the festival of *Samain* was the 'the piglet of *Samain*' (*banb samna*).[157] One particularly eager suitor attempted to woo a young woman in a ninth-century love poem by promising her 'fresh pork' (*muc úr*).[158] This meat also, occasionally, found its way into the diet of the poor; the ninth-century 'Monastery of Tallaght' records that the monks' leftovers should be used to feed 'the poor with flitches of bacon' (*na mbocht de chrocaib saildi*), indicating consumption by both monks and poor people.[159]

Domestic pig, however, was not the only type of pork available in early medieval Ireland; many historical sources also indicate that wild boar commonly appeared in the diet of hunters and, sometimes, commoners. One story survives in which a commoner was directly responsible for the death of a wild boar; a tract, preserved in the *Triads of Ireland*, outlined how a frustrated Finn Mac Cumaill failed to kill the boar of Druim Leithe as it was instead killed by an commoner: 'It is not well that we fed our hounds,/ it is not well that we rode our horses,/ since a little [commoner] from a kiln/ has killed the boar of Druim Leithe' (*Ní mad biadsam ar cono./ ní mad ríadsam ar n-echa/ tan is aithechán átha./ romarb torcc Dromma Letha*).[160] In this tale, the commoner was clearly not actively engaged in the hunt for the boar, and was, in fact, directly associated with the kiln in opposition to the hunter, Finn, but he does end up with the credit for the kill. Furthermore, the law tracts acknowledge that the 'valuables' of the woods were available to all members of the *túath*, to an extent. The eighth-century legal tract *Di Astud Chirt ⁊ Dligid* includes 'The wild animals of every wood' (*fiad cacha feda*) amongst the list of entitlements every freeman in good legal standing enjoyed in the *túath*;[161] an Old Irish gloss enumerates these wild animals as 'badgers, deer and wild pigs' (*bruic, huis, muca aldti*).[162] Smaller wild animals were given a relatively low status in early medieval Ireland as one Middle Irish satire disparaged its target by comparing him to the 'belly meat of a pine marten'(*a feóil tarra togáin*).[163]

The consumption of wild animals was also noted as part of a poor person's and an ecclesiastic's diet. One of the best surviving examples for the consumption of wild animals by the poor can be found in the seventh-century *Life of Columba* by Adomnán.[164] In this tale, Columba blessed a stake for a

---

[157] Kelly, *Early Irish farming*, 461.

[158] Gerard Murphy, *Early Irish lyrics: eighth to twelfth century* (Dublin, 1998), 107, §7.

[159] Gwynn and Purton, 'The monastery of Tallaght', 128, §3.

[160] Text in Kuno Meyer, *The triads of Ireland* (Dublin, 1906), 30, §236; trans. in Kelly, *Early Irish farming*, 281.

[161] '*Cis lir rosuidigead rodilse cacha tuaithe ada comdilsi da cach recht … fiad cacha feda*': Binchy, *Corpus Iuris Hibernici*, vol. i, 241.19–20 and 241.24–5; 'How many (things) have been established as the inherent rights of every territory, and which are equally due to every person? ... the wild animals of each wood', trans. in Hancock *et al.*, *Ancient laws of Ireland*, vol. v, 483; see also Kelly, *A guide to early Irish law*, 106.

[162] Binchy, *Corpus Iuris Hibernici*, vol. iii, 916.40–41; trans. in Kelly, *Early Irish farming*, 282, note 74.

[163] McLaughlin, *Early Irish satire*, 150–51, §46.

[164] Anderson and Anderson, *Adomnán's Life of Columba*, 148–9, book ii (ch. 37).

poor man that had the power to hurt 'neither man nor any cattle', but would instead kill 'only wild animals, and also fish'.[165] After he had affixed the stake, 'in an out-of-the-way part of the district, frequented by wild creatures',[166] it was not long before the beggar and his family were satiated with venison and the meat of other wild animals.[167] Unfortunately, the poor man was ultimately forced to destroy the stake, due to the unfounded anxiety of his wife, and the family became poor and hungry once again. This same focus on wild animals can also be found in a number of ecclesiastical texts. The ninth-century 'Monastery of Tallaght' notes that 'not a morsel of meat was eaten in Tallaght in his [Máel Ruain's] lifetime . . . (unless) it were a deer or a wild swine' (*nicodoes mír feolai dano hi tamlachdai inda bethusom . . . mad oss no muc allaid*).[168] Although the author then qualified this statement to say that whatever meat was eaten was consumed by guests, wild pork and venison appear in another section of the text as part of the relaxations during Easter and, in this case, the monks were the consumers, for 'he [Mael Ruain] does not reckon this as flesh' (*ar ní ar feoil adrime indísin*).[169] The ninth-century 'Prose Rule of the *Céli Dé*' includes a similar relaxation and notes that at Easter 'eggs, and lard, and the flesh of wild deer, and wild hogs' (*oga acas blonoca acas feoil oss n-allaid acas mucc n-allaid*) could be consumed.[170]

This need to seek out additional food sources from the surrounding landscape was particularly important during recurrent periods of famine and scarcity, which were consistently recorded in the early medieval annalistic record. Between AD 600 and 1170 there are over 50 recorded events of famines, scarcities or cattle murrains, many of which led to a significant loss of cattle, other animals and humans. During these scarcities and famines it was likely that woodland and marine resources were sought to supplement the diets.[171]

---

[165] Anderson and Anderson, *Adomnán's Life of Columba*, 149, book ii (ch. 37).

[166] Anderson and Anderson, *Adomnán's Life of Columba*, 149, book ii (ch. 37).

[167] Anderson and Anderson, *Adomnán's Life of Columba*, 149, book ii (ch. 37).

[168] Gwynn and Purton, 'The monastery of Tallaght', 129, §6.

[169] Gwynn and Purton, 'The monastery of Tallaght', 146, §51.

[170] O'Donovan, 'Prose Rule of the Céli Dé', 85.

[171] These records are taken from a total of nine annalistic compilations: John O'Donovan (ed.), *Annala Rioghachta Eireann: annals of the kingdom of Ireland, by the Four Masters, from the earliest period to 1616* (7 vols, Dublin, 1841–51; repr. 1990); Seán Mac Airt and Gearóid Mac Niocaill (eds), *The annals of Ulster (to A.D. 1131)* (Dublin, 1983); Seán Mac Airt (ed.), *The annals of Innisfallen (MS Rawlinson B 503)* (Dublin, 1944; repr. 1988); Whitley Stokes (ed.), 'The Annals of Tigernach', *Revue Celtique* 16 (1895), 374–419; 17 (1896), 6–33, 116–263, 337–420; 18 (1897), 9–59, 150–303, repr. (2 vols, Felinfach, 1993); Conell Mageoghagan, *The annals of Clonmacnoise*, ed. Rev. Denis Murphy (Dublin, 1896); William Hennessy (ed.), *Chronicum Scotorum: a chronicle of Irish affairs, from the earliest times to A.D. 1135* (London, 1866); Joan Newlon Radner (ed.), *Fragmentary annals of Ireland* (Dublin, 1978); William Hennessy (ed.), *The Annals of Loch Cé: a chronicle of Irish affairs from A.D. 1014 to A.D. 1590* (Dublin, 1871); Séamus Ó hInnse (ed.), *Miscellaneous Irish annals (A.D. 1114–1437)* (Dublin, 1947).

Conclusion

At its core, the diet of peasants and commoners consisted mainly of, prime facie, cereals and dairy products; yet, the resourcefulness of these individuals is often overlooked with such a simplification. Depending on the weather and the location, all sorts of fruits, vegetables, fish and fowl were resources, which could be, and, often, were, added to their normal repast. Meat, furthermore, often considered by historians to be the reserve of the nobility, was also a part, albeit minor, of the diet of commoners. Restrictions to their legal entitlements did still apply; certain items were considered relative 'luxuries', such as butter, wheat, honey and sweet apples. Nobles and churches could make it difficult for peasants and commoners to gain access rights to waterways and forests. The amount of food that commoners owed to their lords in base clientship, could, during recurring periods of famines and scarcities, consistently deplete their resources. Yet, variety did still exist. The lists of foods a commoner was allowed to request when dining in another person's home, therefore, should not be considered the entirety of their diet, but they offer a brief glimpse at wider alimentary practices for both peasants and commoners.

Food plants, fruits and foreign foodstuffs: the archaeological evidence from urban medieval Ireland

SUSAN LYONS*

Department of Archaeology, Connolly Building, Dyke Parade,
University College Cork

[Accepted 4 December 2014. Published 15 May 2015.]

Abstract

The historical record is largely used to qualify the consumption of cultivated crops, and other food plants, such as fruits, vegetables, herbs and imported goods in the medieval Irish diet. Despite our rich literary sources, evidence for horticulture as well as the use of collected and exotic foodstuffs in medieval Ireland is still under-represented, and the remains of such plants rarely survive to make any inferences on the subject. The increase in archaeobotanical research in Ireland is producing a valuable archaeological dataset to help assess the nature, composition and variation of food plants in the medieval diet. Botanical remains preserved in anoxic deposits provide a unique snapshot of the diversity of plants consumed at a site, including information on processing techniques, storage and seasonality. With particular reference to urban medieval sites dating from the tenth to the fifteenth centuries, this paper will present and appraise the archaeological evidence for the use and consumption of cultivated, wild and imported foodstuffs, and the areas of research that still need to be addressed.

Introduction

The main source of information for the types of food plants consumed in medieval Ireland, including agricultural production, is documentary evidence.[1] Over the last 20 years however, the increase in archaeobotanical studies has contributed greatly to research in the areas of arable agriculture, diet and food-processing in Ireland.

The main advantage of using documentary sources is the precisely dateable data that exists providing a calendrical marker for the archaeological record. Early medieval law tracts such as the eighth century AD *Bretha Déin*

---

* Author's e-mail: susan.lyons@ipean.ie

doi: 10.3318/PRIAC.2015.115.11

[1] For an example of early medieval references see Fergus Kelly, *Early Irish farming: a study based mainly of the law-tracts of the 7th and 8th centuries AD* (Dublin, 1997); for examples of later medieval references see James Mills (ed.), *The Account Roll of the Priory of the Holy Trinity, Dublin, 1337–46* (Dublin, 1996).

Chécht[2] and literature associated with saints' lives[3] also provides details on crops and food plants based on a hierarchical system. From the thirteenth century records on land use, landholdings, agricultural practices and food liveries featured prominently in the accounts of Anglo–Norman demesnes, manorial holdings and monastic estates in Ireland.[4] While reference to crop yields, and gardens and orchard produce are found in these sources, explicit details on fruit, vegetable and herb consumption is scarcer.[5] These accounts only provide information on land managed directly by the estate rather than on the people who held individual leasings. The content of these records can be selective in what was recorded, with more emphasis on food consumption from rich households and imported goods. Evidence, therefore, for food consumption is more likely to be available for the upper social classes with little regard for other social groups, such as the tenant farmer, the peasantry and urban populations.[6]

Since the 1980s, archaeobotanical studies in Ireland have been on the increase, largely driven by Mick Monk's work on charred macroscopic cereal remains.[7] In the last fifteen years the nature of infrastructural projects and

[2] D. A. Binchy, 'Bretha Déin Chécht', *Ériu* 20 (1966), 1–66; Kelly, *Early Irish farming*, 27; Regina Sexton, 'Porridges, gruels and breads: the cereal foodstuffs of early medieval Ireland', in Michael Monk and John Sheehan (eds), *Early medieval Munster: archaeology, history and society* (Cork, 1998), 76–86.

[3] Edward J. Gwynn and Walter J. Purton (eds), 'The monastery of Tallaght', *Proceedings of the Royal Irish Academy* 29C (1911–12), 115–70; Edward J. Gwynn, 'An Irish penitential', *Ériu* 7 (1914), 121–95; Edward Gwynn, 'The teaching of Máel Ruain', *Hermathena* 44: 2nd suppl. (2 vols, Dublin, 1927), vol. 1, 2–63. Charles Plummer, *Lives of Irish saints* (2 vols, Oxford, 1922), vol. 1, 126–7.

[4] Mills, *Account Roll of the Priory of the Holy Trinity*; James Mills (ed.), *Calendar of Justiciary Rolls, 1295–1303* (Dublin, 1905). James Mills (ed.), *Calendar of Justiciary Rolls, 1305–07* (Dublin, 1914).

[5] Christopher Dyer, 'Gardens and garden produce in the Later Middle Ages', in Christopher Woolgar, Dale Serjeantson and Tony Waldron (eds), *Food in medieval England: diet and nutrition* (Oxford, 2006), 27–40; Terence Reeves-Smyth, *Irish gardens and gardening before Cromwell* (Cork, 1999), reproduced in John Ludlow and Noel Jameson (eds), *Medieval Ireland: the Barryscourt Lectures I–X* (Kinsale, 2004).

[6] Christopher Woolgar (ed.), *Household accounts from medieval England records of social and economic history* (London, 1992–3), 17–18.

[7] Mick Monk, 'Charred grain from Killederdadrum', in Con Manning, 'The excavations of the Early Christian enclosure of Killederdadrum in Lackenavorna, Co. Tipperary', *Proceedings of the Royal Irish Academy* 84C (1984), 265–7; Mick Monk, 'Plant remains', in James Mallory and Peter Woodman, 'Oughtymore: an Early Christian shell midden', *Ulster Journal of Archaeology* 47 (1984), 56; Mick Monk, 'Evidence from macroscopic plant remains for crop husbandry in prehistoric and early historic Ireland: a review', *Journal of Irish Archaeology* 3 (1985–86), 31–6; Mick Monk, 'Excavations at Lisleagh ringfort, north County Cork', *Archaeology Ireland* 2:2 (1988), 57–60; Mick Monk, 'The archaeobotanical evidence for field crop plants in early historic Ireland', in Jane M. Renfrew (ed.), *New light on early farming: recent developments in palaeo-ethnobotany* (Edinburgh, 1991), 315–28.

commercial developments greatly changed archaeological excavation practices in Ireland. These practices included strategic and rigorous sampling of archaeological features and deposits for the recovery of environmental material, such as plant macrofossils.[8] As a result, the archaeobotanical evidence for field crops is now well represented and this new corpus of environmental data has contributed greatly to our knowledge of past agricultural practices. In order to facilitate the analyses and synthesise of this data, research projects such as the Cultivating Societies Project[9] and the Early Medieval Archaeological Project[10] have been influential in disseminating much of this unpublished work. This information is playing a pivotal role in redefining our understanding of past agricultural practices as well as their impact on societal and landscape change.

Archaeobotanical studies also play a vital role in interpreting urban life in medieval Ireland due primarily to the organic matrix[11] of these sites. The Viking Dublin excavations carried out by the National Museum of Ireland[12]

---

[8] Interpretation of archaeobotanical remains is also dictated by archaeological practice, where variation in project constraints, research agendas, sample policies, methodologies and classification all play a part in objectifying the results.

[9] Irish National Strategic Archaeological Research (INSTAR) Programme Awards fund thematic archaeological research, for example, the Cultivating Societies project (2008–2010), INSTAR ref. no.: 16682 and 16717, available at: www.chrono.qub.ac.uk/instar/ (last accessed 14 March 2015). Nikki Whitehouse, Meriel McClatchie, Phil Barrett, Rick Schulting, Rowan McLaughlin and Amy Bogaard, 'INSTAR—Cultivating societies', *Archaeology Ireland* 24:2 (2010), 16–19; Meriel McClatchie, Amy Bogaard, Sue Colledge, Nikki Whitehouse, Rick Schulting, Phil Barrett and Rowan McLaughlin, 'Neolithic farming in north-west Europe: archaeobotanical evidence from Ireland', *Journal of Archaeological Science* 51 (2014), 206–15.

[10] Early Medieval Archaeological Project (EMAP), 2008–2012, INSTAR ref. no.: AR03743. Finbar McCormick, Thom Kerr, Meriel McClatchie and Aidan O'Sullivan, 'The archaeology of livestock and cereal production in early medieval Ireland AD 400–1100', *Reconstructing the early medieval Irish economy. EMAP Report 5.1* (2011), EMAP2, Grant no.: AR02180.

[11] Organic material is preserved by waterlogging in anoxic conditions, as in pits, ditches and wells, where features have been dug below the water table, in low-lying areas and old river channels. In urban medieval centres, successive layers of organic matter from household rubbish, building materials and faecal remains also provide a stable environment for this type of organic preservation. In anoxic conditions, microorganism activity and oxygen is greatly reduced which slows down organic decay.

[12] The National Museum of Ireland carried out ten excavation campaigns ahead of Dublin City Corporation building developments between 1962 and 1981. The best-known of these was Wood Quay, but excavations also took place at Fishamble Street, John's Lane, Christchurch Place, High Street and Winetavern Street. These came to be known collectively as the Dublin Excavations; Brendán Ó Ríordáin, 'Excavations at High Street and Winetavern Street, Dublin', *Medieval Archaeology* 15 (1971), 73–85; Patrick Wallace, 'Wood Quay', in Thomas Delaney (ed.), *Excavations 1975–76* (Belfast, 1977), 31–2; Patrick Wallace, 'Dublin's waterfront at Wood Quay: 900–1317', in Gustav Milne and Brian Hobley (eds), *Waterfront archaeology in Britain and northern Europe*, British Archaeology Report 41 (London, 1981).

represent the most prominent work undertaken in this area. These campaigns provided a unique opportunity to implement sample strategies for the recovery of animal and plant remains in an attempt to interpret the food-processing practices and diet of a growing urban centre in the ninth and tenth centuries AD. Fruits, vegetables, lesser-known field crops and imported foodstuffs, were among the plant remains recorded, offering new insights into the variety of food available and consumed during the medieval period. The archaeobotanical works carried out by Frank Mitchell[13] of Trinity College Dublin and later by Siobhán Geraghty[14] produced a body of archaeological information that was central to understanding daily life in medieval Dublin and became a paradigm for other urban medieval projects that followed.[15]

Archaeobotany is now recognised as an essential component of archaeological interpretation and historical justification, and can complement documentary sources to offer important contributions to the study of medieval agriculture, horticulture and the use of wild food plants. While both sets of evidence suffer from differential survival and varying degrees of preservation, the disparity between these sources must also be appreciated as they will inevitably provide conflicting sets of evidence. Despite this, it has become apparent that a multidisciplinary approach is required in order to fully understand medieval food economy and the theoretical and taphonomical problems facing archaeological interpretation.

The documentary and archaeobotanical evidence presented for cultivated plants has focused predominantly on cereals in the medieval Irish diet. This can result in a poorer understanding of the role of other food plants, such as fruits, vegetables, pulse crops, herbs and imported foodstuffs. Historical sources for food produce from orchards and gardens as well as gathered wild plants are scarce and are often discussed generically as 'fruit' and 'vegetables'.[16] Archaeobotanical evidence has revealed more about the variety of non-cereal food plants and garden produce through the diverse plant remains that have survived in waterlogged and organic deposits in both rural[17] and

---

[13] Frank Mitchell, *Archaeology and environment in early Dublin* (Dublin, 1987).

[14] Siobhán Geraghty, *Viking Dublin: botanical evidence from Fishamble Street* (Dublin, 1996).

[15] John Tierney and Martha Hannon, 'Plant remains', in Maurice Hurley and O. M. B. Scully (eds), *Late Viking and medieval Waterford excavations 1986–1992* (Waterford, 1997), 854–93; Brenda Collins, 'Plant remains', in Claire Walsh, *Archaeological excavations at Patrick, Nicholas and Winetavern Street* (Dublin, 1997), 228–36; Meriel McClatchie, 'The plant remains', in Rose Cleary and Maurice Hurley (eds), *Excavations in Cork City 1984–2000* (Cork, 2003), 391–413.

[16] Margaret Murphy and Michael Potterton, *The Dublin region in the Middle Ages: settlement, land-use and economy* (Dublin, 2010), 355; Dyer, 'Gardens and garden produce', 27.

[17] A cesspit excavated at Athenry Castle contained a variety of edible fruits and the remains of a coprolite, Brenda Collins, 'Plant remains', in Cliona Papazian, Brenda Collins and Margaret McCarthy, 'Excavations at Athenry Castle, Co. Galway', *Journal of the Galway Archaeological and Historical Society* 43 (1991), 1–45: 25–7; waterlogged

urban[18] contexts. Through these physical remains, we can garner a much better understanding of how garden produce, imported fruits and wild plants were processed, utilised and consumed. This is especially significant when charting the diet of the lower classes and urban populations, which often went undocumented.

In order to gain a better understanding of the variety of food plants consumed in medieval Ireland, we need to consider the archaeological evidence that survives which represents these foodstuffs. In particular the evidence for fruit, vegetables, herbs and lesser known field crops, all of which can be under-represented in both the historical and the archaeological records. The emergence of the Norse towns in the ninth and tenth centuries and their subsequent growth during the Anglo–Norman settlement in the late twelfth and the early thirteenth centuries stimulated a growing urban population which required a sustainable source of readily available foodstuffs. The increase in trade also had a major contribution in diversifying food in medieval Ireland where foodstuffs and other commodities were exchanged at a local and international level. To understand the range of food plants consumed by urban dwellers, this paper will present archaeobotanical evidence from known urban medieval sites in Ireland, such as Dublin, Cork, Waterford, Drogheda and Wexford, including new additions from Cashel, Co. Tipperary, and Kilkenny City. The results will be evaluated in order to interpret how harvested, gathered and imported foodstuffs were utilised by urban settlers, and what new information they can contribute to medieval food and drink practices.

Urban living

The period from the late twelfth century to the early fourteenth century saw a vast and rapid increase in the establishment of boroughs and urban markets as

---

deposits at Augherskea, Co. Meath, produced potential evidence for non-cereal food plants in the form of seeds from mint and cabbage/turnip/mustard species, Christine Baker, 'Occam's duck: three early medieval settlement cemeteries or ecclesiastical sites', in Christiaan Corlett and Michael Potterton (eds), *Death and burial in early medieval Ireland in the light of recent archaeological excavations* (Dublin, 2010), 1–21; Apple pips, fig seeds and cherry stones were also recently identified from a waterlogged well and ditch deposit dating to a fourteenth-century well at Doneraile, Co. Cork; Susan Lyons, 'The plant remains', in Patricia Long, 'Assessment report on archaeological excavations on the R581 Doneraile to Newtwopothouse Road Realignment Scheme, Co Cork', unpublished report, Rubicon Heritage Services Ltd, 2013.

[18] Mitchell, *Archaeology and environment*; Geraghty, *Viking Dublin*; McClatchie, 'The plant remains'; Tierney and Hannon, 'Plant remains'; Frank Mitchell and Camilla Dickson, 'Plant remains and other items from medieval Drogheda', *Circaea* 3:1 (1985), 31–7; Edward Bourke, 'Life in the sunny south-east: housing and domestic economy in Viking and medieval Wexford', *Archaeology Ireland* 9:3 (1995), 33–6. For an urban example but not a port town, see Sarah Cobain, 'The plant remains and charcoal macrofossil remains from Navan Gate Street and Mill Street', in Denis Shine and Matthew Seaver, 'Towards the Rogues' Castle: Excavations on Navan Gate Street, Trim', in Michael Potterton and Matthew Seaver (eds), *Uncovering medieval Trim* (Dublin, 2009), 150–3.

a consequence of the economic growth that was developing under the Anglo–Norman administration. Cashel and Kilkenny, which began as early medieval ecclesiastical settlements, were two such towns that grew into prominent urban centres under the new Anglo–Norman economic system.[19] This rise in urban living promoted a commercial economy trading in both local and foreign commodities, which included a variety of foodstuffs. In Cashel, for example, the granting of an eight-day annual fair by King Henry III would have greatly encouraged a market economy, opening up the town to foreign traders.[20] In order to encourage urban settlement, new occupiers were given a burgage plot upon which to build a house, including subsidiary buildings, sheds, cesspits, wells, an orchard, and a garden for herbs and vegetables.[21]

This rise in urban living would have required a strategic system of waste management. While rivers and lakes[22] would have been considered the most convenient way of disposing of domestic refuse, including faecal remains and sewage in urban areas, the main feature to contain a wealth of information concerning diet, waste disposal, health, hygiene and settlement history were cesspits.[23] While the historical record merely mentions their presence as part of a burgage plot, interpreting such features requires a combined understanding of the archaeological and biological record to help with their interpretation.[24] Once they fell into disuse, cesspits were rarely emptied; instead they were

---

[19] The medieval town of Cashel was a planned development founded in a charter by Archbishop Donatus O'Lonergan in 1216. Tadgh O'Keeffe, 'Cashel', in Anngret Simms and John Andrews (eds), *More Irish country towns* (Cork and Dublin, 1994), 161–2: 160. A castle was established in Kilkenny in 1173, but expanded under William Marshall between 1207 and 1225, cited in John Bradley, 'The early development of the medieval town of Kilkenny', in William Nolan and Kevin Whelan (eds) *Kilkenny: historical and society interdisciplinary essays on the history of an Irish county* (Dublin, 1990), 63–74: 66.

[20] Edmond O'Donovan, 'Excavations at Friar Street Cashel: a story of urban settlement AD 1200–1800', *Tipperary Historical Journal* (2004), 3–90: 10.

[21] John Bradley, 'Towns in medieval Ireland', *Archaeology Ireland* 5:3 (1991), 25–8: 26. A typical Anglo–Norman urban design was a system of burgage plots, which were long strips of land set at right angles to the main route ways through the town and adjacent streets.

[22] Ernest Sabine, 'Latrines and cesspools of medieval London', *Speculum* 9 (1934), 303–21.

[23] James Greig, 'Gardrobes, sewers, cesspits and latrines', *Current Archaeology* 85 (1982), 49–52; Lisa Moffett, 'Fruits, vegetables, herbs and other plants from the latrine at Dudley Castle in central England, used by the Royalist Garrison during the Civil War', *Review of Palaeobotany and Palynology* 73 (1992), 271–86; Allan Hall, 'A brief history of plant foods in the city of York: what the cesspits tell us', in Eileen White (ed.), *Feeding a city: York. The provision of food from Roman times to the beginning of the twentieth century* (Totnes, Devon, 2000), 22–41: 24.

[24] David Smith, 'Defining an indicator package to allow identification of "cesspits" in the archaeological record', *Journal of Archaeological Science* 40 (2013), 526–43; Allan Hall, Andrew Jones and Harry Kenward, 'Cereal bran and human faecal remains from archaeological deposits—some preliminary observations', in Bruce Proudfoot (ed.),

covered over to save on the cost of disposal. This accumulation of organic material becomes inert and sterile, providing the perfect anoxic environment for plant preservation. Cesspits could be simple cut features or lined with wood or stone (Pl. I).[25] Since cess material was often dumped into open drains, ditches and pits, and mixed with occupation layers, interpreting medieval plant debris which has accumulated under urban conditions must be done with caution.

As part of this paper, four sites from Cashel and eight sites from Kilkenny City will be referenced and discussed in the context of other urban centres in Ireland (Table 1). The archaeological excavations at these sites were carried out in advance of commercial development, including alterations and extensions to existing buildings. Cashel and Kilkenny are both listed as historic towns in the Record of Monuments and Places[26] and are therefore protected under the National Monuments Acts 1930–2004. This includes their historic core, which contains numerous sub-elements of archaeological and historic interest, as described in the Urban Archaeological Surveys for County Tipperary and County Kilkenny. Any proposed development works within the confines of these areas are, therefore, subject by law to appraisal in order to determine the impact and affect that the works may have on archaeological heritage. To facilitate the archaeological interpretation of these sites and in line with archaeological licensing procedures, strategic sampling of archaeological deposits was undertaken. The programme of post-excavation works from these locations included archaeobotanical analysis of the soils sampled, the results of which have been collated for the purpose of this paper (Table 2).

In Cashel, the sites at Chapel Lane and Bank Place fronted onto the north side of Main Street, Wesley Square on the south side of Main Street and the site at Friar Street located at the eastern side of that Street (Fig. 1). While medieval to post-medieval activity was recorded, the majority of archaeological evidence was centred on thirteenth- and fourteenth-century burgage activity. At Friar Street, the remains of a post-built rectangular structure including a possible cesspit were recorded. At Wesley Square, a series of pits were identified along with the remains of a later stone structure and cemetery. Evidence for industry was found, at Chapel Lane, where a cobbler's workshop and possible occupation was evident, while iron-working or a smithy was located at Bank Place.[27]

Site, environment and economy, British Archaeological Reports International Series 173 (Oxford, 1983), 85–104; Harry Kenward and Allan Hall, 'Enhancing bio-archaeological interpretation using indicator groups: stable manure as a paradigm', *Journal of Archaeological Science* 24 (1997), 663–73.

[25] Evidence from medieval Waterford, where both lined and unlined cess/rubbish pits were recorded, noted that rubbish accumulated quickly which may have resulted in the construction of a new pit, or the emptying and reuse of the pits themselves (Tierney and Hannon, 'Plant remains', 889).

[26] Cashel, Co. Tipperary (RMP TS061-026); Kilkenny City (RMP KK019-026) courtesy of the Archaeological Survey Database, available at: www.archaeology.ie/archaeological-survey-database (14 March 2014).

[27] See www.archaeology.ie/archaeological-survey-database (18 March 2015).

Pit - 1 metre wide

PL. I—*Top left*: a reconstruction of a cess disposal (illustration prepared by Henry Buglass (David Smith, 'Defining an indicator package to allow identification of "cesspits" in the archaeological record', *Journal of Archaeological Science* 40 (2013), 526–43: 540, Fig. 3); *top right*: unlined medieval cesspit (photo: Cóilín Ó Drisceoil, Kilkenny Archaeology); *bottom*: medieval stone-lined cesspit (photo: Cóilín Ó Drisceoil, Kilkenny Archaeology).

TABLE 1—Summary of sites discussed from Cashel and Kilkenny.

Site name	Archaeological reference	Nature of the site	Number of soil samples selected for plant macrofossil remains[a]	Date A.D.	Publication
Friar Street, Cashel	95E0286	Medieval to post-medieval construction phases; urban domestic occupation and property plot alignment; post-built structure burnt in situ dating to the fourteenth century (1280–1408 Cal. A.D. two sigma)	4 samples	13th–18th century	Edmond O'Donovan, 'Excavations at Friar Street, Cashel: a story of urban settlement AD 1200–1800', *Tipperary Historical Journal* (2004), 3–90
Chapel Lane, Cashel	03E0396	Medieval to post-medieval occupation layer; medieval rubbish accumulation; leather off-cuts suggest the remains of a cobbler's workshop; property boundaries; remains of a possible structure	20 samples	12th–17th century	Susan Lyons, 'The environmental remains', in Colm Moloney and Caitríona Gleeson. 'Final report on archaeological excavations at Chapel Lane, Cashel, County Tipperary', unpublished report, Headland Archaeology Ltd. 2005
Bank Place, Cashel	04E0111 (and ext.)	Bowl-furnaces/smithy hearths; series of pits superseded by a timber-framed structure—a possible workshop	25 samples	13th–18th century	Rubicon Heritage Services Ltd. 'New evidence for the form and early development of the medieval town of Cashel from recent excavations', *Tipperary Historical Journal* (2013), 5–24
Wesley Square, Cashel	05E0248	Series of rubbish pits superseded by a stone-built structure and cemetery	17 samples	12th–19th century	Rubicon Heritage Services Ltd. 'New evidence', 5–24
Friary Street/ Garden Row, Kilkenny	01E0569	Medieval to post-medieval burgage plots; refuse pits	18 samples	12th–16th century/ 18th century	Penny Johnston, 'Analysis of the plant remains Friary Street/ Garden Row, Kilkenny (01E0569)', unpublished technical report, Margaret Gowen and Co. Ltd. 2002

TABLE 1 (*cont.*)—Summary of sites discussed from Cashel and Kilkenny.

Site name	Archaeological reference	Nature of the site	Number of soil samples selected for plant macrofossil remains[a]	Date A.D.	Publication
Kilkenny Court house, Parliament Street	08E0462	Medieval pitting/diches/cess pits; burgage plot activity	93 soil samples	12th–17th century A.D.	Susan Lyons, 'The plant macrofossil remains', in Maeve Saundersson, 'Preliminary archaeological report for Kilkenny Courthouse, Parliament Street, Kilkenny, Co. Kilkenny', unpublished technical report, Arch-Tech Ltd, 2009
11 Patrick Street, Kilkenny	06E0230	Medieval pitting and burgage plot activity	13 samples	12th–16th century/ 18th century	Jacinta Kiely and Antonia Doolan, 'Archaeological excavation report 06E0230—11 Patrick Street, Kilkenny, Co. Kilkenny', *Eachtra Journal* 14 (2008), 89–93
12 Patrick Street/ Stratham Street, Kilkenny	99E0757	Medieval to post-medieval pits and ditches; burgage plot activity	12 samples (4 medieval; 8 post-medieval	12th–16th century/ 19th century	Bruce Sutton and Penny Johnston, 'Archaeological excavation report 99E0757 ext-Stratham Street, Patrick Street, Kilkenny, Co. Kilkenny', *Eachtra Journal* 14 (2007), 144–7
26 Patrick Street, Kilkenny	99E0165	Medieval pitting and burgage plot activity	26 samples	12th–16th century	Jacinta Kiely, 'Archaeological excavation report 26 Patrick Street, Kilkenny, County Kilkenny 99E0165', unpublished archaeology report, Eachtra Archaeological Projects, 2000
Irishtown/ Brennan's Yard, Kilkenny	02E1592	Medieval riverside fences; burgage plot activity	10 samples	12th–16th century	Penny Johnston, 'Analysis of the plant remains Irishtown/ Brennan's Yard. Kilkenny (02E1592)'

TABLE 1 (*cont.*)—Summary of sites discussed from Cashel and Kilkenny.

Site name	Archaeological reference	Nature of the site	Number of soil samples selected for plant macrofossil remains[a]	Date A.D.	Publication
Bishop's Palace, Kilkenny	11E157	Medieval pit	2 samples	1000–1140 Cal. A.D.	Nikolah Gilligan, Archaeobotanical analysis, the Robing Room, Bishop's Palace, Kilkenny (11E157), Kilkenny Archaeological Project, 2011, available at: http://www.kkap.ie/assets/bishops-palace-plant-remains.pdf (last accessed 7 April 2015)
Talbot Tower, Kilkenny	E3646	Medieval; earliest evidence for Anglo–Norman defences in the form of an earthen ditch and bank	23 samples	Phase 1: 710–890 Cal. A.D. Phase 2: 9th–11th century A.D. Phase 3: 1220–1280 Cal. A.D. Phase 4: 17th/18th century A.D.	Meriel McClatchie, 'Analysis of non-wood plant macrofossils, Talbot's Tower, Kilkenny', unpublished report, Kilkenny Archaeology Ltd, 2011; Gilligan, 'Archaeobotanical analysis, Talbot's Tower, Kilkenny'

[a] Soil samples averaged 10 litres in volume. Samples were selected and processed in consultation with an archaeobotanist as part of the post-excavation programme for each site. Two types of processing techniques were employed: Dry samples rich in charred remains were processed using a system of flotation. Flots were collected in sieve meshes measuring 300 microns, retents were collected in sieve meshes measuring 1mm; Samples from obvious anoxic deposits or those deemed to be potentially waterlogged were processed using a wet-sieving technique through a bank of sieves, with meshes measuring 250 microns to 2mm, in order to ensure the recovery of small seeds and finer plant parts. Considering other environmental material, such as insect remains, wood, charcoal and mollusca, a subsample of approximately 3–5 litres was processed for the purpose of archaeobotanical analysis. Examinations of these residues were carried out using a stereo microscope ranging in magnification from ×4.8 to ×56. Archaeobotanical material was identified using comparative seed collections and illustrative seed keys (e.g. A-L Anderberg, *Atlas of seeds part 4: Resedaceae-Umbelliferae* (Stockholm, 1994); W. Beijerinck, *Zadenatlas der Netherlandsche Flora* (Wageningen, 1947); N. J. Katz, S.V. Katz and M. G. Kipiani, *Atlas and keys of fruits and seeds occurring in the quaternary deposits of the USSR* (Moscow, 1965). Soil samples were processed in line with industry standards and guidelines as outlined in the Institute of Archaeologists of Ireland (IAI), *Environmental sampling guidelines for archaeologists* (Dublin, 2006); and D. Pearsall, *Palaeoethnobotany: handbook of procedures*, 2nd edn (San Diego, CA, 2000).

TABLE 2—The plant macrofossil remains recovered from sites in Cashel and Kilkenny.[a]

Location			Cashel, County Tipperary				Kilkenny City, County Kilkenny							
Latin binomial	Common names		Friar Street, Cashel	Chapel Lane, Cashel	Bank Place, Cashel	Wesley Square, Cashel	Friary Street Garden Row, Kilkenny	Kilkenny Courthouse, Parliament Street, Kilkenny	11 Patrick Street, Kilkenny	12 Patrick's St./Strathan St., Kilkenny	26 Patrick's Street, Kilkenny	Irishtown/ Brennan's Yard, Kilkenny	Bishop's Palace, Kilkenny	Talbot Tower, Kilkenny
Charred plant macrofossils														
Corylus avellana L.	Hazelnut (nutshell)		++	++++	++	++	–	++	++	+	+	–	+	+
Urtica urens L.	Small nettle		–	–	–	–	–	–	–	–	–	–	–	–
Ranunculus acris L. / R. repens L.	Creeping/ meadow buttercup		–	–	–	–	+	–	–	–	–	–	–	–
Fallopia convolvulus (L.) Á. Löve	Black bindweed		–	–	–	–	–	–	–	–	–	–	–	–
Persicaria lapathifolium L. Delarbre	Pale persicaria		–	–	–	–	–	+	–	–	–	–	–	–
Polygonum spp.	Knotgrass		++	–	–	–	+	–	–	–	–	–	+	–
Rumex acetosa L.	Sorrel		–	–	–	–	+	+	–	–	+	–	–	–
Rumex acetosella L.	Sheep's sorrel		–	–	–	–	–	+	+	–	+	–	–	+
Rumex crispus L. agg.	Curly dock		–	–	–	–	–	–	–	–	+	–	–	+
Rumex spp.	Dock		–	–	–	–	++	++	–	–	–	–	–	–
Polygonaceae (various)	Knotgrass/ Smartweed/ Dock family		+	–	–	–	++	–	+	+	+	–	–	–
Chenopodium album L.	Fat hen		–	–	–	–	–	–	–	–	–	–	+	+
Chenopodium spp.	Goosefoot		–	–	–	–	++	–	–	–	–	–	+	+
Atriplex cf. prostrata L.	Garden orache		–	–	–	–	–	–	–	–	–	–	–	–
Atriplex spp.	Orache		–	–	–	–	–	–	–	–	+	–	–	+
Chenopodiaceae (various)	Goosefoot/ Orache family		–	–	–	–	++	–	+	+	+	–	–	+
Agostemma githago L.	Corn cockle		–	–	–	–	+	–	–	+	–	–	–	+
Silene spp.	Campions		–	–	–	–	–	–	–	–	+	–	–	+
Cerastium spp.	Mouse-ears		–	–	–	–	+	–	–	–	+	–	–	–

TABLE 2 (*cont.*)—The plant macrofossil remains recovered from sites in Cashel and Kilkenny.[a]

Latin binomial	Common names	Cashel, County Tipperary				Kilkenny City, County Kilkenny							
		Friar Street, Cashel	*Chapel Lane, Cashel*	*Bank Place, Cashel*	*Wesley Square, Cashel*	*Friary Street/ Garden Row, Kilkenny*	*Kilkenny Courthouse, Parliament Street, Kilkenny*	*11 Patrick Street, Kilkenny*	*12 Patrick St./Stratham St., Kilkenny*	*26 Patrick's Street, Kilkenny*	*Irishtown/ Brennan's Yard, Kilkenny*	*Bishop's Palace, Kilkenny*	*Talbot Tower, Kilkenny*
Brassica rapa L.	Wild turnip	–	–	–	–	–	–	–	–	+	–	–	–
Brassica/Sinapis spp.	Wild cabbage/radish	–	–	–	–	–	–	–	–	+	–	+	+
Raphanus raphanistrum L.	Wild radish	–	–	–	–	+	–	+	+	–	–	–	+
Sinapis cf. *alba* L.	White mustard	–	–	–	–	–	+	–	–	+	–	–	–
Cruciferae (various)	Cabbage family	–	–	–	–	++	–	–	–	–	–	–	+
Anagallis spp.	Primrose	–	–	–	–	–	–	–	–	–	–	–	–
Vitis vinifera L.	Grape	–	–	–	–	–	–	–	–	–	–	+	–
Prunus avium L.	Wild cherry	–	–	–	–	–	–	–	–	–	–	+	+
Prunus spp.	Cherry (indeterminate)	–	–	–	–	–	–	–	–	–	–	+++	+
Malus spp.	Apple (indeterminate)	–	–	–	–	–	–	–	–	–	–	+	–
Rosaceae (various)	Rose family	+	–	–	–	–	–	–	–	–	–	+	+
Pisum sativum L.	Field pea	+	–	–	–	–	–	+	–	+	–	+	–
Pisum spp.	Pea	–	–	–	–	++	–	+	+	–	–	–	–
Vicia sativa L.	Common vetch	+	–	–	–	+	–	–	+	+	–	–	–
Vicia faba L.	Broad/horse bean	+	–	–	–	+	–	–	–	+	–	–	–
Vicia spp.	Bean	–	–	–	–	–	–	–	+	++	–	–	+
Lathyrus pratensis L.	Meadow vetchling	–	–	–	–	–	–	–	–	+	–	+	–
Lathyrus sylvestris L.	Flat pea/narrow-leafed pea	–	–	–	–	–	–	–	–	–	–	–	+
Lathyrus spp.	Pea	–	–	–	–	–	–	–	–	–	–	–	–
Vicia /Lathyrus spp.	Vetch	++	++	–	–	++	–	–	++	–	–	–	+
Leguminosae/ Fabaceae (various)	Legume (large)	+	+	–	–	++	–	–	–	–	–	–	+
Leguminosae/ Fabaceae (various)	Legumes (small)	+	++	–	–	++++	–	++	++	–	–	+	+
Aethusa cynapium L.	Fool's parsley	–	–	–	–	+	–	–	–	–	–	–	–

TABLE 2 (cont.)—The plant macrofossil remains recovered from sites in Cashel and Kilkenny.[a]

Location			Cashel, County Tipperary				Kilkenny City, County Kilkenny							
Latin binomial	Common names		Friar Street, Cashel	Chapel Lane, Cashel	Bank Place, Cashel	Wesley Square, Cashel	Friary Street Garden Row, Kilkenny	Kilkenny Courthouse, Parliament Street, Kilkenny	11 Patrick Street, Kilkenny	12 Patrick's St./Stratham St., Kilkenny	26 Patrick's Street, Kilkenny	Irishtown/Bremnan's Yard, Kilkenny	Bishop's Palace, Kilkenny	Talbot Tower, Kilkenny
Galeopsis spp.	Hemp-nettle		—	—	—	—	—	—	—	—	—	—	—	+
Lamium spp.	Dead nettle/mint		—	—	—	—	+	—	—	—	—	—	—	—
Plantago spp.	Plantain		—	—	—	—	++	—	—	+	+	—	+	—
Lapsana communis L.	Nipplewort		—	—	—	—	+	—	—	—	+	—	+	—
Chrysanthemum segetum L.	Corn marigold		—	—	—	—	+	—	—	—	—	—	—	—
Asteraceae (various)	Daisy/Marigold family		—	—	—	—	++	—	—	+	—	—	—	+
Apiaceae (various)	Carrot family		—	—	—	—	—	—	—	—	—	—	—	+
Galium aparine L.	Cleavers		—	—	—	—	+	—	+	—	+	—	—	—
Galium spp.	Cleavers		—	+	+	—	+	—	+	+	—	—	—	+
Carex spp.	Sedge		—	—	—	—	+++	—	+	+	+	—	+	+
Cyperaceae (various)	Sedge family		—	—	—	—	+++	—	+	+	—	—	—	+
Luzula spp.	Wood-rush		—	—	—	—	—	—	—	—	—	—	—	+
Iris foetidissima L.	Stinking iris		—	—	—	—	—	—	—	—	—	—	—	+
Bromus spp.	Brome grass		+	—	—	—	—	—	—	—	—	—	—	++
Avena cf. *sativa* L.	Cultivated oat		++++	++++	+	++	—	—	—	—	—	—	+	++
Avena spp.	Oat		+++++	++++	++	++	+++++	++++	+++++	+++++	+	++	+	+++
Avena/Hordeum spp.	Oat/barley		++	+++++	++	—	+	—	—	++	++	++	+	—
Secale cereale L.	Rye		++	+	+	—	+	+	+	++	++	++	+	—
Triticum dicoccum Schrank ex Schübl	Emmer wheat		+++	—	—	—	++	—	—	—	—	—	—	—
Triticum cf. *spelta* L.	Spelt wheat		+	—	—	—	+	—	—	—	—	—	—	+
Triticum aestivum L./ *T. durum* L.	Bread/marconi wheat		—	—	—	—	+++++	—	+++	+++	—	—	—	+
Triticum aestivum L./ *T. compactum* L.	Bread/compact wheat		++	+++	+++	+	+++	++	—	—	—	—	—	—
Triticum spp.	Wheat		+++	+	++	+	++++	++	—	+++++	++++	+	+	—
Triticum spp./*Secale cereale* L.	Wheat/rye		—	—	—	—	—	++	—	++	—	—	—	—

TABLE 2 (*cont.*)—The plant macrofossil remains recovered from sites in Cashel and Kilkenny.[a]

Location		Cashel, County Tipperary				Kilkenny City, County Kilkenny							
Latin binomial	Common names	Friar Street, Cashel	Chapel Lane, Cashel	Bank Place, Cashel	Wesley Square, Cashel	Friary Street/Garden Row, Kilkenny	Kilkenny Courthouse/Parliament Street, Kilkenny	11 Patrick Street, Kilkenny	12 Patrick St./Strabham St., Kilkenny	26 Patrick's Street, Kilkenny	Irishtown/Brennan's Yard, Kilkenny	Bishop's Palace, Kilkenny	Talbot Tower, Kilkenny
Triticum spp. / *Hordeum vulgare* L.	Wheat/barley	–	–	–	–	–	–	–	–	–	–	–	+
Hordeum vulgare L.	Hulled barley	++	++	+	++	+++	+++	–	++++	–	+	+	+
Hordeum vulgare L. var. *nudum* Hook. f.	Naked barley	+	++++	–	–	–	–	–	+	–	–	–	–
Hordeum spp.	Barley	++	+	–	–	+++	–	+	++	++	–	–	–
Cerealia (caryopsis)	Cereal (indeterminate)	+++	+++	++	++	+++	+++	+++	+++	–	++	++	++
Cerealia (chaff)	Culm nodes/internodes/rachis/awns	++++	++	·	–	+++	+++	+	+	–	++++	++	+
Poa spp.	Grass (various)	++	–	–	–	–	–	–	+	–	–	–	+++
Waterlogged macrofossils		–	–	–	–	–	–	–	–	–	–	–	–
Bryophyta (Division)	Mosses (fronds)	–	–	–	–	–	++	–	–	–	+++	–	–
Pteridium aquilinum (L.) Kuhn	Bracken	–	++++	–	–	–	++++	–	–	–	–	–	–
Corylus avellana L.	Hazelnut shell	++	++++	–	–	+++	+++	–	–	–	++	–	–
Papaver spp.	Poppy	+	–	–	–	–	+	–	–	–	–	–	–
Urtica dioica L.	Common nettle	+	++++	–	–	–	++	–	–	–	D	–	–
Humulus lupus L.	Hop	–	–	–	–	–	++	–	–	–	+	–	–
Ficus carica	Fig	–	+++	–	–	–	+++	–	–	–	–	–	–
Persicaria lapathifolium L. Delarbre	Pale persicaria	+	–	–	–	–	–	–	–	–	–	–	–
Persicaria maculosa (L.) Gray	Redshank	–	–	–	–	–	–	–	–	–	+	–	–
Persicaria bistorta Samp.	Common bistort	–	–	–	–	–	+	–	–	–	–	–	–
Persicaria hydropiper (L.) Delabre	Water pepper	–	–	–	–	–	+	–	–	–	–	–	–

TABLE 2 (cont.)—The plant macrofossil remains recovered from sites in Cashel and Kilkenny.[a]

Latin binomial	Common names	Friar Street, Cashel	Chapel Lane, Cashel	Bank Place, Cashel	Wesley Square, Cashel	Friary Street Garden Row, Kilkenny	Kilkenny Courthouse, Parliament Street, Kilkenny	11 Patrick Street, Kilkenny	12 Patrick's St./Stratham St., Kilkenny	26 Patrick's Street, Kilkenny	Irishtown/Bremnan's Yard, Kilkenny	Bishop's Palace, Kilkenny	Talbot Tower, Kilkenny
		Cashel, County Tipperary				*Kilkenny City, County Kilkenny*							
Fallopia convolvulus (L.) Á. Löve	Black bindweed	++	—	—	—	—	++	—	—	—	+	—	—
Polygonum aviculare L.	Knotgrass	+	++	—	—	—	+++	—	—	—	++	—	—
Polygonum spp.	Knotgrass	++	+++	—	—	—	++++	—	—	—	—	—	—
Rumex acetosella L.	Sheep's sorrel	—	++++	—	—	—	+++	—	—	—	—	—	—
Rumex crispus L. agg.	Curly dock	—	—	—	—	—	++	—	—	—	—	—	—
Rumex spp.	Dock	++	++++	—	—	—	+++	—	—	—	—	—	—
Polygonaceae spp.	Knotgrass	+	—	—	—	—	+++	—	—	—	—	—	—
Chenopodium album L.	Fat hen	—	+++	—	—	—	+++	—	—	—	D++++	—	—
Chenopodium glaucum/rubrum	Oak-leaved/red goosefoot	+	—	—	—	—	—	—	—	—	—	—	—
Chenopodium spp.	Goosefoot	—	++	—	—	—	+++	—	—	—	—	—	—
Chenopodium vulvaria L.	Stinging goosefoot	—	—	—	—	—	++	—	—	—	—	—	—
Atriplex cf. *patula* L.	Common orache	++	—	—	—	—	+++	—	—	—	+	—	—
Chenopodiaceae (various)	Orache family	++	—	—	—	—	—	—	—	—	D	—	—
Atriplex spp.	Orache	++	—	—	—	—	++	—	—	—	+++	—	—
Stellaria media (L.) Vill.	Common chickweed	++	+++	—	—	—	++	—	—	—	D	—	—
Agrostemma githago L.	Corn cockle	—	+++	—	—	—	++	—	—	—	+++	—	—
Silene spp.	Campions	—	—	—	—	—	+++	—	—	—	—	—	—
Ranunculus acris L./ *R. repens* L.	Creeping/meadow buttercup	+	—	—	—	—	++	—	—	—	++++	—	—
Ranunculus bulbous L.	Bulbous buttercup	—	—	—	—	—	+	—	—	—	—	—	—
Ranunculus cf. *sceleratus* L.	Celery-leaved buttercup	+	—	—	—	—	++	—	—	—	—	—	—

TABLE 2 (*cont.*)—The plant macrofossil remains recovered from sites in Cashel and Kilkenny.[a]

Location	Cashel, County Tipperary				Kilkenny City, County Kilkenny							
Latin binomial / Common names	Friar Street, Cashel	Chapel Lane, Cashel	Bank Place, Cashel	Wesley Square, Cashel	Friary Street/ Garden Row, Kilkenny	Kilkenny Courthouse, Parliament Street, Kilkenny	11 Patrick Street, Kilkenny	12 Patrick St./Stratham St., Kilkenny	26 Patrick's Street, Kilkenny	Irishtown/ Brennan's Yard, Kilkenny	Bishop's Palace, Kilkenny	Talbot Tower, Kilkenny
Ranunculus spp. — Buttercup	—	++++	—	—	—	+++	—	—	—	—	—	—
Brassica / Sinapis spp. — Wild cabbage/mustard etc.	—	++	—	—	—	—	—	—	—	—	—	—
Raphanus raphanistrum L. — Wild radish	—	++++	—	—	—	—	—	—	—	+	—	—
Prunus spinosa L. — Sloe/blackthorn	—	—	—	—	—	++++	—	—	—	+	—	—
Prunus domestica L. — Plum/bullace	—	—	—	—	—	++++	—	—	—	—	—	—
Prunus avium L. — Wild cherry	—	—	—	—	—	++++	—	—	—	+	—	—
Prunus spp. — Cherry indet	—	+	—	—	—	++++	—	—	—	—	—	—
Malus spp. — Apple	—	—	—	—	—	++	—	—	—	+	—	—
Pyrus L./*Malus* Mill. — Pear/apple	—	—	—	—	—	—	—	—	—	+	—	—
Crataegus monogyna Jacq. — Hawthorn haw	—	—	—	—	—	—	—	—	—	+	—	—
Rubus idaeus L. — Raspberry	—	++	—	—	—	++++	—	—	—	—	—	—
Rubus fruticosus L. — Bramble/blackberry	—	D	—	++++	—	D	—	—	—	+++	—	—
Potentilla spp. — Cinquefoil	—	+++	—	—	—	++	—	—	—	+	—	—
Fragaria vesca L. — Wild strawberry	—	+	—	—	—	++	—	—	—	+	—	—
Rosa spp. — Rose	—	+	—	—	—	+	—	—	—	+	—	—
Trifolium spp. — Clover	—	—	—	—	—	+++	—	—	—	—	—	—
Viola spp. — Violet	—	—	—	—	—	++	—	—	—	—	—	—
Vitis vinifera L. — Grape	—	+	—	—	—	+	—	—	—	—	—	—
Linum usitatissimum L. — Flax	—	+++	—	—	—	—	—	—	—	++	—	—
cf. *Cannabis sativa* L. — Hemp	—	+	—	—	—	—	—	—	—	—	—	—
Mercurialis spp. — Mercuries	—	—	—	—	—	+	—	—	—	+	—	—
Malva silvertris L. — Common mallow	—	—	—	—	—	+	—	—	—	—	—	—
Malva spp. — Mallow	—	—	—	—	—	++	—	—	—	+	—	—
Thlaspi arvense L. — Field-penny	—	—	—	—	—	—	—	—	—	++	—	—
Spergula arvensis L. — Corn spurrey	—	+	—	—	—	—	—	—	—	—	—	—
Prunella vulgaris L. — Self-heal	—	++	—	—	—	+	—	—	—	—	—	—

TABLE 2 (cont.)—The plant macrofossil remains recovered from sites in Cashel and Kilkenny.[a]

		Cashel, County Tipperary				Kilkenny City, County Kilkenny							
Latin binomial	Common names	Friar Street, Cashel	Chapel Lane, Cashel	Bank Place, Cashel	Wesley Square, Cashel	Friary Street/Garden Row, Kilkenny	Kilkenny Courthouse, Parliament Street, Kilkenny	11 Patrick Street, Kilkenny	12 Patrick's St./Strathan St., Kilkenny	26 Patrick's Street, Kilkenny	Irishtown/Brennan's Yard, Kilkenny	Bishop's Palace, Kilkenny	Talbot Tower, Kilkenny
Vaccinium spp.	Whortleberry/cranberry/bilberry	–	+	–	–	–	–	–	–	–	–	–	–
Calluna vulgaris L.	Heather	+	+	–	–	–	++	–	–	–	–	–	–
Lamium spp.	Dead nettle	–	+++	–	–	–	+	–	–	–	–	–	–
Galeopsis cf. tetrahit L.	Common hemp-nettle	+	+++	–	–	–	+	–	–	–	++	–	–
Mentha spp.	Mint	–	–	–	–	–	+	–	–	–	+	–	–
Labiatae/Lamiaceae (various)	Dead-nettle/Mint family	+	–	–	–	–	+	–	–	–	+++	–	–
Plantago spp.	Plantain	–	+	–	–	–	–	–	–	–	+	–	–
Ajuga cf. reptans L.	Bugle/bugleweed	–	+	–	–	–	–	–	–	–	–	–	–
Carduus spp. / Cirsium spp.	Thistles	–	+	–	–	–	–	–	–	–	++	–	–
Lapsana communis L.	Nipplewort	++	–	–	–	–	++	–	–	–	++++	–	–
Picris spp.	Oxtongues	–	+	–	+	–	–	–	–	–	+	–	–
Sambucus nigra L.	Elder	–	–	–	+	–	++++	–	–	–	+	–	–
Chrysanthemum segetum L.	Corn marigold	–	+++++	–	+	–	+	–	–	–	+++	–	–
Asteraceae (various)	Daisy/Marigold family	–	+	–	–	–	–	–	–	–	++++	–	–
Aethusa cynapium L.	Fool's parsley	+	–	–	–	–	+++	–	–	–	–	–	–
Anethum graveolens L.	Dill	+	–	–	–	–	++	–	–	–	–	–	–
Apium cf. graveolens var. duce Mill.	Wild/cultivated celery	–	+	–	+	–	++	–	–	–	++	++	–
Umbelliferae (various)	Carrot family	–	–	–	–	–	–	–	–	–	++	–	–
Pimpinella cf. saxifraga	Burnet saxifrage	–	–	–	–	–	+	–	–	–	–	–	–

TABLE 2 (*cont.*)—The plant macrofossil remains recovered from sites in Cashel and Kilkenny.[a]

Latin binomial	Common names	Cashel, County Tipperary				Kilkenny City, County Kilkenny							
		Friar Street, Cashel	Chapel Lane, Cashel	Bank Place, Cashel	Wesley Square, Cashel	Friary Streetl Garden Row, Kilkenny	Kilkenny Courthouse, Parliament Street, Kilkenny	11 Patrick Street, Kilkenny	12 Patrick's St./Stratham St., Kilkenny	26 Patrick's Street, Kilkenny	Irishtownl Brennan's Yard, Kilkenny	Bishop's Palace, Kilkenny	Talbot Tower, Kilkenny
Torilis spp.	Hedge parsley	–	–	–	–	–	+	–	–	–	–	–	–
Allium spp.	Garlic/onion/ leek	–	+	–	–	–	++	–	–	–	–	–	–
Myosotis spp.	Forget-me-not	–	–	–	–	–	+	–	–	–	–	–	–
Galium aparine L.	Cleavers	–	+	–	–	–	–	–	–	–	+	–	–
Achillea millefolium L.	Yarrow	–	+	–	–	–	–	–	–	–	–	–	–
Apiaceae (various)	Carrot family	–	–	–	–	–	++	–	–	–	–	–	–
Carex spp.	Sedges	–	++++	–	–	–	++	–	–	–	++	–	–
Cerealia indeterminate - bran	Indet. cereal (bran)	–	–	–	–	–	+	–	–	–	–	–	–
Cerealia/Poaceae indeterminate	Straw/grass nodes	++	–	–	–	–	–	–	–	–	–	–	–
Poa spp.	Grass (various)	++	+	+	–	–	++	–	–	–	–	–	–

[a]Nomenclature and taxonomic order follows Clive Stace, *New Flora of the British Isles* (Cambridge, 2010). The identifications refer to seeds unless otherwise stated; 'cf.' denotes a tentative identification; since sampling and methodological procedures differed bewteen each site. For the purpose of this paper, the quantification of individual seeds is based on relative abundance using an abundance key (+, ++, +++, ++++ and D) where + = rare (<10); ++ = occasional (11 – 50); +++ = frequent (51–100); ++++ = abundant (>100); D = dominant (500+).

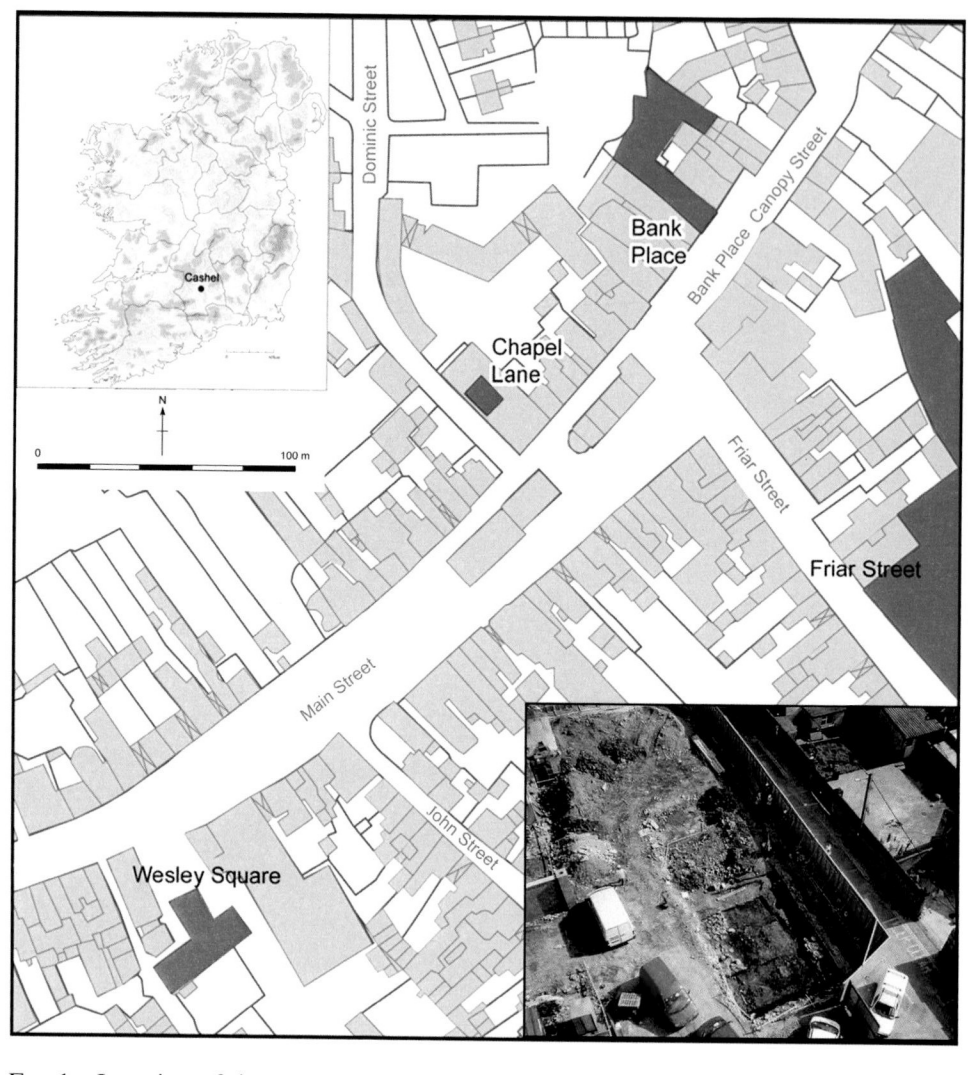

Fɪɢ. 1—Location of sites discussed from Cashel, Co. Tipperary (after Rubicon Heritage Services Ltd./Headland Archaeology Ltd); inset: aerial view of archaeological excavation at Chapel Lane, Cashel (looking south). (Photo: Rubicon Heritage Services Ltd/ Headland Archaeology Ltd.)

The sites from Kilkenny fall within the two main boroughs established in Kilkenny—Irishtown and Hightown. Bishop's Palace and Brennan's Yard were located to the north-west in the borough of Irishtown; Parliament Street was situated adjacent to the commercial High Street at the centre of the borough of Hightown, while Friary Street/Garden Row and 11, 12 and 26 Patrick Street were located to the south-west of Hightown. Talbot Tower formed part of the south-western extremity of the medieval town (Fig. 2). With the exception of Bishop's Palace and Talbot Tower, the sites were characterised as typical medieval burgage plots, where refuse pits and plot boundaries were

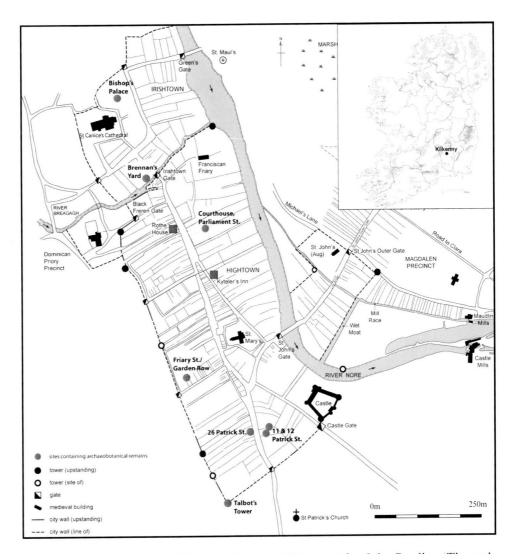

FIG. 2—Location of sites in Kilkenny City, Co. Kilkenny (after John Bradley, 'The early development of the medieval town of Kilkenny', in William Nolan and Kevin Whelan (eds), *Kilkenny: historical and society interdisciplinary essays on the history of an Irish county* (Dublin, 1990), 63–74, Fig. 3.1).

identified. A drying kiln was present at Friary Street/Garden Row, while cess deposits were recorded from Irishtown/Brennan's Yard. The site at Parliament Street, which once housed the thirteenth-century Grace's Castle, later became a gaol in the sixteenth century before its conversion to a courthouse in the eighteenth century. The excavation revealed numerous refuse medieval pits, cesspits, a wood-lined cesspit and long, shallow linears comprising domestic debris and cess material (Pl. II). The programme of environmental analysis from this site included an assessment of the plant macrofossils, insect, pollen

PL. II—*Left*: medieval levels at Parliament Street, Kilkenny; *top right*: series of linear medieval ditches at Parliament Street, Kilkenny; *bottom right*: medieval wooden-lined cesspit at Parliament Street, Kilkenny. (Photos: Arch-Tech Ltd.)

and wood remains, and is the most extensive and comprehensive environmental project undertaken for medieval Kilkenny to date.

Daily fare of starchy staples

Crop harvest and cereal-based products

Irish texts dating from the early medieval period to the later medieval period refer to a well-balanced and healthy diet.[28] This diet comprised bread and milk, providing the main source of carbohydrates and proteins required by the body. Cereals were the principal food consumed from the early to the later medieval period primarily through pot-based dishes, ale and breads[29] and this differed considerably from person to person. The documentary evidence[30] provides

---

[28] Kelly, *Early Irish farming*, 317; A. T. Lucas, 'Irish food before the potato', *Gwerin* 3:2 (1960), 8–43: 8.

[29] Lucas, 'Irish food before the potato', 4–28; Sexton, 'Porridges, gruels and breads', 239.

[30] Plummer, *Lives of Irish saints*.

cultivated during the medieval period, but vary in frequency and composition archaeological sites. Wheat, oat, barley and rye were all typical crops of exposure to fire. The frequency with which they appear to have been exposed to firing events ensures their relative ubiquity and abundance on legumes, commonly survive on archaeological sites in charred form as a result sites.[31] Cereal remains (grains and chaff), including other field crops, such as the growing corpus of archaeobotanical evidence from Irish archaeological extensive information about cereal-based products and this is supported by

with cereal crops in archaeobotanical assemblages. (Photos: Susan Lyons.)

from medieval archaeological sites in Ireland. Wild radish is a wild plant often recorded

Pl. III——Charred macrofossil remains of cultivated cereals and pulse crops recorded

Food plants, fruits and foreign foodstuffs

depending on location, environmental conditions, cultural preference and use (Pl. III).

The archaeological evidence for crops on urban sites is surprisingly less than expected[32] especially considering the frequency of cereal remains in charred assemblages on rural sites.[33] One reason for this may be the plant remains which survived the different stages of food preparation. Since large-scale flour production was carried out in mills located primarily in the rural hinterland, one would expect cereal remains to be a rarity in urban contexts. It has been surmised then that their presence in towns is perhaps for animal fodder, fuel, seed corn or as a consequence of transit.[34] The ubiquity of charred cereal remains on rural sites is particularly associated with features such as kilns and hearths, which can provide insights into crop-processing techniques and potentially cultivation at a local level, something often missing from historical records. The evidence for waste products and cooking debris is also more prolific at these sites, since open features such as ditches, pits and gullies were frequently used as a dumping ground for this material. In contrast, crop-processing within urban centres is more difficult to define and therefore interpret, since the character of rural and urban settlement and their use of space clearly differed. It must be stated, however, that the presence of cereal remains does not in itself indicate if a site was a producer (involved with crop cultivation) or consumer (receiving crops in a processed or semi-processed state) site.[35] While rural settlement would have engaged in producer/consumer activities, it is most likely that urban communities were largely end consumers where evidence for cereal remains reflects predominantly consumption.

Grain-based products, such as breads, porridges and gruels were consumed by grinding the grain into flour or meal. Evidence for this in an urban context is found in faecal remains from cesspits at Fishamble Street, Dublin,[36] Arundel Square, Waterford,[37] and similarly at Coppergate in York[38] which contained frequent fragments of cereal spermoderm (bran), with wheat/rye tentatively identified from Dublin and Waterford. During the medieval

---

[32] Mitchell and Dickson, 'Plant remains and other items'; Collins, 'Plant remains', 1997; Tierney and Hannon, 'Plant remains'; McClatchie, 'The plant remains'; Mitchell, *Archaeology and environment.*

[33] McCormick *et al.*, 'The archaeology of livestock and cereal production'; Penny Johnston, 'Macrofossil plant remains', in O'Donovan, 'Excavations at Friar Street Cashel', 59–67: 61.

[34] James Rackham (ed.), *Environment and economy in Anglo–Saxon England: a review of recent work on the environmental archaeology of rural and urban Anglo–Saxon settlements in England: proceedings of conference held at the Museum of London, 9-10 April, 1990,* British Archaeology Report No. 89 (Oxford, 1994), 115.

[35] McCormick *et al.*, 'The archaeology of livestock and cereal production', 56.

[36] Geraghty, *Viking Dublin,* 31.

[37] Tierney and Hannon, 'Plant remains', 889.

[38] Hall, 'A brief history of plant foods in the city of York', 29.

period the primary use of grain was in bread-making, with most being baked from wheat flour.[39] Wheat, in contrast to oat and barley, has a high gluten content, which determines flour quality and is an essential component for producing leavened bread.[40] The superior quality of wheaten flour was more desired than the heavy flat coarse breads of oat and barley,[41] which were viewed as inferior varieties.[42] Wheat was often thought of as a luxury food of the higher social classes in early Ireland[43] but became a staple crop from the thirteenth century as part of the Anglo–Norman system of intensive cereal production.[44] Monastic/penitential bread, a common staple of the Benedictine rule of the Cistercians and Augustinian orders required coarse flat bread to be consumed.[45] This was made from an inferior flour of barley, oats and pulses baked on ashes or made into dried biscuits.[46] Only the finest wheat flour was permitted on Sundays and in the making of the wafer-thin sacramental Host.[47] Despite the documentary evidence for the use of wheat in bread-making, the recovery of whole wheat grains from urban sites can be low.[48] This is based on the assertion that bulk crop-processing, including milling wheat for flour, was a large-scale operation carried out under seigneurial control on rural demesnes.[49]

While wheat was recorded from most urban medieval deposits, values were generally lower from Hiberno–Norse occupation layers compared to later medieval phases. Instead, barley (six-row) and oat (common, bristle and wild varieties) dominated assemblages from Viking and Hiberno–Norse sites in Dublin, Cork, Waterford and Wexford.[50] With a notable increase in wheat values from thirteenth-century occupation layers in Wexford and at a number of

---

[39] Murphy and Potterton, *The Dublin region in the Middle Ages,* 431.

[40] Regina Sexton, 'Cereals and cereal foodstuffs in the early historic period', unpublished MA thesis, University College Cork, 1993, 98.

[41] Kuno Meyer (ed.), *Betha Colmáin maic Lúacháin: life of Colmáin son of Lúachan,* Todd Lecture Series 17 (Dublin and London, 1911); Sexton, 'Cereals and cereal foodstuffs', 142; Sexton, 'Porridges, gruels and breads', 79.

[42] Kuno Meyer, *The vision of MacConglinne* (London, 1892), 15.

[43] Kelly, *Early Irish farming,* 219.

[44] Kenneth Nicholls, *Gaelic and Gaelicized Ireland in the Middle Ages* (Dublin, 2003), 201.

[45] Maria Dembinska, 'Fasting and working monks: regulations of the fifth to the eleventh centuries', in Alexander Fenton and Eszeter Kisbán (eds), *Food in change: eating habits from the Middle Ages to the present day* (London, 1986), 155.

[46] Sexton, 'Cereals and cereal foodstuffs', 157; Dembinska, 'Fasting and working monks', 155.

[47] Sexton, 'Cereals and cereal foodstuffs', 163.

[48] Penny Johnston, 'Analysis of carbonised plant remains', in Christine Baker, 'Excavations within the manor of Merrion Castle, Dublin', in Seán Duffy (ed.), *Medieval Dublin VIII* (Dublin, 2008), 275–82.

[49] Murphy and Potterton, *The Dublin region in the Middle Ages,* 414.

[50] Geraghty, *Viking Dublin*; McClatchie, 'The plant remains'; McClatchie, 'Non-wood plant macro remains from 36–39 South Main Street, Cork', in Maurice Hurley and

sites in Dublin,[51] oat predominates from similar phases in Waterford and from Washington Street and South Main Street, Cork.[52] Evidence for wheat was low from Cashel, however, it is frequently recorded along with oat from Kilkenny, most notably from a series of thirteenth/fourteenth-century refuse pits on Patrick Street[53] and a later medieval/post-medieval crop-drying kiln on Friary Street.[54] This trend follows a similar pattern emerging from other archae-obotanical datasets in Ireland, where wheat rarely dominants on sites pre-dating *c.* AD 1200,[55] but more prevalent on late twelfth- and thirteenth-century settlements.[56] It was documented as being grown by the Irish population during this period, however it rarely became part of their own diet, instead being used as payment of a tithe or rent to local landlords.[57]

While hulled wheat, such as emmer and possible spelt wheat have been identified from Friary Street, Kilkenny,[58] and Friar Street, Cashel,[59] identifications are tenuously based on grains rather than chaff. In the absence of cereal chaff, it can be difficult to distinguish between different species of wheat in the archaeological record.[60] In most instances, however, it is naked or free-threshing wheat, such as bread wheat (*Triticum aestivum* L.) which are recovered from Irish medieval sites, with some evidence for the bread/club and rivet/durum variety (*T. aestivum/compactum* L.; *T. turgidum/durum* Desf.).[61] Despite the sheer volume of cereal grains being identified from medieval sites in

---

Ciara Brett (eds), *Archaeological excavations at South Main Street 2003–2005 [Cork City]* (Cork, 2014), 429–39, 435; Abi Brewer, 'Archaeobotanical report for Washington Street Cork (02E0034)', unpublished report, University College Cork, 2007; Tierney and Hannon, 'Plant remains'; Bourke, 'Life in the sunny south-east', 35.

[51] Susan Lyons, 'Plant macrofossil remains from Hammond Lane, Dublin (03E0721)', unpublished report, Margaret Gowen and Co. Ltd, 2004; Susan Lyons, 'Plant macrofossil remains from James Joyce Street, Dublin 1 (03E0879)', unpublished report, Margaret Gowen and Co. Ltd, 2004; Abi Brewer, 'Plant remains', in Jacinta Kiely, 'Archaeological excavations at 56–60 South Main Street, Wexford', *Eachtra Journal* 14 (2003), 35–41.

[52] Brewer, 'Archaeobotanical report for Washington Street, Cork'.

[53] Penny Johnston, 'The plant remains', in Jacinta Kiely, 'Archaeological excavation report 26 Patrick Street, Kilkenny, County Kilkenny 99E0165', unpublished report, Eachtra Archaeological Projects, 2000.

[54] Penny Johnston, 'Analysis of the plant remains Friary Street/Garden Row, Kilkenny (01E0569)', unpublished report, Margaret Gowen and Co. Ltd, 2002.

[55] McCormick *et al.*, 'The archaeology of livestock and cereal production', 46.

[56] Monk, 'Evidence from macroscopic plant remains for crop husbandry', 34.

[57] Aidan Clarke, 'The Irish economy 1600–60', in T. W. Moody, F. X. Martin and F. J. Byrne (eds), *Early modern Ireland 1534–1691* (London, 1991), 168–86: 170.

[58] Johnston, 'Analysis of plant remains from Friary Street/Garden Row, Kilkenny'.

[59] Penny Johnston, 'Macrofossil plant remains', in O'Donovan, 'Excavations at Friar Street Cashel', 59–67.

[60] Gordon Hillman, Sarah Mason, Dominique de Moulins and Mark Nesbitt, 'Identification of archaeological remains of wheat: the 1992 London workshop', *Circaea* 12 (1996), 195–209.

[61] McCormick *et al.*, 'The archaeology of livestock and cereal production', 51.

Ireland, spelt wheat and rye are still grossly under-represented, compared to archaeobotanical records from the Continent.[62] In Britain, there is a shift from spelt wheat to naked wheat recorded in Anglo–Scandinavian and later medieval sites, while rye values decrease during this time.[63] This increase in naked wheat could be more cultural than environmentally driven. Taste may have been one factor for wheat preference in different locations. Bread and spelt flour is of high quality, producing a light, white bread, which was favoured by northern and western European regions, while rye bread, common in more easterly areas, was flat and coarse.[64]

From a practical view point, naked wheat requires less processing than hulled wheat, where the grain is difficult to detach from the outer glumes or hulls. In addition, spelt wheat has a lower yield per acre than bread wheat, which would make is less commercially viable.[65] Being less labour intensive, naked wheat would therefore produce a high and stable yield, more suited to the rigors of Anglo–Norman agriculture practices. This could go some way to explaining its frequency in some later medieval archaeobotanical assemblages. More locally, archaeobotanical research in Ireland is revealing that higher incidences of wheat are recorded from sites in Leinster compared to Munster[66] and the data from urban sites in these regions also supports this pattern. This perhaps reflects the breadth of Anglo–Norman settlement within these areas and that cultural preference was also a significant factor in crop variation at different geographical locations within Ireland.

Crop-drying in an urban context was not unusual as kilns and a possible oven were found in back yards of medieval properties on Peter Street and Back Lane, Waterford. Kilns generally represent large-scale crop-drying, so their presence could reflect a commercial activity, such as baking or brewing. This activity is characterised by the number of bakehouses recorded in Dublin[67] in the thirteenth and fourteenth centuries, and in breweries associated with

---

[62] Tanja Märkle, 'Nutrition, aspects of land use and environment in medieval times in Southern Germany: plant macro analysis from latrines (late 11th to 13th centuries AD) at the town of Überlingen, Lake Constance', *Vegetation History and Archaeobotany* 14 (2005), 427–41.

[63] Hall, 'A brief history of plant foods in the city of York', 27.

[64] Märkle, 'Nutrition, aspects of land use and environment in medieval times in Southern Germany', 433; Petr Kocár, Petr Cech, Radka Kozáková and Romana Kocárová, 'Environment and economy of the early medieval settlement at Zatec', *Interdisciplinaria Archaeologica Natural Sciences in Archaeology* 1:1/2 (2010), 45–60.

[65] Märkle, 'Nutrition, aspects of land use and environment in medieval times in Southern Germany', 433.

[66] McCormick *et al.*, 'The archaeology of livestock and cereal production', 51.

[67] Example of a bakehouse is Schoolhouse Lane cited in Murphy and Potterton, *The Dublin region in the Middle Ages*, 431; H. F. Berry, 'History of the religious gild of St. Anne, in St Audeon's Church, Dublin, 1430–1740', *Proceedings of the Royal Irish Academy* 25C (1904–5), 21–106.

religious houses at Holy Trinity and Christ Church Cathedral and Dublin Castle.[68] Bread-baking in Cashel is also documented where a bakehouse is mentioned in a charter dating to 1230.[69] In Kilkenny, the grain from the kiln at Friary Street was interpreted as evidence for brewing. A mixed composition of predominantly wheat and oat displayed signs of germination, a feature of malted grains.[70] While there is some documentary evidence from Dublin that wheat was used in ale-making, oat was the preferred grain for malting and brewing, certainly up until the fourteenth century.[71] Oat was cheap and widely available and used in the brewing of inferior ales, while wheat produced a more superior brew. The preponderance of oat identified from archaeological deposits in Cashel may also signal local ale-making, especially since brewing was a historically attested activity within the town, with some 38 practising brewers recorded.[72] In contrast to the brewing industry in England, barley was the preferred brewing grain at this time, seen perhaps as being superior to oat-brewed ales, as reported by English travellers to Ireland in the seventeenth century: 'scarce outside of Dublin and few other towns will you meet with any good beer or any reasonable bread for your money, only you may have some raw, muddy, unwholesome ale, made solely of oats'.[73]

Another supporting feature for potential brewing at Friary Street, Kilkenny, was the high frequency of cereal chaff and straw present. The use of certain types of fuel in a kiln permeated various flavours into the malted grain, many of which were considered undesirable. While most brewers used wood, straw imparted the least taste, which helped to produce a clean-tasting ale.[74] Since ale was produced without the use of hops, it spoiled quicker particularly ales of ordinary strength. This feature would have greatly affected the trade and transport of ale, prompting ale-making industries, such as those associated with religious houses, to dry malted grains locally. Valued for its nutritional and sustaining abilities,[75] ale became a staple in the diet of medieval people, including penitential orders,[76] so demand was high.

Whether beer was being brewed in Ireland at this time is uncertain. The practice of brewing beer involves the use of hops and in Britain the transition from unhopped ales to hopped beer is documented from the fourteenth

---

[68] Anne Robinson, 'The history of Dublin Castle to 1684', unpublished PhD thesis, University College Dublin, 1994, 73.

[69] Thomas Laffan, 'Abstracts from the ancient records of the corporation of Cashel, 1673–1780', *The Journal of the Royal Society of Antiquaries of Ireland*, ser. 5 XIV (1904), 30–40.

[70] Johnston, 'Analysis of plant remains from Friary Street/Garden Row, Kilkenny'.

[71] Murphy and Potterton, *The Dublin region in the Middle Ages*, 313.

[72] O'Keeffe, 'Cashel', 161–2.

[73] George O'Brien, *Advertisements for Ireland* (Dublin, 1923), 35.

[74] Annie Owen (ed.), *Walter of Bibbesworth, Le Traité de Walter de Bibbesworth* (Paris, 1929), 201.

[75] Sexton, 'Cereals and cereal foodstuffs', 130.

[76] Gwynn and Purton, 'The monastery of Tallaght', 115–80.

century.[77] Archaeological finds of hops do occur but are infrequent and it is difficult to ascertain if they represent a cultivated variety.[78] Hops were included in gardens, although they were also grown as a specialist field crop.[79] Earliest archaeological finds for hops were recovered from tenth- and eleventh-century deposits at Hedeby, Germany, from Birka, Sweden, and Svendborg, Denmark,[80] eleventh- and twelfth-century deposits at Novgorod, Russia,[81] and from Anglo–Scandinavian York,[82] suggesting that hops came into Northern Europe as early as the tenth century. Flavourings such as sweet gale and bog myrtle were found alongside hops from York, Novgorod and fourteenth-century deposits in Aberdeen,[83] however no such combination has been recorded from Ireland to date. The identification of a hop seed from a later medieval cess deposit at Irishtown/Brennan's Yard[84] is an interesting find, since hops were not native to Ireland. At Parliament Street, Kilkenny,[85] evidence for hop/hemp pollen was identified from a medieval cesspit on the site, possibly through human waste or domestic rubbish, suggesting it may have been growing locally. While it is difficult to separate hop from hemp pollen,[86] the presence of the hop seed from Irishtown/Brennan's Yard helps to confidently assume that the pollen could have derived from hops. From this evidence, it is

---

[77] Henry Corran, *A history of brewing* (London, 1975), 24.

[78] James Greig, 'Plant resources', in Grenville Astill and Annie Grant (eds), *The countryside of medieval England* (Oxford, 1988), 109–27: 115.

[79] Greig, 'Plant resources', 115.

[80] Hanne Jensen, 'The Nordic countries', in Willem van Zeist, Krystyna Wasylikowa and Karl-Ernst Behre (eds), *Progress in Old World palaeoethnobotany* (Rotterdam, 1991), 335–46; Grethe Jørgensen, 'Medieval plant remains from the settlements in Mollergade 6', in Grethe Jørgensen, Kristen Jesperen and Kjeld Christensen (eds), *Analyses of medieval plant remains, textiles and wood from Svendborg* (Odense, Denmark, 1986), 45–84.

[81] Mick Monk and Penny Johnston, 'Plants, people and environment: a report on the macro-plant remains within the deposits from Troitsky Site XI in medieval Novgorod', in Mark Brisbane and David Gaimster (eds), *Novgorod: the archaeology of a Russian medieval city and its hinterland*, The British Museum Occasional Paper 141 (2001), 113–17: 114.

[82] Hall, Jones and Kenward, 'Cereal bran and human faecal remains from archaeological deposits'.

[83] James Dickson, 'Plant remains', in John Murray (ed.), *Excavations in the medieval burgh of Aberdeen, 1973–81* (Edinburgh, 1982), 177–81.

[84] Johnston, 'Analysis of plant remains from Friary Street/Garden Row, Kilkenny'.

[85] Bettina Stefanini, 'Preliminary pollen assessment: Kilkenny Court House, Kilkenny', unpublished report, Arch-Tech Ltd, 2009. There is no absolute dating evidence for this feature, but based on relative dating through stratigraphy, it has been postulated that it dates to at least the fifteenth or sixteenth century, Maeve Saundersson, 'Preliminary archaeological report for Kilkenny Courthouse, Parliament Street, Kilkenny, County Kilkenny (08E0462)', unpublished report, Arch-Tech Ltd, 2009.

[86] Benjamin Gearey, Allan Hall, Harry Kenward, M. J. Bunting, M. C. Lillie and John Carrott, 'Palaeoenvironmental assessment of samples from Morton Lane, Beverley', unpublished report, West Yorkshire Archaeological Services, Hull, 2002.

possible to infer that hops were growing in urban gardens in Kilkenny and potentially being consumed. In addition to flavouring beer, hops had medicinal uses such as treating skin ulcers and inflammation.[87]

Since bread and ale were considered the two staples of life, the majority of grain and grain-based products were brought into the towns and sold at city markets for this purpose.[88] The purchase of whole grains would also have been important in order to facilitate food supplies through the winter, especially for urban communities, who depended on seasonal produce. Oat was the most prominent grain recorded from both archaeological and documentary evidence during the medieval period.[89] Since oat could tolerate difficult growing conditions and damp climates, it became the primary foodstuff for all classes, although it was often associated with poorer communities.[90] Oats would have provided more nutrition than wheat or barley, having a higher protein, fibre and amino acid content than any other cereal.[91] The recovery of whole grains from occupational layers on many urban sites in Ireland indicates that cereals were stored in towns without having to be milled. One such example is Friar Street, Cashel,[92] where a mixture of crops and pulses were recovered from a fourteenth-century burnt structure,[93] representing the remains of grains stored for domestic consumption. The presence of oat, barley and wheat in this context may be incidental rather than contamination. Growing a mixed crop, known as dredge or maslin, was well documented in England[94] and suggested by Geraghty[95] for crop assemblages in Viking Dublin. Sowing mixed crops together had an economic incentive, since it ensured the probability of a decent yield. Interestingly, the oat and barley grains from Cashel still had hulls and chaff attached, while the wheat grains did not, evidence that oat and barley were not fully processed. Oat chaff and a variety of arable weed seeds were also plentiful from samples at Chapel Lane, Cashel; Parliament Street, Kilkenny; and medieval Waterford[96] suggesting that oats were being processed within the

[87] Märkle, 'Nutrition, aspects of land use and environment in medieval times in Southern Germany'.

[88] Murphy and Potterton, *The Dublin region in the Middle Ages,* 432.

[89] Monk, 'The archaeobotanical evidence for field crop plants'; Murphy and Potterton, *The Dublin region in the Middle Ages,* 313.

[90] Sexton, 'Cereals and cereal foodstuffs', 142.

[91] Mick Monk, 'Oats: The superfood of early medieval Ireland', *Archaeology Ireland* 25:1 (2011), 36–9: 37.

[92] Johnston, 'Macrofossil plant remains'.

[93] This structure was radiocarbon dated using charcoal and a date of 1280–1408 cal. AD (2 sigma) was obtained, O'Donovan, 'Excavations at Friar Street Cashel', 27.

[94] Herbert Hallam, *Rural England 1066–1348* (Glasgow, 1981).

[95] Geraghty, *Viking Dublin,* 49.

[96] Susan Lyons, 'The environmental remains', in Colm Moloney and Caitriona Gleeson, 'Final report on archaeological excavations at Chapel Lane, Cashel, County Tipperary', unpublished report, Headland Archaeology Ltd, 2005; Susan Lyons, 'The plant macrofossil remains', in Maeve Saundersson, 'Preliminary archaeological report for Kilkenny Courthouse'; Tierney and Hannon, 'Plant remains', 890.

town or were being stored in a semi-clean state. This can be carried out in a domestic context quite easily, using a quern stone, known as 'shelling' or 'graddaning', where the grains are parched in a pot over a fire or rolled with hot pebbles in a basket.[97] Oat had a number of different uses, which depended on availability, use and personal taste. It could be baked into flat cakes, or added to pottage and stews and malted and brewed into inferior ales, as discussed. It was frequently used in making porridge rather than bread as it was easy to digest, and simple and quick to prepare and cook, compared to barley.[98] Porridge was a common dish in the diet of children in medieval Ireland,[99] but oatmeal made of water and buttermilk was viewed as an inferior dish and considered an unhospitable dish to serve to travellers.[100] Since oat was also commonly used for horse fodder (grain and chaff),[101] its preponderance in the archaeological record suggests it was being cultivated for both human and animal consumption. Animals kept in urban areas would have required a constant supply of fodder so unprocessed crops could reflect areas where there was a market for fodder goods, such as poorer consumers and urban hinterlands.[102] Food storage was essential to a stable urban economy given that most food plants, including staples such as crops, were produced seasonally in temperate regions. The ability of cereals to be stored for long periods of time added great value to maintaining a balanced diet throughout the winter. A cache of whole grains was therefore a versatile resource, providing a household with much-needed ingredients for a variety of food and liquid dishes as well as feed for animal stock.

Other field crops—peas, beans, lentils and flax

Other field crops recorded from medieval Ireland are pulse crops or legumes. Traditionally, they were used primarily for animal fodder, especially vetch[103] and as a foodstuff in times of famine or a bad harvest.[104] The historical evidence for peas, beans and vetches is a mention in early medieval Irish law tracts of the eighth century and they are well documented in thirteenth and fourteenth-century manorial accounts for food liveries, maintenance

---

[97] David Robinson, 'Botanical remains [Kirk Close]', in Philip Holdsworth (ed.), *Excavations in the medieval Burgh of Perth 1979–1981*, Society of Antiquaries of Scotland Monograph, ser. 5 (Edinburgh, 1987), 199–209 cited in Tierney and Hannon, 'Plant remains', 890.

[98] Lucas, 'Irish food before the potato', 9; Sexton, 'Cereals and cereal foodstuffs', 143.

[99] Mentioned in the Cáin Iarraith ('The law of the fosterage fee') cited in Kelly, *Early Irish farming*, 331.

[100] Meyer, *The vision of MacConglinne*, 14–6.

[101] James Langdon, 'The economics of horses and oxen in medieval England', *Agricultural History Review* 30:1 (1982), 31–40.

[102] Murphy and Potterton, *The Dublin region in the Middle Ages*, 313.

[103] Langdon, 'The economics of horses and oxen in medieval England', 32.

[104] Murphy and Potterton, *The Dublin region in the Middle Ages*, 314.

agreements and government purveyance records.[105] In fourteenth-century Dublin, 50% of peas and beans recorded from the manor at Clonkeen were given to servants and the remainder were sent to Glasnevin and Grangegorman to be used in horse bread.[106] If Clonkeen is typical of the settlements in the Dublin region at this time, then legumes played an important part in the diet of the poorer classes. Most legumes are toxic in their raw state (have a negative effect on absorbing nutrients in the body), so they require soaking, fermenting or sprouting in order to ensure that they are safe to eat. Once dried, they could be stored easily for the winter months and were a good source of fat, starch, protein and Vitamins B, C and K. Between the twelfth and fourteenth centuries, Spencer's survey of historical documents pertaining to foodstuffs suggests that dried peas and beans were commonly made into flour or as part of a pottage dish consumed by both the rich and poorer classes[107] and archaeological evidence for this practice was recorded from Viking Birka.[108] 'Pottage' by its very meaning translates to: 'that which is cooked in a pot', a common stew-like dish consumed by both the rich and poorer classes.[109] This dish could be made from a variety of different ingredients ranging from the simplest plain-boiled cereal gruels to more luxurious stews which included meats, fish and vegetables.[110] Beans were commonly used in sweet dishes, such as puddings and are mentioned in many medieval recipe books of the thirteenth and fourteenth centuries.[111]

The presence of pulse crops in the archaeological record, however, is less impressive and they rarely survive, possibly as a result of taphonomic factors.[112] Their seeds do not preserve well in waterlogged conditions, especially if ground into flour and since their processing does not require them to be dried, their chances of becoming charred is infrequent. Horse/broad bean and probably field pea were cultivated and eaten in Viking Dublin dating from the eleventh century.[113] In medieval Waterford, charred field pea fragments were recovered

---

[105] Murphy and Potterton, *The Dublin region in the Middle Ages,* 323; Christopher Dyer, 'English diet in the later Middle Ages', in Trevor Aston, Peter Coss, Christopher Dyer and Joan Thirsk (eds), *Social relations and ideas: essays in honour of R H Hilton* (London, 1983), 191–214.

[106] Mills, *Account Roll of the Priory of the Holy Trinity,* 180–1; Murphy and Potterton, *The Dublin region in the Middle Ages,* 315.

[107] Collin Spencer, *British food: an extraordinary thousand years history* (London, 2002), 57.

[108] Peas were ground up like cereals and mixed with other meal in baked bread, cited in Jensen, 'The Nordic countries', 345.

[109] Christopher Dyer, 'Seasonal patterns in food consumption in the latter Middle Ages', in Woolgar, Serjeantson and Waldron, *Food in medieval England,* 201–14: 214.

[110] Peter Brears, *Cooking and dining in medieval England* (London, 2012), 215.

[111] Constance Hieatt and Sharon Butler, *Curye on Inglish: English culinary manuscripts of the fourteenth-century (including the Forme of Cury)* (London, 1985).

[112] Tierney and Hannon, 'Plant remains', 889.

[113] Mitchell, *Archaeology and environment,* 26; Geraghty, *Viking Dublin,* 103.

from deposits dating from the eleventh to the thirteenth century[114] and from thirteenth/fourteenth-century deposits in Drogheda, Co. Louth. Their frequency in the archaeological record increases from the thirteenth century[115] coinciding with the arrival of the Anglo–Norman population, probably as part of their crop-rotation system.[116] Both peas and beans were also recorded charred from medieval deposits associated with cess material, refuse pits and occupational layers at Cashel and Kilkenny. Their occurrence in kiln deposits from Friary Street, Kilkenny,[117] indicates that they were being dried locally prior to storage in seed form. Storage in a domestic context, alongside other whole grains, as in Friar Street, Cashel,[118] represents a cache of foodstuffs for long term use possibly through the winter. As well as cultivated legumes, 'wild' legumes were found at many medieval sites in Ireland, particularly vetches (*Vicia* spp.). While there is no documentary evidence for the cultivation of vetches during this period, there are extensive historical sources for their cultivation in medieval England, principally as fodder and also as famine food.[119] It has been argued that by the fourteenth century, the scale and distribution of vetch cultivation on some English demesnes signal their status as a significant field crop.[120] This also corresponds with the earliest accounts of vetches being used on a large scale to feed draught animals.[121] It is difficult to establish if vetch remains recovered from the Irish archaeological record represent cultivated produce or weeds inadvertently harvested with cultivated legumes, or indeed an uncultivated plant gathered for consumption. Some of the largest vetch assemblages to date (in excess of 100 charred seeds) have been recovered from later medieval settlement sites at Boyerstown, Co. Meath,[122] and Busherstown, Co. Offaly.[123] The absence of chaff makes it difficult to

---

[114] Tierney and Hannon, 'Plant remains', 858.

[115] Susan Lyons and Meriel McClatchie, 'New insights into legume production in early medieval and medieval Ireland', (2012), in the Royal Irish Academy Committee for Archaeology, *Revealing the past: archaeological research in Ireland* (Dublin, 2012).

[116] Monk, 'Evidence from macroscopic plant remains for crop husbandry', 34.

[117] Johnston, 'Analysis of plant remains from Friary Street/Garden Row, Kilkenny'.

[118] Johnston, 'Macrofossil plant remains'.

[119] Bruce Campbell, *English seigniorial agriculture, 1250–1450* (Cambridge, 2000), 228–30.

[120] Bruce Campbell, 'The diffusion of vetches in medieval England', *Economic History Review* 41:2 (1988), 193–208: 196.

[121] Langdon, 'The economics of horses and oxen in medieval England', 32.

[122] Archaeological Services, Durham University, 'Appendix 15: Boyerstown 1: plant macrofossil, charcoal, cremated bone and mollusca analysis', in Kevin Martin, *M3 Clonee—north of Kells Contract 3 Navan Bypass: report on the archaeological excavation of Boyerstown 1, Co. Meath (A023/13, E3105)* (Dublin, 2009), courtesy of the National Road Authority. A large cache of vetch seeds was recovered from a kiln where a charred oat grain was radiocarbon dated to 1650–1950 cal. AD (Beta 247105).

[123] Penny Johnston, 'Appendix 4: Plant remains', in Eachtra Archaeological Projects, *N7 Castletown to Nenagh (Contract 1): archaeological excavation report from Busherstown, Co. Offaly E3661* (2012), 154–71.

identify these seeds to species, however based on the size of the seed and the length of the hilum (seed scar), *Vicia* spp. predominates, with lesser incidences for *Lathyrus* spp. Similar mixed vetch assemblages have also been recorded from later medieval deposits at Carrickmines Castle, Co. Dublin,[124] and the Cistercian Abbey at Bective, Co. Meath.[125] Vetch seeds are recovered together with other cultivated legumes and cereal crops from kiln and hearth deposits and as refuse debris in pits, diches and gully features from these sites. While this indicates that they were dried with mixed crops, potentially to be used in grain-based produce, the distinction between human and animal product is still under-researched. While much is still unknown about the use of vetches in the medieval diet, such assemblages should still be considered when interpreting medieval food economy in the context of other cultivated crops and food plants.

Peas and beans were planted in late spring for harvesting in August or September after they had dried in the pod. While there is documentary evidence for cultivation on large rural demesnes[126] as a cultivated field crop, it is unknown if they formed part of an intensive cropping regime.[127] Other than a foodstuff, legumes have the ability to fix nitrogen in soils, thus making cultivation plots more productive in the long term.[128] Wheat occurs frequently on Irish archaeological sites were legumes are also present,[129] which is interesting because wheat is a rather demanding crop that requires good-quality nitrogenous soils. Recent research in crop-rotation systems has demonstrated that planting legumes in order to increase crop yields can take many years.[130] The apparent association between wheat and legumes in Irish archaeological deposits requires more careful attention, and perhaps further

---

[124] Susan Lyons, 'Analysis of the plant macrofossil remains from Carrickmines Castle, Co. Dublin (00E0525/02E1532)', unpublished report, Valerie Keeley Ltd, 2011. Vetches are recorded with charred oat, wheat, barley and peas from a gully feature which was radiocarbon dated to 1150–1270 cal. AD (SUERC–36184, 835+/–30 BP) and a well radiocarbon dated to 1430–1620 cal. AD (SUERC–36183, 420+/–25 BP). Radiocarbon dates are provided courtesy of Valerie Keeley Ltd.

[125] Susan Lyons, 'Analysis of the plant macrofossil and charcoal remains from Bective Abbey, Co. Meath', unpublished report, Bective Abbey Project, Royal Irish Academy research project (2010–2012), 2013. Vetch seeds were found alongside a large mixed cache of charred cereal crops, peas and beans from a kiln/barn structure, which was radiocarbon dated to the late thirteenth century (date courtesy of Matthew Stout).

[126] John Wynchedon, a Cork landowner who died in 1306, held property including ten acres of barley and peas, cited in Gearóid Mac Niocaill, 'Socio-economic problems of the late medieval Irish town', in David Harkness and Mary O'Dowd (eds), *The town in Ireland* (Belfast, 1981), 7–22: 14.

[127] Murphy and Potterton, *The Dublin region in the Middle Ages*, 314.

[128] Robert Allen, 'The nitrogen hypothesis and the English agricultural revolution: a biological analysis', *Journal of Economic History* 68:1 (2008), 182–210.

[129] Lyons and McClatchie, 'New insights into legume production in early medieval and medieval Ireland'.

[130] Allen, 'The nitrogen hypothesis and the English agricultural revolution', 191.

research before it can be determined if legumes were indeed being cultivated to help to improve crop yields.

Despite their low frequencies in urban contexts, there are archaeological signals for legume storage and possible cultivation at a local level. One biological indicator for their presence on site is the bean weevil (*Bruchus* sp.), a product pest found in stored peas and beans which was identified in cess pits from Parliament Street, Kilkenny,[131] and Temple Bar West, Dublin.[132] Pollen associated with the pea family (*Fabaceae* spp.) was also identified from the cesspits at Parliament Street, Kilkenny;[133] a potential indicator that legumes were growing on a small scale in urban gardens. While these plants would have been very beneficial at a time when grain was in short supply or after a poor harvest,[134] it must also be acknowledged that factors such as seasonality and cultural preference would also have determined how and when legume crops were consumed.

Lentils are extremely rare from Irish archaeobotanical assemblages and to date have been recorded in charred form from just a few medieval sites, namely Clonfad 3, Co. Westmeath,[135] and Naas, Co. Kildare,[136] although their contextual integrity is ambiguous. The largest lentil cache recorded in Ireland to date was identified from a post-medieval pit at Patrick Street in Dublin.[137] While no documentary evidence exists for the cultivation of lentils in Ireland, they are found alongside other pulse crops, which suggest that they may have been grown as part of a mixed legume crop in medieval Ireland. It is also possible that these represent imported crops, as thought to be the case for contemporary lentil finds in Britain.[138]

The presence of flax from medieval sites adds to the diversity of crops cultivated in medieval Ireland. The cultivation of flax would have provided linen obtained from the stalks by retting, animal fodder from the leaves and oil from the crushed seeds, which had uses in cooking and lighting.[139] The presence of flax in cesspits, along with other cess indicators, such as cereal bran, fruit

---

[131] Eileen Murphy, 'Preliminary analysis of insect remains from excavations at the Courthouse, Parliament Street, Kilkenny City (08E0462)', unpublished report, Arch-Tech Ltd, 2009.

[132] Eileen Reilly, 'The contribution of insect remains to an understanding of the environment of Viking age and medieval Dublin', in Seán Duffy (ed.), *Medieval Dublin IV* (Dublin, 2002), 41–62.

[133] Stefanini, 'Preliminary pollen assessment'.

[134] Lucas, 'Irish food before the potato', 15; Sexton, 'Porridges, gruels and breads', 81.

[135] Alison Vaughan-Williams, 'Archaeobotanical analysis', in Paul Stevens (ed.), 'N6 Kinnegad to Kilbeggan Dual Carriageway. Archaeological excavation final report, vol. 2. Ministerial Direction: A001/036. Registration No.: E2723: Clonfad 3, Clonfad Townland, Co Westmeath', unpublished report, Valerie Keeley Ltd, 2009.

[136] Murphy and Potterton, *The Dublin region in the Middle Ages*, 316.

[137] Collins, 'Plant remains', 1997, 230.

[138] Allan Hall and Jacqueline Huntley, *A review of the evidence for macrofossil plant remains from archaeological deposits in northern England*, Research Department Report Series no. 87 (London, 2007), 248.

[139] P. J. Reynolds, *Iron-Age farm: the Butser experiment* (London, 1979), 66–7.

seeds, fish bone and insect ova is a good indication of food debris.[140] Linseed was eaten with grains and pulses in breads and stews as archaeological evidence from Viking Birka[141] and Coppergate[142] can attest. Evidence for flax, together with other food plant remains was recorded from eleventh-century cess deposits at Fishamble Street, Dublin,[143] a thirteenth-century cesspit from John Dillon Street, Dublin,[144] Waterford and South Main Street, Cork.[145] It was also identified from other thirteenth and fourteenth-century sites in Dublin, Cork and Wexford,[146] however, its status as a foodstuff is more difficult to ascertain. Its presence alongside cherry and sloe stones, blackberry pips and a grape seed from thirteenth-century refuse deposits in Chapel Lane, Cashel,[147] hints at potential food debris, as the seeds were crushed in some cases. While documentary evidence for flax cultivation in the medieval period is rare, later medieval sources from England suggest that it grew as a garden crop, indicating small-scale cultivation on individual holdings and in gardens.[148] Flax-drying may have taken place at Friary Street, Kilkenny,[149] along with pulse crops, which could imply that it was growing in urban areas and being stored in seed form. Flax would have grown well and produced higher yields on smaller plots where nutrient-rich loamy soils from organic debris were common.[150]

'To everything there is a season, and a time to every purpose . . .': seasonal contributions to medieval diet

Written evidence for the consumption of fruit, vegetables, nuts and wild plants in the medieval period is largely under-represented and as Christopher Dyer points out, is often dismissed by historians as a marginal or trivial aspect of the medieval diet.[151] Despite the scarcity of horticulture practices in medieval documents, reference to gardens and their produce can be found in many of the later medieval deeds, charters, household accounts, manor surveys and seigneurial records.[152] Gardens and gathered wild produce did not constitute the mainstay of food production but provided the population with a proportion

---

[140] Greig, 'Gardrobes, sewers, cesspits and latrines', 52.

[141] Jensen, 'The Nordic countries', 37.

[142] Hall, 'A brief history of plant foods in the city of York', 29.

[143] Geraghty, *Viking Dublin,* 45.

[144] Penny Johnston, 'Plant remains John Dillon Street, Dublin (98E0158)', unpublished report, Margaret Gowen and Co. Ltd, n.d.

[145] Susan Lyons, 'Plant remains from 40–48 South Main Street, Cork', in Hurley and Brett, *Archaeological excavations at South Main Street,* 250–9; Meriel McClatchie, 'Non-wood plant macro remains'.

[146] Mitchell, *Archaeology and environment;* Collins, 'Plant remains', 1997, 232; Bourke, 'Life in the sunny south-east', 35.

[147] Lyons, 'The environmental remains'.

[148] Geraghty, *Viking Dublin,* 45; Murphy and Potterton, *The Dublin region in the Middle Ages,* 317.

[149] Johnston, 'Analysis of plant remains from Friary Street/Garden Row, Kilkenny'.

[150] Geraghty, *Viking Dublin,* 19.

[151] Dyer, 'Gardens and garden produce', 27.

[152] Murphy and Potterton, *The Dublin region in the Middle Ages,* 351; Dyer, 'Gardens and garden produce', 27.

of their diet on a seasonal basis. The consumption of many plant-based foods (fruit, nuts, vegetables, herbs and wine) during the medieval period was subject to seasonal fluctuation. Functional and economic factors such as weather, cycle of crop growth, and the storage and distribution of commodities also played a part in affecting food supplies.[153] Cultural factors must also be considered, where religious calendars, such as Christmas and Lent, would have impacted on diet and food preferences.

The value of gathered foodstuffs and garden and orchard produce provided both a quantitative and a qualitative element to the medieval diet. In times of food shortage, these natural foodstuffs played a vital role in food production on a seasonal basis. Indeed, this probably led to surplus food supplies, which may have been sold to less self-sufficient consumers, such as the lower classes and urban occupiers. These foodstuffs also supplied people with much-needed nutrition, being a good source of vital vitamins and minerals, which aided balanced eating. The development of an urban market economy and an increase in trade during the later medieval period would have inevitably diversified foodstuffs providing a wider spectrum of fruits and vegetables to a greater number of people.

Historical sources from Ireland document the presence of a vegetable garden outside settlement enclosures as early as the seventh and eighth centuries AD.[154] This is supported in the archaeological record, where small enclosures excavated at a number of early medieval sites, such as Cahercommaun, Co. Clare,[155] and Boyerstown and Castlefarm, Co. Meath,[156] have been interpreted as possible garden plots. Evidence for artificially deepened garden soils has also been identified from early medieval ecclesiastical sites, namely Clonmacnoise, Co. Offaly, and Illaunloughan, Co. Kerry.[157] The function of gardens whether in rural or urban areas was to supply the household with seasonal additions to their diet. From the thirteenth century large secular and ecclesiastical estates would have had well-stocked managed gardens. The lower classes and urban households had access to a small plot for growing vegetables and fruits and would have engaged in small-scale horticulture to facilitate their own dietary needs.[158] In medieval Britain, estates bordering towns were growing

---

[153] Dyer, 'Seasonal patterns in food consumption', 201.

[154] Kelly, *Early Irish farming*, 368.

[155] Hugh O'Neill Hencken, 'Cahercommaun, a stone fort in County Clare', *Journal of the Royal Society of Antiquarians of Ireland* 68 (1938), 1–82.

[156] Linda Clarke, 'M3 Clonee–North of Kells, Contract 3, Navan Bypass. Report on the archaeological excavation of Boyerstown 3, Co. Meath. Ministerial Directions No.A023/015, E3107', excavation report, ACS Ltd, 2009. Available at: www.m3motorway.ie/Archaeology/Section3/Boyerstown3/ (July 2014); Aidan O'Connell and Allister Clark, 'Report on the archaeological excavation of Castlefarm 1, Co. Meath', unpublished report, Archaeological Consultancy Services Ltd, 2009.

[157] Heather King (ed.), *Clonmacnoise studies: seminar papers vol. 2* (2 vols, Dublin, 2003); Jenny White Marshall and Claire Walsh, *Illaunloughan Island: an early medieval monastery in County Kerry* (Bray, 2005).

[158] Murphy and Potterton, *The Dublin region in the Middle Ages*, 349.

garden and orchard produce, which provisioned the urban markets with local fresh supplies.[159] It has also been suggested by Dyer that horticulture was being practised more in urban areas than rural settlements.[160] This would mean that towns were more self-sufficient in providing themselves with garden produce and did not engage to a great extent with the surrounding agrarian economy. Interaction between towns and rural settlement should be reflected in the archaeological record, however, the physical plant remains may not survive to address these questions. Furthermore, preservation conditions may obscure the picture of garden cultivation on agrarian sites, producing a view that garden history is linked to social class and urban environments. Using the current archaeological evidence, more research is needed in the garden plant spectrum from rural settlements in order to assess their place in the medieval food economy. While archaeobotany can provide evidence for the presence of cultivated, wild and collected food plants from urban areas, contextualising this data can sometimes prove difficult, especially in the absence of defined features or well-stratified contexts. It should not be assumed that samples represent in situ deposits. Long periods of occupation will produce multiple layers of middens, increasing the impact of residual and intrusive remains through mixing and disturbance. Identifying sites with limited occupation as well as with a prescribed use of space may yield the best results for interpreting urban food storage, processing activities and horticultural practices.

In the archaeological record, the differential preservation of plant parts is largely based on the part of the plant that has survived. Many non-cereal food plants are rarely exposed to fire and are more likely to be found in wet, anoxic deposits. The edible parts of vegetables and some herbs are soft, so their survival in the archaeological record can be scarce. Food plants valued for their leaves and roots are often under-represented in medieval archaeological deposits as they are generally harvested before the plant goes to seed.[161] In contrast, seeds of herbs and wild plants—where the seed was the part used— fruit stones and nutshells can be over-represented since their robust woody structure ensures that they survive longer (Pl. IV).[162] Even when 'wild' plant seeds are recovered in charred form, they are cautiously interpreted and more often dismissed as arable weed intrusions or fuel debris. One such assemblage from thirteenth/fourteenth-century kilns and a well at Clonfad, Co. West-meath,[163] contained a plethora of wild plants, which historically have both culinary and medicinal qualities. While their presence in these features was

---

[159] Alan Vince, 'Saxon urban economies: an archaeological perspective', in Rackham, *Environment and economy in Anglo–Saxon England*, 108–19: 116.

[160] Christopher Dyer, 'The consumer and the market in the later Middle Ages', *Economic Historical Review* XLII (1989), 305–27.

[161] Tierney and Hannon, 'Plant remains', 856.

[162] Lisa Moffett, 'The archaeology of plant foods', in Woolgar, Serjeantson and Waldron, *Food in medieval England*, 41–55: 54.

[163] Vaughan-Williams, 'Archaeobotanical analysis'.

PL. IV—Examples of typical fruits and herbs recorded from medieval archaeological sites in Ireland. (**a**) blackberry/bramble/raspberry (*Rubus fruticosus/idaeus*); (**b**) wild strawberry (*Fragaria vesca*); (**c**) bilberry (*Vaccinium myrtillus*); (**d**) apple (*Malus* spp.); (**e**) wild cherry (*Prunus avium*); (**f**) blackthorn/sloe (*Prunus spinosa*); (**g**) fig (*Ficus carica*); (**h**) grape (*Vitis vinifera*); (**i**) celery (*Apium graveolens*); (**j**) parsley (*Aethusa cynapium*). (Photos: Susan Lyons.)

interpreted as being the remains of crop-processing waste, perhaps more attention should be given to these plants in the context of other known cultivars and to the possibility that they potentially represent food plant debris rather than crop contaminants. One problem with interpreting vegetables is that they may derive from native wild plants and differentiating cultivated varieties from their wild relatives can be difficult.[164] Their presence in contexts such as cesspits and deposits containing domestic waste together with a series of other biological indicators should also be considered and appropriately evaluated in order to help to establish if they indeed derive from food debris.[165]

Fruits and nuts

One of the most ubiquitous food plants recovered from urban sites, especially from cesspits and cess deposits are fruit remains.[166] Their abundance is partly the result of the high seed content in some fruits, such as blackberry and strawberry but also their robust woody structure can survive well in these environments.[167] The dominance of fruit seeds has coined the expression for this typical assemblage as a 'medieval fruit salad'.[168] Smaller pips are usually swallowed whole with the fruit, such as blackberry, raspberry, strawberry, apple, grape and fig, so they are most likely the remains of food which had passed through the human digestive tract unaltered. Larger fruits such as cherry and plum may be more difficult to swallow and would have been discarded upon eating, so may not be associated with excrement as much as the former fruits.[169] Some of the earliest urban medieval evidence comes from eleventh-century pits at Fishamble Street and Winetavern Street[170] where a wide range of fruits were identified. Cherries, sloes, rose, rowan, blackberry, bilberry, apple and haws were commonly recorded in seed form, with apple endocarp also present from Fishamble Street.[171] A large mass of faecal matter from Winetavern Street contained abundant sloes, blackberry and strawberry seeds, representing direct fruit consumption.[172] Similar fruit assemblage in varying quantities features prominently in later thirteenth and fourteenth-century cesspits and cess

---

[164] Frank Green, 'Problems of interpreting differentially preserved plant remains from excavations of medieval urban sites', in Allan Hall and Harry Kenward (eds), *Environmental archaeology in the urban context* (London, 1982), 40–6; James Greig, 'Archaeobotanical and historical records compared: a new look at the taphonomy of edible and other useful plants from the 11th to the 18th centuries AD', *Circaea* 12 (1996), 211–47: 221.

[165] Smith, 'Defining an indicator package to allow identification of "cesspits"', 537; Greig, 'Gardrobes, sewers, cesspits and latrines', 50.

[166] Greig, 'Gardrobes, sewers, cesspits and latrines', 50; Mitchell, *Archaeology and environment;* Tierney and Hannon, 'Plant remains'; Collins, 'Plant remains', 1997.

[167] James Greig, 'Plant foods in the past: a review of the evidence from Northern Europe', *Journal of Plant Foods* 5 (1983), 179–214: 204; Hall, 'A brief history of plant foods in the city of York', 24.

[168] Robin Dennell, 'Seeds from a medieval sewer in Woolster Street, Plymouth', *Economic Botany* 24:2 (1970), 151–4; James R. A. Greig, 'The investigation of a medieval barrel-latrine from Worcester', *Journal of Archaeological Science* 8 (1981), 265–82: 272.

[169] Greig, 'The investigation of a medieval barrel-latrine from Worcester', 271.

[170] Mitchell, *Archaeology and environment,* 27; Geraghty, *Viking Dublin,* 32.

[171] Geraghty, *Viking Dublin,* 32.

[172] Mitchell, *Archaeology and environment,* 29.

deposits from Chapel Lane, Cashel; Kilkenny; Cork; Drogheda; Athenry, Co. Galway; and Waterford.[173] With the exception of an early thirteenth-century deposit at High Street, Dublin,[174] evidence for bilberry seems confined to earlier Hiberno–Norse occupation in Dublin and Wexford[175] similar to Anglo–Scandinavian sites in England, such as Coppergate.[176] Whether this signifies a cultural preference in the diet of Viking settlers is unknown. Geraghty makes the point that bilberries grow some 10km south of Dublin City, so effort was required to transport them into the town.[177]

Fruit species such as bilberry, bramble, blackberry, haws and elderberry and possibly raspberry were scarcely mentioned in the historical record probably since they were gathered wild. The historical evidence suggests that they were being cultivated from the sixteenth century.[178] Apples were the most frequently mentioned fruit in both the early Irish texts and later medieval sources.[179] Crab/wild apple is native to Ireland and would have provided a good crop of small sour apples.[180] The historical records clearly distinguish between sweet, fragrant and wild apples, and in the *Betha Brigde* from the *Book of Lismore*, apples were stored in a haggard and given as prized gifts.[181] Varieties of apples in later medieval Ireland may have included costards, pearmains and bitter-sweets, the latter being used for cider-making.[182] Pears were rarely recorded prior to the Anglo–Norman period, and varieties included wardens, sorels, caleols and gold knopes.[183] They were usually cooked and eaten in puddings and pies.[184] The use of fruit as relishes and as an accompaniment to dishes is well documented in the early medieval lives of the saints and in the *Aislinge Meic Conglinne*.[185] An eighth-century text *An Irish penitential*,

---

[173] Lyons, 'The environmental remains'; Lyons, 'The plant macrofossil remains'; McClatchie, 'The plant remains'; McClatchie, 'Non-wood plant macro remains'; Lyons, 'Plant remains from 40–48 South Main Street, Cork'; McClatchie, 'Non-wood plant macro remains'; Mitchell and Dickson, 'Plant remains and other items'; Collins, 'Plant remains', 1991; Tierney and Hannon, 'Plant remains'.

[174] Mitchell, *Archaeology and environment,* 27.

[175] Geraghty, *Viking Dublin;* Bourke, 'Life in the sunny south-east', 35.

[176] Hall, 'A brief history of plant foods in the city of York', 31.

[177] Geraghty, *Viking Dublin,* 32.

[178] Greig, 'Archaeobotanical and historical records compared', 215.

[179] Kelly, *Early Irish farming,* 259; Apples were also well referenced in the Rule of Céili Dé, cites in D. A. Binchy, *Corpus Iuris Hibernici* (6 vols, Dublin, 1876), vol. 2, 502–19; Murphy and Potterton, *The Dublin region in the Middle Ages,* 355; Greig, 'Archaeobotanical and historical records compared', 215.

[180] Kelly, *Early Irish farming,* 259.

[181] Meyer, *The vision of MacConglinne,* 38, 79, 100; Gwynn, 'The teaching of Máel Ruain', 31; Sexton, 'Cereals and cereal foodstuffs', 146.

[182] Reeves-Smyth, *Irish gardens and gardening before Cromwell,* 117. Cider-making was more popular in England at this time, cited in Murphy and Potterton, *The Dublin region in the Middle Ages,* 355.

[183] Murphy and Potterton, *The Dublin region in the Middle Ages,* 355.

[184] Murphy and Potterton, *The Dublin region in the Middle Ages,* 355.

[185] Kelly, *Early Irish farming,* 324.

mentions a herbal broth given to the sick known as *brothchán*.[186] *Brothchán* was made with oatmeal and herbs and many texts refer to the health benefits of this dish.[187] This dish was often served with the addition of relishes on Sundays. These relishes included honey or assorted seasonal fruits, an early form of muesli perhaps.[188] It was also viewed as a luxury dish, and was used by penitential monks in lieu of bread and water during times of fasting.[189] In addition to apples, other fruits used in this 'muesli' dish included blackberries/sloes/mulberries/hazelnuts and other nuts. *Aisling Meic Conglinne* mentions purple berries and a little sloe tree, together with cabbage/kale and nuts.[190] This implies that blackberries were stewed in gruel, a mix of oatmeal, honey, fruits and nuts which featured regularly in the diet of all classes.[191] Despite the historical evidence for apples and pears, their presence in the archaeological record is surprisingly low compared to fruits such as blackberry and raspberry. While taphonomy may play a part here, it is also worth considering how different fruits were being consumed, processed and cooked, altering their physical remains and hence distorting their archaeological signal. For example, eating apples raw was frowned upon by medieval physicians, and common practice in England and the Continent was to press them into cider and verjuice (vinegar).[192] In times of surplus supplies, they were also fed to swine.[193]

Nuts in the form of hazelnuts were commonly recorded in both the documentary and archaeological record[194] and their importance in the early medieval diet is highlighted by the numerous historical references to them.[195] They would have been gathered in autumn and suitable for storing through the winter. At Fishamble Street, the recovery of both whole and fragmented nuts suggests they may have been consumed as whole nuts and ground into meal,

---

[186] Comes from the word *bó*, the quality of cow that produced milk for fine boiling, Kelly, *Early Irish farming*, 324.
[187] Kelly, *Early Irish farming*, 349; Patrick Henry, 'A linguistic survey of Ireland: preliminary report', *Lochlann: a review of Celtic studies* 1 (1958), 49–208: 163.
[188] Gwynn, 'The teaching of Máel Ruain', 28, §45; Sexton, 'Cereals and cereal foodstuffs', 146. A recipe for muesli from Richard Barber, *Cooking and recipes from Rome to the Renaissance* (London, 1973). A Renaissance recipe for black muesli: ingredients: ½lb black grapes, 2 apples, 2 pears, 1oz sugar, ½lb oatmeal, ½pt water. Method: boil pears and apples until soft. Peel, core, chop into cubes. Pip and halve grapes. Mix fruit, sugar and oatmeal, and add water. Bring to boil, stirring continuously. Serve with milk and sugar to taste.
[189] Gwynn, 'The teaching of Máel Ruain', 2§1.
[190] Meyer, *The vision of MacConglinne*, 35, 77—'son of fair oatmeal gruel, of sprouty meat-soup, with its purple berries, of the top of effeminate kale, son of soft white midriff, son of bone-nourishing nut-fruit, son of Abel, son of Adam'.
[191] Sexton, 'Cereals and cereal foodstuffs', 146.
[192] Melitta Weiss Adamson, *Food in medieval times: food through history* (London, 2004), 19.
[193] Dennell, 'Seeds from a medieval sewer', 154.
[194] Kelly, *Early Irish farming*, 305; Greig, 'Plant foods in the past', 205.
[195] Kelly, *Early Irish farming*, 305.

known as *maothal*.[196] While well documented as a foodstuff in medieval Ireland, the ubiquity of hazelnut shells from the archaeobotanical record can perhaps be misleading. A good source of Vitamins A and K, they were certainly a nutritious addition to any dish, however, taphanomy must be considered when discussing how certain fruit and nut remains survive and they should be interpreted with caution.

For fruits and vegetables to be enjoyed out of season, they had to be preserved, generally by drying and, depending on the foodstuffs, using honey and brine.[197] Food storage was essential to a stable urban economy given that most food plants, including staples, are produced seasonally in temperate regions. Storage of other plant produce will have been straightforward (hazelnuts, walnuts, linseed, field beans, peas, garlic, parsley and celery) would have been stored dry and could survive for many months. Apples could be harvested slightly later than many other fruits, and were easily dried, which provided a nutritious food source during the winter months.[198] Soft fruits, such as raspberry, blackberry, bilberry and strawberries, could only survive storage beyond a day or two, cooking them would ensure that they kept for several days, but longer term storage would require preserving them in honey or in ferments.[199] Raspberries, elderberries, blackberries and bilberries were not cultivated because they grew quickly and profusely in wild thickets. Cultivation would not have increased their fruit production either making for an unprofitable return.[200] Fruit and berries picked in late summer, could however be preserved in jams and preserves out of season, which can make seasonality difficult to discern in some cases. At Temple Bar West, the fruit stones and insect remains recorded successfully charted the seasonal use of a cesspit at the site.[201] In a similar project, a pit from Parliament Street, Kilkenny,[202] containing abundant cherry, sloe and blackberry represented seasonal fruit produce deposited in late summer or early autumn. At Chapel Lane, Cashel,[203] a deposit of predominantly blackberry and bramble seeds could also reflect

---

[196] Geraghty, *Viking Dublin*, 46; *Maothal* has been interpreted as a dish consumed during fasting. It consisted of nutmeal and milk, but also oatmeal, milk and cheese, cited in Eugene O'Curry, *On the manners and customs of the ancient Irish* (New York, 1873, repr. in 1971), ccclxc–ccclxvi.

[197] Dyer, 'Seasonal patterns in food consumption', 213.

[198] Greig, 'Plant foods in the past', 117.

[199] Allan Hall and Harry Kenward, 'Setting people in their environment: plant and animal remains from Anglo–Scandinavian York', in Richard Hall, David Rollason, Mark Blackburn, David Parsons, Gillian Fellows-Jensen, Harry Kenward, Allan Hall, Thomas O'Connor, Dominic Tweedle, Ailsa Mainman and Nicola Rogers (eds), *The archaeology of York: aspects of Anglo–Scandinavian York* (Oxford, 2004), 400.

[200] Teresa McLean, *Medieval English gardens* (New York, 1982), 238.

[201] Penny Johnston, 'Macroscopic plant remains from excavations at Temple Bar West', unpublished report, Margaret Gowen and Co. Ltd, 2000; Reilly, 'The contribution of insect remains', 41–62: 55.

[202] Lyons, 'The plant macrofossil remains'.

[203] Lyons, 'The environmental remains'.

seasonal food debris. Haws ripened later in the autumn, and although tougher to digest, may have been eaten as a 'last resort' food in the absence of other fruits,[204] which could account for their lower occurrence in the archaeological record. Not all fruit remains should be regarded as human food however. Elder tree stumps, for example, where identified in situ at Coppergate, evidence that they grew as part of the urban vegetation.[205] Their seeds, therefore, would have entered deposits and become part of the archaeological record.

Evidence for fruit-processing was identified from High Street, Dublin, where the remains of an early thirteenth-century fruit press containing the macrofossil remains of cherry, plum, strawberry, fig and bilberry was found. [206] The debris was interpreted as fruit waste for fermentation, a common method of juice extraction documented in many European medieval sources.[207] While juice content can be high (75%), it is a laborious task and may not have been used for large-scale juice production.[208] Many religious houses, manorial estates and high-status residences were recorded as having a cider press so as to facilitate their own personal needs.[209] This suggests, therefore, that the fruit press from High Street could have been providing produce for a wealthy or religious household.

In Winetavern Street, an eleventh-century pit containing an abundance of fruit debris (cherry, sloe, bilberry, blackberry, apple and haws) with pulp still attached, was also considered to be the waste remains of fruit-processing.[210] Whole fruit stones of sloes and cherry identified from medieval Waterford and Parliament Street, Kilkenny, where plums were also identified, were both interpreted as being a possible by-product of food production rather than consumption.[211] Parliament Street's position adjacent to a market on High Street, Kilkenny,[212] would have been at the centre of commercial activity in the thirteenth and fourteenth centuries. Food-processing may have been one such activity carried out to facilitate urban demand, including the growing number of monastic orders, friaries and hospitals that were being established.[213]

The excellent preservation of fruit pulp from Fishamble Street[214] and High Street could be the result of the fruit having been pickled in alcohol or acetic acid.[215] Some fruits, such as sloes were quite bitter and difficult to digest.

---

[204] Listed in James Kelly's *Scottish Proverb* in 1791, cited in John Simpson, *The concise Oxford dictionary of proverbs* (Oxford, 1984), 121.
[205] Hall, 'A brief history of plant foods in the city of York', 32.
[206] Mitchell, *Archaeology and environment*, 26.
[207] Charles Bamforth and Robert Ward, *The Oxford handbook of food fermentations* (Oxford, 2014), 159.
[208] Bamforth and Ward, *The Oxford handbook of food fermentations*, 159.
[209] Christopher Dyer, *Everyday life in medieval England* (London, 2001), 125.
[210] Collins, 'Plant remains', 1997.
[211] Tierney and Hannon, 'Plant remains', 882; Lyons, 'The plant macrofossil remains'.
[212] Bradley, 'The early development of the medieval town of Kilkenny', 67
[213] Bradley, 'The early development of the medieval town of Kilkenny', 73.
[214] Geraghty, *Viking Dublin*, 33; Mitchell, *Archaeology and environment*, 27.
[215] Geraghty, *Viking Dublin*, 37.

It is therefore unusual that they are one of the most ubiquitous fruits found in faecal matter or associated with cess material. Their abundance in the archaeological record therefore deserves some attention. It has been suggested that they are the remains of prunes, rather than sloes in their raw state.[216] While prunes may have been imported from warmer climates, they could be easily kiln or oven dried—a process which is used in making acid fruit, such as sloes and crab apples more palatable.[217] According to James Greig, this made them easier to digest and could explain the high incidence s of *Prunus* (cherry/sloes/plum) type species found in faecal remains. Documentary evidence details the juice of sloes, and sometimes of crab apples, in making verjuice.[218] This unfermented acidic juice was commonly used as a preservant and, in cooking, it was added to sauces.[219] The juice of sloes also had medicinal qualities.[220] A seventeenth-century traveller to Ireland who required a remedy for an ailment documented its use: '... being troubled with an extreme flux ... the syrup and conserve of sloes well boiled, after they have been strained ... boiled in water until they be softened, and then strained ...'[221]

While the preponderance of fruit stones from many urban pits and cess deposits suggests a diet rich in seasonal produce, it is very possible that these remains represent food-processing, in the form of fruit extraction for juices, preserves and verjuice, as much as direct foodstuffs. Such activities would have been carried out in late summer or early autumn when fruits were plentiful. This surplus of fruit stock may not have been so easily conserved, so converting it to juices and preserves would ensure its longevity. The versatility of verjuice as a common cooking ingredient would have kept demand for this condiment high and since sloes and apples were plentiful in season, both elite and non-elite households may have had access to this product or the makings of it. This could

---

[216] Norman Gras, *The early English customs system—a documentary study of the institutional and economic history of the customs from the thirteenth to the sixteenth centuries* (Cambridge, 1918), 45.

[217] Robert Wiltshire, 'The effects of food processing on palpability of wild fruits with a high tannin content', in H. Kroll and R. Pasternak (eds), *Res archaeobotanicae International Workshop for Palaeoethnobotany: Proceedings of the ninth Symposium, Kiel 1992* (Kiel, 1995), 385–97.

[218] McLean, *Medieval English gardens,* 268. In the Account of the Holy Trinity, Dublin, records of the Seneschel mention verjuice bought for 8d, Mills, *Account Roll of the Priory of the Holy Trinity,* 101.

[219] McLean, *Medieval English gardens,* 268; John Russell recommended verjuice to be cooked with chicken, veal and bacon, cited in Frederick Furnivall (ed.), *BABEES book of manners and meals in olden times* (London, 1868), 152.

[220] Nicholas Culpeper, *Complete herbal: consisting of a comprehensive description of nearly all herbs with their medicinal properties and directions from compounding the medicines extracted from them* (London, 1826), 158–9.

[221] William Brereton, *Travels in Holland, the united provinces, England, Scotland and Ireland, 1634–1635* (2 vols, Manchester, 1844), vol. 1, 371.

go some way to explaining the high incidence of sloes in the archaeological record.

It is also worth mentioning that during the medieval period, fruit consumption had a somewhat medicinal fervour and was classified on a sociological scale depending on dietetic considerations. This was borne out of the classical theory that food was categorised by energy patterns which effected general well-being.[222] To maintain health and balance, certain foodstuffs were classified as amicable, while others could cause aggravation. For example, fruits such as plums, cherries, blackberries and grapes were 'cold' foods and difficult to preserve, so should be eaten at the beginning of a meal, and were considered unhealthy for the ill, the young and the elderly.[223] It was believed that different fruits held qualities to treat specific conditions—bilberry was used for blurry vision; cherry and elder for coughs and colds; blackberry for stomach complaints; plum for indigestion; apple pulp was applied to swellings and smallpox scars; while strawberry juice was used to clean teeth.[224]

Herbs, vegetables and edible plants

Since the early medieval period documentary sources mention the use of vegetables such as leek, onion/garlic,[225] celery and cabbage/kale as well as herbs like sorrel, cress and parsley.[226] The importance of vegetables in the diet of the sick and ailing is repeatedly mentioned in the early documents. Celery is particularly valued, as it prevents sickness, relieves thirst and does not affect wounds.[227] The frequency with which these plants are referred to in early medieval texts strongly implies that they may have been subjected to some degree of cultivation.[228] Archaeological evidence for celery, watercress and cabbage/mustard/turnip, and garlic/onion seeds were also recorded from Hiberno–Norse and medieval Dublin, Cork, Waterford, Cashel and Kilkenny sites.[229] Vegetative remains are unusual on archaeological sites, however, leaf tissue of the onion family and cabbage/turnip remains have been recovered from

---

[222] Judith Griffin, *Mother Nature herbal* (Woodbury, MN, 1997), 105.
[223] Griffin, *Mother Nature herbal,* 105.
[224] Griffin, *Mother Nature herbal,* 105.
[225] The word *caineann* is often used interchangeably for garlic and onion in the early medieval text, however, Donnchadh Ó Corráin maintains that *caineann* refers to shallots or Welsh onions, cited in Kelly, *Early Irish farming*, 253; D. A. Binchy, 'Bretha Crólige', *Ériu* 12 (1938), 1–77: 21, 23, 40. Garlic, leek and onion derive from the *Allium* spp., the seeds of which can be difficult to separate in archaeobotany.
[226] Kelly, *Early Irish farming,* 253.
[227] Binchy, 'Bretha Crólige', 36 §45; Whitley Stokes (ed.), *The martyrology of Oengus the Culdee* (London, 1905) cited in Lucas, 'Irish food before the potato', 31.
[228] Lucas, 'Irish food before the potato', 32
[229] Geraghty, *Viking Dublin*; Mitchell, *Archaeology and environment,* 26; McClatchie, 'The plant remains'; Lyons, 'Plant remains from 40–48 South Main Street, Cork'; Tierney and Hannon, 'Plant remains'; Lyons, 'The environmental remains'; Lyons, 'The plant macrofossil remains'.

faecal remains in medieval York[230] and Chester,[231] but not in Ireland to date. Root vegetables such as carrot are cited in *Aislinge Meic Conglinne*, however archaeological evidence is scarcer. Wild carrot was identified from medieval Dublin[232] as at Anglo–Scandinavian York[233] but their status as a root vegetable is dubious. Other wild plants with ethnographic references include goosefoot or fat hen, sorrel, knotgrass, black bindweed, redshank, nettle and wild radish or charlock.[234] Many of these were served as condiments with bread and seasonal foodstuffs.[235] Early medieval documentary sources, such as the saints' lives contain numerous references to the consumption of nettle and sorrel. A. T. Lucas postulates that nettles and charlock may have been a common feature in the diet of the poorer classes, especially in times of severe food shortages, and that this knowledge of famine foods may have been borne out of antiquity.[236] Wild garlic and watercress also get a special mention in the twelfth-century poem *Buile Suibhne*,[237] while cabbage, which features particularly in monastic diets, was frequently mentioned as a foodstuff in *Aisling Meic Conglinne*.[238] During Lent, garlic/onion and celery were permitted and encouraged to be consumed as these would preserve other valuable food stocks, such as butter and salted meats.[239]

Sheep's sorrel is also a common find from these sites and is documented as a salad ingredient and as a flavouring for fish.[240] Cabbage/mustard/turnip was also present in Drogheda. Herbs such as fennel, dill and black mustard were recovered from Drogheda, Wexford and Kilkenny,[241] while mint was identified from Dublin, Kilkenny and Cork.[242] Seeds of marjoram were also present from mid-twelfth to thirteenth-century house deposits at Washington

---

[230] Philippa Tomlinson, 'Vegetative plant remains from waterlogged deposits identified at York', in Jane Renfrew (ed.), *New light on early farming* (Edinburgh, 1991), 109–19.

[231] James Greig, 'Plant remains', in S. W. Ward (ed.), *Excavations at Chester: 12 Watergate Street in 1985: Roman Headquarters building to medieval*, Grosvenor Museum Archaeological Excavation and Survey Reports 5 (1988), 59–69.

[232] Mitchell, *Archaeology and environment*, 26.

[233] Hall, 'A brief history of plant foods in the city of York', 33.

[234] McClatchie, 'The plant remains', 401.

[235] Gwynn, 'An Irish penitential', §3 and 6; Gwynn, 'The teaching of Máel Ruain', 16; D. A. Binchy, 'The old Irish penitential', in Ludwig Bieler (ed.), *The Irish penitentials Scriptores*, Latin Hiberniae (5 vols, Dublin, 1963), vol. 5, 262; Sexton, 'Porridges, gruels and breads'.

[236] A. T. Lucas, 'Nettles and charlock as famine food', *Breifne* 1:2 (1959), 137–46: 146.

[237] James O'Keeffe, *Buile Suibhne* (Dublin, 1931, repr. 1975), 982–3.

[238] Gwynn and Purton, 'The monastery of Tallaght', 132; Kelly, *Early Irish farming*, 256.

[239] Sexton, 'Cereals and cereal foodstuffs', 162.

[240] Lucas, 'Nettles and charlock as famine food', 137; M. F. Moloney, *Irish ethnobotany and the evolution of medicine in Ireland* (Dublin, 1919), 39.

[241] Mitchell and Dickson, 'Plant remains and other items'; Bourke, 'Life in the sunny south-east', 35; Lyons, 'The plant macrofossil remains'; Johnston, 'The plant remains'.

[242] Geraghty, *Viking Dublin*; Lyons, 'The plant remains'; Brewer, 'Archaeobotanical report for Washington Street, Cork'.

Street, Cork.[243] Another common plant recorded from urban deposits in Ireland was yarrow. Although a wild plant, yarrow was grown for medicinal purposes in a vicar's garden in Glasgow in the sixteenth century.[244] In addition, dead nettle species, nettle, plantain, water bistort, cinquefoil and elder are other wild plants that were used in fifteenth-century herbal medicines.[245] Some herbs grown specifically for their leaves, such as parsley, are also represented by their seeds perhaps from herbs gathered in autumn and dried. Since the seeds from many of these herbs provides their distinctive flavours, their occurrence in the archaeological record, especially in cess deposits suggests strongly that they were ingested.[246]

Fat hen and knotgrass were frequently recorded from Dublin, Cork, Waterford, Cashel and Kilkenny.[247] Fat hen has edible leaves similar to spinach and was a common vegetable eaten in Ireland up until the eighteenth century.[248] Another common wild plant recorded from urban deposits is nipplewort and while often interpreted as a weed of cultivation, may have been eaten in salads and used for treating chest complaints.[249] It is possible that fat hen, knotgrass and redshank were being cultivated separately as food grains by the late medieval period,[250] and their preponderance on archaeological sites collectively

---

[243] 'Brewer, 'Archaeobotanical report for Washington Street Cork'.

[244] James Dickson and William Gauld, 'Mark Jameson's physic plants, a sixteenth century garden for gynaecology in Glasgow?', *Scotland Medieval Journal* 32 (1987), 60–2.

[245] W. R. Dawson, *A leechbook or collection of medicinal recipes of the 15th century* (London, 1934).

[246] Hall, 'A brief history of plant foods in the city of York', 29; Greig, 'Gardrobes, sewers, cesspits and latrines', 51.

[247] Mitchell and Dickson, 'Plant remains and other items'; Collins, 'Plant remains', 1997; Mitchell, *Archaeology and environment*; Geraghty, *Viking Dublin;* McClatchie, 'The plant remains'; Tierney and Hannon, 'Plant remains'; Lyons, 'The environmental remains'; Lyons, 'The plant macrofossil remains'; Kiely, 'Archaeological Excavation Report 26 Patrick's Street, Kilkenny 99E0165'; Bruce Sutton and Penny Johnston, 'Archaeological excavation report 99E0757ext—Stratham Street, 12 Patrick Street, Kilkenny, Co. Kilkenny', *Eachtra Journal* 14 (2007), 144–7; Jacinta Kiely and Antonia Doolan, 'Archaeological excavation report (06E0230)—11 Patrick Street, Kilkenny, Co. Kilkenny', *Eachtra Journal* 14 (2008), 89–93; Johnston, 'Analysis of the plant remains Irishtown/Brennan's Yard, Kilkenny', 12–15; Johnston, 'Analysis of the plant remains Friary Street/Garden Row, Kilkenny'; Nikolah Gilligan, 'Archaeobotanical analysis: the Robing Room, Bishop's Palace, Kilkenny (11E157)', Kilkenny Archaeological Project, 2011, available at: www.kkap.ie/assets/bishops-palace-plant-remains.pdf (16 March 2015); Meriel McClatchie, 'Analysis of non-wood plant macrofossils, Talbot's Tower, Kilkenny', unpublished report, Kilkenny Archaeology Ltd, 2011; Gilligan, 'Archaeobotanical analysis'.

[248] John Rutty, *An essay towards a natural history of the county of Dublin* (2 vols, Dublin, 1772), vol. 1, 171.

[249] Dennell, 'Seeds from a medieval sewer Plymouth', 154; Greig, 'Archaeobotanical and historical records compared', 223.

[250] Mitchell, *Archaeology and environment*, 23.

with known cultivars would certainly help to support this. They may have been ground into flour as flavour enhancers,[251] used as a foodstuff to provide gruel or coarse bread for the poorer classes and as a supplement to grain when crop yields were low.[252] Direct evidence for such consumption was found in Dublin, where faecal matter containing a high quantity of fat-hen seeds was recorded from eleventh-century occupation deposits at Fishamble Street, Dublin.[253] Similar remains comprising the crushed seeds of knotgrass, fat hen and chickweed were identified from the pelvic area of a skeleton at High Street, Dublin, both of which were interpreted as the remains of a gruel dish.[254] The term 'condiment' suggests that they were used to add flavour to bland or less palatable foods. Herbs were important in providing flavour to foods prepared with grains or dried legumes.[255]

Another common plant recovered with known foodstuffs from Cork, Dublin, Waterford, Drogheda, Cashel and Kilkenny in the medieval period was corncockle. A former cereal weed, it is now extinct in Ireland, however, its presence from a number of medieval cess deposits shows that it was consumed, possibly in a milled product like bread or flour.[256] Corncockle was often processed with grains during milling probably because its seeds were quite large and may have escaped sieving. This species is also a farinaceous food, containing starch, so it would have been easily incorporated into flour-processing.[257] The remains found in Irishtown, Kilkenny, and Chapel Lane, Cashel,[258] were generally fragmentary, suggesting that they were ground with cereals. Similar results have been obtained in faecal remains from Fishamble Street, Dublin,[259] containing finely ground fragments of corncockle, probably as a result of being milled, consumed with cereal food and passed through the digestive system.[260] Fragments of corncockle were also obtained from pit samples together with other cultivars and wild taxa at Waterford and Temple Bar West.[261] Interestingly, this species contains the toxic githagin which can

[251] Dom Brothwell, *The Bog Man and the archaeology of people* (London, 1986), 92.

[252] Paul Stokes and Peter Rowley-Conway, 'Iron Age cultigen? Experimental return rates for fat-hen (*Chenopodium album* L.)', *Environmental Archaeology* 7 (2002), 95–9; Mitchell, *Archaeology and environment*, 23.

[253] Geraghty, *Viking Dublin*, 29.

[254] Mitchell, *Archaeology and environment*, 23.

[255] Greig, 'Plant resources', 115.

[256] Tierney and Hannon, 'Plant remains', 889.

[257] Sexton, 'Cereals and cereal foodstuffs', 155.

[258] Penny Johnston, 'Analysis of the plant remains Irishtown/Brennan's Yard. Kilkenny (02E1592)', unpublished report, Margaret Gowen and Co. Ltd, 2004; Lyons, 'The environmental remains'.

[259] Geraghty, *Viking Dublin*, 29.

[260] Geraghty, *Viking Dublin*, 29.

[261] Tierney and Hannon, 'Plant remains', 890; Johnston, 'Macroscopic plant remains from excavations at Temple Bar West'.

cause illness, such as gastrointestinal problems, when eaten in large amounts.[262] Its presence in milled products could represent rudimentary cereal-processing associated with domestic rather than industrial milling,[263] however, it may also be intentional, becoming an acquired taste or supplementing grain reserves during periods of bad harvest or food shortages. While it is difficult to establish herb cultivation through archaeobotany, their presence in deposits collectively with known food waste may not be incidental and needs more attention. Their documented use as culinary and medicinal ingredients makes them a credible foodstuff. A statistical approach to interpreting these datasets may help to highlight patterns in the records in order to establish the relationships between different plant communities and their cultivated counterparts.

Foreign foodstuff

Not all sources of garden produce were local, wealthier households enjoyed foods from the Continent and around the Mediterranean, imported in dried or preserved form, such as grapes, dates, figs, raisins, walnuts and almonds. In wealthy households in England, preserved fruits and nuts were often bought in preparation for the Christmas season and before Lent, as these luxuries were a relief to the mundane fish and cereal dishes consumed during this period, making dishes more palatable.[264]

While there is no direct evidence for grape-growing in medieval Ireland, it has been surmised that vines were grown by early medieval monasteries based on historical sources.[265] Documentary sources describe a wine trade between Ireland and Biscay from the seventh century AD[266] and early Irish texts make reference to wine imported from Bordeaux for the celebration of the Eucharist and church feasts.[267] The establishment of the Norse towns in the ninth and tenth centuries stimulated trade, including the importation of wine, however, no archaeological evidence for grape dating to this period is known, despite finds in York and Norwich.[268] The earliest evidence for grape to date has tenuously been recorded from an early twelfth-century pit excavated at Bishop's Palace, Kilkenny,[269] and from late twelfth-century (Hiberno–Norse) pit deposits at South Main Street, Cork,[270] where fig was also identified. These finds were in

---

[262] Gay Wilson, 'Plant foods and poisons from medieval Chester', in Thomas Ward, 'Goldsmith House Site, Goss Street, Chester, 1972', *Journal of the Chester Archaeological Society* 58 (1972), 53–66.

[263] Quern stones were found in Waterford, cited in Tierney and Hannon, 'Plant remains', 891 and Cork, cited in Maurice Hurley, 'Stone artefacts', in Maurice Hurley and Orla Scully, *Excavations at the North Gate, Cork, 1994* (Cork, 1997), 106–14.

[264] Dyer, 'Seasonal patterns in food consumption', 208.

[265] Reeves-Smyth, *Irish gardens and gardening before Cromwell*, 110.

[266] Donnchadh Ó Corráin, *Ireland before the Normans* (Dublin, 1972), 71.

[267] Kelly, *Early Irish farming*, 319.

[268] Brian Ayers and Peter Murphy, 'A waterfront excavation at Whitefriars Street carpark, Norwich', *East Anglian Archaeology* 17 (1983), 1–60.

[269] Gilligan, 'Archaeobotanical analysis'. An antler tine recovered in the same pit as a grape seed was radiocarbon dated to 1000–1140 cal AD.

[270] McClatchie, 'Non-wood plant macro remains', 429.

low numbers so intrusive action cannot be ruled out, especially in light of later occupation, which was recorded at these sites. For the most part, archaeological evidence for grapes dates from the thirteenth and fourteenth centuries and finds have been recorded from Cork, Waterford, Wexford, Drogheda, Cashel and Kilkenny.[271] Interestingly, this coincides with economic prosperity in these areas[272] and the arrival of many European monastic orders.[273] Grapes would have been imported as a luxury product probably in dried form, with wine or cork wood.[274] Late medieval purveyance and administrative records contain abundant information on the wine trade to Ireland.[275] This is also supported by the corpus of ceramic wares from excavations in France and England,[276] a by-product of the flourishing wine trade that existed between the twelfth and fifteenth centuries. Most wine imported into Ireland, as in England would have been consumed within fifteen months of the grape harvest, so consumers would have been influenced by the agricultural cycle and trade on the Continent.[277] In England, wine fleets arrived from Gascony in France in late autumn with households receiving their first barrels around November and then subsequently in spring.[278] Throughout the year wine consumption would fluctuate depending on availability and religious occasion; with high wine consumption at Christmas, Easter and Corpus Christi,[279] while reserves were lower prior to harvest in October and during Lent in February and March.

---

[271] Collins, 'Plant remains', 1997; Mitchell, *Archaeology and environment;* McClatchie, 'The plant remains'; Lyons, 'Plant remains from 40–48 South Main Street, Cork'; Mitchell and Dickson, 'Plant remains and other items'; McClatchie, 'The plant remains'; Bourke, 'Life in the sunny south-east', 35; Lyons, 'The environmental remains'; Gilligan, 'Archaeobotanical analysis'; McClatchie, 'Analysis of non-wood plant macrofossils'; Gilligan, 'Archaeobotanical analysis'.

[272] Alf O'Brien, 'The development of privileges, liberties and immunities of medieval Cork and the growth of an urban economy *c.* 1189 to 1500', *Journal of Cork Historical and Archaeological Society* 90 (1985), 46–64.

[273] Bradley, 'The early development of the medieval town of Kilkenny', 63–73; C. A. Empey, 'The Norman period 1185–1500', in William Nolan and Thomas McGrath (eds), *Tipperary: history and society, interdisciplinary essays on the history of an Irish county* (Dublin, 1985), 71–91: 83–87.

[274] Timothy O'Neill, *Merchants and mariners in medieval Ireland* (Dublin, 1987), 96.

[275] O'Neill, *Merchants and mariners*, 44–57. The Irish wine trade came from France predominantly but trade with Spain and Portugal increased in the late fourteenth century, cited in O'Neill, *Merchants and mariners*, 48.

[276] Clare McCutcheon, 'Pottery', in Cleary and Hurley, *Excavations in Cork City 1984–2000*, 197–235; Cóilín Ó Drisceoil *et al.*, *Kilkenny Archaeological Project (KKAP) Report for the Irish National Strategic Archaeological Research (INSTAR) Programme 2008* (Kilkenny, 2008); Rubicon Heritage Services Ltd, 'New evidence for the form and early development of the medieval town of Cashel from recent excavations'; Clare McCutcheon, 'The medieval pottery of Dublin: some dates and new names,' in Seán Duffy (ed.), *Medieval Dublin I* (Dublin, 2000), 117–25.

[277] Dyer, 'Seasonal patterns in food consumption', 208.

[278] Dyer, 'Seasonal patterns in food consumption', 208.

[279] Dyer, 'Seasonal patterns in food consumption', 210.

Another luxury item frequently recorded from urban sites is fig. While identified from Anglo–Scandinavian York, fig remains from archaeological sites in Ireland emerge at about the same time as grape in the early thirteenth century and often together in the same features.[280] The fig recorded from late twelfth-century deposits at South Main Street, Cork, however, could be one of the earliest finds in Ireland.[281] Based on their frequent recovery from sewage/cess material, it has been suggested that figs may have been more accessible than other luxury foodstuffs at this time.[282] Figs were the cheapest of all food imports from Europe, with the exception of the Lenten period, when demand for fruits and nuts, which were out of season, were higher.[283] They would have been imported dried for long-term storage and records document that they arrived from Europe by the shipload.[284] Furthermore, as a food known for its blood pressure lowering and blood thinning properties, they were eaten after bloodletting, a regular feature of monastic life.[285] Whether they were consumed by all social classes is difficult to interpret, however, using the archaeological evidence alone. Fig, as well as grape, was recovered from largely domestic contexts in Wexford, Drogheda, Cork, Dublin and Waterford, where high status occupation was difficult to define in most cases. In Kilkenny, however, the presence of fig from occupation deposits at Grace's Castle, Parliament Street,[286] and a grape seed from Bishop's Palace strongly signifies high status in both cases. In contrast, fig and grape were absent from Cashel, where more utilitarian settlement was recorded overall. While this could reflect the sampling strategies employed, it is possible that these goods were not as widely consumed here, due, in part perhaps, to their availability but also to distribution. Port towns had more access to foreign goods, so transport to inland centres would have been an onerous and laborious task. Kilkenny's position on the River Nore would have eased the transporting goods from the port of Waterford for example, however, the absence of a river system through Cashel, made imports less readily available, which, in turn, may have increased their market value, allowing access only to those who could afford them.

---

[280] Collins, 'Plant remains', 1997; Mitchell, *Archaeology and environment;* Geraghty, *Viking Dublin;* McClatchie, 'The plant remains'; Lyons, 'Plant remains from 40–48 South Main Street, Cork'; Mitchell and Dickson, 'Plant remains and other items'; Bourke, 'Life in the sunny south-east', 35; Lyons, 'The plant remains from Parliament Street, Kilkenny'.

[281] McClatchie, 'Non-wood plant macro remains', 429.

[282] Greig, 'Gardrobes, sewers, cesspits and latrines', 50.

[283] The supply and demand for figs during this season drove up prices and made it a profitable shipment for merchants, cited in Bridget Ann Henisch, *The medieval calendar year* (University Park, PA, 1999), 43.

[284] Greig, 'Archaeobotanical and historical records compared', 217.

[285] Camilla Dickson, 'Food, medicinal and other plants from the 15th century drain of Paisley Abbey, Scotland', in John Maldon (ed.), *The Monastery & Abbey of Paisley: lectures from the Renfrewshire Local History Forum's Conference 11/12 September 1999, with additional papers* (Paisley, 2000), 213–24.

[286] Lyons, 'The plant macrofossil remains'.

Walnuts were another luxury imported into Ireland during this time, possibly from France or Germany.[287] Archaeological evidence is rare, however, their recovery from eleventh and twelfth-century deposits in Fishamble Street, Dublin,[288] and Waterford[289] suggests that imports to Ireland may have been slightly earlier than fig and grape. Walnut macrofossils were also recorded in a thirteenth-century culvert on Winetavern Street alongside grape and in a sixteenth-century deposit with fig on John's Street, Drogheda.[290] The accumulating evidence for walnut macrofossils and pollen records on many British sites suggests that walnut was grown in Britain during the medieval period,[291] and may have found a market in neighbouring Ireland. Unlike Britain, evidence for walnut in the pollen record is unknown for medieval Ireland, so it is difficult to ascertain if it was growing here. While ground walnuts, recorded as an ingredient in soups and sauces,[292] may not survive in the archaeological record, the scarcity of walnut husks or hulls is more unusual, considering their robust nature. Since it is unknown whether walnuts were imported in their husks or not, it is worth mentioning that their hulls were commonly used in order to produce a brown/black dye, as recorded from Viking sites in Britain and Denmark (Hedeby)[293] and in later medieval documents as a component of ink.[294] This non-culinary use for walnuts could also account for their general absence from archaeological deposits, particularly features containing cess and faecal remains. On a more holistic note, walnuts were documented as a medicinal cure for gallstones and to treat ringworm.[295]

Archaeological evidence for almond is also relatively absent in Ireland and Britain, despite the numerous finds from European sites dating from the thirteenth to the eighteenth centuries.[296] Almond shell recovered from Shrewsbury Abbey and from a drain in Plymouth are just a few published accounts

[287] Greig, 'Plant foods in the past', 205.

[288] Geraghty, *Viking Dublin*, 50.

[289] Tierney and Hannon, 'Plant remains', 889.

[290] Collins, 'Plant remains', 1997; Mitchell and Dickson, 'Plant remains and other items', 73.

[291] Greig, 'Archaeobotanical and historical records compared', 220; Camilla Dickson, 'Macroscopic fossils of garden plants from British Roman and medieval deposits', *Journal of the European Study Group on Physical, Chemical, Biological & Mathematical Techniques Applied to Archaeology* 42 (1994), 47–72.

[292] Adamson, *Food in medieval times*, 25.

[293] Philippa Tomlinson, 'Use of vegetative remains in the identification of dyeplants from waterlogged 9th–10th century AD deposits at York', *Journal of Archaeological Science* 12 (1985), 269–83; Inga Hägg, *Die Textilfunde aus dem Hafen von Haithabu*, Berichte über die Ausgrabungen in Haithabu, Bericht 20 (Neumünster, 1984). Heavily botanical approach, focusing on the identification process for each set of plant specimens.

[294] N. M. McKenna, 'Dyeing with black walnut', *Complex Weavers* 29 (2001), 9.

[295] Griffin, *Mother Nature herbal*, 133.

[296] Greig, 'Archaeobotanical and historical records compared', 221.

from British medieval sites,[297] while the only known archaeological finds from Ireland are from post-medieval Cork.[298] Documentary evidence does exist, however, for almonds being brought into Ireland from the twelfth century, including the purchase of almonds in Kilkenny *c.* 1400.[299] Historically, almond kernels were ground down into flour and milk.[300] Similar to walnut, as a result, these would not be easily identified archaeologically. In addition to their use as a foodstuff, burnt almond shells produce a black pigment, which was highly prized by medieval painters[301] and, while not historically attested may have also been included in animal feed.

While the archaeological evidence for imported foodstuffs is relatively limited, records of grape and fig are steadily increasing, suggesting that these foods were the most common imports. Their presence, largely from cess deposits containing faecal matter, strongly indicates consumption either directly or as processed products. In the case of walnuts and almonds, taphonomy is an unlikely factor as to why they do not survive in anoxic deposits, as demonstrated by the abundance of hazelnut shell and fruit stones frequently recovered. Consideration must therefore be given to how these foodstuffs were transported, processed and consumed, and their alternate uses in the medieval economy. To date recovery of such exotics in Ireland is almost exclusively from urban settlement, where the presence of markets and fairs would have allowed access to a wider variety of local and foreign foods. One exception is a recent find of fig seeds from a fourteenth-century well at Caherduggan Castle, Doneraile, Co. Cork.[302] The presence of an import such as fig is a significant find in the context of a rural settlement and confirmed the high-status nature of this site. Outside of the major urban medieval centres, exotic foodstuffs are rarely identified in the archaeological record. The nature of preservation on urban sites is likely to play a major part in this; however sites like Caherduggan Castle are proving that imported goods were distributed beyond the towns. The high value of these imports reflects increased trading and prosperity, and they would have been seen as social symbols, available to the higher echelons of society and monastic houses.

Differentiating between wealthy and lower-class households in an urban context can be more difficult based on the archaeobotanical evidence alone.

---

[297] James Greig, 'The 13th–18th century plant remains', in Nigel Baker (ed.), *Shrewsbury Abbey,* Shrewsbury Archaeological and Historical Society Monograph Series 2 (2002), 163–77; Dennell, 'Seeds from a medieval sewer'.

[298] Canon Power, 'On a find of ancient jars in Cork City', *Journal of the Cork Historical and Archaeological Society* 33 (1928), 10–11.

[299] In 1171 Henry II came to Ireland with spices, cordial and almonds; in Kilkenny, four pounds of almonds cost 6d *c.* 1400, cited in O'Neill, *Merchants and mariners,* 96.

[300] Adamson, *Food in medieval times,* 45.

[301] Cennino Cennini, *The craftman's handbook,* trans. Daniel Thompson (New York, 1960).

[302] Lyons, 'The plant remains', in Patricia Long, 'Assessment report on archaeological excavations on the R581 Doneraile to Newtwopothouse Road Realignment Scheme, Co Cork', unpublished report, Rubicon Heritage Services Ltd, 2012.

Sampling strategies largely focus on known features, such as cesspits, while sampling of ancillary features like drains and ditches can be less systematic, based on time and budget constraints. This can produce bias assemblages, which in turn distorts interpretations, and can provide misinformation about the site and those who used it. This is certainly another research area that needs to be addressed and can only be undertaken by combining artefactual and contextual evidence with other biological indicators, specifically faunal remains and insect assemblages.

Conclusion

Archaeobotanical datasets offer a unique opportunity to glimpse aspects of past diet and food-processing, albeit an incomplete and distorted one. Taphonomic restrictions, however, can hinder the spectrum of plants identified and so caution is required when interpreting this material. While emphasis is generally on ingredients or raw produce rather than complete dishes, significant information on how food plants were used at the local level can help with archaeological and historical interpretation.

An appraisal of the archaeological evidence for the use of plant remains in urban medieval Ireland has revealed some interesting results. The range of cereal crops and exotic plants recorded in Ireland is somewhat lower than sites in Britain and Europe, influenced perhaps by personal tastes and cultural preference as much as by environmental factors and market resources. The archaeobotanical data has highlighted some chronological and geographical variation in crop use, something that historical sources cannot recognise. Whole grains/seeds were stored and dried on urban sites often in a semi-clean state, implying that there may have been a direct association and interaction with local agrarian suppliers.

Garden produce and gathered foodstuffs were somewhat of a paradox, both cheap and easy to grow, but, historically, not a major component of the medieval diet. Archaeological and palaeoecological evidence shows that low-scale gardening was being practised. The surplus supplied by native seasonal fruits would certainly have promoted the processing of fruit-based products and their abundance in the archaeobotanical record suggests that they were consumed by a large portion of the urban population. It is important to emphasise that leafy vegetables are grossly under-represented in the record, which greatly obscures the range of cultivated garden plants up for discussion. Garden plants, wild plants and fruits are also unevenly distributed, as the greatest diversity survive in the anoxic environment of an urban context. It remains elusive as to what extent these plants were present on agrarian sites and as to what extent the rural economy facilitated the food supplies of neighbouring urban markets. Through archaeobotany, some of the earliest physical evidence for exotic and imported foodstuffs (walnut, fig and grape) has been recorded. To avoid distorting the picture of imported goods, consideration must be given to how nuts such as almonds and walnuts were transported, stored and processed as foodstuffs before eliminating them from any discussion altogether.

Archaeobotany has opened up a number of research avenues for urban sites that require further exploration. The proliferation of urban growth influenced the range of foods available, how foodstuffs were stored and the extent to which they were processed on site. The composition and storage of cereal crops and legumes can potentially help to tease out human supplies from animal feed, something that the historical records cannot extrapolate. Evidence for brewing is still tenuous, however some signals in the record should not be overlooked for malting practices, especially in the context of drying kilns and this is certainly an area of interest that deserves further research. The role of pulse crops in the medieval economy also needs more attention. The extent to which pulse crops were cultivated in the medieval period is still unknown and the use of vetches as a plausible foodstuff also needs to be addressed, especially in the context of known cultivars. Little is known about the cultivation of fruit trees during this time, however, future research on charting changes to stone size and shape could provide a basis for interpreting material derived from wild or domesticated trees. More diligence is also needed when sampling and identifying vegetative parts and cereal bran, an area which would diversify known plant assemblages and broaden the debate on medieval gardens and horticulture. Medieval towns were dependent on the imports of bulk food supplies from their immediate hinterlands or beyond, so developing a relationship with producer sites was vital. Using a statistical approach, a review of the archaeobotanical record for wild species could highlight links between different plant associations, with a view to defining potential food plants. This, in turn, would offer new insights into urban and rural garden and horticulture practices as well as how they differed. Analysing plant macrofossil remains can also go some way to distinguishing between elite and non-elite urban occupation, strengthened particularly by combining this data with faunal assemblages. Conversely, however, sampling and research agendas do militate the information provided by archaeobotanical research. To answer many of the questions posed, a comprehensive evaluation of the data in the context of other biological remains, artefacts and contextual evidence would allow for an informed and overdue discussion on urban living conditions in medieval Ireland to take place.

Acknowledgements

This paper would not have been possible without access to unpublished archaeobotanical reports and results from my environmental archaeology colleagues—Abi Brewer, Mary Dillon, Nikolah Gilligan, Penny Johnston, Dr Meriel McClatchie, Mick Monk, Dr Eileen O'Reilly and Dr Bettina Stefanini— for which I am most grateful. I would like to thank Mick Monk for his thoughts and comments while compiling this paper. Thanks also to Cóilín Ó Drisceoil (Kilkenny Archaeology) and Rubicon Archaeological and Heritage Services Ltd for supplying archaeological reports, site photos and graphics. Permission to use the cesspit illustration in Plate I was granted by the *Journal of Archaeological Science* (courtesy of Dr David Smith of the Classics, Ancient History and Archaeology Department at the University of Birmingham). Finally, I would like to thank the archaeology editor of *Proceedings of the Royal Irish Academy, Section C,* Professor Elizabeth FitzPatrick, and production editor, Lucy Hogan, for their support and patience.

The social significance of game in the diet of later medieval Ireland

FIONA BEGLANE*

School of Science, Institute of Technology, Sligo

[Accepted 1 September 2014. Published 9 March 2015.]

Abstract

While the vast majority of the meat consumed in later medieval Ireland (*c.* 1100–1600) was from domesticates such as cattle, sheep and pig, the hunting of game was important as a social marker. Access to game varied depending on social status, occupation and geographical location, and could be used to mediate social relationships. This paper focuses mainly on the zooarchaeological evidence from eastern Ireland, examining castles, and urban, rural and ecclesiastical sites of mainly Anglo–Norman origin. It will review this evidence for both truly wild mammal species such as red deer, wild pig and hare as well as for species such as fallow deer and rabbits, which were maintained in a managed environment before being hunted for food.

Introduction

In later medieval Ireland, the vast majority of meat consumed—generally well in excess of 95%—came from the three main domesticates: cattle, sheep and pig, regardless of geographical location or social status. Nevertheless, game meat could supplement these everyday foods on an occasional or regular basis and was an important element in the diet of the time. In examining status and social groupings within later medieval society, access to hunted meat is a key marker, both because of the diversity this provided in the diet and because of restrictions in access to such foods.[1] In common with the nobility of both continental Europe and England[2] the Anglo–Norman elite sought to restrict access to hunted foods, by limiting hunting rights for many sections of society. This control over who could hunt, and when and where hunting could take place meant that consumption of game became a status symbol for the elite. The restrictions effectively resulted in venison and other game meats being

---

* Author's e-mail: beglane.fiona@itsligo.ie
doi: 0.3318/PRIAC.2015.115.02
Much of the data utilised was from the author's work as a consultant zooarchaeologist.

[1] H.C. Kuechelmann, 'Noble meals instead of abstinence? A faunal assemblage from the Dominican monastery of Norden, Northern Germany', in Christine Lefèvre (ed.), *Proceedings of the general session of the 11th International Council for Archaeozoology Conference* (Oxford, 2012), 87–97: 88–9.
[2] Aleksander Pluskowski, 'Who ruled the forests? An interdisciplinary approach towards medieval hunting landscapes', in Sieglinde Hartman (ed.), *Fauna and flora in the Middle Ages* (Frankfurt, 2007), 291–323: 291.

possessions that could be gifted to favoured individuals and institutions. The act of giving created cycles of obligation and further gift-giving, so binding members of the elite social group more closely together. Paradoxically, these stringent social controls also made game a potential target for poaching by the lower social classes.

Background

In both Ireland and England, in the later medieval period, there were four types of landscape in which restrictions over hunting were enforced: forests, chases, parks and warrens. 'Forests' were defined as land in which the timber and the hunting of certain game were reserved for the king.[3] The animals protected by forest law were red, fallow and roe deer as well as wild pigs, although roe deer were not found in Ireland. 'Chases' or 'chaces' were similar to forests but were under the control of a member of the nobility who had received a 'right of free chase' from the king; however, the terms 'forest' and 'chase' were sometimes used interchangeably.[4] 'Parks' were relatively small enclosed areas of land in which to keep deer, graze cattle and sheep, raise horses, supply timber for construction and provide a location for fish ponds and rabbit warrens.[5] The word 'warren' had two meanings in the later medieval period: the first relates to an artificial construction for rearing rabbits.[6] The other context in which this word was used was in a 'right of free warren'. This meant that a landowner had the exclusive right to hunt the 'beasts of the warren' on his land and that others were forbidden by law to do so.[7] The 'beasts of the warren' included the hare, rabbit, fox, wild cat, badger, wolf and squirrel.[8] In addition there were a number of 'birds of the warren' including pheasant, partridge and woodcock, and occasionally plover and lark.[9] All species could be hunted at will outside of the bounds of a forest, chase or warren and hence these land designations were hotly sought after.[10] They were seen as marks of royal favour, a way of

---

[3] Oliver Rackham, *The history of the countryside* (London, 1987), 130; N.D.G. James, *A history of English forestry* (Oxford, 1981), 3.

[4] L.M. Cantor and J.D. Wilson, 'The medieval deer-parks of Dorset: III', *Proceedings of the Dorset Natural History and Archaeological Society* 85 (1964), 141–52: 141; James, *A history of English forestry*, 5; Raymond Grant, *The royal forests of England* (Stroud, 1991), 30–1; Leonard M. Cantor, 'Forests, chases, parks and warrens', in Leonard M. Cantor (ed.), *The English medieval landscape* (London, 1982), 56–85: 70.

[5] Rackham, *The history of the countryside*, 125; Fiona Beglane, *Anglo–Norman parks in medieval Ireland* (Dublin, 2015); Fiona Beglane, 'Parks and deer-hunting: evidence from medieval Ireland', unpublished PhD thesis, National University of Ireland, Galway, 2012.

[6] Tom Williamson, *Rabbits, warrens and archaeology* (Stroud, 2007), 17.

[7] James, *A history of English forestry*, 6.

[8] James, *A history of English forestry*, 39.

[9] James, *A history of English forestry*, 39.

[10] James, *A history of English forestry*, 3; C.R. Young, *The royal forests of medieval England* (Philadelphia, PA, 1979), 46.

demonstrating prestige, and also a way of controlling access to hunting activities.[11]

Methodology

Based on these restrictions it would be expected that the zooarchaeological evidence from different site types would show varying levels of wild species and that the relative proportions of the various species would also vary. To test this hypothesis, data from a range of published and unpublished excavations of later medieval sites have been reviewed. These were classified into four categories: castles, ecclesiastical sites, urban sites and rural sites. This review included red deer (*Cervus elaphus*), wild pig (*Sus scrofa*) and hare (*Lepus timidus*) as well as badger (*Meles meles*), hedgehog (*Erinaceus europaeus*), red squirrel (*Sciurus vulgaris*), seal (Pinnipedia) and also cetaceans (Cetacea) such as dolphins and whales, since all of these were considered edible. In addition to the truly wild species, the analysis also included fallow deer (*Dama dama*) and rabbit (*Oryctolagus cuniculus*), which during the medieval period were essentially farmed in parks and warrens respectively. The analysis excluded animals hunted as vermin or for their fur and also amphibians and birds. The number of identified specimens present (NISP) was used throughout this analysis. NISP is a count of bone fragments that can be positively identified as coming from a particular species, genus or order. Sites with phases dated to between the twelfth and sixteenth centuries were included, and some small assemblages were excluded since these were not statistically significant. In some cases it was necessary to estimate the overall site NISP from inferences made in the faunal report if this was not clearly quantified; however, numbers of wild mammals were not estimated.

Unfortunately, the sample sizes and number of sites available in the various categories of site type differed. Urban and castle excavations often produce large animal bone assemblages and due to public interest and the quantity of other material discovered they are most frequently published, so that these site types are well represented. Ecclesiastical sites are also often published; however, as O'Connor[12] noted for England, these sites often yield relatively little animal bone, possibly due to very organised waste disposal within monastic communities, and as a result relatively few zooarchaeological reports have been included in publications on these sites. In this case, the majority of the sites are monastic in character, with one parish church: St Audoen's, Dublin, and one bishop's *cuirt* or palace: Kilteasheen, Co. Roscommon. Also included was Cathedral Hill, Armagh, where various pits and a substantial ditch were found to surround the cathedral. Many rural settlement sites are small, and therefore produce small assemblages; they also have poor above-ground visibility and therefore are often only found during development works. As a result, few have excavation reports published in full

---

[11] Young, *The royal forests of medieval England*, 11.

[12] T.P. O'Connor, 'Bone assemblages from monastic sites: many questions but few data', in Roberta Gilchrist and Harold Mytum (eds), *Advances in monastic archaeology* (Oxford, 1993), 107–11.

TABLE 1—Summary of the recorded presence of edible wild species at later medieval sites.

	No. of samples	No. of excavations	NISP	All edible wild mammals NISP	Total deer NISP	Red deer NISP	Fallow deer NISP	Rabbit NISP	Hare NIISP	All edible wild mammals NISP %	Total deer NISP %	Rabbit NISP %	Hare NISP %
Castle	30	21	32 611	745	316	208	72	263	144	2.3	1.0	0.8	0.4
Ecclesiastical	12	10	4 415	52	6	4	2	27	6	1.2	0.1	0.6	0.1
Urban[a]	40	26	49 069	402	214	207	7	91	78	0.8	0.4	0.2	0.2
Rural	13	11	10 298	53	24	15	0	24	2	0.5	0.2	0.2	0.02
Overall percentages										1.3	0.6	0.4	0.2
Total	95	68	96 393	1 252	560	434	81	405	230				

Abbreviation: NISP = number of identified specimens present.
[a] Note that the urban figures exclude quantified caches of antler-working waste.

and even fewer include zooarchaeological reports of any substance. The sites included here are mainly from the author's own work and from the site reports included on CDs in the National Roads Authority (NRA) Scheme Monograph series, which provide a valuable source of information on these smaller, lower profile excavations. Separate samples from particular excavations were generally from distinct phases of activity or physical areas within the site.

Zooarchaeological and historical data

In all, 95 samples from 68 separate excavations and a total of 96,393 individual bones were considered. From this sample a total of 1,252 bones were from edible wild mammal species, yielding an average of 1.3%. Deer, rabbit and hare made up the vast majority of the wild species, with only occasional examples of the other species (Tables 1 and 2; Fig. 1).

While edible wild mammals constituted an average of 1.3% of the assemblages overall, this rose to 2.3% (745/32,611) on castle sites, where they were the most common (Fig. 2). Ecclesiastical sites were the next most frequent, with an average of 1.2% (52/4,415) of the total assemblage being wild mammals. Surprisingly, urban sites yielded a higher percentage of wild elements than rural sites, with deer elements making up the bulk of the total. In urban sites, antler-working waste is common so where body part distributions have been reported this has been disregarded. However, it was also stated that the majority of the material from the eleventh-century to fourteenth-century excavations in Cork City were antler,[13] but as no figures were given it was not possible to eliminate these. If these sites are disregarded entirely then the 'urban' figure drops from 0.8% (402/49,069) to 0.5% (270/49,069). As a comparison, in England, wild mammal bones were also most likely to come from elite sites, where they

---

[13] Margaret McCarthy, 'The faunal remains', in Rose Cleary and Maurice F. Hurley (eds), *Excavations in Cork City 1984–2000* (Cork, 2003), 375–90: 380.

TABLE 2—Zooarchaeological data for the sites included in the study, classified into castle,[a] ecclesiastical,[b] urban[c] and rural sites.[d]

No.		NISP	Total game NISP	Total deer	Red deer	Fallow deer	Other game NISP	Wild pig	Lagomorph	Rabbit	Hare	Badger	Hedgehog	Squirrel	Seal	Cetacean
	Castle sites															
1	Athenry Castle, 13th to 14th C	1 930	10	10			0									
2	Carlow Castle, 13th C[e]	183	2	2	2		0									
3	Carrickfergus Castle, bridge pit	226	5	5	5		0									
4	Carrickmines Castle, medieval	2 407	20	15	13	1	5			5						
5	Clohamon Castle, late medieval tower house	304	2	2			0									
6	Clough Castle phase I, early 13th C	515	43	4	4		39			21	18					
6	Clough Castle phase III-IV, late 13th to early 14th C	129	7	1	1		6			3	2					1
7	Courthouse Lane Galway, Area 2, high medieval	2 086	41	2	2		39			26	13					
7	Courthouse Lane Galway, Area 2, late medieval	526	4				4			1	3					
8	Drumadoon, Co Antrim phase 3, Motte	37	2	2	2		0									
9	Dunamase Castle, Co. Laois	10 966	306	89	87	2	217			125	92					
10	Ferns Castle early 14th C, S fosse, E section	153	5	5			0									
10	Ferns Castle late 13th to early 14th C, E fosse, S section	3	3	3	2	1	0									
11	Ferrycarrig ringwork, midden dump	1 026	27	6		6	21			21						
12	Glanworth Castle, 13th C	143	5	5	5		0									
13	Grace's Castle, Kilkenny Courthouse, phase 2	663	8	1			7			3	4					
13	Grace's Castle, Kilkenny Courthouse, phase 3	768	12	4	3		8			6	2					

TABLE 2—Zooarchaeological data for the sites included in the study, classified into castle,[a] ecclesiastical,[b] urban[c] and rural sites.[d]

No.		NISP	Total game NISP	Total deer	Red deer	Fallow deer	Other game NISP	Wild pig	Lagomorph	Rabbit	Hare	Badger	Hedgehog	Squirrel	Seal	Cetacean
	Castle sites															
1	Athenry Castle, 13th to 14th C	1 930	10	10			0									
2	Carlow Castle, 13th C[e]	183	2	2	2		0									
3	Carrickfergus Castle, bridge pit	226	5	5	5		0									
4	Carrickmines Castle, medieval	2 407	20	15	13	1	5			5						
5	Clohamon Castle, late medieval tower house	304	2	2			0									
6	Clough Castle phase I, early 13th C	515	43	4	4		39			21	18					
6	Clough Castle phase III-IV, late 13th to early 14th C	129	7	1	1		6			3	2					1
7	Courthouse Lane Galway, Area 2, high medieval	2 086	41	2	2		39			26	13					
7	Courthouse Lane Galway, Area 2, late medieval	526	4				4			1	3					
8	Drumadoon, Co Antrim phase 3, Motte	37	2	2	2		0									
9	Dunamase Castle, Co. Laois	10 966	306	89	87	2	217			125	92					
10	Ferns Castle early 14th C, S fosse, E section	153	5	5			0									
10	Ferns Castle late 13th to early 14th C, E fosse, S section	3	3	3	2	1	0									
11	Ferrycarrig ringwork, midden dump	1 026	27	6		6	21			21						
12	Glanworth Castle, 13th C	143	5	5	5		0									
13	Grace's Castle, Kilkenny Courthouse, phase 2	663	8	1			7			3	4					
13	Grace's Castle, Kilkenny Courthouse, phase 3	768	12	4	3		8			6	2					

TABLE 2 (*cont.*)—Zooarchaeological data for the sites included in the study, classified into castle,[a] ecclesiastical,[b] urban[c] and rural sites.[d]

No.		NISP	Total game NISP	Total deer	Red deer	Fallow deer	Other game NISP	Wild pig	Lagomorph	Rabbit	Hare	Badger	Hedgehog	Squirrel	Seal	Cetacean
14	Greencastle, Co. Down (1952)	24	1	1			0									
14	Greencastle, Co. Down (2007) phase 2, castle construction	339	4	4	3		0									
14	Greencastle, Co. Down (2007) phase 3, occupation	311	26	19	12	5	7		1	3	1				2	
15	Killeen Castle, Anglo–Norman	1 037	1	1	1		0									
15	Killeen Castle, medieval	3 254	5	4	4		1			1						
16	Mahee Castle, Co. Down, occupation	300	5	3	3		2			2						
17	Maynooth Castle, Anglo–Norman	838	46	41	41		5	3		2						
17	Maynooth Castle, F171, mid-13th to 15th C	844	37	24		20	13		1		1				11	
17	Maynooth Castle, F107 early 15th C	111	23	22	4	11	1			1						
18	Parkes Castle, Co. Leitrim, site wide total	329	7	5	5		2			2						
19	Roscrea Castle, 13th C	97	1	1	1		0									
20	Trim Castle S1, late 13th to early 14th C[e]	2 052	47	26	3	23	21	3		13	5					
20	Trim Castle S2, mid-14th to mid-15th C[e]	1 010	40	9	5	3	31			28	3					
	Total NISP **Total NISP %** **for castle sites**	**32 611**	**745** **2.3**	**316** **1.0**	**208** **0.6**	**72** **0.2**	**429** **1.3**	**6** **0.02**	**2** **0.006**	**263** **0.8**	**144** **0.4**	**0** **0.0**	**0** **0.0**	**0** **0.0**	**13** **0.0**	**1** **0.003**
	Ecclesiastical sites															
21	Aghavea, Co. Fermanagh, medieval	58	**0**				**0**									
22	Bective Abbey, Co. Meath, high medieval phases 1 and 2	788	**18**	1	1		**17**		2	12	3					
22	Bective Abbey, Co. Meath, later medieval phases 3–7	1 364	**17**				**17**		7	10						

TABLE 2 (*cont.*)—Zooarchaeological data for the sites included in the study, classified into castle,[a] ecclesiastical,[b] urban[c] and rural sites.[d]

No.		NISP	Total game NISP	Total deer	Red deer	Fallow deer	Other game NISP	Wild pig	Lagomorph	Rabbit	Hare	Badger	Hedgehog	Squirrel	Seal	Cetacean
20	Blackfriary Trim, Co. Meath, phase 1, medieval	18	**0**				**0**									
20	Blackfriary Trim, Co. Meath, phase 2, medieval	11	**0**				**0**									
23	Cathedral Hill, Armagh, later medieval	94	**0**				**0**									
24	Grey Abbey, Co. Kildare, 13th C phase III	70	**0**				**0**									
25	Holy Trinity, Lough Key, Co. Roscommon	262	**1**				**1**					1				
26	Kells Priory, Co. Kilkenny, later medieval totals	250	**4**	2	2		**2**				2					
27	Kilteasheen, Co. Roscommon, 2005–2006 seasons, medieval	496	**6**	1	1		**5**		3	2						
28	St Audoen's Church Cornmarket Dublin, 12th C (excl. antler)	631	**1**				**1**			1						
29	Tintern Abbey, Co. Wexford, 13th and 14th C	373	**5**	2		2	**3**			2	1					
	Total NISP	**4 415**	**52**	**6**	**4**	**2**	**46**	**0**	**12**	**27**	**6**	**1**	**0**	**0**	**0**	**0**
	Total NISP % for ecclesiastical sites		**1.2**	**0.1**	**0.1**	**0.05**	**1.0**	**0.0**	**0.3**	**0.6**	**0.1**	**0.02**	**0.0**	**0.0**	**0.0**	**0.0**
	Urban sites															
30	Cork, 17 Grattan Street, 13th to 14th C	217	**0**				**0**									
30	Cork, Barrack Street, 11th to 12th C	984	**98**	97	97		**1**				1					
30	Cork, Christchurch, F26/27, mid-13th C	1 737	**7**	3	3		**4**			1	2					1
30	Cork, Grattan Street, 13th to 14th C	2 216	**49**	4	4		**45**			43	1					1
30	Cork, Hanover Street, 12th to 13th C	581	**0**				**0**									

TABLE 2 (*cont.*)—Zooarchaeological data for the sites included in the study, classified into castle,[a] ecclesiastical,[b] urban[c] and rural sites.[d]

No.		NISP	Total game NISP	Total deer	Red deer	Fallow deer	Other game NISP	Wild pig	Lagomorph	Rabbit	Hare	Badger	Hedgehog	Squirrel	Seal	Cetacean
30	Cork, North Main Street, 13th to 14th C	384	**2**	2	2		**0**									
30	Cork, North Gate, 13th to 14th C	1 438	**4**	3	3		**1**			1						
30	Cork, North Gate, early to mid-14th C	876	**6**	1	1		**5**			1	4					
30	Cork, Philips' Lane, 13th to 14th C	701	**11**	3	3		**8**			7	1					
30	Cork, Skiddy's Lane, 13th to 14th C	227	**2**	1	1		**1**									1
30	Cork, St Peter's Avenue, 13th to 14th C	1 179	**13**	2	2		**11**			10				1		
30	Cork, Tobin Street, early to mid-13th C	3 120	**27**	2	2		**25**			3	20			1		1
30	Cork, Tuckey Street, 12th to 13th C	1 904	**21**	11	11		**10**			3	7					
30	Cork, Washington Street, early to mid-13th C	1 646	**10**	8	8		**2**				2					
31	Drogheda, Shop Street	727	**8**				**8**			3	5					
28	Dublin, Arran Quay, early to late 14th C	587	**3**				**3**			2	1					
28	Dublin, Arran Quay, late 14th to early–17th C	2 327	**11**	1	1	2	**10**			10						
28	Dublin, Bridge Street Lower	214	**0**				**0**									
28	Dublin, Patrick Street, Site C, 13th C	925	**2**	1	1		**1**									1
28	Dublin, Patrick Street, Site GB, 14th to 16th C	847	**1**				**1**			1						
28	Dublin, Patrick Street, Site B, 13th C	533	**3**	3	3		**0**									
28	Dublin, Patrick Street, Site GA, 12th to 14th C	597	**2**				**2**			2						
13	Kilkenny, Patrick Street/ Pudding Lane	5 324	**10**	5		5	**5**			3	1	1				

Table 2 (*cont.*)—Zooarchaeological data for the sites included in the study, classified into castle,[a] ecclesiastical,[b] urban[c] and rural sites.[d]

No.		NISP	Total game NISP	Total deer	Red deer	Fallow deer	Other game NISP	Wild pig	Lagomorph	Rabbit	Hare	Badger	Hedgehog	Squirrel	Seal	Cetacean
32	Limerick Charlotte's Quay, total of F411/413/414, late 13th to early 14th C	404	0				0									
33	Nobber, Bridgepark, Co. Meath, phases 1–4, 12th – 16th C	839	2				2		2							
20	Trim Townparks, Co. Meath, ad 1027–1290 phase 1	121	1				1	1								
20	Trim Townparks, Co. Meath, ad 1027–1400 phase 1 and 2	11	1	1	1		0									
20	Trim Townparks, Co. Meath, ad1250–1400 phase 2	442	3	2	1		1	1								
20	Trim Townparks, Co. Meath, ad1400–1640 phase 2a	238	1	1	1		0									
20	Trim Townparks, Co. Meath, Castle Street/Lawn, medieval	109	4	3	3		1				1					
20	Trim, 18 Market Street, Co. Meath, 12th to 14th C	150	0				0									
34	Waterford E406:1226, building backfill	299	0				0									
34	Waterford E406:2003, pit	1 943	25	9	9		16				13			3		
34	Waterford E435: 1170/1174, excl. antler	2 175	5	5	5		0									
34	Waterford E435:1161, excl. antler	1 170	4	3	3		1				1					
34	Waterford E435:1163/1168, excl. antler	1 936	11	6	5		5				3				2	
34	Waterford Peter Street, PS2-4 Group 1	1 891	6	5	5		1				1					
34	Waterford Peter Street, PS2-4 Group 2	2 593	8	8	8		0									

TABLE 2 (*cont.*)—Zooarchaeological data for the sites included in the study, classified into castle,[a] ecclesiastical,[b] urban[c] and rural sites.[d]

No.		NISP	Total game NISP	Total deer	Red deer	Fallow deer	Other game NISP	Wild pig	Lagomorph	Rabbit	Hare	Badger	Hedgehog	Squirrel	Seal	Cetacean
34	Waterford Peter Street, PS2-4 Group 3	4 056	**30**	20	20		**10**				9			1		
34	Waterford Peter Street, PS2-4 Group 4	1 401	**11**	4	4		**7**				6			1		
	Total NISP	**49 069**	**402**	**214**	**207**	**7**	**188**	**2**	**2**	**91**	**78**	**0**	**4**	**1**	**5**	**5**
	Total NISP % for urban sites		**0.8**	**0.4**	**0.4**	**0.014**	**0.4**	**0.004**	**0.004**	**0.2**	**0.2**	**0.0**	**0.008**	**0.002**	**0.010**	**0.010**
	Rural sites															
35	Ballintotty 2, Co. Tipperary, later medieval	649	2	2	2		0									
36	Cloncowan II, Co. Meath	688	2	2	1		0									
37	Clonee, Co. Meath, Area 4, drainage ditches, medieval	97	1	1	1		0									
38	Cookstown, Co. Meath, settlement, later medieval	375	0				0									
39	Dunnyneill Island, Co. Down, phase 4, 11th to 14th C	2 150	21	4	4		17			16	1					
40	Johnstown, Co. Meath F124, 1420–1650	3 117	15	7	7		8			7	1					
40	Johnstown, Co. Meath F556, 1420–1640	482	1				1			1						
41	Moone-Timolin Site 45, Co. Kildare	1 456	8	8			0									
42	Portmuck, Island Magee, Co. Antrim	451	3				3							3		
43	Ratoath, Co. Meath, 11th to 14th C	161	0				0									
44	Sheephouse, Donore, Co. Meath, rural ditches medieval	30	0				0									
45	Stalleen, Co. Meath, 3a grange, high medieval	363	0				0									

TABLE 2 (*cont.*)—Zooarchaeological data for the sites included in the study, classified into castle,[a] ecclesiastical,[b] urban[c] and rural sites.[d]

No.		NISP	Total game NISP	Total deer	Red deer	Fallow deer	Other game NISP	Wild pig	Lagomorph	Rabbit	Hare	Badger	Hedgehog	Squirrel	Seal	Cetacean
46	Stalleen, Co. Meath, 3b grange, late medieval	279	0				0									
	Total NISP	10 298	53	24	15	0	29	0	0	24	2	0	0	0	3	0
	Total NISP % for rural sites		0.5	0.2	0.1	0	0.3	0.0	0.0	0.2	0.02	0.0	0.0	0.0	0.03	0.0

Abbreviation: NISP = number of identified specimens present.

[a]Margaret McCarthy, 'Faunal report', in Cliona Papazian, Brenda Collins, and Margaret McCarthy, 'Excavations at Athenry Castle, Co. Galway', *Journal of the Galway Archaeological and Historical Society* 43 (1991), 27–43; Patricia Lynch, 'Animal bone report: Carlow Castle, Co. Carlow 96E105', unpublished report for K.D. O'Conor, n.d.; Margaret Jope, 'Animal bones from Carrickfergus Castle bridge-pit', in D.M. Waterman, 'Excavations at the entrance to Carrickfergus Castle, 1950', *Ulster Journal of Archaeology* 15 (1952) 103–18; Sean Denham and Emily Murray, 'The animal bones from medieval and post-medieval contexts at Carrickmines Castle, Co. Dublin', unpublished report for Margaret Gowen and Co., n.d.; Fiona Beglane, 'Report on faunal material from Clohamon Castle, Castlequarter, Co. Wexford. Licence number: 09E0393', unpublished report for James Lyttleton, 2012; Margaret Jope, 'Animal remains from Clough Castle', in D.M. Waterman, 'Excavations at Clough Castle, County Down', *Ulster Journal of Archaeology* 17 (1954), 150–6; Emily Murray, 'Animal Bone', in Elizabeth FitzPatrick, Madeline O'Brien and Paul Walsh (eds), *Archaeological investigations in Galway City 1987–1998* (Dublin, 2004), 562–601; Fiona Beglane, 'Report on faunal material from Drumadoon: Licence no. AE/03/105', unpublished report for Centre for Archaeological Fieldwork (CAF), Queen's University Belfast, 2005; Vincent Butler, 'Preliminary report on the animal bones from Dunamase, Co. Laois, 93E150. 1994 season', unpublished report for Brian Hodkinson, 1995; Vincent Butler, 'Preliminary report on the animal bones from Dunamase, Co. Laois, 93E150. 1995 season', unpublished report for Brian Hodkinson, 1996; Vincent Butler, 'Preliminary report on the animal bones from Dunamase, Co. Laois, 93E150. 1996 season', unpublished report for Brian Hodkinson, 1996; Vincent Butler, 'Preliminary report on the animal bones from Dunamase, Co. Laois, 93E150. 1997 season', unpublished report for Brian Hodkinson, n.d.; B. Whelan, 'Report on animal bones', in D. Sweetman, 'Archaeological excavations at Ferns Castle, Co. Wexford', *Proceedings of the Royal Irish Academy* 79C (1979), 244–455; Finbar McCormick, 'The mammal bones from Ferrycarrig, Co. Wexford', unpublished report, n.d.; Pam Crabtree and Kathleen Ryan, 'Faunal remains', in Conleth Manning (ed.), *The history and archaeology of Glanworth Castle, Co. Cork: Excavations 1982–4* (Dublin, 2009), 117–22; Margaret Jope, 'Report on animal bones from Greencastle Co. Down', in D.M. Waterman and A.E.P. Collins, 'Excavations at Greencastle, County Down, 1951', *Ulster Journal of Archaeology* 15 (1952), 101–02; Fiona Beglane, 'Report on faunal material from Greencastle, Co. Down, 057:003, Licence no. AE/01/13', unpublished report for CAF, Queen's University Belfast, 2007; Siobhán Duffy, 'From castle to gaol: analysis of the animal bones from Kilkenny Courthouse, Kilkenny, Ireland', unpublished MA thesis, University of Southampton, 2010; Jonny Geber, 'The faunal remains', in Christine Baker (ed.), *The archaeology of Killeen Castle, Co. Meath* (Dublin, 2009), 131–56; Fiona Beglane, 'Report on faunal material from Mahee Castle. Licence nos. AE/01/58 and AE/02/79', unpublished report for CAF, Queen's University Belfast, 2007; Emily Murray, 'Faunal remains from Maynooth Castle', unpublished report, n.d.; Fiona Beglane, 'Animal bone', in Claire Foley and Colm Donnelly (eds), *Parke's Castle, Co. Leitrim: archaeology, history and architecture* (Dublin, 2012), 109–20; Nora Birmingham, 'The animal bones', in Conleth Manning (ed.), *Excavations at Roscrea Castle* (Dublin, 2003), 144–5; F. McCormick and E. Murray, 'Animal bones', in Alan Hayden (ed.), *Trim Castle, Co. Meath: Excavations 1995–8* (Dublin, 2011), 421–33.

[b] Fiona Beglane, 'Report on faunal material from Aghavea, Co. Fermanagh, Ferm 231:036', unpublished report for CAF, Queen's University Belfast, 2007; Fiona Beglane, 'Report on faunal material from Bective Abbey, Co. Meath. Licence no. E4028', unpublished report for Geraldine Stout, 2013; Fiona Beglane, 'Report on faunal material from Blackfriary, Trim, Co. Meath: consent no. C150, licence no. E2398', unpublished report for Cultural Resource Development Services (CRDS), 2009; Valerie Higgins, 'The animal remains', in Cynthia Gaskell Brown and A.E.T. Harper, 'Excavations on Cathedral Hill, Armagh, 1968', *Ulster Journal of Archaeology* 47 (1984), 154–6; Fiona Beglane, 'Report on faunal material from Grey Abbey: licence no. 04E0233', unpublished report for Margaret Gowen and Co. Ltd, 2006; Miriam Clyne, 'Archaeological excavations at Holy Trinity Abbey Lough Key, Co. Roscommon', *Proceedings of the Royal Irish Academy* 105C (2005), 23–98; Finbar McCormick, 'The faunal remains', in Miriam Clyne (ed.), *Kells Priory, Co. Kilkenny: archaeological excavations by T. Fanning and M. Clyne*, Archaeological Monograph Series 3 (Dublin, 2007), 477–82; Fiona Beglane, 'Report on faunal material from Kilteasheen, Co. Roscommon: licence no. 05E0531: 2005', unpublished report for Chris Read, 2006; Vincent Butler, 'Animal bone report', in Mary McMahon (ed.), *St Audoen's Church, Cornmarket, Dublin: archaeology and architecture* (Dublin, 2006), 115–17; Finbar McCormick, 'Appendix IV: the faunal remains', in Ann Lynch (ed.), *Tintern Abbey, Co. Wexford: cistercians and colcloughs. Excavations 1982–2007* (Dublin, 2010), 227–32.

[c] Margaret McCarthy, 'The faunal remains', in Rose Cleary and M.F. Hurley (eds), *Excavations in Cork City 1984–2000* (Cork, 2003), 375–90; Margaret McCarthy, 'Faunal remains: Christchurch', in Rose Cleary, M.F. Hurley and Elizabeth Shee Twohig (eds), *Skiddy's Castle and Christ Church, Cork. Excavations 1974–77 by D.C. Twohig* (Cork, 1997) 349–59; Margaret McCarthy, 'The faunal remains', in M.F. Hurley (ed.), *Excavations at the North Gate, Cork* (Cork, 1997), 154–8; Finbar McCormick, 'The animal bones', in M.F. Hurley and O.M.B. Scully (eds), *Late Viking Age and medieval Waterford* (Waterford, 1997); Finbar McCormick, 'The mammal bone', in Alan Hayden, 'Excavation of the medieval river frontage at Arran Quay, Dublin', in Sean Duffy (ed.), *Medieval Dublin V* (Dublin, 2004), 221–41; Finbar McCormick, The mammal bones from Arran Quay, Dublin, unpublished report, n.d.; Vincent Butler, 'Report on the animal bones from C46, C48, C50, C53, C54, C56, C58, C60 and C62', in Mary McMahon, Vincent Butler and J. Collins, 'Archaeological excavations at Bridge Street Lower, Dublin', *Proceedings of the Royal Irish Academy* 91C (1991), 41–71;

Finbar McCormick and Eileen Murphy, 'Mammal bones', in Claire Walsh (ed.), *Archaeological excavations at Patrick, Nicholas and Winetavern Streets, Dublin* (Dublin, 1997), 199–218; Eileen Murphy, 'Osteological report on the mammal bones from Patrick Street/Pudding Lane, Kilkenny (Licence 98E0092)', unpublished report, 1999; Finbar McCormick, 'Appendix 1: the animal bones', in Ann Lynch, 'Excavations of the medieval town defences at Charlotte's Quay, Limerick', *Proceedings of the Royal Irish Academy* 84C (1984), 322–30; Fiona Beglane, 'Report on faunal material from Bridgepark, Nobber, Co. Meath. Licence no. 07E0345', unpublished report for CRDS Ltd, 2009; Fiona Beglane, 'Meat and craft in medieval and post-medieval Trim', in Michael Potterton and Matthew Seaver (eds), *Uncovering medieval Trim: archaeological excavations in and around Trim, Co. Meath* (Dublin, 2009), 346–70; Fiona Beglane, 'Report on faunal material from Townparks South, Trim, Co. Meath. Excavation licence no. E2016. Ministerial consents C121, C139', unpublished report for CRDS Ltd, 2007).

[d] Margaret McCarthy, 'Faunal analysis Ballintotty E2935 – A026/445', in 'Aegis M7 Limerick to Nenagh animal bone reports', unpublished report for the National Roads Authority (NRA), n.d.; Alan Pipe, 'Report on animal remains', in Christine Baker, 'Excavations at Cloncowan II, Co. Meath', *The Journal of Irish Archaeology* 16 (2007), 98–120; Fiona Beglane, 'Report on faunal material from Clonee Townland, Clonee, Co. Meath. Licence no. 08E0840', unpublished report for Archtech Ltd, 2009; Emily Murray, 'The animal bones', in Richard Clutterbuck, 'Cookstown, Co. Meath: a medieval rural settlement', in Chris Corlett and Michael Potterton (eds), *Rural settlement in medieval Ireland in the light of recent research* (Dubin, 2009), 27–47; Fiona Beglane, 'Report on faunal material from Dunnyneill', unpublished report for CAF, Queen's University Belfast, 2005; Fiona Beglane, The faunal remains from Dunnyneill Island, Strangford Lough, Co. Down, unpublished MSc thesis, Queen's University Belfast, 2004; Catherine Boner, 'Johnstown 1: analysis of mammal bones', in Neil Carlin, Linda Clarke and Fintan Walsh (eds), *The archaeology of life and death in the Boyne floodplain* on CD (Dublin, 2008); Patricia Lynch, 'Bone report', in Valerie Keeley and Hillary Opie, 'Archaeological excavations site 45: N9 realignment Moone–Timolin–Ballintore Hill, Co. Kildare 99E202', unpublished report for NRA, 2001, 121–66; Eileen Murphy, 'The animal bone', in Sue Anderson and A.R. Rees, 'The excavation of a medieval rural settlement at Portmuck, Islandmagee, Co. Antrim', *Ulster Journal of Archaeology* 63 (2004) 76–113; Fiona Beglane, 'Report on faunal material from Ratoath Co. Meath: licence no. 03E1781', unpublished report for Archtech Ltd, 2005; Fiona Beglane, 'Report on faunal material from Sheephouse, Donore, Co. Meath. Licence no. 06E1164', unpublished report for CRDS Ltd, 2008; Fiona Beglane, 'Report on faunal material from Stalleen townland, Donore, Co. Meath. Licence no. 08E0456', unpublished report for CRDS Ltd, 2012.

[e] Modified from the original reports to include re-identification of fallow deer to other species.

constituted 13% of the assemblages[14] so the above-mentioned total figure of 2.3% for Irish castle sites is very low. There are a number of possible reasons for this including the availability of game animals as well as warfare, economics, politics and absenteeism;[15] nevertheless, it is a figure that is considerably higher than that for other site types.

Deer

Throughout medieval Europe the main animals of the hunt were deer, with red and fallow deer relevant to Ireland.[16] Red deer may have arrived in Ireland as early as the Late Glacial period after the Ice Age, although a recent review of the data suggests that they were introduced during the Neolithic period.[17]

---

[14] Naomi Sykes, *The Norman conquest: a zooarchaeological perspective* (Oxford, 2007), 65, App. Ia.

[15] Beglane, *Anglo–Norman parks in medieval Ireland.*

[16] Wilhelm Schlag, *The hunting book of Gaston Phébus. Manuscrit français 616, Paris, Bibliothèque Nationale* (London, 1998), 20–3.

[17] Peter Woodman, Margaret McCarthy and Nigel Monaghan, 'The Irish Quaternary Fauna Project', *Quaternary Science Reviews* 16 (1997), 129–59: 152–4; Finbar McCormick, 'Early evidence for wild animals in Ireland', in Norbert Benecke (ed.), *The Holocene history of the European vertebrate fauna* (Berlin, 1998), 355–71: 360–1. Ruth F. Carden, Allan D. McDevitt, Frank E. Zachos, Peter C. Woodman, Peter O'Toole, Hugh Rose, Nigel T. Monaghan, Michael G. Campana, Daniel G. Bradley and Ceiridwen J. Edwards, 'Phylogeographic, ancient DNA, fossil and morphometric analyses reveal ancient and modern introductions of a large mammal: the complex case of red deer (*Cervus elaphus*) in Ireland', *Quaternary Science Review* 42 (2012), 74–84.

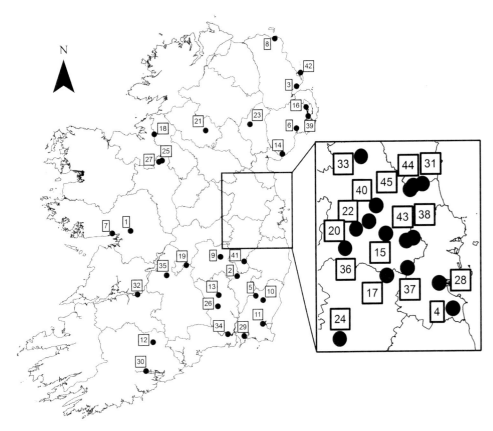

FIG. 1—Location of castles, and urban, rural and ecclesiastical sites discussed in the text. The numbers are cross-referenced in Table 2.

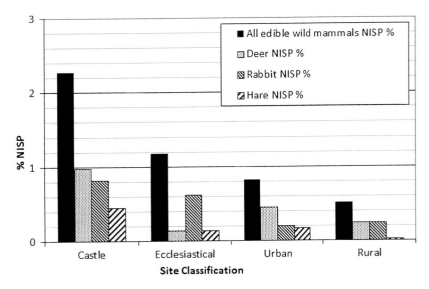

FIG. 2—Number of identified specimens present (NISP) of wild mammals from a range of site types.

By contrast, fallow deer were introduced by the Anglo–Normans in the early thirteenth century.[18] Red deer were essentially wild animals that were hunted in open country, while initially at least, fallow deer were kept in parks that could be used as venues for hunting or as 'live larders' depending on their size and the inclination of their owner.[19]

Giraldus Cambrensis,[20] writing in the twelfth century was uncharacteristically positive in his view of Irish red deer, stating that they 'are not able to escape because of their too great fatness' and that they had particularly impressive heads and antlers. He also noted though, that in common with the other wild species of animals they were small. Four centuries later, Philip O'Sullivan Beare[21] again commented on the 'most dense herds of fat deer' in Ireland and the protection afforded to them by their antlers, which they used against both dogs and people. Red deer are a common image on wall paintings and tapestries and in carvings, and, in Ireland, they appear on a number of hunting scenes. They were tightly bound into a complex symbolism with religious, kingly and erotic connotations. For example the shedding of the blood of the deer was compared to the Blood of Christ which is commemorated in the Eucharist and the blooding of new hunters was compared to the rite of baptism.[22] The death of the deer could symbolise both the consummation of erotic love, with the symbolic shedding of virgin blood, and the capture of the heart,[23] while white deer in particular were associated with immortality and a rightful lineage of kings controlling the land and people back through time.[24]

The Romans first introduced fallow deer to Western Europe from the eastern Mediterranean, as exotica to be kept in parks. Their numbers declined markedly after the fall of the Roman Empire, but with the spread of Norman culture along the Atlantic seaboard, they were reintroduced to north-western

---

[18] McCormick, 'Early evidence', 360–1.

[19] Beglane, *Anglo–Norman parks in medieval Ireland*; Fiona Beglane, 'Deer in medieval Ireland: preliminary evidence from Kilteasheen, Co. Roscommon', in Thomas Finan (ed.), *Medieval Lough Ce: history, archaeology, landscape* (Dublin, 2010), 145–58.

[20] Geraldus Cambrensis, *Topographia Hiberniae: the history and topography of Ireland by Gerald of Wales*, ed. J.J. O'Meara (London, 1982), 47.

[21] Philip O'Sullivan Beare, *The natural history of Ireland c. 1626,* ed. D.C. O'Sullivan, (Cork, 2009), 77.

[22] Richard Almond, *Medieval hunting* (Stroud, 2003), 152; John Cummins, *The hound and the hawk: the art of medieval hunting* (London, 1988), 71–2; J.A. Stuhmiller, 'The hunt in romance and the hunt as romance', unpublished PhD thesis, Cornell University, 2005, 132.

[23] Stuhmiller, 'The hunt in romance', 203.

[24] John Fletcher, *Gardens of earthly delight* (Oxford, 2011), 127–9; Michael Bath, 'King's stag and Caesar's Deer', *Dorset Natural History Society and Archaeological Society* 95 (1974), 80–3; Cummins, *The hound and the hawk*, 69–71.

Europe, again as a park animal.[25] As a result, the species first came to Ireland with the Anglo–Normans. The earliest mention of the species in connection with Ireland was in 1213 when the archbishop of Dublin was granted 30 fallow deer from the king's park of Brewood in England.[26] They are therefore not mentioned by Giraldus Cambrensis who was writing a generation before this, but are discussed briefly by O'Sullivan Beare,[27] writing in the early seventeenth century, who comments that they are smaller than red deer and 'protected by simple, but bigger horns, bent over their foreheads; here, sometimes you may see them fighting bravely'. There was much less symbolism attached to fallow deer than to red deer, and much of this was shared with, or more likely, borrowed from red deer.[28]

The analysis included a total of 560 deer bones, excluding quantified caches of antler-working waste from St Audoen's and from urban Dublin, but including the unspecified quantities of antler from Cork City. Of these, 434 were from red deer, 81 were from fallow deer and the remainder had not been separated into species in the zooarchaeological reports. Deer were uncommon at all site types, but they were found in the greatest numbers at castle sites. While they achieved only an average of 1.0% of the identified bones at castle sites, it is significant that this is more than twice the level achieved at urban sites, and more than four times that at rural sites. All of the castles yielded some deer bones apart from the very small assemblage from the late medieval tower house of Clohamon Castle, Co. Wexford. Nine out of 21 castles yielded fallow deer and all except Clohamon and Ferrycarrig ringwork, Co. Wexford, produced red deer remains.

Ecclesiastical sites were the only site type on which deer were not the largest group of edible wild mammals, with only four out of ten sites yielding deer bones. Tintern Abbey, Co. Wexford, was the only ecclesiastical site to include fallow deer, a metatarsal from the early fourteenth century and a long bone shaft from the thirteenth or early fourteenth century. All other deer bones identified to species were from red deer. Urban sites yielded a large number of deer bones and antler fragments, with the majority of these being from red deer. Only two sites, Patrick Street/Pudding Lane, Kilkenny, and Arran Quay, Dublin, produced fallow deer remains. Six out of eleven rural sites yielded deer, however, these were in small numbers. Only red deer was identified to species, with fallow deer not found, and a total of only 24 specimens was recorded.

---

[25] Naomi Sykes, R.F. Carden and K. Harris, 'Changes in the size and shape of fallow deer: evidence for the movement and management of a species', *International Journal of Osteoarchaeology* 23 (2013), 55–68; Cummins, *The hound and the hawk*, 84; Naomi Sykes, 'European fallow deer', in Terry O'Connor and Naomi Sykes (eds), *Extinctions and invasions: a social history of British fauna* (Oxford, 2010), 51–8: 51–2, 57.

[26] H.S. Sweetman (ed.), *Documents relating to Ireland, 1171–1307* (5 vols, London, 1875–86), vol. 1, no. 477.

[27] O'Sullivan Beare, *The natural history of Ireland*, 77.

[28] Cummins, *The hound and the hawk*, 84.

Deer body part distribution

Having reviewed the overall finds of deer bones, a more detailed analysis can shed further light on social differentiation in food supply. There were a number of methods of deer hunting used during the medieval period, including the *par force* chase, the drive, or bow-and-stable hunting and the use of traps and nets.[29] These often included ritual steps, some of which depended on the method of hunting, and some of which were more generally applicable. The process of dismembering or unmaking the carcass was one of the most ritualised of the stages and in France this was often carried out by the most senior person present. In England, this was more usually delegated to a professional huntsman, or to the person who killed the deer, although in the late sixteenth century, Queen Elizabeth I, a keen hunter, was willing to undertake the feat herself. Special sets of knives were sometimes used and certain organs were reserved for the lord by being set up on display on forked sticks stuck into the ground (Fig. 3).[30]

Hunting manuals of the period state that it was standard practice for the left shoulder of the carcass to be given to the person doing the 'unmaking' or dismembering, the right shoulder to the forester, and the haunches, or back legs, were reserved for the lord.[31] Depending on which source is consulted, the head was either reserved for the lord or given to the *lymer*, or 'scenting hound' that tracked the deer. The *os courbin*, which may have been the pelvis or possibly the sternum, was given to the ravens.[32] By contrast with England, where this introduction of a structured distribution has been dated to the later medieval period,[33] an early Irish judgement that was preserved in a law text and poem refers to similar customs extant in the seventh or eighth centuries:

> the first person who wounds the deer is entitled to the *classach*, which presumably refers to some part of its body, the person who flays the deer gets its shoulder (*lethe*), and the owner of the hounds gets the haunch (*cés*). Another person—perhaps he who actually kills the deer—gets the neck (*muinél*), and the hounds themselves get the legs (*cossa*). The last man on the scene gets the intestines (*inathar*) and the rest of the hunting-party get the liver (*áe*). Finally, the landowner gets the belly (*tarr*).[34]

---

[29] Beglane, 'Deer in medieval Ireland', 150–2.

[30] Cummins, *The hound and the hawk*, 41–3.

[31] Richard Thomas, 'Chasing the ideal? Ritualism, pragmatism and the later medieval hunt in England', in Aleksander Pluskowski (ed.), *Breaking and shaping beastly bodies: animals as material culture in the Middle Ages* (Oxford, 2007), 125–48: 128.

[32] Thomas, 'Chasing the ideal?', 128.

[33] Naomi Sykes, 'Taking sides: the social life of venison in medieval England', in A. Pluskowski (ed.), *Breaking and shaping beastly bodies: animals as material culture in the Middle Ages* (Oxford, 2007), 149–60: 150.

[34] Fergus Kelly, *Early Irish farming: a study based mainly on the law-texts of the 7th and 8th centuries* AD (Dublin, 2000), 275–6.

FIG. 3—Ritual breaking of the stag carcass as shown in BNF MS 619, *Le Livre de chasse*, p. 59r. Reproduced courtesy of the Bibliothèque nationale de France

This would suggest that in both later medieval England and in early medieval Ireland, a shoulder was given to the person dividing up the carcass. In Ireland the owner of the dogs was given the haunches, and in England the lord received this portion, but since dogs were expensive to maintain, they presumably belonged to the lord, and therefore the same distribution can be inferred. This distribution reflects the quality and tenderness of the meat. In cattle, for example, the hind limb includes the topside and silverside whereas the forelimb includes the much tougher clod and shin of beef. Similarly, leg of lamb is much higher quality, more tender meat than the shoulder of lamb from the forelimb.[35] A number of researchers have examined the prevalence of hind limb bones in the zooarchaeological record of England[36] and detailed study has shown that this distribution is valid for both red and fallow deer, with a disproportionate amount of bones from the rear of the animal present at elite sites, and forelimbs over-represented at the homes of foresters, parkers and huntsmen.

---

[35] S.J.M. Davis, *The archaeology of animals* (London, 1987), 25.

[36] Umberto Albarella and S.J.M. Davis, 'Mammals and birds from Launceston Castle, Cornwall: decline in status', *Circaea* 12:1 (1996), 1–156: 32–4; Thomas, 'Chasing the ideal?', 125–48; Richard Thomas, *Animals, economy and status: the integration of zooarchaeological and historical evidence in the study of Dudley Castle, West Midlands (c. 1100–1750)* (Oxford, 2005), 60, 63; Sykes, 'Taking sides', 149–60.

It was therefore to be expected that, given these customs in both early medieval Ireland and later medieval England, a similar tradition was likely to be maintained in later medieval Ireland. Using the Irish data, an analysis was carried out of the body-part distribution. In the rural and ecclesiastical sites small numbers of bones were identified and patterns were mixed so that it was impossible to interpret the results in a meaningful way. Rural sites included some antler fragments, as well as teeth, two radii and a humerus from the forelimb, and an astragalus from the hind limb. The ecclesiastical sites included a metacarpal from the forelimb, a tibia, astragalus and metatarsal from the hind limb and a partial skull.

More useful results were obtained from the castles and urban sites. In total, this involved 28 samples from 16 castle sites and 28 urban samples from Dublin, Kilkenny, Galway, Trim and Waterford. One further limitation is that the summaries included in the published reports of these results do not always include body-part distribution, and so some sites could not be included. The frequency of the four main bones of the front and hind limbs were compared (Fig. 4). In the case of the front limb, the scapula, humerus, radius and metacarpal were included. The ulna was not included since the equivalent bone in the hind leg of a deer is extremely small and rarely quantified by zooarchaeologists. In the case of the hind limb, the pelvis, femur, tibia and metatarsal were used. Most zooarchaeologists do not record all of the individual carpals and tarsals (wrist and ankle bones), however, they do generally record the calcaneus and astragalus, which are the two largest tarsal bones. It was decided to exclude these as otherwise the analysis would be weighted in favour of identifying hind limb bones, purely because more of them are systematically recorded. In addition, the phalanges (toe bones) of the front and hind limbs cannot easily be separated except where they are excavated from an articulated skeleton; therefore these bones were excluded from the measure.

For the castle sites, 73.7% (101/137) of the identified bones were from the hind limb. By contrast, only 50% (25/50) of the bones from urban sites were from the hind limb. The evidence suggests that the general body-part distribution found in English elite sites is mirrored in Irish later medieval castle assemblages, with the majority of bones being from the hind limbs. When the analysis was conducted separately for red and fallow deer it showed that for red deer 71% (64/90) of the identified bones were from the hind limbs, whereas for fallow deer 76% (26/34) were from this part of the body, clearly demonstrating that the same procedure was being undertaken for both species. Although the same general distribution is found on Irish castle sites as on English elite sites, some differences do occur. Thomas[37] demonstrated that forelimbs were either absent or were present only at extremely low levels, arguing that where they were present, this was evidence for occasional lapses in the systematic division of the carcass. By contrast, the Irish evidence is for the presence of approximately three hind limb bones to every one forelimb bone at castle sites.

---

[37] Thomas, 'Chasing the ideal?', 134–8.

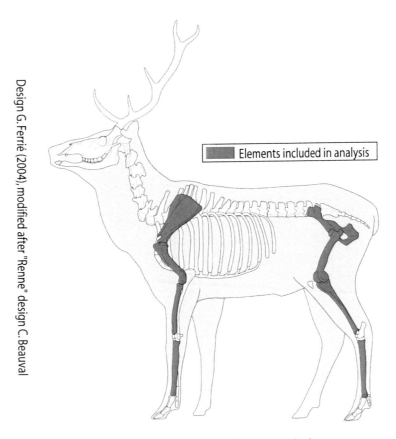

Design G. Ferrié (2004), modified after "Renne" design C. Beauval

Elements included in analysis

FIG. 4—Elements included in the body-part distribution analysis.

The urban results suggest that there are generally equal numbers of fore and hind limbs present in Irish towns. In England, Sykes[38] also found that urban assemblages contained both fore and hind limb bones. She further argued that the other body parts present, including head elements, were evidence of organised poachers who were known to operate out of taverns and alehouses. These poaching gangs worked on a commercial basis, supplying venison to relatively wealthy individuals such as merchants, who did not have official access to this high-status meat. The presence of all body parts in the urban assemblages from Ireland suggests that illicit poaching was also occurring here and there is documentary evidence to support this.[39]

The ability to make a direct comparison between elements from medieval burgage plots at the urban site of Kiely's Yard in Trim Townparks, Co. Meath, and the immediately adjacent Trim Castle is highly revealing, although the sample of deer bones from the burgage plots is small and could therefore be argued to be unrepresentative. Nevertheless, for the castle, 71% (15/21) of the assessed elements were from the hind limb, whereas in Kiely's Yard

---

[38] Sykes, 'Taking sides', 155–7.
[39] See for example, Sweetman, *Documents relating to Ireland*, vol. 1, no. 926.

there was a humerus and a scapula, both of which are from the forelimb. Kiely's Yard also yielded a tooth and a phalanx or toe bone, which could have come from either. An astragalus from the hind limb was found in the 'Castle Lawn' area immediately outside the castle. This area also yielded a scapula from the forelimb, an antler fragment and another phalanx. Given that this location is outside the castle, it may well be that debris produced by the inhabitants of both the town and the castle was deposited there. In a separate excavation at High Street, Trim, Lynch[40] found a single deer metacarpal, which again is from the forelimb.

This comparison of results from the town with those from the castle supports the idea that systematic body-part distribution was being undertaken in Trim. As the town is immediately adjacent to the castle, the forelimb bones found in the burgage plots could potentially have come from poached animals, or could have been legitimate meat. The size of the bones suggests that they were from male red deer. For aristocratic hunting, males would have been deemed to provide the best sport, but for poachers, looking for a simple and quick hunt, a mature male would not necessarily have made the best target as a young individual or a female without antlers would have been easier to capture and kill. Coupled with the presence of only forelimb elements at Kiely's Yard and at High Street, the evidence suggests that this meat had come from huntsmen. This may have been in the form of gifts, or the huntsman's share if he lived in the town, or could potentially have been illicitly sold on by a huntsman who had obtained it legally.

Ireland had far fewer forests and parks than England and communities were smaller.[41] As a result, many professional huntsmen probably lived either in a castle or immediately adjacent to it. In this case, their share of the deer may have been consumed in the castle and/or their refuse may have been disposed of with the castle waste. As a result, it is reasonable that higher proportions of front limb bones are to be found at Irish castle sites than at elite sites in England. Furthermore, this suggestion of the professional hunters living adjacent to the aristocratic hunters is borne out in Trim where forelimb elements were found in urban excavations.

Rabbit

Rabbits and hares are both members of the order Lagomorpha, and the bones of both species are sufficiently similar that, particularly in the case of juvenile elements, some individual toe bones and loose teeth, they cannot always be easily separated. Since their bones are relatively small, they are less likely than those of larger animals to be preserved due to poor soil conditions, destruction by carnivores such as dogs and waste disposal into fires. Furthermore, their small size makes them less likely to be recovered during excavation, especially if

---

[40] Patricia Lynch, 'Human and animal osteoarchaeological bone report: High Street, Trim Co. Meath 06E0148', unpublished report for Carmel Duffy, 2007.
[41] Beglane, *Anglo–Norman parks in medieval Ireland*.

soils are not routinely sieved. This means that rabbit and hare bones are likely to be under-represented in zooarchaeological assemblages compared to those of, for example deer.

Rabbits were not native to Ireland; instead they originated in the western Mediterranean. They were probably originally introduced to Britain by the Romans and then reintroduced by the Normans[42] who subsequently brought them to Ireland. The original rabbits were not the hardy creatures of today, which, through natural selection, have become able to withstand northern European winters. Instead, artificial warrens, often earthen mounds, were constructed to house these delicate creatures, and until the mid-fourteenth century these were usually termed 'coneygarths'.[43] Initially, ownership of a warren was the preserve of the elite, but as the animals multiplied, possession widened to the gentry classes, and as rabbits became naturalised, feral colonies developed, leading to increased availability of wild rabbits. Later medieval coneygarths were often situated in parks or on islands where the rabbits could be protected from predators, with Lambay Island, Co. Dublin, being a good example of the latter.[44] Pillow mounds, which are cigar-shaped earthworks, are a common archaeological feature of the English countryside that have been interpreted as coneygarths, and some may date to the later medieval period, however, many of those that have been excavated have been found to date to the sixteenth to eighteenth centuries.[45] Few, if any, pillow mounds have been found in Ireland, and a search of the database of Irish excavation reports[46] suggests that none have been excavated. O'Conor[47] suggested that in Ireland deserted ringforts and islands may have been used instead. As with deer, rabbits also had a symbolic meaning in medieval iconography. Rabbits were seen as weak creatures that huddled together in communities and were managed by a warrener. Through this they were viewed as emblems of meek, lowly humankind who could be brought to salvation by Christ.[48]

Rabbits were the second most common single species identified in the assemblages, however, since they burrow, it can be difficult to determine whether they were truly present in a context or if the bones were intrusive and the animals had merely burrowed into the context later. There were 405 rabbit bones, and again castle sites yielded the largest number and proportion of these. It is notable, however, that while red and fallow deer combined were the most important food source at castle sites, rabbits were dominant on ecclesiastical

---

[42] Williamson, *Rabbits*, 11.
[43] Williamson, *Rabbits*, 12, 17.
[44] Williamson, *Rabbits*, 11, 17; J.B. Dougbert (ed.), *Report of the deputy keeper of the public records of Ireland* (59 vols, Dublin, 1869–1921), vol. 39, 62.
[45] Williamson, *Rabbits*, 31, 47–53.
[46] www.excavations.ie (17 January 2015).
[47] K.D. O'Conor, 'Medieval rural settlement in Munster', in John Ludlow and Noel Jameson (eds), *Medieval Ireland: the Barryscourt lectures I–X* (Cork, 2004), 225–56: 237.
[48] David Stocker and Margarita Stocker, 'Sacred profanity: the theology of rabbit breeding and the symbolic landscape of the warren', *World Archaeology* 28:2 (1996), 265–72: 267–8.

sites. There are references to rabbit warrens being maintained by monastic communities and by bishops in the thirteenth and fourteenth centuries,[49] and the medieval church considered foetal and newborn rabbits to be acceptable foods for fast days because of their enclosure within the liquid environment of the womb.[50]

Rabbits were also present at moderate levels in urban sites, where small numbers were found in a wide range of excavations. These rabbits are likely to have been brought in from warrens in the countryside. They could have been poached, however, there is also evidence that towns had legitimate access to rabbits either sold as surplus by the manors or produced specifically for sale in the towns. For example, in November 1393 an order was sent 'to the sovereign, provost and community of the town of New Ross' to supply various foodstuffs to James Butler, earl of Ormond and Justiciar of Ireland, who planned to spend Christmas in the town. This included large numbers of cattle and pigs as well as birds, fish and 100 pairs of rabbits.[51] Notably this list did not include deer or hare, as the inhabitants would not have had legitimate access to quantities of these species.

Only two rural sites yielded rabbits: Dunnyneill Island, Co. Down, and the late medieval contexts at Johnstown, Co. Meath, which produced eight bones. Sixteen rabbit bones came from later medieval occupation contexts at Dunnyneill, however *c.* 70 further elements were recovered from the topsoil. Given the island location and the large numbers of elements present in the topsoil, it is quite possible that many of these are intrusive.

Hare

Hares are native to Ireland, they are related to rabbits and have similar skeletons but are larger. They occupy a wide range of habitats, including pasture and arable land as well as uplands and bogs. Unlike rabbits, they do not burrow, but instead they conceal themselves in forms, which are depressions in heather, rushes or hedgerows.[52] Hares were hunted using dogs or by being caught in

---

[49] See for example Charles McNeill (ed.), *Calendar of Archbishop Alen's Register c. 1172–1534* (Dublin, 1950), 30, 44, 178, 180; Paul MacCotter and K.W. Nicholls (eds), *The pipe roll of Cloyne* (*Rotulus pipae Clonensis*) (Middleton, 1996), 249–50; James Mills (ed.), *Account roll of the priory of the Holy Trinity, Dublin, 1337–1346* (Dublin, 1891), 111.

[50] Anton Ervynck, 'Following the rule? Fish and meat consumption in monastic communities in Flanders (Belgium)', in Guy De Boe and Frans Verhaeghe (eds), *Environment and subsistence in medieval Europe. Papers of the medieval Europe Brugge 1997 conference* (Zellik, 1997), 67–81: 76.

[51] Trinity College Dublin, CIRCLE, *A calendar of Irish chancery letters,* CR 17 Rich. II, 11 November 1393.

[52] Stephen Harris and D.W. Yalden, *Mammals of the British Isles: handbook (4th edition)* (Southampton, 2008), 220–8.

nets and traps and were valued for sport, fur and food.[53] Since hares were a beast of the warren, there were restrictions on hunting them, and penalties could be severe. For example, in 1230 Nicholas de Verdun received a right of free warren for his manor of Ferard and it was specifically stated that 'No one is to hunt hare without Nicholas' license on penalty of 10*l*'.[54]

Hares are the third most common edible mammals in the assemblages reviewed and again, the majority are found on castle sites. Relatively few are found on ecclesiastical sites with only a total of six bones identified from Tintern Abbey, Co. Wexford and Bective Abbey and Kells Priory, both Co. Meath. This is very low, especially by comparison with rabbits and suggests that monastic orders did not have regular access to hare meat. By contrast, urban examples of hare bones are almost as common as rabbit bones and although the numbers were small, they were widely distributed. The low numbers of hare bones on rural sites was surprising since they can be caught using nets and so could potentially be targeted relatively easily outside restricted areas or by poachers. It also raises the possibility that hares caught legitimately by rural inhabitants or by poachers were sold in towns for money, rather than being consumed domestically.

Other species

Small numbers of other edible wild species were found. The most common of these were seal bones, which were found at Greencastle, Co. Down; Maynooth Castle, Co. Kildare; Peter Street and E435, Waterford; St Peter's Avenue, Cork; and Portnamuck, Co. Antrim. Apart from Maynooth Castle, all of these are coastal locations where seal bones can reasonably be expected, either as natural intrusions or as a result of deliberate exploitation for food. Since seals live in water, their meat was considered acceptable food to eat during times of fasting. Seal bones were also found at the early medieval monasteries of Ilaunloughan, Co. Kerry, and Iona, Scotland.[55] In 1555 Olaus Magnus recorded that the church in Sweden considered seal meat as acceptable for consumption during Lent.[56] While live seals have been found to have travelled considerable distances

---

[53] Cambrensis, *Topographia Hiberniae*, 48; O'Sullivan Beare, *The natural history of Ireland*, 79; Francois Avril (ed.), *Livre de chasse: the book of the hunt by Gaston Phoebus* (Paris, n.d.), CD-ROM: ff12v–13r.

[54] Sweetman, *Documents relating to Ireland*, vol. 1, no. 1829.

[55] Emily Murray and Finbar McCormick, 'Environmental analysis and the food supply', in Jenny White Marshall and Claire Walsh (eds), *Ilaunloughan Island: an early medieval monastery in County Kerry* (Dublin, 2005), 67–80: 68; Emily Murray, Finbar McCormick and Gillian Plunkett, 'The food economies of Atlantic island monasteries: the documentary and archaeoenvironmental evidence', *Environmental Archaeology* 9 (2004), 179–88: 184.

[56] Alexander Fenton, *The Northern Isles: Orkney and Shetland* (Edinburgh, 1978), 525.

inland,[57] Maynooth Castle is 25km from the sea so that it is likely that this was a definite decision to import seal to the site.

Wild pigs are woodland animals, and are omnivores, eating roots, seeds, fruit, plant material, carrion and eggs.[58] They could be hunted using dogs but could also be trapped, and were considered to be the most dangerous of the animals hunted.[59] There is controversy regarding their fate, since the latest zooarchaeological example of wild pig is from thirteenth century or fourteenth century material at Trim Castle,[60] but O'Sullivan Beare refers to wild pigs.[61] This led Finbar McCormick to suggest that O'Sullivan Beare may have seen feral domesticated pigs, since these are essentially the same species. Since wild and domesticated pigs are the same species, only size can be used to identify the presence of wild pig in an assemblage. Three wild pig bones were found in late thirteenth century to early fourteenth century deposits at Trim Castle, and two possible examples came from the burgage plots at Kiely's Yard in Trim Townparks that also yielded red-deer elements. Three possible wild pig bones were also found in Anglo–Norman contexts at Maynooth Castle.

A small number of cetacean bones were recovered from urban deposits in Cork and Dublin and from Clough Castle, Co. Down, which is less than 2km from Dundrum Bay. These are likely to have come from stranded animals, which were subsequently scavenged for food and craft materials.[62]

One badger bone came from the monastic site at Lough Key, Co. Roscommon, and a single squirrel bone came from Tobin Street in Cork. Both species were considered edible, however they could also be used for their skins. For example, O'Sullivan Beare says of the badger that 'its flesh is not unpleasant to eat nor is its pelt to be despised' and that the blood could be used in a cure for leprosy.[63]

Three hedgehog bones were found in Waterford E406 and one in Patrick Street/Pudding Lane, Kilkenny. Again hedgehogs were considered edible, however, their presence in urban sites may hint at their use in craft-working, as the spiny skins had been used to card wool since at least classical times.[64]

---

[57] Wildlife Extra, *Inland seals: seals reported in Cambridgeshire and Worcester* [Online] (2013). www.wildlifeextra.com/go/news/inland-seals.html#cr (last accessed 10 December 2013); R.W. Baird, 'Status of harbour seals, *Phoca vitulina*, in Canada', *Canadian Field-Naturalist* 115:4 (2001), 663–75: 664.

[58] Harris and Yalden, *Mammals of the British Isles*, 563–4.

[59] Schlag, *The hunting book of Gaston Phébus*, 26.

[60] McCormick, 'Early evidence for wild animals in Ireland', 361.

[61] O'Sullivan Beare, *The natural history of Ireland*, 79.

[62] See for example J.T. Gilbert (ed.), *Chartularies of St. Mary's Abbey, Dublin, with the register of its house at Dunbrody, and annals of Ireland* (Dublin, 1884), 375.

[63] O'Sullivan Beare, *The natural history of Ireland*, 79.

[64] Paula Correa, 'The fox and the hedgehog', *Phaos* 1 (2001), 81–92: 85.

Discussion

Both foods and the animals that are the source of these foods are important aspects of the material culture of any society and therefore their study can shed light on social issues such as identity, status and ideology.[65] The diet of an individual is determined by a number of factors. Firstly, the food must be available within the society being examined, so that, for example, prior to the introduction of rabbits to Ireland, the absence of rabbit from the diet is not useful in differentiating social groups within Ireland. However, in the case of both rabbit and fallow deer these were introduced by the Anglo–Normans, so providing additional food choices for some sections of later medieval society and creating a new way of expressing their identity through food. As such, for the later medieval period, the presence or absence of these foods becomes significant as an indicator of social identity and status. Within the range of foodstuffs potentially available, the position and role of an individual in society can affect the diet in terms of such factors as what foods are acceptable or taboo to consume, what foods are considered to be desirable and the cost of, or ease of access to the particular food of choice. Finally, diet is partly a matter of personal choice or agency, with individuals preferentially selecting different foods from those that are available and socially acceptable. Individual choice can rarely be identified in the archaeological record; however the other factors can be examined and based on the zooarchaeological evidence for the various species, it possible to differentiate the diet of the various groups within society: nobles, ecclesiastics, rural dwellers and urban dwellers, and from this to examine the role of food in expressing these ideas of identity.

For the reasons discussed above, access to game meats was restricted and hence these foods provided opportunities for individuals to accumulate and display both wealth and social capital.[66] In theory, venison could not be sold, so that social capital could be obtained both by the ability to serve venison and by gifting whole carcasses or portions of venison to favoured individuals or institutions. This was true for the lord gifting portions to his retainers or to a nearby abbey, but was also true for the parkers, foresters and huntsmen, who had legal access to this highly prized meat. For them, the opportunity to gift or to illicitly sell this meat was also an opportunity for increased prestige and income. Poachers could gain an income by supplying a willing urban market, with relatively well-to-do individuals keen to sample the meats consumed by the aristocracy and to serve them at feasts as a method of impressing their guests, and in doing so increasing their own social capital.

---

[65] Fiona Beglane, 'Deer and identity in medieval Ireland', in Aleksander Pluskowski, Gunther Karl Kunst, Matthias Kucera, Manfred Bietak and Irmgard Hein (eds), *Viavias 3. Animals as material culture in the Middle Ages 3: bestial mirrors: using animals to construct human identities in medieval Europe* (Vienna, 2010), 77–84; Beglane, *Anglo–Norman parks in medieval Ireland*.

[66] Pierre Bourdieu, 'The forms of capital', in N.W. Biggart (ed.), *Readings in economic sociology* (Oxford, 2008), 46–58: 46–58.

Game in the noble diet

For a medieval aristocrat, hunting primarily served not just to put food on the table, but instead it was a part of elite culture, positioning the individual within society and creating an aristocratic identity.[67] Hunting could be used to create cycles of gift-giving and reciprocal hospitality. There is evidence in Ireland of royal gifts of deer to favoured subjects,[68] and invitations to hunts or to feasts serving venison would have been important occasions at which to demonstrate and create allegiances and alliances.

The nobility sought to control access to hunted foods and one question that this study can answer is whether or not they were successful in this aim. The live animals themselves were part of the material culture of the time, particularly the fallow deer and rabbits that lived in semi-domesticated circumstances in parks and warrens. They were considered to be property and therefore possessing them and being able to serve their flesh was a reflection of the owner's status and position in society. Even wild animals, although not owned as such, were a reflection of the status of the lord, who may have had a right of free warren or free chase on his lands and so had exclusive rights to hunt certain wild animals within certain limits of geography.

Given these restrictions, it is not surprising that castles were the most likely site type to yield wild mammal bones, with 2.3% total game species and 1.0% deer. This equates to approximately 42% of the edible wild mammal bones found at the castle sites being from deer, of which one quarter were from fallow deer. Rabbit (35%) and hare (19%) made up the bulk of the remainder, with other species being found only occasionally. Given the relative size of deer, rabbits and hares, and ignoring differential taphonomic and body part distribution factors, this means that over 96% of the wild meat consumed on castle sites was venison and so it can be stated that venison was the wild meat of choice at these high-status sites.

There is also evidence for the ritual 'breaking' of the carcass along prescribed lines, with predominantly hind limbs found at castle sites, which were the portions of the carcass traditionally reserved for the lord. This would have included the prime cuts of meat, equating to the topside and silverside in beef.[69] By contrast, the forelimbs should have been given to the employed huntsmen, parkers and foresters, and these were under-represented at castle sites. This demonstrates that these traditions were known, understood and practised in Ireland. Nevertheless, the body-part distribution found at Irish castle sites was not as extreme as in England, where forelimb bones are rare on castle sites. This may be linked to the relative size of households, since in Ireland the huntsmen may have lived within the castles.

---

[67] Aleksander Pluskowski, 'The social construction of medieval park ecosystems: an interdisciplinary perspective', in Robert Liddiard (ed.), *The medieval park: new perspectives* (Macclesfield, 2007), 63–78: 63.

[68] See for example Sweetman, *Documents relating to Ireland*, vol. 1, no. 3076.

[69] Davis, *The archaeology of animals*, 25.

Game in the ecclesiastical diet

The ecclesiastical diet was meant to be one of moderation, including regular periods of fasting, and without, or later with only limited consumption of meat.[70] Hunting by clergy or monks was discouraged, however, many high-ranking members of the church were of noble birth and would have hunted since childhood.[71] The ecclesiastic group inhabited an ambiguous position in society in which they were of relatively high status, some of them had parks or warrens stocked with deer and rabbits, they had access to gifts of red and fallow deer from wealthy patrons and may have taken part in hunting on their own account. Nevertheless, they were meant to abstain from meat consumption at least on certain days of the week and on specific holy days and periods during the year.

This ambiguity is reflected in the zooarchaeological results from ecclesiastical sites. At a total of 1.2% they were the second most likely to yield wild mammal bones, but numerically the bones were dominated by rabbit, with only occasional deer bones. Ironically, as a result of the relative size of the animals, approximately 88% of the wild meat again came from deer with rabbit providing 8%, but it is important to restate that the relatively small size of rabbit and hare bones means that they are less likely than those of deer to be represented in zooarchaeological assemblages. All but three of the sites considered here are monastic in character, and of these only three yielded deer bones. This may have meant that few deer carcasses or joints were gifted to the churches and monasteries and that relatively few ecclesiastics had the opportunity to hunt deer or hare. Venison can therefore be considered to be a minor component of the overall ecclesiastical diet, however, it is important to consider that access to game was not necessarily equal within ecclesiastical circles. The situation of a bishop or archbishop was very different to that of a prior or abbot, who would in turn have had access to a wider range of foods than a junior member of his order. For example, while the archbishop of Dublin is documented as having his own deer, a number of parks and also rabbit warrens, the priory of Holmpatrick, Co. Dublin, had a rabbit warren, which also supplied the Priory of the Holy Trinity, Co. Dublin.[72]

---

[70] Ervynck, 'Following the rule', 71–3. Anton Ervynck, '*Orant, pugnant, laborant*. The diet of the three orders in the feudal society of medieval north-western Europe', in Sharyn O'Day Jones, Wim Van Neer and Anton Ervynck (eds), *Behaviour behind bones: the zooarchaeology of ritual, religion, status and identity* (Oxford, 2004); 215–23: 216–17; Barbara Harvey, 'Monastic pittances in the Middle Ages', in C.M. Woolgar, Dale Serjeantson and Tony Waldron (eds), *Food in medieval England: diet and nutrition* (Oxford, 2006), 215–27.

[71] Marcelle Thiebaux, 'The mediaeval chase', *Speculum* 42:2 (1967), 260–74: 264–5; Cummins, *The hound and the hawk*, 10.

[72] See for example McNeill, *Archbishop Alen's register*, 30, 44, 170–2, 173, 178, 180, 195; Mills, *Account roll of the priory of the Holy Trinity*; 111, Sweetman, *Documents relating to Ireland*, vol. 1, nos 316, 477, 1336.

With limited access to wild meat, it can be suggested that at monastic sites this type of meat was often reserved for the abbot's table on the occasion of a feast or for high-ranking visitors rather than for general consumption. For example, the Priory of the Holy Trinity in Dublin regularly bought in pre-cooked food and on one occasion paid 6*d* for 'one roast goose, a rabbit cooked, and pigeons cooked' to be served to the prior and selected guests in the private environment of the sacristy.[73] Nevertheless, given the likely under-representation of rabbit bones in assemblages, this meat may well have provided occasional welcome variety for the monks in a diet otherwise dominated by beef, pork and mutton.[74]

Game in the urban diet

The identification of hunting and venison with the aristocracy raises the issue of venison in the urban environment. Sykes[75] suggests that most of the fallow deer remains from urban sites in England were the result of poaching or of illicit sales of the forester's and hunter's portions. The Irish evidence suggests that poaching was also important in Ireland. Even when antler-working waste is excluded, urban assemblages are second only to castle sites in the number of deer elements found there. Examining the body-part distribution, they have generally similar proportions of forelimb and hind limb bones, as well as containing fragments of skull and mandible. These are indicative of deer that have been slaughtered and dismembered without regard for the formal rules of 'breaking' the carcass. Since venison was regarded as meat for the landed nobility, it would have been highly sought after by wealthy, aspirational townsfolk. These rich merchants would have had the financial means to procure illicit, poached venison, and by doing so, and serving it at feasts and banquets they sought to emulate their social superiors. This demonstration of their cultured regard for fine dining would have increased their standing among their peers and as a result they would have gained cultural capital. Trim was a large town by medieval standards, but was small compared to cities such as Dublin or Waterford, and so employment and trade would have centred on the castle. In this case, there are a number of legitimate reasons why the huntsman's portion of venison could find its way to a burgage plot. This may have been the huntsman's home, or the home of his family, or he could have illicitly sold his portion on the black market.

Urban excavations also yielded significant quantities of rabbit and hare bones, although these made up only a small proportion of the meat sold in the towns. Hares and rabbits were sold by poulterers, who also sold birds such as

---

[73] Mills, *Account roll of the priory of the Holy Trinity*, xiii, 117.
[74] Fiona Beglane, 'Report on faunal material from Bective Abbey, Co. Meath. Licence No. E4028', unpublished report for Geraldine Stout, 2013.
[75] Sykes, 'Taking sides', 156–7.

geese and chickens.[76] While some of their stock may have been legally sourced through sales of surplus rabbits or of hares and feral rabbits hunted outside of restricted areas, some could also have come from poachers. In theory, hunting rabbits and hares was subject to similar restrictions to deer; however, their meat was more accessible than venison. Mature deer are large and can be dangerous to hunt, however, hares and rabbits can be caught legitimately or illegitimately without personal danger using dogs, nets and traps. Having caught them, the smaller carcass sizes made them easier to transport over distances and they required minimal butchery, as a whole hare could be sold to a household. Again, consumption of rabbit and hare would have marked out the urban dweller as aspirational, seeking to emulate the diet of the nobility as far as possible within his means, and certainly in medieval England, urban dwellers served rabbit for feasts and celebrations.[77]

Game in the rural diet

Because of their low archaeological profile, relatively few rural sites have been published and these have yielded only small assemblages of bone, nevertheless, a sample size of 10,298 is significant and should be sufficient in order to identify patterns. These sites yielded the smallest percentages of wild species, which is counter-intuitive given that rural people would have had legal access to hunting outside areas of forest, free warren and chase and that they could potentially also poach wild animals. When antlers are excluded, very few deer bones were identified, as well as negligible quantities of hare bones, suggesting that they did not target these species. The proportion of rabbits is similar to that of deer but with this species a question mark must be raised since most of the examples came from the island site of Dunnyneill, Co. Down. Overall it can be concluded that rural people rarely ate wild mammals, instead consuming the domesticated cattle, sheep and pig that make up the majority of faunal remains from all site types. There are a number of possibilities as to why this was so. Even outside of areas of forest, free warren and free chase, if rural people were found with game in their possession they would have had to prove that it had been obtained legally and this would have discouraged even legitimate hunting. Hunting would also have taken time that could be spent on risk-free routine tasks that were guaranteed to provide food or an income. Finally, as evidenced by the supply of wild meats in urban areas, any hunting that did take place, either legitimately or illicitly would have been more lucrative as a source of money than as a source of food.

Conclusions

Wild meats were a relatively unimportant source of calories in later medieval Ireland, generally providing only a maximum of a few per cent of the meat, but they did have enormous social significance and can be used as indicators of

---

[76] Melitta Weiss Adamson, *Food in medieval times* (Westport, 2004), 102; S.A. Epstein, *Wage labour and guilds in medeval Europe* (Chapel Hill, NC, 1991), 128.
[77] Bridget Henisch, *The medieval cook* (Woodbridge, 2009), 93–5.

social identity and status, so providing important evidence for interpreting later medieval society. In common with elites across Europe, the nobility sought to control access to game and largely succeeded in this, with very few deer, hare or rabbit remains found on other site types. For monastic orders, venison and hare were only occasionally available, however they did have access to rabbits which provided variety in the diet for at least the upper echelons. Both documentary and zooarchaeological evidence show that by contrast with the monks, bishops and archbishops had access to game that was similar in nature to that enjoyed by the nobility. For wealthy urban dwellers, these high-status foods were accessible, for a price, and could be used to emulate the upper orders and increase social standing. Nevertheless, they would have been expensive and evidence for their consumption is limited so that it is likely that these were particularly popular for banquets and celebratory meals rather than for everyday meals. This meat could be supplied by urban dwellers with professional access to the castles, manors and their resources, but could also be supplied by poachers or by rural hunters who saw this market as a lucrative source of extra income, and seem to have rarely eaten wild meats themselves.

Acknowledgements   Many thanks are due to the zooarchaeologists and licence-holders cited and to the NRA for access to unpublished data, without which this paper would not have been possible.

'Whipt with a twig rod': Irish manuscript recipe books as sources for the study of culinary material culture, *c*. 1660 to 1830

MADELINE SHANAHAN*

John Hume Institute for Global Irish Studies, University College Dublin, Belfield, Dublin 4

[Accepted 1 September 2014. Published 12 March 2015.]

Abstract

From the mid- to late seventeenth century on women from the elite classes in Ireland started to write and exchange recipes, which they recorded in domestic manuscripts. Cultural imports to Ireland at this time, these manuscripts are excellent sources for the study of food, giving us a window into the early modern kitchen during a period of great culinary change. This paper will begin by briefly outlining the development of recipe writing as a genre in Ireland, considering issues such as chronology, authorship and content. The second part of the paper will focus more specifically on what these sources can tell us about material culture relating to cookery within high-status Irish homes of this period. By considering the objects mentioned, as well as the way in which they were described, the paper will discuss not simply what people owned, but also, what patterns of naming can tell us about these people's changing relationships with goods, and an emerging consumer identity.

Introduction

During the seventeenth century women from elite backgrounds in Ireland started to write and exchange recipes—a practice which was common over the next 200 years. The manuscripts in which they recorded these recipes are an excellent source for the study of food and the material culture of the kitchen, from the mid-seventeenth century to the close of the Georgian period (1830). Furthermore, they reveal a great deal about the lives of the individuals who wrote these books, their work, concerns and social networks. This paper will briefly outline the development of recipe writing as a genre in Ireland, and what it reveals about material culture relating to cookery within high-status Irish homes. By focusing on the objects mentioned in manuscript recipe books, and the way in which those objects were described, the paper will engage not simply with what people owned, but also with how their relationships with goods and, ultimately, their worldview, evolved. Over the course of the eighteenth century people began to exhibit a heightened

* Author's e-mail: madelineshanahan@gmail.com
doi: 10.3318/PRIAC.2015.115.04

engagement both with food and the objects associated with it. Historical archaeologists have, to date, focused on the material culture associated with dining and food service as evidence of this rise in materialism and consumerism,[1] but, as this analysis will demonstrate, these same patterns are also observable in the production and preparation of food, as instructed by contemporary recipe books.

Food and recipe writing in Restoration and Georgian Ireland

Recipe writing[2] commenced in Irish houses in the mid- to late seventeenth century, and was maintained at a steady pace until the late eighteenth century. From the 1780s their number increased markedly and accelerated further over the course of the nineteenth century.[3] Despite the fact that manuscript recipe books are in many ways a distinct genre, in that they obey a basic cultural template, include similar categories of material and frequently share stylistic norms, it would be wrong to see them as homogenous. Each manuscript is a distinctly personal and flexible object in its own right, and it was structured and written according to its various owners' needs, which may have changed over time. So, manuscript recipe books from Ireland vary dramatically in physical terms, ranging from elaborately decorated organised volumes, which do not show signs of daily use, to rough folders of notes which assisted in the running of a busy kitchen. The manuscripts also vary greatly in terms of their content. They may include writings on a host of subjects beyond food-related recipes, such as cures and prescriptions (an integral part of the genre); beauty, gardening and housekeeping advice; newspaper clippings; scientific, Biblical and literary excerpts; household accounts; table and menu plans; sketches and drawings; and even diary entries.[4]

---

[1] For example, Paul A. Shackel, *Personal discipline and material culture: an archaeology of Annapolis, Maryland, 1685–1870* (Knoxville, TN, 1993); Mark P. Leone, 'Ceramics from Annapolis, Maryland: a measure of time routines and work discipline', in Mark P. Leone and Parker B. Potter Jr (eds), *Historical archaeologies of capitalism* (New York, 1999), 195–216.

[2] It should be noted that the term 'recipe' is anachronistic when discussing manuscripts produced at this time—they were, in fact, called 'receipts' during the period under review—but, for the sake of clarity, I adopt the contemporary term 'recipe'. This decision is in line with other major scholarship in the field, namely Michelle DiMeo and Sara Pennell (eds), *Reading and writing recipe books, 1550–1800* (Manchester, 2013). For a detailed discussion of the history of the genre in Ireland see Madeline Shanahan, 'Dining on words: manuscript recipe books, culinary change and elite food culture in Ireland, 1660–1830', *Irish Architectural and Decorative Studies: The Journal of the Irish Georgian Society* 15 (2012), 82–97; Madeline Shanahan, *Manuscript recipe books as archaeological objects: text and food in the early modern world* (Lanham, MD, 2015). For discussions of the genre in Britain and the United States of America, see DiMeo and Pennell, *Reading and writing recipe books;* Janet Theophano, *Eat my words: reading women's lives through the cookbooks they wrote* (New York, 2002).

[3] Shanahan, 'Dining on words', 84.

[4] Shanahan, 'Dining on words', 89–91.

In terms of authorship, prior to the Victorian period the authors were almost exclusively members of the elite classes, and were predominantly women. Servants and men certainly made contributions, and we see recipes attributed to them, but there is no clear evidence that they were generally the primary authors in Ireland. There are numerous manuscripts written by anonymous hands, so of course there is the possibility that the identity of authors was more diverse, but as the class and gendered pattern observed in Ireland is consistent with studies from Great Britain and the United States of America,[5] it seems fair to say that elite women were the primary producers of recipes in the period under review.

It is generally true to say also that the authors were primarily from 'New English' families, who had settled in Ireland from the sixteenth century on. This is not to say that families of 'Old English' and Gaelic origins did not participate in recipe writing, but it was certainly a new and imported practice for them, as there was no tradition of this in Ireland. It was also an adopted custom which could help them to absorb English culinary norms as necessary. Significantly, the recipe books in the collection of the Inchiquin O'Briens of County Clare, who were one of the most important Gaelic noble families in Ireland, were largely written by English women who married into the family. These women brought their cultural traditions with them at a time when it was necessary for the O'Brien family to adopt central elements of English culture, and food and foodways were fundamental to that process. For example, one of their exquisite volumes, which was in use for generations, was probably started by Catherine O'Brien (née Keightley), who was born in Ireland, but whose family and connections were chiefly English aristocrats. There is also a possibility, based on a later attribution, that this manuscript contains sections transcribed from Catherine's mother, Lady Frances Keightley's (née Hyde) earlier volume.[6] Lady Keightley—the youngest daughter of Edward Hyde, the first earl of Clarendon—came to Ireland after her marriage. Her sister was the duke of York's (later James II) first wife, meaning that Lady Frances was the aunt of both Queen Mary II and Queen Anne.[7]

Jane Ohlmeyer has recently discussed the role of marriage as an important means whereby elite Gaelic and Old English families became both anglicised and 'civilised', and were enabled to retain their position and status at a time of great social flux. According to Ohlmeyer, it was hoped that English

---

[5] Theophano, *Eat my words.*

[6] National Library of Ireland (NLI), Ms 14,786, Inchiquin Papers, A collection of domestic recipes and Medical prescriptions 'started by Lady Frances Keightley about 1660'. Despite the later note attributing this to Lady Frances Keightley, it was more likely to have been started by her daughter, Catherine O'Brien, in the late seventeenth century.

[7] Ivar C. McGrath, 'Keightley, Thomas (c. 1650–1719)', *Oxford Dictionary of National Biography* (Oxford 2012 [2004]). Available online at: oxforddnb.com/view/article/15251 (last accessed 6 May 2012). For a more detailed recent discussion of these individuals see Gabrielle M. Ashford, 'Advice to a daughter: Lady Frances Keightley to her daughter Catherine, September 1681', *Analecta Hibernica* 43 (2012), 17–46.

women would teach the next generation of Irish elites their language, culture, manners and religion; ultimately, that they could 'make Ireland English'.[8] Based on my analysis of surviving family papers in the National Library of Ireland, it is clear that, upon coming to Ireland, many women brought their food culture with them, and that manuscript recipe books, which had been an established genre for generations in Britain, were an important component of that.

The cultural significance of recipe writing in Britain was not limited to manuscript keeping; it can also be seen in the production and consumption of printed texts. While they are by no means a genre unique to England, published recipe books were hugely popular in that country and more titles were produced there from the seventeenth to nineteenth century than elsewhere. The popularity of published recipe books also helped to forge a distinctly and consciously British cuisine.[9] These published models not only influenced food and cookery, but also the writing behaviours of elite women, encouraging a lively manuscript culture within houses. As women's gender roles came to be redefined in Britain, and a less active role in the running of the house was promoted, in line with the genteel and meek model put forward in the Georgian period,[10] writing became a central component of housewifery.[11] A literate and yet passive mistress sitting at her desk was much more desirable than one with her sleeves rolled up sweating away in the kitchen, and so writing household manuals became a central component of this idealised femininity. Considering the identity of the authors, the nature of manuscripts, the distinctly British cuisine that they promote and the chronology of their arrival in Ireland, it seems reasonable to say that recipe writing was an important signifier of class, culture and gendered identity for the new arrivals, and that it subsequently became one for the elite classes already established here.[12]

---

[8] Jane Ohlmeyer, *Making Ireland English: the Irish aristocracy in the seventeenth century* (New Haven, CT, and London, 2012), 169–210.

[9] Stephen Mennell, *All manners of food: eating and taste in England and in France from the Middle Ages to the present* (Urbana and Chicago, IL, 1996), 83–101.

[10] For publications relating to the 'ideology of domesticity' and the 'separating spheres theory' please see Carole Shammas, 'The domestic environment in early modern England and America', *The Journal of Social History* 14:1 (1980), 3–24; Diana. D. Wall, 'Secular dinners and sacred teas: constructing domesticity in mid-19th century New York', *Historical Archaeology* 25:4 (1991), 69–81; Amanda Vickery, 'Golden age to separate spheres? A review of the categories and chronology of English women's history', *The Historical Journal* 36:2 (1993), 383–414; Matthew Johnson, *The archaeology of capitalism* (Oxford, 1996), 155–78; Michael McKeon, *The secret history of domesticity: public, private and the division of knowledge* (Baltimore, MD, 2005); Karen Harvey, 'Barbarity in a teacup? Punch, domesticity and gender in the eighteenth century', *Journal of Design History* 21:3 (2008), 205–21.

[11] Gilly Lehmann, *The British housewife: cookery books, cooking and society in eighteenth century Britain* (Totnes, Devon, 2003), 66–71.

[12] For an extensive discussion of this subject please see Shanahan, *Manuscript recipe books as archaeological objects*.

The recipes

As with the genre itself, the recipes contained within seventeenth- and eighteenth-century manuscripts reflect the close cultural connection that existed between the authors of these manuscripts and the English upper classes.[13] The most important point to make is that the food, tastes and fashions are remarkably similar to those represented in contemporary English recipe manuscripts and published books. There is a basic suite of recipes which are common and obey a general cultural template. Only a few recipes can be seen as particularly 'Irish' in any real sense. One such example appears in the mid- to late eighteenth century section of a volume authored by women from the Inchiquin O'Brien family:

> To make an Irish stew of mutton
> Season the bones of a neck of mutton with pepper and salt, put it down with a layer of onions, put them in covered stewpan, to keep in the steam & as much water as will cover it—the chops must be very tender but as they are all put down together, the potatoes must be taken out first, as they burst.[14]

Notwithstanding examples such as this, the rarity of expressly 'Irish' recipes says much about the nature of the culinary culture of the Anglophone elite of society. The manuscripts depict the cuisine, or at least that which was aspired to, of the elite classes, and they need to be interpreted in that context. Furthermore, the commonalities that they share with English manuscript and printed recipe books indicates that authors from Ireland had access to, and were inspired by, English texts.[15] In some instances we have direct evidence for the influence of printed models. For example, Jane Burton's eighteenth-century manuscript diligently references the original authors of the recipes it contains. Her volume includes recipes attributed to famous published authors such as William Ellis and Hannah Glasse, as well as excerpts from the *Scot's Magazine*.[16]

The chief classes of recipes recorded can be categorised as sweet dishes (a large category which can be broken down further as discussed below), savoury dishes, preserved goods, alcoholic beverages, bread making, dairying advice and substitutes for expensive ingredients. Culinary historians may choose to group these recipes differently and more precisely. Ultimately, there

---

[13] For a detailed discussion of the contents of Irish manuscript recipe books see Shanahan, 'Dining on words', 89–94; Shanahan, *Manuscript recipe books as archaeological objects*.

[14] NLI, Ms 14,786, Inchiquin Papers, A collection of domestic recipes and medical prescriptions 'started by Lady Frances Keightley about 1660', mid- to late seventeenth century, 38.

[15] For a further discussion of the influence of printed works on food culture in Ireland in this period see Alison Fitzgerald, 'Tastes in high life: dining in the Dublin town house', in Christine Casey (ed.), *The eighteenth-century Dublin town house: form, function and finance* (Dublin, 2010), 120–7.

[16] NLI, Ms 19,729, Volume of cookery receipts, medical prescriptions and household hints compiled by Jane Burton [of Buncraggy, Co. Clare?], with index.

are countless ways of breaking down a recipe book depending on the type of questions one seeks to ask. My intention here is to consider the broad 'function' of a recipe in terms of running an efficient and fashionable household. The function may have been to assist in the creation of a rounded and phased meal system based on contemporary fashions, with sweet and savoury flavours required at different stages. Alternatively, a recipe's function may relate to how it assisted with the completion of certain household tasks and provisioning (bread making, distillation, food preservation and dairying). Each of these categories will be outlined below in order of the frequency of their presence. This will help to illustrate the nature of the recipes within the manuscripts, and will demonstrate their similarity with British models.

Sweet dishes are by far the most common category of recipe in Irish manuscript recipe books of this period. This large category can be broken down more meaningfully into baked goods, whipped and set desserts, and confectionery. Sweet baked goods, which were served at breakfast, with tea or at the end of the meal, depending on the recipe, are standard inclusions. Such recipes include cakes, biscuits and macaroons (Pl. I). Although not strictly baked and therefore somewhat distinct, steamed puddings can also be put into this broad grouping in terms of their function within the meal system. The following example, which comes from a seventeenth-century manuscript from the collection of the Smythe family of Barbavilla, Co. Westmeath, demonstrates one such recipe from this category:

A caraway cake
A quarter of a peck of flower dryed [sic] a pound of butter a pound of caraway comfits a pint of cream a pint some sake [sack] of yest [yeast] ye

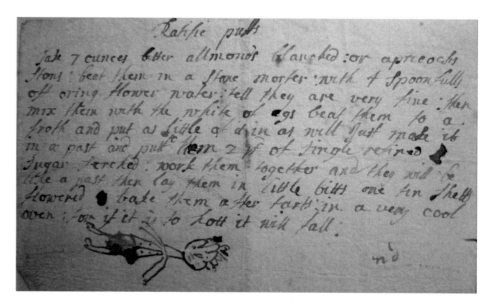

PL. I—Recipe for 'Ratifie puffs' from the National Library of Ireland (NLI), Ms 41,603/2 (2 of 2), Papers of the Smythe family of Barbavilla, Co. Westmeath. Courtesy of the NLI.

yolks of 6 eggs on nutmeg mingle it when you begin to heat your oven and let it rise and when you go to put it in mingle in the caraways.[17]

This example demonstrates a cake very typical to the late seventeenth and eighteenth centuries, both in terms of flavour and method. Such recipes are found throughout the Irish collection and are also common in contemporary British examples.

Whipped and set treats such as blancmanges, jellies, creams, syllabubs, flummeries and possets, which would mostly have been served as desserts at the end of the meal, are also common. A vast range of different types of confectionery such as candied fruits and flowers were familiar, conserves and marmalades ('marmalets') were popular too. These may also be seen as forms of preservation, albeit expensive ones given the high cost of sugar, particularly in the earlier part of the study period.

Recipes associated with food preservation are the second most common category, and they demonstrate the importance of this task. Meat and fish could be salted, smoked, potted and pickled. Fruit and vegetables were preserved as jams, marmalets and conserves (also forms of confectionery), but also as chutneys, pickles and even powders. The following recipe is taken from a second volume written by members of the Smythe family of Barbavilla:

> To pickle cauliflowers
> Take the clossett [sic] and whitest cauliflowers that you can and break them into little knots as you please then put them into salt and water as much as will cover them let it be as strong as will bear an egg and let them stand in it 48 hours then drain them well from the brine and have as much white wine vinegar as will cover them boiled with some nutmeg cut in quarters and some mace so pour it boiling hot upon yr cauliflowers cover them up close and in 3 or 4 days they will be fit to eat.[18]

This example demonstrates just one of the numerous entries for a wide variety of pickled vegetables which appear in manuscripts from the seventeenth century on, most of which use a similar method.

Savoury recipes, which would have formed part of the main meal, are the third most frequently occurring recipe type. Soups, broths, forced meat, roasts, stews, puddings and pies are commonly encountered. 'Ragoos', 'fricassees' and 'cullis' are also regular inclusions and attest to the influence of courtly French food fashions on the cuisine of the elite classes in Britain and Ireland in this period.[19]

---

[17] NLI, Ms 41,603/2 (2 of 2), Papers of the Smythe family of Barbavilla, Co. Westmeath, Box containing two recipe books and four folders of recipes, mid- to late seventeenth century, unpaginated.

[18] See note 17 above.

[19] The complex subject of French culinary influence in Britain and Ireland has been discussed in Fitzgerald, 'Tastes in high life: dining in the Dublin town house'.

Alcoholic beverages are the next major recipe category. These include various types of flavoured wines, liqueurs, mead (or 'meath'), cordials and ales (Pl. II). The proliferation and diversification of such recipes demonstrates that there was an active brewing and even distilling culture within elite Irish houses during the seventeenth and eighteenth centuries.

The final three categories are encountered infrequently. These include recipes for bread making, which appear on occasion, but are not common place. Other sources, such as account books, tell us that many baked goods, but particularly bread, were frequently bought in ready-made. Furthermore, the absence of bread recipes may relate to the purpose and use of recipe books. As Carol Gold has observed in her analysis of Danish published cookery books dating from 1616 to 1901, the recipes found within such manuals tend to record information and directions with respect to recipes that people need assistance with. Gold, one of the only scholars to have written on this subject, suggests persuasively that baking bread was such a commonplace daily task that it did not require written instruction.[20] The next of these infrequent categories is dairying (mostly relating to soft cheeses in this period) (Pl. III), and the rare but intriguing category of creating substitutes for expensive luxury ingredients such as tea, coffee and chocolate.[21] For example, the recipe book by Jane Burton

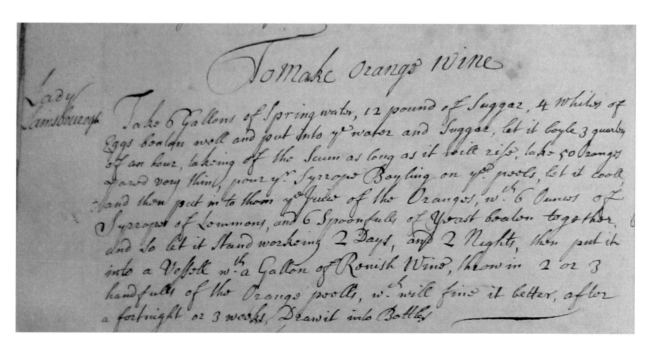

PL. II—'To make orange wine' from the National Library of Ireland (NLI), Ms 14,786, Inchiquin Papers. Courtesy of the NLI.

---

[20] Carol Gold, *Danish cookbooks* (Seattle, WN, 2007), 11–12.

[21] Shanahan, 'Dining on words', 94.

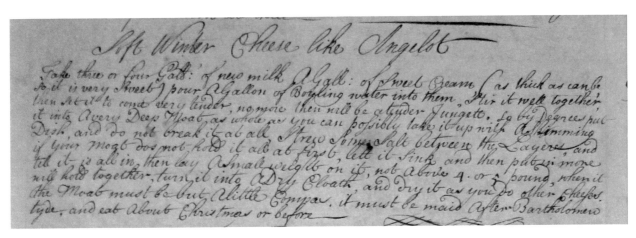

PL. III—'Soft winter cheese like Angelot' from the National Library of Ireland (NLI), Ms 14,786, Inchiquin Papers. Courtesy of the NLI.

includes directions for 'Artificial Coffee' which instructed the reader to burn a piece of bread until it was black, grind it, and add it to hot water.[22]

It is evident from this brief outline of the recipe types recorded in the Irish recipe books that the cuisine represented was broadly similar to that consumed in Britain at the time. The elite classes in Ireland shared a common cuisine with their British counterparts, just as many of them shared ethnicity, marriage bonds, language, religion, architecture and other aspects of culture. This should not be seen as particularly surprising given that they had such close familial and cultural bonds with their counterparts there. What is interesting though, is how the practice of recipe writing was used to articulate this close cultural and class connection across the water. The elite classes did not simply import a cuisine alone, but also an important and fashionable cultural object, which was an integral part of the food system—the recipe book. This was an item closely associated with the British household, foodways and gendered identity. As discussed earlier, recipe writing was a well-established practice in upper-class-British households, and it was one that helped to forge a consciously British cuisine, as well as a new model of idealised femininity characterised by the image of the passive, genteel and literate housewife. In this sense then, both the dishes conveyed within recipe books from this period, as well as the very mode of communication itself, were means through which a definitively English food culture was established in Ireland.

Manuscript recipe books as sources for the study of material culture

Manuscript recipe books contain a high level of detail on life within Irish houses from the mid-seventeenth century. As stated earlier, they contain a range of different types of information in addition to the recipes themselves, and it is perhaps surprising that they have not yet been scrutinised in more detail by

---

[22] NLI, Ms 19,729, *Volume of cookery receipts, medical prescriptions and household hints compiled by Jane Burton [of Buncraggy, Co. Clare?], with index, eighteenth century*, 275.

archaeologists and historians interested in material culture. Manuscript recipe books help us to understand not simply what items were expected to be in the kitchen, but also how they were used. They show us that simple objects often had a variety of functions. Past studies of material culture relating to kitchens have shown that items associated with food processing, not just food service, proliferated during the eighteenth century in England.[23] The analysis that follows demonstrates that a similar pattern can be identified in Ireland. Finally, they also indicate that kitchens contained a range of inexpensive organic and naturally occurring materials which were regularly used in a variety of tasks. As they were of little value, such items would rarely have been mentioned in inventories. They would be difficult to detect archaeologically, making recipe books, which can tell us a great deal about the range of ephemeral, cheap and disposable items not generally discussed elsewhere, an invaluable source.

The remainder of this paper will focus on the objects mentioned in ten recipe books.[24] As the table below, which lists the objects mentioned in a recipe book maintained by members of the Inchiquin O'Brien family between the late seventeenth and mid-eighteenth centuries, demonstrates, manuscript recipe books from this period contain a wealth of information in relation to cookery-related material culture. Comparable lists were made for each of the ten case-study manuscripts, with a view to characterising the contents of kitchens over time.[25] These lists help us to consider how the equipment within kitchens may

---

[23] Lorna Weatherill, *Consumer behaviour & material culture in Britain 1660–1760* (2nd edition, London, 1988), 44, 155, 205.

[24] NLI, Ms 14,786, Inchiquin Papers, A collection of domestic recipes and medical prescriptions 'started by Lady Frances Keightley about 1660', mid- to late seventeenth century; NLI, Ms 14,901, Miss (or Mrs) Barnewall, Collection of domestic recipes and medical prescriptions, late eighteenth to early nineteenth century; NLI, Ms 19,332, A book of recipes and medical remedies, also including some verses. [Compiled by a member of the family of Montgomery, of Convoy, Co. Donegal?], late seventeenth century; NLI, Ms 19,729, Volume of cookery receipts, medical prescriptions and household hints compiled by Jane Burton [of Buncraggy, Co. Clare?], with index, eighteenth century; NLI, Ms 34,110, Doneraile Papers, Notebooks with recipes and health remedies such as an 'elixir for a long life', accounts and household lists, July and August 1798; NLI, Ms 34,953, Cookery book, 1780–1820; NLI, Ms 34,932(1), Culinary and medical recipe books possibly compiled by member(s) of the Pope family of Co. Waterford, 1823; NLI, Ms 41,603/2 (1 of 2), Papers of the Smythe family of Barbavilla, Co. Westmeath, Box containing two recipe books and 4 folders of recipes, early eighteenth century; NLI, Ms 41,603/2 (2 of 2), Papers of the Smythe family of Barbavilla, Co. Westmeath, Box containing two recipe books and four folders of recipes, mid- to late seventeenth century; NLI, Ms 42,008, Ms cookery book belonging to Abigail Jackson, 10 April 1782.

[25] Only one such list has been included here, but for alternative examples please see Shanahan, *Manuscript recipe books as archaeological objects.*

TABLE—List of items mentioned in food-related recipes and inventories in the National Library of Ireland manuscript, Ms 14,786, from the Inchiquin Papers.

Objects mentioned in NLI, Ms 14,786

bag	bag, flannell	bag, jelly
bag, paper	barrel	bason
bason, cheney	bason, earthen or silver	bason, large white
bason, silver	bladder	board, [......] round
boards	bodkin	bottle
bottle, china	bottle, wide mouthed	bottle, wide mouthed glass
bowl	bowl, black and white	bowl, large coulerd
bowl, plain	bowl, small Japend & covers	box
bread basket	candels	candlesticks
canvas	cheese bason	cheese cloath
cheese-vat	chocolet mill	churn vessels
cloth	cloth, coarse	cloth, fine
cloth, straining	cloth, thin	cloth, very thick
coffee pott and plate	cork	crock, glazed
crock, small	cullender	cullender, earthen
cup	cup, chocolate	cup, tea
cups, large chocolate china, netted over	cups, large coulerd burnt china with cover	cups, large with covers
cups, [......] stone	cups, white chocolate cups with raised flowers, china	decanters for water without covers
decanters with covers	dish	dish, broad silver
dish, china	dish, deep	dish, earthen
dish, large coulerd	dish, long lobster china	dish, pewter
dishes of blue china, four different sizes	dishes, round coulerd and gilt	dishes, shallow
drudging box	fish kettle	flannell
flat drying pans	flat iron	forks
frying pan	glass	glass, deep
glass, large	jar, large blue & cover	jar, large coulerd & cover
jar, stone	jug	kettle
knife	knife, very sharp	ladle, punch
ladle, soup	leather	linen, very thin
milk pan	mille	mortar, marble
mortar, stone	muslin	napkin
needle, great	paile	pan
pan, earthen	pan, large	pan, tin
paper, white	papers	papers, brandy
paper coffins, little square	patty pans	pepper box, small
pin	plate, thin	plates
plates, coulerd and gilt	plates for caudle cups	plates, octogon blue and white
plates, square of old china	plates, tin	platter
porringer	pot, deep earthen	pot, earthen & well glazed
pots	pottles	preserving pan
preserving pan, copper	pressing pan	punch bowl, large

TABLE (*cont.*)—List of items mentioned in food-related recipes and inventories in the National Library of Ireland manuscript, Ms 14,786, from the Inchiquin Papers.

Objects mentioned in NLI, Ms 14,786

punch bowl, small	quill	rolling pin
salamander	sallatt dishes, long blue and white	salvers, round
sauce boats	sauce pan	saucers
saucers for chocolate china cups	saucers, small deep	saucers, [. . . . .]stone
sa[u]cers, three cornered	scallop shells	shape
sieve	sieve, coarse	sieve, fine
sieve, hair	sieve, large	sieve, silk
silver knives	silver thing	skillet
skimmer	skimming dish	skimming dish full of holes
soop dish	soop tureen	soup dish, very large coulerd china
soup kettle and cover, large	soup terene with a cover	spoon
spoon, copper or plate	spoon, dessert	spoon, marrow
spoon, table	spoon, tea	stand for middle of table
stew pan	stew pan, broad	stew pan, small
sticks	strainer	strainer, canvas
string	tankards with lids	tea kettle and lamp
tea pot	tea pot, [. . . . .] stone	[tea?] pott, blue and white with a silver spout
tea pot, old brown in the shape of a crab	tea pott, old cracked	tea pot, small old china brown
tea pott, very large brown	[tea?] pott, very small blue with a silver spout	thread
tray for the snuffers	tub	tub, little
tundish	vats, small	vessel
vessel, deep	vessel, earthen	vessel, silver
wafers or papers of any shape you like	water bottle, coarse china	weight
weight, quarter of a hundred	weight, two or three pound	whisk

have changed during the seventeenth and eighteenth centuries, but they also indicate changes in the way in which people described material culture over time, notably an increasing trend towards specification in terms of size, form and composition. However, before continuing in this discussion, some of the challenges of using these sources in this manner must be outlined.

Firstly, a recipe and an inventory are not the same, being compiled for fundamentally different purposes. A recipe book does not necessarily tell us what people owned at a point in time as an inventory does; rather, it tells us what they were expected to own. However, given that these were personal texts, we can be confident that they present a more accurate guide as to what was in the kitchen than published books.[26] An individual may have taken down notes on a recipe which they never subsequently made, but it would be odd for them to have listed a range of expensive items required in their own book if they had no expectation of having access to them. In truth, they are theoretical inventories rather than actual ones. That said, it would be wrong to ignore the information recorded within these books relating to material culture. Food historians have not shied away from using them as sources simply because the food was not necessarily an accurate reflection of everyday meals; they have simply taken cognisance of that fact and used them cautiously.

Secondly, it is difficult to generate a meaningful database of items linking different manuscripts. Many books were kept in use for generations, with the result that the items mentioned in them may demonstrate change over time. Furthermore, as precise dates cannot be ascribed to all entries, it is rarely possible to generate precisely dated lists in the way that it is possible for individually dated inventories. Similarly, recipe books vary dramatically in length. Since some contain merely a handful of recipes, they refer to a few items only. For these reasons, and because these were ultimately profoundly personal items, it is best to interpret any list of material culture within the context of each book and if possible, each house and period in which it was made. With this understanding, we may hope to identify patterns of change from house to house, which are chronologically and socially grounded.

In the account of kitchen artefacts that follows, I have attempted to uncover some broad patterns of change based on the goods mentioned. This is less about quantitative analysis, and more about looking at the way in which people described material culture over time, and what this says about their relationships with those objects. It has been arranged in terms of categories of kitchen tasks: food storage, ingredient measurement, food preparation, cooking and food service.

Food storage

A variety of different types of food storage vessels are mentioned in each of the ten manuscripts, and there is a general consistency in the terms employed to describe them throughout the period. The generic term 'vessel' was commonly used; sometimes with added information regarding material or size, but more specific objects are mentioned as well. Barrels, which are regularly referred to, were used primarily to store alcohol, but stored larger preserved goods like hams as well. Kegs and casks were also used for alcohol storage, but unlike the term barrel, more information is included about their nature. Descriptive terms for casks refer to the type of wood desired, such as oak, or the method of

---

[26] For more on the challenges and the potential uses of published recipe books for the study of material culture see Annie Gray, '"A practical art": an archaeological perspective on the use of recipe books', in DiMeo and Pennell, *Reading & writing recipe books,* 47–67.

manufacture, with some recipes calling for a cask with 'iron hoops'.[27] Other recipes call for casks that are scented or for those suitable for the storage of specific drinks such as sherry or brandy. So, whereas the term 'barrel' appears to have been used as a generic large storage container, 'kegs' and 'casks' are terms which applied to more specialised uses.

Smaller quantities of alcohol and other beverages were stored in bottles, but they were also used to store preserves, pickles and condiments. So, given that bottles were multipurpose small storage containers, more specific advice is often provided to indicate which type was needed. The size and shape of bottles is commonly specified in recipes (such as quart, large, wide mouthed) and sometimes the material that is preferable for a particular recipe is mentioned (such as china, glass, stone). There does not seem to be any remarkable pattern observable here in relation to the recipes themselves, but it is significant that from the later eighteenth century on there is a much wider variety of descriptive terms, with a range of different adjectives applied to bottles from the second-half of the eighteenth century (coarse, china, wide-mouthed, wide-necked, water, glass, stone, quart, large, small). When we consider that seventeenth-century manuscripts rarely employ adjectives for bottles, there is a clear observable pattern here, the meaning of which could be explained in two ways. Firstly, this may be evidence that people had an increasing range of objects in their houses and at their disposal which, given what past studies have shown regarding the proliferation of goods in this period, seems likely.[28] Secondly, this pattern may also demonstrate an increasing fixation with material goods, and a more prescriptive mentality on the part of recipe writers. There was a growing compulsion to specify exactly what type of object should be used, coupled with a raised interest in the different properties of each of the varieties available.

Crocks are another storage item referred to in all the manuscripts and throughout the period under review. They were most commonly associated with butter storage, but they had a variety of other storage uses as well. 'Earthen' is the only descriptive term employed in reference to crocks in seventeenth- and eighteenth-century entries, but by the later eighteenth century they are described both in terms of their composition (earthen, stone), finish (glazed, black-glazed) and form (deep, large, wide-mouthed, closed-mouthed, with cover). So again, there is evidence not only that a greater range may have existed, but also that writers were becoming much more specific. Crocks were also used in cookery, so, like many items, they appear to have been important multifunctional objects in the kitchen. Clare McCutcheon and Roseanne Meenan have discussed the multifunctional use of black-glazed crocks and utilitarian ceramic vessels for storage and preservation purposes in their recent review of domestic pottery. They describe the large black-glazed vessels with heavy rims and horizontal lug handles commonly found on excavations relating

---

[27] NLI, Ms 14,901, Miss (or Mrs) Barnewall, *Collection of domestic recipes and medical prescriptions*, late eighteenth to early nineteenth century, unpaginated.
[28] Weatherill, *Consumer behaviour & material culture*, 44, 155, 205; Johnson, *The archaeology of capitalism*, 179–201.

to this period, citing Dublin Castle as one such example. It is likely that some of the forms mentioned in recipe books correspond to the artefacts found on such sites, both sources informing our understanding of the nature and use of objects in the seventeenth- and eighteenth-century kitchen.[29]

Pots and jars are other frequently mentioned multi-use storage items. Seventeenth-century pots are described as deep, earthen, glass or well-glazed, but the term 'jar' was not employed in manuscripts until the mid- to late eighteenth century. Jars were then described in a variety of ways, including earthen, glazed, large, blue, covered, coloured, small-mouthed, wide-mouthed, stone, sweet and half-pint. Pots from this later period are similarly given a wide range of adjectives relating to their size, material, form and function. 'Gallipots' (also galy pots) are mentioned occasionally as well. These are generally thought of as small earthenware jars for storing ointments and medicine, but as McCutcheon and Meenan have suggested, many were used for food storage as well,[30] and this analysis strongly supports their assessment. Tundishes are also cited throughout the period and, although they are not storage vessels themselves, they were used like a funnel, to fill other containers. Finally, a large variety of vessels and storage containers such as vats, boxes, jugs, pitchers, basins, dishes, pottles, tubs and glasses are encountered. Many of these had a range of functions in the preparation and serving of food. Corks, string, fabric and paper were commonly called upon to seal vessels.

Ingredient measurement

The measurement of ingredients tells us a great deal about the way people used and followed recipes, the cook's assumed skill level, the degree of specification they required, and the level of authority assumed by the author. Units of measurement for weight and volumes such as pounds, ounces, bushels, pints, quarts, gallons, pottles, mutchkins, chopins, naggins and hogsheads were commonly employed. However, the utensils used to measure these amounts are rarely mentioned, although some of the measurement terms were interchangeable as objects in their own right. Physical weights to help measure quantities are referred to very occasionally, but little can be said regarding how frequently they were actually used. The term 'table spoon' is used in seventeenth-century recipes as a unit of measurement, but the term 'tea spoon' does not appear until the mid-eighteenth century. During this period these gradually became formal units of measurement, but it is not clear how standardised they were at this time. Other ingredient quantifications are less formal, but still relatively precise. For example, recipes from the seventeenth and early eighteenth centuries sometimes call for the quantity of spice that

---

[29] Clare McCutcheon and Rosanne Meenan, 'Pots on the hearth: domestic pottery in historic Ireland', *Proceedings of the Royal Irish Academy* 111C (2011), 91–113: 105–06.
[30] McCutcheon and Meenan, 'Pots on the hearth: domestic pottery in historic Ireland', 107.

would cover a shilling. Less precise still are references to generic spoons, cups and glasses, which were not yet standardised measures. Sometimes the recipe quantified the amount of a given ingredient required in terms of cost, such as a penny or shilling's worth of an item, which could have resulted in dramatic variation depending on market fluctuations over time. Finally, recipes from all manuscripts frequently called for 'pinches' and 'handfuls' of an ingredient and for seasoning, spice or sugar simply 'to your taste'.

The principal findings regarding the units and utensils of measurement employed in recipes are that this is a transitional period between a more organic system of quantification, which relied on the cook's discretion and skill, and a modern system which reflected empirical science. The recipes are by no means fully fledged 'modern recipes' with precise measurements for every ingredient, but there was movement in that direction, and terms such as 'tablespoon' and 'teaspoon', which are central to modern cookery, were beginning to appear with increasing regularity. By the mid-Victorian period the changes noticed in this earlier phase had reached their ultimate expression, by which time recipes had become much more prescriptive and authoritative; less knowledge was assumed and more commands and instructions were given.

Food preparation

Common kitchen tasks such as mixing, whisking and whipping are mentioned frequently without guidance being provided regarding the specific utensils that should be used. Presumably, it was obvious what one should use to mix a batter and so on. There are some references to mixing and whisking utensils; these include spoons (sometimes wooden, but also metal), whisks and interestingly, twigs and sticks. The mention of organic objects is particularly important as these are largely undetectable archaeologically, and were too disposable to be mentioned in an inventory or similar historical document. It would also be interesting to know how often hands were used for tasks such as mixing as opposed to utensils, but the absence of specification makes this question difficult to answer.

Chopping, cutting and slicing are again common kitchen tasks for which you may expect a variety of related objects to be mentioned. Again, however, these appear to be so commonplace that recipes rarely suggest which items should be used. Knives and boards are mentioned, but are rarely described in more detail. However, in some instances, knives are described as silver, very sharp or thin.

Grinding and crushing were also important tasks in the kitchen. Mortars and pestles were used to grind a variety of ingredients, including sugar (which was still sold as solid sugarloaves), spices, herbs and nuts (usually almonds). Mortars and pestles were also vital in the preparation of medicines. Mortars are described as both stone and marble, but little more information is provided. Mills are mentioned and were also used to process hard ingredients. It is notable that chocolate mills are mentioned in one late seventeenth-century to early eighteenth-century manuscript, since chocolate was still a relatively new luxury ingredient at the time.[31]

A variety of vessels, many of which were multifunctional, were used to prepare and mix food. It is difficult to establish to what extent certain terms are interchangeable, but they include basons (basins), bowls, dishes and pans. Once again, size (deep, shallow, large, 'common sized slop'[32]); material (wood, earthen, pewter, silver, brass, china); and quality (fine, coarse) are sometimes specified, depending on the recipe and the task at hand. For example, metal bowls made out of materials like brass, pewter and copper react with acidic ingredients, so earthenware was preferable for some recipes. Similarly, metal can be advantageous when whisking egg whites, so it is specifically recommended in other instances. It should be noted that, as observed in other categories thus far, the same pattern of increasing specification in respect to materials, size and form, from the later eighteenth-century on, is noticed in relation to these mixing vessels.

A variety of moulds from the eighteenth century are also listed. These were used to set the various sweet jellies and creams which were popular and fashionable dishes at the time. Moulds may also have held savoury dishes such as terrines, and they demonstrate the fashions for elaborate food presentation. Little information is included in respect of the shape and materials of the moulds themselves, but copper is specified on occasion.

Cloth was used for a wide variety of food preparation tasks and must have been a very common kitchen material. The kinds of tasks in which it was used include straining liquids, cleaning foodstuffs, rubbing during the salting and curing process, holding and steaming puddings, and cheese making. It was also used in storage to form bags and covers for vessels. Sometimes a recipe simply called for the use of a generic 'cloth' or 'rag', but additional information is given in some instances. From the mid-eighteenth century the type of fabric is sometimes specified, including muslin, linen, flannel, crêpe or canvas. In other instances, the quality or texture of the fabric is specified, such as very coarse, coarse, very thick or fine. Sometimes a specific object made of cloth is called for, such as a bag made from a particular type of fabric, a napkin or a salting glove. The criteria specified related to the task for which the cloth/cloth item was needed. For example, fine muslin would be employed when a liquid needed to be carefully sieved, whereas a coarse cloth was more ideal for rubbing salt into hams. Finally, different types of thread or string were used for a variety of tasks, including binding and stuffing meat, tying up bunches of herbs, and sealing containers for storage, amongst a myriad of other uses. The frequency with which cloth and string are mentioned is important, because they are the type of relatively cheap materials that are seldom mentioned in sources such as

---

[31] NLI, Ms 14,786, Inchiquin Papers, A collection of domestic recipes and medical prescriptions 'started by Lady Frances Keightley about 1660', mid- to late seventeenth century, 3.

[32] NLI, Ms 14,901, Miss (or Mrs) Barnewall, Collection of domestic recipes and medical prescriptions, late eighteenth to early nineteenth century, unpaginated.

inventories, and they are rarely visible in the archaeological record. This means that manuscript recipe books give us a much more detailed image of the types of objects always within reach of the cook than we would otherwise be aware of.

Cloth was not the only object used to strain liquids and dishes. Colanders ('cullenders'), strainers and a variety of different types of sieves were used to the same end. 'Cullenders' are sometimes described as earthen, and strainers as cotton, canvas or thin. Sieves are described in more detail as fine, coarse, hair, silk, wire and rod, all of which were called upon in different instances. Once again, the material and quality specified related to the task at hand.

Paper was another very commonly used material in the kitchen and it fulfilled a variety of functions. It could seal containers for storage, form a makeshift lid during cooking, line baking tins and be used as a baking case itself. A variety of different qualities of papers are mentioned, these include fine, white, brown, writing, coarse, strong, brandy and stiff card. Paper bags were also mentioned and were used in similar tasks to fabric bags.

Like cloth and paper, a variety of other organic and naturally occurring materials are mentioned throughout the manuscripts. Organic membranes such as bladders and leather are referred to regularly, and were used for many of the same tasks as the different fabrics. Twigs, sticks and rods were frequently used to mix and whisk. Even bunches of feathers were used on occasion, when extra care was needed in stirring things. Finally, straw, sand and pebbles were used, often in preserving and curing, or to help store perishables safely. References to the use of these naturally occurring and organic materials is significant, in that it helps to create a more detailed image of the contents of seventeenth- and eighteenth-century kitchens. Traditional archaeological evidence and more formal documents rarely provide evidence of these types of objects.

Another category of objects frequently mentioned in relation to food preparation are bodkins, needles, pins and skewers. These had a range of uses, but were commonly employed to test the ripeness of fruits and nuts. Multiple recipes explain that if a pin could be pushed through the centre of the fruit or nut, then it was ready to be used.

Finally, one particularly interesting object involved in food preparation mentioned in the late seventeenth- to early eighteenth-century is a 'drudging box' (dredging box).[33] These were small boxes with a perforated lid that contained breadcrumbs or seasoned flour which could be sprinkled over the top of roasting joints of meat (Pl. IV). It was a method which was rarely used before the start of the eighteenth century,[34] so the mention of this item in a manuscript of this age demonstrates that the kitchen was fitted with up-to-date and fashionable utensils. This same manuscript also contained a reference to a chocolate mill at a relatively early date.

---

[33] NLI, Ms 14,786, Inchiquin Papers, A collection of domestic recipes and medical prescriptions 'started by Lady Frances Keightley about 1660', mid- to late seventeenth century, 8.

[34] Sara Pennell, '"Pots and pans history": the material culture of the kitchen in early modern England', *Journal of Design History* 11:3 (1998), 201–16: 209.

PL. IV—Eighteenth-century brass dredger. © Madeline Shanahan.

Cooking

As we would expect, vessels which needed to withstand the heat of the fire, oven or stove were made of metal or were ceramic. Metal cookware mentioned in recipes throughout the period, from the late seventeenth century on, includes pots ('bellmattle', brass, tin); skillets (small, great, large, copper, brass); griddles; stewpans (broad, small); saucepans; cauldrons; a variety of pans (preserving, frying, brass, tin); and kettles. Fish kettles and omelette (omelet) pans are mentioned only from the mid-eighteenth century, and demonstrate the development of more specialised, highly functionalised forms in the kitchen. Ceramic cookware forms mentioned include earthen pans, crocks, pipkins, and pots in a variety of sizes, colours and finishes.

Vessels and items used for baking specifically are also mentioned. What we would think of as cake tins today were generally called 'shapes' in the manuscripts of this period. These shapes were commonly made out of tin. Copper and tin baking trays or 'sheets' are also mention, as are 'bisket' pans and patty pans, which were used to bake small cakes.

Food service

Given that recipe books focus more on food preparation than on serving, they provide considerably less information on tableware. However, a few types of vessels are described and the findings are consistent with past studies of such objects undertaken by historical archaeologists in Britain.[35] Various vessels such as plates, dishes, trenchers, platters, basons, bowls, ewers, tureens and porringers were used to serve food. However, the references to them

---

[35] Johnson, *The archaeology of capitalism,* 179–202.

demonstrate that many of these terms could be used to refer to multiple, different items. The term 'dish', in particular, filled a variety of functions, being used to prepare, cook and store food. However, while 'dish' may be a general, 'catch-all' term, dishes were not all the same, and they were certainly not used for all purposes. Dishes made out of expensive materials such as silver, pewter and china are listed as serving vessels. Additional details regarding the size, shape and also the colour of ceramic dishes are sometimes provided. Occasionally, the exact food to be served in a dish is specified, so we see butter, soup, trifle and 'sallat' (salad) dishes mentioned from the seventeenth century. Lobster and stew dishes are mentioned in the eighteenth century. A variety of differently sized, shaped and coloured bowls are indicated too; these include cheney (decorated earthenware), and fruit and punch bowls from the mid-eighteenth century. The variety of different types of dishes with specific descriptions increased significantly over the period.

Glasses are another type of serving vessel which is mentioned frequently. They were used to hold a variety of jelly- and cream-based desserts, as well as beverages. 'Jelly glasses' and 'wine glasses' are specifically referred to throughout the period. Silver tankards and goblets are also mentioned, but relate specifically to alcohol consumption.

Chafing dishes were important for ensuring that food arrived to the dining room hot after the sometimes long journey from the kitchen. They also kept the food hot for the length of the meal itself. The manuscripts reviewed here provide little information regarding the material these dishes were made from, but excavated evidence can provide some answers. McCutcheon and Meenan state that ceramic chafing dishes were common from the sixteenth century and were still in use in the seventeenth century. However, there is evidence that metal forms of chafing dishes were in demand from the later seventeenth century.[36]

A variety of utensils for serving food at the table and types of cutlery have been identified. Ladles are referred to throughout the period and particular forms include punch ladles and soup ladles, which are specifically mentioned from the late seventeenth century. Silver cutlery forms such as spoons and knives are mentioned throughout the period, but forks only appear from the eighteenth century. This is consistent with our understanding of when forks came to be used regularly. Bríd Mahon has suggested that despite their earlier adoption elsewhere, they only came to be used in high-status Irish houses from the early eighteenth century.[37] Specific forms of forks are also mentioned from the mid- to late eighteenth century, including dessert, oyster, silver and small forks. Fish, oyster and dessert knives are also mentioned in this same period. There was an even greater variety of spoons, including dessert, marrow, butter, dinner, dishing, egg, gravy, salt and soup spoons.

---

[36] McCutcheon and Meenan, 'Pots on the hearth: domestic pottery in historic Ireland', 107.

[37] Bríd Mahon, *Land of milk and honey: the story of traditional Irish food and drink* (Dublin, 1991), 8.

The emergence of a suite of highly specific serving ware utensils can also be traced over the course of the period in question. While highly specialised tableware such as sauce boats are mentioned in seventeenth-century entries, by the mid-eighteenth century we encounter items such as artichoke cups, asparagus tongs, plates with covers for fish kettles, egg cups and butter boats. Again, this is in keeping with studies which argue that these proliferated in the Georgian period.[38]

Finally, a suite of items associated with tea and coffee, including teacups, saucers, teapots, teaspoons, coffee pots, coffee urns and coffee cups can be identified. Chocolate pots, and chocolate cups and saucers are also mentioned, although less frequently. The early reference to these is interesting because these items and the beverages they were used to serve were relatively new and important luxuries at this time. Identifying the early use of them is significant, particularly as these became hugely important parts of class culture over the next century. Here we see their early use and absorption into the foodways of elite society, at a household and profoundly personal level.

Discussion

Manuscript recipe books are a rich and varied source for the study of food-related material culture in the Restoration and Georgian periods. They can be used to create detailed lists of objects, and to inform us about how those items were used, their multiple functions within the kitchen, the proliferation of forms over time and, significantly, the range of organic, cheap and natural materials that do not show up in excavations or inventories.

Across the categories of objects mentioned, a consistent pattern emerged. Over the course of the eighteenth century recipes mention a wider variety of goods, and they apply more adjectives and descriptive terminology to the goods that are required. This is consistent with a detailed study of seventeenth- and eighteenth-century probate inventories from the United States of America, made by Mary Beaudry. Her study concluded that terms for food-related objects were modified according to their function (mustard pot, posset pot, teapot and so on) with greater frequency by the middle of the eighteenth century in inventories.[39]

The pattern identified in Ireland shows that there was an increasing range of goods at the cook's disposal, and perhaps more importantly, that the increasingly prescriptive terminology employed indicates that the authors were becoming more aware of the range of utensils, and more authoritative in their writing. This change can be interpreted in several ways. Firstly, it has been argued elsewhere that recipes became more authoritative and prescriptive generally, in this period, as there was an increasing loss of culinary knowledge within the house. As a result, cooks began to learn their skills from books

---

[38] Weatherill, *Consumer behaviour & material culture in Britain*, 38–41; Shackel, *Personal discipline and material culture*; Leone, 'Ceramics from Annapolis', 195–216.

[39] Mary C. Beaudry, 'Words for things: linguistic analysis of probate inventories', in Mary C. Beaudry (ed.), *Documentary archaeology in the New World* (Cambridge, 1988), 43–50.

rather than by apprenticeship, and so more instruction was required. This change was supposedly intensified as more and more mistresses took a less active role in the kitchen, and manuals stepped in to take on their instructive duties.[40] As discussed at the start of this paper, as the idealised gender role of the passive and genteel housewife emerged, upper-class women were increasingly urged to distance themselves from 'front-line' duty in the kitchen, and so writing took on a new significance in the management of their homes. In this context we might expect an increasing need for specification in recipe writing, as mistresses could not indicate their precise commands through active demonstration. Usually, this argument is put forward in relation to an increase in precise measurements and more instructions,[41] but the same could apply to more prescriptive language surrounding equipment as well.

While this is interesting, and may have been a factor, I believe that both the proliferation of recipe books, and their increasing exactitude had less to do with a genuine need for instruction, and more to do with a changing relationship with food and material culture, which was in many ways profoundly modern. The recipe books themselves helped to promote modern cuisine, but the conscious fixation with food, the need to write about, define, measure, categorise and standardise it, is both significant and meaningful. We can also look at changes in the way recipes were written as symptomatic of a standardising impulse and a heightened fixation with objects at this time. This interpretation is supported by the work of other historical archaeologists, who have examined a range of different categories of material culture and alternative genres of writing connected to them. For example, inventories and etiquette guides have been interpreted as genres which display a heightened concern with tracing and categorising goods in the first instance, and telling people precisely how to relate to them in the second.[42] These past conceptualisations are crucial to understanding changes in the way recipes were written and how objects are described. In short, the descriptive terms used, and precision which emerged, do not necessarily tell us that cooks did not know what they were doing, but they do tell us that the writer, who was commonly the mistress of the house, was exhibiting greater authority and was more concerned with the cook's methods and precise actions. Whether it was necessary or not, the mistress, who was strongly influenced by published models, increasingly felt the need to mediate the relationship between the cook, the food and the utensils involved in its preparation. In this sense, these manuscripts show us not only that food-related forms of material culture proliferated from the eighteenth century on, but also, and more importantly, that people were more aware of goods and how they should be used, and they articulated and formalised this increasingly.

---

[40] Lehmann, *The British housewife,* 156

[41] Eileen White, 'Domestic English cookery and cookery books, 1575–1675', in Eileen White (ed.), *The English cookery book: historical essays,* Leeds Symposium on Food History: 'Food and Society' Series (Totnes, Devon, 2004), 72–97: 91.

[42] Johnson, *The archaeology of capitalism,* 112.

The consumption and sociable use of alcohol in eighteenth-century Ireland

JAMES KELLY*

Department of History, St Patrick's College, Dublin City University

[Accepted 28 April 2015. Published 19 June 2015.]

Abstract

A tabulation of the amount of duty-paid spirits, wine and beer produced in and imported into Ireland is the starting point for any engagement with the consumption and sociable use of alcohol in Ireland in the eighteenth century. Since a large volume of whiskey and beer, upon which duty was not paid, was also consumed, alcohol was inevitably a subject of much critical contemporary comment. Yet there is another perspective, which is more in keeping with the reality of a world in which alcohol was integral to domestic as well as public life. This paper engages with this subject in two parts. The first seeks, using official figures as its point of departure, to quantify the volume of duty-paid alcohol (specifically spirits, wine and beer) in circulation, and the pattern of illicit distillation. It also seeks to identify the retail structures that merchants, grocers and others evolved in order to meet public demand. The second part engages with consumption. A large proportion of the wine that was imported was consumed in a domestic setting. This was consistent with the view that, consumed in moderation, it was not only an aid to nutrition but also possessed of tangible medicinal benefits. In the public realm, alcohol was imbibed in the inns, taverns, alehouses and dram shops that were to be found in every part of the country. It was also integral to the commemorative, celebratory calendar of the Protestant elite and the popular calendar of the masses. However, it was alcohol's augmented usefulness in the political realm from the 1750s, and its centrality to the rapidly expanding world of male sociability that enabled it to play a central role both as a social lubricant and as a means of forging political and organisational commitment during the remainder of the century.

Introduction

The volume and variety of forms in which alcohol was available are the most tangible evidence of the central place it occupied in Irish life in the eighteenth century. This has generally been portrayed in negative terms. Even before Fr Theobald Mathew embarked in the 1830s on his culturally defining temperance crusade, there was a strong current of commentary—religious, sociological, economic and political—that advanced or echoed the opinion that the patterns

* Author's e-mail: james.kelly@spd.dcu.ie
doi: 10.3318/PRIAC.2015.115.14

of alcohol consumption pursued in Ireland were socially deleterious.[1] Its identification with poverty, violence and anti-social conduct ensured that alcohol was a compelling target for those who promulgated a vision of an improved and economically productive society populated by polite and mannered subjects. Encouraged by this vision, opinion formers at local as well as national level advocated intervention as a means of regulating consumption, and if parliament and the Revenue tended for fiscal reasons to be more reticent, municipal officers, MPs and peers were increasingly disposed from the 1770s to give statutory expression to the contention that regulation would ameliorate the heavy consumption of spirits by the 'lower classes'.[2] The consumption patterns of the elite did not pass unnoticed either as commentators as diverse as Samuel Madden (Fig. 1), George Berkeley and William Henry drew on traditional religious values, the virtues of improvement and the culture of politeness in order to elaborate a powerful condemnation of the patterns of alcohol consumption that were normative in Irish life. However, there is another perspective, which has been overlooked amidst the tsunami of criticism that prevailed in the public sphere. Implicit in the actions of the many who raised a glass either to the 'Glorious Memory' or to 'The Pretender', of those who participated in political gatherings in which toasting was *de rigeur*, and of those who raised a glass on the still more numerous occasions in which people dined in company was an acknowledgement that alcohol was integral to the forms of sociability and the patterns of association that shaped and defined how people interacted in the eighteenth century. This was certainly facilitated by the gustatory, social and mood-altering pleasures it afforded, but it was not the only consideration. Alcohol was a standard accompaniment with meals; while people of all ages and rank, persuaded of its therapeutic value, ingested it as a medicine.

Availability of alcohol: volume and varieties

The import and export figures assembled by Samuel Morewood are a useful starting point to any attempt to establish the order of alcohol consumption in eighteenth-century Ireland.[3] Taking 1720—the second year of Morewood's series—as a starting point and spirits as the focus, duty was paid on 463,157

---

[1] See Elizabeth Malcolm, *Ireland sober, Ireland free: drink and temperance in nineteenth-century Ireland* (Dublin, 1986), 21–55 for an excellent account.
[2] E. B. McGuire, *Irish whiskey: a history of distilling in Ireland* (Dublin, 1973), 91–212 passim; Patrick Given, 'Calico to whiskey: a case study of the development of the distilling industry in the Naas revenue collection district, 1700–1921', unpublished PhD thesis, National University of Ireland, Maynooth, 2011, 66–118.
[3] Samuel Morewood, *A philosophical and statistical history of the inventions and customs of ancient and modern nations in the manufacture and use of inebriating liquors* (Dublin, 1838), 726. Others, notably L. A. Clarkson and E. Margaret Crawford, have tabulated the 'retained imports into Ireland' in wine (tuns) and spirits (gallons) based upon the Ledgers of import and exports, Ireland (CUST15) in The National Archives (TNA). Their table does not allow one to distinguish between domestically produced and imported alcohol: Clarkson and Crawford, *Feast and famine: food and nutrition in Ireland 1500–1920* (Oxford, 2001), 53–5.

Fig. 1—Portrait of Reverend Samuel Madden, by James Brocas, *c.* 1754–80. Reproduced by permission of the National Library of Ireland.

gallons of spirits, 30% (136,075 gallons) of which was domestically distilled and 70% (327,082 gallons) of which was imported.[4] A majority of the duty-paid spirit traded, and consumed, in Ireland was of foreign origin until the late 1770s when the combination of a decline in the availability of foreign produce and a surge in whiskey production signalled the commencement of a phase that was to long endure, when Irish-produced whiskey predominated (see Table 1 and Fig. 2). Unsurprisingly, the primary stimulus of this growth was domestic demand.

---

[4] The precise figures are 29.4% and 70.62% calculated from the data provided in Morewood, *A philosophical and statistical history*, 720.

TABLE 1—Irish alcohol, 1721–1820: spirits (in gallons)—official figures (per quinquennium).

Dates	Volume distilled		Volume imported		Volume exported		Adjusted annual average[a]
	Five-year total	Yearly average	Five-year total	Yearly average	Irish: five-year total	Foreign: five-year total	
1721–5	657 074	131 415	1 801 989	360 398	–	–	491 813
1726–30	807 477	161 496	2 110 064	422 013	–	–	583 509
1731–5	1 062 084	212 417	1 713 606	342 721	–	–	555 138
1736–40	1 092 179	218 436	2 642 141	528 428	–	–	746 864
1741–5	1 729 267	345 854	2 287 651	457 530	–	–	803 384
1746–50	2 431 862	486 372	2 593 609	518 722	–	–	1 005 094
1751–5	2 877 137	575 427	5 311 892	1 062 378	–	–	1 637 805
1756–60	1 616 874	323 375	4 857 317	971 463	–	–	1 294 834
1761–5	3 170 182	634 036	7 504 131	1 500 826	–	–	2 134 862
1766–70	3 294 285	658 857	12 723 812	2 544 762	–	–	3 203 619
1771–5	4 459 447	891 823	11 327 010	2 265 402	330	213 364[b]	3 114 552
1776–80	5 726 247	1 145 247	8 869 812	1 749 158	10	124 024	2 894 405
1781–5	8 522 583	1 704 517	6 045 037	1 209 008	6 837	134 301	2 885 297
1786–90	11 767 754	2 353 551	7 113 479	1 422 696	1 277	109 111	3 754 169
1791–5	18 663 157	3 732 632	3 815 362	763 072	1 874	104 847	4 474 360
1796–1800	20 230 494	4 046 099	1 075 470	215 094	69 904	53 520	4 236 508
1801–05	20 935 789	4 187 158	5 302 359	1 060 472	3 487 177	701 844	4 409 826
1806–10	18 943 044	3 788 609	3 840 458	768 092	1 913 900	399 819	4 093 957
1811–15	23 501 303	4 700 261	3 405 928	681 186	2 428 327	1 586 535	4 578 754
1816–20	20 999 221	4 199 844	674 962	134 992	674 962	418 792	4 116 086

Source: Samuel Morewood, *A philosophical and statistical history of the inventions and customs of ancient and modern nations in the manufacture and use of inebriating liquors* (Dublin, 1838), 726–7.

[a] This figure has been generated by adding the average of the totals of domestically distilled and imported spirits, minus, where the figures are available, the volume of exported spirits.

[b] Export figures are only available from 1772.

During the 1720s, 1730s and 1740s the volume of duty paid on domestically produced and imported spirits both sustained an unspectacular upwards trajectory. The five-year averages presented in Table 1[5] suggest that the volume

---

[5] The preferred temporal measure employed to date has been the decade. The decennial totals generated by Malcolm, *Ireland sober, Ireland free*, 22ff have been cited and used by S. J. Connolly, Toby Barnard and Breandán Mac Suibhne, and her summation that 'during the 1720s … duty was paid on some 5.2 million gallons of spirit, 5.3 million barrels of beer and 12.4 million gallons of wine' has informed the conclusion that alcohol consumption was high. Connolly has described the wine figure as 'astonishing' (*Religion, law and power: the making of Protestant Ireland 1660–1760* (Oxford, 1992), 66); Barnard terms it 'startling' ('Integration or separation? Hospitality and display in Protestant Ireland, 1660–1800', in Laurence Brockliss and David Eastwood (eds), *A union of multiple identities: the British Isles c. 1750–c. 1850* (Manchester, 1997), 137). It has also shaped Breandán Mac Suibhne's interpretation: 'Spirit, spectre, shade: a true story of an Irish haunting or troublesome pasts in the political culture of north-west Ulster 1786–1972', *Field Day Review* 9 (2013), 154–7, and Table 1. By my calculations, duty-paid wine imports in the 1720s amounted to 12.257 million gallons (see Table 1),

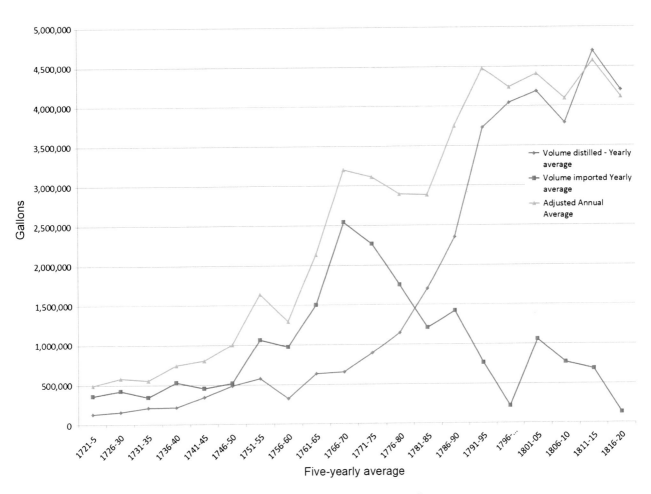

FIG. 2—Ireland's alcohol consumption, 1721–1820: duty-paid spirits (gallons).

of duty-paid spirits rose from just below half a million gallons per annum in the early 1720s to a million gallons in the late 1740s. This increase mirrored broader improvements in the economy,[6] and it is notable that, as well as a significant increase in domestic production, the 'strong upsurge' in economic activity that occurred in the second half of the 1740s sustained the surge in spirit imports, already a decade old, which peaked in the second half of the 1760s when the annual average volume of imported spirits exceeded 2.5 million gallons. The level of demand remained vigorous for several decades thereafter though the

---

which, assuming there were 200,000 wine consumers, amounted to a less than remarkable 1.3 pints (or *c.* 1 bottle a day). Decennial figures tend by reason of their order to encourage the conclusion that Ireland was gripped by a major alcohol problem; I think the evidence is more ambiguous.

[6] See L. M. Cullen, 'Problems in and sources for the study of economic fluctuations 1660–1800', *Irish Economic and Social History* 41 (2014), 8, 18; L. M. Cullen, 'The Irish food crises of the early 1740s; the economic conjuncture', *Irish Economic and Social History* 37 (2010), 1–23.

trajectory was now downwards, as it coincided with record levels of domestic production, which had embarked on a phase of rapid growth in the 1760s. At nearly 4.5 million gallons, domestic spirit production during the five years of 1771–5 accounted for 28% of the total volume of spirits (15.78 million gallons) upon which duty was paid. A decade later, fuelled by a fall in imports and by the Revenue Commissioners' realisation that it was more efficient (from a revenue-raising perspective) to concentrate production in a smaller number of large capacity stills, domestically produced duty-paid spirits exceeded imports.[7] During the quinquennium of 1781–5 more than half (58.5%) of the spirits upon which duty was paid (14.568 million gallons) was home produced, and this trend was sustained. In the late 1790s an imposing 95% of the spirits upon which duty was paid was domestically produced. The volume of spirits imported recovered somewhat in the first decade of the nineteenth century but it was insufficient to alter the balance, as domestic production now comfortably exceeded importation (Table 1; Fig. 2).

Because a proportion (usually small but as high as 46% in 1811–15) of imported foreign spirits was re-exported (see Table 1), the underlying increase in the consumption of duty-paid spirits was less striking than the gross figures suggest, but annual consumption more than doubled, from *c.* 2.1 to *c.* 4.5 million gallons, between the late 1760s and the early 1790s (Table 1). This was not the full story, however. The efficiency with which the revenue service enforced the regulations favouring bigger stills and, by decreeing, first (1732), that licenced producers must be located proximate to, and subsequently (1758) within 'market towns', created an environment in which illicit distillation flourished.[8] It has been conjectured that drunkenness and illicit distillation emerged as a problem together in the second half of the eighteenth century,[9] but, if so, reports from the middle decades of the century to the Revenue

---

[7] McGuire, *Irish whiskey*, 128–34; Malcolm, *Ireland sober, Ireland free*, 23.

[8] Legislation approved in 1758 (31 George II, chap. 6) raised the minimum size of stills to 200 gallons, while greater rebates were offered in 1779 to those with a capacity of over 1,000 gallons (19 and 20 George III, chap. 12). One compelling index of the efficacy of the Revenue Commissioners, and of the impact of regulation on the production of spirits is provided by the decline in the number of licensed stills. According to evidence given to the House of Commons in 1791, the number declined from 1,212 in 1781 to 246 in 1790: *The parliamentary register, of history of the proceedings and debates of the House of Commons of Ireland* (17 vols, Dublin, 1782–1801), vol. xi, 73. The figures assembled by Patrick Given from papers submitted to parliament show some variation from these, but they confirm the trend, and they demonstrate that the pattern of decline continued; by 1800 the number of licensed stills stood at 165, and it had fallen further, to 51, by 1806: Given, 'Calico to whiskey', 200. See McGuire, *Irish whiskey*, 127–32; 5 George II, chap 3, section 13; 11 and 12 George II, chap 3; Malcolm, *Ireland sober, Ireland free*, 23; Minutes of the Revenue Commissioners, 23 February 1733, 17 September 1744, and 10 February and 1 April 1748 (TNA, CUST/1/25, f. 53, 1/38 ff 3, 9, 55v, 1/44 ff 32, 93); Aidan Manning, *Donegal poitín: a history* (Letterkenny, 2003); K. H. Connell, 'Illicit distillation', in Connell, *Irish peasant society* (Oxford, 1968), 1–50.

[9] Mac Suibhne, 'Spirit, spectre, shade: a true story', 154–7.

Commissioners indicate that illicit production was already entrenched. The account conveyed in 1748 by an officer located in the Sligo district of 'some distillers who carry on a clandestine trade ... removing their stills to the mountains' demonstrates that the cat and mouse game in which they were long joined was already under way, but since there were 'upwards of 150 private stills' in that district at that time, and the seizure of 'unstatutable' stills was commonplace, it can be concluded that ('illicit') whiskey was readily available.[10] This is not to suggest that the 1758 act, and the energy with which it was applied, did not push many distillers into illegality, but it served to intensify a trend that was already in being and not to inaugurate a new one.[11] The report of William Parsons, who had charge of the Augher revenue walk in mid-Ulster in 1759, that whiskey was 'the liquor mostly used there, [and] with which the people are supplied in great abundance by sixteen stills, or more, which work in the glinns of the mountain between Augher and Fivemiletown' (both in County Tyrone) is another pointer to its pervasiveness. Parsons could identify, based on visible smoke trails, the proximate locations of these stills, but he was unable to get close 'enough to make a full discovery' because he was prevented from doing so by the 'people in arms'.[12] Others officers had comparable experiences, for though the application of the law progressively reduced the number of enterprises producing spirits legally,[13] demand was sufficient to sustain a vigorous pattern of illicit distilling in rural and in increasingly remote locations.[14]

Clandestine distilling probably accounted for the bulk of the 'illicit' whiskey produced in rural Ireland, but one did not have to be unlicensed in order to produce whiskey upon which duty was not paid. The testimony of the distillers, who gave evidence to a parliamentary inquiry in 1805, that they declared only half their production, not only implies that illicit production was then island-wide, but also that its volume may have equalled that of its 'legal' equivalent.[15] In any event, the conclusion based upon official figures that 'Irish spirit consumption in 1790 was made up of 66% whiskey, 26% rum, 6% brandy

---

[10] Minutes of the Revenue Commissioners, 27 February 1748 and 11 December 1756 (TNA, CUST, 1/44 f. 50, 1/59 f. 84v); *Public Gazetteer*, 30 July and 9 August 1763, and 3 May 21 October and 15 November 1766.

[11] Minutes of the Revenue Commissioners, 20 March, 7 July, 9 August and 11 September 1758 (TNA, CUST, 1/59 f.126v, 1/62 ff 59, 95v, 129v).

[12] Minutes of the Revenue Commissioners, 19 October 1759 (TNA, CUST, 1/63 ff 144v-5).

[13] Sixteen stills were seized by the gauger of Naas district, in Trim and Naas districts in the summer of 1759, for example: TNA, CUST1/63 f. 110.

[14] Manning, *Donegal poitín*, 105–19; Connell, 'Illicit distillation', 1–50; McGuire, *Irish whiskey*, 388–408. For evidence of the endurance of illicit distillation into the 1790s and beyond on the eastern seaboard see: *Dublin Morning Post*, 1 June 1790; *Ennis Chronicle*, 2 February, 20 April and 14 May 1801. It was much more commonplace in County Clare, for example: see the *Ennis Chronicle*, 14 July and 22 December 1796; 19, 22 and 26 January, 2, 9 and 23 February, 23 March and 25 June 1801.

[15] Malcolm, *Ireland sober, Ireland free*, 30.

and 1% gin' is built on insecure foundations. Yet, it does offer some statistical support for claims that increased whiskey production fuelled the surge in spirit consumption that was then taking place. The fact that the respective figures for duty-paid spirits in 1770 were 51% rum, 25% whiskey, 14% brandy and 10% gin is revealing of its impact on consumption patterns.[16]

From the perspective of the sundry moralists, divines, improvers and concerned commentators troubled by these trends, it would have been beneficial if the population replaced whiskey with beer, ale or porter. Each possessed champions, but the pursuit of private and unlicensed brewers by the Revenue and the disadvantageous regulatory environment that had existed since the beginning of the century had taken a heavy toll. As a result, the volume of beer brewed domestically per quinquennium only once exceeded three million barrels in the course of the eighteenth century.[17] The fact that annual production barely exceeded 400,000 barrels per annum in the 1780s (when spirits production surged) indicates that it possessed only modest appeal for the mass of the population which drove the increased demand for Irish whiskey, or for those with more refined palates who accounted for the bulk of the foreign spirits and wines that were consumed. Nor did the enhanced availability of better-quality English imports, which were heavily advertised in the press in the final quarter of the century,[18] alter the picture much. The volume of imported English ales, beers and porter remained modest, exceeding 50,000 barrels per quinquennium for the first time in the early 1770s, and 100,000 barrels for the first time in the early 1790s (Table 2; Fig. 3). Since beer travelled badly, it is tempting to assume that large households and institutions brewed for their own use. Some did, but the observation by a well-informed visitor in 1792 that 'the brewing regulations make it so difficult … that even in great families it is rarely attempted' suggests otherwise.[19] Moreover, the fact that consumption remained at or about half a million barrels annually between the mid-1760s and late 1780s, when the constant endorsement of the virtues of brewed alcohol over spirits registered a (modest) improvement (Table 2; Fig. 3), indicates that demand was largely static.

---

[16] Figures from Malcolm, *Ireland sober, Ireland free*, 23.

[17] See TNA, Minutes of the Revenue Commissioners, 20 March 1717, 2 and 23 June 1742, and 18 April, 16 June and 20 October 1748 (TNA, CUST1/13, 48, 1/34 ff 32v, 42, 1/45 f.114v, 1/61 f. 140v, 1/62 f. 42) for the pursuit of unlicensed brewers, and Public Record Office of Northern Ireland (PRONI), Sheffield Papers, T2965/70, Foster to Sheffield, 23 December [1786] for an admission that official regulations discouraged beer production.

[18] See the *Dublin Morning Post*, 3 April 1788, 3 February 1789 and 3 July 1792; *Hibernian Journal*, 21 August 1789, 2 March and 18 July 1791, 5 April 1790, 18 June 1792, 18 May 1795 and below.

[19] C. J. Woods (ed.), 'Charles Abbot's tour of Ireland in 1792', unpublished manuscript, 2014, appendix. I wish to thank Dr Woods for the opportunity to consult this manuscript. The household of the duke of Abercorn at Baronscourt, Co. Tyrone, did engage in brewing; in 1793 the estate agent reported brewing 6,000 gallons of beer at a cost of 7½d a gallon: Clarkson and Crawford, *Feast and famine*, 55.

TABLE 2—Irish alcohol, 1721–1820: beer and ale (in barrels)—official figures (per quinquennium).

| | Volume brewed | | Imports | Exports | |
Dates	Five-year total	Annual average	Five-year average	Five-year average	Adjusted annual average[a]
1721–5	2 760 600	552 120	264	5 745	546 639
1726–30	2 515 198	503 040	515	4 336	499 219
1731–5	2 536 811	507 362	855	5 724	502 493
1736–40	2 326 608	465 322	1 342	3 789	462 875
1741–5	2 618 078	523 616	4 380	3 796	524 200
1746–50	2 729 071	545 814	10 454	4 604	551 664
1751–5	2 963 299	592 660	18 533	5 173	606 020
1756–60	2 525 469	505 094	13 961	4 157	514 898
1761–5	3 025 550	605 110	23 134	4 810	623 434
1766–70	2 687 621	537 524	37 273	4 263	570 534
1771–5	2 246 595	449 319	51 284	2 787	497 816
1776–80	2 277 214	455 443	59 571	1 200	513 814
1781–5	2 191 346	438 269	54 990	1 423	491 836
1786–90	2 014 339	402 868	79 712	1 561	481 019
1791–5	2 646 572	529 315	100 084	1 102	628 297
1796–1800	2 691 604	538 321	44 346	1 327	581 340
1801–05	2 828 914	565 783	8 941	4 947	569 777
1806–09	3 222 124	805 531	1 701	5 163	802 069

Source: Samuel Morewood, *A philosophical and statistical history of the inventions and customs of ancient and modern nations in the manufacture and use of inebriating liquors* (Dublin, 1838), 726–7.
[a] This column is calculated by adding imports to, and subtracting exports from, the five-year average.

The pattern of wine consumption was comparable, though it was held in much higher esteem because it was the alcohol of choice of the gentry and aristocracy. In contrast to their English peers, Irish wine drinkers favoured French over Portuguese and Spanish wine, and claret over port.[20] Anglo–French rivalry meant that the volume of wine imported fluctuated, but the import figures (Table 3; Fig. 4) suggest that the Irish market required between 1 and 1.5 million gallons per annum until the 1790s when imports, and re-exports, reached record levels, and the strong preference hitherto shown for French wines altered.[21] Wine was also smuggled, of course. Louis Cullen has properly cautioned against assuming that it was a major part of the contraband trade, on the grounds that

---

[20] Writing to Lord Fitzwilliam in 1749, Richard Mathew observed 'we here in Ireland drinke but seldome portwine … the French claret has the ascendant here': National Archives of Ireland, Pembroke Estate Papers, 97/46/1/25/69.

[21] French wine commanded 60% of the Irish market in the mid-1770s, and Portuguese wines a further 30%. By the early 1790s the French share of the market had fallen to 40%, and it fell still further, to a modest 8%, by 1815: Malcolm, *Ireland sober, Ireland free*, 28.

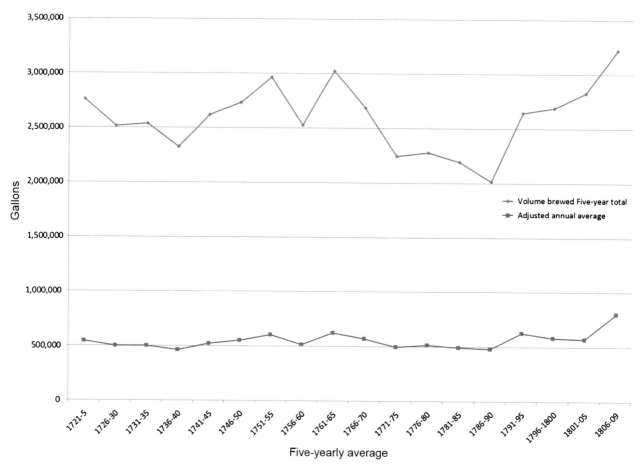

FIG. 3—Ireland's alcohol consumption, 1721–1820: beer (gallons).

'bulky' hogsheads filled with wine were unsuited to surreptitious trading, but this did not discourage all movement of this kind. Wine was certainly a less attractive option for smugglers than brandy, as the seizures reported by Revenue officials attest,[22] but there was a market for those who took the chance, and evidence from the south-west suggests that enough individuals did so to permit the conclusion that some landed families were regularly supplied with quality French wine by

---

[22] Clarkson and Crawford, *Feast and famine*, 53. L. M. Cullen has conjectured that smuggled brandy may have accounted for one-third of spirit consumption between the 1730s and 1770s: 'The smuggling trade in Ireland during the eighteenth century', *Proceedings of the Royal Irish Academy* 67C (1968–9), 169; for examples of brandy seizures, which sustain the point see Minutes of the Revenue Commissioners, 1755–6 (TNA, CUST1/57 ff 6, 7, 20, 16, 19, 30, 49, 82, 92, 1/58 ff 8, 20, 31, 58, 95, 142). A hogshead, which comprised 63 gallons, was one of the standard wine cask units. The others referred to in this paper were a pipe (or butt), which comprised 126 gallons; puncheon, which comprised 84 gallons; a tierce, which comprised 42 gallons, and a barrel or quarter cask, which comprised 31.5 gallons.

TABLE 3—Irish alcohol, 1721–1820: Wine (in gallons)—Official figures (per quinquennium)

Dates	Volume imported		Volume re-exported		
	Five-year total	Yearly average	Five-year total	Adjusted five year volume[a]	Adjusted annual average
1721–5	5 491 524	1 098 305	–	–	–
1726–30	6 766 291	1 353 258	–	–	–
1731–5	5 703 356	1 140 671	–	–	–
1736–40	5 769 102	1 153 820	–	–	–
1741–5	4 815 851	963 170	–	–	–
1746–50	5 529 671	1 105 934	–	–	–
1751–5	7 346 839	1 469 368	–	–	–
1756–60	5 702 163	1 140 433	–	–	–
1761–5	6 857 441	1 371 488	–	–	–
1766–70	7 939 927	1 587 985	–	–	–
1771–5	7 116 640	1 423 328	44 352	7 072 288	1 414 458
1776–80	5 386 147	1 077 230	32 760	5 353 387	1 070 678
1781–5	5 424 052	1 084 811	59 977	5 364 079	1 072 815
1786–90	6 131 002	1 226 201	76 651	6 054 351	1 210 870
1791–5	7 221 981	1 444 352	184 040	7 037 941	1 407 588
1796–1800	9 472 286	1 894 457	188 044	9 284 242	1 856 848
1801–05	9 000 589	1 800 118	352 695	8 647 894	1 729 579
1806–10	8 364 755	1 672 951	673 344	7 691 411	1 538 282
1811–15	5 476 462	1 095 293	1 411 452	4 065 010	813 002
1816–20	3 805 496	761 099	912 240	2 893 256	578 651

Source: Samuel Morewood, *A philosophical and statistical history of the inventions and customs of ancient and modern nations in the manufacture and use of inebriating liquors* (Dublin, 1838), 726–7.
[a] Calculated by subtracting re-exports from the five-year totals.

this means, until targeted interventions by the Revenue upset this traffic.[23] It is likely also that innkeepers and allied retailers, who cultivated the custom and patronage of members of the gentry and middling sort, were also beneficiaries of wine-smuggling, if the recollection of John O'Keeffe (1747–1833), the dramatist, that 'good claret ... was to be had at every thatched ale-house all over the kingdom' possesses even a passing acquaintance with reality.[24]

[23] Malcolm, *Ireland sober, Ireland free*, 30–1; L. M. Cullen, *Anglo–Irish trade, 1660–1800* (Manchester, 1968), 19–20, 139–54; Finola O'Kane, *Ireland and the picturesque: design, landscape painting and tourism in Ireland 1700–1830* (London, 2013), 35, 202; John Ainsworth (ed.), *The Inchiquin manuscripts* (Dublin, 1961), 162; P. Ó Maidin (ed.), 'Pococke's tour of southern and south-west Ireland in 1758', *Journal of the Cork Historical and Archaeological Society* 63 (1958), 86; *Finn's Leinster Journal*, 27 August 1768.
[24] *Recollections of John O'Keeffe* (2 vols, London, 1826), vol. 1, 200; 'Survey of documents in private keeping: Longford papers', *Analecta Hibernica* 15 (1944), 120; *Dublin Morning Post*, 25 November 1794.

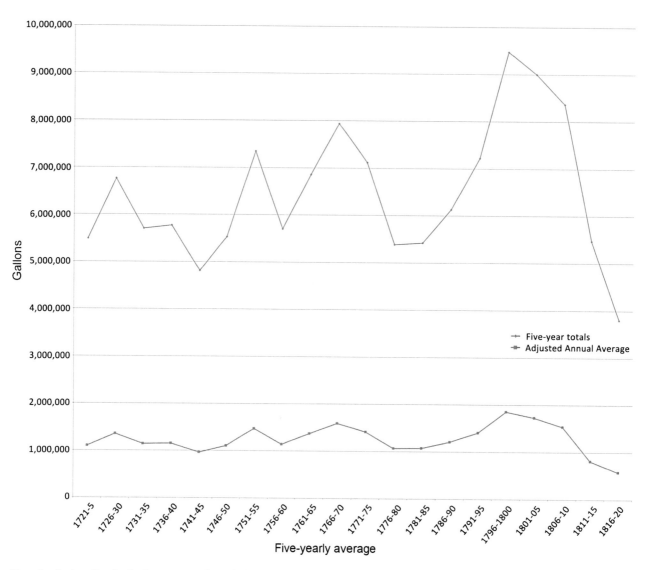

Fig. 4—Ireland's alcohol consumption, 1721–1820: wine imports (gallons).

While the trade in and production of alcohol provide a framework within which the consumption and sociable use of alcohol can be placed, it is necessary to move beyond the figures in order to identify patterns of consumption. This is less than entirely straightforward for though one may locate pertinent contemporary observations, such as those offered by Charles Abbot, the future chief secretary who visited Ireland in 1792, that 'whiskey is the constant drink ... [of] the lower class' in support of this conclusion, whiskey drinking was not exclusive to individuals of this rank.[25] A comparable reservation may be entered with respect to Elizabeth Malcolm's imaginative attempt to calculate per capita wine consumption at the end of the Napoleonic

---

[25] Woods, *Charles Abbot's tour of Ireland in 1792*, appendix.

era. Based on the assumption that the number of wine consumers mirrored that of the 'number of borough and county electors'—220,000, or *c.* 3.2% of the population—Malcolm proposes 'a per capita consumption of five gallons per annum at the very least', which she concludes was 'substantial'. This seems reasonable by modern standards, but it is well in excess of L. A. Clarkson and E. Margaret Crawford's calculation that the pattern of wine consumption among the elite followed an upwards graph from 14 pints per person per annum in 1700 to 24 pints in 1750 only to fall back to 13 pints by 1800.[26] The truth is we are insufficiently informed of the patterns and habits of consumption to sustain much more than general conclusions as to who consumed what. Moreover, conclusions based upon the volumes presented in Tables 1–3 to the effect that consumption was at a (damagingly) high level across Irish society may well be wide of the mark if, as can be argued, consumption was not only less strictly socially determined than it is generally assumed, but was also more fully integrated into the prevailing patterns and habits of dining, recreation and social congregation.

It is possible, using the advertisements placed in the press by auctioneers, merchants and retailers to paint a fuller picture of the range and varieties of alcohol offered for sale, and to show that the patterns of consumption were less firmly socially defined than observers such as Abbot aver. Focusing in the first instance on the marketing of alcohol in early eighteenth-century Dublin, one could in 1711–12 purchase white or red wine (Lisbon white, Barrabar white and Graves claret) by the dozen bottles or by hogshead, and brandy by the gallon from the house of William Hutchinson, a merchant based on Blind Quay.[27] The advertised range available at The Sign of the Ton on Lower Essex Street was larger ('good white', claret, canary, mum, Barcelona wine and brandy), but since it sold primarily by the quart or gallon it evidently functioned as a tavern as well as a retail outlet.[28] This was not unusual. Nearly two decades later one might purchase 'good Graves claret', 'good Margoes [Margeaux]', 'good Canary' and 'good sherry' either by the quart, gallon or in larger volumes at a discount at The Mighty Tun in Smithfield.[29] However, in a more revealing development, echoing that pioneered by the purveyors of patent and proprietary medicine and emulated by the promoters of horse racing, the retailers of alcohol increasingly had recourse to the press as a medium through which to inform the middling sort as well as the elite of the expanding selection of wines and spirits that could be purchased in denominations ranging from a gallon to a pipe.[30] Once this had begun, it was destined to expand, and 40 years

---

[26] Malcolm, *Ireland sober, Ireland free*, 29; Clarkson and Crawford, *Feast and famine*, 53.

[27] *Flying Post*, 28 December 1711 and 23 September 1712.

[28] *Flying Post*, 18 May 1711.

[29] *Faulkner's Dublin Journal*, 14 June 1729.

[30] See *Dublin Gazette*, 17 June 1729, for advertising announcing the availability of arrack, Geneva, brandy, rum, double rum, claret and white wine; for the parallel with

later the retail sector was sufficiently developed to sustain outlets catering for an ever larger portion of society.

The most notable pointer of the extent to which alcohol became a staple commodity for middle- as well as upper-class households in the eighteenth century is provided by the emergence of retailers like Bensons and Hamilton of Cork, where in 1773 one could purchase coffee as well as madeira wine in 'convenient' quantities for 'home consumption', and Dillon (subsequently Duffey) of 43 Castle Street, Dublin, who in the 1790s targeted 'housekeepers' as the most likely consumers of a variety of 'teas, sugars, wines and spirits', the most notable of which was his 'family whiskey'—a 'rectified old spirit whiskey, engaged to bear 7 waters'.[31] Even regular alcohol retailers got in on the act. The Bordeaux Warehouse, which was based on Werburgh Street, Dublin, advertised its blend of 'old spirits of whiskey' as suitable 'for private families use'.[32] A still more compelling insight is provided into the centrality of alcohol in the diet and lifestyle of the households of the 'middling sort' as well as the elite by the presence of alcohol among the stock in trade of grocery outlets. Thus in Cork city, Cornelius Murphy stocked old rum, brandy, Geneva and whiskey alongside 'sugars and teas of all kinds, coffee, raw and ground', and a wide variety of other commodities in his 'grocery business' on Mallow Lane in 1780.[33] John Phelan of Bridge Street, Dublin, maintained a still more extensive selection of teas (seven types), coffees (five) and sugars (eleven) alongside an impressive inventory of wines and spirits; so too did John Leech and John Lee at their premises on Abbey Street, also in Dublin, but the intimacy of the link that had grown between grocery and alcohol is best exemplified by the 'tea, wine, spirit, and grocery warehouse' maintained by Andrew Carr at 71 Dame Street in Dublin where various wines and porters could be purchased in standard quantities of a dozen bottles and spirits by the gallon.[34]

There were, of course, still more dedicated alcohol retailers, catering primarily for the elite, who contrived to broaden their customer base. The most striking feature of the enterprise operated by Charles Carrothers at 6 Lower Jervis Street, Dublin, through the 1770s and 1780s was his attentiveness to price and quality. Able, because he sold for 'ready money' only, to undersell retailers who accepted credit, he maintained an extensive stock of 'superior quality' as

proprietary medicine see James Kelly, 'Health for sale: mountebanks, doctors, printers and the supply of medication in eighteenth-century Ireland', *Proceedings of the Royal Irish Academy* 108C (2008), 1–38, and with horseracing, James Kelly, *Sport in Ireland 1660–1840* (Dublin, 2014), 35–7.

[31] *Hibernian Chronicle*, 29 November 1773; *Hibernian Journal*, 5 January 1791, 9 August 1793, 4 November 1795 and 3 February 1796; *Dublin Morning Post*, 25 February 1792 and 9 January 1794; *Freeman's Journal*, 2 January and 17 April 1800.

[32] *Dublin Morning Post*, 22 October 1791.

[33] *Hibernian Chronicle*, 3 January 1780.

[34] *Finn's Leinster Journal*, 19 August 1767; *Hibernian Journal*, 2 September 1776; *Volunteers Journal*, 19 July 1784. Carr's alcohol stock included red and white port, Malaga, mountain, sherry, claret, calcavella and Lisbon, brandy, cognac, Holland and rich currant Geneva, and Whitbred's London porter.

well as 'choice' wines, amounting in 1779 to '1,000 to 1,500 hogsheads in wood and bottle', which meant he was in a position 'to supply the wholesale buyer as well as the retailer or customer on the very best terms'. It was a formula that worked since his outlet was, with John Wilson's 'vaults' on Grafton Street, one of two major houses in the city in the late 1780s that advertised the availability of 'first growth' (premier cru) wines of the houses of Lafitte, Latour, Chateau Margeaux and Hautbrion; and it is a measure of Carrothers' success that he 'entered into partnership' in 1789 with William Boyd, whose long established house included Dublin Castle among its clients.[35]

Boyd and Carrothers were not the only upper-end wine merchants operating in Dublin in the late 1780s, but equivalent claims were made with less justification by others.[36] It was then commonplace to assert that one stocked wines, port and, increasingly London porter, of 'superior' or 'best' quality, since this was the practice in this competitive sector. Indicatively, the advantage that Charles Carrothers accrued by prioritising 'ready money' customers spawned imitators. Thomas Conroy, who sold wines from his premises on Capel Street through the 1770s and 1780s, emblazoned his advertisement with the slogan 'wines for ready money only', but since he stocked madeira, hock, sherry, claret, port (red and white), mountain, carcavella and other grape varieties 'in pipes, hogsheads, quarter casks and bottles' in the 1790s, it was evidently a successful formula.[37] It certainly helped if the retailer was seen to be responsive to his customer's needs. Conroy's promise that he would supply fourteen bottles for every dozen purchased, and John Wilson's offer to those 'who buy wines in wood, and choose to have it bottled in his vaults' that they would 'be accommodated with clean new bottles at glass-house price' was a well-judged scheme to capitalise on the fact that many householders found the task of bottling wine disagreeable. Promises that wine would be made available in bottles of a standard size, incentives to encourage the purchase, circulation and return of empties, and the availability for purchase of wine labels indicate that those offering 'choice claret' by the hogshead and fine 'old port' by the pipe, hogshead and quarter cask did so in the expectation of making sales.[38]

---

[35] *Hibernian Journal*, 14 April 1774, 29 January 1776, 3 March 1790 and 2 March 1791; *Freeman's Journal*, 24 August 1779 and 10 December 1789; *Dublin Morning Post*, 2 February and 3 April 1788, and 12 February and 10 December 1789; *Dublin Chronicle*, 23 February 1790; L. M. Cullen, 'The Boyds in Bordeaux', unpublished paper, 2013; (PRONI, Wilmot Papers, T3019/5342, 5343, Waite to Wilmot, 14 October 1766, Boyd to Waite, 14 October 1766).

[36] See, for example, *Freeman's Journal*, 11 April 1782 (advertisement for the vaults of Michael Kavanagh, which were located opposite the Linen Hall, proffering 'first quality champagne, best frontigniac [*sic*], best Lisbon, choice claret etc'; and *Dublin Morning Post*, 3 April 1788 promising red port of 'superior quality'.

[37] For Conroy see *Hibernian Journal*, 6 May 1771, 2 September 1776, 20 January 1790, 19 December 1791, 1 August 1792 and 5 August 1793; *Dublin Morning Post*, 27 May 1790, 18 July and 15 November 1791, and 9 January 1794.

[38] *Freeman's Journal*, 29 July 1780; *Hibernian Journal*, 18 June 1792; *Dublin Morning Post*, 3 April 1788.

Moreover, it was not only high-quality wines, and upper-end retailers, that employed such practices in order to ensure that bulk purchasing (in pipes, hogsheads and quarter casks) continued in the face of the increased availability of bottled wine, which was generally sold in units of a dozen bottles.[39] There was certainly enough variety from which to choose. For example, if in the late 1780s one entered the 'vaults' of John Wilson, as well as the claret, port and white wines that were his stock in trade, one could purchase 'claret, burgundy and champagne of the first growths of France, old sherry, Lisbon, carcavella, hock, madeira, frontiniac [*sic*], vin de Grave, white port, Malaga etc equally cheap', and 'best London porter and sweet sparkling English cider in wood and bottle'.[40] Indeed, the demand for wine was perceived as sufficiently robust to justify the establishment, in the 1790s, of a Bordeaux Warehouse on Werburgh Street, and of Birney's Portugal Warehouse on South Great George's Street, though this was evidently a step too far as neither enterprise flourished.[41]

Apart from those at the higher end, few retailers focused exclusively on wine. Most small and medium-sized retailers stocked popular wines as well as spirits (arrack, rum, rum shrub, whiskey of all types, brandy and Geneva) and, increasingly, English beers, ales and porters, and Irish and English cider consistent with their broader customer base.[42] Interestingly, the mounting appeal of porter prompted Birney to rename his flagging Portugal Warehouse the 'London Porter Stores' in 1791, but it did not prove any more successful, and after a short-lived reversion to the Portugal Warehouse, the outlet was known simply as 'Birney's stores' in 1794.[43] Subsequently, John Wilson rebranded his premises as 'Wilson's wholesale wine vaults and London Porter Stores' but it too seems not to have fulfilled its proprietor's expectations.[44] It seems as if the customer base that these retailers appealed to was not sufficiently wealthy to justify this degree of specialisation.

---

[39] See *Saunders' Newsletter*, 25 March and 8 April 1796.

[40] *Dublin Morning Post*, 3 April 1788; *Hibernian Journal*, 21 August 1789, and 27 January and 4 September 1790.

[41] *Hibernian Journal*, 5 April 1790 and 18 June 1792; *Dublin Morning Post*, 3 September 1791 (John Short and son: Bordeaux Warehouse, Werburgh St); *Dublin Morning Post*, 6 November 1790, 7 April and 30 August 1791, 12 July 1792, and 1 April 1794 (Birney Portugal Warehouse, South Great George's Street).

[42] *Freeman's Journal*, 4 October 1774 (George Bruce, Ross Lane, Bride Street); *Hibernian Journal*, 18 June 1792 (Wood's Stores, Abbey St); *Dublin Morning Post*, 30 August 1791, 12 July 1792 and 1 April 1794 (Birney Portugal Warehouse, South Great George's St); *Freeman's Journal*, 13 February 1781 (Berkley Sidney Knox's Porter, wine and cyder store, Great Britain St); *Hibernian Journal*, 23 August 1790 (Minelli's, Bachelor's Walk).

[43] *Dublin Morning Post*, 7 April and 20 August 1791, and 13 February and 1 April 1794.

[44] *Dublin Morning Post*, 3 July 1792, 3 December 1793 and 4 February 1794; *Hibernian Journal*, 9 January 1793 and 18 May 1795.

Though the cultivation by wine merchants such as Charles Carrothers of clients outside Dublin, and the discounts that Dublin-based retailers were prepared to offer, was a factor in accounting for the dominance of the capital in the retail of fine wines in eighteenth-century Ireland, an impressive range of imported alcohol could be purchased in most of the country's larger towns. A survey of the advertisements in *Finn's Leinster Journal* for the late 1760s suggests that the citizenry of Waterford and Carlow had comparable access to Continental wines and West Indian spirits, if not the same choice of outlets in which to make their purchases.[45] This is true also of Clonmel, which was largely supplied through Waterford. The availability at Michael Luther's store in Clonmel in March 1792 of 150 tierces of the 'best London porter', of 'first quality' claret, red and white wine, sherry, and red and white port in 'pipes, hogsheads and quarter casks' and 'in prime order in wood and bottle' provides an indication of the range that he, John O'Keeffe, who operated out of Limerick, and James Sexton, who was based in Ennis, Co. Clare, offered customers.[46] This is not to imply that the quality of the wine available regionally was ordinary, though it is noteworthy that those who engaged in the retail of wine and foreign spirits (Spanish and French brandy, Holland geneva and Jamaica rum) in such locations were more likely to do so as part of a combined 'grocery, wine and spirit business', to target the custom of 'housekeepers', and to 'sell upon the most reasonable terms'.[47] Indicatively, James O'Brien of Limerick, advertised in September 1795 that he could supply 'his friends and the public with [claret] the most capital growth of the years '86, '88, '90 and '91', pipes or hogsheads of vintage red port, and 'a good supply of madeira, frontignaca [*sic*], barsac, vin de Grave, sherry, Lisbon and Mountain'.[48]

As the second city on the island, and an international port that routinely admitted ships from France and Portugal bearing brandy and wine, and from the West Indies carrying rum, the variety of alcohol available for purchase in Cork bore closer comparison to Dublin than any other regional hub.[49] The main identifiable differences between it and the capital was the greater range of rum that was available (Jamaica, Antigua, Barbados, Granada and St Kitts), and the more frequent opportunities to purchase alcohol at auction.[50] It is reasonable to assume that a majority of those who purchased

---

[45] *Finn's Leinster Journal*, 6 June and 19 August 1767, and 19 January 1769.

[46] *Clonmel Gazette*, 17 March 1792; *Ennis Chronicle*, 11 April 1791, 21 September 1795 and 10 January 1800. Similarly, James Roche, who was located in Ennis, advertised claret, port, mountain Lisbon, and Malaga wines in 1795: *Ennis Chronicle*, 12 March 1795.

[47] *Ennis Chronicle*, 6 January 1794, 10 January and 1 December 1800, and 17 September 1801.

[48] *Ennis Chronicle*, 17, 21 September 1795.

[49] See the listing of ships, and their cargoes, admitted to Cork port in July 1773: *Hibernian Chronicle* (Cork), 22 July 1773.

[50] For evidence of the range of rums see the *Hibernian Chronicle*, 2 June 1775, 16 September 1776 and 3 March 1785. Auctions were listed in the *Hibernian Chronicle* and the *Cork Advertiser*; for a selection see the *Hibernian Chronicle*, 26 April 1770;

brandy, wine, rum (perhaps even porter) by the pipe, puncheon, and hogshead (quarter cask) at auction were retailers. Yet, the fact that Hugh Jameson and Sons, of Morrison's Island, who imported wine in significant volumes from France and Portugal for auction, also advertised the sale of 'red and white port wine', Malaga wine, sherry and Cognac brandy by the pipe and hogshead from their cellars, and that others merchants did likewise indicates that the wholesale and retail markets overlapped.[51] The decision of Stephen and Martin Auster, who maintained a wholesale 'grocery, spirit and wine warehouse' on Mallow Lane, to auction 500 dozen bottles of different wines in 1785 is consistent with this, though Dennis Sullivan, Main Street, a 'grocery, wine and spirituous liquor seller', was more representative of this type; he sold a more limited range of wines, brandy and rum alongside sugar, tea, spices and other staples.[52] It is not possible without further inquiry to establish the relative proportions of those who engaged in this dual trade, and those who concentrated on the sale of alcohol, but the impression provided by the local press is that the latter exceeded the former. The closest late eighteenth-century Cork came to the high-end wine specialists to be found in Dublin was the house of Boyd and Maziere whose 'extensive wine cellars' opposite the Custom House were modelled on 'the much approved plan of . . . houses in London and Dublin'. In practice, both they, Samuel Cooper and Co. of Cook Street, and Robert and J. Nettles of George's Street replicated the sales model (in offering discounts and requiring 'ready payment') rather than the inventory of the London and Dublin houses they claimed to emulate, but they did promise those who sought good wine that they could secure the same at 'cheap' prices in units of a dozen bottles.[53]

For those who sought to secure large quantities, there was plenty of opportunity to buy wine and spirits in traditional wood. The flimsy evidential footprint that remains of most of the enterprises that sold wine in bulk in Cork suggests that they operated as general merchants, who moved in and out of the alcohol trade.[54] They also presumably targeted different clients than the retailer. The delightfully named Sober Kent sought out 'private families'; he announced

---

23 January, 19 March, 9 July and 20 August 1772; 22 February and 3 May 1773; 29 May 1777; 2 and 6 December 1779; 29 May 1780; 19 and 22 March, 3 and 21 May 1781; 16 December 1782; 30 June and 8 September 1785; and 2 February and 2 October 1786; and the *Cork Advertiser*, 26 March, 7 and 21 April, 2 May and 2 August 1801; 5 September 1812; and 26 December 1818.

[51] *Hibernian Chronicle*, 30 August 1770; 23 January, 27 February, 2 April and 9 July 1772; 8, 18 March 1773; and 3 February 1783.

[52] See the *Hibernian Chronicle*, 10 September 1772, 22 July 1773, 2 October 1775, 5 and 16 September 1776, 16 March 1777, 5 February 1778, 14 January and 13 December 1779, 11 March 1781, and 13 June and 3 November 1785; *Cork Gazette*, 20 December 1794, *Cork Advertiser*, 7 and 12 May 1801 for other examples.

[53] *Hibernian Chronicle*, 3 December 1781, 17 June and 16 December 1782, 3 February 1783, 5 January and 28 June 1784, and 11 July and 6 October 1785; *Cork Gazette*, 24 March 1792.

[54] See the *Hibernian Chronicle*, 6 April 1772, 21 June 1773, 28 March 1774, and 8 April and 21 October 1776.

in 1770 that he had 'choice claret, rich old sack, Lisbon, frontiniac [*sic*], French white wines, red and white port, genuine Jamaica and Antigua rum, Cognac brandy and choice French cherry brandy' in stock 'at his cellars on the Coal Quay'. Others simply advertised that they had wine for sale and awaited customers.[55] It remains to be established which strategy was most effective, but it is reasonable to conclude that the diversity of retailers identifiable in Cork and Dublin would not have existed if the market was not growing; the surge in advertisements in the final decades of the century announcing the availability of London porter (specifically Whitbred's and Thrale's), Taunton beer (in tierces), spruce beer and Irish cider (in hogsheads), and of locations where they might be purchased is consistent with this. It also cautions against fixedly correlating types of alcohol and social class.[56] This point may be made also in respect of the marketing and consumption of spirits.

The most persuasive evidence that money could be made retailing spirits to those with above average purchasing power is provided by its availability in a variety of outlets. Much of the whiskey consumed by the 'common people' may well have been procured in the 'whiskey shops' that were decried so passionately in the public sphere, but one cannot conclude from this that whiskey was only consumed by those at this social level.[57] Such outlets, and the multiplicity of licensed and unlicensed 'dram shops', were integral to the supply of whiskey, illicit or duty paid, to the populace, and thus to the commercial infrastructure that traded in this commodity; but distillers and others also engaged actively in refining and modifying spirits to suit a broader palate that embraced the elite. There is no information on the proportion of spirits that was consumed in a diluted or softened form. However, the plenitude of retailers who advertised raspberry and cherry brandy, orange and raspberry rum shrub, pineapple rum, blackcurrant Geneva, and raspberry and black-currant whiskey is illustrative of the popularity of these varieties, and of the fact that a proportion of each of the main spirits was consumed in a sweetened or diluted form.[58] This encouraged specialisation by a number of regular and 'compound' distillers in the preparation of 'distilled liquors and cordials'. Some of these 'cordial drams'—notably aniseed, wormwood and tansy

---

[55] *Hibernian Chronicle*, 30 August 1770; 24 August 1775; 6 and 17 January 1785; and 2 January, 16 February and 3 April 1786.

[56] *Hibernian Chronicle*, 9 March 1775; 26 December 1776; 2 July, 27 August, and 16 and 30 November 1778; 14 January, 4 February and 26 April 1779; 27 January and 13 April 1780; 26 July 1781; 21 July 1785; 22 June and 31 July 1786; *Belfast Newsletter*, 27 May 1788 and 17 July 1792.

[57] See, for example, *Volunteer Evening Post*, 9 November 1784.

[58] See, inter alia, *Finn's Leinster Journal*, 21 January, 6 June and 19 August 1767; *Hibernian Journal*, 16 September 1776, 5 January 1791, and 5 and 9 August 1793; *Freeman's Journal*, 4 October 1774 and 13 August 1778; *Dublin Morning Post*, 25 February 1792; *Hibernian Chronicle*, 21 August 1777, 18 March 1779, 4 July 1775 and 21 August 1776; *Volunteers Journal*, 19 July 1784, and Jonah Barrington, *Personal sketches of his own time* (3 vols, London, 1827–32), vol. i, 6 for testimony to the fact that rum shrub in particular was widely consumed.

waters—served a primarily medicinal purpose, though whether that was the focus of the distillery operated by Catherine Higgins at Southgate, Cork, whose output in 1770 embraced 'raspberry brandy, whiskey shrub, aniseed water, wormwood water, hot surfeit water, [and] usquebaugh', is unclear.[59] Usquebaugh was the most famous Irish cordial. Flatteringly described as 'the richest cordial in Europe' in the early eighteenth century, it was perceived to have dis-improved by the 1740s when it was described as 'not so good as it used to be'. Be that as it may, Drogheda usquebaugh was held in sufficiently high esteem for Katherine Conolly, the chatelaine of Castletown, Co. Kildare, to convey it to her sister in England when she was indisposed, and for John, Baron Wainwright, a judge in the Court of Exchequer, to send it to Charles, second duke of Grafton, who had served for a time as lord lieutenant of Ireland.[60] Moreover, though it lost some of its lustre thereafter, it continued to be manufactured and sold, and to evade the criticisms increasingly targeted at punch.[61]

A combination of whiskey, water and sugar, whiskey punch had arrived at such a point of popularity by the 1790s (it was claimed that 'three fourths of the spirits drank in Ireland are consumed in the form of punch') it was condemned as 'pernicious'. This was alarmist, but the popularity of punch, grog (which combined rum and water) and concoctions composed of spirits and fruit served not only to increase the appeal of spirits across social and gender boundaries but also to normalise their usage.[62] The perception of high-end tavern and innkeepers that they required 'the best assortment of all kinds of wines and good liquors' also contributed to the process of normalisation by introducing particular varieties to new consumers. Though the alcohol that was available spoke volumes about the clientele that an inn aspired to attract, the fact that they retailed spirits as well as wines increased the likelihood of their being consumed by a broad social catchment. This was true also of the kingdom's first dining houses which boasted that their 'wines [we]re of the best description' and their port was ideal for 'single gentlemen'.[63]

---

[59] *Hibernian Chronicle*, 18 October 1770, 4 January and 1 April 1773, 6 March 1775 and 20 November 1779.

[60] Rolf Loeber *et al.* (eds), 'Journal of a tour to Dublin and the counties of Dublin and Meath in 1699', *Analecta Hibernica*, no. 43 (2012), 63; Patrick Fagan, *The second city: Dublin 1700–60* (Dublin, 1986), 93; *Pue's Occurrences*, 17 June 1718; Wainwright to [ ], 3 June and 22 August 1737 (TNA, SP63/400); National Library of Ireland (NLI), Smythe of Barbavilla Papers, MS 41578/13, /14, Katherine Conolly to Jane Bonnell, 25 November 1740 and 9 June 1741; Tara Kelleghan, 'Parsnip wine approaches nearest to the malmsey or madeira: a discussion of sweet wines and cordials popular in Georgian Ireland' (2014) available at http://arrow.dit.ie/cgi/viewcontent.cgi?article=1053&context=dgs (last accessed 27 April 2015), 5–8.

[61] See the advertisement for 'usquebagh' in *Hibernian Journal*, 2 January 1795.

[62] Silé Ní Chinneide, 'A Frenchman's impression of County Cork in 1790', *Journal of the Cork Historical and Archaeological Society* 80 (1974), 20; *Dublin Morning Post*, 22 March 1792.

[63] *Hibernian Chronicle*, 26 April and 6 December 1779, and 19 June 1780; *Dublin Morning Post*, 28 November 1793.

This is not to deny the validity of the generalisation that wine was the preferred drink of the elite, and whiskey the preference of the masses. It is rather to suggest that since alcohol was readily available, and society manifested no inclination to embrace temperance, it was not only permitted but also facilitated admission to a prominent place in private as well as public life among all social classes. The negative implications of this, which the appreciating number of critics of alcohol (and particularly whiskey) insistently evoked, included increasing drunkenness, alcohol-fuelled violence and lost productivity, but it also possessed tangible benefits, which contributed in an important way to the well-being of the population at large.

Consuming alcohol

Despite its bounteous availability, and its centrality to life and lifestyle, alcohol consumption was regarded with mounting suspicion by commentators and politicians in eighteenth-century Ireland. Opposition to 'spirituous liquors', specifically whiskey, which the speaker of the House of Commons (John Foster) condemned in memorable terms in 1789 as 'the demolisher of industry, morals and subordination',[64] increased exponentially in the 1780s and 1790s, and informed the attempts by the legislature in the 1790s to reduce the multiplicity of 'dram shops', 'boozing shops', 'whiskey houses' and 'tippling houses', and to confine their hours of opening.[65] Yet, as the preoccupation with the demeanour and deportment of 'the lower class' and the money they 'squander[ed]' on alcohol attests, most comment was from on high, and it echoed the inherent hierarchical assumptions that shaped contemporary attitudes on virtually all questions. Disapproval was expressed on occasion of the violent behaviour of the drunken young 'buckeens' who sometimes terrorised the streets of Dublin, and, still more cautiously, of the 'half mounted gentlemen' (immortalised by Jonah Barrington) whose propensities for over-indulgence was hardly less developed.[66] It is a measure of the fundamentally elitist perspectives that were articulated that there was little or no open discussion of the place of alcohol in life or acknowledgement of the reality, since alcohol was safer than water, that alcohol was consumed daily in most households, and that its provision was a priority for households—domestic and institutional. Indicatively, Dublin Corporation authorised the construction of a brewing facility ('brewhouse') by the Blue Coat School in 1707 'whereby the number of poor boys maintained there may be encouraged by the frugal management of brewing their own drink'.[67] A minority of domestic households also brewed beer, but since beer and cider were normally consumed by servants, and the extant regulations

[64] PRONI, Stanley of Alderley Papers, T3725/3, Foster to Sheffield, 4 January 1789.
[65] McGuire, *Irish whiskey*, 158–63; *Dublin Morning Post*, 2 October 1790, and 21 May and 12 July 1791; *Clonmel Gazette*, 11 June 1791; *Hibernian Journal*, 24 June 1791.
[66] *Freeman's Journal*, 18 February 1794; Barrington, *Personal sketches of his own time*, vol. i, 64–85.
[67] Sir John and Rosa Mulholland Gilbert (eds), *Calendar of ancient records of Dublin* (19 vols, Dublin, 1889–1944), vol. vi, 364.

discouraged the domestic production of beer, it did not liberate them from the need to purchase wine and spirits.

The volume of wine purchased by households varied greatly, but most acquired what they needed to permit its daily consumption. Even the Cosbys of Stradbally, Co. Laois, when the abstemious Pole Cosby was head of the household, consumed two hogsheads annually (or 2.8 pints a day) in the 1710s. By comparison, the £260 spent on wine by the de Vescis of Abbeyleix, Co. Laois, in twelve months over the period 1752–3 would have allowed them to purchase fifteen hogsheads of 'choice claret' which equated to 21 pints daily.[68] This may not seem far removed from the bibulous world of Barrington's 'half mounted gentlemen' but it was not excessive for a household of this size. Saliently, the Bakers of Ballaghtobin, who maintained a palpably smaller household in nearby County Kilkenny at the beginning of the nineteenth century, purchased their claret in bottles; they ordered it ten dozen at a time, along with sherry, madeira and Lisbon in slightly smaller quantities and port by the pipe.[69] This would have provided plenty of opportunity for excess had they been so minded, but like Jonathan Swift, who purchased six hogsheads a year, the most striking feature of their alcohol intake was not its scale but its regularity. Swift drank, he admitted, on occasion 'to encourage cheerfulness' and because he found it eased the vertiginous condition that long bothered him. Yet, his normal daily intake of a bottle (*c.* 1.25 pints) a day, was well within the parameters of what was perceived as normal.[70] Women were assumed to drink less, but since Katherine Conolly advised her sister Jane Bonnell that '2 or 4 glasses a day will nather doe you nor me hurt, for that is my stint at dinner', it is not surprising that a hogshead of wine was a welcome gift or that it was customary to maintain a substantial stock in the home since the consumption of alcohol was almost as routine as tea drinking became in the later nineteenth and twentieth centuries.[71] Moreover, the habit extended well beyond the ranks of the elite. When the household effects of Nicholas Walsh, a medical doctor with a practice in Cork, were auctioned in 1778, they 'included two hogsheads

---

[68] Daniel Beaumont, 'The gentry of Kings and Queen's counties: Protestant landed society, 1690–1760', unpublished PhD thesis, Trinity College Dublin, 1999, 189–90; 'Survey of documents in private keeping: Bowen papers', *Analecta Hibernica*, no. 15 (1944), 16. Some 20 years earlier Katherine Conolly confided that she did not pay 'under 16 or 18 po[u]nd' a hogshead (NLI, Smythe of Barbavilla Papers, MS 41578/7, Conolly to Bonnell, 27 December 1734).

[69] Monica Nevin, 'A County Kilkenny Georgian household notebook', *Journal of the Royal Society of Antiquaries of Ireland* 109 (1979), 9.

[70] Leo Damrosch, *Jonathan Swift: his life and his work* (London, 2013), 271; Carole Fabricant, *Swift's landscape* (London, 1982), 235; Swift to Pope, [25] August 1726 in Harold Williams (ed.), *The correspondence of Jonathan Swift* (5 vols, Oxford, 1963–5), vol. iii, 159.

[71] NLI, Smythe of Barbavilla Papers, MS 41578/12, Katherine Conolly to Jane Bonnell, 4 February 1730, and 16 May and 8 August 1739. For tea drinking in the nineteenth century see Ian Miller, *Reforming food in post-Famine Ireland: medicine, science and improvement 1845–1922* (Manchester, 2014).

of choice claret, one in bottle and one in timber'.[72] Even successful tradesmen prided themselves on the quality of the wines they served: when the traveller Courtney More was invited to dine by a 'wealthy tailor' in Dublin in 1806 his meal included an 'excellent claret'.[73]

The ease and familiarity with which alcohol was treated in the domestic spaces of the elite and middling sort was encouraged by the prevailing perception that, consumed in moderation, it was possessed of therapeutic qualities.[74] Echoing Katherine Conolly's advice to her sister, Richard Lovell Edgeworth alerted Josiah Wedgeworth in 1788, when the latter experienced 'indisposition', that he had twice 'restored myself to tolerable health by relaxation, and by increasing my quantity of daily stimulus in the form of three or four glasses of claret, not port, and half a pint of porter'.[75] Given his dislike of excess, Edgeworth's advice was noteworthy, and it dovetailed with that of some of the best physicians in the land. Some 50 years previously, Edward Barry (1696–1776), who later became the physician general, counselled a patient 'not to exceed' a quart of brandy a day, and though this instruction was offered cautiously as the beneficiary was disposed to greater self-indulgence, Barry's unwillingness to attempt dissuasion was telling.[76] It was indicative of the belief, anchored in humoral medication, that the regulated consumption of alcohol on its own or in tandem with other ingredients was intrinsically beneficial. Significantly, Thomas Sheridan, the author and schoolmaster, imbibed a concoction that included whiskey as well as garlic, bitter orange, gentian root, snake root and wormwood to treat asthma.[77] It is not clear if this remedy relieved Sheridan's pulmonary travails, but the desire for relief that caused him to have resort to it was no different to that which encouraged others

---

[72] *Hibernian Chronicle*, 30 March 1778. The case of Gilbert Mellefont, esq, of Bandonbridge may be similarly instanced; when his house was burgled in 1777 those responsible appropriated 22 dozen bottles of claret: *Hibernian Chronicle*, 15 December 1777.

[73] 'A forgotten tour in Ireland by Courtenay More', *Journal of the Cork Historical and Archaeological Society* 7 (1901), 173.

[74] According to William Buchan, the author of the best-selling medical advice book, wine was 'an excellent cordial medicine ... worth all the rest together': *Domestic medicine*, 12th edition (Dublin, 1792), 634; Clarkson and Crawford, *Feast and famine*, 56.

[75] Edgeworth to Wedgwood, 22 May 1788 in Francis Doherty, 'An eighteenth-century intellectual friendship: the letters of Richard Lovell Edgeworth and Josiah Wedgwood', *Proceedings of the Royal Irish Academy* 86C (1986), 257.

[76] Barry to Orrery, 26 December 1736 in Countess of Cork and Orrery (ed.), *The Orrery Papers* (2 vols, London, 1903), vol. i, 186.

[77] James Woolley, 'Thomas Sheridan and Swift', *Studies in eighteenth-century culture*, ix (1979), 99–100. For a more clear cut illustration of the view that alcohol was of use in maintain the humoral balance see Evans to Barnard, 22 May 1796 in Anthony Powell (ed.), *Barnard letters, 1778–1824* (London, 1928), 60.

to have recourse to usquebaugh, or 'rectified spirits of whiskey for family use' for making into tinctures and other medical potions.[78]

If the alimentary and medical benefits to be derived from alcohol provided a foundation upon which a case in support of its consumption could be constructed, there is no denying that it was also consumed because of its mood-altering qualities. As well as Swift, many were thankful for 'a healing brimmer of claret' at moments of personal difficulty such as the bereavement of a trusted friend or colleague.[79] The inclusion of 'drinking' among the recreations of the 'inhabitants', both native and settler, of County Fermanagh in an account of life in the early eighteenth century demonstrates that this attitude was not exclusive to the elite, but it is also clear that drinking was not simply a recreational activity—it was integral to the familiar occasions and the festive calendar that punctuated the routine cycle of living. It was, for example, appealed to equally to mark birth as well as a death:

> They bury none except a beggar without a good store of dram; and if the deceased be not of substance to order his burial solemnity, his friends and neighbours do meet and make a contribution among themselves to see him buried with credit, these inhabitants generally being so united in manners and customs that a poor cotter would sooner venture the ruin of his poor family before he would see his child christened without a good store of a dram, to see his neighbours and landlord merry with him.[80]

Signally, the empathy manifested by the author of this narrative was rarely present in the accounts of those of a higher social station who commented on Irish funeral customs. Indeed, unease 'with the quantity of whiskey and tobacco consumed upon these occasions' dovetailed over time with specific antipathy to the 'great vice ... [of] drinking spirits'.[81]

It may be that the transition whereby the consumption of alcohol by the population at large evolved from an occasional pursuit, as it was in County Fermanagh in 1718, to become a daily activity, which was the position as the eighteenth century drew to a close, was already underway in the early 1740s when Isaac Butler offers a rare insight into the way in which whiskey was consumed by the rural population of County Cavan:

> Aquavitae or whiskey, which is greatly esteemed by ye inhabitants, as a wholesome balsamic diuretic, they take it here in common at and before their meals. To make it the more agreeable they fill an iron pot with ye

---

[78] *Hibernian Journal*, 2 Jan. 1795; above pp. 237–8.
[79] Above p. 240; Clanricarde and others to Carlingford, 8 January 1677 in *Journal of the Cork Archaeological and Historical Society*, 1896.
[80] P. Ó Maolagáin, 'An early history of Fermanagh', *Clogher Record* 1:4 (1956), 113–14.
[81] Arthur Young, *A tour in Ireland*, ed. A. W. Hutton (2 vols, London, 1890), vol. i, 249; Ó Maidín, 'Pococke's tour of southern and south-west Ireland', 82.

spirit, putting sugar, mint and butter and when it hath seeth'd for some time, they fill their square cans which they call meathers, thus drink out ym to each other.[82]

Though Butler noted that drinking might continue until those present were intoxicated, the reference to the fact that it was consumed in a modified form with food suggests that the population had not entirely forsaken the approach described in 1718. If so, it was not to continue, as reports of the drinking practices of the populace in the second half of the eighteenth century indicate that drinking 'in excess' was endemic in town, city and country. It was made possible by the plentiful supply of 'cheap' whiskey, which was the most striking consequence of the surge in spirit production that characterised the later decades of the eighteenth century.[83] This provides a context for Charles O'Conor's claim, made in his 'statistical account of the parish of Kilronan', Co. Roscommon, in 1773, that annually every cottier 'distilled his oats into spirits, and every cabin became a whiskey house until the spirit was drunk'. Many smallholders doubtlessly followed this pattern and distilled for their own consumption, but others, as 'the inhabitants of Manorhamilton', Co. Leitrim, made clear in 1782 when they protested against the 1779 act 'against distilling', did so 'to support themselves and family ... [as] the distilling of whiskey ... brought an immediate return to them in cash'.[84]

As well as the greater availability of home-produced *poitín* and duty-paid whiskey, popular drinking was facilitated by the greater willingness of those who participated in the rich calendar of festive and celebratory occasions that the populace observed to drink heavily,[85] and by a sharp increase in the number of drinking establishments. The numbers of the latter in contemporary accounts are probably inflated, yet claims by Isaac Butler that 'almost every house' in the early 1740s on the 'great road' between Belturbet, Co. Cavan, and Enniskillen, Co. Fermanagh, 'have for public sale, aquavitae or whiskey' are supported by a similar observation from Strabane, Co. Tyrone, nearly two decades later.[86] Even discounting for hyperbole, these impressions echo accounts that suggest that most of the country's cities and towns sustained large numbers of taverns, alehouses and dram shops. John Rutty's often cited computation that there were 300 taverns, 2,000 alehouses,

[82] Isaac Butler, 'A journey to Lough Derg', *Journal of the Royal Society of Antiquaries of Ireland* 22 (1892), 132–3; see also Mac Suibhne, 'Spirit, spectre, shade', 156.

[83] James Kelly (ed.), *The letters of chief Baron Edward Willes to the earl of Warwick, 1757–1762* (Aberystwyth, 1990), 75; John Bush, *Hibernia Curiosa* (Dublin, 1769), 26.

[84] Charles O'Conor, 'Statistical account of the parish of Kilronan in Ireland, and the neighbouring district' reprinted in Sir John Sinclair, *The statistical account of Scotland* (Edinburgh, 1798), 8; NLI, Killadoon Papers, MS 36030/5, Memorial of the inhabitants of the ... manors of Hamilton and Glenboy ... to Robert Clements, January 1782.

[85] Kevin Danaher, *The year in Ireland* (Cork, 1972); Sean Connolly, *Priests and people in pre-famine Ireland, 1780–1845* (Dublin, 1982), 135–74.

[86] Butler, 'A journey to Lough Derg', 132; Hamilton to Abercorn, 25 May 1759 in J. H. Gebbie (ed.), *An introduction to the Abercorn letters* (Omagh, 1972), 65.

and 1,200 brandy shops in Dublin in 1749 cannot be corroborated but it is not inconsistent with assertions that there were '240 dram shops' in Limerick in 1790 and '500 alehouses and taverns in Cork' in 1806.[87] Furthermore, this was not identified by the populace as a problem; on the contrary, they were more likely to express unease at improving landowners who sought to limit the number of such premises. This was the experience of Sir Thomas Prendergast, 2nd baronet, whose decision to 'allow but six houses to sell liquors' in the town of Gort, Co. Galway, in the 1750s, was regarded as 'a great hardship'.[88]

Given the difference between the prices charged by the retailers of whiskey and claret,[89] and the care that tavern proprietors took to make it known that they stocked 'the nicest wines and spirits',[90] it was inevitable that the venues to which different categories of customers were drawn also varied even if the outcome—intoxication—was shared. Based upon the little that is known of the 'dram shops', and allied low-end alcohol retailers, there is good reason to believe that they were rude establishments that sold alcohol (primarily whiskey and its punch derivatives) at a cheap price without alimentation to the artisans and labourers that were their customers.[91] This was a style of imbibing quite different to that pursued by the elite and middling sort, who when they frequented premises that sold alcohol, were more likely to do so in the company of likeminded individuals that dined together. As the frequent reference in the advertisements inserted in the press by tavern owners to the availability of 'rooms' for 'large or small parties', and to the availability of 'dinner' by arrangement, taverns catered for a clientele that could afford to eat and drink, and which frequently did so as part of a club or society.[92] The consumption of alcohol was, as this suggests, integral to the emergence and growth of the recreational, associational and political world of the elite and middling sort. Moreover, it served a crucial purpose

---

[87] John Rutty, *Natural history of Dublin* (Dublin, 1772), 12; David Dickson (ed.), *The gorgeous mask: Dublin 1700–1850* (Dublin, 1987), 72–3; *Dublin Chronicle*, 26 August 1790; 'A forgotten tour by Courtenay Moore', 174.

[88] Toby Barnard (ed.), 'A description of Gort in 1752, by Thomas Wetherall', *Journal of the Galway Archaeological and Historical Society* 61 (2009), 108.

[89] To compare: in 1736, for 1s 1d, one could purchase a bottle of claret or 2 quarts of whiskey; in 1792 the inn price of claret was 3s 6d; E. Ó hÉideain, 'Leabhair cuntais Teampaill Mhuire 1727–38', *Galvia*, 5 (1958), 9; Woods, 'Charles Abbot's tour of Ireland, 1792', September 1792.

[90] See above, p. 238; *Dublin Morning Post*, 25 November 1794; Arnold Horner, 'In the shadow of the Fitzgeralds: Maynooth *c.* 1700 to *c.* 1900', in Patrick Cosgrave *et al.* (eds), *Aspects of Irish aristocratic life: essays on the Fitzgeralds and Carton* (Dublin, 2014), 162.

[91] Rolf Loeber and Magda Stouthamer-Loeber (eds), 'Dublin and its vicinity in 1797', *Irish Geography* 35:2 (2002), 146.

[92] See the advertisements for the King's Inn Tavern, Fownes's St; the Bagatelle Tavern, Essex St; and the Exchange Tavern, Crane Lane (all Dublin); in the *Dublin Morning Post*, 25 November 1794.

since it was integral to the forging and maintenance of personal relationships that were necessary for the conduct of civil and political activity. These certainly took different forms. In the recreational realm, it can be perceived in operation in the gatherings that filled the long evenings that followed a day's racing, hunting or cockfighting. Much that has survived of these bacchanalian occasions may not always reflect well on the participants. Arthur Stringer's cautionary tale of the 'good huntsman' who 'first drank himself out of his expert sense, secondly out of his money, thirdly out of his service and, consequently, out of his head, fourth, out of his reputation, fifthly, out of his health, and lastly, out of his life' was clearly apocryphal.[93] Yet, accounts of identifiable figures such as John, Lord Eyre, whose gatherings at Eyrecourt, Co. Galway, were famously bibulous, were grounded in real encounters. Moreover, he was not atypical, as individuals such as Eyre bear more than a passing resemblance to the archetype immortalised by Arthur Young, who 'hunt in the morning, get drunk in the evening, and fight the next morning'.[94] Such figures were not unique to Ireland, of course. George Edward Pakenham's observation after a 'delightful' season hunting in County Westmeath in the 1730s that 'the fox hunters [in Ireland] live much after the same manner as in England and drink as hard' offers a proper caution against stereotyping the Irish aristocracy and gentry as exceptional in this respect.[95] Even individuals like Eyre, who was personally very limited (as Richard Cumberland's memorable pen portrait attests), and those who were regular presences at his bacchanals contributed in a practical way to the nurturing of the sports of racing, hunting and cockfighting by combining purposeful recreational association with self-indulgence. This is not how it was seen by contemporaries (who promoted improvement of the self as well as society) and has generally been presented by historians since, but one would be hard pressed to demonstrate that such revelries served a less useful purpose than the bibulous electoral entertainments that punctuated the century, which, for all the criticism properly directed their way, facilitated the operation of the deferential politics that defined the era.[96]

---

[93] Arthur Stringer, *The experienced huntsman* (Belfast, 1714; Dublin, 1780; reprint Belfast, 1978), 33.

[94] Kelly, *Sport in Ireland, 1600–1840*, 168–9; *Memoirs of Richard Cumberland* (2 vols, London, 1807), vol. i, 278–9; Young, *Tour in Ireland*, ii, 79; L. M. Cullen, 'Economic development, 1750–1800', in W. E. Vaughan (ed.), *A new history of Ireland iv: eighteenth-century Ireland, 1691–1800* (Oxford, 1986), 175; *Hibernian Chronicle*, 28 May 1770.

[95] 'Survey of documents in private keeping: Longford papers', *Analecta Hibernica*, no. 15 (1944), 120; see also, Clarkson and Crawford, *Feast and famine*, 54–5.

[96] See A. P. W. Malcomson, 'The parliamentary traffic of the country', in Thomas Bartlett and D. W. Hayton (eds), *Penal era and golden age: essays in Irish history, 1690–1800* (Belfast, 1979), 137–62; and for examples of the use of alcohol in an electoral setting see *Minutes of evidence taken before the select committee of the County Mayo election* (Dublin, 1778), 24, 34, 47, 49, 53, 68–70; *Journal of the House of Commons of the kingdom of Ireland*, 4th edition (21 vols, Dublin, 1796–1802), vol. xi, 28.

One may be less equivocal as to the usefulness of official entertainments mounted to receive visiting dignitaries be they lords lieutenant or judges of assize, or the private celebrations such as greeted the birth of an heir to a landed estate.[97] With respect to the former, the Corporation of Kilkenny was aware that it had exceeded what was proper in 1703 when it directed that 'the conduits [should] run with claret' to mark the arrival of the recently sworn lord lieutenant, James, duke of Ormonde, to the city. However they, and other local authorities, sustained the 'customary' practice of entertaining judges on circuit, while royal anniversaries, military victories and traditional commemorative occasions were often accompanied by the provision of generous amounts of alcohol which, as instanced by the celebration in Dublin of Admiral Edward Vernon's achievements in the War of Jenkins' Ear in 1740–1, might lead to overt displays of public drunkenness.[98] Be that as it may, officials were predisposed to regard these events indulgently, because such exhibitions of public euphoria had manifested their value since they were inaugurated in England in the sixteenth century, and introduced into Ireland in the early seventeenth.[99] Furthermore, they continued to look benignly upon such displays. When Charles Abbot stayed the night at 'the best inn' in Armagh in 1792 he noted that the commissioners in the town for the purpose of 'executing in an Equity cause', 'brought their own piper from Dublin', and that, 'as in England upon such occasions', the night was marked by 'drinking and singing'.[100]

Such events could be difficult for an outsider to comprehend, as evidenced by the angry reaction of an American visitor to successive nights at an inn in Castleisland, Co. Kerry, in August 1797 when 'a parcell of the noiseyest drunken savages ... kept up their dissipate[io]n with carousing and singing, or rather screeching and roaring, 'till break of day'.[101] There was, as this suggests, a lot of socialising and frequenting of taverns that seemed only to result in raucousness and inebriation, but drinking (whether it resulted in

---

[97] For a perspective on these 'private' events, see Toby Barnard, *Making the grand figure: lives and possession in Ireland, 1641–1770* (London, 2004), 350–1.

[98] NLI, Walsh newscuttings, MS 14026, J. G. A. Prim, 'Ancient enactments ... in Kilkenny'; PRONI, Wilmot papers, T3019/293, Waite to Wilmot, 28 May 1741; Richard Caulfield (ed.), *The corporation book of Cork* (Guilford, Surrey, 1876), 348, 398, 414, 420, 434, 445, 466, 470, 603, 604, 610, 637, 750; *Faulkner's Dublin Journal*, 19 August 1732; *Dublin Newsletter*, 4 February 1738.

[99] See David Cressy, *Bonfires and bells: national memory and the calendar in Elizabethan and Stuart England* (London, 1989): Tim Harris, 'The British dilemma', in Tony Claydon and Ian McBride (eds), *Protestantism and national identity: Britain and Ireland c.1650–1850* (Cambridge, 1998), 140; James Kelly, 'The glorious and immortal memory: commemoration and Protestant identity in Ireland, 1660–1800', *Proceedings of the Royal Irish Academy* 94C (1994), 26–31; Sean Connolly, 'The Church of Ireland and the royal martyr: regicide and revolution in Anglican political thought c.1660–1745', *Journal of Ecclesiastical History* 44 (2003), 484–506.

[100] Woods, 'Charles Abbot's tour of Ireland, 1792', 12 September 1792.

[101] Michael Quane (ed.), 'Tour in Ireland by John Harden in 1797', *Journal of the Cork Historical and Archaeological Society* 59 (1954), 74.

intoxication or not) was seldom purposeless or without implication.[102] Shortly after his arrival to take up a law office in Ireland in 1725, the future lord chancellor, John Bowes, observed of those of his peers for whom 'drinking is the business of their leisure hours', that they were incentivised to interact in this manner by an awareness of the value of networking.[103] As someone who preferred to stay at his desk, Bowes identified alternate means 'to preserve my rank in business', but there were many for whom this was either not an option or who (unlike Bowes) found drinking congenial. Major General Thomas Earle was one. As a newly appointed lord justice, it was in his interest to get to know the gentlemen with whom he would have to engage. With this in mind, he reported to his colleagues from County Kilkenny in 1702 that he was 'hard at work "buckhunting" together with an application of as much drink as I am reasonably able to perform in order to familiarise myself in such manner with the gentlemen of the country'.[104]

William Wogan and Katherine Conolly offer still another perspective on the positive usages to which alcohol was put. Both possessed an intimate familiarity with the dining and drinking habits that Earle embraced and Bowes disliked, and both were sufficiently aware of its import to perceive the value of alerting absent friends that they had recently raised a glass to their good health.[105] Toasting was, as this suggests, a matter of consequence in the private as well as the public realm. Calling toasts could be still more significant. It was, for instance, the means by which Henry Boyle demonstrated the sincerity of his apology when, having misread the intentions of the ailing William Conolly, he made it publicly known by calling a toast to the speaker that he had only expressed interest in the speakership of the House of Commons because he believed Conolly was not going to seek re-election.[106]

Though they had much in common when it came to such matters, Irish practices were not always accurately read by officeholders and visitors from England, whose arresting characterisations of the culture of drinking and, in particular, the manner in which toasting seemed to lend itself to egregious excess, has been invoked to support the conclusion that Irish Protestant society was alcohol fuelled. There can be no doubt but that certain English visitors, schooled in the culture of politeness then in the ascendant in Great Britain, were appalled by their encounters with excess. The vivid, and often quoted, descriptions of John Boyle, fifth earl of Orrery (Fig. 5), in the mid-1730s, and the sharply critical observations of the fourth earl of Chesterfield, who was

---

[102] Barnard, *Making the grand figure*, passim.

[103] Bowes to John Ryder, 12 July 1727 in A. P. W. Malcomson (ed.), *Eighteenth-century Irish official papers in Great Britain* (2 vols, Belfast, [1973]–90), vol. ii, 12.

[104] Earle to [Lords justices], 13 July 1702 (NAI, Calendar of miscellaneous letters and papers prior to 1760 f. 23).

[105] Wogan to Southwell, 11 January 1704 (British Library (BL), Southwell Papers, Add. Ms. 37673 f. 40); Conolly to Eustace, 20 June 1723 in M-L. Jennings (ed.), *The letters of Katherine Conolly* (forthcoming), no. 24.

[106] Katherine Conolly to Clothilde Eustace, 23 April 1729 in Jennings (ed.), *Letters of Katherine Conolly*, no. 50.

Fɪɢ. 5—John Boyle, 5th earl of Cork and Orrery, attributed to Isaac Seeman, *c.* 1735–45. © National Portrait Gallery, London.

briefly lord lieutenant in the mid-1740s, of the link then obtaining in Ireland between the 'quantity of claret' that was put on the table and 'mistaken notions of hospitality and dignity', suggest that they had cause.[107] Orrery's accounts are certainly arresting, as the following description of an event in Cork in 1737 attests:

> I have been at a feast. … Nonsense and wine have flowed in plenty, gigantic saddles of mutton and Brobdingnaggian rumps of beef weigh down the table. Bumpers of claret and bowls of white wine were

[107] Malcolm, *Ireland sober, Ireland free*, 39–40; Connolly, *Religion, law and power*, 67; Joep Leerssen, *Mere Irish and fior-ghael: studies in the idea of Irish nationality, its development, and literary expression prior to the nineteenth century* (Amsterdam, 1986), 350; J. G. McCoy, 'Local political culture in the Hanoverian empire: the case of Ireland', unpublished D.Phil. thesis, Oxford University, 1994, 279–81.

perpetually under my nose, till at last, being unable to bear the torture, I took advantage of a health, at which we were all obliged to rise, and slipt away.... This short sketch may give you some faint idea of our entertainments in this part of the world. They are esteemed according to the quantity, not to the quality of the victuals, be the meat good or be it bad, so that there is as much as would feed an army ... I ... cannot help wondering what mansions in the Elysian fields allotted to those heroes whose delight consists in variety of folly, distraction and drunkenness.[108]

Orrery's repugnance at this display is unambiguous. It is also not unique. However, his arresting characterisation of the 'glorious memory Hibernian' as 'a Yahoo that boasts the glorious and immortal memory of King William in a bumper without any other joy in the Revolution [of 1688] than that it has given him a pretence to drink so many more daily quarts of wine' is also a caricature.[109] When William Taylor, Viscount Perceval's agent, addressed this issue in advance of the arrival in Ireland in 1731 of the heir to the Perceval estate he presented a contrary perspective. He advised Viscount Perceval that though Ireland possessed a deserved reputation for 'hard drinking', this was no longer justified: it was, he explained, 'reckon'd churlishness to withhold liquor from a person who likes to drink, yet it is accounted ill manners to press it upon those who show a dislike to it'.[110] Moreover, this remained the case, as both the urbane chief baron of the Court of Exchequer, Edward Willes, and Arthur Young confirmed by their personal experiences.[111] Additionally, when Henry Penruddocke Wyndham visited the country in 1759, he noted that even when the bottle circulated freely, individuals were not required to charge their glass other than at their own pace.[112] Clearly, Orrery's experience was not true of every company.

This is not to suggest that the practice of political toasting did not permit excess, but it may be that Orrery's political as well as behavioural antipathy to what he encountered caused him to exaggerate (Fig. 6). If he was more attuned to the contested nature of political toasting in Ireland, he might have better understood the passion with which the 'glorious memory' was saluted, and the import of so doing. Saliently, Irish Jacobites risked a fine, imprisonment, a stretch in the pillory or assault 'for drinking the Pretender's

---

[108] Orrery to Waynright, 12 April 1737 in Countess of Orrery, *The Orrery Papers*, i, 215–16.
[109] Orrery to [Salkeld], 4 May 1736, in Countess of Orrery, *The Orrery Papers*, i, 157.
[110] Taylor to Perceval, 11 June 1731 (BL, Egmont Papers, Add. MS 46982 f. 52).
[111] Kelly, *Letters of Edward Willes*, 25; Clarkson and Crawford, *Feast and famine*, 53.
[112] Henry Penruddocke Wyndham to Henry Wyndham, 20 October 1759 (Beinecke Library, Osborn Collection, Wyndham file, letter 12). This view was echoed by Thomas Campbell who observed of Ireland that the bottle circulated 'not to the excess we have heard': Thomas Campbell, *A philosophical survey of the south of Ireland* (Dublin, 1778), 39.

Fɪɢ. 6—Gentlemen singing and drinking toasts around a table by Henry Brocas, 1762–1837. Reproduced by permission of the National Library of Ireland.

health' or calling other 'treasonable' toasts,[113] while Irish Tories chose either to avoid toasting altogether or, emboldened by Peter Browne, bishop of Cork, sought to discourage the fast growing cult of William of Orange by questioning the appropriateness 'of drinking in remembrance of the dead'.[114] Irish Whigs, by contrast, used every occasion available to them to assert their identity, and as attested to by the publication in 1712 of an 'exact' list of 'the healths drank' to honour King William's birthday in Dublin in that year, and, following his accession in 1714, of those drank on George I's birthday, they precociously

---

[113] Eamonn Ó Ciardha, *Ireland and the Jacobite cause, c. 1685–1766: a fatal attachment* (Dublin, 2002), 169–71; *Whalley's Newsletter*, 30 November 1715; *Pue's Occurrences*, 6 September 1718; NAI, Calendar of Presentments, f. 123; *Dublin Weekly Journal*, 10 September 1748.

[114] See Kelly, 'The glorious and immortal memory', 31–9; J. G. Simms, 'Celebrating 1690', *Studies* 63 (1974), 235; Peter Browne, *Of drinking in remembrance of the dead* (Dublin, 1713).

perceived the usefulness of publishing lists of the toasts called.[115] Furthermore, in the quarter century following the inauguration of the Hanoverian succession, when their brand of political Protestantism was firmly in the ascendant, the pressure to be seen to conform was so compelling that a man who declined a loyal 'bumper' in public company took the risk of having 'his constant and good affection to the present happy settlement' questioned.[116] As a result, political toasting achieved such symbolic and practical ascendancy in the anglophone public realm in the 1730s and 1740s that when fissures appeared in the 1750s it was logical, such was its usefulness in generating group identity, that the toast was appealed to in a new and novel way.

Though it can reasonably be portrayed as a power struggle in order to determine which faction was in the ascendant politically, the money bill dispute of the mid-1750s stirred ideological currents that were to possess a central place in Irish political discourse for two generations. Questions were posed at the time as to the extent to which the Patriots who seized the political initiative in the 1750s subordinated personal ambition to the virtue they routinely invoked in the toasts they called, but these are of lesser import here than the manner in which the coalition of factions, interests and individuals that rallied round Henry Boyle took political toasting from the preponderantly communal Protestant world in which it had been located since 1715 into the more contested arena of factionalised politics.[117] The key to this was the Patriot Club, a new departure in Irish political life, which provided a structure in which those who supported Boyle could assemble and, through the medium of the political toast, promulgate a political message that served the purposes of advancing a statement of policy and binding those present in a common cause. 'Thus drinking answered two purposes; it united the company and sharpened the wit or malice of the individual against the common enemy', Edmund Sexten Pery noted perceptively.[118] Credit for this has been assigned to Anthony Malone, the MP for County Westmeath, though the reality of the matter is that toasting would not have succeeded so spectacularly but for the fact that it synergised with the burgeoning associational impulse then gathering pace.[119] In any event,

---

[115] *An exact list of the healths drank at the Tholsel, the 4 November 1712* (Dublin, 1712); *Dublin Postman*, 31 May 1715

[116] NAI, Pembroke Estate Papers, 97/46/1/2/5/48, Mathew to Fitzwilliam, 6 October 1747; see also Orrery to [Salkeld], 4 May 1736, in Countess of Orrery, *Orrery Papers*, i, 157.

[117] For accounts of the Money Bill dispute and its impact see Declan O'Donovan, 'The money bill dispute of 1753' in Bartlett and Hayton, *Penal era and golden age*, 55–87; Eoin Magennis, *The Irish political system, 1740–65* (Dublin, 2000), 93–110; James Kelly, 'Patriot politics, 1750–91', in Alvin Jackson (ed.), *Handbook of modern Irish history* (Oxford, 2014), 482–4.

[118] Historical Manuscripts Commission (HMC), *Eighth report, appendix, part 1: Emly Papers* (London, 1881), 178a.

[119] For the impact of the Patriot Clubs and of political toasting see note 115; Bob Harris, *Politics and the nation: Britain in the mid-eighteenth century* (Oxford, 2002), 192–235; idem, 'The patriot clubs of the 1750s', in James Kelly and Martyn Powell

the establishment of Patriot Clubs across the kingdom, and the adoption of the tactic of raising toasts to the individuals, interests and, most importantly of all, to the complex of political convictions, statements of sincerely held principle, and shibboleths that defined contemporary patriotism was an idea that had found its time. Initiated in the febrile atmosphere of the winter of 1753–4, freeholders, 'independent electors' and individuals came together across the kingdom to affirm their traditional commitment to protect and secure their liberties against 'popery and arbitrary power', and their more recently acquired resolve that those whom they unjustifiably defined as 'the enemies of the nation' would not prevail.[120] Given that the toasts, which were the form in which these convictions were conventionally articulated, bore closer comparison to slogans than developed political statements, it can be suggested that this tactic was ideal for a community that was already familiar with this medium, and which was practised at assigning meaning to such phrases as 'the glorious memory' and 'Popery and arbitrary power'. However, this would be to sell these events short. Toasts, then and later, were not called for singly or in isolation. A typical meeting might produce 40, 50 or even 60 toasts. Furthermore, while it is the case that a substantial proportion of those called at a Patriot gathering in the 1750s were little different to those uttered at a typical Williamite anniversary, what gave them a distinct register was the manner in which they combined traditional Whig slogans, loyalty to the Hanoverian monarchy and the Protestant succession, statements of Patriot principle, professions of fellowship, and personalised abuse directed at their opponents into a comprehensive, if not entirely coherent or intellectually subtle, message.[121] It is improbable that those who were present were equally persuaded of the merits of all the toasts to which those who assembled raised their glasses, but it was acknowledged by critics, sympathisers and neutrals alike that the combination of alcohol and toasts served very effectively to unite those present in support of their champions, to reinforce them in their determination to adhere to their position, and to provide them with a corpus of ideologically informed slogans to which they, and those of like mind, could, and did, appeal. Furthermore, the fact that the toasts uttered were the central focus of the reports of those gatherings published in the popular press ensured that the message was not confined to those present.[122]

(eds), *Clubs and societies in eighteenth-century Ireland* (Dublin, 2010), 224–43; M. J. Powell, 'Political toasting in eighteenth-century Ireland', *History* 91 (2006), 508–29; and for the emerging associational culture see Kelly and Powell, *Clubs and societies in eighteenth-century Ireland*, 27–9.

[120] Harris, *Politics and the nation*, 216–17; Powell, 'Political toasting', 514–16.

[121] *An address from the independent freeholders of the p[ro]v[in]ce of M[u]ns[te]r … with a collection of fifty-four original patriot toasts drank at a select assembly of freeholders at Corke, the first of this instance January 1754* ([Dublin], 1754); Conway to Walpole, 8 May 1755, in W. S. Lewis (ed.), *The correspondence of Horace Walpole* (48 vols, New Haven, CT, 1937–83), vol. xxxvii, 392–5.

[122] R. E. Burns, *Irish parliamentary politics in the eighteenth century, 1714–60* (2 vols, Washington, D.C., 1989–90), vol. ii, 135; Powell, 'Political toasting', 509; HMC, *Emly*, i, 178a.

Despite the fact that the money bill concluded in a manner that many of those who engaged in political toasting found disappointing, the episode had a long-term legacy. Traditional loyalist toasting, in the manner of that pursued during the first half of the eighteenth century, continued largely unchanged, but the second half of the century spawned an array of bodies for whom the toast was as one of the key means through which they forged organisational unity and conveyed their views both to their members and to society at large. These included loyal societies of Protestant tradesmen for whom this was a convenient way of recalling the welcome defeat of Jacobitism in the rising of 1745.[123] It was put to still better use by reform-minded organisations such as the Society of Free Citizens and the Volunteers. Each appealed actively to the toast as a means of generating esprit de corps, and elaborating an identifiable political strategy by invoking current as well as historical issues, individuals as well as events, and major issues of principle as well as passing controversies. They also used the toast as a medium to promulgate their message. Given that the Society of Free Citizens subscribed on one occasion to a forbidding 92 toasts, it might seem that such displays were self-defeating, but the enduring capacity of 'improper toasts ... drank at public meetings' to excite disquiet in the highest corridors of power indicates otherwise.[124] Moreover, the practice not only survived, it flourished in the still more participatory milieu of the 1780s and 1790s, and beyond, as organisations as diverse as the Lisburn Constitutional Club, the Aldermen of Skinner's Alley, the Volunteers and the United Irishmen, and following the change of mood in the wake of the 1798 Rebellion, conservative interests perceived the manifold benefits of structured, purposeful drinking.[125]

Occasionally, voices, ill at ease at the connection between toasting and drunkenness were raised in protest, but they were battling against the prevailing behavioural tide.[126] The burgeoning associational impulse, which contributed to the emergence of the Patriot Clubs, also contributed to the foundation of scores of non-political clubs which made dining, and by implication, drinking their raison d'être. Though each possessed its own character and purpose, the evidence of the Bar Club, which was established in 1771 to meet the nutritional and convivial requirements of young barristers in Dublin, indicates the centrality of drinking to male sociability. Given the age, status and comparative wealth of its members, it may be that this club was not typical. There were others, which demanded that their members behaved with greater probity, but

---

[123] *Pue's Occurrences*, 30 October 1768; Kelly, 'The glorious and immortal memory', 41–5.

[124] Powell, 'Political toasting', 516, 519–20; *Hibernian Journal*, 17 January 1776; Beresford to Robinson, 22 November 1779 in William Beresford (ed.), *The correspondence of John Beresford* (2 vols, London, 1854), vol. i, 88.

[125] *Hibernian Chronicle*, 16 September 1783 (The Constitutional Club); *Dublin Morning Post*, 9 February 1788 (Aldermen of Skinner's Alley); *Dublin Morning Post*, 21 August 1790 and 16 July 1791 (Volunteers); *Dublin Morning Post*, 17 July 1792 (United Irishmen); *Freeman's Journal*, 2 August 1798; *Cork Advertiser*, 21 November 1812 (Loyal Societies).

[126] *Hibernian Chronicle*, 13 January 1772; *Hibernian Journal*, 24 May 1773.

the links that one can draw between the conduct of members of the Bar Club and the young men whose revels were chronicled by Jonah Barrington cautions against concluding that these were an unrepresentative minority disposed to bacchanalian excess. What can be stated is that the link, noted by John Bowes in the mid-1720s, between drinking and recreation, and between dining and drinking by Henry Penruddocke Wyndham in 1759, had not just survived, it had been boosted by the proliferation of clubs and societies that made dining and drinking their defining activities. It was increasingly commonplace in the second half of the eighteenth century for bodies of men to assemble in clubs and in societies at 4 p.m. to conduct business, and having done so to commence dining at about 5 p.m. and to continue eating and drinking until 9 or 10 p.m., by which time those who had lasted the pace were as likely as not 'very drunk'.[127] This was how many liked it. It is a fair measure of the depth to which a culture of drinking had penetrated even respectable society by the mid-1780s that it was difficult on occasion, even for those like Lord Charlemont who were studiously proper, to avoid getting drunk.[128] Indicatively, this culture was firmly rooted in the political sphere with the result that lords lieutenant and chief secretaries with little interest in drinking were at a palpable disadvantage by comparison with those who did. The frequency with which senior office holders were called upon to demonstrate their capacity to drink heavily varied from administration to administration, but the fact that one could not draw a clear distinction between the consumption of alcohol and work in spheres as diverse as sport and politics is revealing of the extent to which it had penetrated everyday life.[129] It was possible in England in 1791 to assert that drinking healths was 'growing out of fashion'.[130] It was not possible to make a similar claim for Ireland, for though the elite devoutly wished that the lower classes would forsake whiskey for the good of the country, the patterns of sociability that all classes pursued were too closely bound up with the heavy consumption of alcohol to mean it was practicable at this time.

Conclusion

The volume of alcohol imported into and manufactured in Ireland in the eighteenth century permitted its utilisation by every grade and rank of society. Signally, other than the consumption of spirits associated with the lower classes, this was not perceived as a social problem, since alcohol was regarded as an essentially benign commodity. This was most manifest in its usage as a medication, primarily in the form of cordials. Usquebaugh was the best-known

---

127 M. J. Powell, 'Beef, claret and communication: convivial; clubs in the public sphere, 1750–1800' and James Kelly, 'The Bar Club, 1787–93: a dining club case study' both in Kelly and Powell, *Clubs and societies in eighteenth-century Ireland*, 353–92.
128 Charlemont to Haliday, 27 August 1784 in HMC, *Charlemont*, ii, 5–6.
129 Barnard, *Making the grand figure*, 12, 243–6, 249; Kelly, *Sport in Ireland*, 54–7, 85–7, 106, 133, 146–7; James Kelly, 'Residential and non-residential Lords Lieutenants: the viceroyalty, 1703–90', in Peter Gray and Olwen Purdue (eds), *The Irish lord lieutenancy, c. 1541–1922* (Dublin, 2012), 66–96.
130 [John Trousler], *The honours of the table, or rules for behaviour during meals ...* (London, 1791).

Irish cordial, but since whiskey was also perceived (by the populace at least) to possess therapeutic value, it may also have contributed to its consumption mixed with fruit and medical herbs across society. Moreover, the therapeutic value of alcohol also embraced wine, which helped to insulate it from the harsh criticism targeted at spirits in general, and whiskey in particular, and which sanctioned the daily consumption by women of three to four glasses, and by men of a bottle (1.25 pints) of wine a day. Though more inquiry is required, it can be suggested that because alcohol was safer to drink than water (mineral waters excepted[131]) it was perceived by all classes and interests as a convenient and essentially palatable source of liquid nutrient. The fact that it was also an intoxicant was a complication, but since the stages and implications of intoxication, and its physiological and psychological implications, were far from properly understood, this was insufficient on its own, prior to the surge in whiskey consumption in the later eighteenth century, to inhibit its full integration into private and public life. The alimentary benefits of consuming alcohol in a dining milieu were broadly recognised; its potential as an intoxicant appreciated; its value as a social lubricant acknowledged. In most societies, and at most times, these inducements to consume alcohol are policed, and sometimes kept apart, by law or by custom. This was hardly the case in Ireland in the eighteenth century. One may invoke the impoverishment of the native population, the compelling need for the settler community—Presbyterian as well as Church of Ireland—periodically to affirm their social and political bonds, and new and emerging trends such as associationalism and male sociability in seeking to account for this. However, alcohol's intrinsic appeal should not be overlooked. The fact that society has chosen for nearly two centuries to give precedence to the negative consequences of alcohol consumption, ought not to obscure the reality that, viewed in the round, life in eighteenth-century Ireland was more endurable because of its availability.

---

[131] James Kelly, 'Drinking the waters: balneotherapeutic medicine in Ireland 1660–1850', *Studia Hibernica* 35 (2008–09), 99–146.

Food and culinary cultures in pre-Famine Ireland

REGINA SEXTON*

Adult Continuing Education, The Laurels, University College Cork

[Accepted 1 December 2014. Published 25 May 2015.]

Abstract

This essay investigates how the treatment of food—its acquisition, preparation and consumption, and in particular how food was cooked—can express differences between social classes in pre-Famine Ireland. It describes culinary cultures that range from the singularly simple to the decidedly flamboyant. Drawing on the evidence of estate papers and manuscript receipt (recipe) collections, this paper illustrates how cookery at the upper echelons of Irish society was sophisticated, refined and closely aligned to the norms of British culinary culture. The paper will also briefly describe the stagnant and debased food culture of the rural poor, most especially in the early decades of the nineteenth century. Between these extremes existed a rural 'middling' class for whom food and cookery was varied and imbued with value beyond that dictated by the market. The stratified nature of Irish society suggests the coexistence of a number of food and culinary systems. Questions of how distinct, overlapping and interdependent these systems were deserve investigation. However, of equal concern is the fact that these issues also raise the question as to whether the evidence is substantial enough to frame and support any reliable comparative analysis.

Introduction

Irish diets before the potato have been described as 'retarded ... almost medieval', reflective of 'backwardness more immediately than of poverty in the modern sense' with simplicity compounded by the 'absence of a highly stratified pattern'.[1] This argument is consistent with the view that by the turn of the eighteenth century, the Irish diet lacked complexity and was receptive to change, and was therefore highly prone to absorb new ingredients and new food systems with the associated but selective rejection of older staples. The growing prevalence of the potato in the diet of the rural poor, and its displacement of

---

* Author's e-mail: r.sexton@ucc.ie

doi: 10.3318/PRIAC.2015.115.10

[1] Louis M. Cullen, 'Comparative aspects of the Irish diet, 1550–1850', in Hans J. Teuteberg (ed.), *European food history: a research review* (Leicester, London and New York, 1991), 45–55. Cullen's bleak description of food and culinary culture can be lifted somewhat with reference to Fynes Moryson's textured description of the various food patterns of different groups in seventeenth-century Ireland. His description alludes to a cooking culture aligned to English ways in areas of English influence. In the overall, however, he is critical of the absence of 'sauce'—essentially an ignorance of 'the art of cookery', in a land otherwise well supplied with produce.

traditional foods such as oats, dairy produce and pulses, fits well with this line of argument.

The changing dietary pattern of the rural poor has been analysed extensively and authoritatively and will be revisited but briefly here.[2] The priority of this essay is another change—the emergence of a rich, sophisticated and well-ordered food culture associated with a privileged landed class. Irish manuscript receipt (recipes) books[3] provide a convenient entry point to exploring this culture and the focus here is on five manuscript receipts books from the Townley Hall Papers. Lest such an exploration be accused of perpetuating the idea of Ireland as place of extremes, the second half of the essay looks to food and culinary cultures across different social groups. The focus there is on rural consumption in County Kilkenny in the decades preceding the Great Famine. Three sources,[4] particularly rich in food and culinary detail, inform this discussion—Mrs A. W. Baker's collection of recipes from 1810,[5] the dairy of Humphrey O'Sullivan,[6] and William Tighe's *Statistical observations relative to the County of Kilkenny*.[7] It could be objected that a single-location frame of reference offers a restricted view, but the aim is to identify different cultures and points of divergence or overlap within a local context. This discussion will focus on cookery and it will assess the role and usefulness of the recipe as a means of defining cooking cultures.

Irish manuscript receipt books

Louis Cullen's argument that food inheritance from the past was so weak that it enabled entirely new food systems to grow and establish in Ireland throughout the eighteenth century is evident in the case of the elite food and culinary

---

[2] See for example, L. A. Clarkson and Margaret E. Crawford, *Feast and famine: food and nutrition in Ireland 1500–1920* (Oxford, 2001), 59–88, L. A. Clarkson and Margaret E. Crawford, 'Dietary directions: a topographical survey of Irish diet, 1836', in Rosalind Mitchinson and Peter Roebuck (eds), *Economy and society in Scotland and Ireland 1500–1939* (Edinburgh, 1988).

[3] Irish manuscript receipt books are both problematic in terms of their reliability and valuable as dense cultural artefacts that embody the rich culinary culture of a minority class in eighteenth- and early nineteenth-century Ireland. Measuring reliability and determining value is contingent on a critical reading of the texts and by locating them within the broader contexts of their associated papers and their related material culture. For an analysis of their nature and significance see Madeline Shanahan, '"Whipt with a twig rod": Irish manuscript recipe books as sources for the study of culinary material culture, *c.* 1660 to 1830', *Proceedings of the Royal Irish Academy* 115C (2015), 197–218; and the sources cited in that chapter.

[4] This association of sources was first suggested by Cullen, 'Comparative aspects', 51. Cullen's triad was Humphrey O'Sullivan, Dorothea Herbert and Mrs A. W. Baker.

[5] National Library of Ireland (NLI), MS 34,952, Mrs A. W. Baker's Book Vol. 1st Ballytobin, County Kilkenny, 1810.

[6] Rev. Michael McGrath, S. J. (ed. and trans.), *The diary of Humphrey O'Sullivan, Cinnlae Amhlaoibh Uí Shúileabháin*, parts 1– IV (London, 1929 and Dublin, 1937).

[7] William Tighe, *Statistical observations relative to the country of Kilkenny, made in the years 1800 and 1801* (Dublin, 1802).

cultures of the wealthy landed class which developed during the era of the Protestant ascendancy. The economic environment allowed the Irish gentry of major and minor standing to embrace a more modern food culture as Ireland aligned more closely with external food developments. The effects of the opening up of New World markets and the associated rise in more complex networks of trade and food distribution, while effecting limited food and culinary changes in seventeenth-century Ireland, had more widespread impact on diet during the eighteenth century. This period saw considerable culinary changes and developments: an older order of mixing sweet and savoury ingredients in the one dish and the related practice of serving sweet and savoury dishes in the one course would gradually decline as dishes were increasingly categorised as either one category or the other. The movement to disentangle the sweet/savoury/spice profile of cookery and dishes had its roots in a new European cuisine that 'was born in the middle of the seventeenth century, [and] one which claimed to pay more respect to the intrinsic flavours of food'.[8] Tastes and dishes were refined considerably. These reforming developments were driven largely by the growing availability of, and demand for, exotic luxury goods. Sugar more than any other ingredient changed the face of eighteenth and early nineteenth-century cookery, the structure of the meal and the associated material cultures of food preparation and service.

The manuscript receipt books of the Irish gentry reflected and absorbed these greater changes into the domestic setting of the kitchen complex and the dining room making the food culture of the Irish gentry not only progressive and increasingly complex but also one that ran in line with European patterns of elite consumption with influence mediated through economic and cultural contacts with Britain. Therefore, as Cullen points out, the Irish gentry, was indispensable in 'the transition from medieval to modern'[9] with their food culture just one expression of a more widespread move towards modernity.

As the century progressed, the food habits of the wealthy developed in four main ways. There was a sustained increase in the consumption of luxury and exotic commodities and meat retained its position as a high-status item. Home-grown foods, in particular fruits and vegetables, increased in variety and there was a stronger leaning towards food produced or sourced through specialist suppliers.[10] Essentially, an older order of consumption and food production (self-sufficiency, high consumption of meat, cookery based on strong flavours (sweet/savoury/spice and aromatics) expanded and was refined with greater exposure to commercial activity and culinary experimentation.

This progressive and dynamic food culture was shaped and supported by the increased availability of printed books and an increasingly lavish material

---

[8] Brian Cowan, 'New worlds, new tastes: food fashions after the Renaissance', in Paul Freedman (ed.), *Food: the taste of history* (London, 2007), 197–231. See also Stephen Mennell, *All manners of food: eating and taste in England and France from the middle ages to the present* (Oxford and New York, 1987), 20–39.

[9] Louis Cullen, *The emergence of modern Ireland 1600–1900* (New York, 1981), 35.

[10] Clarkson and Crawford, *Feast and famine*, 29–58.

culture, and from the mid-century onwards by a marked increase in the importation of many individual consumer goods.[11] The allied activities of specialist retailers and purveyors (grocers, seed and nurserymen, and confectioners) resulted in a considerable broadening of the ingredient base that in turn prompted greater culinary experimentation and diversification. Newspaper advertisements, for example, detail the range of goods on offer. A Cork City grocer, Edward Haynes, advertised his extensive stock in the *Hibernian Chronicle* on 13 January 1783 as follows:

> Powder, B.B. Brown, best Lump, common ditto, double refined, single refined, Muscovado, and clayed SUGARS; Sugar Candy, Mace, Cloves, Nutmegs, Cinnamon, white Pepper, black ditto, Allspice, Ginger whole and ground; Hyson, Bloom, Common Green, Congou, and Bohea TEAS; best Pickling Vinegar, Jar Raisins, Cask ditto, Currants, Jordan Almonds, Valentia ditto, Liquorice Ball, Capers, Anchovies, Sallad Oil, Citron, Isinglass, Hartshorn Shavings, Barley, Sage, Rice, best Smalt, Powder, and Stone Blue, Starch, Saltpetre, Hops, Mustard in different sized bottles ...

While Cork may be considered one of the more cosmopolitan Irish cities of the period, the listing of goods is typical of the advertisements placed by grocers in the newspapers in Dublin and other port cities. The variety of goods is striking, as is the emphasis on different varieties of sugar, tea and almonds. Different varieties suggest greater consumer choice while the many grades of sugar indicate a concern with quality and standards. The availability of different grades also points to the different culinary functions and applications of the different types of sugar. In fact, this advertisement references a number of culinary activities, including preserving (sugar, saltpetre), pickling (vinegar), dressing (oil), flavouring (spices, capers and anchovies), setting/moulding (isinglass and hartshorn) and sugar work. Furthermore, the presence of capers, anchovies and citron is evidence of a distinctive English culinary style of flavouring and garnishing 'made dishes'—dishes that were dependent on recipe instruction, were often served in a sauce, and garnished in proscribed way: anchovies and capers were popularly added as a flavour enhancer to meat, fowl and fish dishes, while citron was used as a dish garnish.

Much is also made of the sourcing of ingredients. This marketing initiative that linked goods with place may be seen as a means of authenticating quality. When Denis Sullivan advertised his chocolate manufactory and grocery warehouse in the *Hibernian Chronicle* in 1782, he extends further the place and quality association, intimating that superior quality goods ensure greater customer satisfaction. His advertisement tells readers that he sells 'CHOCOLATE of the very best kinds, particularly some made after the Spanish manner, which is found to be particularly pleasing'.[12]

---

[11] Louis Cullen, *Anglo–Irish trade 1660–1800* (Manchester, 1968), 23.

[12] *Hibernian Chronicle*, 6 May 1782.

The fashion for relatively newly introduced hot beverages (tea, coffee and chocolate) went hand in hand with the increased consumption of sugar. The trade in sugar supported much of this commercial, culinary and consumer activity. The demand for sugar, although small by comparison with Britain, underwent rapid expansion after 1740. By the late eighteenth century imports were five times what they had been in the 1730s.[13] The increased availability of sugar throughout the eighteenth century brought revolutionary culinary changes: it made possible an upsurge in the preservation of garden fruits and the production of an extensive range of wet and dry sweetmeats (jams, jellies, marmalades, clear cakes, comfits, conserves, cordials, syrups, sugar pastes and sugar ornaments). It enabled enriched breads to branch into a larger family of baked goods that included cakes (plum, seed, saffron and ginger), buns, biscuits, tart and pies and when sugar was combined with cream, eggs and flavourings there was a substantial increase in the range of creams, syllabubs, cheesecakes, puddings as well as curd and soft cheese dishes. Printed cookery books supported these developments by providing chapters dedicated to preserving, baking, creams and puddings.

This new system of cookery encouraged specialisation and increasingly dishes were characterised as sweet or savoury. Sugar was the main agent of change and its increased use broke any lingering residue of the medieval practice of mixing sweet and savoury in the one dish. Sugar became a staple ingredient in baking, fruit preserving and sweet dairy dishes but its dominant position in gentry kitchens is best seen in the emergence and rise of the dessert, as a sweet course to follow several courses of savoury dishes.[14] By the close of the eighteenth century, the division of dishes as sweet and savoury was well under way, with some persistent reminders of the earlier tendency of mixing sweet and savoury in the one dish. The mince pie, for example, would linger well into the nineteenth century with the combination of meat, sugar, fruit and spice a clear throwback to old-fashioned tastes and outmoded culinary practice.[15]

This period of culinary innovation brought an increase in the range and type of dishes, which in turn saw a 'growing complexity in the service of refreshments and meals [and] stimulated new utensils' associated with kitchen work and service in the dining and drawing rooms.[16] Utensils and objects of service with a dedicated function now linked to particular dishes and

---

[13] Thomas M. Truxes, *Irish–American Trade, 1660–1783* (Cambridge, 1998 and 2004), 227–8.

[14] See for example, Cowan, 'New worlds, new tastes', 207–22; Gilly Lehmann, *The British housewife: cookery books, cooking and society in eighteenth-century Britain* (Totnes, Devon, 2003), 263–73; Laura Mason, *Sugar-plums and sherbet: the prehistory of sweets* (Totnes, Devon, 1998), 22–8; C. Anne Wilson, *Food and drink in Britain* (London, 1973), 304.

[15] See, for example, Mrs A. Baker's recipe for mince pies with calves' feet: NLI, MS 34,952, vol. i, 31.

[16] Toby Barnard, *Making the grand figure: lives and possessions in Ireland, 1641–1770* (New Haven, CT, and London, 2004), 145. For further detail on the range of service and dining objects see pp. 122–50.

ingredients—sugar tongs, asparagus tongs, syllabub glasses, cake hoops, chocolate pots, fruit and sweetmeat epergnes, cake plates, cream and jelly moulds—bringing decided elaboration to the rituals of dining and food preparation. The upsurge in energy and activities around the commercial and material cultures of food that characterised the second half of the eighteenth century was one expression of 'Irish participation in the feverish consumerism that was griping Western Europe'.[17]

To sustain expenditure on ingredients and material goods, food and cookery were increasingly directed by fashion and as a result were subject to constant change: for instance, a collection of recipes in the Townley Hall Papers includes a brief list of 'fashionable dishes' cooked to particular styles: 'cutlets & cucumber in sorrel sauce, do. rolled up in Bread, Chicken in Crumbs of Bread'.[18] Manuscript receipt collections therefore provide an insight into, perhaps even an index of these diverse commercial and cultural influences. They channelled new ideas transmitted from cookery books, travel and indeed the expansion of the British Empire. The choice and style of dishes reflected not only taste, status and ambition but also how the gentry engaged with modernity and how they kept pace with change. Furthermore, these collections functioned as a source of social and cultural cohesion since the wealthy maintained their collections in ways that permitted them to move with fashions and to emulate the trends of those at the upper levels of wealth in Ireland and Britain.

The corpus of Irish manuscript recipe books share common characteristics in their content, and cookery styles that point to the existence of a distinctive culinary culture amongst the gentry in pre-Famine Ireland: a culture that was heavily influenced by, if not indistinguishable from, English practice. In their assessment of post-Restoration dietary patterns, L. A. Clarkson and Margaret E. Crawford conclude that 'during the long eighteenth century the gentry of Ireland ate and drank in ways that were not greatly different from those of the gentry in England'.[19] Their recipes books confirm that they also promoted and enjoyed a cookery culture that typified that of their English counterparts.

Gilly Lehmann's exemplary treatment of the evolution of culinary styles in Britain between 1700 and 1800, instructs that nothing is as it seems and the recipe operates to its own dynamic: manuscript recipes are taken into print, recipes are liberally transmitted from print to handwritten form; collections hold tenaciously to family traditions, and collections absorb and adapt new culinary styles.[20] Clearly, both printed and manuscript collections were intricately connected[21] and 'played a twofold and contradictory rôle [in

---

17 Barnard, *Making the grand figure*, xxii.
18 NLI, Townley Hall Papers, MS 9,561.
19 Clarkson and Crawford, *Feast and famine*, 57.
20 Lehmann, *The British housewife*, 167–289.
21 The interplay between print and text may also be related to practical concerns such as the size and bulk of many printed books, which makes them difficult to work with in a kitchen setting. A 1796 Dublin edition of Hannah Glasse's, *The art of cookery, made*

contributing] to the diffusion of new dishes, while at the same time perpetuating older ones'.[22] With little exception, Irish receipt collections manifest these same tendencies. Throughout the seventeenth and eighteenth centuries, Britain grappled with the diffusion of cookery styles from the court to the aristocracy to the gentry and it navigated through the emergence of a nouvelle cuisine with a more delicate, seasons-focused and systematic approach to cooking and dining as directed by Francois Pierre La Varenne and François Massialot (and later Marie-Antione Carême). It also considered its relationship with French cookery and dealt with the emergence of a middle class more engaged with cookery and an associated upsurge in printed cookery books. Irish collections mirror these trends in varying levels and to different degrees. What is indisputable is that Irish collections conform to and promulgate British styles of codified cooking, and manifest little influence from a native Irish tradition. Exceptions to this norm are evident in the presence of recipes for local specialities[23]—for instance a 'Lismore recept for pickleing Salmon',[24] a 'Sligo way to Pickle Salmon' (see Pl. I),[25]—and references to 'Soda Bread'[26] Irish mutton stew[27] and Irish stew.[28] On rare occasions, the collections also engage with outside food systems as when they include recipes for soup for the poor,[29]

plain: which far exceeds any thing of the kind yet published, for example, measures 7 × 4.5 × 1.5 inches and it is not practical for kitchen work. The copying and transcribing of recipes into more kitchen-friendly books must have been common. Bishop Edward Synge, for example, has loose recipes for saffron cakes circulating between Roscommon and Dublin (in order to guide in the buying of ingredients) and another two for Canton hams: see Marie-Louise Legg (ed.), *The Synge letters: Bishop Edward Synge to his daughter Alicia, Roscommon to Dublin 1746–1752* (Dublin, 1996), 89, 378.

[22] Lehmann, *The British housewife,* 170.

[23] It is not possible, however, to determine the extent to which these preserving techniques were practised or applied. The connection to place, in these examples, may simply refer to local practice amongst estate communities rather than local custom in a wider community context.

[24] NLI, MS 42,008, 22. Cookery book belonging to Abigail Jackson, inscribed 'Abigail Jackson's book, April 10 1782'.

[25] NLI, MS 34,952. Volume i of this recipe collection references a missing second volume. The recipe appears in the index to vol. ii, 36 (see Table 5).

[26] NLI, Townley Hall Papers, MS 9,560, book of recipes and prescriptions.

[27] NLI, Inchiquin Papers, MS 14,786, late seventeenth/eighteenth century recipe collection associated with the O'Briens of Co. Clare.

[28] NLI, Headfort Papers, MS 25,357. Book containing daily menus served at Headfort House, Kells, Co. Meath, with miscellaneous recipes and notes. Irish stew is a regular dish in the table plans in this eclectic book. The pages with table plans also seem to detail the types and quantities of meats required to support the accompanying plans. It is unclear if these table plans are directed at the family or perhaps the house servants.

[29] See for example, NLI, Leitrim Papers, MS 9,929, Late eighteenth/early nineteenth-century recipe book, with additional loose-leaf recipes; numerous ascribed recipes, for instance, Mrs Taylor, Mrs Vignoles, Mrs Pigott; recipes for soup for the poor and rice for the poor and cheap and nourishing food for the poor.

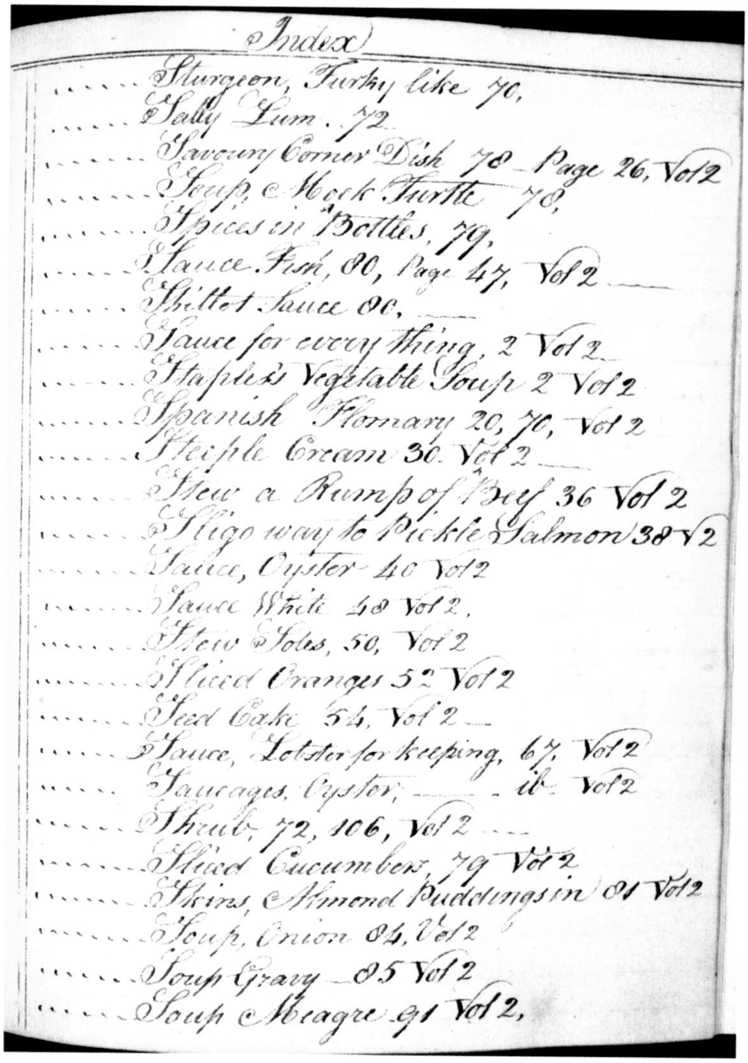
Index
Sturgeon, Turkey like 70,
Sally Lum. 72
Savoury Corner Dish 78 Page 26, Vol 2
Soup, a Mock Turtle 78,
Spices in Bottles, 79,
Sauce Fish, 80, Page 47, Vol 2
Skillet Sauce 80,
Sauce for every thing, 2 Vol 2
Staples's Vegetable Soup 2 Vol 2
Spanish Flomary 20, 70, Vol 2
Steeple Cream 30. Vol 2
Stew a Rump of Beef 36 Vol 2
Sligo way to Pickle Salmon 38 V 2
Sauce, Oyster 40 Vol 2
Sauce White 48 Vol 2,
Stew Soles, 50, Vol 2
Sliced Oranges 52 Vol 2
Seed Cake 54, Vol 2
Sauce, Lobster for keeping, 67, Vol 2
Sausages, Oyster, — ib. Vol 2
Shrub, 72, 106, Vol 2
Sliced Cucumbers, 79 Vol 2
Skins, Almond Puddings in 81 Vol 2
Soup, Onion 84, Vol 2
Soup Gravy 85 Vol 2
Soup Meagre 91 Vol 2,

Pl. I—National Library of Ireland (NLI), MS 34,952, Mrs. A. W. Baker's Book Vol. 1st Ballytobin, Co. Kilkenny, 1810. An index to the missing volume ii is included at the back of the first volume of recipes. Note the recipe for a 'Sligo way to Pickle Salmon'. Volume ii ran to c. 190 and contained other place-specific recipes that held significance for the family like 'Kilbrew Cream Cheese' and 'Bath Cake'. Image reproduced by kind permission of the NLI.

while an un-provenanced late eighteenth-century collection includes a recipe for 'onion Porridge for Catholicks'.[30] Overall, the recipes are open to trends from outside but closed to influences from below.

[30] NLI, MS 42,134. This is more akin to a rich onion sauce than porridge. Onions are softened in butter, added to milk and cream, with three cloves and thickened with breadcrumbs/chips—the rich nature of the dish (perhaps a side or a meat-substitute dish) may suggest an association with wealthy Catholics.

In order to protect the integrity of a collection, access to the recipe was restricted to a select number of individuals. Priority was afforded to the compiler of the collection (the ladies of the house or female relations of the family), and those who executed the recipe (the cooks). The former set the house style and aligned that style with the cultural outlook, mores and tastes of a particular group. Signifiers of judgement and improvement are scattered throughout collections and as a means of defining and improving standards. A late eighteenth-century collection of recipes associated with Mrs Creagh of Creagh Castle, Co. Cork,[31] for example, has pronouncements such as 'The best Receipt That I have Seen for Salter Bisketts', 'A very good Receipt', and the improving addition of toasted fried bread to 'An Onion Soupe by Dr Longfield'. The selection of cooks was often based on their professional training in England[32] and on occasion the upper staff—the cooks, housekeepers or the gentlewomen associated with the family—contributed recipes: for instance 'A Receipt for Walnut Catsup, got by GM [grandmother] from Mrs Costello[?] from My Uncle Desarts[?] House-keeper' is recorded in A. W. Baker's recipe book.[33] Additional characters joined this culinary narrative through the culture of borrowing that was integral to collection-building. Liberal and verbatim copying of recipes from printed sources was also commonplace,[34] and the borrowing culture was extended through the popular

[31] NLI, MS 34,953, Cookery book, Mrs Creagh.

[32] Terence Dooley, *The decline of the big house in Ireland* (Dublin, 2001), 160–3; Mary Dowd, *A history of women in Ireland 1500–1800* (Harlow, Essex, 2005), 133–4.

[33] NLI, MS 34,952, Mrs A. W. Baker's Book Vol. 1st Ballytobin, County Kilkenny, 1810. Sophia Blunden married Abraham White/Whyte Baker of Ballytobin, Co. Kilkenny, in November 1788: *Burke's dictionary of the peerage and baronetage*, 62nd edn (London, 1900), 160; and Monica Nevin, 'A County Kilkenny Georgian household notebook', *Journal of the Royal Society Antiquaries of Ireland* 109 (1979), 5–19: 6. Sophia Blunden was the daughter of Sir John Blunden, first Baronet of Castle Blunden, Co. Kilkenny. He was created a Baronet of Ireland on 12 March, 1766. In 1755 he married his cousin Lucy Susanna Cuffe, daughter of the first Lord Desart of Castle Inch, Co. Kilkenny: *Burke's peerage, baronetage and knightage*, 99th edn (London, 1949), 212. The Cuffes of Desart Court, Co. Kilkenny, were enabled as barons Desart in 1733. Otway Cuffe (1735–1803) third baron Desart was made a viscount in 1781 and an earl in 1793: see George Edward Cokayne, *The complete peerage* (13 vols, London, 1910–59), iv, 228.

[34] See for example NLI, MS 19,729, an un-provenanced collection of 'curious receipts'—relating to cookery, medicine, gardening, household management and crafts like gilding and japanning (a decorative finish applied to paper, wood, tin or leather in the style of Japanese lacquerwork). There are references to Mrs Bindin and Jane Burton but it is unclear if these are associated directly with the compilation. The majority of the recipes are acknowledged and referenced to printed books. Over 20 texts are listed providing a good insight into a late eighteenth-century library collection. The cookery authors referenced include, Martha Bradley, Sarah Harrison and E. Smith. For discussion of the evidence and culture of borrowing and plagiarism in printed cookery books see Lehmann, *The British housewife*, 169–71 and Gilly Lehmann, 'Appendix I: Martha Bradley's borrowings', in *The British housewife: or, the cook, housekeeper's, and*

practice of recipe exchange. For example, a recipe for the 'A Calves Foot Pye' (Pl. II(a)) from Jane Bury's recipe book turns up with minor spelling changes in personal correspondence in the Vigors Papers (see Pl. II(b)).[35] The Creagh collection and Mrs Baker's book are particularly rich in their numbers of attributed recipes: for instance, 'A White Soupe with Meat. the Rec[eip]t given by Leonard Cook to Mr [?] of Doneraile 1778 to Mrs Creagh' is present in the former while Mrs Baker's collection has recipes originating from such eminent personages as Lady Riverston, Lady Blunden, Lady Sydney, Sir William Parsons and Lady Anne Fitzgerald, who commanded a section to herself contributing recipes ranging from preserving oranges to almond soup to pickled oysters.[36] This collection is notable also for the number of inherited recipes which refer to 'My grandmother's book' and 'my grandmother's and Aunt Howth's recipes'[37] thus melding the past with the present and ensuring the continuation of tradition as well as anticipating the delivery of sensory enjoyment into the future. The prestige value that these donors brought to

---

gardiner's companion by Martha Bradley, late of Bath (1756) a facsimile edition and introduction by Gilly Lehmann (6 vols, Totnes, Devon, 1996–8), vol. 1, 51–82. See also Jennifer Stead, 'Quizzing Glasse: or Hannah scrutinized, Part I', *Petits propos culinaires 13* (London, 1983), 9–24 and 'Part II', *Petits propos culinaries 14* (London, 1983), 17–30.

[35] NLI, Vigors Papers, MS 24,979, recipes. (Photocopies, originals in Carlow County Library.)

[36] NLI, MS 34,952, Mrs A. W. Baker's Book Vol. 1st Ballytobin, County Kilkenny, 1810, 67–71. Susanna Catharina Nugent (1685–1763), commonly called Lady Riverston was married to Hyacinth Richard Nugent, styled second baron Nugent of Riverston: Cokayne, *The complete peerage*, ix, 798; possibly Mrs Baker's mother, Lady Lucy Susanna Cuffe, daughter of John, first Lord Desart, who married Sir John Blunden (d. 1783): *Burke's peerage and baronetage*, 76th edn (London, 1905), 173; Isabella St Lawrence (1751–1836), daughter of Thomas first earl of Howth married Dudley Alexander Cosby, first Lord Sydney of Leix in 1773: Cokayne, *The complete peerage*, xii: 1, 593; either William Parsons, 2nd baronet (1661–1741) MP for King's County (1692–1741) or his grandson William (1732–91) who also represented King's County, 1757–91 (E. M. Johnston-Liik, *History of the Irish parliament* (6 vols, Belfast 2002) vol. vi, 27–30; Lady Anne Fitzgerald was possibly Lady Lucy Anne Fitzgerald, daughter of Lord Kildare, 1st duke of Leinster and Lady Emily Lennox, daughter of Charles Lennox, 2nd duke of Richmond: *Burke's dictionary*, 918; or possibly Lady Anne Fitzgerald, wife of Maurice Fitzgerald, knight of Kerry. Lady Anne was the only daughter of William Fitzmaurice, 2nd earl of Kerry. She married Maurice Fitzgerald in 1764: *Burke's dictionary*, 595. A Kerry connection was also established with the Herbert family of Muckross. Two of Mrs Baker's maternal aunts married into the Herbert family. In 1757/59, Hon. Nichola Sophia Cuffe, eldest daughter of John, Lord Desart, married Edward Herbert, MP for Inistioge, Co Kilkenny. Her sister, Hon. Martha Cuffe married Rev. Nicholas Herbert in 1766: *Burke's dictionary,* 452; *Burke's history of the landed gentry of Ireland*, 10th edn (London, 1904), 259.

[37] NLI, MS 34,952, Mrs A. W. Baker's Book Vol. 1st Ballytobin, County Kilkenny, 1810, 1–7. In 1728 William (St Lawrence), Lord Howth, married the seventeen-year-old Lucy, daughter of Nicola Hamilton and Lieut. General Richard Gorges, of Kilbrew, Co. Meath. Lucy was the younger sister of Mrs Baker's grandmother, Dorothea Gorges.

(a)

(b)

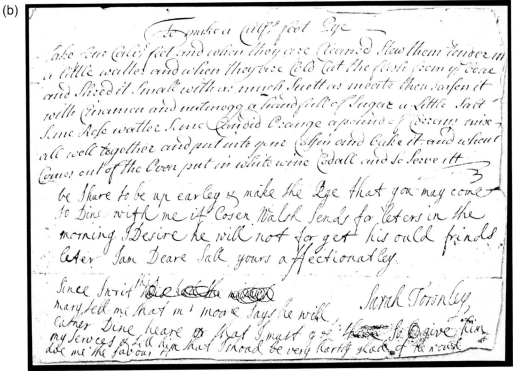

PL. II—(a) National Library of Ireland (NLI), Townley Hall Papers, MS 9,563, Mrs Jane Bury's Receipt Booke, 1700. Four recipes for pies including one for 'skerritt or pottatta pye'. The Townley Hall recipe for 'calves foott pye' appears but with minor spelling changes ('To make a Calf's foot Pye') in (b) NLI, Vigors Papers, MS 24,979 as part of a correspondence from Sarah Townley. Images reproduced by kind permission of the NLI.

the collections invested them with the concept of good taste and assured quality standards.

These powerful and meaning-rich cultural artefacts conveyed the determination of wealthy women to control and direct domestic food culture. Instead of dismissing the collections as the inconsequential, random playthings of women,[38] it is more worthwhile to view the acquisition of recipes, their selection, their circulation, their enactment and the consumption of the final dish, as symbolic acts that build culinary capital within a group. The recipe strengthened networks of influence and engaged the group in reciprocal relationships of borrowing, sharing and consumption. They mixed family inheritance with ideas of fashion brought with change: ultimately they framed a particular and shared identity for those who built, engaged with and guarded the collections. (See Table 1 for common fish/shellfish recipes across eighteenth century and early nineteenth-century collections.)

Manuscript receipt collections, Townley Hall Papers

The Townley Balfours were a family from the gentry who were associated with counties Louth and Fermanagh from the Cromwellian period. With land-holdings extending into counties Meath and Westmeath, the family had their country estate at Townley Hall near Drogheda, Co. Louth. The Francis Johnston-designed house was built in the late 1790s by Blayney Townley Balfour, not long after he returned from his grand tour. Architecturally, the house style and aesthetic can be described as restrained, refined and full of hidden but well-considered details. These characteristics can also be used to describe their food and culinary cultures, which were closely aligned in style and dining rituals to the patterns of elite consumption common to high-standing gentry and aristocratic groups in both Ireland and Britain. Therefore it can be argued that for the Townley-Balfours food, meals and dining were just another expression of what Toby Barnard describes as 'a preoccupation with making the right impression'.[39] And while house, furniture, entertainments and local offices all contributed to the 'making of the grand figure', so too did their choice of meals and dining rituals.[40] Much was invested in the recipe to communicate good character and aesthetic refinement. While in extending hospitality to dinner guests, the choice of dishes made to carefully selected recipes was a stylish though indirect statement of the family's ambitions of status, good standing and good taste.

Cokayne, *The complete peerage, IV* (London, 1916), 609. Many of the recipes attributed to Mrs Baker's grandmother refer to either her maternal grandmother, Dorothea Gorges, daughter of General Gorges of Kilbrew, Co. Meath, or her paternal grandmother, Martha Cuffe of Castle Inch, Co. Kilkenny: *Burke's dictionary*, 160 and 452.

[38] For further discussion of the appraisal of manuscript receipt books as literary texts with semiological and narrative value see Andrea K. Newlyn, 'Redefining "rudimentary" narrative: women's nineteenth-century manuscript cooks', in Janet Floyd and Laurel Forster (eds), *The recipe reader: narratives, contexts, traditions* (Lincoln, NE, and London, 2010), 31–51.

[39] Barnard, *Making the grand figure*, xxi.

[40] See footnote 37.

TABLE 1—Common styles of fish/shellfish cookery and preservation methods across eighteenth and early nineteenth-century recipe collections.

Cooking method	Dish, sauce, enhancers	Preservation (short and long term)
1. National Library of Ireland (NLI), Smythe of Barbavilla Papers, Co. Westmeath, MS 11,688, c. late 17th to early/ mid-18th century		
Carp, to stew	Oyster pottage	Eels, pickled
Mackerel, to broil	Buttered crab	Sturgeon, pickled
Whiting, to fry	Dressed scallops	Oysters, pickled
	Fricassee of lobster or crab	
	Lobster pie	
	Anchovies, oysters and oyster liquor as flavour and texture enhancers in dishes and sauces	
	Oysters in brown fricassee; in white fricassee; in rabbit fricassee	
	Anchovies in catsup; in lobster pie; in ragou (with veal); in pickled mushrooms; in buttered crab; in dressed scallops	
	Anchovies and oysters in Scotch collops; in calf's head pie; in hashed calf's head; with shrimps in sauce for cod's head	
	Anchovy and oyster liquor in to stew carps; in to fry whiting	
	Oyster liquor in sauce for wild fowl	
2. NLI, Smythe of Barbavilla Papers, Co. Westmeath, MS 11,689, c. late 17th to early to mid-18th century		
	Dressed carp x 3	
	Dressed pike	
	Cold salad with anchovies and pickled oysters	
	Anchovies, oysters and oyster liquor as flavour and texture enhancers in dishes and sauces	
	Anchovies and oysters in dressed carp, in Scotch collops	
3. NLI, Townley Hall Papers, MS 9,563, Mrs Jane Bury's Receipt Booke, commencement date 1700		
A cod's head, to boil	Fish sauce	Fish (turbot, pike, base,
Carp, to stew	Eel pie	mullet, salmon), soused
Flounder, trout &	Oyster pie	Souse for bass, mullet,
sole, to stew	Oyster sausages	turbot
Plaice, eels, &	Boiled pullets in oyster sauce	Lobster, potted
flounder, to stew	*Anchovies, oysters and oyster liquor as flavour and texture enhancers in dishes and sauces*	Eels, potted
	Oysters in collared eels	Salmon, potted
	Anchovies in gravy; in Scotch collops; to make cutlets; to stuff a fillet of veal; in stewed carp; in stewed plaice, eels, flounder, sole & trout; in lobster & crab sauce for fish	Eels, collared
	Anchovies & oysters in hash of calf's head; in fricassee of veal, lamb or chicken; in boiled cod's head	Salmon, collared
	Cockles in boiled a cod's head	

TABLE 1 (*cont.*)—Common styles of fish/shellfish cookery and preservation methods across eighteenth and early nineteenth-century recipe collections.

Cooking method	Dish, sauce, enhancers	Preservation (short and long term)
4. NLI, Vigors Papers, MS 24,979, Co. Carlow, c. 1700–99		
		Oysters, pickled x 2
		Oysters, pickled the French way
5. NLI, Fingall Papers, MS 8,041(1), c. 1740–60		
	Lobster soup	Ordinary fish, potted
	Eel pie	Eel, collared
	Salmon pie	Salmon, potted
	Lumber oyster pie	Lobster, potted
	Anchovies, oysters and oyster liquor as flavour and texture enhancers in dishes and sauces	Anchovy in potted wild ducks
	Oysters in lamb pie; in kid pie; in Scotch collops; in dish of boiled pullets; in petty royals; in calf's head hash; in gravy for calf's head	
	Anchovies in ragou of veal; in mutton pie; in royal or? pie; in calf's head pie; in olio pie; in salmon pie; in savoury meatballs; in chestnut pudding in fowls belly; in gravy	
	Oysters and anchovies in fricassee of chicken, rabbits, veal or lamb; in Battally pie; in ragou of ox palates, sweetbreads, lambstones & boiled eggs; in ragou for beef pie; in fish sauce; with cockles in sauce for turkeys and chickens; with cockles in sauce for boiled cod's head	
6. Clonbrock House, Co. Galway, commencement date 1753		
	Dressed eels	Char, potted
	Shoulder of mutton with oysters	
	Petty paste [pastry] for fish	
7. NLI, MS 34,953, Creagh Castle, Co. Cork, c. 1780–1830		
	Oyster sauce	Eels, collared
	Anchovies, oysters and oyster liquor as flavour and texture enhancers in dishes and sauces	Herrings, baked [for keeping?]
	Anchovies in stuffing for hare; in Lady Anderson's stuffing for hare; in? veal; in stewed cucumbers; in stewed rump of beef; in catsup for fish sauce	Pike, soused
		Salmon, pickled, Mr Nathl Wigmore
	Anchovies and oysters in fricassee of eggs	Oysters, pickled
8. NLI, MS 42,008, Abigail Jackson, c. 1782–1849		
Fish, stewed	*Anchovies, oysters and oyster liquor as flavour and texture enhancers in dishes and sauces*	Fish, potted
		Salmon, potted
	Anchovies in royal pasty or stake pie; in Scotch collops	Salmon, pickled x 2
	Anchovies & oysters in a calf's head hash	Salmon, pickled, a Lismore recipe
		Trout, potted
		Herring, potted
		Oyster, pickled

TABLE 1 (*cont.*)—Common styles of fish/shellfish cookery and preservation methods across eighteenth and early nineteenth-century recipe collections.

Cooking method	Dish, sauce, enhancers	Preservation (short and long term)
9. NLI, Leitrim Papers, MS 9,929, c. late 18th to mid-19th century		
Soles, to stew	Fish sauce x 3	Herrings, pickled
Oysters, to fry	Brown sauce for fish	Herrings, to save
	Lobster sauce	Oysters, pickled
	Lobster sauce for keeping	
	Lobster, to dress	
	Oyster sauce for fish	
	Oyster soup	
	Oyster omelette	
	Oyster sausages	
	Oysters in fried bread loaves	
	Fricassee of pike or eel	
	Maître d'hôtel (with cod/haddock)	
	Pepper pot a best Indian dish (lobster, crab, meat & veg.)	
	Anchovies paste in Scotch woodcock	
	Anchovies, oysters and oyster liquor as flavour and texture enhancers in dishes and sauces	
	Anchovies in ragou of breast of veal; in frialote/fiatlote of rabbit; in? of rabbit; in brown fish sauce; in fish sauce x 3; in carp sauce; in lobster sauce for keeping; in sauce for stewed soles; in veal olives; in? blood; in walnut catsup; in camp vinegar; in shoulder of mutton with mince	
	Anchovies & oysters in to dress a mock turtle	
10. NLI, MS 42,134, c. late 18th century/early 19th century, author unknown, provenance uncertain		
Fish, to boil & to boil	Fish sauce x 4	Salmon, soused
in cold water	Lobster sauce	Sturgeon, pickled
Fish, to broil	Fish sauce with lobster, shrimp and oysters	Whiting & haddock, salted
Fish, to fry x 2	Fish sauce with cockles	Cod's tail, salted
Eels, to broil	Sauce for carp or pike; for flounders, sole, pike and tench	Mackerel, soused
Eels, to bake	Oyster sauce	Herring, dried
Eels, to fry	Pike, to dress	Herring & mackerel, potted
Eels, to stew x 2	Pike, dressed with oysters	Anchoives, to keep
Eels, to spitchcock x 3	Pike, baked with a pudding (stuffed)	Oysters, pickled x 2
Pike, to boil	Water souchy with pike	Cockles, pickled x 3
Pike, to bake	Cod's head with shrimps and lobster	Mussels, pickled
Pike, to roast x 3	Crayfish soup x 2	Sole, plaice, smelt or flat
Carp, to stew x 3	Crayfish, to butter	fish, marinated x 2
Carps, to stew in	Lobster soup x 2	
blood	Lobster, to butter	
Tench, to broil	Lobster pie x 3	
Cod's head, to boil	Oyster pie x 3	
Flounder, soles, pike,	Oyster ragou	
tench, to boil	Oyster loaves	
Smelts, to stew	Oyster omlette	
Lobster, to broil	Oyster shells	
Lobster roasted x 3	Oysters fried as dish garnish	

TABLE 1 (*cont.*)—Common styles of fish/shellfish cookery and preservation methods across eighteenth and early nineteenth-century recipe collections.

Cooking method	Dish, sauce, enhancers	Preservation (short and long term)

Oysters, to stew x 3
  Oysters, grilled
  Oysters, fried
	Oysters fried with sauce
	Oysters with fish and bread crust
	Mutton stuffed with oysters x 2
	Boiled pullets with oysters
	Chickens stuffed with oysters
	Stewed morels with fish sauce
	Anchovies, oysters and oyster liquor as flavour and texture enhancers in dishes and sauces
	Oysters in white fricassee of chickens; in fricassee of lamb; in fricassee of eggs; in stuffing for oyster pie; in lear (moistening liquor) for pies; in roasted calf's head; in sauce for boiled or roasted chickens; in roti of sweetbreads; in forcemeat
	Anchovies in fricassee of chickens in vinegar; in fricassee of rabbits; in calf's feet fricassee; in fricassee of patridges; in a fricassee; in neck of veal ragou; in ragou of chickens and pidgeons; in roasted lobsters; in roasted hare; in mutton collops; in Scotch collops; in stewed rump of beef; in fried lambstones and sweetbreads; in sauce for carp or pike; with cockles in roast pike; in gravy; in broth for gravy; in dish of cow's heel; in green pea soup; in roasted shoulder of mutton; in hash of mutton; in mutton cutlets; in collar of beef; in veal olives; in veal collops; in carp stewed in blood; in chickens fried with thick sauce; in stewed eels; in white fish sauce; in soup maigre for Catholics; in sauce for beef steaks; in forcemeat for fowls; in sauce for flounder, sole, pike and tench; in onion soup; in lear for goose pie; in broiled pidgeons
	Anchovies & oysters in hash of calf's head; in ragou of fowls; in stuffing for fowls; in roasted or baked pike; in boiled leg of mutton; in lobster pie; with oyster liquor in boiled turkey
	Oyster liquor in gravy for pie; in lobster pye; with anchoives in sauce for wild fowl; in sauce for pullets or capons; with anchovies in hash of cold mutton; with anchovies in caudle for savoury and fish pies	

11. NLI, Townley Hall Papers, MS 9,560, author unknown, c. late 18th century to early 19th century

Pike, baked	Lobster stewed in cream	

12. NLI, Townley Hall Papers, MS 9,561, Lady Florence Balfour's Receipt Book, c. early to mid-19th century

	Maître D'hôtel with salt fish (haddock or cod)	Herring, potted
	Anchovies, oysters and oyster liquor as flavour and texture enhancers in dishes and sauces	Salmon, pickled
	Oysters in collared eels	
	Anchovies in catsup; in Dutch sauce x2	

The Townley Hall Papers are rich in documentation relating to the food and culinary activities of the Townley-Balfour family in the period spanning the eighteenth and early nineteenth centuries. Account books give an indication of food expenditure, patterns of purchases and reference the suppliers serving the Louth estate; a book of table plans and menus illustrate dining conventions; inventories reveal an elaborate but typical material culture of food preparation and dining, while a collection of recipe books reveals the cookery culture of the house. Five manuscript receipt books[41] (and two loose recipes written in French for '*pour faire une friscasee brune*' and '*pour faire la pate a faire de tourte*'),[42] while typically representative of the genre, hold additional value when analysed as a collection. Compilation of the recipes began in 1700 and continued into the mid-nineteenth century, thereby offering scope to map the evolution of taste and trend across several generations.[43] The diversity of these various food-related sources, while not unique, is quite particular to Townley Hall and their accumulative value provides a rounded view of the food culture of a relatively minor family from the gentry in the pre-Famine period.

The household account books sketch the practical concerns of house-hold management and the dynamics of food procurement. Expenditure was spread across staples (bread, milk, meat and offal) and luxury goods, and there is mention of corresponding suppliers like grocers, bakers, confectioners, butchers and milk sellers. Beef, veal, offal (sweetbreads, tongues and fry) and offcuts (calves' heads and feet) were the dominant meat purchases, followed by fowl (crammed/fattened fowls, chickens, ducks, geese and turkeys) with relatively low purchases of mutton, lamb, pork and bacon. There are occasional accounts of fish (non-specified but with mention of trout and salmon) and shellfish (oysters, lobster and crayfish) purchases with sporadic intakes of fruit (type non-specified) and vegetables (for instance, asparagus, scallions and potatoes). The grocery items are both numerous and various—mustard, raisins, spice, sugar, highly fashionable French sweetmeats, cheese, almonds, anchovies,

---

[41] NLI, Townley Hall Papers: MS 9,563, Mrs Jane Bury's Receipt Booke, 1700; MS 9,560, author unknown, *c.* late eighteenth/early nineteenth century; MS 9,561, Lady Florence Balfour's Receipt Book February 17th 1800; MS 11,925, author unknown, *c.* early to mid-nineteenth century; and Trinity College Dublin, MS 3,649, Anna Maria Leigh, her book, 25 September 1773.

[42] NLI, Townley Hall Papers, MS 10,247.

[43] For instance, the changing status of sugar is evident in NLI, Townley Hall Papers, MS 9,563: in the early recipes, it is used as a seasoning, for instance in the recipe for hare pye, while by the end of the compilation it is a standard ingredient in sweet dishes. NLI, Townley Hall Papers, MS 9,560's recipe for soda bread is witness to the use of chemical leavenings in bread-making. While the recipe for tomato pickle in NLI, Townley Hall Papers, MS 9,561 and TCD, MS 3,649 is evidence of the growing popularity of tomatoes as an ingredient in preserves—tomato was a New World ingredient that was slow to gather a following and was used in preserves before it found favour, in its raw form, as a salad ingredient. It seems that the recipe for tomato pickle was exchanged between members of the family and may indicate both the reliability of the recipe and the growing fashion for the fruit.

isinglass, oranges, lemons, chocolate, tea, coffee, salt, saltpetre and vinegar. Miscellaneous purchases of barm (ale yeast) and rennet suggest on-site bread production and cheese-making. Indeed, the frequent references to dairymaids and purchases of dairy equipment (wooden bowls and skimming dishes) points to the domestic preparation of both butter and cheese.

Account books are most helpful in identifying variety and diversity in the diet. However, they are biased towards goods that could not be produced in a domestic setting (imported luxuries and exotics) and towards those foods where demand exceeded domestic supply and production, as in the case of meat. The consistently low intake of fruit and vegetables indicated suggests that they were largely supplied from home production. Judging by the assortment of seeds supplied to Townley Hall by Daniel Bullen of Dublin in 1755, the cultivation of vegetables was extensive and varied with multiple varieties of the one cultivar grown in their kitchen gardens.[44] The account books, therefore, attest to the existence of a food system balanced between home-produced goods and those bought in commercial commodities. Significantly, the emphasis on meat and grocery purchases in the Townley account books echoes Clarkson and Crawford's assessment of the expenditure patterns of the wealthy based on their analysis of household account books and the retained imports figures from the late seventeenth to the early nineteenth centuries.[45]

This correlation suggests that the wealthy shared a valued system that assigned high status to commercial goods and meat, beef and veal, in the case of Townley Hall, and where value was measured not simply by monetary worth but also by the role and function of particular goods. Goods were not only emblematic of wealth. Access to grocery items in particular, brought consumers into active contact with more progressive and modern food systems. High and frequent consumption of groceries above all characterised the diet of the elite because of the ability of goods like sugar, spice, anchovies and isinglass to transform staple and mainstream ingredients into dishes appropriate to refined dining. The Townley Hall recipe collections are replete with pertinent examples: oatmeal and course brown bread combined with spice, dried fruit and sugar provided the basis for cream and egg-rich puddings; inferior offcuts such as calf's feet together combined with sugar and citrus fruits became delicate but heavily processed jellies; farmyard chicken (fried in butter and simmered in a strong broth with spice, anchovies and capers) became an elaborate fricassee dish of high flavour, of mixed textures (meat and oysters) and embellished for presentation (garnished with lemons and forcemeat balls).

The ingredients, cookery methods, and classification of dishes in the Townley collections conform to a distinctive cookery style that was common across the Irish corpus of receipt books. This style echoed the principles of profusion, diversity and variety. Diversity and variety are well illustrated in the cases of fruit and baked goods. The range of fruits featured in the collections included luxuries (oranges and lemons); hotbed fruit (melons); tree fruit

---

[44] For the full list see Clarkson and Crawford, *Feast and famine*, 49.

[45] Clarkson and Crawford, *Feast and famine*, 51.

(apricots, cherries, apples, pears, plums, damsons and quinces); berries (gooseberries, strawberries, raspberries, barberries, elderberries and black-berries); and currants (red and white), which were variously made into preserves, marmalades, compotes, vinegars, wines and cordials and with some fruits being candied, dried or preserved whole. Recipes for baked goods include cakes (plum, seed, saffron, almond and Shrewsbury); breads and enriched breads (comfortable bread, parapikelets,[46] ginger, saffron and soda); biscuits (saffron, orange and jumbals); and pastry. Profusion is best seen in the classification of dishes by category: pastry, sweet and savoury puddings, sweet and savoury pies, preserves, pickles, fricassees, soups, sauces, jellies, tarts, cakes, creams, custards, candies, sweetmeats, and dried fruits. Luxury imports played a central role in all of these categories. They also imparted distinctive flavours—for instance, the heavy flavouring of anchovies or the perfume of rose water—while mainstream ingredients, especially butter, cream and eggs were commonly used in large quantities making dishes in this convention heavy and rich in fat and flavour. Cooking techniques can be broadly divided between plain cookery; roasting, boiling, broiling and baking—and a more modulated approached in the creation of made dishes.

Incorporated into this complex and progressive food/culinary system, were the older concerns about managing seasonal gluts of fruit and vegetables and protecting perishable fish, meat, offal and game against spoilage. As a result, recipes for preserving feature prominently in recipe collections, and there is corresponding attention accorded to salt, saltpetre, vinegar and sugar. The extensive body of recipes for preserving fruits and vegetables in sweet and savoury forms were effective not only in managing seasonal gluts but they also produced an array of highly flavoured goods that could be incorporated into cookery—preserved fruits for tarts, puddings, cakes and dumplings; pickles, catsups and mushroom powders for seasoning dishes and preserved barberries, lemons and citron as garnishes for dishes. Long-established preservation methods like smoking and dry and wet salt cures remained standard but there was greater emphasis on using sugar to convert fruit into storable goods. Moreover, the recipes are not simply a mix of the old and the new—a close reading will draw out the more nuanced influences that directed developments in preservation methods. For instance, recipes for Dutch beef,[47] hams cured in the Westphalia manner[48] and Polonia sausages cultivated a sense of cosmopolitan sophistication, which tied to the trend linking ingredients to place of origin, but these recipes also encouraged practical dietetic change by introducing

---

46 NLI, Townley Hall Papers, MS 9,560, Parapikelets are barm-raised breads that were enriched with milk and egg whites. The ingredients were mixed to a stiff dough/batter akin to that of a plum cake and the parapikelets were baked on a bake stone. The recipe advises 'to bake one side before you turn them', which suggests that they were individual little breads. In NLI, MS 34,952, Mrs. Baker recommends mixing the ingredients to a stiff batter, which suggests that pikelets were possibly dropped onto a bakestone/griddle to bake.

47 NLI, Townley Hall Papers, MS 9,560.

48 NLI, Townley Hall Papers, MSS 9,563 and 9,561.

new tastes and textures—essentially new food products. The example of the Townley Hall Polonia sausage[49] is a case in point: the recipe is based on a triple-cure method using salt, saltpetre and smoke. It produces a charcuterie-type sausage for quick consumption. Polonia sausages were common across English-printed cookery books from the seventeenth century, but the Townley Hall example has its own peculiarities. It is neither a fresh nor a dry-cured sausage; it has the characteristics of both but eats like products from the European dry-cure tradition.[50]

The cookery style of the Townley Balfours was closely attuned to the rhythms of British culinary culture: dishes were sourced from the English repertoire, recipes evolved and changed in line with English culinary developments but they also embraced donated and family-inherited recipes. In addition, each collection manifests a particular signature of preference in the type and volume of recipes that are included.[51] However, on the whole, recipes for preserving, baking/baked goods, sweet and savoury puddings, and dairy

---

[49] NLI, Townley Hall Papers, MS 9,563. Bologna or Polony smoked sausages were popular in seventeenth-century Britain see Wilson, *Food and drink*, 314 and recipes are common in eighteenth-century printed cookery books. It is believed that the name Polony or Polonia (also sometimes Beloney) is a corruption of Bologna (Bologna sausage). See also see Glasse, *First catch your hare...The art of cookery, made plain easy, by a lady (Hannah Glasse),* a facsimile reprint of the first edition with introductory essays by Jennifer Stead and Priscilla Bain, a glossary by Alan Davidson, notes, and an index (Totnes, Devon, 1995), 126. The Townley Hall version contains chopped beef and pork cured with salt and saltpetre, and the mixture is heavily flavoured with pepper. Red wine and saltpetre give a characteristic red colour. When the beef casings are filled and linked, they are smoked (up the chimney) for a number of days. The sausage is cooked, cooled and thinly sliced for serving.

[50] The author and craft butcher, Jack McCarthy, Kanturk, Co. Cork, made and cooked the Townley Hall Polonia sausages in May 2014 in accordance with the recipe. The recipe was not adapted and worked extremely well.

[51] NLI, Townley Hall Papers, MS 9,563, total recipes: 223/4—culinary: 152/153; medicinal: 49; alcohol/drinks: 15; household: 1; cosmetic; 1; animal management: 1; miscellaneous; 1; unknown: 3. Culinary breakdown: preserves: 45; baked: 27; puddings: 19; dairy: 18/19; meat dishes: 12; fish dishes: 9; pies: 9; cured meat/fish: 4; shellfish: 2; nuts: 2; sauce:1; soup: 1; stuffing: 1; vegetable: 1; jelly/flummery: 1; vinegar: 1. NLI, MS 9,560, total recipes: 211—medicinal: 113; culinary: 75; unknown: 7; alcohol/drinks: 6; household: 6, medicinal, animal/fowl: 3; miscellaneous: 1. Culinary breakdown: preserves: 16; baked: 14; dairy: 9; puddings: 8; barm: 6; cured meat/fish: 5; soups: 5; vinegar: 3; meat dishes: 1; vegetable: 1; fish dishes: 1; shellfish: 1; fruit: 1; pies: 1; jelly/flummery: 1; sugar/confectionery: 1. NLI, MS 9,561, total recipes: 188/9—medicinal: 115/6; culinary: 55; household: 8; alcohol/drinks: 6; miscellaneous: 3; cosmetic: 1. Culinary breakdown: soups: 11; preserves: 10; baked: 8; cured meat/fish: 5; dairy: 4; fruit: 4; barm: 3; meat dishes: 3; fish dishes: 2; sauce: 2; sugar/confectionary: 2; puddings: 1. NLI, MS 11,925, total recipes: *c.* 190—medicinal: 87; culinary: 44; household: 23; craft: 12; alcohol/drinks: 10; unknown: 6; cosmetic: 4; miscellaneous: 2; gardening: 1; newspaper clipping recipe: 1. Culinary breakdown: preserves: 10; jelly/flummery: 8; baked: 7; soup: 6; dairy: 3; cured fish: 2; puddings: 2; vinegar: 2; meat

dishes were especially popular, with National Library of Ireland (NLI) MS 9,560 showing a particular affinity for barm and barm-making (Pl. III), cakes and different cheese dishes, cheese-making and variation of location-specific hard and semi-hard cheeses (Parmesan, Gloucester and Cheshire)[52] and cheeses dishes (potted cheese, ramekins, cheesecakes and amulets).[53]

Jane Bury's book has a commencement date of 1700 but it holds recipes that stretch well into the eighteenth century. Her recipes can be classified into three categories—kitchen, preserving and distilling recipes—and may be taken as evidence of specialisation of work and work space activities (see Table 2). Essentially, the collection suggests that the kitchen, the still room and the bakery were specialised work areas requiring skilled labour and knowledge appropriate and requisite to each. The prominence of preserving recipes and recipes for baked goods is of particular note and may be indicative of the interests of the lady of the house/lady compiler. As Lehmann and others have pointed out,[54] 'the areas where the lady of the house had taken an active role in the past are in sweet dishes and preserves of all kinds ... these are well to the fore in books by women authors'.[55] The association of women with sugar work, distillation and indeed medicinal receipts[56] (often incorporating sugar for its curative properties) was established by the seventeenth century and promoted as a suitable activity for genteel women.[57] With their involvement in refined areas of sweet cookery and medicine, the role of elite women went beyond the economic and operational concerns of household management as they also safeguarded both the physical and reputational well-being of their families.[58] The extension of their activities from the still room to the bakery and dairy is evident outside the recipe collections. Mary Delany, for instance, engaged variously with baking, sweetmeats and the work of the still room: she informed her brother Bernard Granville on 15 July 1750, 'I am preserving, pickling, and

---

dishes: 1; stuffing: 1; barm/yeast: 1; sauce: 1. NLI, MS 10,247, total 2 culinary recipes: baked: 1; meat dish: 1. TCD, MS 3,649, total recipes: 83—medicinal: 63; culinary: 14; alcohol/drinks: 6. Culinary breakdown: baked: 4; preserves: 2; cured meat: 1; meat dishes: 1; fish dishes: 1; soups: 1; sauces: 1; puddings: 1; barm: 1, vinegar: 1.

[52] NLI, Townley Hall Papers, MS 9,560.

[53] See note 49 above.

[54] See also, for example, Pamela A. Sambrook and Peter Brears, *The country house kitchen 1650–1900* (London, 1996), 164–7.

[55] Lehmann, *The British housewife*, 197. See also Mennell, *All manners*, 83–101.

[56] The Irish manuscript receipts collections typically contain recipes for cookery, household/cleaning tips and medicines: for example, medicinal recipes are to the fore in NLI, Townley Hall Papers, MSS 9,560 and 11,925.

[57] See for instance, Sir Hugh Plat's 1609, *Delights for ladies, to adorne their persons, tables, closets, and distillatories: with beauties, banquets, perfumes & waters*, introduced by G. E. Fussell and Kathleen Rosemary Fussell (London, 1948).

[58] For the case of medicine, see James Kelly, 'Domestic medication and medical care in late early modern Ireland', in James Kelly and Fiona Clark (eds), *Ireland and medicine in the seventeenth and eighteenth centuries* (Farnham, Surrey, 2010), 109–35.

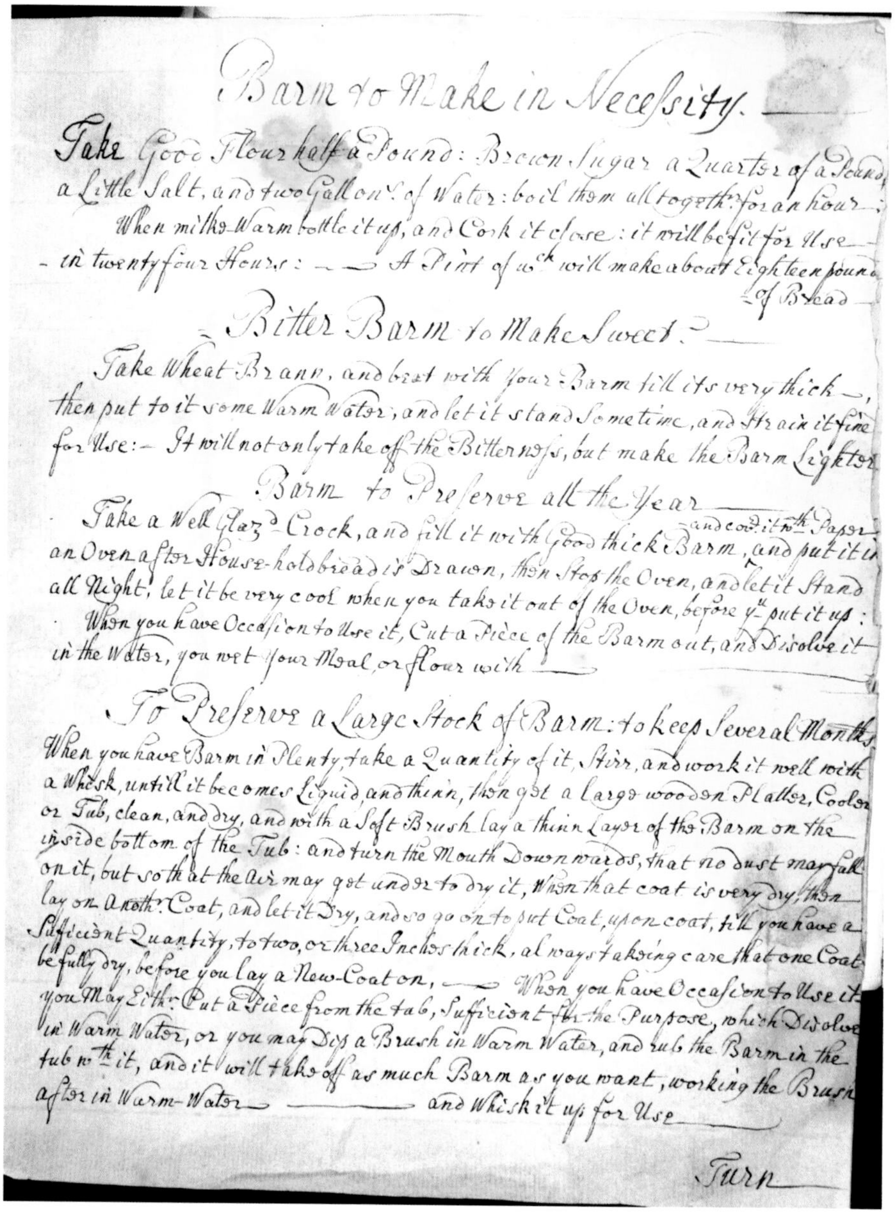

Barm to Make in Necessity.

Take Good Flour half a Pound: Brown Sugar a Quarter of a Pound, a Little Salt, and two Gallons of Water: boil them all togeth.r for an hour; When milk-Warm bottle it up, and Cork it close: it will be fit for Use in twenty four Hours: — A Pint of w.ch will make about Eighteen pounds of Bread

Bitter Barm to Make Sweet.

Take Wheat Brann, and beat with your Barm till its very thick, then put to it some Warm Water, and let it stand Sometime, and Strain it fine for Use:– It will not only take off the Bitterness, but make the Barm Lighter

Barm to Preserve all the Year

Take a Well Glaz.d Crock, and fill it with Good thick Barm, and cov.d it w.th Paper, and put it in an Oven after House-hold bread is Drawn, then Stop the Oven, and let it Stand all Night, let it be very cool when you take it out of the Oven, before y.u put it up: When you have Occasion to Use it, Cut a Piece of the Barm out, and Disolve it in the Water, you wet your Meal, or flour with

To Preserve a Large Stock of Barm: to keep Several Months

When you have Barm in Plenty, take a Quantity of it, Stirr, and work it well with a Whisk, untill it becomes Liquid, and thinn, then get a large wooden Platter, Cooler or Tub, clean, and dry, and with a Soft Brush lay a thinn Layer of the Barm on the inside bottom of the Tub: and turn the Mouth Downwards, that no dust may fall on it, but so that the Air may get under to dry it, When that coat is very dry, then lay on Anoth.r Coat, and let it Dry, and so go on to put Coat, upon coat, till you have a Sufficient Quantity, to two, or three Inches thick, always taking care that one Coat be fully dry, before you lay a New-Coat on, — When you have Occasion to Use it, you May Eith.r Cut a Piece from the tub, Sufficient for the Purpose, which Dissolve in Warm Water, or you may Dip a Brush in Warm Water, and rub the Barm in the tub w.th it, and it will take off as much Barm as you want, working the Brush after in Warm-Water — and Whisk it up for Use

Turn

Pl. III—National Library of Ireland (NLI), Townley Hall Papers, MS 9,560, book of recipes and prescriptions, late eighteenth century. Recipes for making and preserving or keeping barm are common across manuscript receipt collections. Barm is a by-product of beer/ale-making and is used as a leaven in breads and enriched breads. Recipes for home-production of barm are various and can be cereal/bran or flour or potato-based. The prevalence of barm recipes may indicate the decline or absence of home-brewing and it is also an indication of the importance of bread as a staple in the estate community. Image reproduced by kind permission of the NLI.

TABLE 2—Recipes from Mrs Jane Bury's Receipt Booke, 1700. (National Library of Ireland, Townley Hall Papers, MS 9,563.)

A Receipt for the eyes by Thomas Asline?/ Brugh?	M. et. Bury's Eyewater	To make Elderberry Wine	To make Oringe Marmelide	A Receit for ye gravell by Mrs C/Sonnall?
to Make Naple biscite by Heny Posonl/bey?	to Make Elderberry Wine	To Make a very good sack possett	To Make a Whipt Sillibub	To Make Goosebery or curran Wine
To Make Cowslip Wine	A Medicen for the Could	An approved medicen for the Cold or? of the Longs	To hash a Calfes head	To Coller Beefe
An excellent way for aqua mirabilis	Mrs Townlys Orange Pudding	Mrs Townlys Cake	Mrs Caldwells Plum Cake	To Pott Tongues
To make Pancakes	To make Barly Creame	To make sack Creame	To Stuff a Fillitt of veale	To make Almon butor?
To make an Almon Puddin	To Preserve Coddlng Green	To make hartshorne Jolly the best way	To Preserve Oringes in Jolly	To make Almon Creame
To Pickle Mushroon's	To presarve Oringes whole with the Meate in them	To Make Saffron Bread	To Make fine cakes	Aqua Mirabilis
Seed Cake	How to pickell Cowcumbers or purslan	To Make Sett Custards	To Make a fregocy of veale Lamb or Chicken	To make Scotch collips
To presarve Rasberries	To preserve Cherries	To make White Marmallet of Quinces	To make Orange cakes	To make Shrosberrie cakes
To presarve Gosberys	To make Jelly of Pippins	To make Oringe cakes like appry? cakes	To dry Cheryes	To make cleare cakes of Currans Rasberys and goosberries
To make cutlegs	To Boyle a cods head	To coller Eells	To Make an excellent Soope	To Souce fish
To make Chees Cake Meate	To make Angelicoe Cakes	To make Lemon Creame	To make Biskitt	The flower of all Oyntments
What the flower of oyntment is good for	How to make an oringe pudding	An excellent Plaister	A powder for consumptive Coff	Doctor T/Yarnors/ Surfeit Watter
How to Make the Yellow Plaister according to the Lady Meredith? Recept	To Make a Tansey	To Make Almon Butter	To presarve Barberies	To presarve Oringes in Jelly
To Make an egg pye	To Make a Chicken pye	To Make a hare Pye	To Make a Calves foott pye	To Make Sherritt or Pottatta pye
To Make the best Minse pye	What sorts of pyes are to are to [sic] be seasoned with peper and salt only	To Make forced Balls	To pickell kidney Beanes	To make Srosbery Cakes

TABLE 2 (cont.)—Recipes from Mrs Jane Bury's Receipt Booke, 1700. (National Library of Ireland, Townley Hall Papers, MS 9,563.)

To make Makeroons	To make Almon Jumballs	To make Creame Custords/Custards?	Souce for Base Mullett or Turbott?	To pickle purslan [crossed out]
To Make Pickell for Cowcumers	To Make a Saffron Cake? [MS. very faded]	For the pains in the Stomacke	To make an oringe puding by Mrs H? Lady Barkelys? gentlewoman	Lady Elliz? Moores? Receipt for to presarve Goosberries
An Antidote against pogzon [poison]?	For a burn by Mrs/Mst Som…th?	To make a westveliham	To Collar Salmon by M? Stanlay?	To pott Beefe by the same
An Oyster Pye	To pot Lobsters	To pot Eels	brown bread pudding	To make a Cleary? Cake Another
To make Bath Cheese Cakes	Bread Pudding by Mrs Stanley	A Strengthening broath by Mrs Spencer	For a surfeit by the same	To make safran cakes
To prevent impressions of small pox by Mrs Spencer	For ye kings Evil?	Another by Mrs Price	Orange pudding by Mrs Mtgomery?	How to Make A Sego Puding
To make a Jely of Currans	To make an Oatemeale pudding	To make ye plague water	To make Orange Wine	To Stew Carps the?
To Preserve Oranges Whole	To Make oyster Sasages	To make a Westvilliham	To Make Lemon Creame	To Green Plumbs for Tarts
Mrs Lucys fine Creame Cheese	Mrs Leathers? Lemond Puding	Mrs Marvins Creame Cheese	Almond Cheese Cakes	Mutton Pastie to Eat like Vension
Sauce for fish	To Frigasee Musharoons	How to Make a Potteato Puding	To Make a Codlin Toart by Mrs S?	Ginger Bread
To make an apple Pudding	The Sevenhour Pudding	Oyster Sausages	A Calves foot Pudding	To preserve Green Appricock
To Stew plaice, Eells, flounders & Such/Soles?	To preserve Aprriocks?	To Dry Plumes with the Mist on them	To preserve Cherries	To Preserve Walnuts
To Candy Angelica	To Preserve Rasberrys	To preserve Currans or Rasberrys/Barberrys?	Take Make Clear Cakes of Quinces?	To make Spiritt of oranges
To Dry Appricocks	To Dry any kind of Plumes or Cherry's	To Feed Pullets, Capons or Chickens	To recover Beer? sour or turned	To Make Spirit of Clary
To make potatoe pancakes	To Preserve Cherryes	To Make French bread Paste for Apple Pye	To pot salmon	To make Bolle Punch Marmeliet of Quinces
To Make Cow Slip wine	To Make plaine bisketts	To make a Lemon Pudding	To make Balm Wine	
To make Shrubb	To Preserve Lemmons for a Pudding	To Preserve Oranges or Lemons	To Hang Geese	To make a Quaking Puding
To Dry Peares	A neates foot Pudding	A Receipt for the Dropsy?	To Preserve Oranges or for Ballsam Hines? Lemons	To make the Plague watter
To Make a Carret Puding	To Make a Portugale Cake	To Make Shrosberry Cakes	A Receipt for the Dropsy?	

TABLE 2 (*cont.*)—Recipes from Mrs Jane Bury's Receipt Booke, 1700. (National Library of Ireland, Townley Hall Papers, MS 9,563.)

To make aguate Cake [no recipe]	To make Salloop	A Receipt for the biter Drafe/Draft?	A Dyett drinke for Gout or scurvy	Mr Hinds Eye wattor
?	A Receipt to make past for Tarts and?	A Receipt to pickle cowcumbers	Mrs Jane Brunker/ Brinkers?[MS damaged] Poppy Cordial	To Make Angelot Chees/ Mrs Brinker's Angelot Chees
Mrs Sumervills Receipt for Gripes in the Stumack	To make black berry wine	Doctor Cudmores Receipt for a Diet Drink	To Make a Spinge Toart	To Make A Lemon Cake
How to Stew Flounders Trout or Soal	To Boyle Pulits with oyster Sauce	Recipe for ye Ague by Mrs? Ro?	Recipe for a flux by Mrs Clamant?	How to Make a Po/etatoe Pudding
How to Make Rowlands almond Cheese Cakes	A Bitter Draught by Mrs Bury	To preserve Oranges in hony?	Powder for the Teeth by Mrs Loighfield/ Longhfield?	To prevent Moths from Eating of any wooling
A Receipt, by Mrs Price? for a dye/t? Drink ags. the Scurvy?	The Antipestilential Preservation Watter by? Townley	To Make Houghtons Drops	To make wafers	To make Sasages
To make polonia Sasages ? for? [written upside down] a poultes for a Sore breast	To preserve Apricots green For the bloody flux	To preserve damsons / To make hirapicra / For ye gripes	To Scorch Almonds / For ye Country disease? goosberry vinegar	To Stop a bleeding / To stop a vomiting / Lady Moores Drops for a consumption or Cough?
Calves lung water for a consumption? or Heelick fever?	To keep nuts? good & sweet for a whole year [written upside down] / ?	Popes Posset		

papering and giving direction to my maids'.[59] In November of the same year she was called to assist her confectioner in the making of 'orange-flower bread of my own orange flowers, of which I am a little proud', while January 1750/1 she engaged in making orange wine.[60] At a grander level, Emily, duchess of Leinster, (in December 1787) wrote that she was 'very proud of having made fifty cheeses this summer, which next year will nearly keep the family in that particular, my dairy is grown quite an object with me'.[61] These women played a supervisory/advisory role in the kitchen, leaving the laborious work to kitchen staff; thus Jane Bury's recipe for 'Mrs Cadwell's Plum Cake' required the maker to 'take two pounds of fresh butter and in a very Large bowle' but advised the cook to 'let a maid beat it up with her hand for about an hour'.[62] Women's interest and participation in the preparation of sweet goods/dishes can be viewed as occasional leisure activities that declined once sugar became an established ingredient and as staff became increasingly skilled in integrating it into the routines of the kitchen work. However, women's interest in this branch of cookery went well beyond simply an engagement with leisured and productive activities as it brought them into contact with fashionable and emerging trends in confectionery. As this area of cookery became increasingly specialised throughout the eighteenth century, it resulted in a more complex approach to the making, presentation and display of dessert dishes.[63] A corresponding rise in the status of domestic and commercial confectioners was paralleled by an increased output of printed books dedicated to sweet dishes and desserts.[64] These developments in cookery and changes to the meal structure, with increased attention to the dessert course, are evident in the high numbers of recipes for preserving and sweetmeats in the Irish recipe collections. Furthermore, preserving and the production of sweet dishes operated with expensive and exclusive ingredients that were sourced from afar or that demanded expenditure-heavy commitment of resources, energy and skill in their production. These dishes therefore embodied fashion, status and linked with European and cross-Atlantic trade networks, and were the cultural markers of a privileged and outward-looking group.

Women's interest in culinary activities contributed, as Lehmann asserts, to the continuing development of British cookery and to the establishment of a clear and distinctive British association with sweetmeats and sweet dishes:

---

[59] Angelique Day (ed.), *Letters from Georgian Ireland: the correspondence of Mary Delany 1731–68* (Belfast, 1991), 164.

[60] Day, *Letters from Georgian Dublin*, 176.

[61] Fitzgerald, Brian (ed.), *Correspondence of Emily, Duchess of Leinster*, vol. iii, (Dublin, 1957), 436.

[62] NLI, Townley Hall Papers, MS 9,563.

[63] Lehmann, *The British housewife*, 263–73.

[64] See, for example, Hannah Glasse, *The compleat confectioner: or, the whole art of confectionery made plain and easy* (London, *c.* 1760).

puddings, tarts, pancakes, cakes, creams, syllabubs and sweetmeats.[65] By the turn of the eighteenth century these dishes, in particular pies, puddings, creams (and roasts), were emerging as emblems of traditional British cookery. Their prominence in Irish manuscript collections attests to the shared inheritance by the Irish elite of traditional British culinary patterns and styles. Furthermore, as these icons of British food identity evolved throughout the eighteenth century, Irish recipe collections reflect and record these developments thus revealing a consciousness of changing trends and an aspiration to keep in step with culinary fashion. Moreover of course, conforming to the latest food trends also diminished the likelihood of culinary indiscretions that would be injurious on other fronts—attempts to cultivate refinement, gentility and discernment. An entry in the Townley Hall Papers as to the 'proper' means of seasoning pies attests to a willingness to abide by fashion's convention and to conform to the trend of separating sweet from savoury, in decreasing the number of ingredients in individual dishes, and in refining flavouring techniques:

> What sort of pyes are to be seasoned with pepper and salt only
>
> Venison, Mutton, Goose, Turkey Pigeon all manner of fowle Chickons excepted Gibetts Rabitts, all sorts of fish but Eells and? baked currans with them, veale or Lamb if be eaten Could, but if hot it is proper to put fruits in them and a Codall [66]

Equally, the treatment of macaroni as a highly charged item of cosmopolitan eating captures a kitchen trying to come to terms with a new ingredient used in a prescribed way. NLI MS 9,560 contains three macaroni recipes—one with potatoes used in place of pasta and two others, which seem to have grasped the principles of the dish. These developments in culinary styles impacted on dishes in a number of ways and prompted them to change, and evolve or eventually to disappear. The treatment of potato pies and puddings in Jane Bury's collection illustrates these movements (see Table 3). Jane Bury's potato pie is reminiscent of a recipe from Dorothy Parsons' recipe book (see Pl. IV).[67] It is characteristic

---

[65] Lehmann, *The British housewife*, 198.

[66] NLI, Townley Hall Papers, MS 9,563. A codall or caudle was a thick drink made with ale or wine or milk, sugar and spice. The ingredients were heated and thickened with breadcrumbs or oatmeal and eggs. In this instance, 'codall' refers to a moistening liquor made with sack and/or wine, flavoured with sugar and enriched with eggs. The ingredients were heated and added to sweet pies near or at the end of cooking. Lears made with wine, gravy and savoury ingredients were used in savoury pies.

[67] Dorothy Parsons' *The book of choice receipts* has been associated with Birr Castle, Co. Offaly, since 1666. It is possibly the country's oldest extant collection of recipes. Dorothy Parsons was the sister of Sir Laurence Parsons and although she started compiling her recipe book in 1666, many of the recipes predate this commencement, including the recipe for Potata Pie that is attributed to a relative of Dorothy's, Elizabeth Parsons. Many of the recipes are Elizabethan in style: Lady Alison Rosse, pers. comm. 24 March 2014.

TABLE 3—The evolution of potato pies and puddings, a selection of recipes from Irish manuscript books, seventeenth to nineteenth centuries.

Recipe title	Instruction
Dorothy Parsons, The book of choice receipts	
To make a Potata Pie	Take 2 dozen of potatoes boyle them till they will peele, then slit them, being peeled in the middle, then raise your pie, and take 2 pound of butter, and wash it in rose water, and worke it in your hands, then lay it in a thin cake all over the bottom of your pie, then season your potatoes, with half a pound of fine shugar, 2 spoonfulls of cinamon, a little sault place in your pie not to close for you must put between them, a pound a half of yolks of eggs boyled hard and cut in halves, then take 2 ounces of candied oring 2 ounces citron sliced very thin, and stick them in the potatoes, then lay a pound of sweet butter in the same maner as before all over the potatoes, close it up and bake it in a gentle oven half an hour before it is baked, draw it and putt in this Caudle, half a pint of navgis, half a pint of white wine, when it boyles take it from the fire and have a dozen yolks of eggs, and 6 whites ready beaten, stir them in, putting there to half a pound of butter & a quarter of a pound of shugar stirring them together they bee thick then putt it into the pie and set it in the oven tother half hour and scrap hard shugar over it and so serve it.
National Library of Ireland (NLI), Townley Hall Papers, MS 9,563, Mrs Jane Bury's Receipt Booke, 1700	
To Make a Sheritt or Pottatta Pye	Take the largest Sherre/i?tts you can gett and &boile then, peel then and Season them with Suggar & Cinainen sp? then Lay them in yr Coffin with canded Cittron Ringoe rootts good store? of marrow or Sweett Butter & bake it and when it comes out of the oven put in a sack Codall, Soe Searve it
How to Make a Potteato Puding	Take you Poteatoes and boyle ym very well and pound the dryest of them to a peaste then mix Quart/Pint? of Sweet Creame with them till it is as thin as a Batter beat ye yeolks of tenn Eggs and mix with it and half a pound of Pouder Sugar and a greated Nutmegg and half a pound of fresh Butter Some Blanched Almonds and a Little Canded Ornige Laying the marrow of two bones in Pretty Bigg pieces and Soe beake it let your Creame be boyld with some S/C?inainon before you mix it with your Poteatoes

TABLE 3 (*cont.*)—The evolution of potato pies and puddings, a selection of recipes from Irish manuscript books, seventeenth to nineteenth centuries.

Recipe title	Instruction
How to Make a Potatoe Pudding	Take 10 Eggs, Whites and yolks a pint of sweet cream a pound of potatoes peeled and well bruised a quarter of a pound of sugar two spoonfulls of flower a whole nutmegg grated mix all together and put into your Bagg an houre and a half boyleing will serve add to it two spoonfulls of Brandy
NLI, Leitrim Papers, MS 9,929, late 18th/early 19th-century recipe book	
A Potatoe Pudding	A pound of potatoes Boyled an pounded three quarters of a pound of Butter melted without water as much sugar ten Eggs half the whites mix them well together with a little Brandy the peel of a whole limmon grated and the juice squezzed in put a puff peast round the dish three qrs. of an hour will beak it.
NLI MS 5,606, Mary Ponsonby, early to mid-19th-century recipe book	
Potatoe Pudding	Take some potatoes, boil and peel them, pass them through a hair sieve, add the rhind of a Lemon, and four ounces of butter, beat up two eggs, and the juice of two Lemons, add all together, and sweeten them to your taste, put them in a dish or bowl, and bake them in a smart oven.

of an older order of mixing sweet, spice and savoury. In addition, the use of the word 'coffin' to describe the pastry case is a throwback to later medieval cookery, while the fact that skirrets and potatoes are interchangeable base ingredients may suggest that the potato was still a relatively new, and perhaps occasional, ingredient in the kitchen. Potato pies declined in popularity throughout the eighteenth century in contrast to puddings which held strong and developed in line with trends. The pudding recipes appear later in the collection: the first is still a melange of many and contrasting flavours, while the second has refined considerably with sugar and nutmeg as the main flavourings. Similarly a potato pudding recipe from the receipt collection assembled at Killeen Castle displays moderation in the range of ingredients used: the savoury/marrow element has been lost and is it clearly a dish that can be characterised as sweet, although the stalwart flavours of medieval cookery—spices, rose water and almonds—are still present.[68] This process of refinement continued into the nineteenth century, when taste was simplified further. Now potato puddings rely on lemon juice as the main flavouring, the taste is delicate and less cloying; however, the potato remains almost a secret ingredient, lost

---

[68] NLI, Fingall Papers, MS 8,041/1. See also NLI, Pakenham-Mahon Papers, MS 10134, recipe for potato pudding.

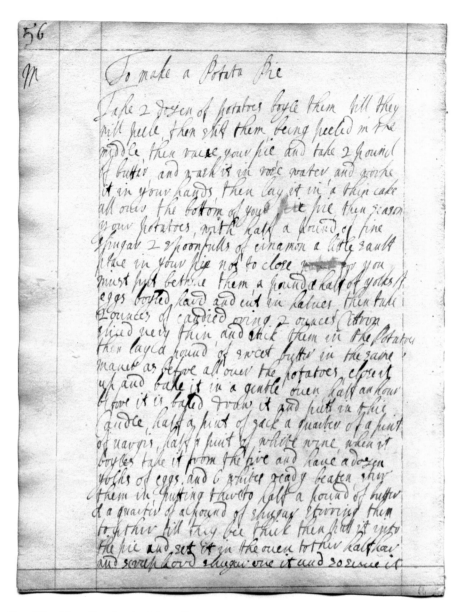

PL. IV—Birr Castle Archive, Dorothy Parsons' receipt book, *The book of choice receipts,* 1666. Dorothy Parsons' recipe for potata pie. Image reproduced by kind permission of Lady Alison Rosse and the Birr Caste Archive.

amongst the others.[69] While the use of fewer ingredients could result in more delicate-tasting dishes, the strength of flavour imparted by the ingredient was determined by cookery methods. The subtle flavour of lemon juice in the potato puddings of a later date contrasts with the intense lemon flavour achieved in a

---

[69] Potato puddings remain popular in nineteenth century recipe books, for instance, NLI, Leitrim Papers, MS 9,929, has 3 recipes (1 of these 3 is contained in Table 3), while University College Cork, MS U59/1 has 5 recipes (4, 11, 26, 41 and 53).

number of contemporary recipes where the fruit was the prime ingredient.[70] Therefore, the objective of the movement to refine tastes was not to produce bland dishes, rather it demonstrated the versatility of individual ingredients to function at different levels of intensity depending on the cookery methods that were employed.

Hidden too from these collections are the more mundane kitchen activities, for instance, cooking procedures such as broiling, boiling and roasting with the associated skills required to manage a spit, to baste meat or fish, and the acts of dredging to seal in juices.[71] In addition, the factors and agents that transform the recipe from text to finished dish remain as outside concerns simply granted passing mention with occasional reference to the maid's work or to a utensil specific to the execution of a particular recipe. The selectivity of the handwritten collections sets them apart from printed cookery books that routinely cover the discipline of cookery in all its dimensions.[72] The collections therefore lean towards more refined cookery; essentially in giving instructions for items and dishes that are heavily processed, and that demand more complexity and the lavish expenditure of resources in their creation.[73]

[70] For example, NLI, MS 34,952, Mrs A. W. Baker's Book Vol. 1st Ballytobin, County Kilkenny, 1810, has three recipes for lemon pudding: 'a lemon pudding', 26; 'a lemon pudding very good', 27; and 'lemon pudding, Lady Anne Fitzgerald', 67. 'A lemon pudding very good' uses the juice and the boiled and pounded rind of lemons in order to achieve an intense lemon flavour in contrast to the more subtle effect of using juice and grated rind in the other two recipes. (Author's experiment with recreating the dishes.)

[71] A notable exception is NLI, MS 42,134, author unknown, provenance uncertain. This extensive (*c.* 402 pages), well-ordered, well-planned and indexed recipe book includes cookery instruction together with direction for basic cooking methods; boiling, broiling, roasting, etc. In addition, the book provides a guide to foods in season. The mix of instruction for more complex cookery, basic cookery methods and market and provisioning information is typical of printed books and may indicate that parts of this collection were transcribed from printed cookery/household books and compendiums. The references to Thames salmon and Hampshire custom for burnt bacon would seem to support this suggestion.

[72] See, for example, Martha Bradley, *The British housewife: or, the cook, housekeeper's, and gardiner's companion by Martha Bradley, late of Bath* (1756) a facsimile edition (6 vols, Totnes, Devon, 1996–8). These volumes cover cookery techniques, recipes, bills of fare, the art of carving, medicinal recipes, animal husbandry, how to shop at market and seasonal produce. See also Ann Bagnall (ed.), introduction by Roy Shipperbottom (Lewes, East Sussex, 1997), *The experienced English housekeeper Elizabeth Raffald* which divides into part I (soups, fish, roasting and boiling, made dishes, pies and batters and puddings); part II (table decorations, preserving, drying and candying, creams, custards, cheesecakes, cakes and little savoury dishes); and part III (potting and collaring, possets and gruels, wines, catchups, vinegars, pickling, keeping garden stuff and distilling). The Irish collections are a pick and mix of these categories and, depending on the collection, emphasise particular or personal preference.

[73] The treatment, presence and profile of certain foods, therefore, are frequently neglected and under-represented in the manuscript recipe books. This bias is corrected somewhat with references to associated estate papers: for instance, the market books in

This is cookery of a higher order that extends to include made dishes—dishes that require an assembly of ingredients to a set convention either in line with an older order (hashes, collops and pies) or, as was more typical in the eighteenth century, dishes in sauces influenced by French styles of cookery (for instance in the inclusion of fricassees and ragouts).[74] The lower orders of cookery are given more attention outside the recipe collections, for instance in kitchen inventories that list spits, dredgers and dripping trays.[75] In addition, this type of cookery was not wholly dependent on the skills of a cook. Mrs Delany's letter of 23 January 1753, to her sister in England, explains that her husband's simple tastes make it convenient for her to travel without taking her 'very indifferent cook' as 'D. D.' (Doctor Patrick Delany) 'loves only roast, boiled and broiled and if all fails, the greatest feast to him is a fired [fried] egg and bacon'.[76]

These less than delicate cooking procedures were associated with the less affluent and, within the confines of the estate, with the diet of the servants. The marquis of Kildare's household book of 1758, for example, details the diet of the upper and lower servants as one characterised by boiled meats with special days marked with roasts and pies.[77] Indulgence, therefore, was linked to more expensive cuts of meat (roasting) and to a more complex system of cookery and an assortment of ingredients (pies). However, while the servants'

---

the Headfort Hall Papers record the importance and prevalence of meat in the diet. NLI, MS 25,306 is a series of 34 market books that detail the purchase of butcher's meat from 1759 to 1794. The books are remarkable on a number of fronts: in illustrating the range of meats consumed—mutton (in quantity), lamb, beef, kid and veal, purchased in carcass, side or quarter; offal and off-cut being equally typical and various in range—tongues, tripe, heads, feet, liver, crow, tongue and suet. The culinary treatment of offal as described in the manuscript receipt books sees its overt animal nature disguised through heavy and, at times, protracted cookery. Calves' feet, for instance, form the basis for elaborate jellies. The market books also detail the purchase of sheep's heads for distribution to the poor. These are a routine part of each meat order. For further discussion see Regina Sexton, 'Heads and feet, liver and lights: refining the objectionable', in *Cattle in Ireland: proceedings of the Agricultural History Society of Ireland conference 2014* (forthcoming).

[74] While it is not strictly correct to group pies amongst made dishes, they are included for this discussion in order to distinguish complex cookery from basic techniques. To appreciate more fully the nature of made dishes see Glasse, *The art of cookery*. A Dublin edition of 1796 has over 200 recipes for made dishes, including one for '*Tripe á la Kilkenny*'.

[75] See NLI, Townley Hall Papers, MS 10,249, Inventories, lists of furniture and plate, household goods, etc. of members of the Balfour family, mid-eighteenth to mid-nineteenth century. The inventory was first published by Rosemary ffolliott, 'An inventory of Reynella, Co. Westmeath in 1827', *The Irish ancestor* xii:1 and 2 (1980), 10–13.

[76] Day, *Letters from Georgian Ireland*, 170.

[77] Terence Dooley, 'A copy of the marquis of Kildare's household book, 1758', *Archivium Hibernicum* 62 (2009), 183–220.

diet was generous and various in its composition, it was 'ordinary'[78] in comparison to the style (and recipes) associated with the dining room and possessed an inbuilt tendency to privilege the steward's hall above the servants with the dishes served in both halls ranked with boiling as commonplace and roasting the technique of Sundays (see Table 4).

The collections, therefore, to varying degrees magnify the culinary interests and activities of wealthy women and promote a gentlewoman's country house style of cookery. Indeed with their emphasis on preserves as well as sweet, baked and dairy items, they may also reflect female taste preferences or at least tastes that were perceived to have a closer association with women. Bishop Edward Synge, for example, in expressing his frustration at the shortcomings of his kitchen staff, asserted that 'it is natural to expect Jelly on Sunday, especially for ladies'.[79] Selective and biased towards more refined culinary operations, the collections also conceal the ordered, disciplined and hierarchical world of work that scaffolded the culinary culture of the wealthy in late eighteenth and early nineteenth-century Ireland. The farm, the demesne, the kitchen complex and the *batterie de cuisine* supported the instruction of the recipe (see Fig. 1 and Pl. V). The climax of this extravagant expenditure in labour and resource was the dining room where presentation and consumption followed stylised and ritualised codes of behaviour with the dining convention to *service à la française*. A notebook of table settings from Townley Hall details the symmetrical patterning of named dishes on the table for eleven dinners that were prepared between 1811 and 1815 (see Pl. VI).[80] All bar one of these dinners were for two courses with parties ranging from six to sixteen people. This structure of two courses followed by a dessert course seems to have been typical and it is the structure often referred to by Mrs Delany[81] and Bishop Edward Synge.[82] The first table setting may be illustrated by a note dated 3 July 1811, 'a family party no 2 d course but tarts'.[83] This family dinner had nine or ten dishes (soup removed)—at the bottom of the table, green pea soup removed to roast beef and at the top end duck, and salmon and sole. At one side was fricassee of rabbit, boiled lamb, ham and bits, and at the other Buckingham Raised Meat Pies, fowl, and veal cutlets. The dinner ended with tarts in place of an elaborate dessert course, with a related recipe, 'to preserve fruit for tarts and family desserts' included in the Townley Hall Papers.[84] The substitution of tarts for a dessert course indicates a degree of difference between the meal plans for family dinners and more formal dinners with invited guests. Therefore the dessert course, where the skills of the confectioner were evident in intricate

[78] See for example NLI, MS 42,134: a recipe for boiled black pudding states that in order 'to make it more ordinary for servants you may add meal to thicken it'.
[79] Legg, *The Synge letters*, 69.
[80] NLI, Townley Hall Papers, MS 10,247, Recipes, menus, notes of household duties.
[81] Day, *Letters from Georgian Ireland*, 40, 53, 84.
[82] Legg, *The Synge letters*, 468.
[83] NLI, Townley Hall Papers, MS 10,247, Recipes.
[84] NLI, Townley Hall Papers, MS 11,925.

TABLE 4—Diet in the steward's and servants' halls. 'Rules to be observed at Carton in the absence of Lord or Lady Kildare in Regard to feeding of the Family', *Marquis of Kildare's household book, 1758.*

Meals	Time	Food	Cooking/Dish	Additional comments
Steward's Hall				
Breakfast	?	As for supper		
Dinner	4 pm	1 or 2 dishes	Mutton and broth	
Everyday		Mutton, pork, peas, veal, garden stuff	Mutton chops Harrico or flashed roast or boiled pork and pease pudding and garden things or stakes, roast or boiled veal with garden things (when veal is killed at Carton)	
Sunday		Beef and pudding	Roast beef and plumb pudding or any other kind of pudding	
Once a week			Mutton or beef pye	
Supper	?	Leftover meat from dinner, potatoes or garden stuff, eggs or cheese	Meat—cold, flashed, or broiled as they like	
Servants' Hall				
Breakfast	?			
Dinner Everyday	1pm	Beef, cabbage, roots	Boiled beef	Meat 1 ½ lbs per person. Housekeeper to have a contant supply of fattened chickens and fowl for the young ladies. Ducks, turkeys or pigeons only when convenient
Sunday		Beef and pudding	Roast beef and plumb pudding or any other kind of pudding	
Every Thursday		Mutton and turnips etc. or pork, pease, potatoes	Boiled mutton and turnips. Boiled pork or pease pudding and potatoes instead of mutton	
Once a week		Salt fish	Salted fish with potaotes and cheese	
Supper	?	Bread and cheese		Quarter pound of cheese. Butter a patt per man 1 oz (12 patts to the pound)
Vistors				
Any tenant, tradesman or stranger to Carton		Beef, mutton or cheese	Beef stakes, mutton chop, cold meat or cheese	Food to visitors as desired by Mr Bere (estate manager). Servants do not eat with visitors unless they are present at the servants'mealtime

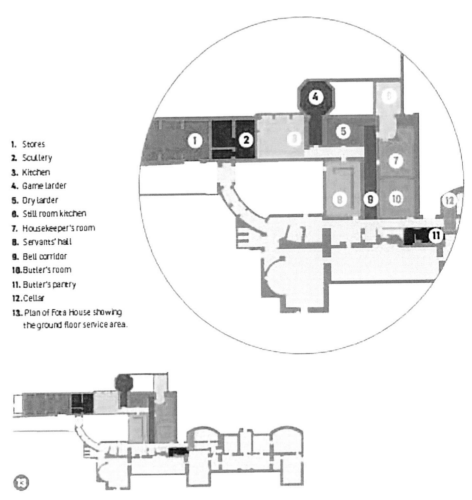

1. Stores
2. Scullery
3. Kitchen
4. Game larder
5. Dry larder
6. Still room kitchen
7. Housekeeper's room
8. Servants' hall
9. Bell corridor
10. Butler's room
11. Butler's pantry
12. Cellar
13. Plan of Fota House showing the ground floor service area.

FIG. 1—Kitchen complex, Fota House, Carrigtwohill, Co. Cork. The country's best preserved kitchen complex illustrates the journey and touch points of the recipe from storerooms to its final destination, the dining room. The kitchen complex deals not only in cookery but in the storage (storerooms, wet/game larder and dry larder), preparation (scullery), cooking (kitchen) and preservation of food (still room for preserves and wet larder for salting and pickling). The scullery connects directly to the passage way that leads to the house's kitchen gardens and orchard. Image reproduced by kind permission of the Irish Heritage Trust.

sweet and sugar creations, augmented the sense of ceremony and display associated with grand occasions of dining.

On occasion, the receipt collections signal the table status of a dish, for instance 'To fricassee Artichoke-bottoms, for a side-dish'[85], and a savoury side dish[86], but for the most part the function of the dishes is understood or else is

---

[85] NLI, MS 34,953, Cookery book *c.* 1780–1820, Mrs Creagh.
[86] NLI, MS 34,952, Mrs A. W. Baker's Book Vol. 1st Ballytobin, County Kilkenny, 1810.

PL. V—The restored kitchen (*c.* 1820s) at Fota House, Carrigtwohill, Co. Cork. The kitchen is designed in order to provide five different cooking areas: from left to right, charcoal-fired broiling range, built-in wall oven, simmering range, horizontal spit/ basket spit that can accommodate smaller vertical spits or bottle jacks, (warming cupboard) and built-in boiling pot (out of view). Image reproduced by kind permission of the Irish Heritage Trust.

guided by ample instruction supplied in printed cookery books.[87] This structure allowed for the element of display as the quality and quantity of dishes produced was a tangible measure of the capabilities of the kitchen and the skill of its staff. In addition, the menu design also demonstrated the taste (or otherwise) of the dinner planner, with her choice of dishes bringing sensory enjoyment (or otherwise) to guests. Hosting and planning a dinner for guests was therefore an inherently risky undertaking that encouraged critique and reputation evaluation, which explains the safeguards that attended the culture of recipe-keeping and the selection of kitchen staff.

County Kilkenny: William Tighe, Mrs Baker and Humphrey O'Sullivan

By the turn of the nineteenth century a number of different dietary systems coexisted in rural Ireland: the lavishly flamboyant food culture of the landed gentry, the comfortable and secure diet of the middling classes, and the debased and weak pattern of the rural poor. In the case of rural County Kilkenny, the complex food patterns of the gentry, typified by the Baker family of Ballytobin contrasted greatly with the debased one-pot cookery of the poor as outlined by

---

[87] See for example, *The modern cook, or housewife's directory* (Dublin, 1766), 61–6. A copy of this publication can be found in the NLI (LO 7000).

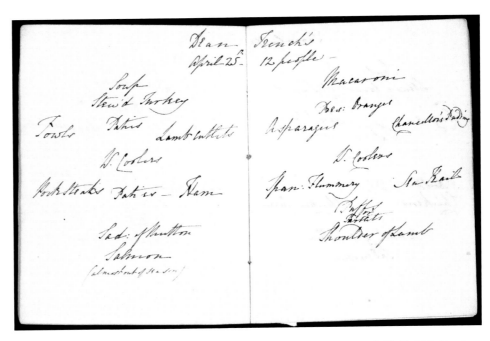

PL. VI—National Library of Ireland (NLI), Townley Hall Papers, MS 10,247, Recipes, menus, notes of household duties. A more elaborate table setting for a dinner for a party of 12 *á la française*, 25 April 1812? with the note for salmon 'almost out of season'. Image reproduced by kind permission of the NLI.

William Tighe, which some commentators believed was deteriorating further as a result of the increasing consumption of tea, sugar and baker's white bread. Therefore, the drivers of changes—changing market conditions and the increased availability of commercial goods in rural areas—worked either to weaken an already insecure system or else to elevate further an already elaborate one.

The Baker Papers[88] contain an account book spanning the years 1799 to 1838, and one of a two-volume set of recipe books, inscribed as 'Mrs A. Baker's Book Vol. 1st, Ballytobin, County Kilkenny, 1810'. Tastes and aspirations were shaped by visits to Bath and by contacts with Europe and the British Empire.[89] A network of more local suppliers provided staple and luxury ingredients, and supported home industry in planting, preserving and fattening farm animals and fowl.[90] The contents of the extant recipe book

---

[88] For discussion of Mrs Baker and the Baker Papers see Nevin, 'A County Kilkenny Georgian household notebook', 5–19.

[89] See, for example, Mrs Baker's recipe for preserved ginger 'as good as Indian ginger' (NLI, MS 34,952, vol. i, 12) and Indian Pickle (NLI, MS 34,952, vol. i, 13).

[90] Various suppliers' bills, with dates between 1799 and 1810/11 detail the purchase of garden seed, butter, salt, meat, game, poultry and groceries (tea, sugar and spices—nutmeg in quantity and lesser weights of cinnamon and mace). The poulter's bill (c. 1800–38) lists rabbits, venison, pheasant, partridge, snipe, woodcock, wild duck and teale alongside more usual farmyard fowl.

follow the pattern identified in other collections with recipes for preserving fruits and vegetables to the fore.[91] A body of recipes for sugar work (for example, orange cakes, snow drops and a hedgehog[92]) together with the large volume of preserving recipes, point to the utilisation and consumption of sugar of different grades. A large number of recipes for dairy produce in the second (lost) volume of recipes, in particular for homemade cheeses and extravagant moulded creams (see Table 5) contrasts sharply with Tighe's description of the food of the labouring poor of potatoes and seasonal residue milks (sour and buttermilk).[93]

Between these extremes, the rural middle class was economically resilient enough to withstand the vagaries of the market, which made its diet secure in the staples and open on occasion to engaging in elaborate systems of cookery and dining. The prevalence of mainstream foods (potatoes, bread, butter and meat) gave its diet a conservative character that dovetailed to some extent with the consumption patterns of the lower classes. However, security in the supply of staples gave a rural middle class confidence to aspire to the tastes and culinary mores of the upper classes. This is evident from the diary of the Callan-based schoolmaster and shopkeeper, Humphrey O' Sullivan. His work stands 'unrivalled in Irish as a source of information on the *mentalité* of the Catholic middle class'[94] and it is singular in the detail it provides on the food culture of a small rural town and its environs in the decades before the Famine. Described as a 'man of no small culture' with interests extending to literature, botany and folklore, O'Sullivan was also prominent in local politics as an O'Connellite leader.[95] His personal background was touched by poverty, which informed his understanding of the food culture of the poor.[96] His interests in food, therefore, were wide-ranging and comprehensive extending from descriptions of meals to wild foods to market prices. In line with Tighe, he also addressed the impact or otherwise of agricultural improvement on food quality and supply.

Recorded between 1827 and 1835, the diary details the range of available food and ingredients. His entries also reference a number of different

---

[91] The categorised breakdown of the over 180 recipes is as follows: total recipes *c.* 184—culinary: 178; alcohol/drinks: 3; household: 1; miscellaneous: 2. Culinary breakdown: preserves: 54; puddings: 19; dairy: 18; baked: 17; meat dishes: 11; sugar/sugar work: 8; soup: 7; fish: 6; shellfish: 5; barm: 5; vegetable: 4; fruit: 4; sauce: 4; meat cure: 3; pies: 3; jelly/flummery: 3; stuffing: 2; fish cure: 2; vinegar: 2; colouring: 1.

[92] These various sugar confections used refined sugar, pounded to a powder and made into a paste. For the hedgehog, powdered sugar was made to a paste and shaped to resemble a hedgehog; almonds were used to mimic the spines: NLI, MS 34,952, vol. i, 21.

[93] Tighe, *Statistical observations*, 474, 483.

[94] Proinsias Ó Drisceoil, 'Ó Súilleabháin, Amhlaoidh', in Brian Lalor (ed.), *The encyclopaedia of Ireland* (Dublin, 2003), 847. For further reading see also Liam P. Ó Murchú (ed.), *Cinnlae Amhlaoibh Uí Shúileabháin: reassessments* (Dublin, 2004).

[95] McGrath, *The diary*, vol. i, ix.

[96] See McGrath, *The diary*, vol. i, vii–xi.

TABLE 5—A list of the recipes contained in Mrs A. W. Baker's Book, volume ii. The collection has a high number of recipes for preserving fruit, vegetables, meat and fish, together with dairy-based and cheese recipes. The concern with the routine of bread-making, evident in the inclusion of six recipes for barm, a leavening agent, contrasts with more intricate activities of creating elaborate moulded cream dishes (in recipes for steeple cream and raspberry cream in shapes). It is not known if this collection is extant. The list of recipes is indexed in Mrs Baker's first volume (National Library of Ireland, MS 34,952).

Almond Cheese Cakes	Almond Puddings in Skins	Apricots preserved	Almond flomary	Almond Cream
Apple Puddings baked (×2)	Almonds Parched	Angelica Preserved	Barm [× 6 recipes]	Black Currant Jelly
Bath Cake	Brandy Peaches	Burnt Cream (×2)	Blanch Monge (×2)	Beef du Chasse
Black Caps	Butter Milk Cheese	Best baked Custards (×2)	Bacon Made	Black Currant Wine
Blanch Walnuts	Barberries Preserved	Beef Hung	Cream Spanish	Yellow lemon Cream
Cheese Cakes	Custards Baked with snow	Curd Pudding	Catsup	Cucumbers Pickled (×2)
Cherries preserved	Calfs Head Collar	Cream, Devonshire	Camp Vinegar	Collar a Turkey
Cream, Steeple	Chickens & Onions	Compot of Apples	Cherries, Dried	Cream Cheese
Cheese, New Milk	Cherry Brandy	Cucumbers Sliced	Cakes Queen	Cream, Whipt
Collar Beef	Cucumbers Preserved	Cheese, Dutch	Cheese, Slip coat	Codlings to keep for Winter
Carp or Tench, to Stew	Catsup, Oyster	Damacine Paste	Dry Salmon	Dutch way to Pickle Herrings
Egg Cheese	Flomary, Rice or Rattilie Cream	Flumary	Flomary, Spanish (×2)	Fricasy of Lobsters
Frost Tort	Fish Sauce	Fricasy of Chicken	French Rolls	Fasting Soup
Fatten a Veal	Figgs Preserved	Fatten Old Turkeys	Fatten Young Turkeys	Ginger Preserved
Gooseberry Wine	Ginger Wine	Goose berry Paste	Gooseberry Vinegar	Goffers
Green Pea Soup	Green Walnuts Preserved	Gravy Soup, very good	Good Woman's Pye	Green Plumbs Preserved
Green Apricots Preserved	Green Mogul Plumbs Preserved	Golden or Lemon Pippins Preserved	Gooseberries the whole year to keep	Ham Pye
Jelly, Red Currant	Jelly, Orange	Jam, Rasberry	Kilbrew Cream Cheese	Lemon Cakes
London Lemon Cheese Cakes	Lemon & Orange Cheese Cakes	Lady Riverston's Orange Custards	Lady Blunden's Sollid Whipt Cream	Lemonade
Mushrooms, Pickle Brown	Mince Pies	Mrs Cole Hamilton's Sauce for everything	Mead [×2]	Matrimony
Macaroon Cheese Cakes	Mushrooms to keep a year	Mock Brawn	Morella Cherries Preserved	Mushrooms Preserved
Nectarines, to Preserve	Nuns Biscuits	Noyau Peach leaf	Ox Cheek to Stew	Oranges Preserved Whole
Oyster Sauce	Onions Ragout	Oranges Sliced	Oyster Sausages	Onion Soup
Orange Brandy	Orgeat	Oyster Catsup	Pickle Walnuts	Pudding, Raw rice
Pudding, A	Pears red & Clear	Plumb Pudding Light	Paste Royal	Pancakes [×2]
Pigots Cakes	Pot Mackerel	Puddings, College	Potatoe Pudding	Pickle for Tongues
Pickle Beef	Potted Turkey	Preserved Pippins Whole	Pot Salmon To	Puff Paste
Plumb Cake, Mrs Wade	Icing for Ditto	Rasberry Brandy	Rasberry Jam, the Very Best	Rasberry Cream in Shapes

TABLE 5 (*cont.*)—A list of the recipes contained in Mrs A. W. Baker's Book, volume ii. The collection has a high number of recipes for preserving fruit, vegetables, meat and fish, together with dairy-based and cheese recipes. The concern with the routine of bread-making, evident in the inclusion of six recipes for barm, a leavening agent, contrasts with more intricate activities of creating elaborate moulded cream dishes (in recipes for steeple cream and raspberry cream in shapes). It is not known if this collection is extant. The list of recipes is indexed in Mrs Baker's first volume (National Library of Ireland, MS 34,952).

Rattifie Cheese Cakes	Rump of Beef Stewed	Rigby's, Mrs, Turnip Soup	Roussals/Roufsals? (×2)	Rusks
Shrewsberry/bury? Cakes (×2)	Savoury Corner Dish	Staple's Vegetable Soup	Sligo Way to Pickle Salmon	Sauce White
Stew Soles	Seed Cake	Sauce, Lobster for keeping	Shrub (×2)	Soup Meagre
Vinegar, King's Fort	White Currant Wine	Wade's, Mrs. Cheese Cakes	White Soup	Weafors
Yeast				

dietary systems,[97] the seasonal nature of the diet,[98] special occasion foods,[99] Famine relief foods,[100] feasting and fasting foods[101] and hotel food.[102] Furthermore, from the descriptions of the meals that he consumed, it is possible to make guarded inference to styles of cookery and dining rituals. In addition, the mixed nature of his entries, which range from observational to reflective, provides food-related details that range from day-to-day market conditions to long-term pronouncements on how diet had changed, particularly for the poor, within a generation from the turn of the nineteenth century.[103]

The food and ingredients mentioned throughout the diary range from the home-produced or market staples of meat, offal, off-cuts, grain, potatoes

[97] McGrath, *The diary,* reference, for example, to servants' diet: vol. i, 151.

[98] McGrath, *The diary*, reference to soft berry summer fruits: vol. i, 93; vol. ii, 155; blackberries: vol. i, 123 and nuts: vol. i, 135.

[99] McGrath, *The diary*, reference to fair/patron day foods (gingerbread, currants, cherries, gooseberries): vol. ii, 183; wake food/bread and butter: vol. 1. 57; vol. iii, 225; and possible reference to three kinds of bread (leavened bread, brack/fruit cake and seed cake) at a country christening: vol. ii, 361.

[100] McGrath, *The diary*, reference to maize as relief food: vol. i, 61; vol. ii, 185–6, 315; vol. iv, 41; and to oatmeal for the poor: vol. i, 29; vol. ii, 293.

[101] McGrath, *The diary,* reference to Shrove Tuesday meat: vol. i. 229; vol. iii, 19; Shrove Tuesday pancakes: vol. iii, 19; Easter food/eggs: vol, i 21, 247; vol. ii, 263; meat for Christmas season: vol. i, 197; vol. ii, 77; Christmas pig: vol. iii, 267; Martinmas food: vol. ii, 356–9 vol. ii, 357; Halloween food: vol. ii, 47; vol. iii, 87; probation of white meats for fast days: vol. i, 231, 241; vol. ii, 119, 263; vol. iii, 21, 117; New Year's Eve/Little Christmas Eve custom of throwing bread at the door: vol. ii, 99; and Good Friday food: vol. ii, 141, 263.

[102] McGrath, *The diary,* Rose Hotel, Kilkenny, hake, salmon and new potatoes, vol. i, 309.

[103] McGrath, *The diary,* vol. i, 277

and dairy foods to luxury goods such as tea, sugar and spices. Game is rarely mentioned; fish is a secondary concern to meat, and largely associated with days of fasting, while wild foods are mentioned largely in the context of their role as need foods for the poor. In the diary these categories—fish, game and wild foods—possess peripheral status as O'Sullivan devotes most emphasis and attention to market conditions and how fluctuations in price impact on the circulation of meat, grain, potatoes and dairy produce most especially as it impacted on the diet of the poor.

Seasonal scarcity in the availability of foods[104] and in the reduced demand for paid labour,[105] and the impact of bad weather[106] affected food supply as did the management of farm animals and the availability or otherwise of winter fodder. O'Sullivan linked methods of animal husbandry and food quality to disparities in the range and standard of food at the market at different times of the year and by association, to the different farm practices of those open or closed to improvement, 'Cattle have no grass and hay does not give them milk; but only very few children of the Gael yet know how to put up green winter crops; consequently only a pint of sour milk is [to be got] for a penny now'.[107]

The seasonal disruption in supply, which resulted in poor quality milk and, particularly, meat were features that often coincided with two significant meat points of the religious calendar—Shrove Tuesday and Easter Sunday. A feast of meat on Shrove Tuesday and the procurement of meat at this time to put to salt or smoke for Easter Sunday were two aspects of feasting rituals that bookended the Lenten fasting period. For the poor, these meat-eating/procurement rituals held additional significance as two of the three calendar days when meat was the aspired to item of celebratory eating.[108] O'Sullivan notes the paucity of supply, the expense, and the poor quality of both meat and off-cut available for Shrove Tuesday in 1829, 'Shove Tuesday, ... little meat on the market, and that little bad and dear, five pence for pickled pork, five pence halfpenny for tortured mutton: four pence halfpenny for carcass beef: three pence [a lb] for pigs' heads'.[109] For Shrove Tuesday, 1831, he recorded his stockpiling of meat, most likely in anticipation of Easter Sunday, when he referred to hanging up 'five pieces of beef, six neats' tongues, and a half hogshead'.[110] Setting aside also secured against a hike in price at times of seasonal meat scarcity as indicated on Good Friday, 1832, 'Callan butchers have very little meat today. It will be dear on Easter Saturday. I will buy no meat, for I have bacon and "landrae" that is, smoked beef, in plenty'.[111] The

---

[104] McGrath, *The diary*, vol. i, 7; vol. ii, 117–18, 133.

[105] McGrath, *The diary*, vol. i, 7.

[106] See note 98 above.

[107] McGrath, *The diary*, vol. ii, 133.

[108] McGrath, *The diary*, vol. i, 19–21, vol. ii, 133 and Tighe, *Statistical observations*, 490.

[109] McGrath, *The diary*, vol. ii, 117–19

[110] McGrath, *The diary*, vol. iii, 19.

[111] McGrath, *The diary*, vol. iii, 137

ability, therefore, to set aside meat to cure and smoke in times when the quality was good and the supply large enough to make prices reasonable were features of the foodways of the more economically secure. In this sense, economic security brought a sense of food security; furthermore, economic security allowed for future planning, and this orderly approach to food procurement and storage contrasted with the system of leaving to chance, goodwill or alms-giving that characterised the food patterns of the poorer classes.

In this precarious and weakened food system, meat was an expensive and rare commodity, which held luxury status and gave more meaning to times of celebratory and festive eating.[112] Tighe's comment that the poor will distress themselves to secure meat 'in plenty as pork and geese for christenings'[113] indicates that the priority for the poor was the acquisition of meat in quantity above concerns of quality. The determinants of quality were many: O'Sullivan for instance equated it with the type of meat cut as his entry for Christmas Eve, 1828, made clear, 'Many a pork steak, and pig's head; many a "little market joint" of lean, tough beef; many a large fat junk of an old sow's groin; many a remnant bit of a little old ram being bought by the poor people; for the wealthy prosperous folk have already bought choice meat'.[114]

For his part, Tighe used the issue of quality as a recommendation for the adoption of improving methods over the older system of animal husbandry, implying that new and improved breeds of cattle and sheep produced better quality food: in the case of cattle, milk with a higher fat content for butter-making and for sheep, meat of finer grade.[115] However, the disparity between old and new farming methods, and the associated divergence in product quality was not simply based on a willingness to adopt principles of betterment and advancement through enlightened thinking and practice but rather related to market conditions. Therefore, as Tighe highlighted, preference for different cattle breeds, improved or otherwise, was determined by how the farmers supplied the market with either raw or processed product, 'Here the little farmers who sell milk prefer the Irish cow from the quantity it gives, independent of quality; and the dairy men approve of the rather half bred cattle'.[116]

The relationship between improving methods and a more intensive system of production was developed further by Tighe in his advocacy of the improved Leicestershire breed of sheep because they fattened early and fattened well on less feed with 'the grain of the meat [being] very fine'.[117] Additional desirable characteristics above unimproved sheep were the heavier carcass weight, lighter weight offal and by-product.[118] This is a case of improvement giving quicker profit at the expense of taste and quality. A slower and older

---

[112] See notes 101 and 104 above.
[113] Tighe, *Statistical observations*, 504.
[114] McGrath, *The diary*, vol. ii, 77.
[115] Tighe, *Statistical observations*, 309–12 and 325.
[116] Tighe, *Statistical observations*, 310–11.
[117] Tighe, *Statistical observations*, 325.
[118] Tighe, *Statistical observations*, 327.

system of sheep-rearing produced more intensely flavoured mutton and quantities of offal/by-products (blood, guts, head and pluck), which were a cheap source of protein for the poor.[119] Tighe was unconvinced:

> Those who have been accustomed to eat six year old mutton, say the Leicestershire sheep are not good at two year old, but the farmer feeds for the butcher, who buys his meat when fat, and it is a doubt whether many would know the difference on the table, provided the meat is kept a day or two longer before it is dressed: the gravy of the former may be higher coloured, but they will not know it by taste[120]

The sacrifice of taste for profit was ameliorated somewhat by the advice to hang meat longer before cooking, leaving only the lightness of the resulting gravy as objectionable to the discerning consumer. In culinary terms, improving agriculture may be said to have brought refinement in both taste and texture rather that acting as an agent of destruction to taste; this new approach paralleled a similar movement in cookery styles. New styles of cookery developed and encouraged a scaled down combination of ingredients to produce more refined and nuanced-flavoured dishes. The move to a more refined system of cookery encouraged taste, in the physiological sense, to discriminate between strong and more subtle flavouring techniques. Culinary refinement expressed in changes to the composition, flavouring and presentation of dishes gained ground on the premise that less was more. Good taste expressed through a more refined and simpler approach to cookery was a matter of choice for the more affluent classes.

For the poorer classes, however, a stagnant culinary culture linked simplicity with debasement making inevitable the advice of improvers that dietary advance was contingent on the development of cookery skills and a diversification of the ingredient base. For advocates of improvement, the transmission of recipes and the promotion of basic cookery skills were seen as means of bringing moral, nutritional and economic benefits to the poor household. In a middle-class context, the consumption of recipe-inspired dishes also had particular meaning. O'Sullivan's diet while stable in character and representative of a mainstream, rural middle ground is touched on occasion by luxury and recipe-inspired dishes. It operated to a rhythm that saw the everyday broken by periods of fasting and feasting. Within this structure the recipe made occasional appearance bringing complexity to dishes associated with celebratory dining. Aspects of this culinary and dining culture are identifiable in his descriptions of the meals that he consumed both at home and in the homes of neighbours and the priest, Fr James Hennebry. Between the years 1827 and 1832 of the diary, he records 25 occasions of dining at different levels of formality in both domestic and social contexts (see Table 6). The slight number

---

[119] For offal/off-cut eating amongst the poor see McGrath, *The diary,* vol., ii, 77; Tighe, *Statistical observations,* 386. For the consumption of sheep's heads by the poor see NLI, Headfort Papers MS 25,306 (1–34), market books 1759–97.

[120] Tighe, *Statistical observations,* 326.

TABLE 6—The festive, everyday and special occasion meals of Humphrey O' Sullivan, Callan, Co. Kilkenny, 1827–32.

Date	Entry
Easter Sunday, 15 April 1827	to Butler's where we got white baker's/loaf bread (*builín bán*) fat/juicy pork, sweet/tender mutton, whitish pudding, and a drop of whiskey, or barley juice
Thursday, 12 July 1827	… to Mockler's, where I got a junk/thick slice of bread (*ceapaire*), baker's/loaf bread (*builín*) and butter, and a strong drop of spirits
Thursday, 19 July 1827	We got a good dinner from Mr Power … fat smoked swine flesh-bacon, white cabbage, magnificent potatoes and hot-mixed whiskey or punch
Thursday, 11 October 1827	We got whiskey, cold and hot, baker's/loaf bread, broiled beef/steaks, cooked colt's foot (*adhann brúite*) and tea [at funeral/wake]
Tuesday, 25 December 1827	I have a roast goose for dinner, stuffed with potato/potato pudding
Sunday, 30 December 1827	I have pigs feet and fat pork for dinner
Thursday, 21 February 1828	I have *coimhbleidhe* (*comhbleide*) for dinner today. It is not correct to call it calecannon for there is neither kale nor cabbage nor white cabbage in it, but white potatoes / 'lumpers'? (*bocairighe bána*) full-white new milk, good salted butter, salt on top of that, pepper to heat it for me onions if I were to mention them, and myself and the children and my beloved wife eating it to our hearts' content without shortage or superfluity
Easter Sunday, 6 April, 1828	Easter Sunday and Christmas Day: the two best days for the stomach. I had today smoked pork or bacon and biped-flesh or chicken for dinner
Friday, 20 June, 1828	I had dinner with Father James Hennebry. We had two fine fat sweet substantial trout, one of them as big as a small salmon. We had hard boiled hen eggs and cooked vegetable/asparagus? (*creamh muc bhfiadhain i. lus praicidh.i lus súghach i. moighnian*) soaked in melted butter on boiled new milk and salt. We had port wine, and punch as good as I ever drank, on the table
Friday, 18 July 1828	Seven of us had dinner at the Rose hotel [Kilkenny]. We had salmon and fresh hake and new potatoes, bread, beer and punch. It cost us three shilling a man
Tuesday, 22 July 1828	I had dinner with the parish priest, Father James Hennebry. We had a boiled leg of mutton, and roast fowl with spiced stuffing/spiced pudding (*putóg spiosartha*). We had punch, tea and songs in Irish till ten o'clock

TABLE 6 (*cont.*)—The festive, everyday and special occasion meals of Humphrey O' Sullivan, Callan, Co. Kilkenny, 1827–32.

Date	Entry
Thursday, 31 July 1828	I went to Kilkenny in Keating's car. I ate my share of a leg of mutton and flour bread for sixpence halfpenny
Sunday, 14 September 1828	Patron Day of Cooliagh. Four of us dined with Father James Hennebry. We had a boiled leg of mutton with carrots/parsnips? (*meacain*) and turnips; we had a roast goose with green peas and stuffing/pudding; we had a dish of tripe smothered in new milk; we had port and wine and punch; we had tea and sweet Irish songs
Sunday, 28 September 1828	I spent the evening and part of the night at the house of the parish priest, Fr. James Hennebry. We had three dishes, cow entrails, that is tripe smothered in butter and new milk; bacon with cow's kidney and white cabbage; roast duck with green peas. We had punch and songs till ten at night
Sunday, 5 October, 1828	We had a splendid dinner at the parish priest's . . .We had a leg of mutton, bacon, chickens and white cabbage; two roast duck and green peas. We had sherry/white wine and port wine, and lots of punch till eleven o'clock
Tuesday, 17 March, 1829	A group of us drank our Patrick's Pot at the parish priest's, Father James Hennebry. We had for dinner fresh cod's head, salt ling softened by steeping, smoke - dried salmon and fresh trout, with fragrant/sweet/tender cheese and green cabbage. We had sherry and port wine, whiskey and punch enough
Sunday, 27 December 1829	An splendid dinner was ready for me [at Mullinabro, county Waterford with Father Simon Walsh and Mary Walsh] a chine of beef new-salted and white cabbage, roast goose with bread stuffing/pudding (*putóg aráin*) in it; a leg of mutton and turnips, bacon and chickens and roast snipe. There were port wine and whiskey turned into punch
Friday, 30 July 1830	The diet of my family and myself is as follows: -a hot breakfast, consisting of oat-meal stirabout made on milk; wheaten bread and milk at one o'clock, this is a cool midday meal; and potatoes and meat, or butter, towards late evening, as a meal in the cool of the evening
Tuesday, 19 October 1830	A mild night which I passed happily at Michael Hickey's, eating juicy/fat/dainty beef and tender/sweet mutton, and merrily drinking sweet strong punch, till midnight, in the company of the parish priest, and Richard Culleton and the host and his wife, who is a cousin of the priest's

TABLE 6 (*cont.*)—The festive, everyday and special occasion meals of Humphrey O' Sullivan, Callan, Co. Kilkenny, 1827–32.

Date	Entry
Thursday, 11 August 1831	I had ox-tongue and white cabbage for dinner
Michaelmas Thursday, 29 September 1831	I had a dinner-beef and potatoes—for four pence halfpenny. I also had a share of Michaelmas goose [in Dublin]
Friday, 30 September 1831	I had dinner, bread and butter, at Eileen Delahunty's, my sister-in-law
Tuesday, 4 October 1831	I got bread and butter and punch in plenty [at Patrick Phelan's]
Monday, 31 October 1831	November, or Hallow Eve. I spent the night…eating apples, drinking tea, roasting nuts, drinking punch and eating speckled/fruit apple loaf/cake? (*breac-bholg ubhla*)
Friday, 31 August 1832	I had salmon for dinner

of dining references relative to the time period covered is problematic but qualified somewhat by the fact that his entries refer predominantly to festive and special occasion meals. Most usually, Christmas Day and Easter Sunday dinner, as 'the two best days for the stomach',[121] were consumed at home, while Sunday and special occasion meals were typically taken with Fr Hennebry. Indeed, the meals at the priest's house possessed a higher level of complexity in terms of preparation and meal structure.

Meals were characterised by an ample variety of ingredients and composed of several dishes. An additional feature is the high prevalence of meat (two or three varieties at most meals) relative to fish, which was reserved for Fridays and fast days. Fresh and preserved meats were often presented at the same meal, and the combining of meat with offal was common. Of note is the reference to newly salted chine of beef that was part of the meal O'Sullivan enjoyed with Fr Simon Walsh on 27 December 1829 after travelling to Mullinabro, Co. Waterford, to meet Mary Walsh with a view to making her his second wife,[122] and may indicate a taste preference on special occasions for more lightly salted meats as distinct from those of a heavy, wet or dry-salt cure.

Dishes that characterise more affluent tables, for instance soups and sweet courses, or indeed elaborate dairy dishes requiring stepped preparation are not mentioned. A soup and a dessert/sweet course were boundary markers to a meal with the nature of both determined by style conventions that direct their composition and their location within the structure of the meal. Depending on type, soups needed stepped preparation or a modular approach

---

[121] McGrath, *The diary*, vol. i, 245.
[122] McGrath, *The diary*, vol. ii, 219.

to cooking, while the sweet course demanded expensive, and at times exotic, ingredients. Furthermore, as Lehmann points out, the sweet or dessert achieved new heights of flamboyance from the mid-eighteenth century[123]—a development which found expression in the manuscript recipe collections and their references to moulds, steeple creams and sugar work. These developments made no impression on O'Sullivan's cooking and dining culture. From the meal descriptions, devoid as they are of recipe-style instruction, it might be inferred that the cookery style alluded to by O'Sullivan varied from the basic of the everyday to more complex for special occasions. Boiling and roasting were the main cooking techniques; there is evidence of composed or made dishes in the stuffings for roast birds, and the milk and butter sauces for tripe and vegetables. Puddings were of indeterminable variety, with *putóg banbreac* possibly a savoury white/speckled pudding. However, his diary entry-style, where dishes were simply named rather than detailed may mask more complicated culinary work. His mention of a dish of cod's head is a case in point. What might be taken from the description to be no more than an insipid dish of boiled fish was in practice a quite detailed culinary operation involving many ingredients combined together to produce quite a lavish and rich dish:[124] one that John Rutty describes as 'a dish that Apicius might envy us'.[125] This point can also extend to his reference to a dish of duck and peas. It is possible to speculate therefore, that the meals O'Sullivan consumed on special occasions and especially those taken with Fr Hennebry were prepared by a cook and invested with a degree of culinary skill. Indeed the dish of cod's head was part of the festive Saint Patrick's Day dinner of 1829. It comprised four fish dishes, two fresh, one salted, and one smoked together with cheese and green cabbage. The similarities and relationship between this cooking and dining style and that of the affluent classes can be seen in the meal structure, the inclusion of a number of dishes in each course, in the element of variety and in the high representation of meat in meals. If these features suggest the percolation downwards of influence and a corresponding willingness to emulate this received approach to food, it was but an occasional incursion and not part of the daily routine. O'Sullivan's reference to his summertime diet is, in all

---

[123] Lehmann, *The British housewife*, 134–7 and 263–73.

[124] See, for example, NLI, Townley Hall Papers, MS 9,563, recipe: 'To Boyle a cod's head: When the watter boyles put in yr fish having put in a hand full of salt and a pint of vinegar in the watter you boyle it in, Let it not boil too fast, 3 quarters of an hour will boyle it, if it be a piece of cod boyle the peas with it and when they are hard cut it in thin slices flower it & fry it till it browns, then take up yr fish & draine it very well from the water and lay it in yr Dish then take a little wine, whole pepers, mace and cloves some horse Radish scraped, two anchovies a shallot small cut, a pint of oysters, a pint of cockles with the liquor of the oysters and let them stew till they are almost dry, then put them to your butter being/very? thick drawn power all over you fish with a lemon slicet and the peas all laid in the dish and soe it and some fried oysters'.

[125] John Rutty, *An essay towards a natural history of the county of Dublin, accommodated by the noble designs of the Dublin Society* (2 vols, Dublin, 1772), vol. i, 353.

likelihood, an indication of an everyday pattern dominated by carbohydrates—potatoes, oatmeal and wheaten bread—with meat and butter interchangeable and confined to dinner.[126] When his home dinners are described, they invariably include meat and at times in its stead butter as in the case of his dinner of *coimhbleidhe* (mashed potatoes). His description of *coimhbleidhe* and the related dish, colcannon is the closest he comes to supplying a recipe.[127]

If the culinary culture described by O'Sullivan is a scaled down and modified version of a richer pattern appealed to on special occasions, it also possessed its own peculiarities with luxury or novel status goods hived off to particular eating and social rituals. From O'Sullivan's descriptions, the conclusion to a meal or the immediate post-meal marker was not a sweet course but punch made with alcohol, sugar, spice and citrus fruit such as orange or lemon.[128] Punch, therefore holds the ingredients of luxury—the ingredients used in grander kitchens to made dessert items and enriched puddings. However, with O'Sullivan they are combined in a straightforward manner to serve particular roles. Punch is used to promote congeniality and extend hospitality to guests; on his house visits to friends, for instance, O'Sullivan is received with punch and bread and butter.[129] In this instance, what separates the different classes is not simply confined to the frequency with which luxury goods are used and consumed but difference was marked by how they are used.

When taken together, the evidence of Tighe and O'Sullivan suggests that the core ingredients in the diet of the rural middling to more secure lower classes were meat, offal, potatoes, oatmeal and bread together with milk and butter. The low profile of fruits and vegetables (apart from roots, cabbages and onions) is worthy of attention as these are foods of infrequent consumption. Dietary variety in fruits and vegetables was traditionally emblematic of a class wealthy enough to support the labour and skills required to service the kitchen garden, the orchard and the stillroom. In the late eighteenth and early nineteenth centuries interest in fruit and vegetable production and consumption is evident especially amongst the middling and the wealthy urban classes.[130] Supporting these developments were the activities of a growing number of seedsmen, nurserymen, and culinary commercial gardens and gardeners who supplied fruit and vegetable seed/cultivar in impressive variety. Tighe's reference to produce at the Kilkenny market—where meat and fowl, and fish from Dungarvan, and English and Waterford cheeses were offered with a wide variety of vegetables and fruit including melons, peaches, grapes and pineapples—reflects the work of commercial gardener and pomologist, Mr John Robertson,

---

[126] McGrath, *The diary*, vol. ii, 315.

[127] McGrath, *The diary*, vol. i, 230–3.

[128] For reference to the ingredients of punch see Liam Kennedy and Clare Murphy (eds), *The account books of the Franciscan House, Broad Lane, Cork, 1764–1921* (Dublin, 2012).

[129] McGrath, *The diary*, see, for example, vol. i, 87.

[130] Keith Lamb and Patrick Bowe, *A history of gardening in Ireland* (Dublin, 1985), 54, 59.

but also related to the rise of commercial gardening in Kilkenny from the 1780s onwards.[131] Growing middle-class interest in fruit and vegetables was linked with a corresponding growth in interest in cookery, in a general sense, attested by the upsurge in printed books in the second half of the eighteenth century.[132] O'Sullivan's duck and peas and cod's head may be one small expression of this movement. However, where, how far and in what way these largely urban middle-class trends migrated to rural areas is a discussion for elsewhere.

Conclusion

The food and culinary changes that marked the eighteenth and early nineteenth centuries brought Ireland in line with the more modern food systems that had been developing in Britain and Europe since the early modern period. The diffusion of new ingredients and the emergence of more complex systems of food production and distribution were made possible by the favourable economic conditions that characterised the second half of the eighteenth century. The effects of these changes were felt variously across the different social classes. The rate and depth of change also varied in accordance with location, which produced particular rural and urban patterns. The case of rural Kilkenny in the opening decades of the nineteenth century has been used here to profile not only the diversity of food and culinary cultures in pre-Famine Ireland, but also to illustrate how Ireland transitioned from what Cullen described as medieval backwardness at the close of the seventeenth century to a more market-orientated, commercially driven and hierarchical food system. However, discussion of the extent and nature of this reform is hampered by the lack of scholarly attention to the nature of food and culinary cultures in Ireland of the sixteenth and seventeenth centuries.[133] It is impossible, therefore, to determine reliably how food and culinary systems from the past carried over and adapted to change especially for the lower and middle classes.

---

[131] Tighe, *Statistical observations*, 498–500.

[132] Between the 1720s and 1800 at least 27 cookery and household management/economy books were produced by Dublin printers. All but two would appear to be of Irish origin or authorship but are simply recipe collections of the well-established British repertoire. The rest are Dublin editions of English cookery books. Notables in the English food scene are listed here, for instance Raffald, *The experienced English housewife*, going to two print runs in 1772 and 1778. And of course Hannah Glasse, *The art of cookery* has four print runs in Dublin between 1748 and 1799. Her *compleat confectioner* (1760) and her *The servant's directory or housekeeper's companion* (1760) were also printed in Dublin. Printing activity increases from *c.* 1740s reflective of trends in Britain which saw increased demand for educational books on gardening, medicine, spas, hygiene, geography, travel, marriage, children, etiquette and agriculture. For cookery books in the context of educational works in general see Stead, 'Quizzing Glasse: or Hannah scrutinized'. For Irish cookery book print activity see Virginia Maclean, *A short-title catalogue of household and cookery books published in the English tongue 1701–1800* (London, 1981). For English cookery book print activity see Gilly Lehmann, *The British housewife*.

[133] For new work in this area see Susan Flavin, *Consumption and culture in sixteenth-century Ireland: saffron, stockings and silk* (Woodbridge, Suffolk, 2014).

The elite consumption cultures of the wealthy classes were received, directed and guided by British, and to a lesser extent, European norms. Wealthy gentry women embraced British styles of cookery and brought dishes that were strongly imbued with a British sense of identity and tradition to their homes and estates. It was this model of cookery that the emerging middle classes aspired to emulate at times of special meaning and celebration. For others food identity was shaped by the vagaries and demands of the market, which soaked up quality ingredients which in turn encouraged the food and culinary cultures of the lower classes to displace certain ingredients and to substitute foods thereby disrupting traditional patterns. On the eve of the Great Famine, Irish food and culinary cultures were diverse, dynamic and various but they also lacked any enduring and developed sense of a distinctive Irish identity. As Cullen points out this 'was a society [and a food culture] that suffered acute problems of identity precisely because of the limitation of their traditions'.[134] The borrowing culture so characteristic of Irish food and culinary practices in the pre-Famine period would continue to direct developments and the Irish relationship with food well beyond the Great Famine.

Acknowledgements   I would like to extend my gratitude to a number of people who gave generously of their time and resources in the undertaking of this research. Thank you to Lady Alison Rosse, Birr Castle, Co. Offaly, for permission to publish Dorothy Parsons' seventeenth-century recipe for Potata Pie. To George Gossip, who back in August 1999 introduced me to the 1753 Clonbrock receipt book from Clonbrock House, Co. Galway. Thank you to craft butcher, Jack McCarthy, for his time and expertise in making the Townley Hall Polonia sausage and his faithful adherence to the original recipe and to the Irish Heritage Trust for its permission to published the floor plans of the Fota House kitchen complex.

---

[134] Cullen, *The emergence of modern Ireland,* 137–9.

Nutritional decline in post-Famine Ireland, *c.* 1851–1922

IAN MILLER*

Centre for the History of Medicine in Ireland, University of Ulster, Coleraine Campus, Cromore Road, Coleraine, Co. Derry~Londonderry, BT52 1SA

[Accepted 4 July 2014. Published 6 February 2015.]

Abstract

Irish dietary practice changed dramatically after the Famine. Families began to consume a more varied diet instead of relying on the potato. Prior to the Famine, this change would have been greeted positively. Most political economists advocated ending Ireland's monocrop culture as they associated the potato diet with a lack of socio-economic development. This paper explores the meanings attached to dietary change and argues that concerns were raised after the Famine about the failure of the Irish poor to obtain a diet as nutritious as the potato diet had previously been. By the turn of the twentieth century, many commentators agreed that the national dietary adjustment, which had followed the Famine, had not been an improvement. On the contrary, the Irish poor seemed undernourished and underfed as they now subsisted upon nutritionally insufficient diets dominated by tea and white bread. In addition, this chapter explores the new ways in which food was thought about after the Famine with particular emphasis on how the new sciences of food impacted on the discussion of the Irish diet. It investigates state and voluntary interventions in Irish dietary health and maintains that these were relatively ineffective. In summary, this chapter problematises the post-Famine Irish diet by emphasising a sense of decline in nutritional well-being debated in contemporary commentary on the national diet set against a backdrop of shifting expert ideas on food.

Post-Famine dietary change

In his evidence to the Inter-Departmental Committee of Physical Deterioration of 1904, the bishop of Ross, Denis Kelly, recalled:

> When I was a boy, looking back to the period of the late fifties and early sixties the food of the peasantry consisted of potatoes for one meal, Indian meal and oatmeal for two other meals, as a rule, and there was very little bread used. Now in some sense the food has been improved, and hence I am going to propound the paradox that while the food used

* Author's e-mail: i.miller@ulster.ac.uk
doi: 10.3318/PRIAC.2015.115.01

is a better class of food, yet the people are worse fed. Wheaten bread has become of very common use in Ireland, and has almost entirely superseded the use of both Indian meal and oatmeal, and to a very large extent the use of the potato.[1]

At the Committee, Irish physicians echoed the thrust of Bishop Kelly's remarks by warning of the deleterious effects of excessive tea-drinking habits among the poor. They blamed tea for the rising incidence of neuroses and for making Irish housewives, who on average consumed at least twelve cups of strong black tea per day, chronically dyspeptic.[2] Further medical evidence drew attention to an additional problem: there was a remarkably limited knowledge of cookery across Ireland. Speaking of the situation in Dublin, the physician, chemist and food analyst Charles Cameron asserted: 'cookery amongst the working classes is at an extremely low ebb; you can hardly call it cookery at all'. Cameron lamented that:

> They [the poor] have nothing except cabbage and Swedish turnips, and they hardly ever use peas or beans or celery, or any of those things. It is always cabbage. In fact, for the Sunday dinner, very often, the meal consists of bacon and cabbage. I do not know any country in the world where so much bacon and cabbage is eaten.[3]

These statements raise important questions about post-Famine food cultures. Why did contemporaries perceive Irish dietary change so negatively? To what extent did they view the potato as a significant cultural loss? And why did food continue to feature as a troubling, controversial element of Irish society long after debates on the predominantly potato diet had subsided?

Irish dietary practice changed dramatically following the Famine. The less affluent gradually replaced a potato diet with one containing more variety. This change in dietary customs was rapid and inherently complex.[4] The new diet shielded the poor from a further major famine, although localised minor famines occurred sporadically.[5] Nonetheless, the Irish diet remained controversial well into the twentieth century despite this positive development. Leslie A. Clarkson and E. M. Crawford have argued that diminishing reliance on the nutritious potato resulted in an observable decline in nutritional health; a fact

---

[1] *Minutes of evidence taken before the Inter-Departmental Committee on Physical Deterioration Volume II*, Reports of Commissioners, Commons, 1904 [Cd.2201], vol. xxxii.45, 412.

[2] *Minutes of evidence*, 452.

[3] *Minutes of evidence*, 402.

[4] For a full discussion, see Ian Miller, *Reforming food in post-Famine Ireland: medicine, science and improvement, 1845–1922* (Manchester, 2014).

[5] Timothy O. O'Neill, 'The food crisis of the 1890s', in E. Margaret Crawford (ed.), *Famine: the Irish experience 900–1900: subsistence crises and famines in Ireland* (Edinburgh, 1989), 176–97.

recognised by contemporaries such as the bishop of Ross.[6] This unwelcome consequence of dietary change formed the basis of a new set of food-related anxieties.

Post-Famine dietary adjustment coincided with significant changes in the understanding and knowledge of food. The Irish public came to appreciate food differently after the Famine. From the mid-nineteenth century experts in nutrition and public health rigorously subjected food to scientific investigation. New exploratory techniques emerged that encouraged food to be considered for the first time with reference to factors such as nutritional value, as well as hygiene and purity. It was no longer acceptable to view food solely as a means of subsistence, as had often been the case prior to the Famine. Instead, food was seen as consisting of particular chemical components, and as potentially contaminated with harmful germs in certain circumstances. Scientists also gradated diet on a new scale of 'healthy' and 'unhealthy'. In many ways, understandings of food were revolutionised in the period between the Great Famine and Irish independence. In light of this, shifting expert knowledge of food intake fuelled greater public understandings of diet. An emerging attention to the content of food and the health consequences of subsisting on a nutritionally insufficient diet ensured that conditions such as under-nutrition took centre stage in a new set of food-based anxieties. Arising out of this, this essay will address the dietary concerns that arose in relation to the poor as it was on this social grouping that anxieties typically coalesced. It also explores the effectiveness of the educational strategies that emerged in response to mounting anxiety in the post-Famine period about the Irish diet.

Nutritional knowledge and the post-Famine Irish body

In the 1840s, critics of the potato diet often emphasised its apparent excessiveness. This concern was vividly and forcefully articulated in their depictions of the engorged, enlarged and gluttonous Irish stomach. Thomas Campbell Foster, a travel writer and contributor to the *Times*, asserted in 1846 that by subsisting on excessive quantities of food, the Irish peasant's stomach had become overindulged, craving quantity constantly. Foster even claimed that pathological investigation had revealed the potato-fed Irish peasant's stomach to be double the size of the average human stomach.[7] The historian Helen O'Connell has also identified contemporary apprehension about the reckless, hedonistic and excessive consumption of tea by the poor.[8] These sources indicate that until the Famine, Irish dietary intake was considered primarily in terms of excess. It was the quantity of food being consumed that caused

---

[6] Leslie A. Clarkson and E. Margaret Crawford, *Feast and famine: food and nutrition in Ireland, 1500–1920* (Oxford, 2001), 109–10.

[7] Thomas C. Foster, *Letters on the condition of the people of Ireland* (London, 1846), 558–9.

[8] Helen O'Connell, '"A raking pot of tea": consumption and excess in early nineteenth-century Ireland', *Literature and History* 21:2 (2012), 32–47: 36.

concern. In this context, excessive food consumption appeared indicative of a lack of self-restraint and moderation inherent in the Irish character itself.[9]

This emphasis on excess became increasingly redundant as new scientific imperatives encouraged a more nuanced discussion of diet. Between 1845 and 1922 ideas on food changed dramatically. A new vocabulary featuring protein, fats, starch and carbohydrates and, later vitamins and calories, increasingly informed public understandings of food. Importantly, this new language stressed the importance of food quality. How much the Irish ate now seemed of less importance than what they ate. By the mid-twentieth-century, nutritional scientists had identified various ways of assessing the chemical consistency of meats, vegetables and other foodstuffs empirically. They were able to classify food into its constituent chemical parts to determine which diets possessed the most nutritional value.[10]

Food quality and nutrition were seriously debated for the first time in Ireland during the Famine. At the same time that political economists were suggesting that the catastrophe was an opportunity to change Ireland's monocrop culture, scientists investigating the blight were confirming the nutritional value of the potato.[11] In the 1840s political economists identified the potato as emblematic of all that seemed wrong with Ireland; the potato was synonymous with national idleness and economic underachievement. In their view, bringing Ireland's monocrop culture to an end could not fail to generate economic prosperity and social development.[12] At the same time, this was a period when nutritional science was developing a new framework for understanding food intake; and food chemistry had evolved into a recognisably distinct scientific sub-discipline. The German chemist Justus von Liebig and his supporters significantly raised the public profile of nutritional science from the 1830s by promoting the value of analysing the chemistry of food to identify healthy and unhealthy diets.[13]

The onset of blight encouraged chemists to investigate its cause (normally hypothesised as chemical rather than mycological) and the chemical consistency of the potato.[14] In 1845 the British chemist George Phillips published a detailed account of the biochemistry of the potato. In *The potato*

---

[9] Helen O'Connell, *Ireland and the fiction of improvement* (Oxford, 2006), 6.

[10] For an overview of scientific developments in nutrition, see Harmke Kamminga and Andrew Cunningham (eds), *The science and culture of nutrition, 1840–1940* (Amsterdam, 1995).

[11] See Peter Gray, 'Potatoes and providence: British government responses to the Great Famine', *Bullán: An Irish Studies Journal* 1:1 (1994), 75–90.

[12] Ian Miller, 'The chemistry of famine: nutritional controversies and the Irish Famine, *c.* 1845–7', *Medical History* 56:4 (2012), 444–62: 447–9.

[13] Justus von Liebig, *Research on the chemistry of food*, trans. W. Gregory (Lowell, 1848).

[14] Thomas P. O'Neill, 'The scientific investigation of the failure of the potato crop in Ireland 1845–6', *Irish Historical Studies* 5 (1946), 123–38.

disease: its origin, nature and development, he broke the potato down into its constituent parts: water, starch, sugar, potateine, gum, albumen and so on.[15] Researchers such as Phillips specified that human health depended upon ingesting correct mixtures of chemical elements such as protein and fat, which the potato contained in sufficient quantity to provide the basis for a healthy diet. The physician William Wilde announced in 1854:

> [during the Famine] the fact became evident to the chemists, which had long ago been practically demonstrated by the people, that the potato, bad as it was, contained more life-sustaining elements, added to more palatable qualities, and less deleterious constituents, when taken for any length of time into the system, than any other vegetable that could be procured.[16]

As an alternative to the potato, individuals such as Wilde promoted a diet consisting primarily of oatmeal, Indian meal, vegetables and meats.[17]

In the decades that followed the Famine, various other considerations informed new public understandings of food, with the result that by the end of the century, social investigators had forged more precise definitions of nutritional health and under-nutrition.[18] Individuals, social groups—even nations—could now be diagnosed as nutritionally vulnerable. In the early twentieth century social researchers worldwide developed a refined under-standing of calories and vitamins that radically altered expert and public conceptions of food.[19] Public health also played an important role. From the 1850s public health officials began to make greater use of microscopial analysis to expose, and warn of, the potential presence of germs in impure, contaminated foodstuffs.[20] Combined, these developments helped to reshape how the Irish thought about what they ate (or, perhaps more precisely, what critics and physicians thought about the dietary habits of the poor). At the same time, new notions of a nutritionally 'ideal' diet and the 'pure' food product—sterilised and free from germs—generated alarm about the extent to which post-Famine diets deviated from these new norms. The laying out of new food standards in itself created apprehension about how far the dietary customs that

---

[15] George Phillips, *The potato disease: its origin, nature and prevention* (London, 1845), 7–10.

[16] William Wilde, 'The food of the Irish', *Dublin University Magazine* 43 (1854), 127–46: 138.

[17] See, for instance, *Report of the Commissioners of Health, on the Epidemics of 1846 to 1850*, H. C. 1852–3 [1562] xli, 25.

[18] For instance, an important nutritional survey was published in Anthony M. MacSweeney, *Poverty in Cork* (Cork, 1917).

[19] Rima Apple, *Vitamania: vitamins in American culture* (New Brunswick, NJ, 1996), 1–4; Anson Rabinbach, *The human motor: energy, fatigue and the origins of modernity* (Berkley, CA, 1992), 130–3.

[20] Bee Wilson, *Swindled: from poison sweets to counterfeit coffee—the dark history of the food cheats* (London, 2009), 1–45.

evolved after the Famine diverged from the ideals outlined in contemporary nutritional science. For reasons such as these, food remained remarkably central to post-Famine discussion on Irish health.

Food, illness and the Irish

Post-Famine optimism about the potential for a new Irish diet was short-lived. The potato certainly figured less prominently in the Irish diet after the Famine. However, new concerns were soon raised about the foodstuffs being consumed by the poor in its stead. Scientists had established the high nutritional value of the potato, but the desirability of banishing the potato diet encouraged physicians to demand that the population obtain nutrition from an array of other healthy foodstuffs. Institutions were important sites in which physicians could intervene directly in inmates' diets and suggest changes. Physicians investigating institutional conditions played an important role in shaping ideas on nutrition after the Famine as many of them examined links between nutritionally insufficient diets and the onset of various physical and mental conditions.[21] In the late 1840s Arthur Jacob, the editor of the *Dublin Medical Press*, established that feeding workhouse children with a nutritionally inadequate diet for sustained periods caused high incidences of ophthalmia (or conjunctivitis).[22] John Lentaigne, physician and inspector of the Irish reformatory and industrial school system, took steps in the 1850s to address childhood problems such as scrofula (or tuberculosis of the neck) in the institutions under his inspectorate by promoting healthy, nutritious feeding.[23] In 1859, the lord mayor of Cork, John Arnott, sparked a heated public debate on the quality of food supplied in the city's workhouses. The workhouse diet of watery soups containing few vegetables and sparse amounts of meat was, he maintained, the source of an alarmingly high scrofula incidence among the young inmates. With the backing of local physicians, Arnott argued that workhouse diets wasted the blood, reduced vigour and rendered the institutionalised susceptible to disease.[24]

During the late nineteenth century institutional managers gradually improved institutional diets. Fewer possibilities existed, however, for regulating dietary behaviour in the general community. An additional debate on nutrition emerged that focused on the relationship between nervousness and diet. According to political economists and socio-economic reformers, the abandonment of the potato diet was to usher in a new era of socio-economic advancement in Ireland. They foresaw a post-Famine population producing

---

[21] The issue of institutional diets is discussed in Miller, *Reforming food in post-Famine Ireland*, 65–84.

[22] Philomena Gorey, 'Childhood ophthalmia in Irish workhouses, 1849–1861', in Anne Mac Lellan and Alice Mauger (eds), *Growing pains: childhood illness in Ireland, 1750–1950* (Dublin, 2013), 71–88.

[23] Ian Miller, 'Constructing moral hospitals: childhood health in Irish reformatories and industrial schools, *c.* 1851–90', in Mac Lellan and Mauger (eds), *Growing pains*, 105–22.

[24] John Arnott, *The investigation into the condition of the children in the Cork Workhouse* (Cork, 1859), 6–7.

and consuming combinations of meats and vegetables, generating a self-sustaining community no longer exposed to the potentially devastating effects of blight and famine.[25] The consumption of a varied diet was also commonly understood as a step towards civilising the Irish and raising them into more sophisticated beings. As the German travel writer and geographer Johan George Kohl asserted in 1841:

> Many Irishmen have but one day on which they eat flesh, namely, on Christmas day. Every other day they feed on potatoes and nothing but potatoes. Now this is inhuman; for the appetite and stomach of man claim variety in food, and nowhere else do we find human beings gnawing from year's end to year's end, at the same root, berry or weed. There are animals who do so, but human beings, nowhere except in Ireland.[26]

Embedded in Kohl's powerful statement was a sense that dietary change was part of a civilising process; that the adoption of a diverse, sophisticated diet would signal personal and social advancement in Ireland.[27] In Kohl's view, the potato diet was unrefined and uncivilised; a remnant of a less sophisticated, primitive inheritance. Initially, the Irish diet seemed to develop in a more positive direction. In 1863 the prominent British physician and nutritional expert Edward Smith investigated the diets of the labouring classes across the British Isles, including Ireland. Using nutritional analysis, he concluded that the rural Irish were never so healthy, as they complemented the potato with oatmeal, vegetables and meat.[28] Smith concluded that 'throughout the country I found them [the Irish] a fine, well-built, and often athletic race, with children sufficiently fleshy and rosy and bearing all the marks of health'; even 'the wife, however, was usually more robust and healthy looking than is observed in England'.[29]

Smith failed to anticipate the role that an advancing consumerism in the late nineteenth century would play in determining national dietary customs. From the 1870s Ireland suffered from an economic depression that impacted on the ability of families to procure nutritious food.[30] In the same period a national network of urban and rural retailing was established that encouraged the less

---

[25] See, for instance, Robert Kane's discussion of how Ireland's food resources could be maximised in Robert Kane, *The industrial resources of Ireland* (Dublin, 1844), 236–327.

[26] Johan George Kohl, *Ireland* (New York, 1844), 24.

[27] Norbert Elias has persuasively outlined links between consumption habits and middle-class civility in Norbert Elias, *The civilising process*, trans. E. Jephcott (Oxford, 1978–82).

[28] For more on Smith's dietary surveys, see T.C. Barker, Derek J. Oddy and John Yudkin, *The dietary surveys of Dr Edward Smith 1862–3* (London, 1970).

[29] Barker, Oddy and Yudkin, *Dietary surveys of Dr Edward Smith*, 283.

[30] For the relationship between economic cycles, and agrarian and urban economies, see Mary E. Daly, *Dublin, the deposed capital: a social and economic history, 1860–1914* (Cork, 1984), 53–64.

affluent to rely increasingly upon food purchased from shopkeepers and, in many instances, to accumulate considerable debt.[31] By the 1890s the Irish poor once again appeared worryingly underfed. When members of the Congested Districts Board investigated the day-to-day life of the rural poor in the 1890s, they discovered that the poor were consuming high levels of bread and tea while purchasing less frequently nutritious foodstuffs such as Indian meal, bacon, potatoes, milk, fish, eggs, oatmeal, butter, sugar, cabbage and meat.[32] The food items which the poor used to barter with shopkeepers tended to be more nutritious than the items that they received in their place. Many mothers exchanged their home-produced eggs for tea.[33] In addition, late-century technological developments, which made certain foodstuffs cheaper, contributed to a general downturn in nutritional health. White bread became particularly popular from the 1880s onward as gradual-reduction roller milling steadily replaced traditional flour-milling practices; the bread produced using these modern techniques was less nutritious despite its cheaper cost.[34]

In many ways, excessive tea drinking exemplified all that seemed to have gone wrong with the Irish diet in the decades after the Famine. Tea was an imported product containing relatively little nutrition. Physicians dismissed it as a stimulant that was used by the lower classes for the purposes of exhilaration and hedonism. They mostly refused to consider that over-reliance on tea and white bread was a consequence of social conditions such as poverty, not individual recklessness.[35] In the 1890s concerned members of the Congested Districts Board warned that families were purchasing as much as a pound of tea per week in some regions of Connacht.[36] Clarkson and Crawford also point to a startling rise in tea drinking per family which, in 1904, averaged nine ounces a week in rural communities and close to twelve ounces in urban centres.[37]

---

[31] Liam Kennedy, 'Traders in the Irish rural economy, 1880–1914', *Economic History Review* 32:2 (1979), 201–10; Samuel Clark, *Social origins of the Irish Land War* (Princeton, NJ, 1979), 126; Michael D. Higgins and John P. Gibbons, 'Shopkeeper-graziers and land agitation in Ireland, 1895–1900', in P.J. Drudy, *Ireland: land, politics, and people* (Cambridge, 1982).

[32] Leslie Clarkson, 'The modernisation of Irish diet', in John Davis (ed.), *Rural change in Ireland* (Belfast, 1999).

[33] Ciara Breathnach, *The Congested Districts Board of Ireland, 1891–1923: poverty and development in the west of Ireland* (Dublin and Portland, OR, 2005), 38–9.

[34] Glyn Jones, 'The introduction and establishment of roller milling in Ireland', in Andrew Bielenberg (ed.), *Irish flour milling: a history, 600–2000* (Dublin, 2003).

[35] For comparison between different regions of the United Kingdom and Ireland, see Ian Miller, '"A dangerous revolutionary force amongst us": conceptualising working-class tea drinking in the British Isles, *c.* 1860–1900', *Cultural and Social History* 10:3 (2013), 419–38.

[36] Breathnach, *Congested Districts Board*, 40.

[37] Clarkson and Crawford, *Feast and famine*, 103.

The problem of tea drinking prompted a new moral panic about Irish dietary customs that was as alarmist in nature as condemnations of the potato diet once had been. In 1893 the *Freeman's Journal* asserted that:

> Evidence is overwhelming that the food now partaken of by the people, though of more refined quality and more in accordance with modern ideas, is not nearly so strengthening and in consequence the actual physical capacity of the people is now deteriorating. White bread and tea have now taken the place of the humble but more strengthening oatmeal, stirabout and milk. The tea drinking is especially condemned by the doctors as injurious to health. Dyspepsia and its allied diseases, and also mental diseases, are said to be traceable to it. The people seem to take tea at all their meals, not only because they use a great deal of it, but because they let it stand so long before the fire.[38]

Three years later, the newspaper warned that:

> Tea is slowly conquering the world. It is an insidious beverage, and the desire for it grows by what it feeds on. Its popularity has created a new repast in modern society—afternoon tea—to with, which has two distinct and deteriorating tendencies: the one towards dyspepsia and the other towards the abominable form of mental indigestion, scandal-mongering.[39]

These alarmist sentiments were echoed by physicians and psychiatrists. In the 1890s physicians noticed a startling rise in asylum admissions by comparison with the levels reached in the 1880s. Some believed that the Irish were particularly prone to developing insanity because their constitutions predisposed them to nervous and psychiatric conditions. In 1894 Thomas Drapes, the leading Irish psychiatrist and resident medical superintendent at Enniscorthy District Asylum, published an article in the *Journal of Mental Science* on the subject of this apparent national increase of insanity. Drapes identified the poor quality of the post-Famine diet as a driving force behind this regrettable trend. He also expressed concern that excessive tea drinking was overstimulating the nervous systems of the Irish, rendering them susceptible to mental and physical illnesses. Drapes asserted that 'we see its [tea's] effects in the number of pale-faced children who are brought up on it instead of the old time-honoured, but now nearly abandoned, porridge and milk'.[40]

The issue of excessive tea drinking was not confined to sensationalistic newspaper editorials or limited to the alarmist writings of a small but vocal number of doctors. On the contrary, the adverse effects of tea drinking were

---

[38] 'The Irish agricultural labourer', *Freeman's Journal*, 6 December 1893.
[39] 'Tea and tea drinkers', *Freeman's Journal*, 10 January 1896.
[40] Thomas Drapes, 'On the alleged increase of insanity in Ireland', *Journal of Mental Science* 40 (1894), 519–48: 535–6.

addressed in a range of forums. The theme featured particularly prominently in the Inter-Departmental Committee of Physical Deterioration of 1904, considered above.[41] Diet—tea in particular—also occupied a pivotal place in an official investigation made in the 1890s by the Irish Inspectors of Lunatics, George Plunkett O'Farrell and E. Maziere Courtenay, into the national increase in insanity. O'Farrell and Courtenay agreed that tea was as a key contributory factor. Diet, they suggested, had unquestionably contributed to increasing insanity levels as large numbers of the insane bore the scars of 'scant, improper food'— 'the insanity of malnutrition'.[42] The inspectors concluded that poor diets had resulted in alarmingly high levels of anaemia, constitutional weakness, scrofula and neurotic disease. Excessive tea drinking, in particular, was identified as the cause of a national outbreak of dyspepsia with severe symptoms of neurotic disturbance, mental depression and psychological decline.[43] The debate on the relationship between tea drinking and nerves facilitated the entry of terms such as 'tea drunkards' and 'tea mania' into the Irish vocabulary. The latter condition was characterised by symptoms, including headache, vertigo, insomnia, palpitation of the heart, mental confusion, nightmare, nausea, hallucinations, morbid depression of the spirit and even suicidal impulses.

Evidently, nutrition provided a key framework for understanding diet and its potential relationship to bodily complaints after the Famine. The nineteenth century saw a shift in priorities in the discussion of food in Ireland. Pre-Famine critiques of the Irish diet had emphasised excess and monotony; post-Famine critiques focused on food chemistry and nutritional content. Although this formed part of an international trend, the issue of nutrition seemed particularly pertinent in Ireland given that a decline in nutrition was traceable back to the Great Famine. It could be seen as having directly resulted from the dramatic shift in dietary patterns that had followed the catastrophe. The scientific establishment of the potato as a nutritional food allowed late-century commentators to refer to the pre-Famine era as one when the population had enjoyed a nutritional diet, even if they had been exposed to the fatal implications of relying upon a single dietary staple.

In addition, from the 1860s public health officials amplified the discussion of food by drawing attention to the potential of working-class diets to be adulterated and contaminated. They encouraged consumers to consider food in terms of purity and hygiene, highlighting a further way in which science impacted on public perceptions of food. Prior to the late nineteenth-century common sense—coupled with humoral understanding of diet and constitution—dictated that it was unwise to eat food that smelled putrid, tasted unsavoury or appeared rotten. The development of microscopical techniques of examining foodstuffs, the commencement of a concerted drive to end

---

[41] *Alleged increasing prevalence of insanity in Ireland: special report from the Inspectors of Lunatics to the Chief Secretary*, H.C. 1894 [C.7331] xliii.647, 4.
[42] *Alleged increasing prevalence of insanity*, 4–5.
[43] *Alleged increasing prevalence of insanity*, 16.

adulteration practices in the 1860s and the realisation that ingesting germs caused illness combined to emphasise purity and hygiene in food. From the 1860s medical scientists began, first, to hypothesise and then, to prove that diseases such as tuberculosis could pass from animals to humans through meat consumption.[44] However, the ability to inspect meat for contamination remained limited.[45] A sustained assault on traditional butchering practices emerged in urban centres such as Dublin, which saw urban butchers demonised for their allegedly unsanitary and unscrupulous business practices that threatened the health of unsuspecting working-class consumers.[46]

Various controversies sustained this increasingly critical attitude, which was encouraged by legislation enacted in 1860 to tackle food adulteration. Public health officials in 1863 discovered that workhouse sugar supplies in South Dublin Union were contaminated with thousands of seemingly harmful sugar mites.[47] The selling of poisoned sweets to children also incited public anger. In 1873 James Dunne of the Royal College of Surgeons wrote to the *Freeman's Journal* on the matter arguing that:

> No wonder that the children of trades people and the poor are sickly, and frequently of immature development, when, besides all the other evils of a crowded city, they are beset on all sides of the street by unripe or rotten fruit, unwholesomely prepared sweets, and advocates of plaster of Paris as a juvenile luxury.[48]

Further concerns about hygiene were raised once medical scientists began in the 1870s to suspect that diseases such as typhoid were transmitted through the consumption of milk and water.[49] In 1879 Charles Cameron sought firmly to establish the connection between fever and the consumption of infected milk, although his ideas that Dublin's dairy yards needed to be hygienically managed took time to be fully accepted.[50] Debates on the poor hygienic quality of Irish-produced food raised the appeal of food produced by (particularly Denmark); a concern depicted by the *Irish Homestead* in 1896 (see Fig. 1). This discussion of hygiene added important new perspectives on the Irish working-class diet. The poor not only needed to secure nutritionally sufficient diets but had to be aware

---

[44] For discussion of this development, see Michael Worboys, 'Germ theories of disease and British veterinary medicine, 1860–1890', *Medical History* 35 (1991), 308–27.

[45] Keir Waddington, *The bovine scourge: meat, tuberculosis and public health, 1850–1914* (Woodbridge, 2006), 9.

[46] Miller, *Reforming food in post-Famine Ireland*, 105–29.

[47] Anon., 'The sugar contract for the North Dublin Union', *Dublin Medical Press*, 8 July 1863, 256.

[48] James Dunne, 'Bitter sweets', *Irish Times*, 28 January 1873.

[49] Jacob Steere-Williams, 'The perfect food and the filth disease: milk-borne typhoid and epidemiological practice in late-Victorian Britain', *Journal of the History of Medicine and Allied Sciences* 65:4 (2010), 514–45.

[50] Charles A. Cameron, 'On an epidemic of fever caused by infected milk', *Dublin Journal of Medical Science* 91 (1879), 1–23.

JOHN BULL'S BREAKFAST.

Fɪɢ. 1—'Bull's Breakfast', *Irish Homestead* 2:40 (1896), 642. Courtesy of the National Library of Ireland.

that foods could be contaminated or impure and had to be cooked in accordance with hygienic practices.

Tackling nutritional decline

State bodies made serious efforts to tackle nutritional decline from around 1900, but their interventions were inadequate. One key strategy was the extension of national school cookery instruction provision through the reform of the national education system. In the closing decades of the nineteenth century demand for domestic instruction rose dramatically in Ireland. However, most national schools were small and lacked the space required to instruct children on cooking.[51] In 1892 the Unionist MP for South Tyrone Thomas Wallace Russell declared in the House of Commons that the Irish education system 'wants to be taken to pieces and re-modelled', and lamented the inherent limitations of pre-existing arrangements given that, in his view, 'in Dublin,

---

[51] See, for instance, the discussion between a headmistress and the Commissioners in National Education in the Public Record Office of Northern Ireland, ED/8/1/212, communication relating to the erection of a cookery room at Newry Model School, 1898–1900.

Limerick and Cork the people are not fed, and they are not fed because their wives and daughters do not know anything of cookery'.[52] In the absence of appropriate facilities, cookery tended to be taught theoretically using scientifically informed but impractical and dry text-books such as Fannie M. Gallaher's *Short lessons in domestic science.*[53]

The moral panic about excessive tea drinking and poor nutrition across much of Ireland lent urgency to the discussion of domestic instruction. In 1900 domestic education was made into a compulsory subject for girls throughout Ireland. From 1900 a large number of teachers were trained by the department of agriculture and technical instruction. Municipal technical schools also offered training, as photographed in Plate I. Yet these teachers returned to encounter a lack of equipment and the space necessary for cookery instruction.[54] If space was unavailable in schools, then it had to be sought elsewhere. In Kilkenny, teachers delivered cookery classes in rented rooms and poorly ventilated abandoned houses. In County Wexford, they taught cookery in unoccupied homes, courthouses, a security room attached to a church,

Pl. I—'Municipal Technical School Cookery Class, *c.* 1910'. Courtesy of the Deputy Keeper of Records, Public Record Office of Northern Ireland. Ref: D2886/A/1/4/53.

---

[52] 'Motion for leave', *House of Commons Debates* (22 February 1892), vol. 1, cc968–99.

[53] Fannie M. Gallaher, *Short lessons in domestic science* (Dublin, 1894).

[54] See the criticism recorded in *Appendix to sixty-seventh report of Commissioners of National Education*, H.C. 1902 [Cd.954] xxx.1, 89–91.

a stockroom, a spare room in a disused mill, a joiner's workshop and even in barns and coach houses.[55] More positively, new text-books (such as Kathleen Ferguson's *Advanced lessons in cookery* and Josephine Redington's *Economic cookery book*) distributed to national schools discussed cookery, nutrition and hygiene in a clearer, more pragmatic style than earlier text-books. Even if teachers struggled to secure practical and financial resources, the new text-books contributed to increasing knowledge of the importance of a nutritionally balanced diet, hygienic cookery and cautious purchasing.[56]

The reluctance of state bodies to feed schoolchildren also encouraged public debate. The Irish Education Act of 1892 made school attendance compulsory but failed to take into consideration how the young were to be fed during the school day. The implementation of school meals provision in England and Wales in 1906 raised questions about why the policy was not extended to Ireland. A fear that state help would diminish parental responsibility for feeding their children was a consideration but it did not inhibit the sustained campaign led by Maud Gonne through her Ladies School Dinners Committee in 1910.[57] As part of her public campaign for school meals provision, Gonne penned emotive statements such as 'hundreds of child lives are being sacrificed; thousands of Irish boys and girls are being condemned to life-long physical suffering and mental inefficiency by school-day starvation'.[58] She also attracted physicians such as John O'Conor Donelan, assistant medical officer of Richmond Asylum, Dublin, to her scheme. These physicians confirmed that numerous incidences of mental breakdown among the Irish young were due to the excessive strain and long hours of schooling without feeding.[59] Oliver St John Gogarty added to the debate by warning that:

> Lunacy is increasing in this country. The unfit are being propagated and preserved. There is neither law to protect the children nor law to save the future generation from unfit parents. Soon there will be no one healthy. But we must not deliberately hasten this morbid millennium. It may be in some way delayed, and the most important way of delaying it is to protect the rising generation. Feed the school children. The school children must be fed.[60]

The activities of Maud Gonne's committee focused on distributing 450 meals per day to two Dublin schools: St Audoen's and John's Lane, two of the poorest

---

[55] National Archives of Ireland, Department of Agriculture, 92/1/26, Building Grants for Technical Instruction, 1906.

[56] Kathleen Ferguson, *Advanced lessons in cookery* (Athlone, 1903); Josephine Redington, *The economic cookery book* (Dublin, 1906).

[57] Lindsey Earner-Byrne, *Mother and child: maternity and child welfare in Dublin, 1920s–1960s* (Manchester, 2007), 12.

[58] Maude Gonne, 'Responsibility', *Irish Review* 1:10 (December 1911), 483–5: 483.

[59] Gonne, 'Responsibility', 484.

[60] Oliver St John Gogarty, 'The need of medical inspection of school children in Ireland', *Irish Review* 2:13 (1912), 12–9: 18.

schools in Dublin,[61] though Dublin Corporation refused to provide a grant to aid this work.[62] The issue was finally resolved when the Education (Provision of Meals) (Ireland) Act of 1914 allowed local authorities to provide school meals and purchase cooking equipment. The implementation of this measure was encouraged by the visibility of starving, underfed children during the Dublin Lockout of 1913.[63]

The most efficient interventions in dietary concerns were made in the voluntary sector. The Women's National Health Association (WNHA) adopted a particularly pro-active role in tackling tuberculosis, high infant mortality levels and the relative lack of knowledge among working-class mothers on infant feeding. Founded in 1907 by Lady Aberdeen, wife of the Lord Lieutenant John Campbell Hamilton-Gordon, 7th earl of Aberdeen, the association established 150 branches nationwide.[64] Through their public lectures and publications such as *Sláinte*, the association promoted the need to feed children with milk, not tea, to ensure their healthy growth. In addition, it encouraged the consumption of pasteurised milk.[65] Milk depots were intended to play an important role in popularising milk consumption. Milk supplies dispatched from these depots were guaranteed to be pasteurised and to have originated from healthy cows. Mothers received education on nutrition, hygiene and infant feeding when they collected their milk.[66] Yet the association reached a barrier when its members campaigned for the initiation of a systematic state-supported scheme at the Vice-Regal Commission on the Irish Milk Supply of 1911.[67]

It was only in the early twentieth century that post-Famine concerns about under-nutrition and a general lack of knowledge of hygiene and cookery were tackled in a sustained manner in Ireland, although with limited efficacy. This development stemmed in part from an international rise in sensitivity to the health of infants and children, diet and nutrition-related concerns. Yet this issue seemed particularly pronounced and emotive in Ireland given that the country had proportionately higher infant mortality than most other European countries and that under-nutrition seemed to have resulted, in part, from changes stemming from a momentous national catastrophe: the Great Famine. The early twentieth century saw the development of new ways of investigating food, digestion and diet. In the opening decades of the century, laboratory

---

[61] Maude Gonne, 'Meals for school children', *Irish Times,* 16 October 1912.

[62] 'State-aid or Irish self-help', *Irish Times,* 9 December 1911.

[63] Padraig Yeates, *Lockout: Dublin 1913* (Dublin, 2000), 366.

[64] See A. Evans, 'The Countess of Aberdeen's health promotion caravans', *Journal of the Irish Colleges of Physicians and Surgeons* 24:3 (1995), 211–18; Greta Jones, *'Captain of all these men of death': the history of tuberculosis in nineteenth- and twentieth-century Ireland* (Amsterdam, 2001), 101.

[65] 'Why children's milk should be pasteurised', *Sláinte* 1 (January 1909), 39–40.

[66] 'The result of six months' experience of Dublin pasteurised milk depot', *Sláinte* 1:3 (March 1909), 41–8.

[67] *Vice-Regal Commission on the Irish Milk Supply: the final report of the Irish Milk Commission,* H.C. 1914 [Cd.7129] xxxvi.601, 8.

scientists isolated vitamins for the first time and drew connections between vitamin deficiency and the onset of conditions such as rickets, although it was only after independence that vitamins were widely discussed in Ireland.[68] Prior to independence, calories and the idea that food intake was related to physical energy impacted more forcefully on expert thought on diet in Ireland. Studies such as William Henry Thomas's *Food problems: supplies and demand in Ireland* (1916) sought to determine the levels of energy that Dublin's labourers obtained from their diets as part of an effort to prove that wartime food shortages were impacting adversely on the ability of the Irish labour force to sustain productivity in the workplace. In particular, Thompson lamented the fact that Irish producers exported large amounts of nutritious foodstuffs, such as beef, while the Irish poor tended to derive energy from potatoes and bread in addition to imported goods such as tea.[69] The introduction of further ways of measuring dietary health did little to alleviate problems in the Irish diet. In the decades after the Famine physicians seemed to have found new ways of investigating and diagnosing nutritional problems. Yet state action remained limited, which was exploited to effect during Sinn Féin's wartime propaganda campaign, which claimed that Britain was pursuing a policy once again of starving Ireland by refusing to stop nutritious foodstuffs, such as meat, being exported out of Ireland to feed England.[70]

Conclusion

In the period after the Famine food was thought about in new ways. An increasingly sophisticated science of food and diet gradually informed food choices. A new vocabulary of nutrition, hygiene, nervousness and calories steadily impacted on attitudes towards food intake. This development allowed physicians and other critics to problematise dietary customs that failed to conform to the new dietary ideals outlined by medical scientists. A moral panic about post-Famine customs such as heavy tea drinking replaced the negative preoccupation with the large quantities of potatoes consumed in pre-Famine Ireland. Concern also arose about the institutionalised young as physicians established firm links between nutritionally inadequate feeding regimes and the onset of conditions such as scrofula. This development also reflected a palpable shift in the debate on food that emphasised the importance of obtaining nutritional quality instead of condemning the large quantity of food seemingly consumed by the Irish. This expert language on food increasingly informed how the dietary and nutritional problems shared by the Irish poor were understood, interpreted and discussed.

How best to resolve the dietary problems shared by the less affluent remained a thorny issue. State bodies introduced measures such as domestic education. However, these proved relatively ineffectual due to a lack of financial

---

[68] Apple, *Vitamania*, 1–4.

[69] William H. Thompson, *Food problems: supplies and demand in Ireland* (London, 1916).

[70] The National Archives, London, CAB 24/29; 'Food shortage in Ireland', *Irish Times,* 7 December 1917.

and practical resources. The issue of 'school-day starvation' proved particularly emotive and it encouraged individuals such as Maud Gonne to campaign against the large numbers of hungry schoolchildren that she encountered in Irish schools. Yet children were also underfed at home. Groups such as the WNHA believed that mothers failed to feed their children due to ignorance, not neglect. Accordingly, they sought to educate working-class mothers on matters such as infant feeding. Despite these activities, a profound sense existed in post-Famine Ireland that the Irish had been healthier and stronger when fed on the nutritious potato. Diet may have been revolutionised after the Famine, as political economists and critics of Ireland's monocrop culture had long advocated. Yet the consumption of a more varied diet failed to bolster nutritional well-being. On the contrary, it seemed to some that the Irish had never been so poorly fed.

Towards a new domestic architecture: homes, kitchens and food in rural Ireland during the long 1950s[1]

RHONA RICHMAN KENNEALLY*

Department of Design and Computation Arts, School of Canadian Irish Studies, Concordia University, Montreal, Quebec, H3G 1M8, Canada

[Accepted 16 November 2014. Published 22 May 2015.]

Abstract

An understanding of food habits and rituals is deeply enriched by factoring in the impact of the spaces in which they take place. This study explores the effects on the domestic foodscape—the physical built environment of home including its contents—primarily during the 1950s, when rural Irish households were in the midst of transformations to the visual, material and spatial experiences of the kitchen brought on by new foods and/or technologies. The life-changing potential of this modernised environment was acknowledged by certain influential public agents such as the Electricity Supply Board of Ireland, the Irish Department of Agriculture, the Irish Countrywomen's Association, and the Royal Institute of the Architects of Ireland, and they actively sought to ameliorate housing conditions in order to address quality-of-life issues, contribute to agricultural productivity and help to curb the flow of emigration. This modernisation strategy necessarily took into account certain proclivities in terms of food choices or preparation methods as well as wider cultural practices that were deeply embedded in Irish everyday life. Hence what emerges is a juxtaposition of the traditional, with new tastes, practices and expectations.

Introduction

Readers of the *REO News* (published by Ireland's Electricity Supply Board (ESB)) were treated, in December 1950, to an updated version of the Cinderella story in image and verse (see Fig. 1). The scene opens with the unfortunate maiden in her traditional Irish dwelling, with its small window, shadowy kerosene lamp and a three-legged iron pot hung over an open fire. She is '[w]orn with all the work to do' and hence '[s]taying home without a fella', which would

* Author's e-mail: rrk@concordia.ca

doi: 10.3318/PRIAC.2015.115.12

[1] Research for this essay was funded by the Social Sciences and Humanities Research Council of Canada. I am grateful to Gerard Hampson, Pat Yeates and Brendan Delany of the Archive of the Electricity Supply Board for their expertise and for permission to access this collection, and to my research assistant Gabrielle Machnik-Kékesi for her enthusiastic and meticulous work on this project.

FIG. 1—'The Adventures of Johnny Hotfoot: No. 2. The Transformation of Cinderella' (*REO News* IV: 1 (December 1950), 14). Reproduced by permission of the Electricity Supply Board.

have been read as an unfortunate circumstance in 1950s rural Ireland.[2] Hope is at hand, however, as the Prince Charming of this edition, the cartoon mascot of the ESB, Johnny Hotfoot, is both 'elegant' and 'quite fond of farming', and his vast and fertile acreage, proof of his stature and prowess, is picturesquely portrayed complete with castle ruins in the distance. A perfect specimen of the traditional male hero, then, he nevertheless also subscribes to the most up-to-date principles of domestic modernity, evidenced by his kitchen replete with mod cons: electric light, an electric kettle, a cooker, an iron and a washing machine, and an enormous refrigerator by the standards of the time. Such entangled hybridity of traditional and modern ethos—surprising even to the cow that ventures into this idyllic domestic scenario—drives the happy-ever-after narrative. Johnny's fondness for 'labour saving' has precipitated a lavish use of electricity, and '[p]lugs and sockets around the place' enable Cinderella to transform into a kind of mid-twentieth-century domestic icon, a glamorous, affluent, comfortable, married, lady of leisure.[3]

Given that this essay sits within a volume devoted to food and drink in Ireland, what is most relevant in the aforementioned parable is its depiction of an idealised transition brought on by modernisation impulses, from hearth (or other solid-fuel cooking) to electric (or gas), and from the multipurpose living space of the kitchen in the vernacular Irish 'cottage' to the specialisation, in the modern home, of zones for food preparation and the separation of domestic spaces related to eating and leisure. This study explores the effects on the domestic built environment brought on by evolving Irish and international food systems during the 1950s (a momentum that continued through to the 1970s), when families throughout Ireland were experiencing—if not necessarily to Mr and Mrs Hotfoot's advanced degree—the life-changing alterations that new technology brought to their dwellings, especially their kitchens.[4] Electric or gas cookers, refrigerators, fitted (built-in) cabinets, running cold, and, later, hot water made their way into and transformed the visual, material, and spatial experience of the kitchen and, in the wider context, what Seamus Heaney called

---

[2] For a description and analysis of the domestic circumstances (particularly in terms of the absence of running water in most rural households of this time) that Irish rural women experienced during the 1950s, see Mary E. Daly, '"Turn on the tap": the state, Irish women, and running water', in Maryann Gialanella Valiulis and Mary O'Dowd (eds), *Women and Irish history: essays in honour of Margaret MacCurtain* (Dublin, 1997), 206–19. Low marriage rates and high rates of permanent celibacy are explored in Caitriona Clear, '"Too fond of going": female emigration and change for women in Ireland, 1946–61', in Dermot Keogh, Finbarr O'Shea and Carmel Quinlan (eds), *The lost decade: Ireland in the 1950s* (Cork, 2004), 135–46: 141–3.

[3] Anonymous, 'The adventures of Johnny Hotfoot, no. 2: the transformation of Cinderella', *REO News* IV: 1 (December 1950), 14.

[4] See, for example, Michael Shiel, *The quiet revolution: the electrification of rural Ireland, 1946–76* (Dublin, 2003); and Maurice Manning and Moore McDowell, *Electricity supply in Ireland: the history of the ESB* (Dublin, 1984).

'[t]he rooms where we come to consciousness', that most essential space that humans occupy out of the womb—home.[5]

Food-related interactions within the household fundamentally motivate the practices of everyday life. An understanding of food habits and rituals is deeply enriched by taking into consideration the impact of the spaces in which they take place. In mid-twentieth-century Ireland virtually every family (except those in the most remote areas) gained the capacity to alter food and drink traditions honed over generations, if only through the purchase of an electric kettle: most homes were electrified by the 1970s and this small appliance was a very popular and early electrical purchase even in the most modest households.[6] In a country where the phrase 'put on the kettle' still ubiquitously rings through kitchens, and where hospitality to visitors often begins with a cup of tea, the true magnitude of even this seemingly small change deserves contemplation.

The Cinderella story of the ESB is only one of a myriad of advertisements, pamphlets, lectures, demonstrations, contests and other attention-gathering phenomena in circulation in the Irish popular culture of the period, and these echoed parallel campaigns in Europe, North America and Australia.[7] The Rural Electrification Scheme that began after the end of the Second World War was an additional driving force, and so were initiatives to pipe running water into rural homes.[8] Carried into the public consciousness by a variety of stakeholders including the ESB, were modifications in food-related thinking and activity at a range of scales: tools and other aids to facilitate new cooking methods and new foods were popularised and made available for appropriation; new food-related performances—how and where to cook, what to cook, and how and what to eat—were routinely discussed and demonstrated; and a broader culinary gaze, a curiosity about what and how, for example, American women were cooking in their appliance-laden kitchens, was valorised and activated.[9]

---

[5] Seamus Heaney, 'The sense of the past', *History Ireland* 1:4 (winter 1993), 33–7: 33.

[6] Shiel, *The quiet revolution*, 166.

[7] See June Freeman, *The making of the modern kitchen: a cultural history* (Oxford, 2004); Klaus Spechtenhauser (ed.), *The kitchen: life world, usage, perspectives* (Basel, 2006 and 2013); and two special issues (issues 13:2 and 13:6) of *Gender, Place and Culture: A Journal of Feminist Geography* edited by Louise C. Johnson in 2006.

[8] Indeed, the *REO News* was a monthly publication that reported on the progress of this countrywide project, primarily aimed at the Board's own executive, technical and sales force.

[9] For an introduction to such changes, see Rhona Richman Kenneally, 'Cooking at the hearth: the "Irish cottage" and women's lived experience', in Oona Frawley (ed.), *Memory Ireland* (4 vols, Syracuse, NY, 2012), vol. 2, 224–41; and Rhona Richman Kenneally, 'Tastes of home in mid-twentieth-century Ireland: food, design, and the refrigerator', *Food and Foodways* 23:1–2 (2015), 1–24. To provide additional context, see Joanna Bourke, *Husbandry to housewifery: women, economic change, and housework in Ireland, 1890–1914* (Oxford, 1993); and Caitriona Clear, *Women of the house: women's household work in Ireland, 1922–1961: discourses, experiences, memories* (Dublin, 2000) as well as *Social change and everyday life In Ireland, 1850–1922* (Manchester, 2007).

There is compelling evidence that the life-changing potential of the modernised domestic foodscape was acknowledged by at least some influential public agents in Ireland during this period. This term takes as its point of departure the assumption that the physical space of the home and the objects which it contains—the layout of rooms and furniture; the juxtaposition and intermingling of spaces for work and leisure; or the selection and arrangement of the contents of the home, for example—play a dynamic role in the food-related experiences of members of the household. Working from the perspective that Ireland was predominantly a rural and agricultural society and economy, organisations and bodies, such as the ESB, the Irish Department of Agriculture, the Irish Countrywomen's Association (ICA), and the Royal Institute of the Architects of Ireland (RIAI), initiated and supported projects aimed at rural dwellers, that showed a perceptive appreciation of the inextricable link between the acts of cooking and eating, and the environment in which they occurred. Moreover, these agents recognised that the quality of that environment had a significant bearing on the well-being of Irish families especially in rural parts of the country. Consequently, the narrative of Irish culinary modernity that these stakeholders appropriated from the international models with which they were acquainted, and strove to activate, was carefully and consciously mediated through a range of projects in order to try to accommodate the widest array of households of the time. Equally worth examining is the fact that this modernisation strategy for food in Ireland necessarily took into account certain proclivities in terms of food choices or preparation methods as well as wider cultural practices which were deeply embedded in Irish everyday life, and these vestiges are reflected in fascinating ways in the output of the campaigners. Hence what emerges is a juxtaposition of the traditional with new tastes, practices and expectations. Mid-twentieth-century Irish domestic food culture was a domain of 'and', rather than 'or'; indeed, that one can still find an Aga-type stove sitting next to the electric or gas cooker in a few present-day Irish kitchens is testament to the durability, in the nation's collective domestic foodscape, of tradition within the paradigm of the modern.[10]

Irish domestic foodscapes and the 'spatial turn'

Key stakeholders who promoted change in the Irish domestic foodscape during the 1950s and 1960s were cognisant of the crucial relationship between the nature of those physical spaces as sites of food (and other kinds of) activity and fundamental quality-of-life issues of their inhabitants. The very sensitivity of these agents to the spatially and materially driven stimuli of everyday life in rural Ireland deserves careful investigation, and resonates with recent work by researchers in architecture and design studies (and other fields) who have

---

[10] An Aga is a cooker that gives continuous heat for both cooking and the warming of rooms. Usually associated with solid-fuel energy (coal, anthracite or wood), it can now be fuelled by gas or electricity.

devoted attention to what has been called the 'spatial turn'.[11] For scholars undertaking such investigation, architecture is not simply a passive backdrop of walls, floor and ceiling within which people go about their everyday lives— not simply a 'collection of preexisting points set out in a fixed geometry, a container, as it were, for matter to inhabit' as Karen Barad puts it. Instead, a particular building may be explored as an 'iterative (re)structuring of spatial relations', as a universe dynamically comprised of the relationships, or interactions, between the people who occupy a particular space, the objects it contains, and the forces that operate within it.[12] Arising out of the spatial turn, then, is a conceptual framework through which to study the continuous engagement through which each of these elements both gives and receives stimuli in a continuous exchange. It allows us to think about how the physical properties of a kitchen, for example, induce particular behaviours or reactions on the part of those who occupy it—different reactions at different times, under different circumstances, by different people. Branko Kolarevic takes this analytical approach one step further by highlighting two variables that stimulate interactions in the built environment, namely pervading cultural practices and existing technological infrastructures. From his perspective, then, 'culture, technology, and space form a complex *active* web of connections, a network of interrelated constructs that affect each other simultaneously and continually'.[13] Understanding space in this way, as continually made and remade in a (re)active web of connections that transpire between people, material culture, energies such as light, heat and electricity, and so on, allows us to appreciate in a granular way the implications of mid-twentieth-century efforts to address the link between home, food, comfort and cultural aspirations. Such an understanding thus creates opportunities, in turn, to ponder the complexity of food-related activities in Irish domestic space.

---

[11] Examples of works that explore Irish spatiality and materiality include F. H. A. Aalen, Kevin Whelan and Matthew Stout (eds), *Atlas of the Irish rural landscape* (Toronto, Ont., 1997, second edition 2011); Gerry Smyth, *Space and the Irish cultural imagination* (London, 2001); Jim Hourihane (ed.), *Engaging spaces: people, place and space from an Irish perspective* (Dublin, 2003); Elizabeth FitzPatrick and James Kelly (eds), *Domestic life in Ireland, Proceedings of the Royal Irish Academy* 111C (2011); and Vera Kreilkamp (ed.), *Rural Ireland: the inside story* (Boston, MA, 2012). Earlier, pioneering advocates were Kevin Danaher (Caoimhín Ó Danachair), E. Estyn Evans and Henry Glassie.

[12] Karen Barad, *Meeting the universe halfway: quantum physics and the entanglement of matter and meaning* (Durham, NC, 2007), 180–1.

[13] Branko Kolarevic, 'Towards the performative in architecture,' in Branko Kolarevic and Ali M. Malkawi (eds), *Performative architecture: beyond instrumentality* (New York, 2005), 204–13: 205.

Incentives toward modern kitchen design with particular attention to rural areas

The temporal focus of this essay is primarily the 1950s, a period of social and economic hardship for many in Ireland, especially in rural areas. For most of the decade the Irish economy was stagnant.[14] In addition, according to Enda Delaney, '[e]xpectations, aspirations and other elements of socio-cultural change'—such as real as well as anticipated standards of living amongst young people—were such that emigration seemed the most reasonable alternative to remaining in rural Ireland.[15] The result was the highest emigration rate of Irish citizens, during this decade, in both absolute and relative terms, since the 1880s.[16] Rosemary Cullen Owens points out that '[t]he effects of post-Famine marriage patterns involving late and low rates of marriage, allied to high celibacy and female emigration rates, [the highest of any European country between 1945 and 1960] were still being felt in rural Ireland into the 1960s'.[17] Moreover, Caitriona Clear explains that at this time most women gainfully occupied by working on farms were employed by relatives; she concludes that '[o]ral and other evidence suggests that women who were working as assisting relatives [sisters, daughters and daughters-in-law of farmers, for example] up to the 1950s felt themselves to be unusually disadvantaged'.[18]

Inferior housing conditions were deemed to have played a role, and various social agencies sought to remedy matters. As Mary McCarthy observes, 'from 1942 onward both northern and southern Ireland began to consider housing as an issue that required serious attention', and '[b]oth governments were willing to improve housing conditions, took steps to quantify the problem and focused on the best way to achieve set targets'.[19] Rural electrification in the Republic was one consequence, and the rhetoric of the ESB, as we have already seen, reflected strategies to enhance facilities in the farmhouse itself through electrical interventions, in addition to promoting inducements to install electrical apparatuses in barns or dairies. Two other agencies with social and cultural obligations stand out in this regard, namely the RIAI and the ICA. Working together, these bodies were instrumental in proposing adaptations to the rural domestic foodscape that would raise the quality of life in rural

---

[14] See Gerry O'Hanlon, 'Population change in the 1950s: a statistical review', in Keogh, O'Shea and Quinlan (eds), *The lost decade*, 72–9: 74. Diarmaid Ferriter has noted that historians of the period have used words like '"doom", "drift", "stagnation", "crisis", and "malaise" to describe Ireland south of the border in the 1950s'. Ferriter, *The transformation of Ireland* (New York, 2005), 462.

[15] Enda Delaney, 'The vanishing Irish? The exodus from Ireland in the 1950s', in Keogh, O'Shea and Quinlan (eds), *The lost decade,* 80–6: 82–3.

[16] O'Hanlon, 'Population change', 72.

[17] Rosemary Cullen Owens, *A social history of women in Ireland 1870–1970* (Dublin, 2005), 165, 323. For a wider sense of the position of the Irish Government on 1950s emigration see Mary E. Daly, *The slow failure: population decline and independent Ireland, 1920–1973* (Madison, WI, 2006), especially 183–221.

[18] Clear, '"Too fond of going"', 135–46: 139.

[19] Mary McCarthy, 'The provision of rural local-authority housing and domestic space: a comparative North–South study, 1942–60', *Proceedings of the Royal Irish Academy* 111C (2011), 287–309: 308.

households and augment the experience of women undertaking domestic duties including cooking.

The Royal Institute of the Architects of Ireland and its members participated in important strategies to recast the experience of the domestic foodscape, by offering advice about and encouraging architectural and design-based remedies. Predominant in this regard was Patrick Delany, an architect with a Dublin practice but an interest in rural issues. In a five-part series of articles on rural housing that appeared in 1953–4, in a magazine called *Homeplanning* meant for a general (rather than professional-architectural) audience, Delany argued that '[i]f within the term "Housing" we agree to include not only four walls and a roof, but also decent services such as piped water, sewerage, electricity, telephone and transport, then lack of housing amenities [in rural areas] is one of the prime causes of the Drift from the Land'.[20] Having elicited and received feedback from readers of his series, Delany was further disheartened by what he learned. '[F]ar too many of our people are living in the country without even the essential minimum of services', he wrote, 'and at great distances from their shops, their neighbours and their work. It is as one would suspect; but the picture painted by their replies is one of deep gloom'.[21] Delany consequently set out to offer readers succinct and basic advice regarding how best to undertake new construction in the countryside. Issues that were addressed included the orientation of the dwelling for optimal sunlight and warmth as well as techniques of insulation, and these instructions were meant to stimulate reflection on the part of homeowner and builder alike. It goes without saying that these issues of utility as well as comfort also fundamentally affected the house as a food workspace or site of commensality.

Delany's next intervention in *Homeplanning* was a five-part series entirely devoted to kitchen design (not confined to rural homes), called 'Planned kitchen'. The series was conceptualised as an analysis of general subject matter in the first two parts, with special attention being given to kitchen design in which the cooker was electric, gas and solid-fuel, respectively, in parts three to five. Delany opened the series by asserting that

> No one needs to be reminded of the importance of good kitchen design for the comfort and convenience both of the housewife and of her family, no matter how large or how small that family's income may be. Directly or indirectly, the kitchen affects family nutrition and family life as a whole in a way that no other part of the house can—as is recognized in the clichés 'the woman's workshop,' 'the hub of the house,' and so on.[22]

---

[20] Patrick Delany, 'Rural housing: the vicious circle', *Homeplanning* 1:3 (September 1953), 4–5: 4. *Homeplanning* was a monthly journal published by Harpers Ltd, College Green, Dublin. Its first issue appeared in July 1953, and it ran until at least April 1954.

[21] Patrick Delany, 'Rural housing: a final word', *Homeplanning* 1:7 (January 1954), 4–5: 4.

[22] Patrick Delany, 'Planned kitchen', *Homeplanning* 1:8 (February 1954), 4–5: 4.

Kitchen size, layout, storage, lighting and finishes were discussed, and complemented by an illustration on the cover of the February 1954 issue, the one in which the first instalment of his series of articles appeared (see Fig. 2). The image's caption outlines the kitchen's pivotal features: a Rayburn cooker embedded in a sleek and efficient space, with '[b]uilt-in presses from floor to ceiling [to] avoid dust traps', and a 'working table top runs from wall to wall [...] bordered by [a] tile surround to avoid splashes'. Storage is made possible through 'enamel kitchen cabinet[s]' and a 'glass-doored china press' as well as shelves hung under the table surface. On a third wall, not shown, a hanging place rack plus an additional 'hanging china cupboard with folding table below and a storage cabinet from floor to ceiling' also helped keep the kitchen

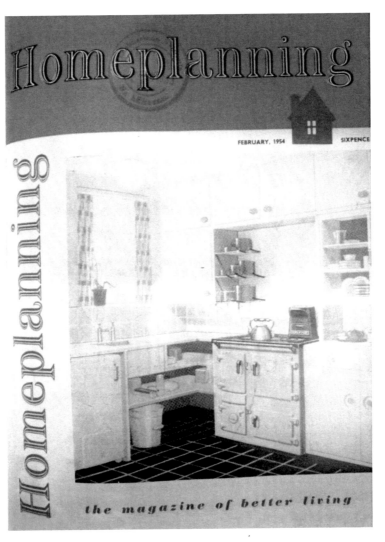

Fig. 2—Front cover of *Homeplanning*, February 1954.

organised and efficient. The refrigerator is visible in the image, and the 'sink with mixer tap' implies hot and cold running water. Aesthetic features may also be discerned: patterned window curtains are in view, a plant sits on the windowsill, and the reader was advised that the cabinets are cream-coloured and the floor made of red tiles.[23]

Notwithstanding this definitive rendering of an idealised foodscape, Delany took a surprisingly flexible view on kitchen planning, thereby making his articles more accommodating to a wider audience in need of design advice. With regard to kitchen layout, for example, he pushed back against the extreme views of international experts who advocated the compartmentalisation of kitchens into discrete and rigid zones, and argued instead that the:

> saving of steps, while undoubtedly important, is an aspect [of design] that tends to be over stressed by the 'scientific' designer who will quote impressive statistics to show that a housewife can walk 4 miles per day in a badly laid out kitchen and only 2½ miles per day in the same kitchen if well laid out.[24]

In the article devoted to the all-electric kitchen, Delany offered readers one sample architectural plan, a small kitchen of 10 feet 9 inches × 8 feet 6 inches, realistically intended for a family of four or five of limited budget (see Fig. 3(a) and (b)). In his breakdown of the drawings, Delany created an opportunity for readers to negotiate, for themselves, pragmatic rather than perfect kitchen design, by listing both the advantages and disadvantages of this compromise. Hived off from the other living areas of the house rather than part of an open plan, this space 'can be small enough to be kept tidy easily', was 'planned to secure almost a "laboratory" degree of efficiency', and 'takes up a relatively small area, so that in the limited area of the modern small home, more space is left over for other rooms'. However, its 'chief disadvantage is psychological rather than practical—that is, it is rarely large enough to seem like a room at all, and can be a little depressing to work in for long periods', although this can be 'mitigated by giving the window a pleasant outlook'. Also problematic is that it offered no room at all for even the 'most hurried' meal, and so 'the apparent saving of total floor-space is something of an illusion'. Delany also admitted that there was a limited amount of food storage allowed in the design, which had 'little room for reserve stocks of anything', and would therefore require '[c]areful budgeting [*sic*] and ordering'. He also warned that while 'the general lighting is good, the positions of window and cooker make it difficult to see what is in the oven'. Readers may have been left bewildered by this ultimately

---

[23] Anon., 'Our cover design', *Homeplanning* 1:8 (February 1954), 5.

[24] Patrick Delany, 'Planned kitchen', *Homeplanning* 1:9 (March 1954), 4–5: 4. For a discussion of prescriptives targeting kitchen efficiency see, for example, Ellen Lupton and J. Abbott Miller, *The bathroom, the kitchen, and the aesthetics of waste* (Princeton, NJ, 1992).

Fig. 3(a)—Axonometric drawing of a small all-electric kitchen designed by Patrick Delany, *Homeplanning*, April 1954.

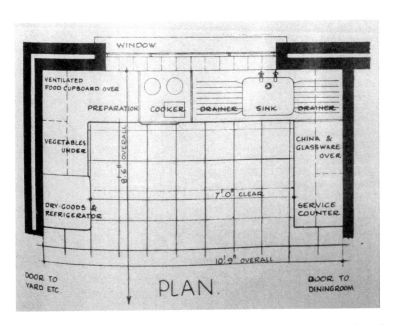

Fig. 3(b)—Plan of a small all-electric kitchen designed by Patrick Delany, *Homeplanning*, April 1954.

unresolved kitchen plan, but this approach seems to have been an intentional encouragement to take matters into one's own hands and to consider the unique needs and particularities of one's own household. As Delany reminded his audience; '[t]here is of course no "ideal" kitchen any more than there can be an "ideal" house'.[25] A year later, by the summer of 1955, Delany was broadening

---

[25] Patrick Delany, 'Planned kitchen', *Homeplanning* 1:10 (April 1954), 4–5.

his own knowledge by working with members of the Irish Countrywomen's Association as a representative of the RIAI studying rural kitchen design, and listening to the experiences and recommendations of this team of highly experienced collaborators.

The ICA took a leadership position vis-à-vis rural housing that included extensive attention to the introduction of modern methods of cooking and new foods into the kitchen.[26] This was achieved through a variety of means. The association was instrumental, for example, in advocating the introduction of running water in rural homes, a necessity that was far from commonplace at the time: even in 1961 only one rural household in eight had running water according to Mary E. Daly.[27] In 1954—the same year that Delany prepared his articles for *Homeplanning*—the organisation obtained financial support from the W. K. Kellogg Foundation in the United States of America, and opened An Grianán, its residential campus located in Termonfechin, Co. Louth. As its ICA organisers proudly noted, 'through An Grianán, we look forward to promoting national and international co-operation in the field of rural betterment'.[28] The agenda included lectures and courses of several days' duration, and, amongst other facilities, there was a 'demonstration kitchen . . . to encourage members in the use of electrical and other labour saving equipment, for courses in fruit and vegetable preservation, in dietetics, and in general household cookery'.[29]

If ICA members now had a destination away from their homes at which demonstrations of modern methods could be taught, the existence of that facility did not preclude extensive measures to take their message out on the road, to the very doorstep of women on their farms. The goal was to be proactive in making direct contact with households throughout the country in an effort to enhance conditions in the home place—including those related to food—by supplementing the knowledge that was available through more passive means such as newspapers or magazines. In 1956 (after at least five years of discussion with the Irish minister for agriculture) the association received funding from the United States Government through cooperation with the Irish Department of Agriculture under what was known as the Grant

---

[26] The ICA, a non-sectarian association of women, was established in 1910. It operated at the local level through guilds of members in towns and villages; these were clustered into federations at the county level and administered nationally from Dublin. For further information see, for example, Patrick Bolger (ed.), *And see her beauty shining there: the story of the Irish Countrywomen's Association* (Dublin, 1986), and Aileen Heverin, *The Irish Countrywomen's Association: a history 1910–2000* (Dublin, 2000).

[27] Daly, '"Turn on the tap"', 207. For further information regarding the role of the ICA (and the ESB) in promoting piped-in water see Shiel, *The quiet revolution*, 194–212 and Heverin, *The ICA: a history*, 105–14.

[28] Anon, 'Grianan committee report', *Farmers' Gazette* CXII:15 (10 April 1954), 407–08: 408.

[29] Anon, 'Grianan committee report', 408.

Counterpart Scheme.[30] The mandate of the ICA was to 'to advance materially the productivity and amenities of Irish agriculture' by hiring advisors to criss-cross the country for the duration of the project, which lasted into the early 1960s.[31] Eleanor Butler, a qualified architect and member of the RIAI, was employed by the ICA as a home planning advisor with the responsibility to 'make the women of Ireland "Housing Conscious" and this she certainly succeeded in doing' according to Esther Bishop, the Chair of the Grant Counterpart Committee.[32] Butler was called upon to help to develop housing policy and practice, for example the design of three houses at the request of 'one Agricultural officer' to be used as residences on three pilot farms.[33] However, she considered herself at her most effective when visiting local ICA guilds rather than advising at more remote levels, partly because, as she noted, members of other rural-based organisations such as the Macra na Feirme and Muintir na Tíre would also be present, and also because '[v]ery often I am invited to visit the homes and advise on the spot'.[34] While dedicated, then, to cut as large a swath as possible through the Irish countryside, she nevertheless took a very realistic view of the impact of her consultations with rural families. Her ambition was to 'try to ensure that every member of the [ICA] could carry out at least one planning improvement in her home during the period of my service', keeping in mind the financial and social constraints that she knew would have to be overcome.[35]

Margaret Crowley, a qualified domestic science instructor, began work as the ICA home economics advisor in 1958. Her first task, funded by the Kellogg Foundation, was to complete a year of additional training at the University of Kentucky and elsewhere in the United States, where she was given the opportunity to learn 'in particular how the field workers reach the woman in her home, there to advise her on her own specific problems'.[36] The report Crowley submitted on the completion of the scheme in 1962 is an impressive account of her activities in all 26 counties of the Republic, and it notes substantial attendance at her lectures, many of which addressed kitchen planning, home decoration (including the kitchen) and cooking methods.[37]

---

30 National Library of Ireland (NLI), MS 39,876/8, Esther Bishop, Typescript report of the work of the Grant Counterpart Fund Committee of the ICA entitled 'Better living', 1962, 1.

31 NLI, MS 39,876/8, Bishop, 'Better living', 1962, 2.

32 NLI, MS 39,876/8, Bishop, 'Better living', 1962, 4.

33 NLI, MS 39,876/8, Report of Miss Butler, 'Better living', 1962, 30.

34 NLI, MS 39,876/8, Butler, 'Better living', 1962, 29–30.

35 NLI, MS 39,876/8, Butler, 'Better living', 1962, 19.

36 NLI, MS 39,876/8, Bishop, 'Better living', 1962, 5.

37 Recognition of the significance of comfort and aesthetics within Irish domestic space can be noted as early as the turn of the twentieth century, in *The Irish Homestead*, the publication of the Irish Agricultural Organisation Society. See James MacPherson, '"Ireland begins in the home": women, Irish national identity, and the domestic sphere in the *Irish Homestead*, 1896–1912', *Éire-Ireland* 36:3–4 (2001), 131–52: 138–42.

Crowley worked systematically, county by county, through the auspices of local foundations and guilds that organised events at venues such as schools or town halls. Her audience was not confined to ICA members: students, local members of the Macra na Feirme and Muintir na Tíre as well as other interested parties sat in on her sessions. Additionally, Crowley undertook numerous home visits by invitation of their inhabitants in order to offer even more specific advice, and often regretted, in her report, not having had enough time to respond to all such requests; she was estimated to have declined fully half of those who wished to receive this personalised advice.[38] Her reports provide a few opportunities by which to learn more about the nature of such consultations: a visit to a home in Co. Monaghan in October 1959, for example, was a '[r]e-planning of kitchen to cut off draughts', while she advised, in Co. Mayo, regarding the 're-organisation of the kitchen to make working conditions simpler'.[39]

The work and reports of both these women shed light on the overarching goals of the ICA. Butler, like Crowley, began her tenure with a reconnaissance mission, travelling in her case to Scandinavia and West Germany in order to study domestic conditions in other nations whose economies were based on agricultural exports. She noted that agricultural productivity there 'was in direct proportion to a rise in the standard of home conditions'.[40] Indeed, '[i]n other countries, where production is low on a farm, the Agricultural Advisor is not allowed to suggest outside improvements until the planning and amenities of the house have been looked into, beginning with the kitchen'.[41] By contrast, Irish women suffered and were often forced to emigrate because:

> [t]he quite common attitude of farmers of 'what was good enough for my Mother is good enough for any woman coming into my house' has confirmed many girls in their opinion that there is no hope of improved living conditions in rural Ireland, and so they often refuse to marry into what they consider primitive conditions.[42]

Evidence that numerous farm women echoed Butler's dissatisfaction regarding domestic cooking and other household tasks is demonstrated by those women's enthusiasm in attending lectures and requesting home visits. It is also suggested qualitatively, for example through the comments of the president of the Corofin, Co. Clare, Guild of the ICA, Proinseas, Bean Mhic Cafaid, who provided an account, in Margaret Crowley's report, of a series of Crowley's

---

38 NLI, MS 39,876/8, Bishop, 'Better living', 1962, 7.
39 NLI, MS 39,876/8, Report of Miss Margaret Crowley, 'Better living', 1962, 120, 123.
40 NLI, MS 39,876/8, Butler, 'Better living', 1962, 21.
41 NLI, MS 39,876/8, Butler, 'Better living', 1962, 32.
42 NLI, MS 39,876/8, Butler, 'Better living', 1962, 32.

lectures attended by members of five guilds in March 1960. Pronouncing the lectures a great success, the president wrote:

> Special attention was paid to kitchen planning and a receptive audience proved that they took all the points. Apart from the practical value of the lecture, I felt that it was a sound psychology to bring what are usually ones' private domestic torments and irritations into the open and show that they can be beaten, or treated intelligently, as merely unescapable [*sic*] monotonies which can be relieved.[43]

An important outgrowth of concerns about the domestic foodscape that emanated from both Patrick Delany's work and that of the ICA was a collaboration, beginning in 1955 and continuing into the 1960s, between the ICA and the RIAI (with Delany part of a three-person team representing the architectural institute) in which the ESB also participated.[44] Its genesis was at the request of James Dillon, minister for agriculture, and the goal was to design a model farm kitchen that could be visited by anyone curious about rural housing improvements. The kitchen was to be constructed full-scale at the 1956 Spring Show, an annual event hosted by the Royal Dublin Society (RDS), routinely visited by thousands of people from across Ireland. The most remarkable characteristic of this farm kitchen was its blend of traditional and modern elements, no doubt an outcome derived from the experience and aspirations of all participating bodies. As the *Homeplanning* series suggests, Delany was already predisposed to taking an open approach to kitchen design subject to individual needs; one assumes that this helped to make him responsive to what was described in the *Farmers' Gazette* as the 'critical demand of the farmhouse wife as represented by the [ICA]'.[45] Extant information suggests that the collaboration involved a give-and-take approach on both sides: ICA representatives requested modifications to certain design details initially laid down by the RIAI subcommittee, and at least some of these are evident in the final design.[46] Compatibility is also implied in a letter of thanks that the honorary secretary of the ICA, Kathleen Delap, wrote to the president of the RIAI, in which she pronounced that 'we could not have

---

[43] NLI, MS 39,876/8, Cited in Crowley, 'Better living', 1962, 93.

[44] Irish Architectural Archive (IAA), Basement E2, Irish Countrywomen's Association Kitchen Exhibition 1956, Wilfrid Cantwell (honorary secretary of the RIAI) to Francis J. Barry and Patrick M. Delany, 3 August 1955.

[45] 'A modern farmyard at the Spring Show: plenty of ideas for electrification', *Farmers' Gazette* CXV:18 (4 May 1957), 494.

[46] Examples of adjustments to the design made on the recommendation of the ICA are the inclusion of two windows on the north wall of the kitchen and the location of the cooker to the left of the sink. IAA, Basement E2, ICA kitchen exhibition 1956, Kathleen A. Delap (honorary secretary of the ICA) to Wilfrid Cantwell, 31 October 1955.

achieved such good results without such generous co-operation from the Architects'.[47]

The kitchen as built in 1957 is fascinating inasmuch as it reflects a deliberate hybridity that took into account and maintained key characteristics of vernacular domestic design, while striving to create an efficient and pleasant modern zone for food production.[48] As the *Farmers' Gazette* explained:

> [a]ttention here has been paid not alone to work saving, but also to the saving the [*sic*] thousands of footsteps which is the burden that badly planned kitchens impose on the housewife. Hot and cold water are, of course, an essential feature, but the modernisation has not lost any of the comfort and charm of the good type country kitchen.[49]

A study of the kitchen design (see Pl. I) reveals elements of the modern that were to be expected at the time, many of which had been addressed by

PL. I—Photo of model farm kitchen exhibit at the Spring Show of the Royal Dublin Society, 1957. Reproduced by permission of the Electricity Supply Board.

---

[47] IAA, Basement E2, ICA kitchen exhibition 1956, letter from Kathleen Delap to the President of the RIAI, 14 May 1956.

[48] The 1956 RDS farm kitchen was the same design as that which was erected a year later (for which substantial documentation remains): this is indicated in an ICA memorandum: see NLI, MS 39,877/3 b, ICA memorandum to the Department of Agriculture, 16 July 1957, 3.

[49] 'A modern farmyard at the Spring Show', 494.

Delany in his *Homeplanning* series: fitted cabinets, taps for hot and cold running water, a large refrigerator and electrical appliances, including a cooker, a toaster and a kettle are included, while extensive fenestration is provided to complement the electric lighting, the latter consisting of at least one ceiling fixture as well as an additional fluorescent unit above the countertop that separated the cooking and eating areas. However, unlike Delany's sample plan with its small, isolated kitchen, this one is open to an eating and leisure area and, as a report on the kitchen in the *Irish Press* both explained and illustrated (see Pl. II):

> still retains the large open fire place which has now been fitted with a boiler grate which gives constant hot water. Even the old settle still remains in the corner and a large turf box is fitted beside the fire. The old and new are beautifully combined with the traditional furnishings by the I.C.A. and the modern electrical fitments by the E.S.B.[50]

The plan was conceived as a modification of a typical existing farm kitchen (and therefore 16×16 square feet in size) that could be retrofitted either by a builder or as a do-it-yourself project by a handy farmer. Architectural drawings of the design were also made available to interested parties for that purpose.[51]

PL. II—Photo of model farm kitchen exhibit reproduced in the *Irish Press*, May 1957. Reproduced by permission of the Electricity Supply Board.

---

[50] RK, 'All electric farm kitchen', *Irish Press*, 8 May 1957, 3.
[51] RK, 'All electric farm kitchen', 3.

The RDS farm kitchen was deemed a great success by many observers. The ESB estimated that if the number of leaflets that were made available at the kitchen was any indication of attendance by the public, then some 30,000 people visited the display.[52] So well received was this initiative, in fact, that the decision was taken a year later to erect one, and, later, a second mobile version. These were designed to be collapsible and thus transportable on a trailer (see Pl. III showing the interior of one of the units). The mobile kitchens were almost exact replicas of the 1957 Spring Show design (and of each other), and were large enough to accommodate 40 visitors who could either explore the design on their own, or attend the lectures and demonstrations held by the ESB, the ICA or other instructors, usually in the evenings. Whereas the units were usually tended by ESB employees, both Butler and Crowley gave demonstrations in them, to enthusiastic audiences. The first model took to the road in March 1958, the second in August 1959, and they were still mobile through to November 1961 at least, having been displayed at some 150 venues throughout the towns and villages of Ireland.[53] Accounts of visits from ICA members, and newspaper reports of the arrival of the mobile kitchen were consistently

PL. III—Photo of the interior of the mobile farm kitchen. Reproduced by permission of the Electricity Supply Board.

---

[52] 'News items', *REO News* X:6 (May 1957), 13.

[53] 'A mobile farm kitchen', *REO News* XI:4 (March 1958), 4–5; 'ESB mobile kitchen' on the Irish Countrywomen's Association page, *Farmers' Gazette* CXIX:47 (25 November 1961), 18. Dates and places of mobile kitchen venues were tracked through *Farmers' Gazette* reports, and ICA and ESB documentation. The ideal kitchens displayed at the RDS and their mobile counterparts are the subjects of a future monograph by the author.

positive. The anticipated visit of the mobile kitchen to Castlebar, Co. Mayo, in September 1958 was deemed by the *Connacht Telegraph* to be '[o]f tremendous interest to all householders'.[54] The *Irish Independent* gave the design a more detailed imprimatur: '[e]mbodying many of the essential items and geared to modern standards of efficiency, the kitchen, if even in part transferred to a farmhouse, would be a decided benefit to the housewife'. The popularity of the design was at least in part due to its blend of traditional and contemporary: 'no matter what new gadgets are purchased, the housewife will be reluctant to part with her keepsakes. It is with this in mind that the travelling kitchen has been planned. A pleasant blending of old and new is embodied in the general aspect with pleasing results'.[55] In 1960 the model farm kitchen was replaced, at the RDS Spring Show, by a full-scale all-electric house, the product of another collaboration principally between the ESB and, this time, An Foras Talúntais (The Agricultural Institute). Whereas the updated design was yet a further iteration of electrical and time-saving features embedded in what appeared to be a sleek modern bungalow, the connection between working zone and leisure zone, and the adjacent open hearth, were retained.[56]

Food within the domestic foodscape of mid-twentieth-century rural Ireland

It is not the intention of this essay to track the implementation of modern kitchen design in mid-twentieth-century Ireland from the perspective of homeowners, or to elaborate on the individual homeowners' reception of these models or indeed of modern cooking, except to say that the women who were interviewed by this author about their experiences in mid-twentieth-century Irish domestic space expressed enthusiasm about the convenience associated with the new paradigm—especially running water.[57] Ethnographic evidence of this nature serves as confirmation of the efficacy of the ICA and others' work to bring modern practices to the domestic foodscape in Ireland. Such findings are further supplemented and enriched by studies of the architecture itself and the interactions that took place within it, to gain a more complex understanding of how 'progress' unfolded in rural Ireland, and how that technological evolution was tempered and mediated by the vicissitudes of time and place. For example, it seems significant that the open fire, while no longer promoted as a site for cooking, remained an integral element of the kitchens proposed by the ESB/RIAI/ICA collaboration. This reflected an anticipated reluctance of Irish household members to give up sensory-based or historically based experiences of comfort and pleasure, heat and light, disbursed throughout the work and

---

[54] 'All-electric exhibition kitchen in Castlebar', *Connacht Telegraph*, 13 September 1958, 2.

[55] 'Mobile modern farm kitchen', *Irish Independent*, 19 February 1958, 4. The article also noted the aesthetic qualities of the unit, which is described as having 'delicately off-white walls, with blue flooring' in order to 'dispense with the usual dark interior and make the kitchen bright and airy'.

[56] 'Spring Show—1960', *REO News* XIII:6 (May 1960), 2. The architect on this project was P. J. Tuite. See ESB, 'Better living for the farm family' [1960].

[57] These interviews and conversations took place between 2010 and 2014, in counties Cork, Clare, Galway and Kilkenny.

leisure space of the hearth, as compared with the confined heat of a gas or electric cooker that is turned off when not in use (that residual Aga comes to mind here).[58] A hesitation about sacrificing the gustatory qualities and indeed heritage value of open-hearth cooking seems also to be a factor for some.[59] A profound example of such sentiments can be found in one segment of a weekly column called 'Cooks' causerie: By Clare' that ran during the early 1950s in the *Farmers' Gazette*. The author recounted a recent visit to the Wicklow Mountains, and an encounter with a man out hunting rabbit, and it set her into a reverie about what she would have liked to do with the meat:

> I'd cook that rabbit and glory be but he'd taste good. I'd have to rake out the turf ashes until they were just nicely hot, then into the pot-oven I'd put the bacon cut in dice t'would sizzle and the smell would be exquisite. In with the rabbit cut in joints I'd poke the pieces around and about until they were all brown, then the little pinch of nutmeg, the salt and pepper and about two tablespoons of water, stir again and put the lid on. 'Tis a young rabbit I'm cooking, so he won't take long, half-an-hour—just time for me to wash and cook some new potatoes. Just when the potatoes are cooked and sizzling a minute in a little butter and chopped parsley I'll take the lid off the pot-oven and add my cup of cream, another good stir and onto a hot dish with the lot ... If I had a rabbit and a pot-oven I'd do all that. But I haven't a pot-oven. No! Not any more. I've a brightly shining most modern and up-to-date electric cooker, one that would turn up its nose at a 'black as night pot-oven,' but I'll tell you a secret, that cooker would be green with envy if it could only taste the bread baked in the 'black as night pot-oven' and if it could but smell the rabbit cooking away on the turf ashes. Ah, well, fair is fair. The electric monarch is a wonder for biscuits and as I'm very fond of biscuits I'll make some[.]

Not only is the sense of taste engaged in this imagined performance, but those of sight (dicing the bacon), smell, touch (poking the pieces) and sound (sizzling). Nostalgia aside, coming back to present-day reality is still a worthwhile compromise for Clare, and recipes for Florentines and 'Little Biscuits' follow.[60] Several months later, she invoked another touching replay of

---

[58] Eleanor Butler confirms this in her rationale for keeping the open fire in the 1957 RDS kitchen design: 'This adaptation of an old kitchen allowed for the continued use of the open fire which forms the focal point of rural home life, but extending its use beyond that of conversation [by adding a system to heat water]'. NLI, MS 39,876/8, Butler, 'Better living', 1962, 22.

[59] For an analysis of a fictional account of the significance of traditional cooking methods see Rhona Richman Kenneally, 'The elusive landscape of history: food and empowerment in Sebastian Barry's *Annie Dunne*', in Máirtín Mac Con Iomaire and Eamon Maher (eds), *'Tickling the palate': gastronomy in Irish literature and culture* (Oxford, 2014), 79–98.

[60] Clare [surname unknown], 'Cooks' causerie: By Clare', *Farmers' Gazette* CXI:22 (30 May 1953), 658.

a traditional kitchen experience that demonstrated just how essential that space was as an anchor to country life. Especially in the early morning, she recounts,

> when I come downstairs and open the door of my neat, spick-and-span kitchen with its gleaming cooker and its scarlet polished floor, I turn the page and look back to a country kitchen I remember years ago, and sometimes in the quiet of the early morning while the electric kettle boils I wink back a tear.

Clare attributes her present-day dismay to a kind of loneliness: 'My kitchen of to-day is so quiet in the morning and I am so alone. My kitchen of the past was such a bustly [*sic*] place at 7 a.m.', and she narrates the various activities of family members criss-crossing the space to undertake their various pursuits. The boiling kettle brings her back to reality, her 'kitchen of the past melts into the morning sunshine and I hurry upstairs to call the family. All day long I'll be a city dweller but at night and in the kitchen to-morrow morning I'll have my dreams and I'll slip to the country'.[61]

What other traits and characteristics can be discerned about food habits and precedents brought on by these inducements regarding modern kitchens? Clare herself included, in a number of her weekly columns, prompts to entice readers to try new or unfamiliar foods and techniques, including recipes such as 'Chartreuse of Fish' requiring tarragon vinegar and 'Chilli' vinegar, instructions on how to cook the frankfurters that appeared in the 'delicatessen shop windows' of the time, and a recipe for 'Spaghetti in Tomato Sauce', which she promoted as 'a very nourishing and very cheap dish'.[62] Irish 'women's' magazines such as *Model Housekeeping* showed similar tendencies, by publishing for example, a conversion table of cooking temperatures for solid-fuel, electric and gas ovens (slow/moderate/hot to degrees Fahrenheit to regulo settings), and explaining what a marinade, and paprika, were to readers who sent in requests for such information.[63] Articles in *Homeplanning* amongst other magazines explored nutritional and hygiene issues, thus locking both food selection and manipulation into the scientific paradigm that also underscored efficient kitchen design.[64] Moreover, American and Continental recipes and

---

[61] Clare, 'Cooks' causerie', *Farmers' Gazette* CXII:7 (13 February 1954), 174. Similar linkages of cooking proficiency acquired in a traditional kitchen with the skills necessary in a modern kitchen appear in the introductions to cookbooks by Maura Laverty and Theodora FitzGibbon, written in the 1950s and 1960s. See Richman Kenneally, 'Cooking at the hearth', 236–7.

[62] Clare, 'Cooks' causerie', *Farmers' Gazette* CXI:1 (3 January 1953), 22; CXI:12 (21 March 1953), 318; and CXI:43 (24 October 1953), 1226.

[63] The conversion chart and question about paprika appear in the anonymous 'My cookery postbag', *Model Housekeeping* (February 1952), 255; the request about marinades is in the April 1952 'My cookery postbag', 379.

[64] Regarding nutritional issues see Mary de R. Swanton, 'Your kitchen: the foods you really need', *Homeplanning* 1:7 (January 1954), 9. She addressed hygiene a month later in 'Your kitchen: waste not food want not food', *Homeplanning* 1:8 (February 1954), 9.

cooking techniques proliferated, through publications by the ICA, columns such as Clare's and in cookery books of the time.[65]

It certainly would be wrong, however, to assume that everyone switched over to modern methods during this period, that they could afford to or even wanted to do so. Nor should the pleasure or satisfaction gleaned by some women using traditional methods be ignored. When the distinguished folklorist Henry Glassie visited Ballymenone, Co. Fermanagh, in the 1970s to study that Northern Irish community, Ellen Cutler was still proudly cooking over a hearth fire, and joyfully exclaimed over the glorious taste of boiled cabbage 'and it is boiled right'.[66] Reluctance to change food tastes and methods stemmed from long-standing habits, reflected for example in the letter sent in to *Woman's Way* by one frustrated woman whose husband refused to eat the vegetables she tried to serve him for the sake of good nutrition.[67] That the cook of the house could not always unilaterally select the foods for consumption has been recognised by researchers in other areas, and so, inevitably, if incentives to new cooking and eating were to work, they had to be directed at men as well as women.[68] Eleanor Butler knew this, and reported requests, 'at almost every place', for men-only demonstrations in the mobile kitchen, in the hopes that the males would be more receptive to their contents if they did not have their female relations present.[69] The amazing Margaret Crowley knew this too. Even before she was hired by the ICA, in 1953 when teaching at the new vocational school in Banagher, Co. Offaly, she insisted on introducing the male students to cooking. She turned off the running water supply and insisted that they fetch water from the village well; they had weekly classes to learn to cook simple dishes; they were given a voice in planning the menu of the annual Christmas party for the school; and they helped to serve the foods that were prepared by the girls, for more than 80 guests. All the pupils dined, in rotation, in small groups with the teacher to learn proper manners, and they had a school kitchen garden to prove, as an article in the *Irish Independent* put it, 'that there are other edible vegetables in Ireland besides cabbage, turnips and potatoes'.[70]

So mid-twentieth-century incentives to revise the Irish rural domestic foodscape propelled a movement toward a series of goals: a more comfortable and welcoming home that would help to inspire the young generation to stay on

---

[65] See, for example, the Danish 'Foreign recipes' on the ICA page of the *Farmers' Gazette* CXI:16 (18 April 1953), 423; American tart, in Clare, 'Cooks' causerie', *Farmers' Gazette* CXI:41 (10 October 1953), 1,178, and a chapter on American-inspired convenience foods in Maura Laverty, *Maura Laverty's cookbook* (New York and Toronto, Ont., 1947), 117–23.

[66] Henry Glassie, *Passing the time in Ballymenone: culture and history of an Ulster community* (Philadelphia, PA, 1982), 445.

[67] Maura Laverty, 'Maura Laverty's letters page', *Woman's Way* (15 May 1963), 58.

[68] See Wm. Alex McIntosh and Mary Zey, 'Women as gatekeepers of food consumption: a sociological critique', in Carole Counihan and Steven L. Kaplan (eds), *Food and gender: identity and power* (Amsterdam, 1998), 125–44.

[69] NLI, MS 39,876/8, Butler, 'Better living', 1962, 23.

[70] IM, 'Answer to your questions', *Irish Independent*, 15 February 1958, 9.

the farm; an efficient and hygienic kitchen, in keeping with the latest labour-saving designs emerging from America and elsewhere; a revitalised interest in the taste, nourishing qualities and varieties of foods; and, at the same time, a reappraisal of what was intrinsically Irish about the Irish domestic foodscape, particularly the abiding centrality of the open fire and its continuing capacity to radiate warmth, serve as a nucleus to household activity, and physically as well as symbolically anchor memories of past kitchens, meals and foods. Whereas most Irish kitchens today emerged from a linear progression built on this enthusiasm generated half a century or so ago, that crucially eliminated such physically arduous tasks as fetching water from a well, we know now that some of its promises could not be kept. Rather than precipitate a life of leisure and turn every Irish homemaker into Cinderella Hotfoot, such environments often increased the demands made on the woman of the house and the time she devoted to food-work, through expectations that she would become capable of more lavish homemade treats with all the assistance that new technology could provide—refrigerators, powerful new cookers, electric mixers and blenders, and so on.[71] Convenience foods became a factor enabling women to pursue careers elsewhere, but the *bean an tí* remained the primary food caregiver in the household (the efforts of Margaret Crowley notwithstanding).

This essay on the domestic foodscape was intended to underscore the complexity inherent in cultural and technological transformation, complexity teased out by looking at the anything-but-mute architecture and material culture of the built environment of the home. That complexity certainly adds powerful resonance to the word 'almost' in a remarkable report on the arrival of the mobile kitchen to Rathdowney, in February 1960. The article in the *Kilkenny People* offered a decidedly international perspective in summing up local impressions:

> Farmers returning from a fair on Monday and the Mart on Tuesday regaled their womenfolk with the wonders of the mobile all-electric farm kitchen [....] Housewives turned up in big numbers to view with envious eyes the ideal layout, the gleaming paintwork, the built-in cupboards, and the numerous electrical appliances in this labour-saving model kitchen. From the general remarks heard at the exhibition one could almost conclude that modern Irish housewives agree with Carbusiers' [*sic*] definition of a house as 'a machine for living in'.[72]

Almost, but not quite.

---

[71] See Ruth Schwartz Cowan, *More work for mother: the ironies of household technology from the open hearth to the microwave* (New York, 1985).

[72] Anon., 'All-electric kitchen', *Kilkenny People,* 13 February 1960, 8. The reference is to Le Corbusier, the famed modernist architect who did indeed argue that the house is 'a machine for living in'. This idea was captured in his book *Vers une architecture* (Paris, 1923), commonly known in English as *Towards a new architecture.*

Drink and society in twentieth-century Ireland

DIARMAID FERRITER*

School of History and Archives, Newman Building, University College Dublin, Belfield, Dublin 4,

[Accepted 5 November 2014. Published 24 April 2015.]

Abstract

This chapter examines debates, controversies and trends in relation to the consumption of alcoholic drink in twentieth-century Ireland, and explores the difficulties and ambiguities associated with characterising the consumption of alcohol in Ireland and defining the Irish drinking culture during this period. In doing so, it includes reflections on drunkenness, temperance, alcoholism, licensing legislation, the drinks industry, the impact of the Catholic Church, the extent to which debate about alcohol was gendered and the role of alcohol in stereotyping Irish identity. Numerous examples of the range of social, political and cultural comment on Irish alcohol consumption are cited, and the chapter also looks at the connections between alcohol consumption and the economy, the impact of modernisation on consumption and the range of alcoholic drinks consumed, and the difficulties associated with alcohol consumption statistics and the comparative analysis of moderate and excessive drinking.

Introduction

In June 1949, on one of the hottest days of the summer, 80,000 members of the Pioneer Total Abstinence Association (PTAA) crammed into the Gaelic Athletic Association stadium at Croke Park in Dublin for the golden jubilee celebrations of the PTAA. By that stage the PTAA was the largest Catholic lay association in the Irish Republic with an estimated membership of 500,000. Established in 1898 its members took a pledge to abstain from alcohol (what was termed a 'heroic offering') in devotion to the Sacred Heart of Jesus.

The Croke Park celebrations in 1949 provoked the ire of the brilliant writer and alcoholic Flann O'Brien, who lambasted members of the PTAA for bringing Dublin City to a standstill by taking over its transport network in order, as he saw it, to parade their piety. In his *Irish Times* column published a day after the event, he remarked:

> Dublin's working man with his wife or four children intent on spending a day at the seaside does not have to journey to Croke Park to prove that he is not a slave to whiskey. If he can manage a pint of porter a day it is the best he can do ... I can call nothing comparable to yesterday's

* Author's e-mail: diarmaid.ferriter@ucd.ie
doi: 10.3318/PRIAC.2015.115.08

procedure and I hope somebody will examine the legality of it. If the abstainers are entitled to disrupt transport in their own peculiar and selfish interest, there is in our democratic mode no reason in the world why the drinking men of Ireland should not demand and be given the same right. Let everybody stay at home because the boozers are in town! I would advise these Pioneer characters that there is more in life than the bottle, that fair play to others is important and that temperance—taking the word in its big and general value—is a thing they might strive to cultivate a bit better.[1]

The PTAA rally and O'Brien's response to it underlined some aspects of Ireland's tortured relationship with alcohol by the middle of the twentieth century, and the difficulty of finding a middle ground with regard to its consumption. In the same year writer John D. Sheridan depicted the dilemma of the moderate drinker in such a country. Moderate consumers of alcohol, he suggested:

resent the sneers of the heavy drinker—that prince of bigots—who looks down on us as cute, penny-watching apron-slaves, and is forever trying to raise us to his mighty stature. Our case against the total abstainer is not so easy to put into words, since we envy his high motives and admire his self-control, but we think it unfair that we who carry the heavier end of the cross should be denied a share of the halo.[2]

I

The contributions of O'Brien and Sheridan regarding the place of alcohol in Irish society were a continuation of debates that had been aired, spasmodically, for over a century. The Capuchin friar Fr Theobald Mathew (Fig. 1) made a considerable impact with his temperance crusade in the late 1830s—estimates of the number of pledges administered during his dominance vary from 700,000 to over 2 million—reflecting the transition from moderation to teetotal in mid-1830s temperance societies, a departure which was accompanied by increased working-class involvement. The Fr Mathew episode highlighted the relative ease with which a temperance crusade could be transformed into a temporary mass movement, but it also exposed a multitude of difficulties, including indifference on the part of the Catholic hierarchy and hostility from Protestants. Its link with nationalist politics and the failure to establish a national structure to provide durable foundations for the future of the movement were also problematic.[3]

---

[1] *Irish Times*, 27 June 1949.

[2] Diarmaid Ferriter, *A nation of extremes: the pioneers in twentieth century Ireland*, 2nd edn (Dublin, 2008), 207.

[3] Colm Kerrigan, *Father Mathew and the Irish Temperance Movement* (Cork, 1992), 80. See also Paul A. Townsend, *Father Mathew, temperance and Irish identity* (Dublin, 2002), 260–89.

THE VERY REV? THEOBALD MATHEW

THE GREAT APOSTLE OF TEMPERANCE.

Extract of a letter from Father Mathew dated Cork Sept? 18 1848, to his friend Col. J.H. Sherburne at London in transmitting his Portrait for his acceptance &c.

FIG. 1—'The very revd. Theobald Mathew the great apostle of temperance', *c.* 17 April 1849. Reproduction Number: LC-USZ62-1727 (b&w film copy neg.). Repository: Library of Congress Prints and Photographs Division Washington, D.C. 20540 USA.

The consumption of alcohol in the nineteenth century militated against political support for temperance; consumption of spirits was in decline from the 1850s due to hefty tax increases, while beer-drinking increased, which created substantial tax revenue; the greater prosperity of rural Ireland after the Famine also contributed to an increase in beer consumption but economic decline from the late 1870s reduced overall alcohol consumption. Although many of the statistics regarding alcohol consumption in the nineteenth century are less than comprehensive, partly because of the extent of illicit distillation, general trends are traceable. Consumption of spirits plummeted in the early 1840s, late 1850s and early 1860s and stagnated after the mid-1870s; by that stage, Irish spirit consumption was lower than Scotland and the United States of America. In relation to per capita beer consumption, a measure that is problematic (see below), the figure for Ireland in 1851 was estimated at 3.5 gallons, which rose to 26 gallons by 1901; these figures 'were always exceeded, often two to four times, by figures from the United Kingdom as a whole'. Economic forces were clearly a major determining factor in beer and spirit consumption and wine consumption was minimal.[4]

What was unique about Ireland was its identification with Guinness porter; its iconic St James's Gate Brewery had been located in Dublin since 1759. The output of the Irish brewing industry trebled between the 1850s and 1914, by which time 40% of its production was exported, and that success was largely associated with Guinness, at that stage the largest brewery in the world.[5] Between 1850 and 1875 its sales increased by 600% and the Irish rural market was a key factor in this expansion. By the time of the First World War the Guinness Company, with capital of £5 million, employed 2,000 people and had a reputation as an enlightened and socially progressive employer.

The licensing laws governing the availability of alcohol in Ireland caused much comment as they were distributed over 25 acts of parliament, which seemed to reinforce a liberal interpretation of their provisions, if not ignorance of their content. This was one reason for the House of Lords 1898 Commission on Intoxicating Liquor, which in common with other such commissions was good at highlighting and specifying abuse and wrongdoing, but rather weak on proposing solutions. The commission exposed much malpractice in relation to the operating of the licensing laws, the deplorable condition and excessive number of public houses, and the vigorous canvassing of Justices and packing of benches when the granting of licences was being decided.

Despite per capita consumption figures that suggested relative moderation, the contention that Ireland was shaming itself, morally, politically and culturally by its heavy drinking achieved widespread currency in the late nineteenth and early twentieth centuries. What lay behind such assertions and a seemingly Irish tolerance of and ambivalence to excess? Many reasons have been suggested, including the idea that it was a product of colonisation, or in the words of nineteenth-century nationalist Thomas Davis, there was a destructive desire 'to achieve liberty and luxury for an hour by the magic of intoxication' (an argument later used by Irish nationalists, in the words of A. M. Sullivan, MP, was that 'Ireland sober' would be 'Ireland free').[6] The use of drink for medicinal purposes in a cold and damp climate was also cited, as were dietary gaps being filled with drink and payment for work through alcohol in the absence of an advanced cash society. It has also been maintained that heavy drinking was a form of solace to counteract emigration and exile, a facilitator of group identity and an affirmation of male identity.[7] A new post-Famine single

---

[4] Elizabeth Malcolm, *Ireland sober, Ireland free: drink and temperance in nineteenth-century Ireland* (Dublin, 1986), 323–5.

[5] Cormac Ó Gráda, *Ireland: a new economic history 1780–1939* (Oxford, 1994), 304.

[6] Elizabeth Malcolm, 'Temperance and Irish nationalism', in F. S. L. Lyons (ed.), *Ireland under the union: varieties of tension* (Oxford, 1980), 70–5.

[7] Richard Stivers, *A hair of the dog: Irish drinking and American stereotype* (New York, 1976), 13–14. See also Roger Swift and Sheridan Gilley, *The Irish in Britain 1815–1939* (London, 1989), 1–10.

inheritance farm economy, lower marriage rates and a cultural remission, or 'a release from sexual Puritanism' have also been cited as reasons for Irish excess[8] as have the power of Irish breweries which needed to operate on a large scale in order to compete with English brewers' expansion of their trade as a result of the English industrial revolution and cheaper imports. There was also the peculiarly Irish system of buying 'rounds' of drinks, seen by its critics as the bane of Irish social life.[9]

In the early twentieth century it was widely agreed that the country was drinking excessively; over £15 million a year was being spent on drink in Ireland at the time of the First World War and there were over 15,000 licensed premises.[10] In tandem, public health reformers and moral crusaders were vocal in linking alcohol abuse to a variety of tragedies, including lost childhoods. Reports from the Dublin branch of the National Society for the Prevention of Cruelty to Children, for example, identified excessive drinking as the chief cause of child neglect and there were numerous references in its reports to women addicted to alcohol, or 'confirmed drunkards' as they were labelled.[11] But there were such a variety of vested interests in the alcohol industry that a cynicism existed about the extent to which politicians would be prepared to enact legislation or help foster a climate that would reduce consumption.

A problem that has faced all chroniclers of Irish alcohol consumption is that official figures, in so far as they were available, told only part of the story because they were meta rather than micro snapshots and did not factor in abstainers, which, given the impact of the PTAA, were a very sizeable cohort. In the absence of reliable consumption figures it is difficult to establish the veracity of assertions about the extent of excessive drinking, but it was undoubtedly the case that after the creation of the Irish Free State in 1922, critics of Irish alcohol consumption saw this time of transition as an opportunity to tackle excess. In 1925, for example, the writer and poet George Russell (AE) noted acerbically:

> It is merely absurd that a country struggling desperately to find its feet should attempt to maintain in proportion to its population twice as many licensed houses as England and three times as many as Scotland. The statistics for individual towns are still more startling. In Charlestown and Ballaghadereen every third house is licensed to sell liquor; Ballyhaunis, with a total population of a thousand, has a drink shop for every twenty of its inhabitants and Strokestown and Mohill run it close with one for every twenty six ... how many of these towns can boast a bookshop, a gymnasium, a public swimming bath or a village hall? Throughout the greater part of a rural Ireland such things are still looked on as ridiculous

---

8 Stivers, *A hair of the dog*, 90.
9 Ferriter, *A nation of extremes*, 43.
10 Ferriter, *A nation of extremes*, 38–83.
11 Diarmaid Ferriter, *Occasions of sin: sex and society in modern Ireland* (London, 2009), 46–7.

luxuries, and the mark of social progress is demonstrated by the opening of two public houses where one would normally suffice . . .[12]

Cumann na nGaedheal, which governed the new Free State until 1932, was urged to tackle the licensed vintners, to restrict pub opening hours and to decrease the number of pub licences. It responded quite vigorously, through an intoxicating liquor commission and licensing acts in 1924 and 1927. By that stage the government was particularly conscious of figures which revealed that in England and Wales there were 86,722 licensed premises (a ratio of 1 for every 415 of the population), in Scotland 56,841 (1:695) and in Ireland 16,396 (1:263). An important factor in the promotion of new legislation was the determination of Kevin O'Higgins, minister for home affairs (subsequently minister for justice), who stated in 1923 that:

> we need a genuine licensing code, not a bewildering maze of statutes and decisions, which, while creating offences also provided ingenious means of escape for unscrupulous people, and for people otherwise honest but who were driven to lie and worse in the struggle for existence.[13]

For the government, such sentiments were indicative of the need not only to negotiate a middle path through the licensing maze, but also a tacit acceptance that any restrictive legislation would arouse the ire of the licensed trade, a powerful lobbying group, which was politically influential. In an internal government memorandum, it was accepted that 'they are now vested and not to be disturbed'.[14] It took a forceful politician like O'Higgins to do just that. As Madeleine Humphreys has noted, while revenue was of paramount importance, there was still a determination to regularise the trade, despite the fact that the 15,339 recorded convictions for drunkenness in 1914 had been reduced to 6,862 by 1925.[15]

The 1924 Licensing Act, particularly the sections dealing with a reduction in trading hours, compulsory endorsement of licences after conviction for an offence and the position of district justices in their application of this law (they had been far too lenient) 'clearly symbolizes O'Higgins' acute anxiety that the judiciary should understand its subservience to the state while the publicans would know their privileged monopoly demanded exceptional responsibility'.[16] The Intoxicating Liquor Act of 1927 reduced the number of licensed premises and prohibited general openings on Sundays.

---

[12] Terence Brown, *Ireland: a social and cultural history, 1922–79*, 2nd edn (London, 1986), 43.

[13] Ferriter, *A nation of extremes*, 93.

[14] National Archives of Ireland (NAI), Department of Justice (DJ), H47 A, Licensing law reform, March 1923.

[15] Madeleine Humphreys, 'Jansenists in high places: a study of the relationship between the liquor trade and manufacturing industry and the Cumann na nGaedheal government 1922–32', unpublished MA thesis, University College Dublin, 1991.

[16] Humphreys, 'Jansenists in high places', 178.

Nevertheless, O'Higgins was careful in the language that he used, insisting he was not hostile to the licensed trade or indulging prohibitionists masquerading as temperance reformers. He was also deliberately vague in addressing the question of whether Ireland was a nation of drunks. Speaking in the Dáil in 1927 he commented

> That of course is a question of angles. What is excessive drinking? I do not take it that excessive drinking means that you fall over a man every five yards on your way home. If we are drinking beyond our resources there is excessive drinking. £17.5 million was spent across the counter on drink in the financial year 1925–6. Is that excessive drinking? Some people would say no. Some people would say very differently. At any rate I object to the criterion that drunkenness and drunkenness alone is to be the test of whether or not there is excessive drinking.[17]

The licensed vintners, who had formed an association as early as 1817—the Licensed Vintners Association (LVA)—to safeguard their interests, in bemoaning in the 1920s what they saw as punitive legislation, were defensive, and frequently identified their own targets. In particular, they singled out chemists who sold spirits, illicit distillers and private clubs which they characterised as 'gigantic drinking shops with the difference that they had no restrictions or limitations of any sort or kind'. The LVA also criticised excessive duties on spirits, and its chairman in 1925 expressed the view that the government was 'travelling too fast on a subject which the old regime avoided as long as possible'. At a licensed trade conference the following year, its chairman J. P. O'Neill condemned Irish licensing legislation as 'harsh, unjust and ill-conceived'. Following the general election of June 1927, after which Fianna Fáil TDS took their seats in the Dáil for the first time, J. P. O'Neill expressed satisfaction that the Dáil was now representative of the whole state with the result that the 'prohibitionist mindset will not be allowed to prevail'. Few subsequent governments had the appetite to confront the vintners.[18]

II   The extent to which the Catholic Church assumed control over the moral and religious climate of the new Free State has been well-documented, and it is unsurprising that advocates of sobriety felt they had an unprecedented opportunity to link the question of alcohol abuse to the preoccupation with eradicating other perceived moral abuses. Given the wider debates in Ireland in the 1920s and 1930s concerning the impact of foreign social imports, including motor cars, 'company keeping', jazz music and what was termed the 'dance craze', it was inconceivable that Catholic activists on the drink question, dedicated as they were to domestic moral purity, would not make their voices heard.[19]

---

[17] Ferriter, *A nation of extremes*, 87.
[18] Ferriter, *A nation of extremes*, 95.
[19] James Smyth, 'Dancing, depravity and all that jazz: the Public Dance Halls Act of 1935', *History Ireland* 1:2 (1993), 51–5.

Much of the focus remained gendered, with women being regarded as both more vulnerable to excess and their abuse of alcohol more transgressive than that of their male counterparts. The Irish Bishops' Lenten Pastoral of 1924 referred to the 'existence of many abuses' in the context of morality and decency. Maintaining this trend in 1926, a sermon by Dr Thomas Gilmartin, archbishop of Tuam, referred to the trend in women's immodest dress and suggested 'the future of the country is bound up with the dignity and purity of the women of Ireland'.[20] Part of this future, it seemed, involved more female sobriety. In the early 1930s a prominent Dundalk priest decried the advent of the 'modern girl':

> You know the type I mean, a feather-headed immature creature who talks a lot about being independent, emancipated and nap-doodle of that sort. She deems it essential to throw—to use no stronger word—conventionality to the winds, to toss off as many glasses of champagne as her befuddled admirers, and swallow cocktails with the best of the simpering hobbledehoys who are the young bloods of this age. Fortunately, the modern girl with her boasted independence and emancipation from parental and other control is alien to the Catholic and Irish mind. That safeguard, great though it is, in many cases does not suffice, for quite a number of foreign influences have found their way into our midst and made themselves felt. At all events the modern girl is a cross-channel importation, and you will be well advised to place upon her a protective tariff ... the man who enters the matrimonial state with the modern girl and hopes to make a success of it needs to be more than a magician. For one thing, he is an incurable optimist.[21]

Writers of fiction also broached the issue of male abuse of drink, though in less bombastic terms. In his 1932 novel *The saint and Mary Kate*, Frank O'Connor drew attention to the havoc the abuse of alcohol wreaked on Irish family life, and the character Mary Kate's realisation that the truth of an Irish adage—'behind all the love of women for man lies a secret sorrow'—was that of excessive drinking. Alcohol abuse also created a sexual incapacity, suggested O'Connor, to the point that 'where the charms of women are concerned, a son of Erin couldn't care less'.[22]

There also was much hypocrisy evident in relation to the castigation of excessive Irish drinking. Eoin O'Duffy, for example, the leader of the Irish fascist Blueshirt movement in the 1930s, and a successful Garda commissioner in the 1920s, devoted much attention to preaching what has been termed 'the gospel of national virility' by promoting fitness and athleticism and denouncing vices, especially smoking and drinking. Yet, O'Duffy 'never exercised, smoked

---

[20] Maria Luddy, 'Sex and the single girl in 1920s and 1930s Ireland', *The Irish Review* 35 (2007), 79–92.

[21] *Irish Catholic*, 3 December 1932.

[22] Frank O'Connor, *The saint and Mary Kate* (London, 1932), 47.

eighty Sweet Aftons a day and developed a serious alcohol problem'. His biographer Fearghal McGarry has reasonably suggested that O'Duffy identi-fied his own shortcomings with those of the general population, 'a process of transference which may have been reinforced by the gulf between his idealized and real identities'.[23] But what was more common than condemnation was acceptance, ambivalence or a tolerance of excess wrapped up in a charitable disposition; the idea of drunkenness as 'the weakness of the good man'. Like other shortcomings in the Irish character, according to Joe Lee, drink abuse was afforded a 'reassuringly venial status in the hierarchy of morality'.[24]

But in parallel, it was reported in the early 1930s that since 1921 'there had been a general marked decrease in the consumption of alcoholic liquor of all kinds'[25] and there had been a further decline in spirits consumption after 1900. It is also estimated that there was a 20% drop in deaths from cirrhosis of the liver between 1908 and 1949.[26] There is little doubt that the Guinness Company was affected by a reduction in its domestic market; what was significant was its expansion and internationalisation, partly because during the interwar years the Irish market contracted sharply, though 'the decline in Irish sales in absolute terms was partly compensated by the advance of extra stout at the expense of the less profitable porter'.[27] All brewing was seriously impeded by the First World War, with a consistent decline in sales throughout Ireland and Britain, and Guinness reacted by launching its first advertising campaign in the late 1920s, stressing the alleged medical benefits of Guinness, and using the subsequently famous slogan 'Guinness is good for you'. These advertisements led to a rise in sales and resulted in future campaigns with ever increasing budgets.

The Guinness Company, along with a reputation for philanthropy and social initiatives, proved remarkably adaptable in business terms. It steered 'a wise course' through political unrest and two world wars, deciding to brew Guinness stout for the first time outside of Ireland by opening a huge plant at Park Royal, west London, in 1936, and after 1945 the company's breweries multiplied and diversified into other branches of the beer and drink industries.[28] But the linking of Irishness with Guinness remained central to the company's marketing strategy.

In relation to alcohol addiction, a notable development was the arrival of the first European branch of Alcoholics Anonymous (AA) to Dublin in 1946, which encouraged discussion in the following decades about the nature of drink addiction. Shane Butler, author of a book on how AA fared in Ireland,

---

[23] Fearghal McGarry, *Eoin O'Duffy: a self-made hero* (Oxford, 2005), 162–3.
[24] Joe Lee, *Ireland: politics and society, 1912–1985* (Cambridge, 1989), 645.
[25] See, for example, 'Consumption of alcohol', *Irish Times*, 9 May 1933.
[26] *Irish Times*, 9 November 1972, and *Irish Independent*, 7 December 1972.
[27] S. R. Dennison and Oliver Mac Donagh, *Guinness 1886–1939: from incorporation to the Second World War* (Cork, 1998), 264–6.
[28] Tony Corcoran, *The goodness of Guinness* (Dublin, 2005), 143–6.

describes AA as 'loosely structured and largely leaderless', its promoters believing that ultimately, for all the debate about defining alcoholism as a disease, the only diagnosis that mattered was self-diagnosis. Particularly during times when the 'ownership of drinking problems' was still such a contested affair, AA was shrewd in maintaining an official position of neutrality in relation to the concept of alcoholism as a disease. Distaste for top-down authority and for facilitating the autonomy of individual AA groups was also essential to its longevity in Ireland.[29]

AA arrived in Ireland at a time when some saw its philosophy as a threat to the homogeneity of the medical profession and the Catholic Church, and in overcoming these difficulties, the persistence and the abilities of key AA organisers like Conor Flynn, Richard Perceval and in particular Sackville O'Conor Mallins, who devoted 30 years of his life to organising AA in Ireland, were instrumental. He insisted 'either the Catholic Church in Ireland was made an ally or AA in Ireland was sunk' and demonstrated considerable skill and energy in ensuring that it stayed afloat. The Catholic archbishop of Dublin, John Charles McQuaid, did not give it his blessing or denounce it; Butler refers to this as 'the curious incident of the dog that didn't bark',[30] and AA must stand alone as something that provoked neutrality from the exceptionally opinionated and interfering McQuaid.

This did not mean that individual AA organisers did not have to build contacts and alliances, whilst retaining the association's independence. Building these networks was no easy task, as seen, for example, in its relationship with the National Council on Alcoholism, established in 1966 by the minister for health, and about which O'Conor Mallins became disillusioned and somewhat cynical, criticising 'the circle of so-called experts' globetrotting to various conferences.[31]

Although it is impossible to give a realistic estimate of the number of alcoholics in Ireland during this era, it is clear that ignorance at all levels of society existed concerning the condition. The Intoxicating Liquor Commission, which reported in 1957, formed the basis for the Intoxicating Liquor Act of 1959 that sought to further liberalise the Irish licensing laws. Although there was opposition to the 1959 legislation, particularly from Archbishop McQuaid, politicians, including Taoiseach Seán Lemass, rejected the requests of those who sought a free vote in the Dáil on grounds of conscience, and were able to cleverly square the circle of episcopal disapproval by claiming, in the words of Lemass, that 'drunkenness is a sin for which men are responsible to a higher court than ours'.[32]

The Intoxicating Liquor Bill episode was interesting for other reasons. The report of the commission had stated baldly that drunkenness was no longer a serious problem in Irish society. As someone who was deeply involved in the provision of Catholic social services in Dublin, McQuaid was justified in challenging this fallacious contention. In a letter to the Department of the

---

[29] Shane Butler, *Benign anarchy: Alcoholics Anonymous in Ireland* (Dublin, 2010), 32–58.
[30] Butler, *Benign anarchy*, 89–92.
[31] Butler, *Benign anarchy*, 124–32.
[32] *Dáil debates*, vol. 178, cols 384–6, 25 November 1959.

Taoiseach in May 1959, McQuaid expressed regret that 'in the report, consideration is given to drunkenness, not to alcoholism' and suggested that, given the continued increase in the consumption of drink, aligned with a falling population and high percentage of abstainers, it was surely obvious that there was heavier drinking by fewer people. As a result of his comments, the Department of Justice queried the Department of Health as to the scale of alcoholism in Ireland. The reply was an indictment of the prevailing ignorance concerning alcohol abuse, and characteristic of an ambivalent official attitude to the Irish drinking culture: 'Off hand the Department of Health have said it is not a problem in this country: that fewer than 400 persons are received into institutions (public or private) for treatment in any year'.[33]

III

Despite the pace of change in Ireland in the 1960s there was a certain stagnation associated with some Irish drinking practices and the drinking environment. Assertions about the Irish drink 'culture' became more negative. This was the analysis of writer Michael Sheehy:

> Intoxicating drink is the Irish anodyne. A fondness for drink, like religion and patriotism, unites and characterises the Catholic Irish. It is evident everywhere, in city, town and country, in all social classes rich and poor, educated and ignorant, and, in recent decades in women as well as in men. Irish drinking is heaviest in the country towns where addicts excuse themselves by saying 'there's nothing else to do'. The clergy themselves are apt to share in this 'good man's weakness' and turn a blind eye on Irish drinking habits.[34]

In his study of the (fictional) western parish of Inishkillane, Hugh Brody wrote of drinking patterns and habits being closely aligned to the seasons, with heavy but happy drinking in the summer and more despondency in the winter among the alcoholic bachelors:

> A drunken man in winter leans more heavily on the bar. He often seeks to draw another drinker or two to his side. Such a group creates a tight circle of privacy around itself—a privacy physically expressed by the arms they lay across another's shoulders. Then, with faces almost touching, they appear to join closely in evident despair. This despair is not expressed in discussion among the drinkers. Rather, they exchange silence as if it were words, and words in brief expression of the lonesomeness.[35]

---

[33] NAI, Department of the Taoiseach (DT) S16524, Memorandum from the Department of Justice, 5 June 1959.

[34] Michael Sheehy, *Is Ireland dying? Culture and the church in modern Ireland* (London, 1968), 204–06.

[35] Hugh Brody, *Inishkillane: change and decline in the west of Ireland* (London, 1973), 33.

There were however, alternative observations, such as the following from Donal Connery, an American journalist writing in 1969, who concluded that alcoholism was a problem, and that it had a seriously negative effect on relations between the sexes, yet he cautioned:

> The pub is a booby-trap however, for anyone trying to take a true measure of Irish life. The fact is that the majority of adults hardly ever set foot in a pub. Most Irish females simply do not drink in public and many never touch a drop in their lives, and among the men there are more total abstainers than heavy drinkers . . . I will admit, as I write this that it is painful to go against form and portray the Irishman as something other than a glorious drinker and an altogether devil of a fellow. None the less, there are far more homes than pubs in Ireland and it is in the homes that one must look for the Irishman as he is most of the time. Away from the conviviality of the pub he's revealed as someone who is extraordinarily ordinary. He leads a far simpler and certainly less sophisticated life than most other Europeans.[36]

These observations are a reminder that there was no adequate or agreed definition of the 'Irish drinking culture'. While it has frequently been asserted that 'Ireland is synonymous with pubs'; that 'the importance of the pub to community life cannot easily be overstated'; that 'there is something quintessentially Irish about the country's relationship with alcohol' and that heavy consumption 'is viewed as the heroic preservation of a famous oral culture', what caused counter comment was an identification of 'extreme ambivalence about drinking' as 'part of the national psyche'.[37]

But there was a high proportion of Irish adults who abstained from drink—one estimate from 1968 was that they accounted for 42% of the adult population—and those intent on promoting more sobriety or seeking to prevent alcohol abuse received increasing publicity and were provided with new forums in the 1960s and international research, which provided verifiable evidence of the harm of excessive consumption. In 1967, the year after the government announced the establishment of the National Council on Alcoholism, it was suggested in the *Sunday Press* that there were up to 60,000 alcoholics in Ireland, and that perhaps the prevalence of alcoholism and the concomitant call for a more ecumenical approach to a problem which had for so long remained underground, represented a challenge to those who saw it as primarily a moral failing. Modern research on the issue generated new perspectives which suggested that traditional attitudes to alcoholism were not only lacking in

---

[36] Donal Connery, *The Irish* (London, 1969), 97–100.
[37] Shane Kilcommins and Ian O'Donnell (eds), *Alcohol, society and law* (Chichester, West Sussex, 2003), xix; James Fennell and Turtle Bunbury, *The Irish pub* (London, 2008), 6.

scientific and medical accuracy but were also devoid of basic charity.[38] European sociological research, which suggested that inculcating children with an exceptionally negative view of alcohol was not conducive to a healthy and balanced approach to alcohol in later life, was also cited. Particularly influential was the Plaut report, published by the French government in 1967, which condemned therapeutic nihilism (the belief that problem drinkers could not be helped), and criticised the confusion of disapproval of dangerous drinking with opposition to all drinking.[39]

The enduring identification of Irishness with drinking to excess was, however, bolstered by the antics of well-known Irish personalities who were famed for their drunkenness. These included the playwright, Brendan Behan (Pl. I), who used his drinking to establish himself as a 'character'; a hard drinker 'who could enthrall any gathering with a stream of songs, parodies and grotesquely dramatized incidents'. But this 'roaring boy' persona masked a

Pʟ. I —Brendan Behan being asked to sing again at the Jager house Ballroom 85st & lex av [sic]/World Telegram & Sun photo by Phil Stanziola, 1960. Reproduction Number: LC-USZ62-108030 (b&w film copy neg.). Repository: Library of Congress Prints and Photographs Division Washington, D.C. 20540 USA.

---

[38] Ferriter, *A nation of extremes*, 216ff.
[39] Thomas Plaut, *Alcohol problems: a report to the nation by the co-operative commission on the study of alcoholism* (New York, 1967), 8.

tragedy: 'his failure to face up to the solitary discipline of writing filled him with guilt and self-disgust which led in turn to heavier drinking in order to obliterate his demons, although as a diabetic he knew that such drinking was suicidal'.[40] He died in 1964 at the age of just 41.

Behan also achieved international recognition due to his television appearances in Britain and the United States, but broadcasts relying on the theme of the drunken Irish were a source of concern for those seeking to project a more sophisticated image of Irishness internationally. In June 1960 an article in *Time* magazine which made reference to the unlikeliness of an Irishman attending a temperance meeting, provoked the ire of the Department of External Affairs. In response, the Taoiseach, Seán Lemass, addressed a community group in County Tipperary and suggested that the stereotypes of the drunken Irish fuelled racial prejudice:

> One of the most persistent and irritating falsehoods about the Irish is that they are excessive consumers of alcoholic drink. The lie has gone very far afield. Even the BBC Television service rarely, if ever presents a play about Ireland without the characters moving around in clouds of alcoholic vapour. The simple truth is ignored and the truth is that the per capita consumption of alcoholic drink in Ireland is one of the lowest for all countries for which reliable statistics are available ... the consumption of beer per head in Britain is about the same as in Ireland, and of wines considerably higher. Of all the spirit drinking countries, Irish per capita consumption is nearly the lowest.[41]

The contentions of Lemass were a result of details furnished by the Central Statistics Office, which had been established in 1949; the figures he received, based on the year 1958, showed that in bulk litres of alcohol, Ireland's per capita consumption was 64.3 litres of beer and 1.2 litres of spirits, while the figures in Britain were 79.1 and 1.1, respectively.[42]

Whatever about sensitivity regarding racial stereotypes, successive Irish governments virtually ignored many of the social problems associated with underage drinking and alcohol-induced poverty and crime. Alcohol consumption rose dramatically in the 1960s and 1970s. Between 1963 and 1972 consumption of spirits, for example, rose by 66%. Brewers, notably Guinness, continued to innovate and adapt to cater for new markets; one of the successful episodes in brewing during this period was the creation by Guinness of Harp Lager in 1961; sales of this new product rose to 1 million barrels by 1970

---

[40] Colbert Kearney, 'Brendan Francis Behan', in James McGuire and James Quinn (eds), *Dictionary of Irish biography: from the earliest times to the year 2002* (9 vols, Cambridge and Dublin, 2009), vol. 1, 415–17.

[41] NAI, DT S16920A, 'Statistics re: consumption of drink in Ireland', 8 July 1960 and text of a speech by Seán Lemass at the Muinitir na Tíre rural week at Rockwell College, Co. Tipperary, 1960.

[42] See note 41 above.

and 2 million in 1976, while by 1979 pre-tax profits at Guinness were £52 million.[43] In 1971 £147 million was spent on alcohol in Ireland, accounting for 11.5% of total consumer expenditure, and by then there were an estimated 66,000 alcoholics in Ireland. Ten years later, 1.5 million drinkers consumed £700 million worth of drink, with a conservative estimate of 75,000 suffering from alcoholism. In the mid-1970s a report by the National Council on Alcoholism maintained:

> The most important step in the prevention of alcoholism and excessive drinking is to change attitudes. This change can only be achieved gradually by a broad based programme of propaganda, information and education in which certain departments of state, regional health boards, voluntary organisations, schools, management, trade unions and the medical profession co-operate. Above all, the state must be seen to be concerned and must give the lead in preventative measures.[44]

These desired collaborations did not materialise to any significant extent. The chairman of the National Off Licence Traders Association, Patrick McDonnell, who owned an off licence on Dorset Street, Dublin, wrote to the government in 1970 to complain that the minister for justice, Des O'Malley:

> is not taking any notice of the serious problem of teenagers consuming alcoholic drinks. The situation is ready to erupt into a national scandal and will, if not erased now, have disastrous effects on the physical, mental and moral conditions of the children of Ireland

He maintained that the licensing laws were out of date (the last intoxicating liquor act had been in 1962) and that 'it has become the in-thing with over 14 year olds to get half stoned before they attend the "baby dances" on Friday and Saturday nights' and that cider was being sold by those with 'sweet licences' that allowed shopkeepers to sell wine of Irish manufacture. What was needed, he argued, was 'maturity regarding their drinking as the European children have'.[45] Taoiseach Jack Lynch expressed his regret that McDonnell's letter 'should be couched in rather intemperate terms'. At that time there were only 256 off licence holders (spirit grocers) in the republic but there were 11,000 publicans.

W. Herlihy, a Garda inspector, was asked to investigate McDonnell's claims that well-known Dublin pubs were serving teenagers alcohol, and while he accepted that McDonnell was genuinely concerned about teenage drinking, he also saw him as championing his own trade 'and that of the other spirit grocers who he feels are being squeezed out of business by the larger combines'.

---

[43] Michelle Guinness, *The Guinness spirit* (London, 1999), 495.

[44] Ferriter, *A nation of extremes*, 251.

[45] NAI, DT 2009/135/117, Intoxicating Liquor Acts, Patrick McDonnell to Jack Lynch, 3 February 1970.

O'Malley refused to meet with McDonnell and told Lynch he was not representative; O'Malley found the tone of some of McDonnell's statements 'grossly offensive'. He was also 'far from satisfied that the problem of drinking by young persons, in so far as it exists, can be materially reduced by any practicable change in the law or by increased Garda action'.[46]

When asked in the Dáil that month by Dublin Fine Gael TD Hugh Byrne, a district medical officer, if he would consider raising the legal drinking age from 18 to 21 on the grounds that 'nowadays a 14 year old can pass for a person of 18 years', O'Malley was dismissive: 'Surely a 20 year old can pass even more easily for a 22 year old. I consider Deputy Byrne's suggestion ridiculous'. Byrne also suggested that 'in a certain area of Dublin, firelighters, which contain a high content of methylated spirits, are being mixed with cider and cheap wine'.[47] Concerns about young people 'physically maturing at an earlier age' continued to be raised in the late 1970s to which the response from the Department of Justice was that it was the job of parents and not the state to police underage drinking.

There was also much comment during that decade on the lack of social alternatives to the pub; Ivor Browne, chief psychiatrist to the Eastern Health Board, was vocal in this regard, as was Dr Michael Browne, the Catholic bishop of Galway ('there is nothing else for young people to do on Friday nights than to start drinking'). The National Council on Alcoholism also reported to the minister for health about the lack of alternative facilities for youth.[48] Joseph Adams, the director of the Council, pointed to the irony of the linkages made between the economic well-being of Ireland and alcohol consumption; while historically, poverty had been blamed for excessive drinking, now increased affluence was deemed to be the reason.[49]

By 1975 Irish annual per capita consumption of alcohol was 0.42 gallons of spirits and 19.1 gallons of beer (the beer consumption levels were similar to those of the 1880s), figures that were not excessive internationally. In a list ranking consumption figures for 29 western countries, Ireland came twentieth in spirits consumption and tenth in beer consumption.[50] Nonetheless, it was asserted in the current affairs magazine *Magill* in December 1977 that 'the country has been on a massive drinking rampage'. Sales of alcohol 'rocketed by 15%' in the three months of June to September 1977 compared to the same period in 1976. In 1968 58% of the adult population were estimated to have drunk alcohol; by 1975 this figure had increased to 65% and it was maintained by the end of 1977 that this had risen further to 70%, with women and younger people accounting for the majority of the increase. But the point

---

[46] NAI, DT 2009/135/117, Intoxicating Liquor Acts, letter of W. Herlihy, 24 July 1971, and Des O'Malley to Jack Lynch, 13 August 1971.

[47] NAI, DT 2009/135/117, Intoxicating Liquor Acts, *Dáil debates*, vol. 255, cols 3520–23, 5 August 1971.

[48] *Irish Times,* 5 October 1976 and 16 April 1973.

[49] *Irish Independent,* 7 December 1972.

[50] Malcolm, *Ireland sober, Ireland free*, 324–5.

was also made in *Magill* that Irish consumption figures were still not high by international standards as expressed by per capita consumption; in the late 1970s the per capita consumption expressed in litres of 100% alcohol for France was 16.5, West Germany 12.5, Denmark 9.2, United Kingdom 8.4 and Ireland 8.7.

What did mark Ireland out as different was that 75% of all drinking was done in pubs or clubs. In addition, Ireland spent more of its consumed expenditure on alcohol than other European Economic Community countries (12%); this 'anomaly is explained by the very high duties on drink in Ireland and the relatively low income per capita'. There had also been a doubling of the consumption of spirits in a decade due in large part to its appeal to young women: 'Every Saturday night in the 26 counties … 195,000 Vodka drinks are consumed by women under 30 years of age and these same women drink 4,500 cases of vodka a week. The social consequences of these consumption patterns bear investigation'.[51]

Those involved in the licensed trade remained more concerned about the burden of taxation that their products had to bear, informing Minister for Finance Richie Ryan in 1973 that it was 'excessive and out of scale'. Wages had gone up 82% in four years in the Dublin area, they maintained, and profit margins were 30–50% higher in Britain and other European countries: 'we have the highest taxed pint of beer in Europe'. Revealingly, the number of special exemption orders granted by the courts—to allow drink to be served outside normal licensing hours—increased from 6,342 in 1967 to 14,814 in 1972, to 34,300 in 1978.[52]

In the last two decades of the twentieth century there was mounting evidence of excessive alcohol consumption amongst particular cohorts and of the problems to which it gave rise; while Irish alcohol consumption stabilised or reduced in the late 1970s and early 1980s, this was after consumption had doubled between 1960 and 1979. Alcohol problems among the under 25 age group in the republic increased by 360% between 1970 and 1985, and between 1989 and 1999 there was a 41% increase in overall alcohol consumption in Ireland, whereas in ten other European countries its consumption decreased during that ten-year period.[53] In 1970 the Irish drank 7 litres of pure alcohol per adult; that increased to 10.1 by 1986, and to 14.1 litres by 2001. Overall alcohol consumption per head of population showed an increase of 48% from 1986 to 2006 and alcohol consumption peaked in 2001. Mortality rates for liver cirrhosis among Irishmen of all ages doubled from 5.4 per 100,000 per year in 1957–61 to 11.1 per 100,000 in 1997–2001.[54]

[51] *Magill*, 7 December 1977.
[52] NAI, DT 2009/135/117, Memorandum submitted to Richie Ryan in May 1973 and a Department of Justice memorandum, 30 September 1977, and a memorandum on special exemptions, March 1979.
[53] Ferriter, *A nation of extremes*, 248ff.
[54] *Irish Times*, 29 April 2006.

The distribution of average weekly expenditure at different stages of the second half of the twentieth century also indicated the continuity of increased expenditure on alcohol. Accounting for 1.1% of the average urban household in 1951–2, it rose to 3.7% in 1965–6 and 5.5% in 1994–5.[55] Increased consumption in the very late twentieth century made it clear that modernisation and prosperity were factors in facilitating alcohol abuse, just as recession had been a factor in temporarily reducing or stabilising it. The earlier stages of the Celtic Tiger economy in the mid-1990s saw a particular hike in consumption, although per capita consumption had been increasing for far longer.[56]

But the international 'league tables' of drinking continued to give solace to those who maintained that the Irish drinking problem was exaggerated. In the mid-1990s, while it was accepted that Ireland's alcohol consumption was rising, this was to a level that was approximately the same as the European average, according to a World Drink Trends report in 1995 (see the table below).

In 1996 the Department of Health's *National alcohol policy* statement insisted that 'there is evidence that the description of the Irish as a particularly alcohol-prone race is a myth. Indeed it is doubtful whether Ireland ever occupied a prominent role with regard to alcohol use or misuse'.[57] Such an assertion was erroneous, overlooked specific drinking patterns, practices and attitudes (see below) and perhaps proves the veracity of the assertion that at the heart of the Irish relationship with alcohol is a deep ambivalence, where there is an eagerness to admit alcohol as:

> both a positive and negative feature of political, social and economic life. Alcohol is tolerated and censured, often by the same people, in a way that reveals, paradoxically, the stability and resilience of a particular social system. The ability of the Irish people … to admit and accommodate contradictory attitudes towards this most socially defining of activities is evidence of Ireland's wider success as an ambivalent nation of abstainers and swallowers[58]

There was also a noticeable nostalgia for the decline of the traditional pub, which, it was maintained, had epitomised 'the essential charm of old Ireland', provided a focus for community life or a place to imbibe involving 'an emigration of the soul from sometimes unhappy realities', a very deceptive euphemism.[59]

---

[55] Adrian Redmond (ed.), *That was then this is now, change in Ireland, 1949–1999* (Dublin, 2000), 73–85.

[56] Tony Fahey, Helen Russell and Christopher T. Whelan, *Best of times? The social impact of the Celtic Tiger* (Dublin, 2007), 106.

[57] Department of Health, *National alcohol policy* (Dublin, 1996), iv.

[58] Tanya Cassidy, 'Society and alcohol', in Kilcommins and O'Donnell (eds), *Alcohol, society and law*, 33–59.

[59] Fennell and Bunbury, *The Irish pub*, 6.

Advertising also increased exposure to drink, notably the highly successful advertisements for Guinness; in 1997 the company became part of the huge multinational Diageo Company, though stout was still produced at the St James Gate Brewery in Dublin at the level of about 18 million pints a week.[60] But what was also striking was the increase in the consumption of wine; while between 1986 and 2006, the sale of alcohol in all beverage categories increased, with beer sales increasing by 32% and spirits by 46%, 'the most dramatic increase in volume was in wine sales with an increase of 8,121,225 litres of pure alcohol representing a 523% increase, although this was from a relatively low base'.[61] Beer continued to be the most popular drink but its market share declined to 51% in 2006 from 69% in 1986, while for wine, the market share increased from 6% in 1986 to 21% in 2006 and there were an estimated 1.45 million wine drinkers in Ireland by 2004. While Irish wine consumption remained 30% below that of Italy or France, much more effort and resources were put into marketing wine which had previously been regarded as a more inaccessible drink due to high prices, limited selections and complex labelling.[62]

The promotion of alcohol however, was also countered in the late twentieth century by commentary on the social, economic, physical and mental health consequences of excessive drinking. One of the most striking features of Irish alcohol consumption was the high rate of psychiatric hospital admission for alcohol-related disorders. The average age of first drinking also fell steadily and this change was 'significantly greater' in females.[63] Alcohol abuse was also implicated in rapid increases in sexually transmitted infections from 1989 onwards.[64] Increases in street disorder and violence were other consequences of excessive drinking and in 1994 legislation was passed to deal with public drunkenness under the title the Criminal Justice (Public Order) Act, sections of which dealt with intoxication in a public place.[65]

But it was still maintained that there were too many 'myths and misconceptions' about the Irish being excessive drinkers; in the mid-1990s, Ireland still had the highest percentage of teetotallers in Europe at 20% of the population, compared to between 5 and 7% in southern Europe.[66] This was one of the reasons for considerable debate about 'objective definitions of excessive alcohol consumption' in specialist literature, but 'of equal importance is the

---

[60] Corcoran, *The goodness of Guinness*, 143–6.
[61] Ann Hope, *Alcohol consumption in Ireland, 1986–2006, report for the Health Executive Alcohol Implementation Group* (Dublin, 2007), 1.
[62] Hope, *Alcohol consumption in Ireland*, 4 and Drinks Industry Group of Ireland, *The drinks market performance in 2009*, Report prepared by Anthony Foley (Dublin, 2010), 1–18.
[63] Gemma Cox, Alan Kelly and Bobby Smyth, 'Decline in age of drinking onset in Ireland', in *Alcohol and alcoholism* 46:4 (2011), 478.
[64] Fahey, Russell and Whelan, *Best of times?*, 346.
[65] Kilcommins and O'Donnell, *Alcohol, society and law*, 189.
[66] *Irish Times*, 27 March 2010.

subjective definition of excessive drinking used by individuals in their normal environments'.[67] This was yet another reminder of the shortcomings of international comparisons that did nothing to shed light on the context, experience and historical backdrop of drink consumption or drinking patterns within particular groups. In the early twenty-first century, a joint committee of the houses of the Oireachtas heard that the incidence of intoxication of teenagers had increased by 370% since 1996.[68] It was also clear that binge drinking (75 grams of pure alcohol in one sitting) at least once a week was common amongst Irish college students in the early twenty-first century; one male student's definition of excessive drinking was 'when you're stumbling all over the place and you can't get your words out'.

What was notable in the surveys of student drinking patterns was the high threshold that for them qualified as excess, and 'a clear disregard for the concept of alcohol guidelines', and, because they associated excessive intake with intoxication, they felt that recommended levels of safe drinking were unrealistic. But crucially, there was also the culture they had inherited and what they had observed of their parent's generation ('whom the students do not perceive to be particularly heavy drinkers'), which also undermined the validity of alcohol guidelines and warnings.[69] Furthermore, while Ireland's overall alcohol consumption, as crudely measured by the league tables, may have been slightly below the European average, Ireland's consumption of beer was much higher than other European countries; beer, white wine and vodka remained the drinks of choice for most Irish consumers.[70] By 2006 while alcohol consumption decreased from a peak of 14.3 litres of pure alcohol per adult in 2001 to 13.3 litres:

> Ireland continues to be among the highest consumers of alcohol in Europe. The average consumption per adult in the enlarged European Union is 10.2 litres of pure alcohol. Ireland ranks third in per adult alcohol consumption when compared with other international countries. Taking the EU 15 countries, Ireland ranks second after Luxembourg.[71]

Waves of publicity over the problems of alcohol abuse continued, as did promises of taskforces and measures to tackle the problems such as stricter regulation of marketing, but ultimately it was decided to allow the industry to

---

[67] Liam Delaney, Colm Harmon, Claire Milner, Lorna Sweeney and Patrick Wall, 'Perception of excessive drinking among Irish college students', *UCD Geary Institute Discussion Paper Series*, May 2007, 1–36.

[68] Terence Brown, *Ireland: a social and cultural history, 1922–2002* (London, 2004), 385.

[69] Delaney *et al.*, 'Perception of excessive drinking', 22.

[70] Kilcommins and O'Donnell, *Alcohol, society and law*, 183.

[71] Hope, *Alcohol consumption in Ireland*, 5.

regulate itself. The influence of the drinks industry was regarded as 'one of the biggest barriers to change',[72] a charge it rejected, but experts on alcohol abuse agreed that a change in the drinking culture and targeting alcohol as a major public health problem rather than the use of legislative measures was the key to transforming attitudes, a message that had also been propounded in the late nineteenth and early twentieth centuries, to little avail.

---

[72] *Irish Times*, 15 March 2008.

Haute cuisine restaurants in nineteenth and twentieth century Ireland

Máirtín Mac Con Iomaire

School of Culinary Arts and Food Technology, Dublin Institute of Technology, Cathal Brugha Street, Dublin 1

[Accepted 13 October 2014. Published 13 March 2015.]

Abstract

Historically, Ireland has not been associated with dining excellence. However, in 2011, the editor of *Le Guide du Routard*, Pierre Josse, noted that the Irish dining experience was as good, if not better, than anywhere in the world. This was a signal achievement for, as Josse also observed the disastrous nature of Irish public dining thirty years ago, when they first started the Irish edition. Thus it may come as a surprise to many that Ireland had a previous 'golden age' of haute cuisine—the benchmark for which was set by Restaurant Jammet which traded in Dublin between 1901 and 1967. Indeed, Ireland experienced an influx of gastro-tourists during 'the Emergency' (1939–45), and in the 1950s, The Russell Restaurant joined Restaurant Jammet as one of the most outstanding restaurants in Europe. In addition, both Dublin and Shannon airports housed two of Ireland's finest restaurants in the early 1960s. Cashel, Co. Tipperary, had two Michelin-starred restaurants during the early 1980s. From 1975 to 1988 Cork was the centre of fine dining in Ireland. The opening of Roscoffs in Belfast in 1989 spawned a cluster of Michelin-starred restaurants in Northern Ireland. Restaurant Patrick Guilbaud in Dublin was awarded its first Michelin star also in 1989, signalling a rebirth of fine-dining restaurants in the capital. This paper will discuss the history of Ireland's haute cuisine restaurants, identifying the various phases that led to our current standing: equal to if not better than any global competitors.

Introduction

Historically, Ireland has not been associated with dining excellence. However, in 2011, the editor of *Le Guide du Routard*, Pierre Josse, noted that 'the Irish dining experience is now as good, if not better, than anywhere in the world'. This was a signal achievement for, as Josse also observed, 'thirty years ago, when we first started the Irish edition, the food here was a disaster'.[1] This paper begins with a brief outline of the development of French haute cuisine and the

---

* Author's e-mail: mairtin.macconiomaire@dit.ie

doi: 10.3318/PRIAC.2015.115.06

[1] Nick Bramhill, 'Irish chefs best in world', *Sunday Independent*, 9 January 2011, available at: www.independent.ie/irish-news/irish-chefs-best-in-world-26612329.html (last accessed 8 February 2015).

emergence of restaurants in Paris. Its main focus is to track the emergence and development of haute cuisine restaurants in Ireland which began in the second half of the nineteenth century. The influence of foreign-born chefs and restaurateurs will be discussed drawing on evidence from trade directories, advertisements, oral histories, material culture and the 1901 and 1911 Censuses.

Key players such as the Jammet family will be profiled and a little-known 'golden age' of haute cuisine (1949–74) centred on Dublin will be discussed.[2] Dublin was home to two of the most outstanding restaurants in Europe during this period.[3] From 1975–88 Cork emerged as the new 'gourmet capital' as the focus of fine dining shifted from Dublin to country house hotels such as Arbutus Lodge and Ballymaloe House. The arrival of the *Egon Ronay guide* in 1963 and the *Michelin guide* in 1974 allows for patterns in Ireland to be compared with Great Britain and Europe. From the 1960s, a number of trends and culinary movements challenged the Georges Auguste Escoffier orthodoxy which had pervaded since the Edwardian era. Irish haute cuisine restaurants negotiated yet never fully embraced trends such as nouvelle cuisine, fusion cuisine and molecular gastronomy in order to arrive at a new 'golden age' (1994–2014) when the Irish dining experience was described in 2011 by the editor of *Le Guide du Routard* as being 'as good if not better, than anywhere in the world'.[4]

Origins and spread of French haute cuisine

French haute cuisine originated in the large kitchens of the aristocracy during the seventeenth century, and the pattern spread from there in the eighteenth century to the kitchens of wealthy households across the European continent. It is noteworthy that in most of Europe, up until the development of restaurants, food served in public premises was less spectacular than the fare available in the houses of the wealthy. This was the pattern also in Dublin where the restaurant was preceded by taverns, coffee houses and clubs.[5]

Haute cuisine has experienced a number of paradigm shifts since its inception. This paper uses the term to cover the evolving styles of elite cuisine produced and served in restaurants by professional staff spanning the Escoffier orthodoxy of the early twentieth century through the 'nouvelle cuisine' movement of the 1970s and 1980s, to the 'molecular gastronomy' or 'modernist' movement of the early twenty-first century. French haute cuisine in the public realm can be said to have originated in Paris with the appearance of restaurants during the second half of the eighteenth century. This phenomenon was greatly

---

[2] Máirtín Mac Con Iomaire, 'Louis Jammet', in James McGuire and James Quinn (eds), *Dictionary of Irish Biography* (9 vols, Cambridge, 2009), vol. 4, 956–8.
[3] *Irish Times*, 7 February 1956, 11.
[4] Bramhill, *'Irish chefs'*.
[5] For a detailed discussion on Dublin taverns, coffee houses and clubs see Máirtín Mac Con Iomaire, 'Public dining in Dublin: the history and evolution of gastronomy and commercial dining 1700–1900', *International Journal of Contemporary Hospitality Management* 25:2 (2013), 227–46.

boosted during the French Revolution when the number of restaurants increased dramatically.[6] Restaurants have been differentiated from a tavern, inn or a *table d'hôte* by a number of factors. Firstly, they provided private tables for customers; secondly, they offered a choice of individually priced dishes in the form of a carte or bill of fare; and thirdly, they offered food at times that suited the customer, not at one fixed time as in the case of the *table d'hôte*.[7] The spread of restaurants from Paris to London, Belfast and Dublin was slow, due primarily to the abundance of gentlemen's clubs which siphoned off much of the prospective clientele for restaurants in these cities.[8] A number of factors helped to create a more congenial environment for the opening of restaurants in both Ireland and England in the second half of the nineteenth century. They include the widespread adoption of *service à la Russe,* and the introduction of the Refreshment Houses and Wine Licences (Ireland) Act 1860.[9] *Service à la Française* was the method of service practised at the aristocratic upper end of French and other European cuisine from medieval times until the mid-nineteenth century in which food was served not in courses as it is now, but in services. Each service could comprise a choice of dishes from which each guest could select what appealed to him or her most. The service subordinated flavour and the enjoyment of food to making an impression of wealth and power. *Service à la Russe* replaced *service à la Française* in Britain and elsewhere in Europe in the course of the nineteenth century. This new style of table service provided for dishes being served to guests at their seats by servants who handed them round. The meal was served in courses starting with hors d'oeuvres, soup, fish, entrée, etc. and required more servants, and also table decorations to fill the spaces which the dishes themselves would have occupied under the old system.

Restaurants such as the Café Royal in London and The Burlington in Dublin, which both opened in the 1860s, were male bastions. Separate ladies rooms appeared in certain restaurants during the final decades of the nineteenth century but it was not until French chef Georges Auguste Escoffier (1846–1935) and Swiss hotelier César Ritz (1850–1918) developed the Savoy Hotel dining room in London in 1890 that it became acceptable and fashionable for genteel ladies to dine out publicly in mixed company.

The emergence of restaurants in Ireland

The first specific evidence of a French restaurant serving haute cuisine in Ireland is provided by an advertisement in the *Irish Times* for the Café de Paris, Lincoln Place, Dublin, in 1861. Establishments using the term 'restaurant' became common in the second half of the nineteenth century but the term was

---

[6] Rebecca L. Spang, *The invention of the restaurant: Paris and modern gastronomic culture* (Cambridge, 2000), 130–3; Stephen Mennell, *All manners of food*, 2nd edn (Chicago, IL, 1996), 141–2.

[7] Jean-Anthelme Brillat-Savarin, *The physiology of taste,* trans. A. Drayton (London, 1994), 267.

[8] Mennell, *All manners*, 155.

[9] Mac Con Iomaire, 'Public dining in Dublin', 227.

not used by *Thom's directory* until 1909 in which the category 'Restaurants and Tea Rooms' was first listed. There is one listing for the Imperial Hotel Restaurant, Donegall Place, Belfast, in *Henderson's directory for 1846–7*, and *The Belfast directory* for 1887 lists fourteen establishments under the heading 'Restaurants' although only three use the word restaurant in their title.[10] Over 26 different Dublin-based restaurants advertised in the *Irish Times* between 1865 and 1900, which notices included an advertisement announcing the opening of a 'High-Class Vegetarian Restaurant' at 3 and 4 College Street.[11] There was also a vegetarian restaurant in Belfast at this time and in 1908 an 'Indian Restaurant and Tea Rooms' opened in Dublin predating by three years the first twentieth-century Indian restaurant in London.[12] The establishment of The Hotel and Restaurant Proprietors' Association of Ireland (1890) also predates its English equivalent by a number of years.[13] The Irish Tourist Association was established in 1893 by F. W. Crossley, the Irish manager of Thomas Cook and Sons in order to develop Ireland as a tourist destination.[14] Growth in tourism, enabled by the expansion of railways, assisted the emergence of the hospitality sector by providing more customers for restaurants and hotels. One English-born chef, G. Frederick Macro, is given credit by *The Chef* in 1896 'for the part he has taken in raising the status of Irish hotels in the estimation of the English public'.[15] Macro trained in Paris and later at the Russian Embassy in London. He travelled widely prior to becoming chef at the newly opened Grand Hotel in Belfast in the 1890s and taking the position of chef de cuisine at the Imperial Hotel in Cork. The twelve-course Christmas dinner that he served in Cork in 1897 (Fig. 1) is a good example of *service à la Russe* and of Escoffier-style French haute cuisine with the accompanying wines.[16]

---

[10] *Henderson's Belfast directory and Northern repository 1846–7* (Belfast, 1846), 80; *The Belfast directory 1887* (Belfast, 1887), 155, both available at http://streetdirectories. proni.gov.uk/ (8 February 2015).

[11] *Irish Times*, 22 June 1899, 1.

[12] The X.L. Vegetarian Restaurant, 27 Cornmarket, Belfast, see the *Belfast and Ulster directory* (1900), 235, available at: http://streetdirectories.proni.gov.uk/ (8 February 2015); Michael Kennedy, '"Where's the Taj Mahal?": Indian restaurants in Dublin since 1908', *History Ireland* (July/August 2010), 50–2; the venture lasted less than a year. Note that London's first ever Indian restaurant was opened in 1810 by a Bengali, Sake Dean Mahomet, who had lived in Cork for 25 years and had an Irish wife, Jane Daly.

[13] A photo of 39 members of the Hotel and Restaurant Proprietors Association of Ireland appeared in the British trade journal *The Chef* on 23 May 1896; see also D. J. Wilson, 'The tourist movement in Ireland', *Journal of the Statistical and Social Science Society of Ireland* XI (1901), 56–63.

[14] Frank Corr, *Hotels in Ireland* (Dublin, 1987), 58.

[15] 'Celebrated chefs—No. XL: G. Frederick Macro', *The Chef: A Journal for Cooks, Caterers and Hotel Keepers* II:44 (1896), 1–2.

[16] Note the 'Braized Ham à la Irlandaise' on the menu.

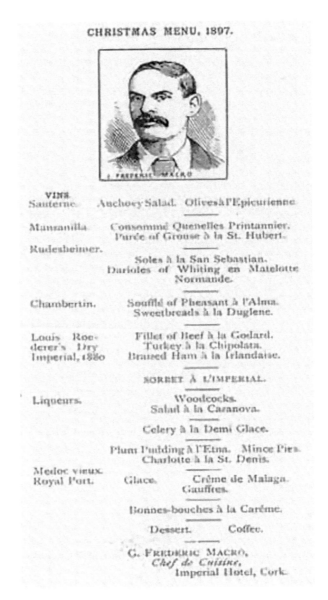

FIG. 1—Christmas Menu, 1897, from G. Frederic Macro, Imperial Hotel, Cork. (Source: *The Chef and Connoisseur*, 18 December 1897.)

Trade directories such as *Thom's*, *Guy's* and the *Belfast and Ulster directory* give listings but the fact that catering premises are listed under different headings makes direct comparison between cities difficult (Table 1).[17]

---

[17] Direct comparison between cities is exacerbated by the fact that the listings are no indication of the type or quality of food served. For Dublin, see Máirtín Mac Con Iomaire, 'The emergence, development and influence of French Haute Cuisine on public dining in Dublin restaurants 1900-2000: an oral history', unpublished PhD thesis, Dublin Institute of Technology, 2009, 3 vols, vol. 2, 81–2, 140–4, 185–6.

TABLE 1—Dublin food dining premises listed in *Thom's directory* 1850–1951. (Source: *Thom's directory* (Dublin, 1850–1951).)

Year	Hotel and taverns	Hotel and proprietors	Inns	Taverns and inns	Dining rooms	Refreshment rooms	Restaurant and tea rooms	*Total*
1850	134		10					**144**
1860	174		12					**186**
1870		133		74	12			**219**
1880		145		33	20	19		**217**
1890		130		25	23	22		**200**
1900		111		24	20	17		**172**
1911		143			22		32	**197**
1931		149					45	**194**
1941		191					57	**248**
1951		188					64	**252**

Despite possessing a smaller population than Belfast, Dublin's position as the focal point for the elite who ruled the country from Dublin Castle meant that it possessed a higher proportion than the former of haute cuisine restaurants by the early twentieth century.[18] The 1901 and 1911 Censuses indicate that Dublin, Belfast and Cork were the urban centres with the largest number of restaurants and that smaller clusters were to be found in Killarney (Co. Kerry), Limerick, Londonderry, Waterford and Galway.[19] Of the 24 establishments listed under 'Restaurant, Tea, Luncheon and Dining Rooms' in Cork for 1910, only two (The Mall, Tivoli) use the word restaurant, although an advertisement appears for Leech's Hotel and Restaurant on a separate page. Also listed is the famous Oyster Tavern and Dining Rooms in Market Lane.[20] Cross-referencing *Guy's* with the 1911 Census shows a German manager, Henry J. Koenigs, in the Great Southern Hotel in Killarney, and reveals an Austrian assistant manager, Italian chef, and both Austrian and German waiters. It also reveals an English manager in the Imperial Hotel in Cork with Swiss, German and French chefs listed as 'Hotel Cook', and waiters from Austria and Germany. For much of the twentieth century, haute cuisine restaurants were associated with grand hotels.[21]

---

[18] Nearly half of the 32 restaurants listed in the *Belfast and Ulster directory 1924* were affiliated with the Irish Temperance League.

[19] Based on analysis of the 1901 and 1911 censuses' search options, see www.census. nationalarchives.ie/search/#searchmore (8 February 2015).

[20] *Guy's Cork City and county almanac and directory for 1910* (Cork [1910]), 178, 273, available at: www.corkpastandpresent.ie/places/streetandtradedirectories/1910directory/ 1910directoryguys/#/273/ (8 February 2015).

[21] The most famous chef and hotelier partnership began in 1890 when Escoffier and Ritz accepted an invitation from Richard D'Oyly Carte to his newly opened Savoy Hotel in London.

Data from census
reports

The 1911 Census shows that the leading chefs, waiters and restaurateurs in Dublin during the first decades of the twentieth century were predominantly foreign-born. Most had trained in the leading restaurants, hotels and clubs of Europe.[22] On the assumption that foreign chefs and waiters are potential indicators of haute cuisine in Irish restaurants, a thorough search was made of the 1901 and 1911 Censuses. Of the 89 chefs listed in the 1901 Census, nearly half were foreign-born. The main countries of origin were England (14), France (9), Switzerland (9), Germany (7), Scotland (3), and one each from Austria and Holland. The 1911 Census lists 168 chefs more than half of whom were foreign-born. They came from England (33), France (18), Switzerland (12), Germany (8), Scotland (6), Italy (4), and one each from India, Belgium, Malta and Jersey. Within Ireland in 1911, Dublin was the birthplace of 37 chefs; 8 chefs were born in both Cork and Belfast, and the remainder were born elsewhere in the country. The keyword 'waiter' yielded 1,106 results in the 1901 Census and 1,200 results in the 1911 Census. The foreign-born waiters in 1901 came from England (111), Germany (49), Scotland (14), Austria (12), and Switzerland (5). In 1911 the foreign-born waiters came from England (137), Germany (37), Austria (26), Scotland (29) and France (6).

Gender is another method of differentiating haute cuisine restaurants from other restaurants, particularly in the first half of the twentieth century. Searching the 1901 and 1911 Censuses using 'restaurant' as a keyword revealed 195 and 211 results, respectively, but this masked a broad array of employment categories. These embraced restaurant proprietor, keeper, manager and cook, waitress and porter. The vast majority were female as most restaurants at the lower level of the market, as opposed to haute cuisine restaurants, were owned, managed or run by Irish women. Similarly, a search for 'café' revealed 58 entries, the majority of which embraced female café attendants, managers, superintendents, waitress or assistants. In 1901 there were 531 waitresses listed in Ireland; this had risen to 821 by 1911.[23] The word 'cook' was associated more with women, and when associated with men it was usually in the context of ship's cooks or army cooks. Indicatively, only 561 of the 15,878 cooks listed in the 1901 Census, and only 635 of 14,592 listed in the 1911 Census were male.

Influence of
foreign chefs/
restaurateurs

Haute cuisine was advertised as being available in the dining rooms of the best hotels in Dublin (Gresham, Shelbourne, Metropole and Royal Hibernian), Belfast (Royal Avenue, Grand Central and Midland), Cork (Imperial, Metropole and Victoria) and elsewhere in the country (Slieve Donard, Co.

---

[22] Máirtín Mac Con Iomaire, 'Searching for chefs, waiters and restaurateurs in Edwardian Dublin: a culinary historian's experience of the 1911 Dublin Census online', *Petits Propos Culinaires* 86 (2008), 92–126.

[23] German chefs and waiters were interned during the First World War and this provided opportunities for both Swiss hospitality workers and also for waitresses to serve in hotels and restaurants that had previously been male bastions. See Mac Con Iomaire, 'The emergence', vol. 2, 133–82.

Down, and Great Southern, Killarney) in the first half of the twentieth century. These premises, along with select restaurants, were the preferred workplaces of immigrant chefs and waiters. The 1911 Census return for 47 Royal Avenue, Belfast (Avenue Hotel) is illustrative. It reveals an American, Ernest Everest, as head of the family (hotel manager) living with his English wife (hotel manageress), and 20 staff which embraced hotel waiters from Germany, Bohemia, Austria and France, and a night porter from Switzerland.[24] The Grand Central Hotel, 9 Royal Avenue, Belfast, had an English manager, a Swiss pastry chef and an Italian second chef. Head chefs and senior chefs often did not live-in which complicates issues. Triangulating with other sources (newspaper reports, advertisements and material culture) reveals patterns of movement throughout the country. For example, M. Geller who wrote a reference for the Belgian chef, Zenon Geldof, before resigning as manager of the Central Hotel in Dublin (Fig. 2) in 1910, re-emerges as Martin Geller, the German-born hotel manager in 16 Donegall Place, Belfast, where he oversaw 20 live-in staff which included a German chef, and waiters from Germany and Switzerland. The 1901 Census lists Geller as 'Hotel Proprietor' on Main Street, Cavan Town, with six live-in staff (all Irish-born). Sources such as directories and the census can provide the answers to the who, where, and when questions, but it requires associated information from oral histories, interviews and obituaries to reveal the how and why?[25]

Along with the Jammet brothers, other European families, such as the Geldofs, Oppermanns, Gygaxs, and Bessons, were influential in developing the restaurant business in Ireland.[26] Paul Besson came to Dublin from the Hotel Cecil, London, in 1905 to serve as manager of The Royal Hibernian Hotel on Dawson Street. Over a number of decades, Paul Besson, his son Kenneth and other members of his family took control of The Royal Hibernian Hotel, The Russell Hotel, The Bailey Restaurant in Dublin and the Old Conna Hill Hotel in Wicklow.[27]

The most notable foreign chefs were the Jammet brothers. Michel (1858–1931) and François (1853–1940) Jammet were born in St Julia de Bec, near Quillan, in the French Pyrenees. Michel first came to Dublin in 1887 as chef to Henry Roe, the distiller. Following four years working in London for George Henry, sixth earl Cadogan, he returned to Dublin in 1895, becoming head chef at the Vice-regal Lodge when Cadogan became Lord Lieutenant of

24 The 1901 Census shows Everest as a restaurant manager living in Belfast; for more detailed examples of Dublin see Mac Con Iomaire, 'Searching for chefs', 92–106.
25 Mac Con Iomaire, 'The emergence', vol. 2, 271–325.
26 For more information see Máirtín Mac Con Iomaire, 'Zenon Geldof', in McGuire and Quinn (eds), *Dictionary of Irish biography*, vol. 4, 46–7; for details on the Gygax and Opperman families, see Mac Con Iomaire, 'The emergence', vol. 3, 269–94 and 332–8 (interviews with Fred Gygax and Johnny Opperman).
27 For a full analysis of these establishments see Mac Con Iomaire, 'The emergence', vol. 2, 133–398.

FIG. 2—Reference for Zenon Geldof, March 1910, signed M. Geller. (Source: Geldof Family Private Collection.)

Ireland.[28] In 1888 François became head chef of the Café de Deux Mondes, rue de La Paix, Paris; he subsequently moved to the Boeuf à la Mode, Rue de Valois, Palais Royal, where he married the owner's daughter, Eugenie. In 1900 Michel and François Jammet bought the Burlington Restaurant and Oyster

---

[28] Other notable chefs who worked for various Lord Lieutenants in the vice-regal lodge in Dublin include Alfred Suzanne, Reginald Bateman and Signor Lama, see Mac Con Iomaire, 'The emergence', vol. 2, 71–182.

Saloons at 27 St Andrew Street, Dublin, from Tom Corless. They refitted, and renamed it The Jammet Hotel and Restaurant in 1901, and it became pre-eminent among the restaurants of Dublin. Its clientele included leading politicians, nobility, actors, writers and artists. These included Harry Kernoff, whose painting of the restaurant (Pl. I) now hangs in Dublin's Restaurant Patrick Guilbaud. Jammet's Hotel and Restaurant traded at 26–27 Andrew Street and 6 Church Lane until the lease reverted to the Hibernian Bank in 1926. Michel Jammet acquired Kidd's Empire Restaurant and Tea Rooms at 45–46 Nassau Street at this time and brought some of the fittings from the original premises. When he retired in 1927, his son Louis took over the running of the business while Michel returned to Paris where he was a director and the principal shareholder of the Hotel Bristol until his death in 1931. The new Restaurant Jammet on Nassau Street traded successfully from 1927 until its closure in 1967. It became the haunt of artists and the literary set, and the Jammet's took pride in the fact that it was Dublin's only French restaurant.[29]

Pl. I—The Jammet Hotel and Restaurant (Andrew Street) by Harry Kernoff. (Source: Restaurant Patrick Guilbaud—The Merrion Hotel, Dublin.)

---

[29] For more detailed information on Restaurant Jammet, see Mac Con Iomaire, 'The emergence', vol. 2 or Alison Maxwell, *Jammet's of Dublin* (Dublin, 2012).

The interwar
years and the
'Emergency'

During the interwar years, growth in the restaurant sector in Dublin took the form primarily of large-scale dining rooms similar to those of the Lyons Group in London. An advertisement for Clery's Restaurant in January 1928 claimed that it was 'The Largest and Most Popular Restaurant in Ireland'.[30] In November 1928 The Plaza Restaurant opened on Middle Abbey Street with six French chefs, with the capacity to serve between 600 and 1,000 diners at one time.[31] The Plaza was managed by Zenon Geldof, a Belgian chef and confectioner who owned the Café Belge on Dame Street and the Patisserie Belge on Leinster Street. An advertisement for The Plaza in 1929 pronounced that it was 'The Largest and Most Luxurious Restaurant in Ireland'.[32] If so, it soon encountered difficulties and may have closed as in October 1929 it was advertised as a roller-skating rink though the *Irish Times* carried an advertisement in January 1930 of the reopening of the Plaza Restaurant.[33] By 1934 foreign visitors were becoming noticeably more numerous in Dublin. The Red Bank Restaurant's Ernest J. Hess belonged to the new school of maître d'hôtel; 'keen, alert, of cosmopolitan outlook, and fluent linguist', he was ideally adapted to welcoming these visitors from different countries.[34] Large restaurants were also attached to theatres and cinemas such as the Savoy, Metropole and Capitol.[35] The Irish Transport and General Workers Union (ITGWU) had a hotels and restaurants branch which was active at this period and had members in most of the leading establishments (Fig. 3).

The *Belfast and Ulster directory* of 1924 lists 32 restaurants in Belfast. This publication also carried a full-page advertisement for Thompsons (Belfast) Ltd. Located at 14 Donegall Place, established in 1847, it was heralded as the 'Premier Restaurant in Belfast'.[36] There appears to have been a cluster of restaurants on Donegall Place (Carlton, Shaftsbury Tea Rooms, The Savoy), with the Grand Metropole Hotel on Donegall Street. The onset of the Second World War must have affected business in Belfast restaurants but the Belfast Blitz by the Luftwaffe in April and May 1941 was catastrophic. In neutral Dublin, restaurants thrived during the 'Emergency' and indeed for a number of years later as diners crossed the border or came over from England to enjoy a solid meal.[37] John Ryan recalled that a customer described the 'fabulous' fare available in Jammet's as 'the finest French cooking between the fall of France

[30] *Irish Times*, 6 January 1928.
[31] 'One thousand diners in a restaurant', *Dublin Evening Mail*, 8 November 1928.
[32] Corporation of Dublin, *A book of Dublin* (Dublin, 1929).
[33] *Irish Times*, 18 January 1930.
[34] *The Irish Hotel and Club Manager*, May 1934.
[35] The Regal Rooms opened attached to the reopened Theatre Royal, Dublin; *Irish Times*, 23 September 1935; see Mac Con Iomaire, 'The emergence', vol. 2, 183–245.
[36] The *Belfast and Ulster directory* (Belfast, 1924) was compiled at the Belfast News-letter office.
[37] For oral evidence of 'gastro-tourists' to Dublin at this time see Mac Con Iomaire, 'The emergence', vol. 3, 176–88 and 313–31. (Interviews with Jimmy Kilbride, Tony and Annie Sweeney, and Garret Fitzgerald.)

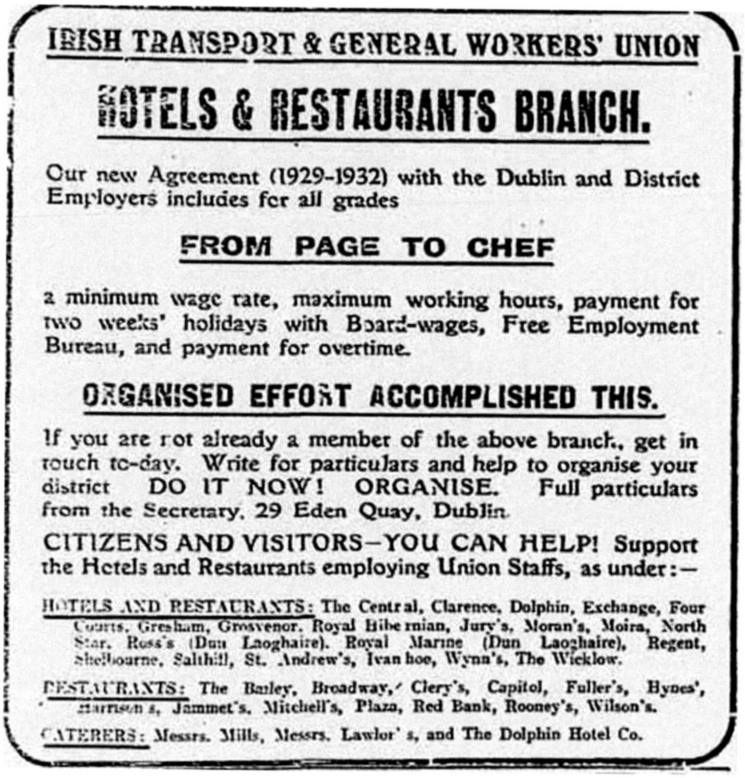

FIG. 3—Advertisement for the Irish Transport & General Workers' Union, Hotels and Restaurants Branch. (Source: *Irish Times*, 8 August 1929, 7.)

and the Liberation of Paris'.[38] American servicemen, according to Ryan 'cigar chomping and in full uniform', streamed across the border to sample the quality food in the prodigious quantities that it was available here. Tony Sweeney recalled Jammet's 'packed with military people during the war'. Garret Fitzgerald remembered American soldiers coming to Dublin as late as 1949 but did not recall them in uniform. Jimmy Kilbride noted that The Gresham Hotel, Dublin, had no shortage of food thanks to the black market activities of its manager Toddy O' Sullivan. When in 1943 the *Daily Express* published one of the Gresham's extensive à la carte menus on its front page, to illustrate how neutral Ireland was not suffering from the effects of war, it unintentionally increased the numbers of off-duty servicemen who dined at the Gresham.[39] Such was the Gresham's reputation that Eleanor Roosevelt once turned up unexpectedly with an entourage of ten airmen.[40]

---

[38] John Ryan, 'There'll never be another Jammet's', *Irish Times*, 11 April 1987, Weekend, 3.

[39] *Daily Express*, 14 November 1943, 1; Christopher Sands, *The Gresham for style* (Dublin, 1994), 40–1.

[40] Shaun Boylan, 'Timothy "Toddy" O'Sullivan', in McGuire and Quinn (eds), *Dictionary of Irish biography*, vol. 7, 983–5.

Over many years, Restaurant Jammet maintained its position as the finest restaurant producing haute cuisine in Ireland. Until the appointment of Pierre Rolland as head chef of The Russell in 1949, Jammet's was also 'the only restaurant in Dublin with an international reputation'. Indeed, according to *Journal l'Epoque* in June 1947, Jammet's was the only place in the British Isles where one could eat well in the grand French tradition, *'A Dublin, . . . on trouve une cuisine digne de la grande tradition française'*.[41]

A golden age of haute cuisine in Dublin

The 1949–74 period can be viewed as a 'golden age' of haute cuisine in Dublin, since more award-winning world-class restaurants traded in Dublin during this period than at any previous time. In the late 1940s, The Red Bank Restaurant reopened as a fine-dining restaurant with a French head chef producing haute cuisine. Newspaper reports of gastronomic dinners held by the Irish branch of André L. Simon's Food and Wine Society attest to the growing interest in haute cuisine at this time. Both The Russell Restaurant and Restaurant Jammet received awards from the American magazine *Holiday* in the 1950s for being 'outstanding restaurants in Europe'.[42] Further evidence of Dublin restaurants' as culinary leaders is provided by the *Egon Ronay guide* which first covered Ireland in 1963. By 1965 Ronay suggested that The Russell Restaurant 'must rank amongst the best in the world'.[43] A menu from The Russell in 1966 is shown in Figure 4, and it is notable that when Rolland left full-time employment in The Russell in 1966 to work winters in the Bahamas, the restaurant dropped to two Egon Ronay stars in 1967. The majority of the award-winning Dublin restaurants produced a form of haute cuisine that had been codified by Escoffier; it was labour-intensive and it was silver-served by large teams of waiters in elegant dining rooms.

The beginnings of expertise transfer to Irish chefs can be dated to the early 1950s when an agreement between Ken Besson and the ITGWU allowed foreign-born chefs and waiters to work in Ireland in return for Irish apprentices being indentured in the Besson-owned Russell and Royal Hibernian Hotels under the guidance of chefs Pierre Rolland and Roger Noblet.[44] *The Irish Hotelier* described Rolland as 'numbered among the ten most distinguished culinary experts in France'.[45] Under his leadership, The Russell Hotel kitchen became a training ground for generations of Irish chefs (Pl. II). The number of foreign chefs and waiters working in Ireland fell during the late 1950s and early

---

[41] Charles Graves, *Ireland revisited* (London, New York, 1949); R. Lacoste, 'Les Cuisiniers Francais Partis: Les Anglais ne mangent plus que des conserves et des soupes en poudre', *Journal l'Epoque*, 22 June 1947.

[42] *Irish Times*, 7 February 1956, 11.

[43] Egon Ronay, *Egon Ronay's 1965 guide to hotels and restaurants in Great Britain and Ireland with 32 motoring maps* (London, 1965), 464.

[44] For more information see Máirtín Mac Con Iomaire, 'Kenneth George Besson', in McGuire and Quinn (eds), *Dictionary of Irish biography*, vol. 1, 505–06; for more information see Máirtín Mac Con Iomaire, 'Pierre Rolland', in McGuire and Quinn (eds), *Dictionary of Irish biography*, vol. 8, 594–5.

[45] Anon., 'The Russell Hotel', *The Irish Hotelier* (February 1954), 13.

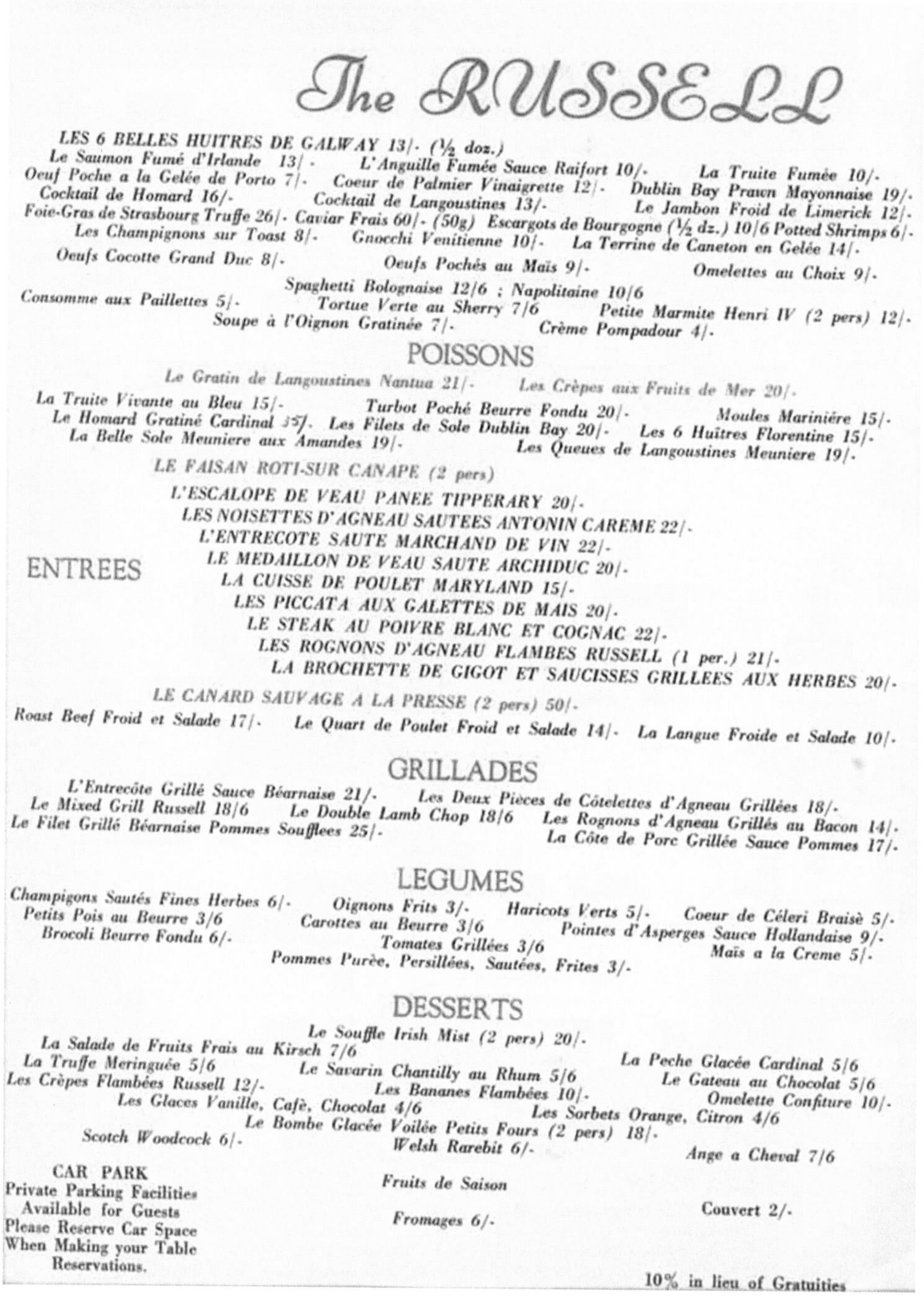

The RUSSELL

LES 6 BELLES HUITRES DE GALWAY 13/- (½ doz.)

Le Saumon Fumé d'Irlande 13/-   *L'Anguille Fumée Sauce Raifort* 10/-   *La Truite Fumée* 10/-

Oeuf Poche a la Gelée de Porto 7/-   *Coeur de Palmier Vinaigrette* 12/-   *Dublin Bay Prawn Mayonnaise* 19/-

Cocktail de Homard 16/-   *Cocktail de Langoustines* 13/-   *Le Jambon Froid de Limerick* 12/-

Foie-Gras de Strasbourg Truffe 26/- *Caviar Frais* 60/- (50g) *Escargots de Bourgogne* (½ dz.) 10/6 *Potted Shrimps* 6/-

Les Champignons sur Toast 8/-   *Gnocchi Venitienne* 10/-   *La Terrine de Caneton en Gelée* 14/-

Oeufs Cocotte Grand Duc 8/-   *Oeufs Pochés au Maïs* 9/-   *Omelettes au Choix* 9/-

Spaghetti Bolognaise 12/6 ; *Napolitaine* 10/6

Consomme aux Paillettes 5/-   *Tortue Verte au Sherry* 7/6   *Petite Marmite Henri IV* (2 pers) 12/-

Soupe à l'Oignon Gratinée 7/-   *Crème Pompadour* 4/-

POISSONS

Le Gratin de Langoustines Nantua 21/-   *Les Crêpes aux Fruits de Mer* 20/-

La Truite Vivante au Bleu 15/-   *Turbot Poché Beurre Fondu* 20/-   *Moules Marinière* 15/-

Le Homard Gratiné Cardinal 35/- *Les Filets de Sole Dublin Bay* 20/-   *Les 6 Huîtres Florentine* 15/-

La Belle Sole Meuniere aux Amandes 19/-   *Les Queues de Langoustines Meuniere* 19/-

ENTREES

LE FAISAN ROTI SUR CANAPE (2 pers)

L'ESCALOPE DE VEAU PANEE TIPPERARY 20/-

LES NOISETTES D'AGNEAU SAUTEES ANTONIN CAREME 22/-

L'ENTRECOTE SAUTE MARCHAND DE VIN 22/-

LE MEDAILLON DE VEAU SAUTE ARCHIDUC 20/-

LA CUISSE DE POULET MARYLAND 15/-

LES PICCATA AUX GALETTES DE MAIS 20/-

LE STEAK AU POIVRE BLANC ET COGNAC 22/-

LES ROGNONS D'AGNEAU FLAMBES RUSSELL (1 per.) 21/-

LA BROCHETTE DE GIGOT ET SAUCISSES GRILLEES AUX HERBES 20/-

LE CANARD SAUVAGE A LA PRESSE (2 pers) 50/-

Roast Beef Froid et Salade 17/-   *Le Quart de Poulet Froid et Salade* 14/-   *La Langue Froide et Salade* 10/-

GRILLADES

L'Entrecôte Grillé Sauce Béarnaise 21/-   *Les Deux Pièces de Côtelettes d'Agneau Grillées* 18/-

Le Mixed Grill Russell 18/6   *Le Double Lamb Chop* 18/6   *Les Rognons d'Agneau Grillés au Bacon* 14/-

Le Filet Grillé Béarnaise Pommes Soufflees 25/-   *La Côte de Porc Grillée Sauce Pommes* 17/-

LEGUMES

Champigons Sautés Fines Herbes 6/-   *Oignons Frits* 3/-   *Haricots Verts* 5/-   *Coeur de Céleri Braisè* 5/-

Petits Pois au Beurre 3/6   *Carottes au Beurre* 3/6   *Pointes d'Asperges Sauce Hollandaise* 9/-

Brocoli Beurre Fondu 6/-   *Tomates Grillées* 3/6   *Maïs a la Creme* 5/-

Pommes Purèe, Persillées, Sautées, Frites 3/-

DESSERTS

Le Souffle Irish Mist (2 pers) 20/-

La Salade de Fruits Frais au Kirsch 7/6   *La Peche Glacée Cardinal* 5/6

La Truffe Meringuée 5/6   *Le Savarin Chantilly au Rhum* 5/6   *Le Gateau au Chocolat* 5/6

Les Crèpes Flambées Russell 12/-   *Les Bananes Flambées* 10/-   *Omelette Confiture* 10/-

Les Glaces Vanille, Café, Chocolat 4/6   *Les Sorbets Orange, Citron* 4/6

Le Bombe Glacée Voilée Petits Fours (2 pers) 18/-

Scotch Woodcock 6/-   *Welsh Rarebit* 6/-   *Ange a Cheval* 7/6

CAR PARK
Private Parking Facilities
Available for Guests
Please Reserve Car Space
When Making your Table
Reservations.

Fruits de Saison

Fromages 6/-

Couvert 2/-

10% in lieu of Gratuities

Fig. 4—Menu from The Russell, 13 December 1966. (Source: Arthur McGee Private Collection.)

1960s. They were replaced by foreign-trained Irish chefs and waiters. During this period the catering branch of the ITGWU strongly opposed the employment of foreign staff. Oral evidence suggests that some Irish chefs and waiters

Pl. II—Pierre Rolland with the Russell Hotel Kitchen Brigade *c.* 1958. *Front row (left to right):* Nicky O'Neill, Jackie Needham, unnamed French chef, Monsieur Petrel (general manager), Pierre Rolland (head chef), Monsiuer Maurice (restaurant manager), Roger Noblet (sous chef), Henri Rolland, Arthur McGee. *Middle Row (left to right):* unnamed trainee manager, Brian Loughrey, Charlie O'Neill, Brendan Egan, Johnny Kilbride, Louis Corrigan, unnamed trainee manager. *Back row (left to right):* Michael (kitchen porter), unnamed commis, commis Mansfield, Eamon (Ned) Ingram, Mary (vegetable maid). *Note:* Arthur McGee notes that both Willie Woods and Jimmy Doyle are missing from the photo but were part of the brigade at that time. (Source: Arthur McGee Private Collection.)

were pressurised by the union to take senior positions, in order to exclude suitable foreign-born candidates.[46] Two Irish chefs, Vincent Dowling in Restaurant Jammet, and Joe Collins in Jury's Hotel, Dame Street, were sent abroad for training—to Paris and Switzerland—before returning to become chef de cuisine in their respective restaurants. The move from French to Irish head chefs, combined with a new Irish culinary aesthetic inspired by *An Tóstal,* may have influenced the change in listings of certain Dublin restaurants published in the 1965 *Egon Ronay guide.* In that year the classification of the Shelbourne Hotel Restaurant, The Red Bank Restaurant, Haddington House Hotel Restaurant, Metropole Georgian Room, Intercontinental Embassy Restaurant and Gresham Hotel Grill Room was changed from 'French' cuisine

---

[46] Mac Con Iomaire, 'The emergence', vol. 3, 147–75 and 189–218. (Interviews with Christy Sands and Arthur McGee.)

to 'Franco–Irish' cuisine. Restaurant Jammet and the Royal Hibernian's Lafayette Restaurant remained listed as 'French', whereas The Russell was listed as 'Haute Cuisine'. However, restaurants such as the Old Ground Hotel in Ennis, Co. Clare, and The Pontoon Bridge Hotel in County Mayo were listed as 'Plain Cooking'.[47]

Decline of haute cuisine in Dublin and rise of country house restaurants

Dublin's golden age of haute cuisine ended with the closure of Restaurant Jammet in 1967; and the subsequent closures of The Red Bank Restaurant in 1969 and The Russell Hotel in 1974. Dublin had seven starred restaurants in 1963 (Table 2), a number not equalled for more than 40 years (see Table 6). The pattern that emerges from the Egon Ronay and Michelin guides is that haute cuisine restaurants moved thereafter from the capital to country house hotels such as Arbutus, Ballymaloe and Ballylicky in County Cork; The Tower Hotel Glenbeigh, The Park Hotel Kenmare and Sheen Falls in Co. Kerry; Ashford Castle, Streamstown Bay and Newport House Hotels in County Mayo; and to restaurants such as Dunderry Lodge in County Meath, Shiro in County Cork and the Barn in Saintfield, Co. Down, where it remained until a resurgence recommenced in Dublin and Belfast from 1990 onwards.

Two reasons given for the closure of Restaurant Jammet in 1967 were the growing trend towards suburban living and the rising importance of car parking.[48] A number of factors led to the demise of the traditional Escoffier style haute cuisine in the 1970s. Political and economic factors such as the Organization of the Petroleum Exporting Countries oil crisis, the Dublin bombings and banking strikes, all contributed. It has also been suggested that the introduction of a 'wealth tax' by the coalition government in 1973, resulted in a mass exodus of landed gentry from Ireland. The Shelbourne Hotel, Dublin, witnessed an instant 20% drop in business in 1973,[49] and The Russell Hotel was also affected. The latter closed in 1974 after which The Royal Hibernian Hotel then assumed the mantle of Dublin's last bastion of 'Escoffier style' haute cuisine until it too closed its doors in 1982.[50] It is more than coincidental that some of the country house hotels

---

[47] Ronay, *1965 guide*; the 1950s witnessed efforts to boost tourism such as *An Tóstal*, a festival to promote Irish culture and heritage (see Irene Furlong, 'Tourism and the Irish State in the 1950s', in Dermot Keogh *et al.* (eds), *Ireland in the 1950s: the lost decade* (Cork, 2004), 164–86). Part of this movement was the promotion of traditional Irish food. In 1958 *Bord Fáilte Éireann*, working with Michael Mullen (ITGWU), suggested the inauguration of an Irish Food Festival Week. To bring this idea to fruition, a panel of Dublin's leading chefs were formed—and named *Seanad Cócaire na hEireann*: Panel of Chefs of Ireland—see Panel-of-Chefs, *Jubilee Stockpot 1958–1983* (Galway, 1983).
[48] Mac Con Iomaire, 'The emergence', vol. 3, 339–62. (Interview with Róisín Hood.)
[49] Michael O'Sullivan and Bernardine O'Neill, *The Shelbourne and its people* (Dublin, 1999), 161.
[50] The building was subsequently redeveloped into offices and a shopping arcade—The Royal Hibernian Way.

TABLE 2—Irish restaurants awarded stars (*) by the *Egon Ronay guide* in 1963–74. (Source: *Egon Ronay guide* (London, 1963–74).)

Name of establishment	1963	1964	1965	1966	1967	1968	1969	1970	1971	1972	1973	1974
Dublin												
The Russell Hotel Rest.	3*	3*	3*	3*	2*	2*	2*	2*	2*	2*	2*	1*
The Royal Hibernian Lafayette Rest.	1*	1*	1*	1*	1*	1*	1*	1*	1*	1*	1*	1*
The Shelbourne Hotel Rest.	1*	1*										
Intercontinental Hotel Embassy Rest.		1*	1*	1*								
Jammet's Rest., Nassau Street	2*	2*	1*	1*	1*							
The Red Bank Rest., D'Olier Street	1*	1*	1*	1*	1*							
Snaffles Rest., Leeson Street										1*	1*	
The Soup Bowl, Molesworth Lane										1*	1*	
The Gresham Hotel, O'Connell Street	1*											
Haddington House, Dun Laoghaire	1*	1*	1*									
Cork												
Arbutus Lodge, Cork City							1*					
Ballymaloe House, Yeats Room, Co. Cork					2*	2*	2*	1*	1*	1*	1*	1*
Ballylickey House Hotel, Co. Cork			1*	1*		1*	1*	1*	1*	1*	1*	1*
Mayo and Galway												
Newport House Hotel, Co. Mayo			1*	1*	1*	1*	1*	1*	1*	1*	1*	1*
Streamstown House, Priory, Clifton, Co. Mayo				1*	1*	1*	1*	1*	1*	1*		
Ashford Castle, Cong, Co. Mayo		1*	1*	1*	1*	1*	1*	1*				
Renvyle House, Co. Galway										1*	1*	
Zetland Hotel, Cashel Bay, Co. Galway	1*	1*	1*	1*	1*	1*						
Egan's Lake Hotel, Oughterard, Co. Galway	1*	1*										
Kerry, Clare and Wicklow												
Dunloe Castle, Co. Kerry								1*	1*			
Great Southern Hotel, Parknasilla, Co. Kerry				1*								
Butler Arms Hotel, Waterville, Co. Kerry	1*											
Glenbeigh Hotel (Towers 1965), Co. Kerry	1*		1*	1*	1*	1*						
Hotel Europe Rest., Killarney, Co. Kerry				1*	1*							
Shannon Airport Hotel, Shannon, Co. Clare	1*	1*										
Dromoland Hotel, Co. Clare			1*	1*								
Glenview Hotel, Delgany, Co. Wicklow			1*	1*	1*							

TABLE 2 (*cont.*)—Irish restaurants awarded stars (*) by the *Egon Ronay guide* in 1963–74. (Source: *Egon Ronay guide* (London, 1963–74).)

Name of establishment	1963	1964	1965	1966	1967	1968	1969	1970	1971	1972	1973	1974
Northern Ireland												
Ballygally Castle Candlelight Inn, Larne, Co. Antrim	1*											
Old Inn, Crawfordsburn, Co. Down	1*	1*										
King's Arms Hotel, Larne, Co. Antrim	1*											
Mondello Rest., North Street, Belfast, Co. Antrim			1*	1*	1*							
Dunadry Hotel, Co. Antrim							1*	1*				
Culloden Hotel Rest., Hollywood, Co. Down							1*	1*				
Ardmore Hotel Rest., Newry, Co. Down							1*	1*				

and restaurants around the country which became locations of haute cuisine in the following decades belonged to the landed gentry who had departed.[51]

The decline in haute cuisine also reflected changes in social attitudes which reflected the emergence of a deferential but respectful outlook that did not leave dining untouched. Egon Ronay's 1965 guide discussed emerging trends: the rise in Italian restaurants; the decline in the top end of the market, and a rise in the bottom end; and particularly the rise in younger clientele visiting restaurants:

> A new type of restaurant clientele is being born—this is the most significant development in our catering scene. Young people eat out very much more often than years ago. They are more critical and outspoken, have less of a complex about walking into restaurants, and a large proportion have palates un-poisoned by public school feeding.[52]

A new phenomenon appeared towards the end of the 1960s when enthusiastic amateurs opened restaurants such as Snaffles on Leeson Street (Nicholas Tinne) and The Soup Bowl on Molesworth Lane (Peter Powrie), both in Dublin. These restaurants proved popular with a new generation of Irish restaurant clientele typified by emerging businessmen like Michael Smurfit and politicians like Charles Haughey. In Shanagarry, Co. Cork, another enthusiastic amateur, Myrtle Allen, a farmer's wife, opened up Ballymaloe House in 1964, but she soon became an enthusiastic professional as shall be discussed later. This amateur phenomenon reflected a similar trend that had occurred slightly earlier in England.[53]

[51] For examples see www.irelands-blue-book.ie/ (8 February 2015) which includes properties throughout the whole island of Ireland.
[52] Ronay, *1965 guide*, 16.
[53] Gregory Houston-Bowden, *British gastronomy: the rise of great restaurants* (London, 1975), 127.

Guidebooks—
Egon Ronay and
Michelin

Since the advent of the motor car there has been a link between tyre companies and guidebooks. Maurice Edmond Sailland or Curnonsky (1872–1956) is considered the inventor of gastronomic motor-tourism when he encouraged French 'gastro-nomads' to explore the regional cookery of their country by automobile. He wrote a weekly column for Michelin in *Le Journal* from 1907. The introduction of these guidebooks to Ireland brought new discerning customers to Irish restaurants. With the arrival of the *Egon Ronay guide* in 1963 and the *Michelin guide* in 1974, it is easier to identify which restaurants were producing haute cuisine within the island and also how they compared to the United Kingdom, and the rest of Europe. Both guides used a one-, two- and three-star rating system, with three-star restaurants considered to be worth a special journey indicating exceptional cuisine. In 1963 Dublin was described by Egon Ronay as a 'city of good restaurants', noting that Jammet's would have had three stars but for the fact that the patissiere was on a day off, and that both the Gresham and the Royal Hibernian would have had two stars except for poor desserts and the over use of table lamps in the Gresham.[54] The guide expressed 'our appreciation of the result an Irish–French team can produce in a kitchen. The Irish touch, we find has a peculiar, mellowing effect on the—sometimes too fancy—French cooking'. In 1963 the *Egon Ronay Guide* awarded The Russell three stars, the highest possible award, and in the 1965 guide, Egon Ronay wrote: 'words fail us in describing the brilliance of the cuisine at this elegant and luxurious restaurant which must rank amongst the best in the world'.[55] However, by 1974, when the *Michelin guide to Great Britain and Ireland* was first published, the only star awarded in Dublin appropriate to an exceptional restaurant was to The Russell Restaurant, which closed its doors that very year (Tables 2 and 3).

There are links, however, between the old and the new. For example, Declan Ryan, who achieved stars from both Egon Ronay and Michelin in Arbutus Lodge, Cork, trained for a while under Pierre Rolland in The Russell in Dublin. He and his brother Michael also trained in France with Jean and Pierre Troisgros whose restaurant in Roanne was awarded three Michelin stars in 1968, and voted 'best restaurant in the world' in 1972.[56] Pierre Troisgros's son Claude worked as sauce chef in Arbutus for a year.[57] The Ryans trained

---

[54] Egon Ronay, *Egon Ronay's guide to 1,000 eating places in Great Britain and Ireland including 250 London pubs* (London, 1963), 362, 367.

[55] See Tables 2 and 3 for a list of Irish restaurants awarded stars by Egon Ronay from 1963–1994; Ronay, *1965 guide*, 464.

[56] Mac Con Iomaire, 'The emergence', vol. 3, 295–312 (interview with Declan Ryan); voted the best restaurant in 1972 by the Gault Millau restaurant guide *Le Nouveau Guide* (Paris, 1972).

[57] For Claude Troisgros mastery of sauces see Máirtín Mac Con Iomaire, 'Identified by taste: the chef as artist?', *TEXT* Special Issue Website Series No. 26 (April 2014), 1–8, available at: www.textjournal.com.au/speciss/issue26/MacConIomaire.pdf (8 February 2015).

TABLE 3—Irish restaurants awarded stars from the *Egon Ronay guide*[a] in 1975–94. (Source: *Egon Ronay guide* (London, 1975–94).)

Name of establishment	1975	1976	1977	1978	1979	1980	1981	1982	1983	1984	1985	1987	1988	1989	1991	1993	1994
Dublin																	
Rest. Rolland, Killiney	1*																
Rest. Patrick Guilbaud, Dublin									1*	1*	1*	1*			1*	1*	1*
Colin O'Daly's Park Rest., Blackrock														1*	1*		
Cork																	
Ballymaloe House, Co. Cork	1*	1*	1*	1*	1*	1*	1*		1*	1*		1*	1*				↑
Ballylickey House, Co. Cork	1*	1*	1*	1*	1*	1*	1*	1*									
Arbutus Lodge, Cork City	1*	1*	1*	1*	2*	2*	2*	3*	1*	2*	2*	1*			1*		
Vintage, Kinsale, Co. Cork					1*	1*	1*										
Shiro, Ahakista, Co. Cork													1*	1*	1*	1*	1*
Clifford's, Cork City																	1*
Republic of Ireland (continued)																	
Ashford Castle, Cong, Co. Mayo	1*	1*	1*	1*	1*	1*		1*									
Blue Bull, Sneem, Co. Kerry					1*	1*											
Park Hotel, Kenmare, Co. Kerry									1*	1*							
Slane Castle Rest., Co. Meath					1*	1*											
Dunderry Lodge, Co. Meath									1*	1*	1*	1*	1*				
Cashel Palace Hotel, Co. Tipperary								1*									
Chez Hans, Cashel, Co. Tipperary								1*									
Armstrong's Barn, Co. Wicklow	1*																
Tree of Idleness, Bray, Co. Wicklow													1*				
Drimcong House, Moycullen, Co. Galway													1*	1*	1*	1*	1*
Jockey Hall, Curragh, Co. Kildare							1*										
Dromoland Castle, Co. Clare														1*↑			
Cromleach Lodge, Co. Sligo																	1*
Northern Ireland																	
Barn, Saintfield, Co. Down		1*	1*	1*	1*	1*	1*	1*	1*								
Ramore, Portrush, Co. Antrim												1*	1*	1*	1*	1*	1*
Roscoff, Belfast, Co Antrim															1*	1*	1*

[a] Egon Ronay sold the rights to his guides to the Automobile Association in 1985. The rights were subsequently sold to Leading Guides International, a company that went bankrupt in 1997. Comparisons in this table stop at 1994 because consistency in awards is lacking under the new owners. By 1994 there is a separate *Egon Ronay Jameson Guide for Ireland* with Georgina Campbell as the regional editor, which eventually becomes the *Georgina Campbell guide* in 1997 when Egon Ronay Publications ceased publication.

Michael Clifford who would earn them another Michelin star when they took the lease of the Cashel Palace Hotel in County Tipperary in the 1980s. Another Russell-trained chef, Ken Wade, was responsible for the fine cooking in Ashford Castle. Colin O'Daly, the head chef who first won a Michelin star in the Park Hotel Kenmare in 1983, trained under Bill Ryan, another ex-Russell chef, in the

Dublin Airport Restaurant and later under Ken Wade in Ashford Castle. When Shannon Airport Restaurant was awarded an Egon Ronay star in 1963 and 1964, the chef was Willie Ryan who had trained in the Besson-owned Royal Hibernian Hotel in Dublin.[58]

Three Michelin-starred Irish restaurants were run by women who had no formal training. The most significant and influential was Myrtle Allen, whose arrival was announced in 1964 with an advertisement in the *Cork Examiner*—'Dine in a country house'. The Irish chef Gerry Galvin, of the Vintage, Kinsale, and Drimcong House, Galway, was greatly influenced by Allen. He once said:

> Myrtle served home cooking in a refined environment, using whatever fresh, local foods were available. This is commonplace now, but it was fairly revolutionary then. At the time, anything really good was expected to have been imported. We were still suffering from the notion that anything that was our own was inferior.[59]

Myrtle Allen published *The Ballymaloe cookbook* in 1977,[60] and in 1981 accepted an invitation to run a restaurant *La Ferme Irlandaise* in Paris which brought modern Irish food to the French capital.[61] In 1986 she became a founding member of the European chef organisation, Eurotoques International. She has arguably been one of the most influential Irish people to date in promoting Irish food.[62] Myrtle's son Tim and daughter-in-law Darina opened the Ballymaloe Cookery School in 1983, and have trained and influenced generations of chefs and restaurateurs.

The second amateur, Catherine Healy, was dubbed 'Ireland's greatest female chef'.[63] She was running a playgroup, and, when her husband Nicholas was made redundant, they opened Dunderry Lodge, which was tremendously successful throughout the 1980s and only closed when Catherine became

---

[58] Shannon Airport Restaurant and later the Shannon School of Hotel Management were set up by Brendan O'Regan, a waiter in the Stephen's Green Club, following a request by Séan Lemass. See Corr, *Hotels in Ireland*, 46–51.

[59] Joe McNamee, 'Myrtle Allen's recipe for success', *Irish Examiner*, 2 December 2013, available at: www.irishexaminer.com/lifestyle/features/myrtle-allens-recipe-for-success-251259.html (8 February 2015).

[60] Myrtle Allen, *The Ballymaloe Cookbook* (London, 1977)

[61] It is interesting to note that the loss of the Egon Ronay star in 1982 seems to arise from Myrtle focusing her energy on the Parisian restaurant. The same happened to the Ryan brothers when they were awarded a star in Cashel Palace in 1982 only to lose their three-star rating Arbutus in 1983.

[62] For further details see Mac Con Iomaire, 'The emergence', vol. 3, 92–119. (Interview with Myrtle Allen.)

[63] See www.independent.ie/lifestyle/where-to-eat-without-it-costing-an-arm-and-a-leg-26518881.html (8 February 2015).

terminally ill.[64] The third Michelin-starred restaurant, Shiro, was run by Japanese-born Kei Pilz and her German husband Werner Pilz in their house in Ahakista, Co. Cork, and again the restaurant closed following her death in 2001.[65] Other award-winning female chefs/restaurateurs include Mary Bowe (Marfield House), Maura Tighe (Cromleach Lodge), Cath Gradwell (Aldens), Mercy Fenton (Jacobs on the Mall), and 'three well-travelled ladies' (the Barn in Saintfield, Co. Down).[66]

Declan Ryan credits discerning French tourists with being the arbiters of taste at his Cork City restaurant and their arrival was facilitated by the establishment of a direct Rosslare–Le Havre ferry link in 1973. It is important also not to overlook the impact that President and Madame Charles de Gaulle's Irish holiday in Killarney and Cashel House in Galway in 1968 had on encouraging growing numbers of discerning French diners to visit Ireland in the early 1970s. Georgina Campbell notes that leading French chefs such as Paul Bocuse and Jean Troisgros came on regular fishing holidays and that Bocuse once related that a slightly undercooked dish of wild salmon served in Ernie Evans Towers Hotel in Glenbeigh was 'the birth of *Nouvelle Cuisine*'.[67]

Nouvelle cuisine and the rise of the chef/proprietor

The nouvelle cuisine movement was rooted in the '*cuisine de marché*' which originated with Fernand Point as a rebellion against the Escoffier orthodoxy, particularly as it was practised in international hotel cuisine. Point trained a generation of young French chefs such as Paul Bocuse and the Troisgros brothers after the Second World War who went on to become chef/proprietors championing this new aesthetic. In many ways, Myrtle Allen was following many of the rules of 'nouvelle cuisine' by composing her Ballymaloe menu daily based on the best local available market ingredients. By the mid-1970s and early 1980s, however, the term '*nouvelle cuisine*' had acquired a pejorative meaning of small portions artistically presented and of inflated prices. This artistic aspect reflected Japanese influence following French chefs' experience at the Tokyo Olympics in 1964 and at the Osaka Expo in 1970. This latter aesthetic reached Ireland in the early 1980s.

A synopsis of Henri Gault's 'ten commandments' of nouvelle cuisine includes: reduced cooking time for fish, game, vegetables and pasta; smaller menus based on market-fresh ingredients; new dishes; advanced technology; the aesthetics of simplicity; and a knowledge of dietetics. Stephen Mennell has pointed out that Gault and Millau omitted one key characteristic common to most *nouveaux cuisiniers*, that they were mostly chef/proprietors of their own

---

[64] 'Nick Healy—accomplished chef and front of house man acclaimed at Dunderry Lodge', *Irish Times*, 9 June 2012, obituary, 14.

[65] The background to Shiro is available in Mac Con Iomaire, 'The emergence', vol. 3, 363–83. (Interview with Frank Corr.)

[66] Egon Ronay, *Egon Ronay's Dunlop 1975 guide to Great Britain and Ireland* (London, 1974), 721.

[67] Georgina Campbell, 'Development of Irish food and hospitality', in Georgina Campbell (ed.), *Egon Ronay's Jameson guide 1994 Ireland* (London, 1994), 97.

restaurants. The significance of chef/proprietors mirrors the gradual rise in the status of chefs and their changing public profile. This would culminate in the 1990s with the cult of the 'celebrity chef'. In cities, many of the new restaurants opened not in the centre but in the affluent suburbs.[68] Analysis of both the Egon Ronay and Michelin guides show that many of the award winners were either chef/proprietors, and/or grew much of the produce they cooked in their kitchen garden, often attached to a country house hotel. One may instance, Egon Ronay's description of Armstrong's Barn in Wicklow in 1975:

> the chef owes his training and success to the proprietor, Peter Robinson, who spent ten years in France and Switzerland before buying the Barn two years ago. ... Everything is fresh and Mr Robinson scours the countryside for produce; even driving daily to meet trawlers landing their catch. The result is the best local materials available with meticulous care and attention to detail.[69]

Robinson subsequently moved to Sneem, Co. Kerry, and was awarded stars for the Blue Bull in 1979 and 1980 (Table 3).

The magic combination seems to have been Irish ingredients, French culinary practice, and warm Irish hospitality. Ballylickey House Hotel at the head of Bantry Bay in County Cork developed from the Franco–Irish Graves family's seventeenth-century private home. Egon Ronay noted that Mrs Graves's French touch showed in the chic décor, the antique furniture, flower arrangements and exquisite lighting. He concluded 'where three French chefs set to work on fine ingredients so plentiful in Ireland the results are likely to be memorable: that is what happens here.... Things like fresh salmon in sorrel sauce, terrines, soups, follow each other from the kitchen in a tantalising procession, served by charming, gentle girls'. In Newport House in County Mayo, 'young French and Irish chefs under the close supervision of the proprietor's wife Mrs. Momford-Smith' cooked locally caught salmon and trout, the hotel's own livestock and garden produce.[70] Few city restaurants possessed kitchen gardens but specialist suppliers of game, fish and herbs began to respond to demand from haute cuisine restaurants both urban and rural.[71]

One of the first Dublin restaurants to be opened by a chef/proprietor was The King Sitric (Aidan McManus) in Howth (1971 to the present). This was followed by The Mirabeau (Sean Kinsella) in Sandycove (1972–84), Johnny's (Johnny Opperman) in Malahide (1974–89), Le Coq Hardi (John

---

[68] Henri Gault, 'Nouvelle Cuisine', in Harlan Walker (ed.), *Cooks and other people: proceedings of the Oxford Symposium on Food and Cookery 1995* (Devon, 1996), 123–7. Mennell, *All manners*, 164; Máirtín Mac Con Iomaire, 'The changing geography and fortunes of Dublin's *haute cuisine* restaurants 1958–2008', *Food, Culture & Society* 14:4 (2011), 525–45.

[69] Ronay, *1975 guide*, 721–2.

[70] Ronay, *1975 guide*, 722; Egon Ronay, *Egon Ronay's 1974 guide* (London, 1974), 679.

[71] La Rousse Foods was set up in the early 1990s by Marc Amand, while working as sous chef in Restaurant Patrick Guilbaud; see www.laroussefoods.ie (8 February 2015).

Howard) in Ballsbridge (1977–2001), The Guinea Pig (Mervyn Stewart) in Dalkey (1977 to the present), and Rolland (Henri Rolland) in Killiney (1974–*c.* 1986).[72] Most of these chef/proprietors were classically trained in Dublin and abroad. Sean Kinsella is widely regarded as Ireland's first 'celebrity chef' as he actively courted media attention. His style was emulated by Mervyn Stewart who realised that restaurateurs also needed to be active in marketing their business.[73] Three restaurants, all of which opened in the 1980s, can be said to best represent the nouvelle cuisine movement in Dublin. They are Restaurant Patrick Guilbaud, The Park (Colin O'Daly), and White's on the Green (Michael Clifford) (Table 3). The 1980s were a difficult time for fine-dining restaurants in Ireland, as cheaper establishments such as pizzerias and ethnic restaurants became popular.

Patrick Guilbaud, a French-born chef, trained in the leading restaurants in Paris before moving to the Egon Ronay one-starred Midland Hotel, Manchester, in order to learn English. He eventually opened his own restaurant in Cheshire where one of his customers, Barton Kilcoyne, invited him to visit Dublin. He soon moved to Dublin and opened a purpose-built restaurant, designed by architect Arthur Gibney, which set standards in dining that had been missing since the Jammet era.[74] A description of Restaurant Patrick Guilbaud in the *Irish Times* in 1982 is brief: 'the restaurant is bright and elegant with French staff serving French food'.[75] The restaurant did not enjoy immediate commercial success; it took a while for the Irish clientele to become accustomed to the small portions and *la nouvelle cuisine d'Irlande* served by Guilbaud. However, the restaurant did receive critical acclaim, being awarded an Egon Ronay star in 1983. The early 1980s proved to be a difficult time for Irish restaurateurs due to a combination of general economic conditions and fiscal changes made by the government (23% value added tax on meals). Restaurant Patrick Guilbaud ran into financial difficulties in the mid-1980s, but an investment by two wealthy clients cleared the restaurant's debts. Their trust was rewarded when the restaurant won its first Michelin star in 1989—the first Dublin Michelin star since the closure of The Russell Hotel in 1974 (Table 4). The restaurant was awarded two Michelin stars in 1996 and it moved premises in 1997 to the five-star Merrion Hotel where it is now located.[76] During the last two decades of the twentieth century Restaurant Patrick Guilbaud set the standard of haute cuisine that other restaurants emulated. Its kitchen and

---

[72] Henri Rolland was the son of the famous Pierre Rolland from The Russell Hotel.

[73] Mac Con Iomaire, 'The emergence', vol. 3, 627–47. (Interviews with Sean Kinsella and Mervyn Stewart.)

[74] For a more detailed discussion of Guilbaud's and the other Dublin Restaurants, see Mac Con Iomaire, 'The emergence', vol. 2, 326–98; vol. 3, 593–603 (interview with Patrick Guilbaud).

[75] *Irish Times*, 2 June 1982, 7.

[76] A trend re-emerged towards the end of the twentieth century for five-star hotels to entice Michelin-starred chefs to locate their restaurants in the hotels. This was the case with Peacock Alley which moved from South William Street to the Fitzwilliam Hotel. It was eventually replaced by Thornton's Restaurant which moved from Portobello.

TABLE 4—Irish restaurants awarded Michelin star (*) or red 'M' 1974–89. (Source: *Michelin Guide to Great Britain and Ireland* (Watford, Herts, 1974–89).)

Name of establishment	1974	1975	1976	1977	1978	1979	1980	1981	1982	1983	1984	1985	1986	1987	1988	1989
Cork																
Ballylickey House, Co. Cork		*														
Arbutus Lodge, Cork City	*	*	*	*	*	*	*	*	*	*				*	*	
Ballymaloe House, Co. Cork		*	*	*	*	*	*	M	M	M	M	M	M	M	M	M
Shiro, Ahakista, Co. Cork															M	M
Vintage, Kinsale, Co. Cork										M	M					
Longueville House, Co. Cork								M	M	M	M	M	M	M	M	M
Lovetts, Cork City								M	M	M	M	M	M			
Dublin																
Russell Hotel, Dublin	*															
Rolland, Killiney, Co. Dublin					M	M	M									
Restaurant Patrick Guilbaud, Dublin															*	
Kerry																
Park Hotel Kenmare, Co. Kerry										*	*	*	*	*	*	*
Doyle's Dingle, Co. Kerry										M	M	M	M	M	M	M
Towers Glenbeigh, Co. Kerry					M	M										
Republic of Ireland (continued)																
Cashel Palace, Co. Tipperary									*	*						
Chez Hans, Cashel, Co. Tipperary								M	M	*		M	M			
Dunderry Lodge, Co. Meath								M	M	M	M	M	*	*	*	*
Marlfield House, Co. Wexford								M	M	M	M	M	M	M	M	M
Armstrong's Barn, Co. Wicklow					*		M	M								
Mustard Seed, Co. Limerick																M
Drimcong House, Co. Galway													M	M	M	M
MacCloskey's, Bunratty, Co. Clare														M	M	M
Northern Ireland																
Blades, Comber, Co. Down					M	M	M									
Ramore, Portrush, Co. Antrim													M	M	M	M

dining room also acted as nurseries for young talent, both Irish and foreign-born. Some restaurants even advertised that their chef was 'ex-Patrick Guilbaud's' as a marker of the high standard of food that they served.

Many young Irish chefs and waiters emigrated during the 1980s although some, such as Kevin Thornton, Michael Clifford, Ross Lewis, Robbie Millar and Paul Rankin, returned during the late 1980s and early 1990s with knowledge of nouvelle cuisine and fusion cuisine gained in the leading restaurants of London, Paris, New York, California and Canada.[77] They

---

[77] Paul and Jeanne Rankin built a restaurant empire which once employed 500 staff but by 2008 they had been forced to sell all but one establishment, named 'Cayenne', which replaced Roscoff around 2000 (see Table 6).

brought a new energy and confidence to the Irish restaurant industry on their return. Both Rankin and Clifford trained with the Roux Brothers in London, and Thornton with Paul Bocuse in Lyon.[78] In 1988 Clifford left White's on the Green to open his own restaurant in Cork. The late 1980s and early 1990s saw the opening of exciting new restaurants in Dublin such as The Wine Epergne (Kevin Thornton) and Clarets (Alan O'Reilly), both of which produced fine dining in difficult economic conditions. They were joined by Ernie Evans of the Towers Hotel in Glenbeigh, who opened Ernie's in Donnybrook. During the 1990s clusters of award-winning restaurants appeared in Dublin, Cork, Kerry and Belfast with individual restaurants emerging in a number of other counties around Ireland (Table 5). Restaurants run by a chef/proprietor were now the norm, though not all were financially successful.[79] One factor, which led to the growing popularity of dining out in Irish restaurants and the rising status of Irish chefs, was the growth in food writing in the national press from the 1980s. Restaurant reviewers such as Helen Lucy Burke in the *Sunday Tribune* became powerfully influential in the industry. Publications such as *Food and Wine Magazine* also profiled Irish chefs and reviewed restaurants and presided over annual award ceremonies.[80]

'New Irish cooking': a second 'golden age' of haute cuisine restaurants (1994–2014)

The *Irish Times* reported in 1996 that Ireland had the most dynamic cuisine of any European country, a place where in the last decade 'a vibrant almost unlikely style of cooking has emerged'.[81] This dynamism was manifesting on both sides of the border. Restaurant Roscoff, opened by Paul and Jeanne Rankin in 1989, won its first Michelin star in 1991.[82] According to Rankin, 'Roscoff was really the first proper restaurant in Belfast. It gave people an excuse to come back to the city—to forget about the Troubles and feel like they could be dining in London or New York'.[83] Factors influencing this new dynamism included the rising wealth of Irish citizens which made dining in

---

[78] Sandy O'Byrne, 'Cooking come home: is it time for Irish cuisine to come of age?', *Irish Times,* 3 December 1988, 23.

[79] Both O'Daly and Clifford's restaurants went bankrupt; Café Paradiso, a world renowned vegetarian restaurant opened in October 1993 in the Lancaster Quay building that once housed Clifford's. O'Daly went on to success with Roly's Bistro in Dublin.

[80] The Irish Food Writers Guild was formed in 1990 to promote high professional standards of knowledge and practice among food writers—see www.irishfoodwriters-guild.ie (8 February 2015).

[81] John McKenna, 'Euro nosh', *Irish Times,* 26 June 1996, 44.

[82] The couple had worked in Albert Roux's Michelin-starred London restaurant, *Le Gavroche.* They attracted young keen chefs from all over Ireland, such as Neven Maguire, Robbie Millar and Dylan McGrath, who went on to work or open some of the restaurants listed in Tables 5 and 6. They closed Roscoff and relaunched it as a more casual restaurant Cayenne which won a Michelin red 'M' from 2001until it closed in 2013.

[83] Interview with Paul Rankin in *Daily Mail,* 18 March 2010, available at: www.dailymail.co.uk/travel/article-1258134/St-Patricks-Day-Its-Guinness-Belfast-Irish-chef-Paul-Rankin.html#ixzz2qWANN100 (8 February 2015).

TABLE 5—Restaurants awarded a Michelin red 'M' in 1990–2014. (Source: *Michelin Guide to Great Britain and Ireland* (Watford, Herts, 1990–2014).)

Name of establishment	1990	1991	1993	1994	1995	1996	1997	1998	1999	2000	2001	2002	2003	2004	2005	2006	2007	2008	2009	2010	2011	2012	2013	2014
Dublin																								
Ernie's, Donnybrook	M			M		M	M	M	M	M	M													
The Park, Blackrock		M	M	M	M																			
Clarets, Blackrock			M	M	M																			
Blueberry's, Blackrock																								
Jacobs Ladder (The Pigs Ear 2010), D.2									M	M	M	M		M	M	M			M	M	M	M	M	M
Lloyd's Brasserie, D.2									M	M	M													
Mermaid Café, Dame Street									M	M	M	M												
Morel's at Stephens Hall, Leeson Street									M	M	M													
Roly's Bistro, Ballsbridge, D. 4						M	M	M																
Morels (Duzy's Café in 2001), Glasthule							M	M	M	M	M	M	M											
La Maison (de Gourmet until 2010)														M	M	M	M	M	M	M	M			
Bang Café, Merrion Row, D. 2														M	M	M	M	M						
The Winding Stair, D. 1																		M	M	M	M	M	M	M
Pichet, D. 2																					M	M	M	
Box Tree, Stepaside, Co. Dublin																							M	M
Downstairs at Gilbert & Wright, Clontarf																								
Brasserie at Bon Appétit, Malahide																								M
Republic of Ireland (continued)																								
Longueville House, Co. Cork	M	M	M																					
Ballymaloe House, Co. Cork	M	M	M	M																				
Cliffords, Cork City	M	M	M	M	M																			
Skippers, Kinsale, Co. Cork		M																						
Rectory, Glandore, Co. Cork						M																		
Jacobs on the Mall, Cork City										M	M	M	M	M										
Casino House, Kilbrittain, Co. Cork										M	M	M	M	M	M	M	M	M	M	M				
Fishy Fishy Café, Kinsale, Co. Cork												M	M	M	M	M	M	M	M	M	M	M	M	M

TABLE 5 (*cont.*)—Restaurants awarded a Michelin red 'M' in 1990–2014. (Source: *Michelin Guide to Great Britain and Ireland* (Watford, Herts, 1990–2014).)

Name of establishment	1990	1991	1992	1993	1994	1995	1996	1997	1998	1999	2000	2001	2002	2003	2004	2005	2006	2007	2008	2009	2010	2011	2012	2013	2014
Customs House, Baltimore, Co. Cork											M	M	M	M	M	M	M	M	M	M					
Good Things Café, Durrus, Co. Cork																M	M	M	M	M	M	M	M		
Deasy's, Clonakilty, Co. Cork																								M	M
Doyle's Seafood, Dingle, Co. Kerry	M	M		M	M	M	M	M	M																
The Chart House, Dingle, Co. Kerry											M		M	M	M	M	M	M	M	M	M	M	M	M	M
The Lime Tree, Kenmare, Co. Kerry			M	M				M	M							M	M	M	M	M					
D'Arcys, Kenmare, Co. Kerry						M	M	M	M																
An Leath Phingin, Kenmare, Co. Kerry										M	M	M	M	M		M	M								
Loaves and Fishes, Caherdaniel, Co. Kerry							M																		
Drimcong House, Co. Galway	M	M		M	M																				
Archway, Galway City											M	M													
O'Dowds, Roundstone, Co. Galway																					M	M	M		
Mustard Seed, Adare, Co. Limerick	M	M		M	M	M																			
White Sage, Adare, Co. Limerick																					M	M	M	M	
MacCloskey's, Bunratty, Co. Clare	M	M		M	M	M	M																		
Wild Honey Inn, Lisdoonvarna, Co. Clare																					M	M	M	M	M
Marfield House, Gorey, Co. Wexford	M	M		M	M																				
Aldridge Lodge, Duncannon, Co. Wexford																		M	M	M	M	M	M	M	M
The Tannery, Dungarvan, Co. Waterford										M	M	M	M	M	M	M									
O'Brien Chop House, Lismore, Co. Waterford																					M	M	M	M	
Tyrells, Edenderry, Co. Offaly														M											

TABLE 5 (*cont.*)—Restaurants awarded a Michelin red 'M' in 1990–2014. (Source: *Michelin Guide to Great Britain and Ireland* (Watford, Herts, 1990–2014).)

Name of establishment	1990	1991	1993	1994	1995	1996	1997	1998	1999	2000	2001	2002	2003	2004	2005	2006	2007	2008	2009	2010	2011	2012	2013	2014
Sha Roe Bistro, Clonegall, Co. Offaly																		M	M	M	M	M	M	M
Zuni, Kilkenny City												M	M											
Cromleach Lodge, Co. Sligo			M	M	M	M	M	M	M															
Chez Hans (Café Hans 2005), Co. Tipperary						M									M	M	M	M	M	M	M			
Rosso, Dundalk, Co. Louth																			M	M	M			
Courthouse, Carrickmacross, Co. Monaghan																							M	M
Northern Ireland																								
Ramore, Portrush, Co. Antrim	M	M	M	M	M	M	M	M	M	M	M													
Deanes Brasserie, Belfast, Co. Antrim										M	M	M	M	M	M	M	M							
Aldens, Belfast, Co. Antrim										M	M	M	M	M	M	M								
Fontana, Hollywood, Co. Down										M	M	M	M	M	M	M	M	M	M					
Distillers Arms, Bushmills, Co. Antrim														M										
Restaurant 23, Warrenpoint, Co. Down																		M	M	M	M	M	M	
Oregano, Ballyclare, Co. Antrim																				M	M	M	M	M
Home, Belfast, Co. Antrim																							M	
Coppi, Belfast, Co. Antrim																								M

restaurants a regular pastime rather than an occasional treat, and also the changing tastes of a public who were more widely travelled than any previous Irish generation. In 1996 the year Michelin awarded two stars to Restaurant Patrick Guilbaud; Thornton's Restaurant in Portobello received its first star. New stars awarded to Shanks and Deane's in Northern Ireland coincided with an air of hope that emerged following the beginning of the peace process (Table 6). In 1998 another Michelin star was awarded to Conrad Gallagher's Peacock Alley. By 1999 the chief executive of the Restaurant Association of Ireland declared 'we have a dining culture now, which we never did before'.[84]

In 2001 Kevin Thornton became the first Irish chef to be awarded two Michelin stars. In the first years of the new millennium Michelin stars were awarded in Dublin to L'Écrivain (Derry Clarke) and to Chapter One (Ross Lewis) which had both held Red 'M's from the mid-1990s. Two new Michelin stars were awarded in 2008 to Bon Appétit (Oliver Dunne) in Malahide, and to Mint (Dylan McGrath) in Ranelagh. Both Dunne and McGrath trained in Ireland's best restaurants, such as The Commons, and Roscoff, then in London with Gordon Ramsay, Tom Aikens and John Burton Race. The food of these award-winning Irish chefs is often described as 'new Irish cooking' in that it champions local, seasonal, often artisan ingredients or food and presents them using their own individual flair.

In January 2011 *Le Guide du Routard*, the travel bible for the French-speaking world, praised Ireland's restaurants for being unmatched the world over for the combination of quality of food, value and service.[85] This second 'golden age' has been maintained despite the current difficult economic environment. The 2014 Michelin Guide not only awarded stars to five Dublin restaurants, but also awarded stars to four restaurants outside Dublin—the highest number of starred restaurants in Ireland since the guide was first published in 1974. In 2013, however, a number of Michelin Red 'M' restaurants closed; these included O'Brien Chop House in Lismore, Co. Waterford; White Sage in Adare, Co. Limerick; and most notably Paul Rankin's Cayenne in Belfast which had traded since 1989. The closure of the latter was blamed on Union flag protests and on the change in the Shaftsbury Square area over the last number of years.[86]

Conclusion

The projection and presentation of Irish cuisine, both foreign-influenced and home-inspired, have given it a notable public profile. Its beginnings were in French haute cuisine; its further progress came in the development of restaurants, especially in the early golden age of Dublin restaurants, the ones

---

[84] Katherine Holmquist, 'Take a top chef, place in a swanky location and stir well for a winning restaurant', *Irish Times*, 20 October 1999, 43.

[85] Bramhill, 'Irish chefs'.

[86] Lesley-Anne McKeown, 'Celebrity chef Paul Rankin blames flag protests on restaurant closure', *Irish Independent*, 26 March 2013, available at: www.independent.ie/irish-news/celebrity-chef-paul-rankin-blames-flag-protests-for-belfast-restaurant-closure-29155782.html (8 February 2015).

TABLE 6—Restaurants awarded Michelin stars in Ireland 1990–2014. (Source: *Michelin Guide to Great Britain and Ireland* (Watford, Herts, 1990–2014).)

Name of establishment	1990	1991	1992	1993	1994	1995	1996	1997	1998	1999	2000	2001	2002	2003	2004	2005	2006	2007	2008	2009	2010	2011	2012	2013	2014
Dublin																									
Rest. Patrick Guilbaud, Baggot St. (later The Merrion Hotel)	*	*	*	*	*	*	2*	2*	2*	2*	2*	2*	2*	2*	2*	2*	2*	2*	2*	2*	2*	2*	2*	2*	2*
The Commons, St Stephen's Green					*	*	*	*					*												
Thornton's, Portobello (later Fitzwilliam Hotel)										*	*	2*	2*	2*	2*	2*	*	*	*	*	*	*	*	*	*
L'Ecrivain, Baggot St.							M	M	M	M	*	*	*	*	*	*	*	*	*	*	*	*	*	*	*
Peacock Alley, SthWilliam St. (Fitzwilliam)									*	*	*	*	*												
Chapter One, Parnell Square, D. 1							M	M	M	M	M	M						*	*	*	*	*	*	*	*
Bon Appétit, Malahide																			*	*	*	*	*	*	*
Mint, Ranelagh, D. 6																			*	*					
Locks Brasserie, Portobello																			M	M					
Republic of Ireland (continued)																									
The Park Hotel, Kenmare, Co. Kerry	*								*																
Sheen Falls, Kenmare, Co. Kerry				M	*	*	*	*	*																
The K Club, Straffan, Co. Kildare				M	*	*	*	*	*																
Dromoland Castle, Co. Clare						*																			
Shiro, Ahakista, Co. Cork	M	M	M	M	M	M	*	*	*	*	*	*													
Erriseask House, Co. Galway									M	M	*	*													
Cliff House, Ardmore, Co. Waterford																					*	*	*	*	*
Aniar, Galway City																								*	*
Lady Helen Rest., Mount Juliet, Co. Kilkenny																								*	*
Campagne, Kilkenny City																									*

Table 6 (*cont.*)—Restaurants awarded Michelin stars in Ireland 1990–2014. (Source: *Michelin Guide to Great Britain and Ireland* (Watford, Herts, 1990–2014).)

Name of establishment	1990	1991	1992	1993	1994	1995	1996	1997	1998	1999	2000	2001	2002	2003	2004	2005	2006	2007	2008	2009	2010	2011	2012	2013	2014
Northern Ireland																									
Roscoff (Cayenne), Belfast, Co. Antrim		*	*	*	*	*	*	*	*			M	M	M	M	M	M	M	M	M	M	M	M	M	M
Shanks, Bangor, Co. Down							*	*	*	*	*	*	*	*	*	*									
Deanes, Belfast, Co. Antrim								*	*	*	*	*	*	*	*	*	*	*	*	*	*				
Oriel, Gilford, Co. Down															*	*									

so strongly influenced by French families such as the Jammets, Bessons and Rollands, all of whom adopted Ireland as home. The latest important French influence is prospering: Patrick Guilbaud was advised that if his restaurant was half as successful as Jammet's had been, he would be doing extremely well. Restaurant Patrick Guilbaud, now in its thirtieth year in business, has already outlasted The Russell Restaurant in longevity but has another 37 years to go to equal Jammet's as the most influential and successful haute cuisine restaurant Ireland has had. There is a neat symbolism involved in Patrick Guilbaud's purchase of the Harry Kernoff painting of Jammet's: it signifies both continuity and tradition; it ties haute cuisine to Irish imagery, and it reflects the degree to which French influence has dominated Irish public imagination in that most important area over two centuries.

Beef with potatoes: food, agriculture and sustainability in modern Ireland

FRANK ARMSTRONG*

[Accepted 19 September 2014. Published 17 June 2015.]

Abstract

Shared consumption of food can generate a sense of belonging among a group with those eating together developing a sense of 'we', as opposed to 'they'. The content of the shared meal can then emerge as a metaphor for a wider social formation. We call this cultural institution commensality. Shared meals are evolving rituals that form and reproduce families, confessional groups and social classes. Until recently Irish identity was not expressed overtly through food. This is a legacy of inter alia painful famine, stoic Catholicism and the enduring influence of a wider British culture. The nineteenth century shift in agriculture from tillage to pasture, due to a change in British demand, shaped not only our food culture but also the wider economy and demographic patterns. Priorities have not changed since then. The development of 'alternative agriculture', drawing on a variety of international toolkits, has the potential to increase employment, lower agricultural emissions and perhaps improve the health of the population, thereby producing a food culture in which we can take pride.

Food on the mind

It may be an exaggeration to say that interest in food in Ireland has never been higher. Its acquisition was a far greater preoccupation in the past. Nonetheless, it is probably accurate to say that interest in food as a source of identity, health and entertainment has never been so significant. The Irish population enjoys unparalleled access to an unprecedented array of comestibles and coverage of issues pertaining to food in print journalism, television and across the internet shows no sign of abating. Restaurants continue to be major employers as food emporia and farmers' markets burgeon, and the number of recipe books written by Irish-based chefs since the 1980s has grown exponentially. Food production is a mainstay of the economy with Ireland's agri-food sector generating significant export revenue.

Yet, most farms in Ireland actually lose money while food poverty now affects over 10% of the population.[1] Conversely, on average two in five adults

---

* Author's e-mail: frankarmstrong2@yahoo.com

doi: 10.3318/PRIAC.2015.115.05

[1] Mandate, *Hungry for action: mapping food poverty in Ireland* (Dublin, 2013), available at: www.mandate.ie/Documents/104355_food_poverty_document4.pdf (last accessed 5 February 2015).

are defined as clinically obese[2] with this condition projected to afflict as much as 90% of the country's population by 2030.[3] Furthermore, the estimated proportion of greenhouse gas emissions in Ireland emanating from agriculture is second only to New Zealand's. This is primarily due to long-term emphasis on and heavy subsidisation of foods derived from cattle (meat and dairy), predominantly for export. Grants to pastoral farmers drives up the cost of land inhibiting the cultivation of a diverse range of crops for direct human consumption. Horticulture and tillage enjoy little support from the state.

Allowing for how interest in food is at an all-time high, there is general acknowledgment that Ireland has an undeveloped culture of food compared to most European countries. This has been attributed simplistically to colonisation (as earlier papers in this collection attest), and it has been suggested that a 'heroic' food tradition could have been recovered.[4] The identification and celebration of specifically 'Irish' food did not figure prominently in the construction of Irishness that occurred at the end of the nineteenth century. Crucially, with the inception of the state, agriculture was identified as a primary source of export revenue thereby perpetuating a pattern of development that can be traced to the end of the Napoleonic wars when a reduction in the price of grain on the British market created economic conditions in Ireland favouring cattle over corn. The potato has long been identified with the Irish people but it is not a cherished foodstuff and early nationalists were more concerned with promoting self-sufficiency in wheat, perhaps due to some extent to the latter's symbolic association with Christianity. The Great Famine remains a largely unexplored trauma in terms of the Irish relationship with food and the land.

The nation plate

Consumption of food is never simply a matter of ingesting calories: 'nutrition can always to some extent be explained in cultural and sociological terms'.[5] Human beings survive on a wide variety of available foodstuffs, and 'taste' is the product of culture. 'Commensality', according to Emiko Ohnuki-Tierney, is 'a crucial cultural institution whereby people who eat together become, "we," as opposed to "they," and the food shared becomes a metaphor for the social group'.[6] This common appreciation for particular dishes and individual foodstuffs plays an important role in an individual's 'belonging' to a family,

---

[2] Irish Heart Foundation, *Obesity fact sheet* (Dublin, 2011), available at: www. irishheart.ie/iopen24/pub/factsheets/obesity_fact_sheet.pdf (5 February 2015).

[3] L. Keaver, L. Webber, A. Dee, F. Shiely, T. Marsh, K. Balanda and I. J. Perry, 'Application of the UK foresight obesity model in Ireland: the health and economic consequences of projected obesity trends in Ireland', *PLos One* 8:11 (2013), available at: www.ncbi.nlm.nih.gov/pubmed/24236162 (5 February 2015).

[4] See A. T. Lucas, 'Irish food before the Famine', *Gwerin* 3 (1960–2), 8–43 and Hasia R. Diner, *Hungering for America: Italian, Irish, and Jewish foodways in the age of migration* (Cambridge, 2002), 103–04.

[5] Hans J. Teuteberg, 'Agenda for a comparative European history of diet', in Hans J. Teuteberg (ed.), *European food history: a research review* (Leicester, 1992), 4.

[6] Emiko Ohnuki-Tierney, *Rice as self—Japanese identities through time* (Princeton, NJ, 1993), 9.

confessional group, social class or nation. Indeed a social formation can also maintain a perceived integrity through renunciation of external, alien food-stuffs. A meal confers more than mere sustenance, creating intimacy 'for which it is hard to find parallels in the natural world'.[7] It forges close bonds, as does the idea of entire communities consuming similar food even in the absence of direct encounters.

The consumption of certain foodstuffs also expresses social rank. Jack Goody notes that hautes cuisines only develop in highly stratified, highly differentiated, socially unequal, complex societies.[8] Stephen Mennell concurs, suggesting: 'People have always used foods in their attempts to climb the social ladder themselves, and to push other people down the ladder'.[9]

The status of foodstuffs varies radically, some cultures prizing staple cereal crops others esteeming animal products. In Europe, meat consumption was identified with aristocracy, but elsewhere elite groups such as Brahmans in India, the highest Hindu caste, avoid it altogether. As Sidney Mintz puts it: 'What constitutes "good food", like what constitutes good weather, a good spouse, or a fulfilling life, is a social, not a biological matter'.[10]

Anderson defined the nation as:

> an imagined political community—and imagined as both inherently limited and sovereign . . . it is imagined because the members of even the smallest nation will know most of their fellow members, meet them, or even hear of them, yet in the minds of each lives the image of the communion.[11]

[7] Martin Jones, *Feast* (Oxford, 2007), 24.

[8] Jack Goody, *Cooking cuisine and class: a study in comparative sociology* (Cambridge, 1982), 105.

[9] Stephen Mennell, *All manners of food: eating and taste in England and France from the Middle Ages to the present* (Oxford, 1996), 17.

[10] Sidney Mintz, *Sweetness and power: the place of sugar in modern history* (New York and London, 1985), 8.

[11] Benedict Anderson, *Imagined communities: reflections on the origin and spread of nationalism* (London, 1991), 6. Anderson's interpretation is countered by the idea of an 'ethnie' espoused by Anthony Smith defined in the following terms: 'named units of population with common ancestry myths and historical memories, elements of shared culture and a shared link with a historical territory and some measure of solidarity, at least among their elites'. Such ethnies, Smith argues, form the raw material of nations. But Smith's definition throws up more questions than it answers, not least of which being: how are firm dividing lines drawn between these 'cultures' and therefore between ethnies? The indecisive language (the use of words such as 'elements' and 'some') employed in Smith's description is indicative of the difficulty of providing a satisfactory definition. Moreover, it is important to understand the extent to which ethnies are generated for exploitation by political elites: the 'cultures it [nationalism] claims to defend and revive are often its own inventions, or are modified out of all recognition' (see Ernest Gellner, *Thought and change* (London, 1964), 158–69). Anderson's model along with that articulated by Gellner and Eric Hobsbawm is therefore preferred.

A discourse of national food, where accumulated culinary skill connects to agricultural production within a defined geographic area, has emerged as an important source of identity in many national contexts. Thus, so important was Japanese-grown rice to being Japanese that during the Second World War it was sent to soldiers at far distant fronts. Yet, until the seventeenth century, it was not a widespread staple[12] and the crop is not indigenous.[13] Interestingly, these are two features it shares with the potato in Ireland.

The development of national dishes is also closely connected to the advance of a written culture facilitated by the invention of movable type. This allowed recipe books to be easily printed homogenising previously more haphazard combinations: 'the standardization of typography also spelt out the standardization of food'.[14] This process is apparent in Italy where a national cuisine owes a considerable debt to the writings of Pellegrino Artusi, especially *La Scienza in Cucina e l'Arte di Mangiar Bene* (1891), which 'deemphasised regional styles and elevated the cuisine of the middle classes as the embodiment of Italian food';[15] in the process defining an archetypal Italian cuisine. It is a mark of the novelty and flexibility of Italian cuisine that the word pizzeria is not recorded in an Italian dictionary until 1958,[16] while the beloved pomodoro is, like the potato, a member of the nightshade (*Solanaceae*) family that originates in South America.[17] The invention of Italian food was one way of differentiating the idea of Italy from that of France considering their close linguistic, political and geographical proximity. According to Dickie: 'Italian food would not be Italian food without the French'.[18] But even French cuisine as we now perceive it is a recent and constantly evolving idea. Stephen Mennell writes: 'There is a great deal of evidence that until into the twentieth century, soup was the staple dish of every meal (including breakfast) for the majority of Frenchmen'.[19] National cuisines evolve continuously.

Eating Irish

For much of the twentieth century Irish mealtimes seem to have been functional affairs. Families sat down together—to a greater extent than today—generally to a meal featuring potatoes, bread or other carbohydrate-rich staple, and perhaps a narrow range of vegetables and meat, though in some families the

---

[12] Fernand Braudel, *The structures of everyday life* (3 vols, Berkeley, CA, 1979), vol. 1, 147.

[13] Ohnuki-Tierney, *Rice as self*, 8.

[14] Jack Goody, 'Recipe, prescription and experiment', in Carole Counihan and Penny van Esterik (eds), *Food and culture: a reader*, 2nd edition (New York, 2008), 338.

[15] Diner, *Hungering for America*, 28.

[16] John Dickie, *Delizia: the epic history of Italians and their food* (London, 2007), 209.

[17] This affirms David Inglis and Debra Gimlin's contention that 'supposedly authentically "national" food cultures were made possible by a collective amnesia as to the originally non-indigenous origins of certain foods': David Inglis and Debra Gimlin, 'Food globalizations: ironies and ambivalences of food, cuisine and globality', in David Inglis and Debra Gimlin (eds), *The globalization of food* (Oxford, 2009), 12.

[18] Dickie, *Delizia*, 191.

[19] Mennell, *All manners of food*, 48.

presence of the latter would depend on the time of the month. Fish was penitential food consumed on Fridays. Tony Kiely describes Dublin working-class meals in the 1950s as follows: 'Family diets were very basic, consisting in the main of bread, tea, oatmeal, cocoa, potatoes, cabbage, herrings and pairings of cheap meat pieces for stews and soups ... Bread was both a staple, and a constant companion at all meals'.[20] The contents seem to have elicited little critical appraisal though, importantly, many women drew considerable pride from preparing home-cooked meals and felt a sense of loss when this task was denied to them. One of the leading light of Irish cookery Darina Allen admits of her childhood: 'It was rare at that time for people to talk about food—they just ate it'.[21] Anthony Farmar suggests that an absolute rule among the Irish middle class in the 1960s was never to talk about food: 'to enjoy eating as such was unbecoming to a serious person'. He quotes an American commentator who claimed cooking in Ireland was 'a necessary chore rather than an artistic ceremony, and that in restaurants "nine out of ten ordered steak every time with nine out of ten ordering chips with it"'.[22] Although most professional chefs at the time were male, in the domestic arena, overwhelmingly, it was women who prepared meals. The absence of men from domestic kitchens may be a sign of a culture in which food preparation is awarded a low status.

From the formation of the Irish state until as late of the 1990s, the majority of the Irish population adhered to a devout and often austere form of Catholicism where the original meaning of the sin of gluttony, which encompassed both excessive eating and of the wider appreciation of food, dwelt in the collective consciousness. Moreover, the impoverishing effects of prolonged colonisation sustained a reduced domestic market for sophisticated cuisine and stymied 'alternative agriculture'.[23] Alternative agriculture is here defined as the cultivation of foodstuffs originally for reasons of gastronomic pleasure and/or health as opposed to basic sustenance though, over time, such foodstuffs can occupy a more central nourishing role. This probably occurred with the potato. It is argued that the level of agricultural experimentation that this entails is a prerequisite for the development of a native gastronomy. To a large extent this did not occur in Ireland: since the incorporation of Ireland into the British political orbit in the seventeenth century the country's produce was a resource to be exploited. Brutally satirised by Jonathan Swift in *A modest proposal*, this resulted in the development of a commercial relationship with food in the advanced market economy of the British Empire. The Act of Union 1801 accelerated this process as a substantial number of landlords, a class who

[20] Tony Kiely, '"We managed": reflections on the culinary practices of Dublin's working class poor in the 1950s', in Máirtín Mac Con Iomaire and Eamon Maher (eds), *'Tickling the palate', gastronomy in Irish literature and culture* (Oxford, 2014), 108.

[21] Darina Allen, *Forgotten skills of cookery: the time-honoured ways are best—over 700 recipes show you why* (London, 2007) 2.

[22] Anthony Farmar, *Privileged lives: a social history of middle class Ireland 1882–1989* (Dublin, 1991), 180–2.

[23] For a history of alternative agriculture in Britain and beyond see Joan Thirsk, *Alternative agriculture: a history from the Black Death to the present day* (Oxford 1997).

could have encouraged and supported this kind of agriculture, left the country.[24]

Among the post-Great Famine diaspora, there is little evidence of recreation or reinvention of native dishes. Panikos Panayi claims that in Britain: 'Irish food did not have enough distinction from that of the ethnic majority to warrant the opening of specifically designated food shops'.[25] According to Henry Mayhew, the newcomers began to move away from potato-eating and to adopt the same food patterns as the rest of the working class.[26] Poverty alone does not explain this phenomenon as other impoverished immigrant groups reinvented their 'national' cuisines, especially in the New World. Regarding nineteenth-century Irish–American immigrants, Hasia R. Diner says: 'They rarely talked about food, neither did they sing about it, nor did it contribute to community institutions and rituals'.[27]

It appears that before the Great Famine Irish immigrants showed a greater attachment to the foods of their homeland, or at least the dominant staple: consignments of potatoes were frequently advertised in colonial newspapers and there are accounts of immigrants longing for the taste of home.[28] It may be that the Great Famine not only changed the Irish relationship with their primary staple, but also stunted a wider appreciation of food.

Aping appreciation

The Irish nationalist 'awakening' of the late nineteenth and early twentieth century sought to recover Ireland's native language, and sponsored a literary and later a musical dynamism that earned a global reputation. The Gaelic Athletic Association devised new sporting codes that countered the influence of so-called 'garrison games'. But the idea of food conferring identity did not register in this narrative.[29] Self consciously, Irish recipe books emerged only after independence. Most Irish nationalists did not view eating distinctively Irish food as an important cultural marker, except perhaps when it came to eating bread made from home-grown wheat. Thus, in a pamphlet addressed to the women of Ireland, the writer and Irish-language activist Mary Butler crafted a list of fifteen ways in which to foster authentic Irishness in their homes.[30]

---

[24] In 1870 there were some 130,000 landlords, one-third of whom lived outside of the country. John Feehan, *Farming in Ireland* (Dublin, 2003), 124. Máirtín Mac Con Iomaire, 'The emergence, development and influence of French haute cuisine on public dining in Dublin restaurants 1990–2000: an oral history', unpublished PhD thesis, Dublin Institute of Technology, 2009 (3 vols), vol. 2, 52.

[25] Panikos Panayi, *The multicultural history of British food* (London, 2008), 43.

[26] Panayi, *The multicultural history of British food*, 44.

[27] Diner, *Hungering for America*, 114.

[28] Louis M. Cullen, *The emergence of modern Ireland 1600–1900* (London, 1981), 159.

[29] In Bruce Nelson's *Irish nationalists and the making of the Irish race* (Princeton, NJ, 2012), the subject of food is not mentioned as a marker of identity.

[30] Alan O'Day and John Stevenson, *Irish historical documents since 1800* (Dublin, 1992), 133.

Revealingly, 'no traditional recipes, foodways, food names, or food practices as instruments for building Irish identity were included'.[31]

According to Anderson, 'by the second decade of the nineteenth century if not earlier a "model" of "the" independent nation state was available for pirating'.[32] This is important in the Irish context as the model most readily accessible was English or British, a society that prized letters and sporting prowess, and in which a native culinary tradition had been 'decapitated' by the end of the nineteenth century.[33] In 1880 the surgeon and polymath Sir Henry Thompson observed:

> On questioning the average middle-class Englishman as to the nature of his food, the all but universal answer is, 'My living is plain, always roast and boiled'—words which but too clearly indicate the dreary monotony, not to say unwholesomeness, of his daily food; while they furthermore express his satisfaction, such as it is, that he is no luxurious feeder.[34]

The disinterest exhibited by the English middle and upper classes in cookery and the discussion of food was compounded by the nutritional impoverishment of its working class. Mintz estimates that by 1900 nearly one-fifth of average caloric intake came in the form of refined sugar, which was mainly consumed in tea or jam.[35] Apart from being nutritionally deficient, this diet lacked variety and bred conservatism as older traditions of food preparation yielded to bland industrial approaches. George Orwell tartly observed in *The road to Wigan pier* that: 'The English palate, especially the working class palate, now rejects good food almost automatically'.[36]

One might expect a predominantly rural people such as the Irish to manifest significant dietary diversity but from the late nineteenth century their diet corresponded ever more closely to British working fare with an emphasis on white bread or potatoes, sugar[37] and occasional cheap cuts of meat.[38] According to Margaret Crawford and Leslie Clarkson, 'Fruit and vegetables apart from potatoes, made very little impact on the labouring diets'.[39] A witness to the Commission on Irish Industry in 1884 affirmed that the primary staple of the Irish was white bread,[40] and by the eve of the First World War Irish flour

---

[31] Diner, *Hungering for America*, 84.

[32] Anderson, *Imagined communities*, 81.

[33] Mennell, *All manners of taste*, 204.

[34] Mennell, *All manners of taste*, 296.

[35] Mintz, *Sweetness and power*, 6.

[36] George Orwell, *The road to Wigan pier* (London, 1933), 132.

[37] During the second half of the nineteenth century sugar consumption increased tenfold: see Leslie Clarkson and Margaret Crawford, *Feast and famine* (Oxford, 2001), 3.

[38] Clarkson and Crawford, *Feast and famine*, 88.

[39] Clarkson and Crawford, *Feast and famine*, 107.

[40] Andy Bielenberg, 'A survey of Irish flour milling 1801–1922', in Andy Bielenberg (ed.), *Irish flour milling a history 600–2000* (Dublin, 2003), 69.

consumption was slightly higher per capita than in the rest of the United Kingdom.[41] The effect of a diet laden with white bread and sugar was a 'striking' increase in mortality from diabetes.[42]

The pre-eminent foodstuff from which social status was derived in England was beef. By the eighteenth century 'England was already the beef-eating capital of the world',[43] a significant proportion of which was imported from Ireland where most of the population was too poor to eat it.[44] The adoption of small quantities of beef and other meat in working-class diets may be interpreted, according to Mennell, as a way of 'climbing the social ladder'. One regrettable consequences of this was that purchase of expensive meat left little for the purchase of fruit and vegetables. Mintz argues: 'There are reasons to believe that the late nineteenth century diet was ... unhealthy and uneconomical' due to a 'disproportionately high expenditure on meat'. This set in train an enduring pattern: by the end of the twentieth century vegetable consumption in the United Kingdom remained the lowest in Europe.[45]

Beef's popularity among the English upper classes contributed to its high status in Ireland as manifested by 1950s dining preferences. In the absence of a gastronomic culture where subtlety and variety are prized, a foodstuff containing concentrated macronutrients (protein and fat) and micronutrients (vitamin B12, iron, selenium, and zinc) may confer a physiologically-induced satisfaction redolent of wealth and satisfaction, reinforced by an association with the machismo of the popular cinematic 'cowboy' archetype of that period. Myrtle Allen observed of dining habits in restaurants before she opened her own Ballymalloe House: 'I mean the thing was steak then, to have a steak'.[46]

With no sophisticated model of food consumption to compete against, the Irish cultural elite were not drawn to food as an expression of identity. Unlike Italians, situated within the domineering cultural orbit of French cuisine, there was little beyond an appetite for meat, beef in particular, in English gastronomic culture for Irish nationalists to pirate. This was compounded by the near extinction of many traditional foods as a result of poverty and changes to agricultural production during the Agricultural Revolution. Dickson 'suspects that much of what is today regarded as traditional Irish cuisine—soda bread, barm brack, boxty, champ, colcannon etc' was only developed in the nineteenth century 'in the kitchens of the solid farming class'.[47]

---

[41] Bielenberg, 'A survey of Irish flour milling', 70.

[42] Clarkson and Crawford, *Feast and famine*, 246.

[43] Jeremy Rifkin, *Beyond beef: the rise and fall of the cattle culture* (New York, 1992), 54.

[44] 'Beef was not an important item in the Irish diet and it is unlikely that more than 25,000 mature cattle were consumed annually on the home market': Raymond Crotty, *Irish agricultural production* (Cork, 1966), 17.

[45] Thirsk, *Alternative agriculture*, 238.

[46] Mac Con Iomaire, 'French haute cuisine on public dining in Dublin restaurants 1990–2000', 97.

[47] David Dickson, 'The potato and the Irish diet before the Great Famine', in Cormac Ó Gráda (ed.), *Famine 150 commemorative lecture series* (Dublin, 1997), 19.

The potato eaters

Exploring Irish food's cultural inheritance one cannot understate the dominance of the potato. It 'has in the minds of more than half the world, an inalienable and time-honoured association with Ireland, comparable to the age-long dependence of many Asiatic peoples on rice'.[48] Dependence culminated in the Great Famine after the failure of successive harvests from 1845 to 1849 owing to the fungus *phytophthora infestans*. Many nations are given nicknames from preferred foodstuffs from *les rosbifs*, to 'krauts' and 'frogs', but few have the deadening historical weight of the term 'potato eater'.

Ireland was the first European country to adopt the potato as a serious food crop.[49] This was an inauspicious development, according to John Reader, as 'the innocent potato has facilitated exploitation wherever it has been introduced and cultivated'.[50] The catalyst for the potato's successful adoption was the traumatic wars of the seventeenth century especially Oliver Cromwell's subjugation of Ireland (1649–53) since 'the potato could both be cultivated and stored in a manner which might intuit the spirit of destruction, and the malevolence of the enemy'.[51] If its durability contributed to its appeal, it was not without negative implications. Henry Hobhouse argues that 'of all the havoc wrought by [Oliver] Cromwell in Ireland, the by-product, the lazybed, was in the end the most damaging'.[52] A. T. Lucas denigrated the 'dark reign of the potato' for 'banishing' most other foods from the table.[53]

For the individual small farmer the advantages of the potato far outweighed any disadvantages, and the impressive growth of the Irish population in the eighteenth and early nineteenth centuries[54] would hardly have been achieved but for the availability of this crop whose yields exceeded wheat and which was suited to Ireland's moist, friable soil. The potato has a nutritional profile that allows for almost exclusive long-term consumption—unlike most cereals which lack the essential amino acid lysine—though the tuber has the drawback of a high glycaemic load.[55] The agronomist Arthur

---

[48] Radcliffe Salaman, *The history and social influence of the potato* (Cambridge, 1949), 188.

[49] Máirtín Mac Con Iomaire and Pádraic Óg Gallagher, 'The potato in Irish cuisine and culture', *Journal of Culinary Science and Technology* 7:2–3 (2009), 152–67.

[50] John Reader, *The untold history of the potato* (London, 2009), 14.

[51] Salaman, *The history and social influence of the potato*, 215.

[52] Henry Hobhouse, *Seeds of change: six plants that changed mankind* (London, 1985), 253.

[53] Cullen, *The emergence of modern Ireland*, 140.

[54] The Irish population increased from about 2 million in 1687 to 3.5 million in 1760 without 'any decline in living standards', see Crotty, *Irish agricultural production*, 15.

[55] A 2006 nurses' health study states: 'Our findings suggest a modest positive association between the consumption of potatoes and the risk of type 2 diabetes in women. This association was more pronounced when potatoes were substituted for whole grains', see Thomas L. Halton, Walter C. Willett, Simin Liu, JoAnn E. Manson, Meir J. Stampfer and Frank B. Hu, 'Potato and French fry consumption and risk of type 2 diabetes in women', *The American Journal of Clinical Nutrition* 83:2 (2006), 284–90, available at: http://ajcn.nutrition.org/content/83/2/284.full (5 February 2015).

Young who spent a number of years in Ireland in the late eighteenth century was impressed by the vitality of Irish peasants compared to their English counterparts: 'When I see the people of a country ... with well-formed vigorous bodies, and their cottages swarming with children; when I see their men athletic, and their women beautiful, I know not how to believe them subsisting on unwholesome food'.[56] Indeed, at the start of the nineteenth century Irishmen's heights were greater than those of equivalent Englishmen in a variety of occupations and situations, and life expectancy was higher than most Europeans of that time.[57] Latterly, Mary Daly has described it as 'a wonder crop—the only subsistence foodstuff which provides a nearly perfect diet, a crop which would feed a family on very little land, in almost all types of Irish soil, irrespective of rain or lack of sunshine'.[58]

However, from its position as dominant staple of the nineteenth and early twentieth centuries, the production of the potato has fallen steadily in the last half century. Small-scale agricultural cultivation is rare and regions are not associated with particular varieties. Only one Protected Geographical Indication has been awarded for a variety known as 'Comber Earlies', and this in Northern Ireland where reliance on the potato was traditionally less acute than elsewhere on the island.[59] The range cultivated has shrunk considerably since the turn of the twentieth century.[60] Irish consumers have long accepted imported potatoes while the successful application by Teagasc to trial a genetically modified variant in 2012 encountered little opposition. The Irish relationship with the potato is now a marriage of convenience.

Diner has argued that 'had the Irish celebrated the potato as the symbol of identity, they would in essence have celebrated the English stranglehold on the native lands',[61] though she fails to adduce compelling evidence to support this somewhat bombastic contention. In fact, the original name for the potato, *an spainneach*,[62] suggests some awareness of a non-English provenance. The potato has not been banished from the Irish table, it is just not the subject of gastronomic musing. This is dissimilar to polenta in Italy, which was the

---

[56] Salaman, *The history and social influence of the potato*, 260.

[57] William J. Smyth, '"Mapping the people": the growth and distribution of the population', in John Crawley, William J. Smyth and Mike Murphy (eds), *Atlas of the Great Irish Famine 1845–52* (Cork, 2012), 17.

[58] Mary Daly, 'Farming and the Famine', in Ó Gráda, *Famine 150 commemorative lecture series*, 39.

[59] European Commission Implementing Regulation No. 148/2012 of 20 February 2012.

[60] According to Feehan in *Farming in Ireland*, 512: 'In the opening years of the last century 124 varieties of potato were being grown in trials at Glasnevin: the number had dropped to 51 as early as 1916. Today no more than half a dozen varieties are grown commercially in Ireland'.

[61] Diner, *Hungering for America*, 106.

[62] Crawford and Clarkson, *Feast and famine*, 61.

primary staple for most Italians until the 1950s after which it virtually disappeared, because it was considered a sign of poverty.[63]

The absence of a devotion to the potato that might have been conveyed through dining rituals or popular sayings and superstitions is bound up with the rupture of the Great Famine, one among many periods of sustained deprivation due to the failure of the crop. Timothy O'Neill claimed in 1977: 'In no other western European country is starvation caused by crop failure so fresh in the folk memory, and many older people, are very much aware of the terror of famine'.[64] The Great Famine was devastating for the 3 million out of a population of 8 million almost exclusively dependent on it. According to Amartyra Sen: 'In no other famine in the world [was] the proportion of people killed ... as large as in the Irish famine of the 1840s'.[65]

Those unaffected by starvation bore witness to suffering on a scale that is hard for those of us living in contemporary Ireland to fathom. Joseph Lee likens its effects to the Jewish experience of the Holocaust and explores its psychological legacy:

> They will have seen corpses, if not in their own dwellings, then on the roads and in the ditches. Many are likely to have felt a degree of guilt, of the type that often afflicts survivors of tragedies, not only of the Holocaust, but of events like earthquakes and mining catastrophes. Why did you survive when others in your family did not? A sense of guilt can simmer below the surface, to perhaps breakout in uncontrollable and, to uncomprehending outside observers, in apparently inexplicable ways.[66]

Crawford and Clarkson concur; they have suggested that survivors carried psychological scars and that their physical and intellectual developments were stunted.[67]

Disturbingly, many survivors took advantage of the opportunities that the Famine presented which may have accentuated their guilt. Kerby A. Miller writes:

> an unknown but surely very large proportion of Famine sufferers were not evicted by Protestant landlords but by Catholic strong and middling farmers, who drove off their subtenants and cottiers, and dismissed their labourers and servants, both to save themselves from ruin and to consolidate their own properties.[68]

---

[63] Dickie, *Delizia*, 294.

[64] Timothy O'Neill, *Life and tradition in rural Ireland* (London, 1977), 62.

[65] Amartyra Sen, *Identity and violence: the delusions of destiny* (New York, 2006), 105.

[66] Joseph Lee, 'The Famine as history', in Ó Gráda, *Famine 150 commemorative lectures*, 168–9.

[67] Crawford and Clarkson, *Feast and famine*, 134.

[68] Kerby Miller, 'Emigration to North America in the era of the Great Famine', in Crawley, Smyth and Murphy, *Atlas of the Great Irish Famine*, 221.

Just as guilt seems to have altered Irish sexual consciousness,[69] this may have been the case also with the Irish food tradition.

It is instructive that nationalists in the first half of the twentieth century dreamed of making bread from Irish-grown wheat, thereby reducing reliance on the potato, and embracing a crop that resonated with a proudly Catholic people. Wheat may also have been considered the staple crop of a 'mature' nation. In 1935 the department of agriculture expressed the hope that: 'the time is not far distant when wholesome bread, baked at home from home-grown wheat, will form the staple food of our rural population'.[70] But the Irish relationship to domestic wheat then and now is incomparable to the symbolic importance of Japanese rice in Japan where a 778% tariff is today imposed on imported rice.[71] In Ireland, price supports for wheat-growing were phased out after the Second World War.

Commercialisation

Another reason it seems for the absence of discernible Irish gastronomic tradition is the legacy of the systematic commercialisation of agriculture. According to Hobhouse the rich, high-born in Ireland were not 'in organic unity with the countryside'. 'The Emerald Isle was a source of income, a country to be exploited'.[72] Crotty noted 'the general absence of any semblance of feudal paternalism in landlord-tenant relationships',[73] by comparison with England. The consequence was a countryside denuded of native produce, with Ireland supplying 70% of England's food imports in the early nineteenth century.[74] L. M. Cullen concurs; writing of the period prior to the Famine he has observed: 'What is most striking about the Irish economy is its high degree of commercialization and how increasingly foods which in other societies were consumed within the family were sold'.[75] Alexis de Toqueville who travelled through Ireland in the 1830s observed this in operation: 'The Irishman raises beautiful crops, carries his harvest to the nearest port, puts it on board an English vessel, and returns home to subsist on potatoes. He rears cattle, sends

---

[69] Indicative of this was the eightfold increase in the number of nuns between 1841 and 1901 (see John Crawley, William J. Smyth and Mike Murphy, 'Introduction', in Crawley, Smyth and Murphy, *Atlas of the Great Irish Famine*, xvi).

[70] Mary E. Daly, *The first department: a history of the department of agriculture* (Dublin, 2002), 162.

[71] Hiroko Tabuchi, 'Japanese begin to question protections given to homegrown rice', *New York Times*, 9 January 2014, available at: www.nytimes.com/2014/01/10/business/international/japanese-begin-to-question-rices-sacred-place.html?_r=0 (5 February 2015).

[72] Hobhouse, *Seeds of change*, 264.

[73] Crotty, *Irish agricultural production*, 44.

[74] Reader, *The untold history of the potato*, 159.

[75] L. M. Cullen, 'Population growth and diet 1600–1850', in J. M. Goldstrom and L. A. Clarkson (eds), *Irish population, economy and society: essays in honour of the late K. H. Connell* (Oxford, 1981), 96.

them to the London, and never eats meat'.[76] The French consul in Dublin in 1834 contrasted the abundance of food at local level in France with the sale of so much of what was produced in Ireland.[77] Often a farm comprised a small plot of potatoes which offered a precarious subsistence with the remainder of the land used to grow cereals or graze a cow for butter to raise money for the rent.

The dominance of the market generated a snobbery directed against foraged foods which according to Cullen acquired a 'stigma'.[78] Kevin Myers has identified a modern resonance stating: 'It's almost as if those who live on the land here are culturally and emotionally disengaged from its essence as a living thing'.[79] Loss of the native agriculture may have played a role, according to John Feehan: 'it seems more than likely that the loss of the Gaelic tradition of farming was accompanied by a decline in the lore of wild plants and animals as food or medicine'.[80] The decline of the Gaelic language could also have led to a corresponding loss of knowledge of native plants.

Furthermore, the absence of a substantial 'improving' native gentry reduced experimentation in and demand for 'alternative' crops: fruit and vegetable varieties with limited market value. This differed to England where, from the seventeenth century, an intellectual passion for horticulture emerged among gentlemen-farmers inspired by classical authors.[81] Tom Nairn argues that 'blatant, deliberately preserved inequities of class were the striking feature of the English social order',[82] which explains why the enjoyment of many of these foods did not diffuse widely there; in Ireland class distinctions were compounded by sectarian divisions and absenteeism.

Crotty has highlighted the responsiveness of Irish agriculture to demand from external markets.[83] During the eighteenth century demand for grain and salted beef and other processed animal products generated high employment. This was bound up with the Cattle Acts (1663–1667) which prohibited the export of live cattle, leading farmers to focus on tillage and on producing livestock for processing. Combined with the relative peace that reigned in the eighteenth century and the increased cultivation of the potato, unprecedented population growth ensued, much of it in the poorest cottier class. By the eve of the Great Famine 3 million (out of a population of 8 million) were living on 1 million acres of land which represented but 5% of the total acreage of 20 million. Poverty was worsened by a shift from tillage to pasture as, after the Battle of Waterloo, British 'demand swung from cereals to livestock

---

[76] Emmet Larkin, *Alexis de Toqueville's journey in Ireland, July–August 1835* (Washington, DC, 1990), 29.

[77] Louis Michael Cullen, 'Comparative aspects of Irish diet 1550–1850', in Teuteberg, *European food history: a research review*, 47.

[78] Cullen, *The emergence of modern Ireland*, 173.

[79] *Irish Times*, 30 January 2001.

[80] Feehan, *Farming in Ireland*, 201.

[81] Thirsk, *Alternative agriculture*, 27.

[82] Tom Nairn, *The break up of Britain: crisis and neo-nationalism* (London, 1977), 13.

[83] Crotty, *Irish agricultural production*, 55.

products, causing cattle, sheep and butter prices to rise further relative to cereal prices'.[84] This led to a contraction in seasonal employment. Crotty argues that 'with twenty million, instead of one million, acres of land available for the production of the population's food requirements even with the worst conceivable crop failures, an abundance of food could have been grown to feed eight or more millions of people'.[85] This view is endorsed by Joel Mokyr who argued that Ireland was not overpopulated on the eve of the Great Famine.[86]

The Great Famine is presented by Crotty as facilitating an acceleration in an inexorable shift from tillage to pasture taking its cue from increased British demand for beef after the Napoleonic wars when Britain could resume importing grain from the continent. The repeal in 1846 of the Corn Laws, which imposed tariffs on the import of wheat and other staples, made tillage farming uneconomical across the British Isles (Fig. 1). The major outcomes in Ireland were a significant decline in the rural population which emigrated in vast

FIG. 1—*The stone bridge, Blarney Castle (dry bridge at Blarney)* by James Mahoney, 1850. (© Crawford Art Gallery, Cork.)

---

[84] Crotty, *Irish agricultural production*, 37.

[85] Crotty, *Irish agricultural production*, 63.

[86] Joel Mokyr, *Why Ireland starved: an analytical and quantitative history of the Irish economy 1840–1850* (New York, 1985), 291.

numbers, and the emergence of a petit bourgeois class of pastoralists who took possession of most of the land at the end of the nineteenth and the start of the twentieth centuries through government redistribution schemes culminating in Wyndham's Land Act of 1903.

Surprisingly, Crotty laments these tenant land purchase schemes as: '[t]he abandonment of competitive rent in favour of a system of peasant proprietorship naturally introduces an element of immobility into the allocation of land among farmers'. He argues that: '[t]here are reasons to believe that under Irish conditions this immobility is likely to be particularly severe, leading in turn to serious misallocation of land', and so it has proved.[87] Mary E. Daly disputes Crotty's claim that this was detrimental to the development of Irish farming though she concedes that 'between 1900 and 1914 productivity growth was lower than anywhere in Europe except Britain'.[88]

Between 1850 and 1900 the number of cattle on Irish farms increased by over 60% and the number of sheep more than doubled. The area under tillage declined from 4.3 to 2.4 million acres and the rural population from 5.3 to 3 million.[89] James Connolly identified its effect on parts of rural Ireland: 'Where a hundred families had reaped a sustenance from their small farms, or by hiring out their labour to the owners of large farms, a dozen shepherds now occupied their places'.[90] Raymond Crotty reached a similar conclusion:

> concentration on cattle and sheep ... has had an extremely harmful effect on Irish agriculture and on the whole Irish economy. While on the one hand is has led to the enrichment of the numerically small landed interest, on the other it has given rise first to famine and subsequently to chronic emigration and to very slow economic progress for the numerically much greater non-land-owning section of the population.[91]

Connolly and Crotty notwithstanding, the consequence of Ireland's shift to a cattle-based agricultural modernity is under-acknowledged in Irish historiography. The successful movement for land reform in the late nineteenth century created a society with a preponderance of peasant proprietors who maintained a model of production that offered few employment or investment opportunities. According to Crotty: 'The structure of the agriculture, characterized by the predominance of beef-cattle and sheep, provided little opportunity for the employment of labour or capital and with a static volume of output these opportunities did not improve'.[92]

Reduction in tillage coincided with a decline in the indigenous flour milling industry, consistent with E. O'Malley's contention that 'the main causes

---

[87] Crotty, *Irish agricultural production*, 93.

[88] Daly, *First department*, 46–7.

[89] Crotty, *Irish agricultural production*, 84.

[90] James Connolly, *Labour in Irish history* (Dublin, 1973), 15–16.

[91] Crotty, *Irish agricultural production*, 236.

[92] Crotty, *Irish agricultural production*, 108.

of decline lay in the strong tendencies to industrial centralization, or agglomeration, within the United Kingdom'.[93] An independent state might have protected the interests of Irish industry and reordered the priorities of Irish agriculture in favour of higher employment and lower food prices along lines similar to what occurred in Denmark where property taxes discouraged the amassing of property, leading to more productive use of land.[94]

Independence daze

In the 1920s the economist George O'Brien offered an opinion, still widely assumed that: 'In the Irish Free State the interests of the farmers and of the nation are, at least prima facie, identical and the best uses of the resources of the country is that which maximises the prosperity of the farming classes'. In fact, a strong case can be made in support of the opposite conclusion; for as Crotty has pointed out, Irish agriculture's mode of production was contrary to the country's economic and social interests: while unemployment and emigration 'were serious problems, these [O'Brien's] views were far from axiomatic and an entirely different approach might have been justifiable'. Crotty argues that the interests of farmers, or landowners, and the nation 'are essentially conflicting'; because: '[t]he scope for intensifying grassland beef production is very limited. The profitability of the system depends on a low rate of expenditure'.[95] Thus the Irish population did not increase after independence and the price of food tended to be at least as high as in Britain,[96] despite far lower population density, and greater scope for local production.

Independence brought little change in agricultural priorities with Ireland remaining a primary producer of livestock products and cattle often exported 'on the hoof' to Britain. This was driven by the first minister for agriculture Patrick Hogan (1922–32) whose sympathy lay with large cattle farmers who present in his own family background. It ran contrary to an earlier trend among Irish nationalists such as Robert Barton who favoured reviving labour-intensive tillage. Hogan's preference for an agriculture based on the export of livestock products, primarily for the British market, might be justified on the basis that this was the main source of export revenue for a fledgling state and that grain or other field crops could not have found such a ready market. But the exploitation of this opportunity was at the cost of continued rural depopulation and reliance on imported foodstuffs.

A partial swing to tillage occurred after Eamon de Valera's Fianna Fáil party came to power in 1932 and pursued policies that encouraged self-sufficiency. To an extent this was prompted by external events: firstly, the so-called 'Economic War' (1933–38) occasioned by the withholding of annuities owed on land purchased under the aforementioned land redistribution schemes;

---

[93] E. O'Malley, 'The decline of Irish industry in the nineteenth century', *The Economic and Social Review* 13:1 (1981), 21–42.

[94] Crotty, *Irish agricultural production*, 70.

[95] Crotty, *Irish agricultural production*, 117.

[96] Crotty, *Irish agricultural production*, 136.

and secondly, the 'Emergency' (1939–45) which Ireland survived without food shortages through reversion to tillage.

The post-war period witnessed a returned emphasis on livestock exports, although the structure of agriculture changed with the introduction of intensive methods connected to the so-called Green Revolution. Thus Ireland's once substantial egg export trade declined dramatically as small farms became uncompetitive once British agriculture adopted what is known as 'factory farming'. Irish farming has since adopted such approaches with poultry, egg and pork production now overwhelmingly industrial activities. Today these facilities usually depend on imported grain and soya often cultivated on land that was previously rainforest; while animal welfare standards rarely, if ever, live up to the five freedoms.[97] Over time industrial methods have also entered dairy farming and dry cattle farming although grass-feeding remains more prevalent in both for much of the year.

The global mechanisation of agriculture after the Second World War put Irish tillage farmers at a distinct disadvantage compared to competitors in drier conditions. Wheat cut by a combine harvester at high moisture content must be dried immediately while 'bindered' wheat (the traditional harvesting method) can dry out gradually over months in stacks. Ironically, in Irish conditions the effect of the combine harvester has been 'to change wheat from being a manageable and predictable crop into one of risk and doubt'.[98] This brought Ireland from self-sufficiency to almost complete reliance on import of this dominant staple. It would be worthwhile researching how different technologies or alternative crop varieties suited to Irish conditions could be employed to promote self-sufficiency in cereal staples in the event of future energy 'shocks' or dramatic climate change.

The early commercialisation of agriculture has cast a long shadow as farmers have continued to devote their land to the production of commodities for the international market, and purchased their own food from the same anonymous source. In an address to Macra na Feirme in 1974, the psychiatrist Ivor Browne observed the irrational scenario of: 'a small farmer in Mayo taking his calf to the town to sell and his wife asking him to pick up a chicken for dinner in the supermarket while he is there; he manages to sell his calf for £1 and pays £1.50 for the chicken for dinner'.[99] Widespread indifference to provenance suggests that, by and large, food continued to be seen as simply fuel for the body, largely, though never entirely, divorced from ritual celebration. Rosemary Fennel writing in 1971 bemoaned the demise of country markets and how a 'frequent complaint in Ireland is the lack of variety of in vegetables for

---

[97] See John Webster, 'Food from the dairy: husbandry regained', in Joyce D'Silva and John Webster (eds), *The meat crisis: developing sustainable production and consumption* (London, 2010), 101.

[98] J. B. Ruane, 'The farmer in a changing industry', in Baillie and Sheehy, *Irish agriculture in a changing world*, 133.

[99] Ivor Brown, *The writings of Ivor Browne: steps along the road: the evolution of a slow learner* (Cork, 2013), 90.

sale and the high prices charged'.[100] Media coverage of the subject of food in the form of recipes, reviews and features only really took off in the 1990s. What little elite dining there was remained rooted in the conservative haute cuisine tradition of Georges Auguste Escoffier.[101]

It may be that the enduring absence of alternative agriculture and gastronomy owes something to the rejection of the 'Big Houses' that once dominated the countryside, and in whose walled gardens, orchards and hothouses most horticultural experimentation had occurred prior to independence and the departure of a significant proportion of the landlord class. The absence of a paternalistic relationship between peasantry and landlords sustained suspicion of these properties in an independent state dominated by a petit bourgeois farmer class. In 1944 Minister for Lands Sean Moylan condemned them as 'tombstones of a departed aristocracy' remarking 'the sooner they go down the better. They are no use'.[102] More recently Nuala O'Faolain admitted: 'We cannot, or at least I cannot, look at the Big House without some degree of rage'.[103]

In 1958 T. K. Whittaker's seminal 'Economic Development' paper advocated further specialisation in beef production, as it was the sector where perceived comparative advantage lay.[104] In contrast attempts to develop farming cooperatives that would produce a wider variety of foodstuffs in the 1960s floundered largely for want of government support.[105] From 1972 the European Community's Common Agricultural Policy (CAP) perpetuated this pastoral model, generating further specialisation and reducing the unprotected horticultural sector which struggled, as a result, to compete with cheap and often subsidised imports that the removal of trade barriers brought. Farm supports did allow large farmers to earn incomes comparable often to urban dwellers but generated further imbalance: a mere 3.8% of Irish farmland is now devoted to tillage, much of it used as animal feed; there are almost 7 million cattle and over 5 million sheep in the country.[106] Government policy as outlined in *Food harvest 2020* places an increased emphasis on livestock production.[107]

---

[100] Rosemary Fennell, 'The domestic market for Irish agricultural produce', in Baillie and Sheehy, *Irish agriculture in a changing world*, 106.
[101] Máirtín Mac Con Iomaire, 'Haute cuisine restaurants in nineteenth and twentieth century Ireland', *Proceedings of the Royal Irish Academy* 115C (2015), 371–403.
[102] Terence Dooley, 'The Big House and Famine memory: Strokestown Park House', in Crawley, Smith and Murphy, *Atlas of the Great Irish Famine*, 625.
[103] Dooley, 'The Big House and Famine memory', 628.
[104] Crotty, *Irish agricultural production*, 192.
[105] See Daly, *First department*, 428–41.
[106] Central Statistics Office (CSO), *Crops and livestock survey June provisional estimates* (Dublin, 2013), available at: www.cso.ie/en/releasesandpublications/er/clsjp/cropsandlivestocksurveyjuneprovisional2013/#.UukV9_uqE1I (5 February 2015).
[107] Department of agriculture, fisheries and food, *Food harvest 2020: a vision for agri-food and fisheries* (Dublin, 2010), available at: www.agriculture.gov.ie/media/migration/agri-foodindustry/foodharvest2020/2020FoodHarvestExeSummary240810.pdf (5 February 2015).

Another long-term legacy of the dominant pastoral mode of production has been a significant loss of native biodiversity. By the second half of the nineteenth century Ireland had 'the sad distinction of being the European country with least forest cover'.[108] Increased emphasis on livestock production has accelerated damage to the natural environment and biodiversity. During the 1980s European Community 'headage' payments subsidised smallholders to increase sheep flocks[109] with no regard for the carrying capacity of their land. Paddy Woodworth has identified the damage caused to the unique ecosystems of blanket bogs:

> Their increasingly anxious hooves, scrabbling for any little bit of sustenance, broke up the surface peat into unstable fragments, then to dust. These bogs turned into true wastelands, black and bleak ... river systems became so acidified that precious populations of trout and salmon collapsed.[110]

Moreover, since 1985, the demands of Irish agriculture have prompted a 'cull' of almost 100,000 badgers due to a perceived threat of bovine tuberculosis, despite the existence of an effective badger vaccine.[111]

Irish food today

The 'elephant in the room' for Irish agriculture is the scale of its anthropogenic greenhouse gas emissions, especially the methane released by ruminant animals through enteric fermentation. The agriculture sector now accounts for over 30% of total national emissions,[112] which is second only to that of New Zealand's among developed countries. The Climate Change Bill 2013 targets a voluntary 80% reduction in emissions by 2050, leaving 11 million tonnes of carbon dioxide equivalent.[113] But agriculture alone accounts for 19 million tonnes. The current minister for agriculture and food Simon Coveney has argued that Irish farmers should be exempted from reducing emissions because these are lower than EU average[114] but this assumes that consumption is static and discounts the success

---

[108] Paddy Woodworth, *Our once and future planet: restoring the world in the climate change century* (Chicago, IL, 2013), 191.

[109] Sheep numbers rose from 3.3 million in 1980 to 8.8 million in 1991 see Frank Mitchell and Michael Ryan, *Reading the Irish landscape* (Dublin, 1997), 351.

[110] Woodworth, *Our once and future planet*, 357.

[111] See http://iwt.ie/what-we-do/iwt-badger-campaign/ for more details (5 February 2015).

[112] Agriculture accounted for 32% of overall emissions in 2011, the biggest share of any sector see: Environmental Protection Agency, *Greenhouse gas emissions by sector* (Dublin, 2015), available at: www.epa.ie/irelandsenvironment/environmentalindicators-dashboard/greenhousegasemissionsbysector/# (5 February 2015).

[113] Irish Government, Climate Change Bill 2013, available at: www.oireachtas.ie/documents/bills28/bills/2013/813/b813d.pdf (5 February 2015).

[114] European Commission Joint Research Centre, *Evaluation of the livestock sector's contribution to the EU greenhouse gas emissions (GGELS)* (Ispra, 2010), available at: http://ec.europa.eu/agriculture/analysis/external/livestock-gas/exec_sum_en.pdf (5 February 2015).

of marketing campaigns (such as 'Origin Green') trumpeting Irish agriculture's 'green' credentials which maintain consumption.

Consideration of emissions might prompt exclusion or at least radical reduction of animal products. A 2014 Oxford University study of British consumers (who share much the same supply chain as most Irish consumers) showed that a heavy meat eater generates more than twice the emissions of a dietary vegan.[115] Global meat consumption (including dairy and fish) accounts for a greater proportion of anthropogenic emissions than the entire transport sector. Even the transport of food is an insignificant emission contributor compared to production meaning simply eating locally as some conscientious consumers choose, is generally worse in terms of emissions than choosing a plant-based alternative, even if many of the foodstuffs in that diet are (at present) imported. According to Ireland's leading climate scientist, John Sweeney, the objective of intensifying production as outlined in *Food harvest 2020* cannot be achieved without increasing emissions. He also points out that the type of high-protein food that Ireland produces is not used to feed the global poor as has been argued.[116]

The objectives of the Irish agricultural authorities run contrary to a growing consensus that predominantly plant-based nutrition improves health outcomes.[117] This seems likely to drive future consumer choice and health policy.[118] Indeed, it may be that we are witnessing a break in the age-old association between wealth and meat consumption in Britain and Ireland with growing awareness of the impact of diet on personal health and planetary well-being, complimenting longer-standing revulsion among a growing minority at the exploitation of animals for food. In time these trends may diffuse more widely as other social classes seek to climb the 'social ladder'. But this outcome contends with powerful lobbies promoting the consumption of animal products

---

[115] Peter Scarborough, Paul N. Appleby, Anja Mizdrak, Adam D. M. Briggs, Ruth C. Travis, Kathryn E. Bradbury, Timothy J. Key, 'Dietary greenhouse gas emissions of meat-eaters, fish-eaters, vegetarians and vegans in the UK', *Climate Change* 125:2 (2014), 179–92, available at: http://link.springer.com/article/10.1007%2Fs10584-014-1169-1#close (5 February 2015).

[116] Interview with Damien English on the RTÉ Radio 1 programme *CountryWide* on 11 March 2014.

[117] See: Joyce D'Silva, and John Webster (eds), *The meat crisis: developing more sustained production and consumption* (London, 2010), 161–206; and Kirk R. Smith, Michael Jerrett, H. Ross Anderson *et al.*, 'Public health benefits of strategies to reduce greenhouse-gas emissions: health implications of short-lived greenhouse pollutants', *The Lancet* 374:9707 (2009), 2091–103.

[118] For example, the United States of America healthcare provider Kaiser Permanente recommends the adoption of a plant-based diet as 'cost-effective, low-risk interventions that may lower body mass index, blood pressure, HbA1C, and cholesterol levels to improve health outcomes', see Philip J. Tuso, Mohamed H. Ismail, Benjamin P. Ha and Carole Bartolotto, 'Nutritional update for physicians: plant-based diets', *The Permanente Journal* 17:2 (2013), 61–6, available at: www.ncbi.nlm.nih.gov/pmc/articles/PMC3662288/ (5 February 2015).

both directly through advertising, and indirectly through the exertion of influence on government nutritional advice.[119] Daly argues that 'it is evident that the Department [of Agriculture] has traditionally looked at agricultural matters from the perspective of the producer rather than the consumer'. She cautions that the identity of interests between farmers and the Irish nation 'does not necessarily apply on issues such as food policy, or the environment'.[120]

Irish cattle producers may become increasingly reliant on markets in developing countries where, in contrast to developed countries, meat consumption is growing in parallel with increasing affluence. But the political instability of markets such as the Middle East makes this policy risky. The experience of the late 1980s should not be forgotten when the Irish taxpayer was obliged to pay export credit insurance to Goodman International in the wake of Iraq's invasion of Kuwait. Similarly, in 2014 Irish farmers lost access to the Russian market due to EU trade sanctions. Another threat to the continued viability of the sector comes from the development of analogue and laboratory grown 'meat' which is attracting large investment, especially in Silicon Valley.

Also, the national emergency arising out of the food-and-mouth disease crisis of 2001 exhibited the ecological risk of dependence on monoculture livestock farming. Ireland's agricultural authorities would do well to heed Evan Fraser and Andrew Rimas's advice that 'nature is most resilient when it's diverse'.[121] More recently the fodder crisis of 2013 revealed how an increasingly unpredictable climate threatens the viability of the sector. The latter crisis was accentuated by the high cost of animal feed owing to drought in the United States of America in 2012 with climate change implicated. A lesson from the Great Famine is that specialisation may confer short-term advantage but the long-term consequences can be catastrophic.

Moreover, 'reputational' damage from the horsemeat crisis of 2013 and the earlier bovine spongiform encephalopathy (BSE) crisis of 1996 reveal the potential for a far-reaching shift in consumer preference. Today scientists are drawing attention to the grave danger posed by the extensive use of antibiotics in animal agriculture in Ireland and elsewhere which has already brought antimicrobial-resistant bacteria into the food chain.[122] It is rare for a year to pass without a public health scare emanating from animal agriculture emerging.

---

[119] For instance government advice to consume between and three and five portions of dairy (depending upon a person's age) is inconsistent with the advice of the Harvard School of Public Health which says that 'milk isn't the only or the best source of calcium'; see Harvard School of Public Health, *Calcium and milk*, available at: www.hsph.harvard.edu/nutritionsource/what-should-you-eat/calcium-and-milk/ (5 February 2015). For an examination of the political influence exerted on dietary advice of the United States of America see Marion Nestle's *Food politics* (Berkeley, CA, 2002)

[120] Daly, *First department*, 548.

[121] Evan D. G. Fraser and Andrew Rimas, *Empires of food* (London, 2010), 19.

[122] Martin Blaser, *Missing microbes: how killing bacteria creates modern plagues* (London, 2014), 79–87.

Since the economic crash of 2008 the relative importance of agriculture to the economy has increased. Recent figures claim export revenues of almost €10 billion.[123] But imports of food to a value of almost €5 billion include many products, such as potatoes, apples and carrots, that could easily be grown in Ireland. Moreover, high production costs in agriculture are not accounted for, among these are feedstuffs for livestock, fertilisers derived from natural gas and oil for machinery. The net profits are a fraction of the gross figure,[124] and the benefit to most farmers and the wider economy can be questioned if we consider the opportunity cost of the subsidies. Certainly it has been argued that small rural town are disconnected from any uplift.[125] Moreover, the *National farm survey 2012* found that despite EU CAP payments to farmers of €2.39 billion, a mere 37% of Irish farms were economically viable as 58% of incomes derive from the Single Farm Payment. This amounted to 80% and 33% of income for dry cattle farmers and dairy farmers, respectively.[126] It appears that the beneficiaries of Irish agriculture are the multinational companies such as the Kerry Group, Glanbia and the ABP Food Group (formerly Goodman International) whose shareholders have assumed the role of absentee landlords.

The adoption of agricultural alternatives from a variety of international 'toolkits' could confer significant advantages through reduced dependency on imported food, and increased employment in labour-intensive tillage and horticulture at a time of high unemployment. Interestingly, quinoa, another Andean staple, which due to undersupply retailed at the time of writing at almost €9 for 500 grams. Like potatoes quinoa offers a 'complete' protein package of all essential amino acids, is already being grown commercially in the United Kingdom and one variety has been trialled successfully as far north as Fife in Scotland.[127] Thus, potentially, cheaper and healthier food can be grown in Ireland, an important consideration given the scale of food poverty and the obesity epidemic.

---

[123] See www.bordbia.ie/eventsnews/press/pages/ExportPerformanceProspects2014. aspx (27 January 2014).

[124] According to the CSO, 'intermediate consumption', including feeding stuffs, fertilisers, energy and lubricants, forage plants and contract work cost €5,494.1 million in 2013, see CSO, *Output, input and income in agriculture—advance estimate* (Dublin, 2013), available at: www.cso.ie/en/releasesandpublications/er/oiiaa/outputinputandinco meinagriculture-advanceestimate2013/#.VAXn5aPEnFI (5 February 2015). If subsidies are included, net profit for agriculture appears to be in the region of €2 billion, putting the balance of Irish agricultural trade a €3 billion in deficit.

[125] Diarmuid Ó Gráda, 'Problems of the Irish village require immediate action', *Irish Times*, 11 July 2014, available at: www.irishtimes.com/news/social-affairs/problems-of-the-irish-village-require-immediate-action-1.1862154 (2 September 2014).

[126] Teagasc, *National farm survey 2012: preliminary estimates* (Dublin 2013), available at: www.teagasc.ie/publications/2013/1935/NFSIncomeEstimates2012.pdf (5 February 2015).

[127] 'The popular Fife Diet has reached another milestone', *Fife Today*, 9 June 2009, available at: www.fifetoday.co.uk/news/local-headlines/diet-reaches-milestone-1-159707 (2 March 2015).

One challenge for alternative agriculture is the historic inflexibility in the land market which thwarts diversification. Frank Mitchell and Michael Ryan observed: 'In Ireland it is still next to impossible to rent land on a lease of sufficient length to make improvements and where land can be bought it is often in small parcels at too high a price'.[128] Unfortunately, the CAP subsidy regime serves to increases the cost of land as farmers are guaranteed incomes from privileged pastoral farming.

Any alternative agriculture should involve far wider direct participation than is the case today, many working on a part-time or seasonal basis perhaps. The hinterland of cities would be especially important. Crotty argued that: 'A land-tax offers the only means of reconciling future increases in cattle and sheep prices, relative to those of other farm products, with the general welfare'.[129] This could involve the broadening of the property tax to encompass agricultural land, a project envisioned in the 1980s through the Farm Assessment Office, which was disbanded in 1987 as a result of an agreement between Charles J. Haughey and the Irish Farmers' Association. Taxation revenue emanating from any land tax could be redistributed in the form of low-interest loans allowing enterprising individuals or cooperatives to acquire land.

While it could be argued that this was an unfortunate decision, the involvement of government agencies should be restricted according to Joan Thirsk:

> [T]he strong assumption of our age that omniscient governments will lead the way out of economic problems will not in practice serve. The solutions are more likely to come from below, from the initiatives of individuals, singly or in groups, groping their way, after many trials and errors, towards fresh undertakings. They will follow their own hunches, ideals and inspirations, and obsessions, and along the way some will even be dismissed as harmless lunatics. The state may help indirectly, but it is unlikely to initiate, or select for support the best strategies; and, out of ignorance or lack of imagination, it may positively hinder.[130]

The state should, nonetheless, retain an environmental watchdog role in order that 'the tragedy of the commons' should be avoided. And if Irish farmers are to shift direction and compete on the domestic and international markets, state financial assistance will be required perhaps prioritising the construction of greenhouses and other hothouse facilities. This could be linked to establishing a greater connection between farmers and consumers through community-assisted agriculture. Farmers can draw from a global seed bank alongside traditional crops as well as utilising agroforestry. Climate change is likely to

---

128 Mitchell and Ryan, *Reading the Irish landscape*, 356.
129 Crotty, *Irish agricultural production*, 236.
130 Thirsk, *Alternative agriculture*, 256.

make a shift towards tillage more economically attractive,[131] and, assuming less land is used in food production, restored biodiversity can bring tangible economic benefits.[132] Ireland's dubious reputation as a 'green' island could have real foundation.

Improvements in diet through the development of alternative agriculture could also help to confront the obesity pandemic especially through the appeal of increased variety, freshness and a reduction in the cost of fruit and vegetables. Imbalances in the present system are revealed in the 2011 healthy eating guidelines of the Food Safety Authority of Ireland (FSAI),[133] which found that foods high in fat and sugar were generally a far cheaper source of calories and that fruits and vegetables were in the most expensive category. Damningly, the report noted that 'healthy eating was less affordable for families dependent on social welfare'. The authors identified a need 'for more work to be carried out on how families on limited incomes can best put healthy eating into practice'. They argue that this 'should focus on developing advice on healthy eating using cheaper food options, e.g. 1) pulses (peas, beans and lentils) and eggs,[134] as a cheaper alternative to meat and 2) using fruit and vegetables in season'.[135] But the authors note the difficulty of achieving this 'due to lack of familiarity with, and the acceptability of, these food options'.

The findings of the FSAI show that Mintz's observations regarding the poor value for money of the food choices of the English working class in the nineteenth century still apply to many on low incomes in Ireland today. Sadly, the aspiration of shifting diets towards a greater consumption of plant-based 'alternatives' identified in the authority's guidelines are not shared by another government agency: An Bord Bia's website contains no category of plant-based recipes.[136]

The challenge of shifting diet is associated with the inheritance of a food culture. In childhood we are habituated to the taste of certain foods. Pierre

[131] Stephen Flood, *Projected economic impacts of climate change on Irish agriculture* (Dublin, 2013), available at: www.stopclimatechaos.ie/download/pdf/projected_economic_impacts_of_climate_change_on_irish_agriculture_oct_2013.pdf (5 February 2015). Also Feehan, *Farming in Ireland*, 515.

[132] For example, New York City managed to save an estimated €1 billion in capital costs as well as major annual savings in operating costs through the restoration of natural capital see Woodworth, *Our one and future planet*, 37.

[133] Food Safety Authority of Ireland, *Scientific recommendations for healthy eating guidelines in Ireland* (Dublin, 2011).

[134] The desirability of eating eggs is also doubtful. In the nurses' health study and health professionals follow-up study, heart disease risk was increased among men and women with diabetes who ate one or more eggs a day; see F. B. Hu, M. J. Stampfer, E. B. Rimm *et al.*, 'A prospective study of egg consumption and risk of cardiovascular disease in men and women', *The Journal of the American Medical Association* 281:15 (1999), 1387–94.

[135] Surprisingly, the authority omits nuts and seeds as a potential source of protein and healthy fats.

[136] See www.bordbia.ie/aboutfood/recipes/pages/recipehome.aspx (5 February 2015).

Bourdieu claims that 'it is probably in tastes in food that one would find the strongest and most indelible mark of infant learning'.[137] This may also be connected to the strains of bacteria in our gut that we develop after consuming specific nutrients.[138] Developing a taste for new foods, especially vegetables, is also constrained by an innate suspicion, born of evolutionary experience that makes us wary of the poisonous nature of some bitter-tasting substances.[139] One way of bringing about change is to acquaint children with novel flavours as part of their education. This already occurs in France.[140] Also, a grow-it-yourself approach increases what Michael Kelly, chairman of GIY Ireland, describes as food 'empathy'. He wrote: 'Research has shown that food empathetic people make healthier food choices'.[141]

The absence of a discernible gastronomic culture has offered little resistance to the advance of American-style fast food designed for compulsive eating.[142] But equally the lack of a dominant national cuisine may create more openness to healthier and more environmentally beneficial food choices.

This paper has attempted to draw a connection in Irish culture between dysfunctional food consumption and the food production system that emerged in the wake of the Great Famine. The recent upsurge in interest in food is a positive sign, and the presence of a significant number of non-nationals in the country is making once exotic ingredients increasingly familiar. Agricultural reform in Ireland can bring significant benefits by confronting the obesity pandemic and reducing anthropogenic greenhouse gas emissions. It is apparent that the optimum solutions lie in successful adaptation rather than wholesale restoration of primitive, anachronistic methods or reversion to narrow self-sufficiency. The state of Indiana in the United States, comparable in size to Ireland, does not seek full self-sufficiency, so why should a country the size of Ireland aspire to it? Significant local production makes sense, but as part of a wider European community which includes commensality. Many more Irish crops should become European-wide delicacies: a unique climate and moist, friable soil can nourish a bounteous array. The undoubted skills and knowledge of farmers must be harnessed to reform Irish agriculture, and we should

---

[137] Pierre Bourdieu, *Distinction: a social critique of the judgment of taste,* trans. by Richard Nice (London, 2010), 71.

[138] Vic Norris, Franck Molina and Andrew T. Gewirtz, 'Hypothesis: bacteria control host appetites', *Journal of Bacteriology* 195:3 (2013), 411–16, available at: www.ncbi. nlm.nih.gov/pmc/articles/PMC3554020/ (5 February 2015).

[139] According to Mintz: 'sweet-tasting substances appear to insinuate themselves more quickly into the preferences of new consumers while bitter substances are "bitter-specific"'. Thus, 'liking watercress has nothing to do with liking eggplant [aubergine] for instance'. See Mintz, *Sweetness and power,* 109.

[140] Alan Warde, 'Globalisation and the challenge of variety: a comparison of eating in Britain and France', in Inglis and Gamlin, *The globalization of food,* 237.

[141] *Irish Times,* 2 September 2013.

[142] David Kessler identifies five key influences on insatiable eating: 'calories, flavour hits, ease of eating, meltdown and early hit', see David A. Kessler, *The end of overeating—taking control of our insatiable appetites* (London, 2010), 105.

continue to pay a fair price for food, but the interests of farmers and the rest of the country need to be aligned. Any suggestion that individual farmers are to blame for a systemic failing is denied. Irish farmers have long been forced to produce what the market has demanded. Wider popular engagement with our agricultural model should make its reform a progressive cause, with the aspiration of generating healthy, delicious food, affordable to all. In so doing we can forge a food identity to be proud of.

INSTRUCTIONS TO AUTHORS

Papers may be submitted by members or non-members of the Royal Irish Academy and should be e-mailed to submissions@ria.ie. Alternatively, they can be sent (in duplicate) to the Secretary, Royal Irish Academy, 19 Dawson Street, Dublin 2, or to the editors.

Abstract—Each paper must be preceded by an abstract not exceeding 150 words, which should be intelligible in itself without reference to the paper.

Text—Papers submitted for publication should be within the range of 8,000 to 12,000 words. Longer submissions will be permitted in exceptional circumstances. The text should be presented in double spacing, with wide margins and the right-hand margin left unjustified. Low-resolution scans or photocopies of any line figures or maps should accompany the paper at the initial submission stage. If submitting in hard copy, two copies of the paper (including photocopies of illustrations) are required.

Illustrations—Original figures or plates should not be submitted until requested by the Publications Office. The maximum space available for illustrations (including captions) is 180mm by 215mm, and care should be taken that any lettering or decoration will accept the necessary reduction. Line drawings should be in black drawing ink on smooth white card or good quality tracing material. Authors are requested to consult the Publications Office for further instructions, also regarding the requirements for electronic artwork. Authors will be required to pay the cost of large maps that have to be reproduced as folder plates. When submitted, such maps must not exceed 750mm by 1000mm, and should, if possible, be drawn to reduce to 200mm in height so as to avoid folding two ways. Figures and plates should be numbered in separate sequences (Fig. 1, Fig. 2; Pl. I, Pl. II). Where appropriate a scale should be used. Captions for illustrations should be given in separate lists at the end of the paper.

Tables—Legends should be typed at the top of the tables, which should be presented separately from the text. Vertical rules should be avoided.

References—Authors alone are responsible for the accuracy of their references. Either footnote (history papers) or author–date system (archaeology papers) may be used. Authors are advised to consult a recent paper in the relevant field for reference style or to view the style guidelines on the journal home page (http://www.ria.ie/publications/journals/procci/instauth.html).

Proofs—Authors normally receive first proofs only and are requested to return them without delay.

Subventions—Subventions to assist with costs of publication of papers are welcomed by the Royal Irish Academy and should be sought by authors in a position to obtain them. The Royal Irish Academy gratefully acknowledges subventions from the following institutions towards the publication costs of papers by members of their staff: University College Cork; University College Dublin; National University of Ireland, Galway; National University of Ireland, Maynooth; Trinity College Dublin.

AUTHOR CHECK LIST

To avoid any delay in the processing of your paper please go through this list prior to submission to ensure that your paper meets each of these technical requirements.

Abstract
- Present
- Approximately 150 words
- No footnotes or references

Text
- Paper divided into logical headed sections, including introduction and conclusion
- All abbreviations given in full at first mention
- Few or no typographical errors

References
- Author–date style for archaeology papers; footnote style for history papers; no mixing of the two styles
- Format for the journal correctly followed (e.g. punctuation, order, capitalisation style for titles)
- Complete reference supplied in all cases (e.g. page spans of articles in books and journals, full first names if required)
- All quotations accompanied by a reference
- No use of 'ibid.', 'op. cit.' etc.
- Archaeology: all items on the reference list cited in the text; all works cited in the text included on the reference list
- History: second and subsequent citations of a work given as 'Surname, *Short title*'

Tables (if applicable)
- Each table referred to in the text *in sequence*
- Each table labelled according to the submission instructions and guidelines for authors
- Each table saved in a separate file, with a name in the format 'AuthorSurname-Table01'

Illustrations (if applicable)
- Author should aim to include at least one illustration per paper
- Each illustration referred to in the text *in sequence*, as 'Fig.' or 'Pl.'
- Separate sequences for figures (line drawings, maps) and plates (photographs)
- Figures numbered in arabic and plates in roman
- Plates in black and white unless colour has been approved
- Supplied in .jpeg format when requested by Publications Office; minimum resolution of 300 dpi
- Each image saved in a separate file, with a name in the format 'AuthorSurname-Figure01', 'AuthorSurname-Plate01'
- Separate file listing captions for illustrations provided

Author information
- Affiliation
- Email address
- Phone number
- Postal address

PROCEEDINGS OF THE ROYAL IRISH ACADEMY, SECTION C

Section C—archaeology, Celtic studies, history, linguistics, literature

The Royal Irish Academy was founded in 1785 to promote the study of science, polite literature and antiquities. It publishes a number of journals in which a large body of research papers appears each year. Its first journal was the *Transactions* of the Academy, which appeared in 1787. This was supplemented in 1836, and eventually replaced by the *Proceedings*.

Section C of the *Proceedings* publishes original research papers primarily in the fields of archaeology and history, although submissions in Celtic studies, linguistics and literature will also be considered. Papers should focus on Ireland or have a strong Irish relevance. Scholarly editions of short historical documents of Irish origin or interest are also published.

Authors of papers in archaeology are encouraged to relate their findings, where possible and appropriate, to wider themes, in order to connect ideas about Irish local, regional and national material with the outside world. Papers on non-Irish material housed in collections within Ireland, and sites, settlements and cultural landscapes outside of Ireland with significant Irish connections, will also be considered for publication. All submissions are refereed and only papers of a high academic standard are accepted.

ANNUAL SUBSCRIPTION RATES (single annual volume):
Individual (print & online) €35/£30/$45
Institutional (online only) €125 /£100/$250
Institutional (print & online) €137/£110/$270
Fascicles prior to volume 106C may also be purchased individually.

SUBSCRIPTIONS/ORDERS SHOULD BE SENT TO:
Publications Office
Royal Irish Academy
19 Dawson Street
Dublin 2
Ireland
Tel. +353-1-676 2570

Orders and enquiries may also be emailed to: publications@ria.ie